ADVANCES IN THEORY AND APPLICATIONS OF STEREO VISION

Edited by **Asim Bhatti**

Advances in Theory and Applications of Stereo Vision
Edited by Asim Bhatti

Published by InTech
Janeza Trdine 9, 51000 Rijeka, Croatia

Publishing Process Manager Iva Lipovic

Technical Editor Teodora Smiljanic

Cover Designer InTech Design Team

Additional hard copies can be obtained from orders@intechopen.com

Advances in Theory and Applications of Stereo Vision, Edited by Asim Bhatti
p. cm.
ISBN 978-953-307-516-7

For EU product safety concerns:
IN TECH d.o.o., Prolaz Marije Krucifikse Kozulić 3, 51000 Rijeka, Croatia,
info@intechopen.com or visit our website at intechopen.com.

Meet the editor

Dr. Bhatti is affiliated with Centre for Intelligent Systems Research, Deakin University, Australia. He has been actively involved in Research and development in the areas of Computer Vision and Image/Signal processing as well as Haptics and human machine interfaces. Dr. Bhatti has authored two books on the theory and applications of wavelets and multiwavelets analysis in signal and image process and has edited one book on stereo vision. Dr. Bhatti has published over 45 peer reviewed research papers and is awarded a worldwide patent on haptics. He has been part of number of successful competitive research grants and R&D funding through industrial collaboration.

Contents

Preface

Computer vision is one of the most studied and researched subjects of recent times and has gained paramount attention over the last two decades with exponentially grown focus on stereo vision. Lot of activities in the context of stereo vision are getting reported and published on the vast research spectrum, including novel mathematical ideas, new theoretical aspects, state of the art techniques and diverse range of applications. These reported ideas and published texts serve as fine introductions and references to individual mathematical ideas, however, they do not educate research trends of the overall field. This book addresses the aforementioned concerns in a unified manner by presenting diverse range of current research ideas and applications, providing an insight into the current research trends and advances in the field of stereo vision.

The book presents wide range of innovative research ideas and current trends in stereo vision. The topics covered in this book encapsulate research trends from fundamental theoretical aspects of robust stereo correspondence estimation to the establishment of novel and robust algorithms, as well as the applications in wide range of disciplines. The book consists of 17 chapters addressing different aspects of stereo vision. Research work presented in these chapters tries to establish either the correspondence problem from a unique perspective or new constraints to keep the estimation process robust. Understanding of the theoretical aspects and the algorithm development in solving for the robust solutions are connected. Algorithm development and the relevant applications are also tightly coupled as generally algorithms are customised to achieve optimum performance for specific applications. Despite of this tight coupling between theory, algorithms and applications, presented ideas in this book could be classified into three distinct streams.

First five chapters (1 to 5) discuss correspondence estimation problem from theoretical perspective. New ideas employing approaches such as evolutionary, wavelets and multiwavelets theories, Markov random fields and type-2 fuzzy sets are introduced. For instance, Chapter 2 proposes the use of multiwavelets in addressing the correspondence estimation problem and initiates a new debate by discussing the implicit potential of multiwavelets theory and embedded attributes of multiwavelets bases in the context of stereo vision. Chapter 3 discusses the consideration of local interactions to define Markov random fields to recover 3D structure from stereo images. Chapter 4 proposes fuzzy information theoretical approach based on type-2 fuzzy sets for the estimation and extraction of features of interest. Chapter 5 proposes novel combination of matching constraints to address the correspondence estimation problem.

Similarly, chapters 6 to 10 present innovative algorithms employing novel ideas and technologies inspired by the nature. Particularly interesting are biologically inspired technologies and techniques, such as address-event based stereo vision with bio-inspired silicon retina imagers and dimensional measurement using fisheye stereo vision. Chapter 10 presents a novel idea of measurement of objects in liquids by making use of refractive index of liquid. These unique ideas and algorithms truly inspire new researchers to look outside the box and redefine the current research problems and trends.

Chapters 11 to 17 provide a diverse range of applications, including human activity detection, 3D terrain mapping, navigation, obstacle detection and bio-inspired autonomous guidance. Although these applications are targeted to the domains of surveillance, agriculture, mobile robotics, manufacturing and unmanned air vehicles, presented techniques can easily be applied to other disciplines. A major problem with robust stereo vision algorithms is the computational complexity, which compromises their real time performance. This issue is addressed in chapter 17 by introducing FPGA-based architecture to execute stereo vision algorithms at 100 Hz, much faster than real time.

In summary, this book comprehensively covers almost all aspects of stereo vision and highlights the current trends. Diverse range of topics covered in this book, from fundamental theoretical aspects to novel algorithms and diverse range of applications, makes it equally essential for established researchers as well as experts in the field.

At this stage of the book completion, I would like to extend my gratitude and appreciation to all the authors who contributed their invaluable research to this book to make it a valuable piece of work. Finally, from all research community, I would like to extend my admiration to INTECH Publisher for creating this open access platform to promote research and innovation and making it freely available to the community.

Dr. Asim Bhatti
Centre for Intelligent Systems Research
Institute of Technology Research Innovation
Deakin University
Vic 3217, Australia

1

Evolutionary Approach to Epipolar Geometry Estimation

Sergio Taraglio and Stefano Chiesa
ENEA, Robotics Lab, Rome
Italy

1. Introduction

An image is a two dimensional projection of a three dimensional scene. Hence a degeneration is introduced since no information is retained on the distance of a given point in the space. In order to extract information on the three dimensional contents of a scene from a single image it is necessary to exploit some *a priori* knowledge either on the features of the scene, i.e. presence/absence of architectural lines, objects sizes, or on the general behaviour of shades, textures, etc. Everything becomes much simpler if more than a single image is available. Whenever more viewpoints and images are available, several geometric relations can be derived among the three dimensional real points and their projections onto the various two dimensional images. These relations can be mathematically described under the assumption of pinhole cameras and furnish constraints among the various image points. If only two images are considered, this research topic is usually referred to as epipolar geometry. Naturally there is no mathematical difference whether the considered images are taken at the same time by two different cameras (the stereoscopic vision problem) or at different times by a single moving camera (optical flow or structure from motion problem). In Robotics both these cases are of great significance. Stereoscopy yields the knowledge of objects and obstacles positions providing a useful key to obtain the safe navigation of a robot in any environment (Zanela & Taraglio, 2002). On the other hand the estimation of the *ego-motion*, i.e. the measure of camera motion, can be exploited to the end of computing robot odometry and thus spatial position, see e.g. (Caballero et al., 2009). In addition the visual sensing of the environment is becoming ubiquitous out of the ever decreasing costs of both cameras and processors and the cooperative coordination of more cameras can be exploited in many applicative fields such as surveillance or multimedia applications (Arghaian & Cavallaro, 2009). Epipolar geometry is then the geometry of two cameras, i.e. two images, and it is usually represented by a 3 x 3 *fundamental* matrix, from which it is possible to retrieve all the relevant geometrical information, namely the rigid roto-translation between camera positions. The estimation of the fundamental matrix is based on a set of corresponding features present in both the images of the same scene. Naturally the error in the process is directly linked to the accuracy in the computation of these correspondences. In the following a novel genetic approach to epipolar geometry estimation is presented. This algorithm searches an optimal or sub-optimal solution for the rigid roto-translation between two camera positions in a evolutionary framework. The fitness of the tentative solutions is measured against the full set of correspondences through a function that is able to correctly cope with outliers, i.e. the incorrectly matched points usually due to errors in feature detection and/or in matching. Finally the evolution of the solution is granted through a reproduction and mutation scheme. In Section 2 the relevant geometrical concepts of epipolar geometry are recalled, while in Section 3 a review of some of the algorithms devised for the estimation of epipolar geometry is presented. In Section 4 the details of the proposed epipolar geometry estimation based on evolutionary strategies is given. In Section 5 some experimental data relative to both ego-motion and stereoscopy are shown and in Section 6 discussion and conclusions are presented.

2. Theoretical background

Let us briefly review the relevant geometrical concepts of the pinhole camera model and of epipolar geometry.

2.1 Pinhole camera

A point $M = (X,Y,Z,1)^T$ in homogeneous coordinates in a world frame reference and the correspondent point $m = (x,y,1)^T$ on the image plane of a camera are related by a projective transformation matrix:

$$sm = \mathbf{P}M \tag{1}$$

here s is a scale factor and $\mathbf{P}$ is a 3x4 projective matrix that can be decomposed as:

$$\mathbf{P} = \mathbf{A}[\mathbf{R}|\mathbf{t}] \tag{2}$$

where $\mathbf{A}$ is the 3x4 matrix of the internal parameters of the camera:

$$\mathbf{A} = \begin{bmatrix} f\alpha & \gamma & c_x & 0 \\ 0 & f\beta & c_y & 0 \\ 0 & 0 & f & 0 \end{bmatrix} \tag{3}$$

with (c_x, c_y) the optical centre of the camera, f its focal length, α and β take into account the pixel physical dimensions and γ encodes the angle between x and y axis of the CCD (skew) and is usually set at 0, i.e. perpendicular axes. The matrix $[\mathbf{R}|\mathbf{t}]$ is a matrix relating the camera coordinate system with the world coordinate one, i.e. the camera position $\mathbf{t}$ and rotation matrix $\mathbf{R}$:

$$[\mathbf{R}|\mathbf{t}] = \begin{bmatrix} \mathbf{R} & \mathbf{t} \\ \mathbf{0}_3^T & 1 \end{bmatrix}. \tag{4}$$

2.2 Epipolar geometry

Let's now consider two images of the same three dimensional scene as taken by two cameras at two different viewpoints (see Fig. 1). Epipolar geometry defines the imaging geometry of two cameras, either a stereoscopic system or a single moving camera. Given a three dimensional point M and its projections m and m' on the two focal planes of the cameras, the three points define a plane Π which intersects the two image planes at the epipolar lines l_m and $l_{m'}$ while e and e' are the epipoles, i.e. the image point where the optical centre of the other camera projects itself. The key point is the so called epipolar constraint which simply states that if the object point in one of the two images is in m, then its corresponding image point in the other image should lay along the epipolar line $l_{m'}$ Such a constraint can be described in terms of a 3x3 fundamental matrix through the:

$$m'^T \mathbf{F} m = 0. \tag{5}$$

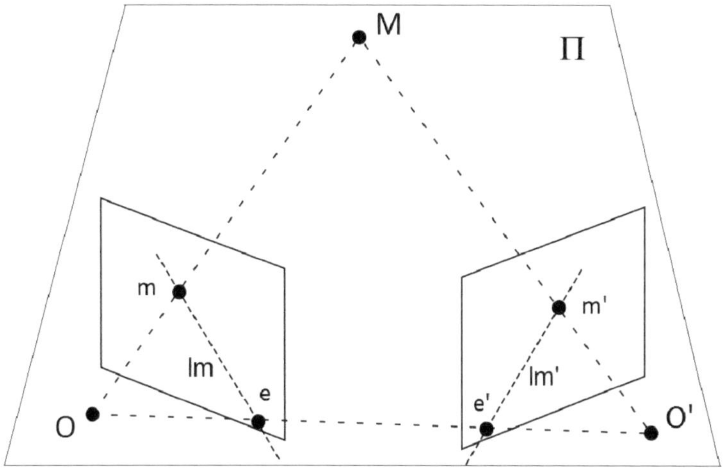

Fig. 1. Epipolar geometry.

The fundamental matrix **F** contains the intrinsic parameters of both cameras and the rigid transform of one camera with respect to the other and thus describes the relation between correspondences in terms of pixel coordinates. A similar relation can be found for the so called essential matrix where the intrinsic parameters of the cameras are not considered and the relation between correspondences is in terms of homogeneous coordinates. The algorithms for the estimation of epipolar geometry deal with actual pixel positions as produced by actual lenses and cameras. Therefore the interest of such algorithms is in the fundamental matrix rather than in the essential one. The standard approach for the computation of the fundamental matrix is based on the solution of a homogeneous system of equations in terms of the nine unknowns of the matrix **F**:

$$\mathbf{Zf} = 0 \tag{6}$$

where

$$\mathbf{f} = (f_1, f_2, f_3, f_4, f_5, f_6, f_7, f_8, f_9)^T \tag{7}$$

and

$$Z = \begin{pmatrix} x'_1x_1 & x'_1y_1 & x'_1 & y'_1x_1 & y'_1y_1 & y'_1 & x_1 & y_1 & 1 \\ \vdots & \vdots & \vdots & \vdots & \vdots & \vdots & \vdots & \vdots & \vdots \\ x'_nx_n & x'_ny_n & x'_n & y'_nx_n & y'_ny_n & y'_n & x_n & y_n & 1 \end{pmatrix}. \tag{8}$$

If nine or more correspondences are known the system is overdetermined and a solution can be sought in a least square sense; in a subsequent step, from the found fundamental matrix, the geometrical information is derived, exploiting the knowledge about the two camera matrices (equation 3). The number of independent unknowns varies among the different approaches employed for the computation. Some approaches don't take into account the additional rank-two constraint on the fundamental matrix (8 point algorithms) and some do (7 point algorithms). Naturally the former considers the rank constraint in a subsequent phase; finally the solution is derived with an unknown scale factor. Let us now suppose that the rigid motion of one camera with respect to the other is *a-priori* known, it is then possible to build directly the fundamental matrix. Let us consider the essential matrix **E** defined as (Huang & Faugeras, 1989):

$$\mathbf{E} = \mathbf{TR} \tag{9}$$

and

$$\mathbf{T} = \begin{pmatrix} 0 & -t_z & t_y \\ t_z & 0 & -t_x \\ -t_y & t_x & 0 \end{pmatrix} \tag{10}$$

here (t_x, t_y, t_z) is the translation vector and **R** the rotation matrix. It is possible to rewrite the equation for the fundamental matrix using **E** and taking into account the intrinsic parameters matrix **A**, as

$$\mathbf{F} = (\mathbf{A}^T)^{-1}\mathbf{TRA}^{-1}. \tag{11}$$

This equation holds if the intrinsic parameters matrix is equal for both cameras, i.e. a single moving camera is considered as in the ego-motion problem. In the case of stereoscopic imaging, there will be two different matrices ($\mathbf{A}_L$, $\mathbf{A}_R$), one for each of the cameras considered and the equation would be:

$$\mathbf{F} = (\mathbf{A}_L^T)^{-1}\mathbf{TRA}_R^{-1}. \tag{12}$$

In practical terms the relation linking the correspondences to the epipolar lines can be considered from two different perspectives. On one side it helps in correctly finding a correspondence to a given pixel since it will lay along the relative epipolar line, on the other side if a given match, obtained with some matching algorithm, is far from the epipolar line relative to the considered pixel, it will be incorrect, i.e. an outlier.

3. State of the art

As described in Section 2 the starting point for epipolar geometry estimation is represented by a set of correspondences between two images of the same scene as taken from different viewpoints. The existing techniques to exploit this pairwise information for fundamental matrix estimation can be classified in three broad classes: linear, iterative and robust. Longuet-Higgins in 1981 (Longuet-Higgins, 1981) opened the way to the computation of scene reconstruction from epipolar geometry through a linear approach. The basic procedure is the so called Eight-Point Algorithm, an algorithm of low complexity but prone to great sensitivity to noise in the data, i.e. error in the pixel position of the correspondences, and to the possible presence of outliers, i.e. incorrectly matched points. The outliers are usually due to error in feature detection and in matching and are in large disagreement with the inliers, i.e. the correctly matched points. Further refinement by Hartley (Hartley, 1995) allowed a sensible amelioration of the original algorithm through a simple normalization of image data. The linear approach solves a set of linear equations relating the correspondences through the fundamental matrix, i.e. solves equation (6). If a large number of correspondences is available, the solution is sought in a least square sense or through eigen analysis determining the fundamental matrix through eigen values and vectors, see (Torr & Murray, 1997). The iterative methods basically try to minimize some kind of error signal and can be classified in two groups: those minimizing a geometrical distance between points, and their is corresponding epipolar lines and those based on the gradient. The most widely used geometrical distances are the Euclidean distance and the Sampson one. They both measure with slightly different means the distance between a correspondence and its relative epipolar line in a symmetric way. Since two are the correspondences, the distance from the first one to the epipolar line originating from the other is computed and then the positions are reversed and the distance of the second from the epipolar line originating from the first one is computed and added to the former. Finally all the contribution are added up and considered in an average value. The minimization can be carried out with different approaches: classical gradient descent, Levenberg-Marquardt or more refined ones such as the Newton-Raphson technique (Chojnacki et al., 2000; 2004) The main drawback of iterative methods is represented by their incapability to correctly treat outliers. Moreover the iterative methods compute in a intensive way, even if with more accuracy than the linear methods. Finally robust methods are those methods able to cope with outliers and noise, maintaining a relative good accuracy. Most of them are based on statistical methods used to pick a subset of all the available correspondences yielding the best linear or iterative estimation of the fundamental matrix. The basic idea is that if a sufficient number of random extractions of correspondences subsets is performed, eventually a good one, i.e. one composed of inliers only with a limited noise, will be picked out. This implies a large number of linear or iterative estimations, but on a limited number of correspondences. Following (Hu et al., 2008) the best known robust methods are LMedS (Least Median of Squares) (Zhang, 1998), RANSAC (RANdom SAmple Consensus) (Torr & Murray, 1997), MLESAC (Maximum Likelihood Estimation SAmple Consensus) (Torr & Zisserman, 2000) and MAPSAC (Maximum A Posteriori SAmple Consensus) (Torr, 2002). LMedS and RANSAC randomly sample some subset of seven matching points in order to estimate, with a linear approach, the model parameters and use additional statistical methods to derive a minimal number of samples needed since all possible subset can not be considered to save time; the difference between the two is the technique used to determine the best result: on one side the median distance between points and epipolar lines on the other the number of inliers. MLESAC is an improvement over RANSAC and MAPSAC is a further improvement over MLESAC. It must be here noted that there is an important drawback in robust methods: they are usually not repeatable. Since they aleatorily select points there is no certainty that any of these algorithms on a given pair of images will yield the same result if made run more than once. A side effect of this is that it sometimes happens that even if accurate from a numerical point of view (error value) a robust algorithm does not always properly model the epipolar geometry. In (Armangué & Salvi, 2003) a full comparison both theoretical and experimental among many approaches of the three different categories is presented in depth. Besides these classical algorithms, more recently a philosophically different approach has been proposed. Several authors (Chai & De Ma, 1998; Hu et al., 2002; 2004; 2008) have employed a genetic computing paradigm to estimate epipolar geometry. The main idea is to employ an evolutionary approach in order to choose, among the available correspondences, the optimal, or sub-optimal, set of eight points by which the epipolar geometry estimation can be carried out with minimal error. In these genetic approaches each individual is represented by a set of pairs and the algorithm is able to change a subset of these during the temporal evolution, measuring the fitness of each individual with the already mentioned geometrical distance functions. Therefore these evolutionary approaches can be considered part of the robust algorithms family. In conclusion all of the algorithms in literature start with the the available correspondences and try to estimate the fundamental matrix solving the epipolar constraint equation, trying to avoid with different means the faulty matches. The roto-translation between the cameras is then computed with a single value decomposition (SVD) method. It is interesting to note that no constraints are placed on the fundamental matrix from geometrical considerations on the final roto-translation. In other words the fundamental matrix is computed regardless to the possibility that the resulting roto-translation between the cameras may be physically incorrect or even impossible.

4. Epipolar geometry estimation using a genetic approach

As briefly reminded in Section 3 the genetic approaches found in the literature evolve their characteristics in order to pin out the set of correspondences data point able to perform best in a standard computation of the geometric parameters. The idea underlying the present algorithm is different, the evolutionary approach is exploited in a more *natural* way. A set of solutions for the epipolar geometry estimation (i.e. a set of roto-translations) is hypothesized, then it is tested against the available experimental data points, genetically evolving the initial hypotheses into better and better ones until an optimal or near optimal solution is reached. The evolutionary algorithm goes through the standard logical steps of any genetic approach. An individual is defined and a fitness function is designed in order to measure the individual ability to solve the task. Finally a reproduction phase is implemented inserting some kind of variability in the genetic pool.

4.1 The individual

Each individual of the population of N estimators of the epipolar geometry is implicitly a possible fundamental matrix and is implemented by a vector of six real values representing the chromosomes:

$$i_i = [\theta, \phi, \psi, t_\alpha, t_\beta, \sigma] \tag{13}$$

these chromosomes are the three angles of a three dimensional rotation (the pitch, roll and yaw angles), two direction cosines for the translation and a sixth value that is the standard deviation of a normal distribution used for the chromosome mutation, as it will be explained in more detail later. The translation is here described with the two direction cosine only, since the solution for any epipolar geometry estimation is always found with an unknown scale factor. In other words the epipolar geometry is insensitive to scale, a scene can be viewed either at a close distance with a short translation between cameras or at far with a large translation, with no difference on the fundamental matrix. In order to superimpose a metric to the environment a simple calibration step considering a known distance measurement about the image must be added.

4.2 The fitness function

Each individual is used to compute a fundamental matrix following equation (11) if considering an ego-motion case or equation (12) for stereoscopy. Each individual must be tested against the environment, i.e. the correspondences, employing a fitness function, whose design is critical for the success of the algorithm. The implemented function takes into account the following two aspects of the problem: on one side the interest in having a low geometric error between correspondences and their relative epipolar lines and on the other in maximizing the number of correct correspondences, i.e. the inliers. Thus the fitness function has been defined as the ratio between the number of inliers found and the total symmetric transfer error:

$$f = \frac{n_{inliers}}{E} \tag{14}$$

where

$$E = \sum_{i=0}^{N} [d(x'_i, Fx_i) + d(x_i, F^T x'_i)] \tag{15}$$

is the symmetric transfer error and $d(x,y)$ is the standard Euclidean distance. This error is the sum of the distances between a given point and the epipolar line relative to its corresponding point plus the symmetric distance obtained switching the points; finally it is summed over the full set of available correspondences. Naturally it may be convenient to use a relative error measure in order to weight in an opportune way those correspondences which are very close to each other and that may be less reliable in the geometry estimation, using:

$$E = \sum_{i=0}^{N} \frac{d(x_i', Fx_i) + d(x_i, F^T x_i')}{d(x_i, x_i')}. \tag{16}$$

The number of inliers is defined as the number of correspondences for which

$$[d(x_i', Fx_i) + d(x_i, F^T x_i')] < \lambda \tag{17}$$

where λ is a threshold, empirically determined. As an alternative it can be also employed the Sampson distance, defined as:

$$E = \sum_{i=0}^{N} \frac{(x_i' F x_i)^2}{(Fx_i')_1^2 + (Fx_i)_2^2 + (F^T x_i')_1^2 + (F^T x_i)_2^2} \tag{18}$$

here the subscripts indicate the k-th entry of the vector. The experiments have shown that the results in the algorithm performance are practically insensitive to the used error distance.

4.3 Reproduction

At each time step a subset of individuals, represented by the best 20%, is allowed to reproduce. This subset gives rise to a new generation of full 100% individuals through a five fold replication of the chosen subset, affected by a mutation mechanism in order to search further in the solution space. This mechanism is implemented with a random extraction of a number from a normal distribution as the displacement around the current value of a single chromosome of the individual. The standard deviation of the normal distribution employed is that of the sixth chromosome in the individual, see equation (13). Thus this mutation amplitude becomes itself part of the genetic algorithm optimization strategy. In more detail, of the six chromosomes one of the five geometrically meaningful is chosen with equal probability. This is mutated adding a value randomly extracted with a normal distribution of zero mean value and standard deviation as indicated by the sixth chromosome,

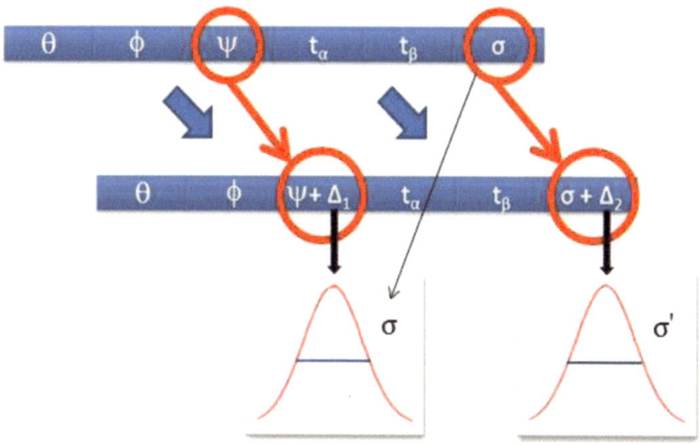

Fig. 2. Mutation implementation.

see Figure 2. The sixth chromosome is then itself updated through a similar mutation with a random extraction of normal distribution with zero mean and a fixed $\sigma' = 0.4$. The individual with the overall best fitness is always retained at each time step.

4.4 Outliers detection and exclusion

A very important issue to discuss here is relative to the outliers. As seen in Section 3 one of the main concerns of the algorithms in literature is the individuation of outliers and their elimination for an accurate estimation of epipolar geometry. These outliers originate from inaccurate performance of the image processing algorithms resulting in errors in feature detection and in matching. In the presented approach the fitness function computation (equation (14)) easily and naturally shows which of the point pairs are outliers, as it will be experimentally presented in Section 5. After a few iterations the error distribution over the experimental pairs relative to the best individual, computed with equation (15), clearly shows which of the points are inliers and which outliers, permitting the limitation, in the following time steps, of the number of pairs used for the fitness function computation. In other words the algorithm is capable to perform the detection and exclusion of outliers in a fully automatic way. This detection is performed through a threshold value to isolate those correspondences yielding a too large error in the best individual. The cutoff value can be chosen as three times the standard deviation in the error distribution, since the expected value for the error is null.

4.5 Algorithm flow

The algorithm flow is as follows.

Initialization: a population of 100 individuals is created with random values for θ, ϕ, ψ, t_α, t_β and $\sigma = 10$.

Main loop:

1. For each individual
   (a) compute **F** (equation (11) or (12))
   (b) compute fitness on the available number of N correspondences (equation (14))
2. order the population with ascending fitness
3. take the 20 best individuals and reproduce with mutation, keeping the best individual
4. goto 1

After a given number of iterations the outliers are removed (K) and the set of used correspondences reduced to $M = N - K$. The genetic algorithm then restarts with this reduced set of correspondences. Presently the genetic algorithm removes its outliers only once and is stopped after a given number of iterations has passed without an improvement in error.

5. Experimental data

In the following experimental data in the two cases of ego-motion computation and stereoscopy are provided. The proposed algorithm has been tested on both synthetic and real images. The synthetic data have been prepared projecting a grid of three dimensional points onto two image planes displaced one with respect to the other via equations (1) and (2), inserting given amounts of Gaussian noise when needed. Also for the purpose of

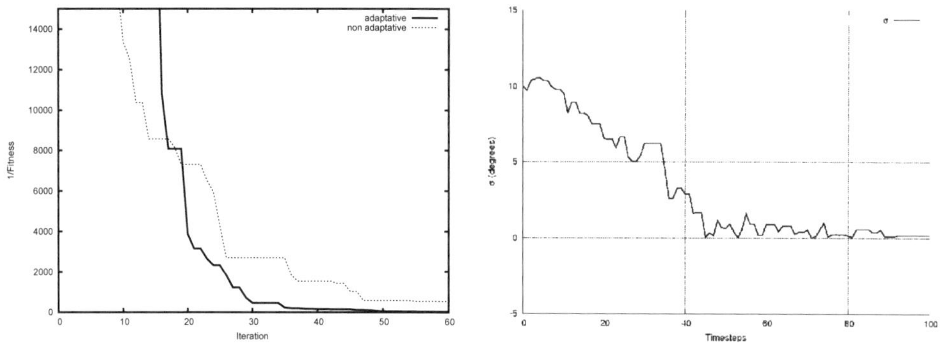

(a) Adaptative vs non adaptative. (b) Mutation amplitude (σ) as a function of time.

Fig. 3. Algorithm convergence and mutation amplitude.

testing, different quantities of inliers have been added. The real images data come from different sources: some of them derive from a paper (Armangué & Salvi, 2003) presenting a comparative study on epipolar geometry estimation, some have been acquired in the ENEA Robotics Lab using different kinds of calibrated cameras and of moving robots, some are from publicly available data-sets and finally one has been shot in everyday life.

Let us first consider the features of the present approach. The rapid convergence of the genetic algorithm is plotted in Fig. 3(a) where the inverse of the average fitness of the entire population is shown as a function of time for a typical run over synthetic data. Here two different modes are compared: one plot is relative to an adaptive σ in the individual, i.e. undergoing a genetic optimisazion as described in Section 4, while the second is relative to a fixed σ value. It is evident that the adaptivity is an advantage in terms of speed of convergence. The reason for such a behaviour can be understood examining Figure 3(b). Here the time evolution of the mutation amplitude σ is plotted as a function of time for the former of the two modes described. The decreasing behaviour shows how the algorithm searches the solution space at first in a coarse way, with large *jumps* and, as the error decreases, the search becomes finer and finer. This variability accounts for a more efficient search in the solution space, while a constant amplitude in the mutation algorithm forces the algorithm to *jump away* from a good solution, rendering the convergence much longer. In (Armangué & Salvi, 2003) a very interesting comparison is presented among most of the epipolar geometry estimators. Since the relative experimental data are freely available over the Internet a direct comparison of the presented algorithm is possible. In Fig. 4 is shown the robustness of the algorithm against the adding of Gaussian noise to the data point location. The error of the best individual increases linearly with the amount of added noise. These data are compared to the available results relative to the two best performing robust algorithms reviewed in (Armangué & Salvi, 2003), i.e. MAPSAC and LMedS. The presented approach performs better. The capability of the algorithm to identify and remove outliers is evidenced in Figure 5. Here it is plotted the ordered error value for the best individual as a function of the correspondence pair. The plot can be easily divided in two parts: on the left the inliers, with a limited amount of error, on the right the outliers, with a large error. From this plot appears evident how it is possible to separate the two sets via an opportune threshold. If it is assumed that the expected value for the error should be null and that a Gaussian distribution may describe the behaviour, a tentative threshold can be placed at three times the standard deviation in the error distribution. Naturally a limited number of outliers must be assumed. The robustness

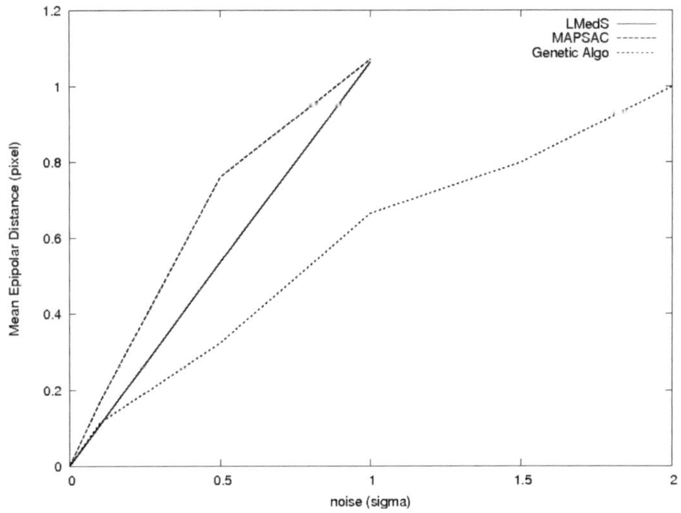

Fig. 4. Performance as a function of noise.

against the presence of outliers is further shown in Table 1 where the algorithm insensitivity is evident. In Figure 6 is shown the relevant data to assess the repeatability of the presented approach. The graphs are relative to 100 runs of the algorithm with different random seeds, i.e. initial conditions, in a real image case (the *kitchen* one, Figure 7(f)). They present the distributions of differences from the average value for the five physically meaningful values of the approach, namely θ, ϕ, ψ, t_α and t_β. Even if the number of runs is not large, the distributions can be considered Gaussians with a null expected value, moreover the spread of the differences is very limited, less than one hundredth of degree for the rotation angles and half a degree for the direction cosines of the translation vector. These data show that the found

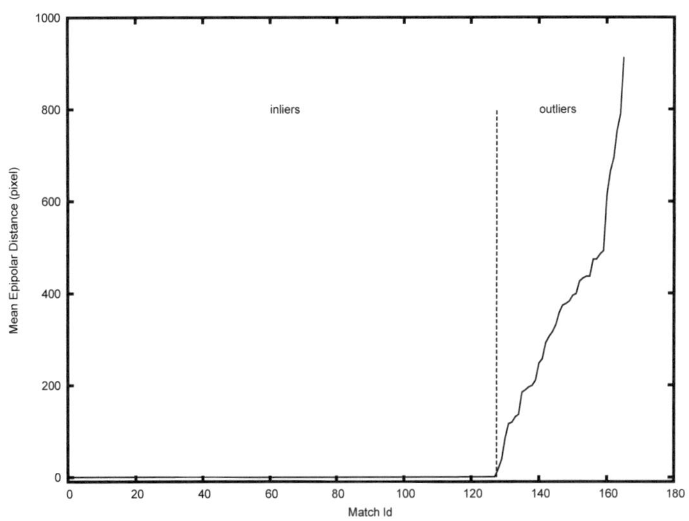

Fig. 5. Error as a function of correspondences for the best individual. The outliers are clearly visible.

Outliers	GeneticAlgo
10%	0.193
	0.123
20%	0.236
	0.120
30%	0.169
	0.116

Table 1. Performance as a function of percentage of outliers. Every cell show the mean and standard deviation of the error between points and epipolar lines in pixels.

solution is always the same, i.e. that repeatability is no concern for this approach. While robust approaches may found different subsets of correspondences for a given error limit, yielding different fundamental matrices, this algorithm when repeated simply changes the starting point for the search for an extremisation of the same error function (or fitness function), always yielding a near optimal solution in a limited neighbourhood of the actual optimum, properly modelling epipolar geometry. In Table 2 it is presented the algorithm performance on the real images shown in Figure 7. The data are compared to those of the LMeds and MAPSAC robust algorithms. The performance of the presented approach is similar in most cases with that of the published algorithms and with markedly better performances on the *mobile robot* image (Figure 7(b)). The reason of the choice of these two algorithms among those in (Armangué & Salvi, 2003) is the combination of two positive features: they performed well and they yielded the correct epipolar geometry for the used images. As above pointed out, it may actually happen that a robust algorithm gives a good performance in terms of error but with a mistaken geometry. In Figure 8 an example on real images taken by one of the surface robots is shown together with the capability of the algorithm to remove outliers. In this figure most of them are in the central part of the image. In Figure 9 an example of an everyday life, large baseline stereogram is shown. In Figure 9(a) and 9(b) are visible the epipolar lines. In

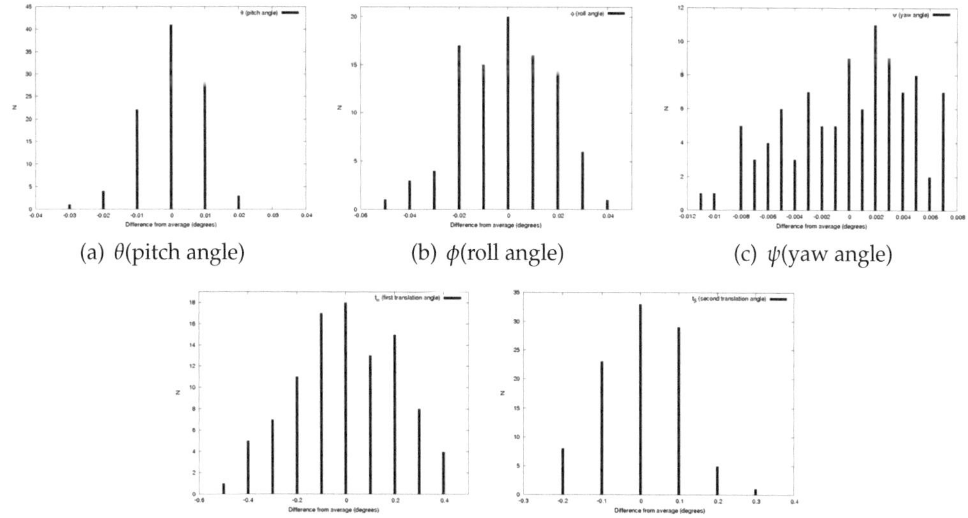

(a) θ(pitch angle) (b) ϕ(roll angle) (c) ψ(yaw angle)

(d) t_α (first direction cosine) (e) t_β (second direction cosine)

Fig. 6. The distributions of distances in pixels from average values over 100 runs.

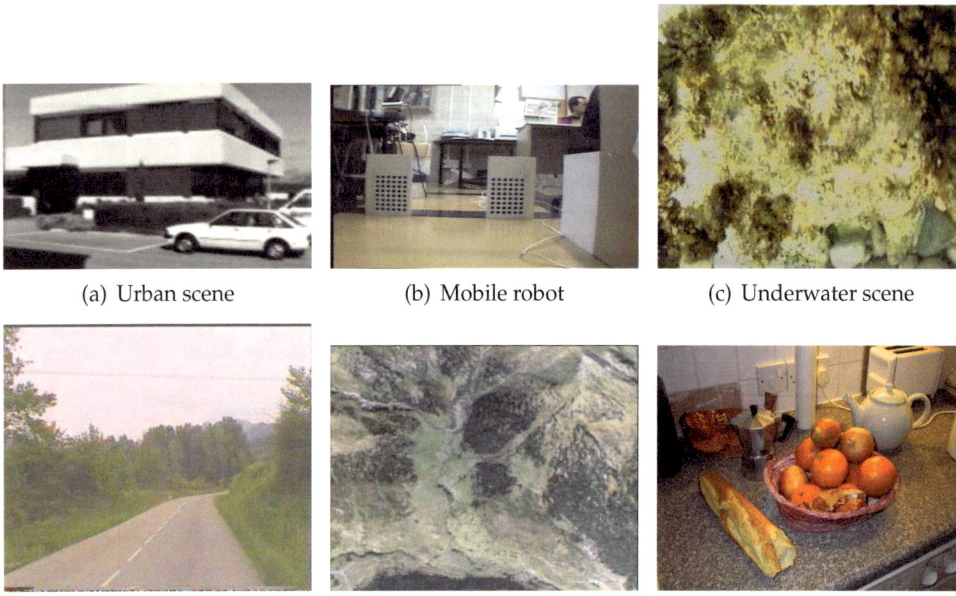

(a) Urban scene (b) Mobile robot (c) Underwater scene

(d) Road scene (e) Aerial view (f) Kitchen scene

Fig. 7. The real images set from (Armangué & Salvi, 2003)

the second one is also visible the epipole, i.e. the actual location of the centre of projection of the other camera. In Figure 9(c) are shown the displacements of the correspondences from one image to the other. In Figure 10 two classical stereograms and their epipolar lines are presented as computed by the presented approach. The algorithm computed data for Figure 10(b) are: $\theta = 0.0000$, $\phi = 0.0049$, $\psi = 0.0000$, $t_\alpha = 90.0373$ and $t_\beta = -0.0003$ with an average symmetric transfer error of $E = 0.1819$ pixels, in optimal agreement with the actual values, representing a perfect lateral shift.

Image	LMedS	MAPSAC	GeneticAlgo
urban	0.319	0.440	0.393
	0.269	0.348	0.314
mobile robot	1.559	1.274	0.490
	2.715	2.036	0.715
underwater	0.847	1.000	0.848
	0.740	0.761	0.792
road	0.609	0.471	0.433
	0.734	0.403	0.491
aerial	0.149	0.257	0.432
	0.142	0.197	0.308
kitchen	0.545	0.582	0.543
	0.686	0.717	0.571

Table 2. Real images results. Comparison with Lmeds and MAPSAC from (Armangué & Salvi, 2003). Every cell show the mean and standard deviation of the average discrepancy between points and epipolar lines in pixels.

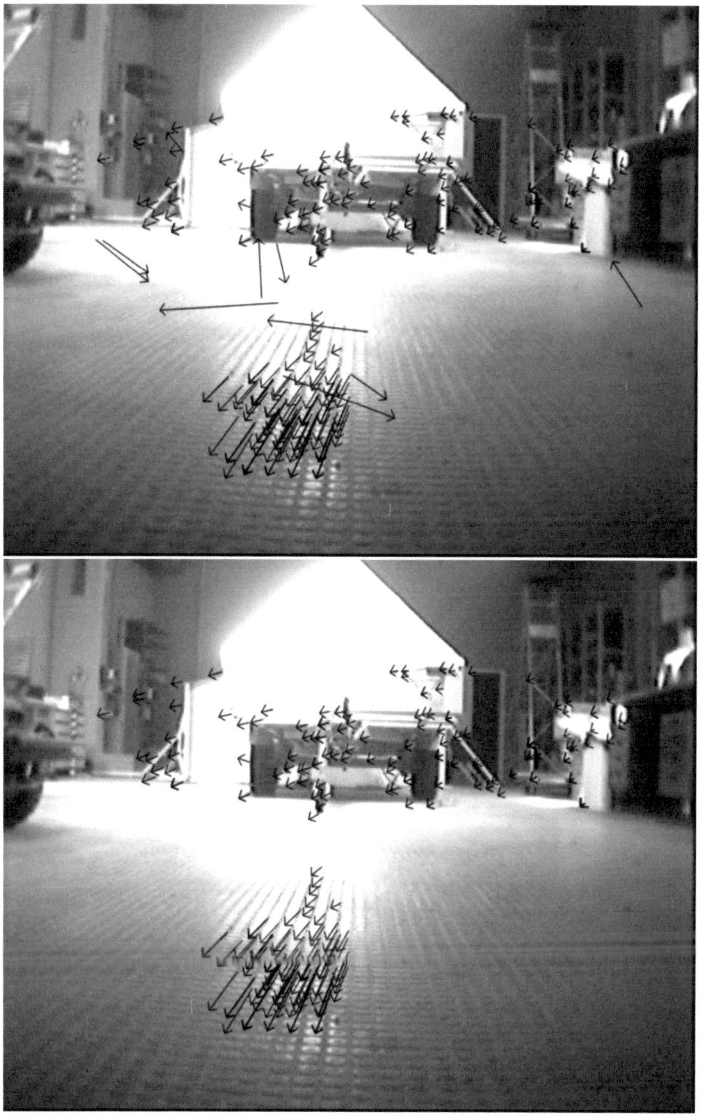

Fig. 8. An example of real image and the outliers removal.

6. Discussion and conclusions

A novel genetic approach for the estimation of epipolar geometry has been here presented. The classical algorithms take as input the whole experimental data, the correspondences, and from them compute the fundamental matrix and then the rigid roto-translation from one camera to the other. The presented approach, instead, tackles the problem in the opposite way, it hypothesize an initial set of random roto-translations and then genetically optimise it against a fitness function computed over the correspondences set. The advantages of the described approach are represented by the following points. The algorithm is sensibly simpler than the ones in literature allowing a more limited computing intensiveness. The convergence is quickly reached. This is especially true if considering the ego-motion problem. If the

(a) Left image

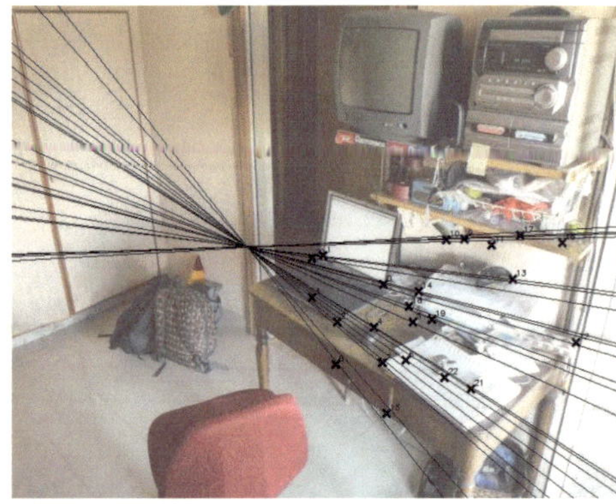

(b) Right image

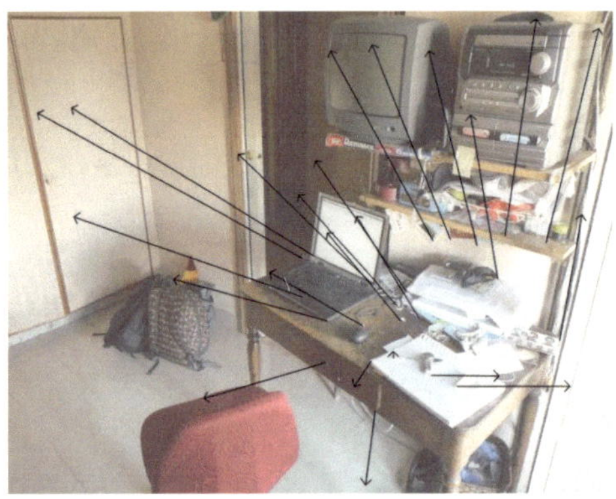

(c) Optical flow

Fig. 9. An example of large baseline stereoscopy on real images.

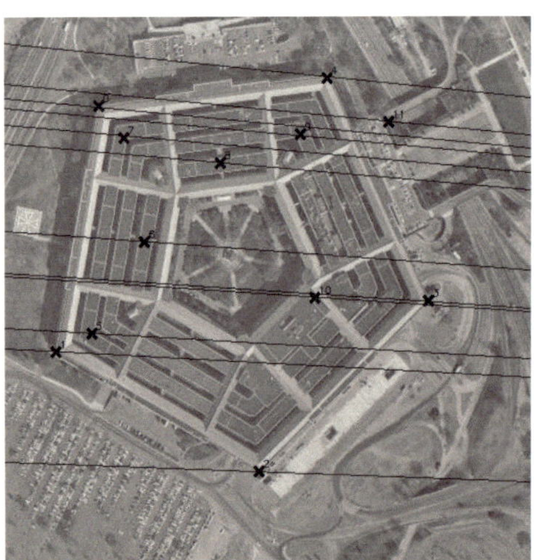

(a) Aerial view of Pentagon.

(b) A synthetic corridor.

Fig. 10. Two classical examples of stereograms.

epipolar geometry is exploited to measure the motion of a camera in the three dimensional space, the solution search space of the genetic algorithm can be dramatically reduced. If the camera at the preceding time step was heading in a given direction with a given pose, at the following one will head toward a direction and with a pose not much dissimilar from the preceding ones, with a very high probability. This means that the initial population of roto-translation can be tuned on the basis of the near motion history of the camera and the algorithm will quickly converge to the right solution. With a standard approach the motion information would have been of no use, since the epipolar geometry estimation would have been performed blindly, processing all the data points. In different words, using the present approach it is possible to add constraints on the geometry of the camera system. The genetic design of the algorithm is responsible for the capability to automatically ignore outliers during the computation. The fitness computation is based on the geometric distance between points and epipolar lines relative to their correspondences. If a given roto-translation is the one accurately describing the geometry, then all the correct correspondences will have a quasi null distance and the outliers will yield a large one. This mechanism can be exploited to automatically pin out the outliers from the set of available experimental correspondences also implying the possibility to reduce the data set to the inliers only, gaining in precision and on the quantity of data to process. The results in terms of performance are good. In Section 5 it has been shown that the error is not larger than that of the best performing algorithm presently available in literature, that the robustness against noise in the data is good and also the insensitivity against the presence of outliers among the data point is high naturally. The algorithm has a high degree of repeatability, reaching the same solution even if started from different initial conditions. This feature must be compared to some difficulties in the robust approaches to the same end. Future work will be carried out in the direction of tuning the genetic components of the algorithm and of code optimisation in order to obtain real time performances in the processing of video streams from PAL cameras. This in order to compute visual odometry for underwater robotic platforms, where such a solution may be of help since the number of exploitable sensors is limited. Under water the electromagnetic radio signals are rapidly damped and GPS can't be used, accelerometers or gyroscopes need numerical integration and thus present large errors, unless using expensive ones. Naturally also underwater video sequences are blurred and noisy and need some kind of pre processing, but still this may be a viable solution. Further work will be dedicated to the implementation of a full visual odometry system as a standalone device composed of a camera of the webcam class and of an embeddable computer of the genre of the Gumstix computer-on-module. This means the implementation of a feature extraction stage (e.g. using Harris angles), of an optical flow model (e.g. Lucas Kanade algorithm) and finally of the present algorithm completed with a metric calibration. From the point of view of epipolar geometry estimation in the stereoscopy field of application, further efforts will be devoted towards the exploitation of the computed geometry in order to match targets across different cameras for the purpose of video surveillance and target tracking in cluttered environments.

7. References

Zanela, A. & Taraglio, S. (2002). A Cellular Neural Network Based Optical Range Finder, *Int. J. of Circuit Theory and Applications*, vol 30, pp 271 – 285.

Caballero, F., Merino, L., Ferruz, J., Ollero, A. (2009). "Vision-based odometry and SLAM for medium and high altitude flying UAVs", *J. Intell. Robot Syst.*, vol 54, pp 137 – 161.

Arghaian, H & Cavallaro, A. (2009). "Multi-Camera Networks", *Academic Press*, Burlington

MA.
Longuet-Higgins, H.C. (1981). "A computer algorithm for reconstructing a scene from two projections",*Nature*, vol. 293, pp 133 – 135.
Hartley, R.I. (1995). "In defence of the 8-point algorithm", in *Proc. of the Intl. Conf. on Computer Vision*, pp 1064 – 1070.
Torr, P.H.S. & Murray, D.W. (1997). "The development and comparison of robust methods for estimating the fundamental matrix", *Int. J. Comput. Vision*, vol 24 (3), pp 271 – 300.
Chojnacki, W, Brooks, M.J., van den Hengel, A., Gawley, D. (2000). "On the fitting of surfaces to data with covariances", *IEEE Trans. PAMI*, vol. 22 (11), pp 1294 – 1303.
Chojnacki, W, Brooks, M.J., van den Hengel, A., Gawley, D. (2004). "A new constrained parameter estimator for computer vision applications", *Image Vision Comput.*, vol. 22 (2), pp 85 – 91.
Hu, M., McMenemy, K., Ferguson, S., Dodds, G., Yuan, B. (2008). "Epipolar geometry estimation based on evolutionary agents", *Pattern Recognition*, vol 41, pp 575 – 591.
Zhang, Z. (1998). "Determining the epipolar geometry and its uncertainty: a review", *Int. J. Comput. Vision*, vol 27 (2), pp 161 – 198.
Torr, P.H.S., Zisserman, A. (2000)."MLESAC: a new robust estimator with application to estimating image geometry", *Comput. Vision Image Understanding*, vol 78, pp 138 – 156.
Torr, P.H.S. (2002). "Bayesian model estimation and selection for epipolar geometry and generic manifold fitting", *Int. J. Comput. Vision*, vol 50 (1), pp 35 – 61.
Armangué, X., Salvi, J. (2003). "Overall view regarding fundamental matrix estimation", *Image and Vision Comp.*, vol 21, pp 205 – 220.
Chai, J., De Ma, S. (1998). "Robust epipolar geometry estimation using genetic algorithm", *Pattern Recognition Letters*, Vol 19, pp 829 – 838.
Hu, M., Xing, Q., Yuan, B., Tang, X. (2002). "Epipolar geometry estimation based on genetic algorithm under different strategies", in *Proc. of 6th Intl Conf. on Signal Processing*, pp 885 – 888.
Hu, M., Yuan, B., Dodds, G., Tang, X.(2004). "Robust method of recovering epipolar geometry using messy genetic algorithm", in *Proc. of the First Canadian Conf. on Comp. and Robot Vision*, pp 164 – 171.
Huang, T.S., Faugeras, O.D. (1989). "Some properties of the E matrix in two-view motion estimation", *IEEE Trans. PAMI*, vol 11 (12), pp 1310 – 1312.

2

Impact of Wavelets and Multiwavelets Bases on Stereo Correspondence Estimation Problem

Asim Bhatti and Saeid Nahavandi
Centre for Intelligent Systems Research, Deakin University
Australia

1. Introduction

Finding correct corresponding points from more than one perspective views in stereo vision is subject to number of potential problems, such as occlusion, ambiguity, illuminative variations and radial distortions. A number of algorithms has been proposed to address the problems as well as the solutions, in the context of stereo correspondence estimation. The majority of them can be categorized into three broad classes i.e. local search algorithms (LA) L. Di Stefano (2004); T. S. Huang (1994); Wang et al. (2006), global search algorithms (GA) Y. Boykov & Zabih (2001); Scharstein & Szeliski (1998) and hierarchical iterative search algorithms (HA) A. Bhatti (2008); C. L. Zitnick (2000). The algorithms belonging to the LA class try to establish correspondences over locally defined regions within the image space. Correlations techniques are commonly employed to estimate the similarities between the stereo image pair using pixel intensities, sensitive to illuminative variations. LA perform well in the presence of rich textured areas but have tendency of relatively lower performance in the featureless regions. Furthermore, local search using correlation windows usually lead to poor performance across the boundaries of image regions. On the other hand, algorithms belonging to GA group deals with the stereo correspondence estimation as a global cost-function optimization problem. These algorithms usually do not perform local search but rather try to find a correspondence assignment that minimizes a global objective function. GA group algorithms are generally considered to possess better performance over the rest of the algorithms. Despite of the fact of their overall better performance, these algorithms are not free of shortcomings and are dependent on how well the cost function represents the relationship between the disparity and some of its properties like smoothness, regularity. Moreover, how close that cost function representation is to the real world scenarios. Furthermore, the smoothness parameters makes disparity map smooth everywhere which may lead to poor performance at image discontinuities. Another disadvantage of these algorithms is their computational complexity, which makes them unsuitable for real-time and close-to-realtime applications. Third group of algorithms uses the concept of multi-resolution analysis Mallat (1999) in addressing the problem of stereo correspondence. In multi-resolution analysis, as is obvious from the name, the input signal (*image*) is divided into different resolutions, i.e. *scales and spaces* Mallat (1999); A. Witkin & Kass (1987), before estimation of the correspondence. This group of algorithms do not explicitly state a global function that is to be minimized, but rather try to establishes correspondences in a hierarchical manner J. R. Bergen & Hingorani (1992); Q'ingxiong Yang & Nister (2006), similar to iterative optimization algorithms Daubechies (1992). Generally, stereo correspondences established in lower resolutions are propagated to higher resolutions in an iterative manner with mechanisms to estimate and correct errors along the way. This iterative error correction minimizes the requirements for explicit post processing of the estimated outcomes. In this work, the goal is to provide a brief overview of the techniques reported within the context of stereo correspondence estimation and wavelets/multiwavelets theory and highlight the deficiencies inherited in those techniques. Using this knowledge of inherited shortcomings, we propose a comprehensive algorithm addressing the aforementioned issues in detailed manner. The presented work also focuses on the use of multiwavelets basis that simultaneously posses properties of orthogonality, symmetry, high approximation order and short support, which is not possible in the wavelets case A. Bhatti (2002); Ozkaramanli et al. (2002). The presentation of this work is organized by providing some background knowledge and techniques using multiresolution analysis enforced by wavelets and multiwavelets theories. Introduction of wavelets/ multiwavelets transformation modulus maxima will be presented in section 3. A simple, however, comprehensive algorithm is presented next, followed by the presentation of some results using different wavelets and multiwavelets bases.

2. Wavelets / multiwavelets analysis in stereo vision: background

The multi-resolution analysis is generally performed by either Wavelets or Fourier analysis Mallat (1999; 1989; 1991). Wavelets analysis is relatively newer way of scale space representation of the signals and considered to be as fundamental as Fourier and a better alternative A. Mehmood (2001). One of the reasons that makes wavelet analysis more attractive to researchers is the availability and simultaneous involvement of a number of compactly supported bases for scale-space representation of signals, rather than infinitely long sine and cosine bases as in Fourier analysis David Capel (2003). Approximation order of the scaling and wavelet filters provide better approximation capabilities and can be adjusted according to input signal and image by selecting the appropriate bases. Other features of wavelet bases that play an important role in signal/ image processing application are their shape parameters, such as symmetric and asymmetric, and orthogonality (i.e. $\langle f_i, f_j \rangle = 0$ if $i \neq j$) and orthonormality (i.e. $\langle f_i, f_j \rangle = 1$ if $i = j$). All these parameters can be enforced at the same time in multiwavelets bases however is not possible in scaler wavelets case A. Bhatti (2002). Wavelet theory has been explored very little up to now in the context of stereo vision. To the best of author's knowledge, Mallat Mallat (1991); S. Mallat & Zhang (1993) was the first who used wavelet theory concept for image matching by using the zero-crossings of the wavelet transform coefficients to seek correspondence in image pairs. In S. Mallat & Zhang (1993) he also explored the the signal decomposition into linear waveforms and signal energy distribution in time-frequency plane. Afterwards, Unser M. Unser & Aldroubi (1993) used the concept of multi-resolution (coarse to fine) for image pattern registration using orthogonal wavelet pyramids with spline bases. Olive-Deubler-Boulin J. C. Olive & Boulin (1994) introduced a block matching method using orthogonal wavelet transform coefficients whereas X. Zhou & Dorrer (1994) performed image matching using orthogonal Haar wavelet bases. Haar wavelet bases are one of the first and simplest wavelet basis and posses very basic properties in terms of smoothness, approximation order Haar (1910), therefore are not well adapted for correspondence problem. In aforementioned algorithms, the common methodology adopted for stereo correspondence cost aggregation was based on the difference between the wavelet coefficients in the perspective views. This correspondence estimation suffers due to inherent problem of translation variance with the discrete wavelet transform. This means that wavelet transform coefficients of two shifted versions of the same image may not exhibit exactly similar pattern Cohen et al. (1998); Coifman & Donoho (1995). A more comprehensive use of wavelet theory based multi-resolution analysis for image matching was done by He-Pan in 1996 Pan (1996a;b). He took the application of wavelet theory bit further by introducing a complete stereo image matching algorithm using complex wavelet basis. In Pan (1996a) He-Pan explored many different properties of wavelet basis that can be well suited and adaptive to the stereo matching problem. One of the major weaknesses of his approach was the use of point to point similarity distance as a measure of stereo correspondences between wavelet coefficients as

$$SB_j((x,y),(\acute{x},\acute{y})) = |B_j(x,y) - \acute{B}_j(\acute{x},\acute{y})| \tag{1}$$

Similarity measure using point to point difference is very sensitive to noise that could be introduced due to many factors such as difference in gain, illumination, lens distortion, etc. A number of real and complex wavelet bases were used in both Pan (1996a;b) and transformation is performed using wavelet pyramid, commonly known by the name Mallat's dyadic wavelet filter tree (DWFT) Mallat (1999). Common problem with DWFT is the lack of translation and rotation invariance Cohen et al. (1998); Coifman & Donoho (1995) inherited due to the involvement of factor 2 down-sampling as is obvious from expressions 2 and 3.

$$S_A[n] = \sum_{-\infty}^{\infty} x[k]L[2n-k] \tag{2}$$

$$S_W[n] = \sum_{-\infty}^{\infty} x[k]H[2n+1-k] \tag{3}$$

Where L and H represent filters based on scaling function and wavelet coefficients Mallat (1999); Bhatti (2009). Furthermore similarity measures were applied on individual wavelet coefficients which is very sensitive to noise. In Esteban (2004), conjugate pairs of complex wavelet basis were used to address the issue of translation variance. Conjugate pairs of complex wavelet coefficients are claimed to provide translation invariant outcome, however increases the search space by twofold. Similarly, Magarey J. Magarey & Kingsbury (1998); J. Margary & dick (1998) introduced algorithms for motion estimation and image matching, respectively, using complex discrete *Gabor-like* quadrature mirror filters. Afterwards, Shi J. Margary & dick (1998) applied *sum of squared difference* technique on wavelet coefficients to estimate stereo correspondences. Shi uses translation invariant wavelet transformation for matching purposes, which is a step forward in the context of stereo vision and applications of wavelet. More to the wavelet theory, multi-wavelet theory evolved Shi et al. (2001) in early 1990s from wavelet theory and enhanced for more than a decade. Success of multiwavelets bases over scalar ones, stems from the fact that they can simultaneously posses the good properties of orthogonality, symmetry, high approximation order and short support, which is not possible in the scalar case Mallat (1999); A. Bhatti (2002); Ozkaramanli et al. (2002). Being a new theoretical evolution, multi-wavelets are still new and are not yet applied in many applications. In this work we will devise a new and generalized correspondence estimation technique based wavelets and multiwavelets analysis to provide a framework for further research in this particular context.

3. Wavelet and multiwavelets fundamentals

Classical wavelet theory is based on the dilation equations as given below

$$\phi(t) = \sum_h c_h \phi(Mt - h) \tag{4}$$

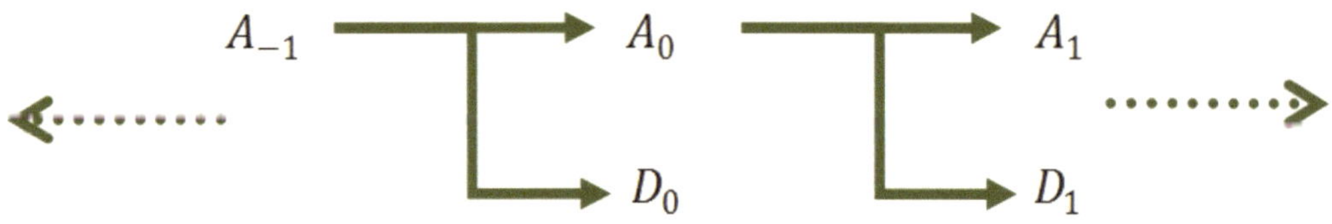

Fig. 1. wavelet theory based Multiresolution analysis

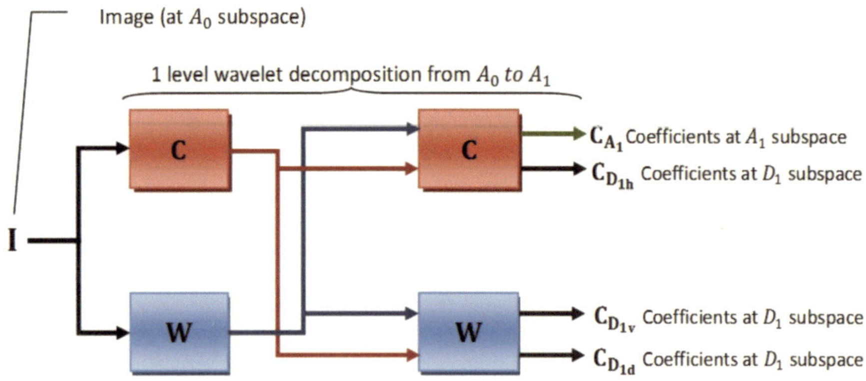

Fig. 2. Mallat's dyadic wavelet filter bank

$$\psi(t) = \sum_h w_h \phi(Mt - h) \tag{5}$$

Expressions (4) and (5) define that scaling and wavelet functions can be represented by the combination of scaled and translated version of the scaling function. Where c_h and w_h represents the scaling and wavelet coefficients which are used to perform discrete wavelet transforms using wavelet filter banks. Similar to scalar wavelet, multi-scaling functions satisfy the matrix dilation equation as

$$\Phi(t) = \sum_h C_h \Phi(Mt - h) \tag{6}$$

Similarly, for the multi-wavelets the matrix dilation equation can be expressed as

$$\Psi(t) = \sum_h W_h \Phi(Mt - h) \tag{7}$$

In equations 6 and 7, C_h and W_h are real and matrices of multi-filter coefficients. Generally only two band multiwavelets, i.e. $M = 2$, defining equal number of multi-wavelets as multi-scaling functions are used for simplicity. For more information, about the generation and applications of multi-wavelets with, desired approximation order and orthogonality, interested readers are referred to Mallat (1999); A. Bhatti (2002).

3.1 Multiresolution analysis

Wavelet transformation produces scale-space representation of the input signal by generating scaled version of the approximation space and the detail space possessing the properties as

$$\cdots A_{-1} \supset A_0 \supset A_1 \cdots \tag{8}$$

$$\overline{\bigcup_{-\infty}^{\infty} A_s} = L^2(R) \tag{9}$$

$$\bigcap_{-\infty}^{\infty} A_s = 0 \tag{10}$$

$$A_0 = A_1 \bigoplus D_1 \tag{11}$$

In expression (8) subspaces A_s are generated by the dilates of $\phi(Mt-h)$, whereas translates of $\phi(t-h)$ produces basis of the subspace A_0 that are linearly independent. A_s and D_s represents approximation and detail subspaces at lower scales and by direct sum constitutes the higher scale space A_{s-1}. In other words A_s and D_s are the sub-spaces of A_{s-1}. Expression (11) can be better visualize by the Figure 1. Multi-resolution can be generated not just in the scalar context, i.e. with just one scaling function and one wavelet, but also in the vector case where there is more than one scaling functions and wavelets are involved. A multi-wavelet basis is characterized by r scaling and r wavelet functions. Here r denotes the multiplicity of the scaling functions and wavelets in the vector setting with $r > 1$. In case of multiwavelets, the notion of multiresolution changes as the basis for A_0 is now generated by the translates of r scaling functions as

$$\Phi(t) = \begin{bmatrix} \phi_0(t) \\ \phi_1(t) \\ \vdots \\ \phi_{r-1}(t) \end{bmatrix} \tag{12}$$

and

$$\Psi(t) = \begin{bmatrix} \psi_0(t) \\ \psi_1(t) \\ \vdots \\ \psi_{r-1}(t) \end{bmatrix} \tag{13}$$

The use of Mallat's dyadic filter-bank Abhir Bhalerao & Wilson (2001) results in three different detail space components, which are the horizontal, vertical and diagonal. Figure 2 can best visualize the graphical representation of the used filter-bank, where C and W represents the coefficients of the scaling functions and wavelets, respectively, as in 6 and 7. Figure 3 shows transformation of Lena image using filter bank of Figure 2 and Daubechies-4 B. Chebaro & Castan (1993) wavelet coefficients.

3.2 Translation invariance

Discrete wavelets and multiwavelets transformations inherently suffer from lack of translation invariance. In the context of stereo vision, translation invariant representation of the signal is of extreme importance. The translation of the signal should only translates the numerical descriptors of the signal but should not modify it, otherwise recognition of the similar features within the translated representation of the signal could be extremely difficult. The problem of translation variance arises, in discrete dyadic wavelet transform, due to the factor−2 decimation which stands for the disposal of every other coefficient without considering its significance. To address this inherent shortcoming of translation invariance we have adopted the approach of utilizing wavelet transformation modulus maxima coefficients instead of simple transformation coefficients. The filter bank proposed by Mallat Mallat (1999) is modified in this work by removing the decimation of factor 2, which discards every

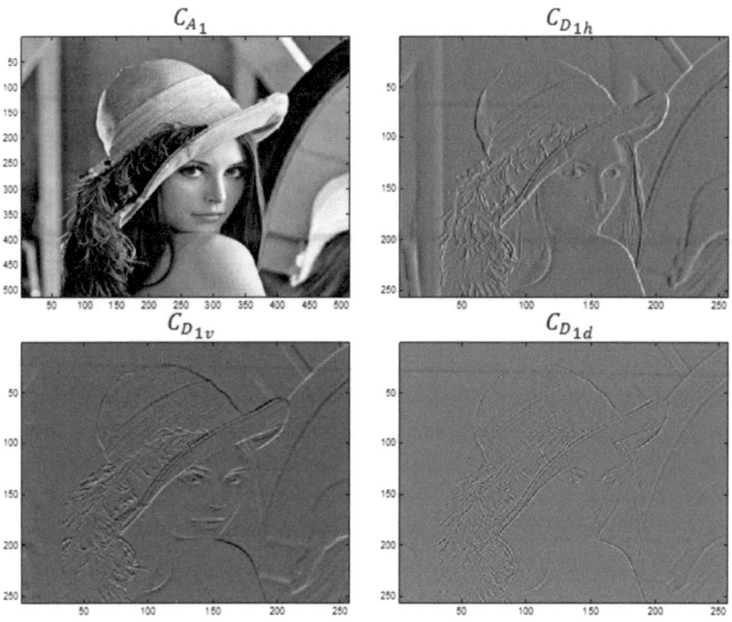

Fig. 3. 1-level discrete wavelet transform of Lena image using figure 2 filter bank

second coefficient, consequently creating an over complete representation of coefficients at subspaces (D_j). Instead, zero padding is performed for coefficients that are not transform modulus maxima. For correspondence estimation between stereo pair of images wavelet transform modulus maxima coefficients are employed to provide translation invariance representation. The proposed approach in achieving translation invariance is motivated by Mallat's approach of introducing critical down sampling Mallat (1999; 1991) into the filter bank instead of factor-2. Before proceeding to translation invariant representation of wavelets and multiwavelets transformation, concept of scale normalization is adopted (Figure 2) as

$$\zeta_s = \left| \frac{C_{D_{s,j}}}{C_{A_s}} \right| \qquad \forall\, s \text{ and } j \in \{h, v, d\} \tag{14}$$

$|.|$ defines the absolute values of the coefficients' magnitudes at scale s. The benefit of wavelets and multiwavelets scale normalization is two fold. Firstly, it normalizes the variations in coefficients, at each transformation level, either introduced due to illuminative variations or by filters gain. Secondly, if the wavelets and multiwavelets filters are perfectly orthogonal, the features in the detail space become more prominent. Let wavelet transform modulus (WTM) coefficients in polar representation be expressed as

$$\Xi_s = \zeta_s \angle \Theta_{\zeta_s} \tag{15}$$

Where ζ_s defines the magnitude of (WTM) coefficients and can be further expanded by referring to (2) as

$$\zeta_s = \frac{1}{3}\left(\sqrt{C^2_{D_{sh}} + C^2_{D_{sv}} + C^2_{D_{sd}}}\right) \tag{16}$$

Where D_{jh}, D_{jv} and D_{jd} represents D_1 subspace coefficients, which in visual terms represent discontinuities of the input image **I** along horizontal, vertical and diagonal dimensions. The

Fig. 4. Top Left: Original image, Top Right: Wavelet Transform Modulus, Bottom Left: wavelet transform modulus phase, Bottom Right: Wavelet Transform Modulus Maxima with Phase vectors

phase of (WTM) coefficients (Θ_{ζ_s}), which in fact is the phase of the discontinuities (edges) pointing to the normal of the plan that edge lies in, can be expressed as

$$\Theta_{\zeta_s} = \begin{cases} \alpha & \text{if} \quad C_{D_{sh}} > 0 \\ \pi - \alpha & \text{if} \quad C_{D_{sh}} < 0 \end{cases} \tag{17}$$

where

$$\alpha = tan^{-1}\left(\frac{C_{D_{jv}}}{C_{D_{jh}}}\right) \tag{18}$$

These discontinuities are referred by Mallat as multi-scale edges Mallat (1999) (section 6.3, page 189).The vector $\vec{n}(k)$ points to the direction, normal to the plan where the discontinuity lies in, as

$$n(k) = [cos(\Theta_{\zeta_s}), sin(\Theta_{\zeta_s})] \tag{19}$$

A discontinuity is the point p at scale s such that Ξ_s is locally maximum at $k = p$ and $k = p + \varepsilon n(k)$ for $|\varepsilon|$ small enough. These points are known as wavelet transform modulus maxima Ξ_n, and are translation invariant through the wavelet transformation and can be expressed by reorganizing expression 15 as

$$\Xi_{ns} = \zeta_{ns} \angle \Theta_{\zeta_{ns}} \tag{20}$$

Through out the rest of presentation, **coefficients** term will be used for wavelet transform modulus maxima coefficients instead of wavelets and multiwavelets coefficients, as in 20. An example of wavelet transform modulus maxima coefficients can be visualized by Figure 4. For further details in reference to wavelet modulus maxima and its translation invariance, reader is kindly referred to Abhir Bhalerao & Wilson (2001) (section 6).

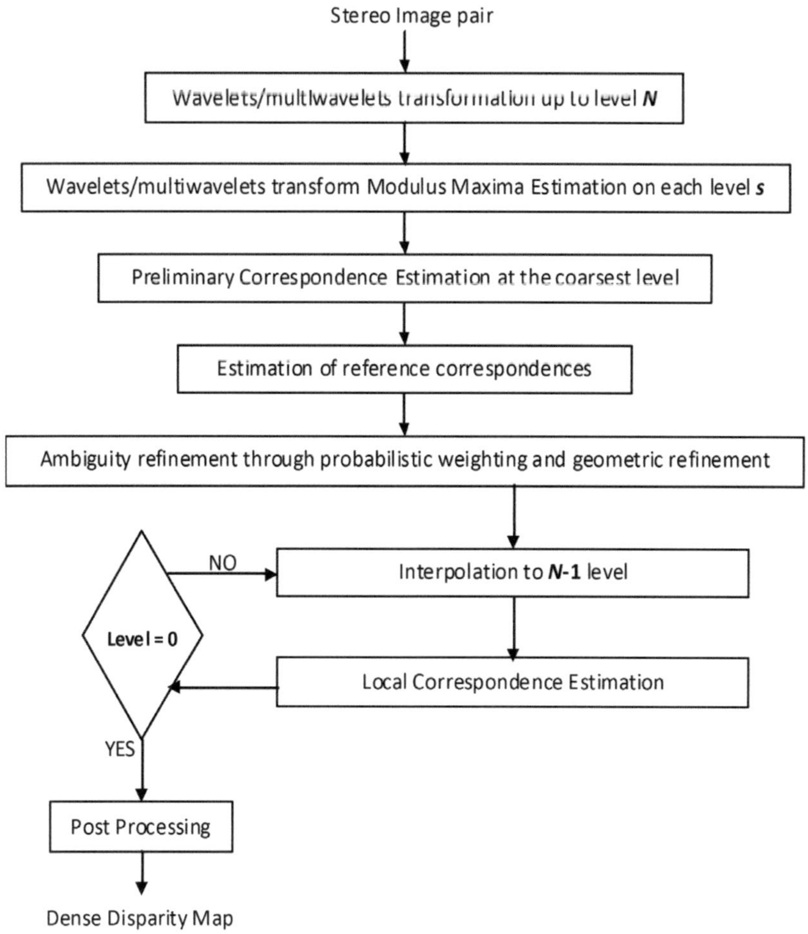

Fig. 5. A simple block representation of the proposed algorithm

4. Correspondence estimation

In the light of multiresolution techniques, presented in section 2 and their inherited shortcomings, we propose a novel wavelets and multiwavelets analysis based stereo correspondence estimation algorithm. The algorithm is developed to serve two distinct purposes; 1) to exploit the potential of wavelet and multiwavelets scale-space representation in solving correspondence estimation problem; and 2) providing a test-bed to explore the correlations of embedded properties of wavelets and multiwavelets basis, such as approximation order, shape and orthogonality/orthonormality with the quality of stereo correspondence estimation. The correspondence estimation process of the proposed algorithm is categorized into two distinct steps. First part of the algorithm defines the correspondence estimation at the coarsest transformation level, i.e. at signal decomposition level N. Figure 2 can facilitate visualization of signal decomposition considering the presented filter bank decomposes the signal up to level 1. Second phase of the algorithm defines the iterative matching process from finer $(N-1)$ to finest (0) transformation level, which according to Figure 1 refers to subspace A_0. Correspondence estimation at the coarsest level is the most important part of the proposed algorithm due to its hierarchical nature and dependance of finer correspondences on the outcomes of coarser level establishments. Estimation of correspondences at finer levels use local search methodology searching only at locations where correspondences have already been established in the coarser level search. A block diagram representing the process of the proposed algorithm is shown in Figure 5.

4.1 Similarity measure

To establish initial correspondences, similarity measure is performed on modulus maxima coefficients (Ξ_s) using correlation measure Medioni & Nevatia (1985) enforced by multi-window approach Alejandro Gallegos-Hernandez (2002) (Figure 6) as

$$C_\Xi = \overline{C_{\Xi,W_0} + \sum_{i=1}^{n_W/2} C_{\Xi,W_i}} \tag{21}$$

Where C_Ξ represents the correlation score of wavelets transform modulus maxima, under investigation and n_W represents the number of surrounding windows, usually taken as 9, without considering W_0. The second summation term in (21) represent the summation of best $n_W/2$ windows out of n_W. An average of the correlation scores from these windows is taken to keep the score normalized i.e. within the range of [0 1].

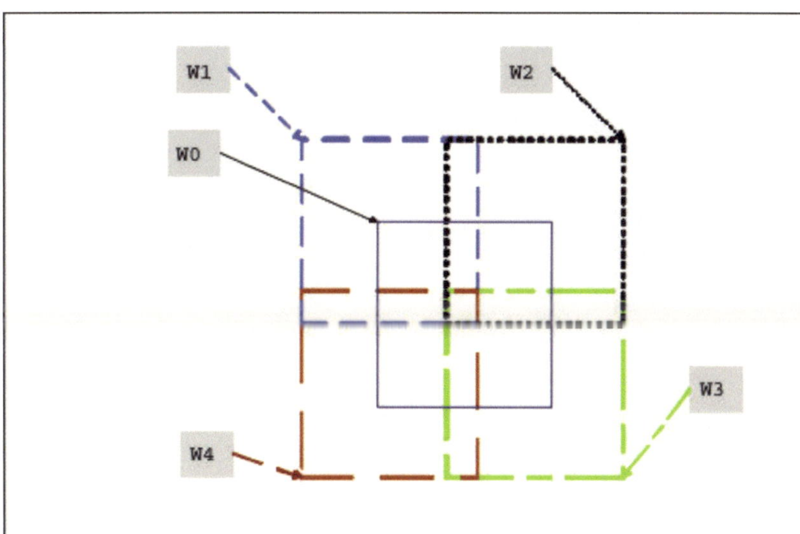

Fig. 6. Multi-window approach for correlation estimation

4.2 Probabilistic weighting

Wavelets and multiwavelets transformations, using filter-bank (Figure 2), produce r^2 sub-spaces for each bank at each scale. r defines the multiplicity of scaling functions and wavelets, which is one (i.e. $r = 1$) for wavelets, whereas $r > 1$ in case of multiwavelets, as illustrated in (12 and 13). Figure 7 represents one level multiwavelets transformation using GHM basis C. Baillard & Fitzgibbon (1999) with $r = 2$, therefore each subspace $(C_{A_1}, C_{D_{sh}}, C_{D_{sv}}, C_{D_{sd}})$ has produced 4 subspaces in contrast to one subspace as shown in Figure 3. Consequently, multiwavelets transform modulus maxima representation will consists of r^2 subspaces (16) for correspondence estimation process at each scale s. To ensure the contribution of all coefficients from r^2 subspaces, probabilistic weighting is introduced to strengthen correlation measure of (21). In case of wavelets with $r = 1$, this step is bypassed. Probabilistic weighting defines the probability of optimality for any corresponding pair of coefficients. To define this probability; let Ξ_{c1} be the reference coefficient that belongs to one image of the stereo pair and Ξ_{c2_j} be the corresponding coefficients from the other image. The term j in Ξ_{c2_j} is due to the fact that sometimes different coefficients from r^2 subspace of the other image appear to be the potential correspondences for Ξ_{c1} coefficient. This phenomena is generally referred to as ambiguity Baker & Binford (1981).

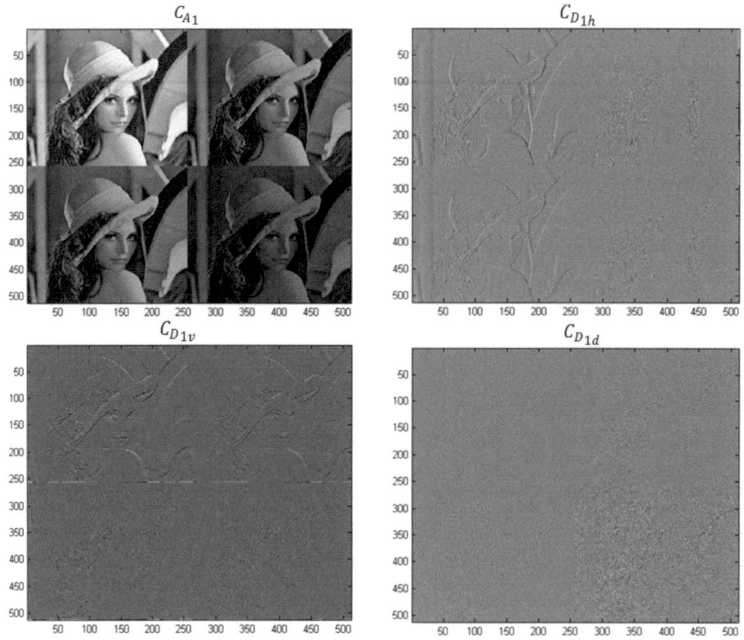

Fig. 7. 1-level discrete multiwavelets transform of Lena image using figure 2 filter bank and GHM multiwavelets C. Baillard & Fitzgibbon (1999)

The probability expression for corresponding pair (Ξ_{c1}, Ξ_{c2_j}) is defined as

$$P_{\Xi_{c2_j}} = n_{\Xi_{c2j}}/r^2 \quad \text{where} \quad 1 \leq n_{\Xi_{c2_j}} \leq r^2, \ \forall j \tag{22}$$

where $n_{\Xi_{c2_j}}$ is the number of times coefficient Ξ_{c2_j} is appeared as potential correspondence for Ξ_{c1}. In case of no ambiguity, Ξ_{c2} will appear as corresponding coefficient for Ξ_{c1} throughout r^2 subspaces, producing the $P_{\Xi_{c2}} = \frac{r^2}{r^2} = 1$. It is obvious from expression (22) that the P_{Ξ_c} lies between the range of $[1/r^2 \ \ 1]$. The correlation score in expression (21) is then weighted with P_{Ξ_c} as

$$\aleph_{\Xi_{c2_j}} = \frac{P_{\Xi_{c2_j}}}{r^2} \sum_{n_{\Xi_{c2j}}} C_{\Xi_{c2_j}} \tag{23}$$

r^2 term in expression (23) is for normalization of the correlation scores which will be accumulated over r^2 subspaces. In case of no ambiguity between the correspondence of Ξ_{c1}

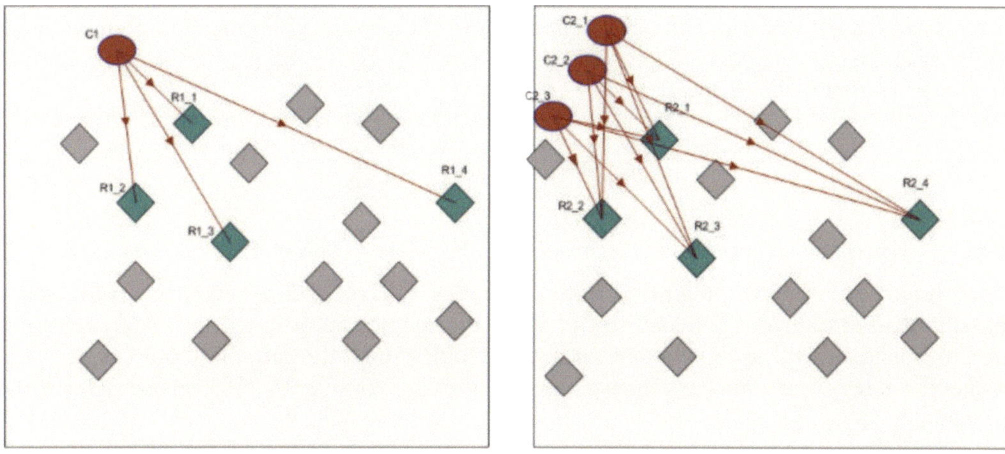

Wavelet Modulus maxima coefficients of Image 1 | Wavelet Modulus maxima coefficients of Image 2

Fig. 8. Geometric refinement procedure

and Ξ_{c2} throughout r^2 subspaces, expression 23 will be simplified to C_Ξ as in expression 21 as

$$\aleph_{\Xi_{c2}} = \frac{1}{r^2}\left(r^2 \times C_{\Xi_{c2}}\right) = C_{\Xi_{c2}} \tag{24}$$

Simplification of expressions from 23 to 24 is of course under the assumption that C_Ξ is constant for the corresponding pair trough out the r^2 subspace, which is found to be true majority of the times. Corresponding pairs with $P_\Xi = 1$ and C_Ξ above predefined threshold, usually within the range of $[0.6 \quad 0.7]$, are used as references in addressing the ambiguity problem for rest of the correspondences. These reference coefficients provide a test ground to measure the credibility of rest of the correspondences by employing geometric refinement technique, presented in the following section.

4.3 Geometric refinement

Geometric refinement is employed to filter credible coefficients' correspondences, out of the ambiguous ones, using established reference correspondences from previous section-4.2. Three geometric features, relative distance difference (*RDD*), absolute distance difference (*ADD*) and relative slope difference (*RSD*), are employed to perform geometric refinement. The selection of these geometric features is influenced by their invariant nature through geometric transformations, such as Projective, Affine, Matric and Euclidean Siebert (1998). Geometric refinement procedure can be best visualized by Figure 8 where red circles represent candidate coefficient correspondences and squares represent reference coefficients. In Figure 8, $C1$ represents the coefficients from first image with potential corresponding coefficients $C2\_i$ from second image. Similarly, $R1$ and $R2$ represents reference corresponding coefficients with respect to first and second images, respectively. Small number of randomly chosen reference correspondences are employed in this phase to keep the process computationally less expansive. Let n_r be the number of randomly chosen reference correspondences out of N_r total reference correspondences and n_c be the number of candidate corresponding coefficients represented by $C2_j$ in Figure 8. With trial and error it has been found that n_r within the range $[3 \quad 5]$ produces desired outcome. Let Ξ_{n_r} and $\acute{\Xi}_{n_r}$ be the reference corresponding coefficients and Ξ_{n_c} and $\acute{\Xi}_{n_c}$ be the corresponding candidate coefficients for left and right images, respectively. According to Figure 8 aforementioned coefficients can be mapped as $(\Xi_{n_r} : R1)$, $(\acute{\Xi}_{n_r} : R2)$, $(\Xi_{n_c} : C1)$ and $(\acute{\Xi}_{n_c} : C2)$. To calculate *ADD*, we can define the expression as

$$D_{A_{\Xi_{c_j}}} = \left[\left| \frac{d_{\Xi_{c_j}} - d_{\Xi_r}}{d_{\Xi_{c_j}} + d_{\Xi_r}} \right| \right]_m \tag{25}$$

Where $|.|$ represents the absolute values and $D_{A_{\Xi_{c_j}}}$ defines *ADD* for *j*th candidate coefficient of second image corresponding to d_{Ξ_r} from first image. Process of 25 is averaged over m times repetitions to minimize any bias introduced by the coefficients belonging to any particular area of image as well as involvement of any wrong candidate pair that could have been assigned the tag of reference coefficients as $\Xi_{n_{r_j}}$ and $\acute{\Xi}_{n_{r_j}}$. Similarly, *RDD* can be defined by the following expression

$$D_{R_{\Xi_{c_j}}} = \left[\left| \frac{d_{\Xi_c r} - d_{\acute{\Xi}_{cr_j}}}{d_{\Xi_{cr_j}} + d_{\acute{\Xi}_{cr_j}}} \right| \right]_n \tag{26}$$

Similar to *ADD* (25), (26) is repeated n times. Finally, *RSD* is calculated by defining relative slopes between candidate and reference coefficients as

$$S_{\Xi_{c_j}} = \left[\left| \frac{s_{\Xi_c r} - s_{\acute{\Xi}_{cr_j}}}{s_{\Xi_c r} + s_{\acute{\Xi}_{cr_j}}} \right| \right]_n \tag{27}$$

The term $(.)_n$ defines the average over n repetitions for each *j*th candidate coefficient. Employing expressions (25), (26) and (27), a generalized expression of geometric refinement is defined for each *j*th candidate correspondence by weighting the established correlation score from (23) as

$$F_{\Xi_{c_j}} = \frac{\aleph_{\Xi_{c_j}}}{3} \left(e^{-D_{A_{\Xi_{c_j}}}} + e^{-D_{R_{\Xi_{c_j}}}} + e^{-S_{\Xi_{c_j}}} \right) \tag{28}$$

It is obvious from expression (28), $\acute{\Xi}_{n_{c_j}}$ with highest score will be the one having closest geometrical topology with respect to the reference coefficients Ξ_{n_r} and $\acute{\Xi}_{n_r}$. For instance, for an optimal correspondence between Ξ_{n_c} and $\acute{\Xi}_{n_c}$, expression $(F_{\Xi_{c_j}})$ will boil down to simple correlation score $\aleph_{\Xi_{c_j}}$ from (23) as the term $\left[\frac{1}{3} \left(e^{-D_{A_{\Xi_{c_j}}}} + e^{-D_{R_{\Xi_{c_j}}}} + e^{-S_{\Xi_{c_j}}} \right) \right]$ will become 1.

5. Finer levels correspondence estimation

Correspondence estimation process (section-4) at coarsest wavelet transformation level, i.e. level N, produces set of optimal correspondences between coefficients belonging to first and second images. These correspondences are then projected to finer level, i.e. level $N-1$, where a local search is performed to authenticate correspondences, established at coarsest level N, as well as to estimate new ones. Referring back to section (3.1) and (3.2), transform modulus maxima that belongs to lower frequency components disappear at higher transformation levels. Authentication of correspondences at $N-1$ level, using the information of N level correspondences, provides a structured ground to constraint the search of new coefficient correspondences to local search regions. This local search eliminates the need of computationally expansive geometric refinements leaving the processes

Basis	r	$[C_s, C_w]$	A_p	Orth	Shape
Haar Haar (1910)	1	[2 , 2]	1	o	s
D-4 Daubechies (1988)	1	[4 , 4]	2	o	as
D-8 I. Daubechies & Lagarias (1992)	1	[8 , 8]	4	o	as
BI9 Strela (1998)	1	[9 , 7]	4	bo	s
BI7 Strela (1998)	1	[7 , 9]	4	bo	s
BI5 Strela (1998)	1	[5 , 3]	2	bo	s
BI3 Strela (1998)	1	[3 , 5]	2	bo	s
GHM Gernimo et al. (1994)	2	[4 , 4]	2	o	s
CL Chui & Lian (1996); Chui (1992)	2	[3 , 3]	2	o	s
SA4 Strela (1996)	2	[4 , 4]	1	o	s
BIH52S Strela (1998)	2	[5 , 3]	2	bo	s
BIH32S Strela (1998)	2	[3 , 5]	4	bo	s
BIH54N Strela (1998)	2	[5 , 3]	4	bo	s
MW1 A. Bhatti (2002); Ozkaramanli et al. (2002)	3	[6 , 6]	2	o	s
MW2 A. Bhatti (2002); Ozkaramanli et al. (2002)	3	[6 , 6]	3	o	as
MW3 A. Bhatti (2002); Ozkaramanli et al. (2002)	3	[8 , 8]	4	o	s

Table 1. Employed wavelets and multiwavelets bases with embedded attributes

of sections (4.1) and (4.2) necessary and sufficient to achieve desired quality of correspondence estimation. This procedure can be considered as iterative optimization process Daubechies (1992).

6. Analysis of the effect of different wavelet and multi-wavelet bases

To address the influence of wavelets and multiwavelets bases on the quality of correspondence estimation, 16 wavelets and multiwavelets bases are employed. These bases are carefully chosen to cover range of properties such as orthogonality, bi-orthogonality, symmetry, asymmetry, multiplicity and approximation order Asim Bhatti & Zheng (2003) as presented in Table 1.

Referring to Table 1, parameters *o* and *bo*, in the Orth column represents orthogonality and bi-orthogonality ,respectively, of the bases. *s* and *as* are the shape parameters, representing symmetric and asymmetric, whereas r defines the multiplicity. It is obvious from the Table 1 that scalar wavelets possess unit multiplicity, i.e. one scaling function and one wavelet. The coefficients related to wavelets and multiwavelets bases presented, in Table 1, can be found in Bhatti (2009). Statistical analysis is performed using *root mean squared error* (RMS) and *percentage of bad discrete pixel disparities* (BPD), employed from D. Scharstein & Szeliski (n.d.), for qualitative measure of the correspondences estimation. Disparity maps generated using

Basis	r	$[C_s, C_w]$	A_p	Orth	Shape
CL Chui & Lian (1996); Chui (1992)	2	[3 , 3]	2	o	s
MW2 A. Bhatti (2002); Ozkaramanli et al. (2002)	3	[6 , 6]	3	o	as
MW3 A. Bhatti (2002); Ozkaramanli et al. (2002)	3	[8 , 8]	4	o	s

Table 2. Selected multiwavelets basis

estimated correspondences are compared with the ground truth disparity maps.

$$RMS = \sqrt{\frac{1}{N}\sum_{x,\,y} |d_E(x,y) - d_G(x,y)|^2} \tag{29}$$

and

$$PBD = \frac{1}{N} \sum_{(x,y)} |d_E(x,y) - d_G(x,y)| > \xi \tag{30}$$

where d_E and d_G are the estimated and ground truth disparity maps, N is the total number of discrete disparity values in the disparity map whereas ξ represents the disparity error tolerance, taken as 1. In other words any difference greater than 1 between ground truth disparity maps and the estimated disparity is considered as bad discrete disparity. These statistics are related to the images *Map, Bull, Teddy, Cones* and *Venus,* taken from D. Scharstein & Szeliski (n.d.). Referring to visual representation in Figures 9 and 10, a distinguished higher performance of multi-wavelets bases can be observed throughout the set of employed images. This statistical behavior of the estimated data strengthens earlier established understanding about the superior performance of multiwavelets bases over the scalar ones Strela (1996). Their success stems from the fact that they can simultaneously posses the good properties of orthogonality, symmetry, high approximation order and short support G. Strang & Strela (1995; 1994), which is not possible in the scalar wavelets case G. Strang & Strela (1994); Daubechies (1992). Out of 9 multiwavelets bases, CL, MW2 and MW3 has outperformed rest of the bases with major contribution from *MW2*. Analyzing embedded attributes of these multiwavelets bases, separated in Table 2, we see a clear pattern of commonality in terms of multiplicity and orthogonality contributing into the higher performance of these multiwavelets bases. Although it is hard to visualize a clear correlation pattern, explicitly, between the attributes of presented wavelets and multiwavelets bases and the quality of correspondences, however we would initiate a short discussion to address some possible effects of these attributes to correspondence estimation problem as:

Orthogonality dictates that coefficients in subspaces of D_{sj} and A_s and linearly independent, as in Figures 1 and 2, and their direct sum produces the subspace A_{s-1} (11). In classical signal processing terms, subspace A_s contains lower frequency components of the input signal whereas D_{sj} contains higher frequency components depending on the approximation order of the scaling functions. Perfect separation, due to orthogonality, between lower and higher frequency components and into scales and subspaces provides a sparse representation of high value features that are easier to track.

Multiplicity influences the size of search space by producing r^2 subspaces of coefficients (sections (3.1) and (4.2)). Consequently producing expanded search space to establish and authenticate coefficient correspondences. In general, multiplicity and orthogonality together, influences the separation of signal components into distinct subspaces making it easier to establish robust correspondences. This leads to the notion of scale-space representation Chui & Lian (1996). In this particular study employing wavelet transform modulus maxima coefficients with higher multiplicity and orthogonality ensured the involvement of high profile features at different scales and spaces making the algorithm robust and resistant to errors.

Approximation order defines the approximation capabilities of the scaling functions. Multiwavelets bases are set to have approximation order p if a linear combination of the scaling functions can produce polynomials up to degree $p - 1$. In other words, polynomials up degree $p - 1$ are in linear span of scaling space spanned by the shifts of scaling functions $\phi_0(t), \phi_1(t), \cdots \phi_{r-1}(t)$. This means polynomials up to degree 1, i.e. $f = t$ are in the linear span of multiscaling functions of D4, BI5, BI3, GHM, BIH52S and MW1 (Table 1). Similarly, $f = t^2$ and $f = t^3$ polynomials are in the linear span of MW2 and MW3 bases, respectively. In the context of image processing, polynomials can be represented by the gradient intensity change. Single color without any intensity variations can be represented as polynomial of degree zero ($f = t^0 = 1$), that is a constant function. A constant intensity variation would refer to polynomial of degree 1, i.e. $f = t$. Based on this understanding of approximation order, we can say, higher approximation order leads to higher order modulus maxima coefficients in $D_s j$ subspaces (Figure 1 and 2). In other words higher approximation order ensures the separation of higher order features or modulus maxima coefficients from lower order features, consequently allowing the algorithm to focus on global aspects rather than getting stuck into local minima introduced by low value coefficients. Considering, very high approximation order could also result in filtering the important coefficients into the approximation space rather than detail space, which is used for correspondence estimation, it can be argued; what is the optimal approximation order? It is very hard to conclude at this stage however our future work involves the extension of statistical analysis utilizing bigger data base of images and multiwavelets bases.

7. Conclusion

In this presentation we have tried to initiate a discussion about the potential of multiwavelets bases into the domain of robust correspondence estimation. We have addressed some embedded attributes of wavelets and multiwavelets bases that could play a key role in establishing highly robust correspondences between two and more views. Seven wavelets and nine multiwavelets bases were employed covering a range of well known attributes including orthogonality, approximations order, support and shape. For statistical performance analysis, five well known images with diverse range of intensity complexities were employed. In addition, a novel and robust correspondence estimation algorithm is presented to provide a test bed to exploit the potential of wavelets and multiwavelets bases. The proposed algorithm uses multi-resolution analysis to estimate correspondences. The translation invariant multiwavelets transform modulus maxima (WTMM) are used as matching features. To keep the whole matching process consistent and resistant to errors an optimized selection criterion is introduced involving the contribution of probabilistic weighted normalized correlation and geometric refinement. Probabilistic weighting involves the contribution of more than one search spaces, whereas geometric refinement addresses the problem of geometric distortion between the perspective views. Moreover, beside that comprehensive selection criterion

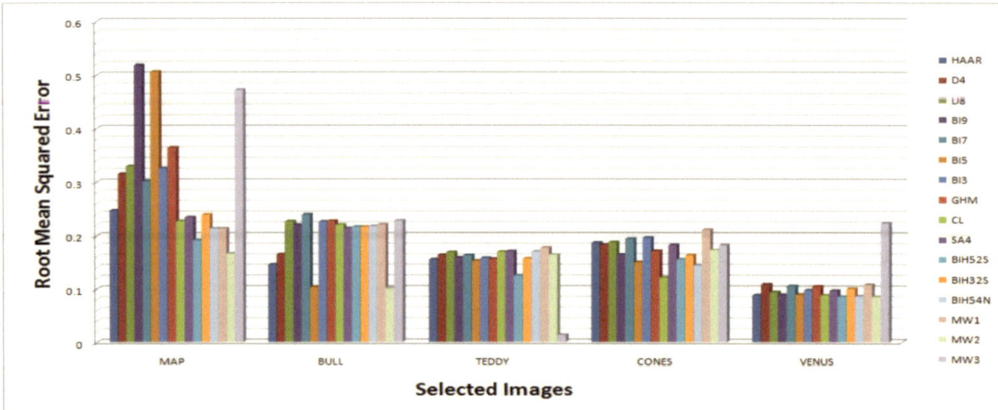

Fig. 9. Root Mean Square Error (RMS) for number of images

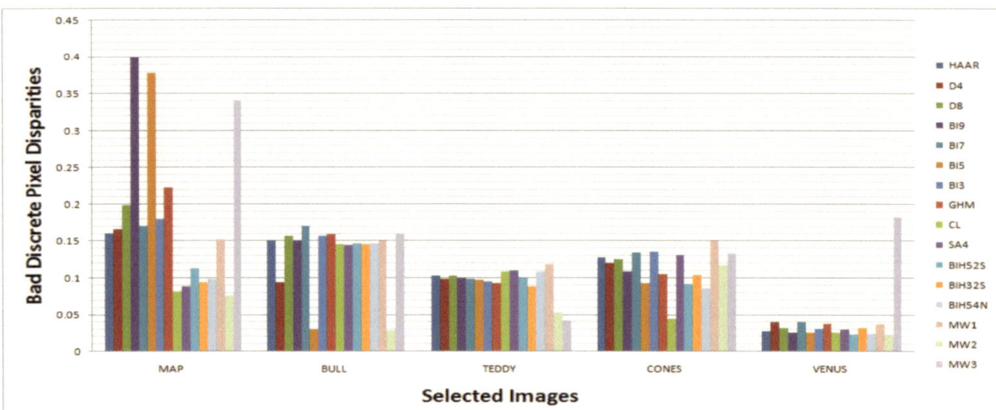

Fig. 10. Percentage of Bad Pixel Disparity (BPD) for number of images

the whole matching process is constrained to uniqueness, continuity and smoothness. We are currently in the process of expanding the experimental envelope and would hope to present clearer picture of correlations between the embedded attributes of the bases and correspondence problem in future presentations.

8. References

A. Bhatti, ., H. . (2002). M-band multiwavelets from spline super functions with approximation order, *in* IEEE (ed.), *International Conference on Acoustics Speech and Signal Processing, (ICASSP 2002)*, Vol. 4, IEEE, pp. 4169–4172.

A. Bhatti, ., S. N. (2008). Stereo correspondence estimation using multiwavelets scale-space representation based multiresolution analysis, *Cybernetic and Systems* 39(6): 641–665.

A. Mehmood, ., A. S. (2001). Digital reconstruction of buddhist historical sites (6th b.c-2nd a.d) at taxila, pakistan (unesco, world heritage site), *in* IEEE (ed.), *Proceedings of the Seventh International Conference on Virtual Systems and Multimedia (VSMM01)*.

A. Witkin, D. T. & Kass, M. (1987). Signal matching through scale space, *Int. J. of Computer Vision* 1: 133–144.

Abhir Bhalerao, . & Wilson, R. (2001). A fourier approach to 3d local feature estimation from volume data, *Proc. of British Machine Vision Conference*, Vol. 2, pp. 461–470.

Alejandro Gallegos-Hernandez, Francisco J. Ruiz-Sanchez, J. R. V.-C. (2002). 2d automated visual inspection system for the remote quality control of smd assembly, *in* IEEE (ed.), *28th Annual Conference of Industrial Electronics Society (IECON 02)*, Vol. 3, IEEE, pp. 2219–2224.

Asim Bhatti, S. N. & Zheng, H. (2003). Disparity estimation using ti multi-wavelet transform, *Fourth International Conference on Intelligent Technologies (Intech'03)*.

B. Chebaro, A. Crouzil, L. M.-P. & Castan, S. (1993). Fusion of the stereoscopic and temporal matching results by an algorithm of coherence control and conflicts management, *Int. Conf. on Computer Analysis of Images and Patterns*, pp. 486–493.

Baker, H. & Binford, T. (1981). Depth from edge and intensity based stereo, *Int. Joint Conf. on Artificial Intelligence*, Vancouver, Canada, pp. 631–636.

Bhatti, A. (2009). *Stereo Vision and Wavelets/Multiwavelets Analysis*, Lambert Academic Publishing.

C. Baillard, C. Schmid, A. Z. & Fitzgibbon, A. (1999). Automatic line matching and 3d reconstruction of buildings from multiple views, p. 12.

C. L. Zitnick, T. K. (2000). A cooperative algorithm for stereo matching and occlusion detection, *IEEE PAMI* 22(7): 675–684.

Chui, C. K. (1992). *Wavelets: A tutorial in theory and applications*, Acadmic press.

Chui, C. K. & Lian, J. (1996). A study of orthonormal multi-wavelets, *J. Applied Numerical Math* 20(3): 273–298.

Cohen, I., Raz, S. & Malah, D. (1998). Adaptive time-frequency distributions via the shiftinvariant wavelet packet decomposition, *Proc. of the 4th IEEE-SP Int. Symposium on Time-Frequency and Time-Scale Analysis*, Pittsburgh, Pennsylvania.

Coifman, R. R. & Donoho, D. L. (1995). Translation-invariant de-noising, *Wavelet and Statistics, Lecture Notes in Statistics*, a. antoniadis and g. oppenheim, ed. edn, Springer-Verlag, pp. 125–150.

D. Scharstein, . & Szeliski, R. (n.d.). www.middlebury.edu/stereo.

Daubechies, I. (1988). Orthonormal bases of compactly supported wavelets, *Comm. Pure Appl. Math.* 41: 309–996.

Daubechies, I. (1992). *Ten Lectures on Wavelets*, Philadelphia.

David Capel, A. Z. (2003). Computer vision applied to super-resolution, p. 10.

Esteban, C. H. (2004). *Stereo and Silhouette Fusion for 3D Object Modeling from Uncalibrated Images Under Circular Motion*, Ph.d. dissertation.

G. Strang, . & Strela, V. (1994). Orthogonal multiwavelets with vanishing moments, *J. Optical Eng.* 33: 2104–2107.

G. Strang, . & Strela, V. (1995). Short wavelets and matrix dilation equations, *IEEE Trans. on SP* 43: 108–115.

Gernimo, J., Hardin, D. & Massopust, P. R. (1994). Fractal functions and wavelet expansions based on several functions, *J. Approx. Theory* 78: 373–401.

Haar, A. (1910). Zur theorie der orthogonalen funktionen-systeme, *Math* 69: 331–371.

I. Daubechies, . & Lagarias, J. (1992). Two-scale difference equations i. existence and global regularity of solutions, *SIAM J. Math. Anal.* 22: 1388–1410.

J. C. Olive, ., J. D. & Boulin, C. (1994). Automatic registration of images by a wavelet-based multiresolution approach, *SPIE*, Vol. 2569, pp. 234–244.

J. Magarey, . & Kingsbury, N. (1998). Motion estimation using a complex-valued wavelet transform, *IEEE Transections on signal proceessings* 46(4): 1069–1084.

J. Margary, . & dick, A. (1998). Multiresolution stereo image matching using complex wavelets, *Proc. 14th Int. Conf. on Pattern Recognition (ICPR)*, Vol. 1, pp. 4–7.

J. R. Bergen, P. Anandan, K. J. H. & Hingorani, R. (1992). Hierarchical model-based motion estimation, *ECCV*, pp. 237–252.

L. Di Stefano, ., M. M. S. M. G. N. (2004). A fast area-based stereo matching algorithm, *Image and Vision Computing* 22(12): 938–1005.

M. Unser, . & Aldroubi, A. (1993). A multiresolution image registration procedure using spline pyramids, *SPIE Mathematical Imaging* 2034: 160–170.

Mallat, S. (1989). A theory for multiresolution signal decomposition: the wavelet representation, *IEEE Trans. PAMI* (11): 674–693.

Mallat, S. (1991). Zero-crossings of a wavelet transform,, *IEEE Transactions on Information Theory* 37: 1019–1033.

Mallat, S. (1999). *A Wavelet Tour of Signal Processing*, Vol. 2nd edition, Academic Press.

Medioni, G. & Nevatia, R. (1985). Segment based stereo matching, *Computer Vision, Graphics and Image Processing* 31(1): 2–18.

Ozkaramanli, H., Bhatti, A. & Bilgehan, B. (2002). Multi wavelets from b-spline super functions with approximation order, *International Journal of Signal Processing, Elsevier Science* 82(8): 1029–1046.

Pan, H.-P. (1996a). General stereo matching using symmetric complex wavelets, *Wavelet Applications in Signal and Image Processing* 2825.

Pan, H.-P. (1996b). Uniform full-information image matching using complex conjugate wavelet pyramids, *XVIII ISPRS Congress, International Archives of Photogrammetry and Remote Sensing*, Vol. 31.

Q'ingxiong Yang, ., L. W. R. Y. H. S. & Nister, D. (2006). Stereo matching with color-weighted correlation, hierarchical belief propagation and occlusion handling, *CVPR*, Vol. 2, pp. 2347–2354.

S. Mallat, . & Zhang, S. (1993). Matching pursuits with time-frequency dictionaries, *IEEE Transactions on Signal Processing* 41(12): 3397–3415.

Scharstein, D. & Szeliski, R. (1998). Stereo matching with nonlinear diffusion, *Int. J. of Computer Vision* 28(2): 155–174.

Shi, F., Hughes, N. R. & Robert, G. (2001). Ssd matching using shift-invariant wavelet transform, *British Machine Vision Conference*, pp. 113–122.

Siebert, A. (1998). A linear shift invariant multiscale transform, *in* IEEE (ed.), *International Conference on Image Processing*.

Strela, V. (1996). *Multiwavelets: Theory and Applications*, Phd.

Strela, V. (1998). *A note on construction of Biorthogonal Multi-scaling functions*, Contemporary Mathematics, A. Aaldoubi and E. B. Lin (eds.),.

T. S. Huang, ., A. N. N. (1994). Motion and structure from feature correspondences: A review, *in* IEEE (ed.), *Proc. of the IEEE*, Vol. 82, pp. 252–268.

Wang, L., Liao, M., Gong, M., Yang, R. & Nister, D. (2006). High-quality real-time stereo using adaptive cost aggregation and dynamic programming, *International Symposium on 3D Data Processing, Visualization, and Transmission (3DPVT'06)*, pp. 798–805.

X. Zhou, . & Dorrer, E. (1994). Automatic image-matching algorithm based on wavelet decomposition, *IAPRS* 30(1): 951–960.

Y. Boykov, ., O. V. & Zabih, R. (2001). Fast approximate energy minimization via graph cuts, *IEEE Transections of Pattern Analysis and Machine Intelligence* 23(11): 1222–1239.

3

Markov Random Fields in the Context of Stereo Vision

Lorenzo J. Tardón[1], Isabel Barbancho[1] and Carlos Alberola[2]
[1]*Dept. Ingeniería de Comunicaciones, ETSI Telecomunicación-University of Malaga*
[2]*Dept. Teoría de la Señal y Comunicaciones e Ingeniería Telemática, ETSI Telecomunicación-University of Valladolid*
Spain

1. Introduction

The term *stereo vision* refers to the ability of an observer (either a human or a machine) to recover the three-dimensional information of a scene by means of (at least) two images taken from different viewpoints. Under the scope of this problem—and provided that cameras are calibrated—two subproblems are typically considered, namely, the correspondence problem, and the reconstruction problem (Trucco & Verri, 1998). The former refers to the search for points in the two images that are projections of the same physical point in space. Since the images are taken from different viewpoints, every point in the scene will project onto different image points, i.e, onto points with different coordinates in every image coordinate system. It is precisely this *disparity* in the location of image points that gives the information needed to reconstruct the point position in space. The second problem, i.e., the reconstruction problem, deals with calculating the disparity between a set of corresponding points in the two images to create a disparity map, and to convert this into a three-dimensional map.

In this context, we will show how Markov Random Fields (MRFs) can be effectively used. It is well known that MRFs constitute a powerful tool to incorporate spatial local interactions in a global context (Geman & Geman, 1984). So, in this chapter, we will consider local interactions that define proper MRFs to develop a model that can be applied in the process of recovery of the 3D structure of the real world using stereo pairs of images.

To this end, we will briefly describe the whole stereo reconstruction process (Fig. 1), including the process of selection of features, some important aspects regarding the calibration of the camera system and related geometric transformations of the images and, finally, probabilistic analyses usable in the definition of MRFs to solve the correspondence problem.

In the model to describe, both a priori and a posteriori probabilities will be separately considered and derived making use of reasonable selections of the potentials (Winkler, 1995) that define the MRFs on the basis of specific analytic models.

In the next section, a general overview of a stereo system will be shown. In Sec. 3, a brief overview of some well known stereo correspondence algorithms is given. Sec. 4 describes the main stages of a stereo correspondence system in which MRFS can be applied. Sec. 5 describes the camera model that will be considered in this chapter together with some important related issues like: camera calibration, the epipolar constraint and image rectification. Sec. 6 describes the concept of Markov random fields, and related procedures, like simulated annealing. Sec. 7 introduces MRFs for the edge detection problem. Sec. 8 describes, in detail, how MRFs can

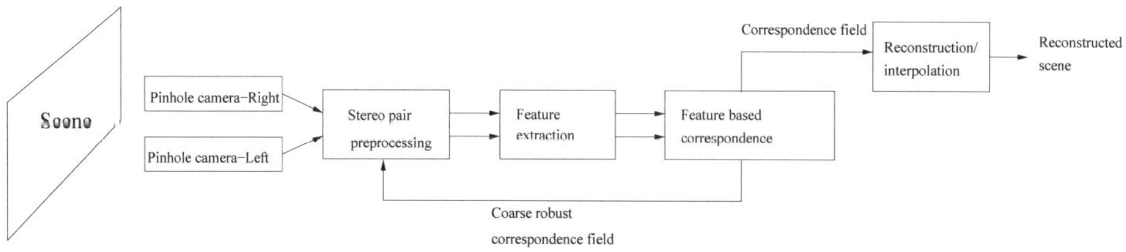

Fig. 1. Scheme of a stereo image reconstruction system.

be modeled using probabilistic analyses in the stereo correspondence context. Sec. 9 describes the implementation of the MRF based stereo system from the point of view of object models. Sec. 10 presents some illustrative experiments done with the MRF described. Finally, Sec. 11 draws some conclusions.

2. Processing stages in three-dimensional stereo

Now, we will briefly describe the main stages of a stereo system (Fig. 1).

Preprocessing: the images acquired by the camera system may require the application of some techniques to allow the reconstruction of three-dimensional scenes and/or to improve the performance of other stages. These techniques refer to many different aspects related to low level vision like: noise reduction, image enhancement, edge sharpening or geometrical transformations.

Feature extraction: this stage is required by feature based stereo systems, like the approach we will present. So, we will briefly introduce MRFs for the detection of edge pixels.

Matching: this stage refers to the process of resolution of the correspondence problem of the selected features. This stage will make use of a MRF defined upon specific probabilistic models.

Reconstruction/interpolation: after the correspondence problem is solved, the 3D scene can be reconstructed using information of the setup of the camera system and interpolating (if necessary) matched points or features.

Regarding these stages, stereo matching is often considered the most important and most difficult problem to solve. So, now, we are going to briefly overview some main ideas on solving the correspondence problem.

3. Solving the correspondence problem

The correspondence problem in stereo vision refers to the search for points in the two images that are projections of the same physical point in space (Trucco & Verri, 1998).
Correspondence methods can be broadly classified within two categories (Brown et al., 2003), namely, *local* and *global* methods. Local methods find the correspondence of a pixel using solely local information about that pixel. They can be very efficient, but also highly sensitive to local ambiguities. On the other hand, global methods provide global constraints on the image that may resolve these ambiguities, at the expense of a higher computational load. However, the following classification: area-based and feature-based methods is also widely used and accepted.
Area-based methods establish the correspondence mainly on the basis of the cross-correlation of image patches from each of the two images of a stereo pair. These techniques allow to obtain

dense disparity maps, but these are rather sensitive to noise and to perspective distortions although their efficiency matching images that contain natural elements solely.
Feature-based methods use specific similarity measures between pairs of selected features together with local and global restrictions regarding the disparity maps to obtain. These methods are often more robust but more difficult to implement and with higher computational burden. Regarding the features to match, it has been observed that edges are very important for the human visual system which makes these elements to be the most widely used features employed in stereo matching algorithms (observe the Fig. 9 b) which contains only detected edges. In this figure, the face of a woman is easily recognized).
A very short review of some main correspondence methods is given below.

3.1 Area-based methods

In (Cochran & Medioni, 1992), a deterministic and robust area-based correspondence method is proposed that used three levels of resolution to obtain dense disparity maps. The method defined is used in each of the three levels of resolution considered. The resolution levels are defined performing a Gaussian filtering and subsampling. The algorithm starts by cutting the image so that the disparity is zero at a fixed point and performing an epipolar alineation process. Then an area-based matching process starts which provides correspondence using a local measure of texture
Lane, Thacker and Seed (Lane et al., 1994) rely on the search of maxima of the correlation cross the pixel blocks previously deformed and the application of global constraints to eliminate the ambiguity due to the search of local maxima. The algorithm starts by aligning and correcting images according to the epipolar constraint.
Kanade (Kanade & Okutomi, 1994) proposed a model of the statistical distribution of the disparity at a point about the center. Such distribution is assumed to be Gaussian with variance proportional to the distance between the points.
Nishihara (Faugeras, 1993, sec. 6.4.2) proposed an improvement of area-based techniques introducing the use of sign of the Laplacian of Gaussian to reduce the sensitive to noise.

3.2 Feature-based methods

Pollard, Mayhew and Frisby (Pollard et al., 1985), (Pollard et al., 1986) proposed an algorithm to solve the problem of correspondence on the basis of the limits of the disparity gradient, derived from experiments performed on the human visual system's (HVS) ability to fuse stereograms.
According to their approach, the cyclopean separation is defined on the cyclopean image as (Fig: 2):

$$S = \sqrt{\left(\frac{x + x'}{2}\right)^2 + y^2} \tag{1}$$

and the disparity gradient is:

$$DG = \frac{|x' - x|}{S} \tag{2}$$

It is checked that a disparity gradient of 1 approximates the limit found for the human visual system (although it is also observed that when the matching dots are nearer the cameras, then it is more unlikely that this condition is maintained (Pollard et al., 1985)).

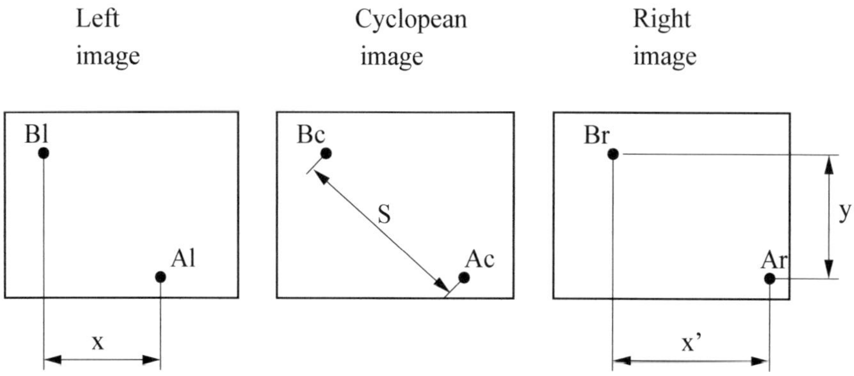

Fig. 2. Projections of the points A and B on the left and right image planes of a stereo system. Cyclopean image and cyclopean separation.

The disparity gradient is a main concept that will be used in the definition of the MRFs involved to solve the correspondence problem.

Barnard and Thompson (Barnard & Thompson, 1980) select the points to match using the Moravec operator (Moravec, 1977), which calculates the sum of squared differences of the intensity of adjacent pixels in the four directions at each position in windows of size 5×5 pixels; the minimum of these measures is stored. Then local maxima are found.

Ohta and Kanade (Ohta & Kanade, 1985) introduced a method based on dynamic programming to obtain optimal correlation paths between pairs of selected features.

On the basis of computational and psychophysical studies, Marr and Poggio (Grimson, 1985, sec. II), (Faugeras, 1993, sec. 6.5.1) develop a correspondence technique according to a hierarchical strategy to match zero crossings of the result of the application of the Lapacian of Gaussian filter to the images. Then, the continuity of the surfaces is imposed to solve the ambiguity the matchings. The matching process is repeated at different resolutions.

Marapane and Trivedi (Marapane & Trivedi, 1989), (Marapane & Trivedi, 1994) propose a hierarchical method in which at each stage of the correspondence process correspondence the most appropriate features should be used. Three main stages are considered to match: regions, line segments and edge pixels.

4. MRFs in a stereo correspondence system

Now, we describe the general stereo matching process. Note that MRFs can be used in two main stages: selection of features to match and resolution of the correspondence process. However, in this chapter, we pay special attention to the correspondence problem. The features that will be matched are edge pixels. Also, our process is supported by the calibration and the rectification processes. The complete scheme, with indication of the stages in which MRFs can be applied, is shown in Fig. 3.

Two stages are made to establish the correspondence in static scenes: the first one is used to rectify the images to apply the epipolar restriction (Faugeras, 1993) to help to simplify and to reduce the computational burden of the process of establishing true correspondences. The second one corresponds to the final stereo matching process.

The process of detection of edges will use the Nalwa-Binford (Nalwa & Binford, 1986) edge detector, but MRFs can also be defined to solve this stage (Tardón et al., 2006). Only edge pixels will be considered as features.

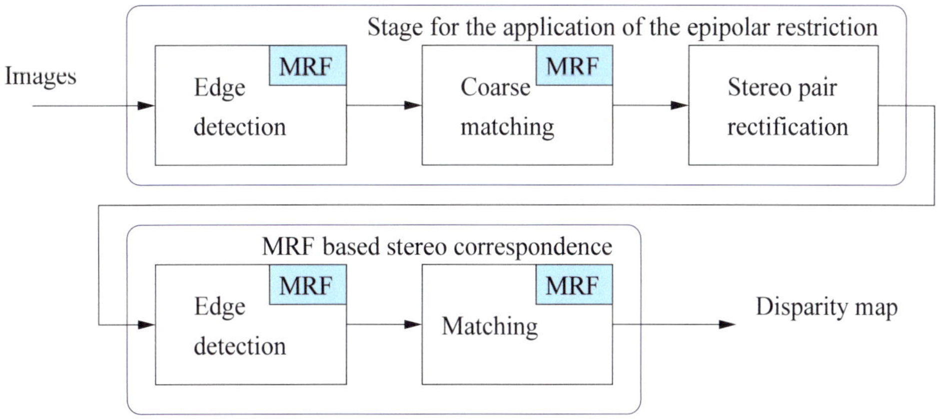

Fig. 3. An example of suitable application of MRFs in a stereo correspondence system.

After the edges are extracted, an initial matching stage is performed before image rectification:

- Area-based matching, using the normalized cross-covariance, is performed.
- Then, our iterative matching algorithm is employed to increase the reliability of the previous result by eliminating inconsistencies between correspondences and establishing new robust correspondences.

After obtaining a first map of correspondences, these are used to estimate the fundamental matrix (Mohr & Triggs, 1996). Once the fundamental matrix is estimated, the process of image rectification is done to easily apply the epipolar restriction.
Now, using the images properly rectified, the edges will be found again and then, the final matching process starts. Area-based matching using the normalized cross-covariance is employed and, then, the full MRF model is used to obtain the final disparity map for the selected features because of the modeling capability of MRFs (Li, 2001; Winkler, 1995) and their robust optimization capabilities (Boykov et al., 2001; Geman & Geman, 1984).
To begin with, we will make a description of MRFs and related concepts. Then, we must describe the camera model and the geometrical relations involved in the camera system considered because of their influence in the probabilities that help to define the MRFs involved in the formulation of the correspondence problem. Afterwards, we will describe the different stages in our stereo correspondence system.

5. Model of the binocular camera system

In this chapter, we consider a binocular system. One of the important factors involved is the main geometry of the system regarding the orientation of the optical axes. If the optical axes are parallel, then there exists a simple relation in the disparity (difference in the coordinates in the different images) between matching points (Barnard & Fischler, 1982) and depth (Bensrhair et al., 1992). This is a convenient case and it is usable in multitude of real cases.
The behavior of the cameras of the system must be described. We will consider the *pinhole* camera model (Faugeras, 1993, cap. 3), (Foley et al., 1992, cap. 6) (Fig. 4). Then a number of transformations expressed in homogeneous coordinates can be used to describe the relations between the real world coordinates and the image coordinate systems (Faugeras, 1993, cap. 3), (Foley et al., 1992, cap. 6), (Duda & Hart, 1973, cap. 10).

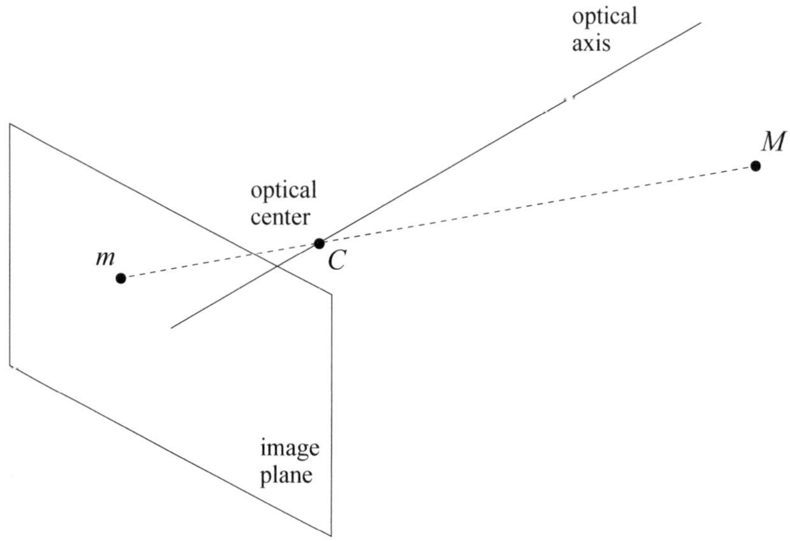

Fig. 4. The pinhole camera model.

According to the pinhole model, the camera is represented by a small point (hole), the optical center C, and an image plane at a distance F behind the hole (Duda & Hart, 1973) (Fig. 4). This model has a small drawback which is to reverse the images, so it is common to replace it by an equivalent one in which the optical center C is located behind the image plane. Then, the orthogonal projection that passes through the optical center is called the optical axis.
Homogeneous coordinates are suitable to describe the projection process in this model (Vince, 1995). First, consider the center of coordinates of the real world at the optical center and the following axes: Z orthogonal to the image plane and the axes X and Y orthogonal and, also orthogonal to Z. The origin of coordinates in the image plane will be the intersection of the Z axes with this plane and the axes u and v in the image plane will be orthogonal to each other and parallel to X and Y, respectively, then, the projected coordinates in the image plane $[U,V,S]^T$ of a point at $[x,y,z,1]^T$ will be given by (Faugeras, 1993, cap. 3):

$$\begin{bmatrix} U \\ V \\ S \end{bmatrix} = \begin{bmatrix} -f & 0 & 0 & 0 \\ 0 & -f & 0 & 0 \\ 0 & 0 & 1 & 0 \end{bmatrix} \cdot \begin{bmatrix} x \\ y \\ z \\ 1 \end{bmatrix} \qquad \vec{m} = P_0 \vec{M} \tag{3}$$

Now, we must also take into account all the possible transformations that can happen between the coordinates of a point in the space and a projection in the image plane. Consider a modification of the coordinates system in the image plane: a scaling of the axes and a translation. These operations, in the 2D space of projections, can be represented by:

$$H = \begin{bmatrix} k_u & 0 & t_u \\ 0 & k_v & t_v \\ 0 & 0 & 1 \end{bmatrix} \tag{4}$$

so that we can obtain a new matrix $P_1 = H * P_0$ that takes into account these transformations. The parameters $\alpha_u = -fk_u$, $\alpha_v = -fk_v$, t_u y t_v are called the *intrinsic parameters* and they depend only on the camera itself.

Of course, we will probably desire to modify the usable coordinates system in the real world. Often, a rotation and a translation of the coordinates system is considered (Faugeras, 1993, sec. 3.3.2). These operations can be represented by the 4×4 matrix:

$$K = \begin{bmatrix} & R & & T \\ 0 & 0 & 0 & 1 \end{bmatrix} = \begin{bmatrix} r_{11} & r_{12} & r_{13} & t_x \\ r_{21} & r_{22} & r_{23} & t_y \\ r_{31} & r_{32} & r_{33} & t_z \\ 0 & 0 & 0 & 1 \end{bmatrix} \tag{5}$$

This matrix describes the position and the orientation of the camera with respect to the reference system and it defines the *extrinsic parameters*.
With all this, the projection matrix becomes:

$$P = P_1 * K = H * P_0 * K = \begin{bmatrix} \alpha_u \vec{r}_1 + t_u \vec{r}_3 & \alpha_u t_x + t_u t_z \\ \alpha_v \vec{r}_2 + t_v \vec{r}_3 & \alpha_v t_y + t_v t_z \\ \vec{r}_3 & t_z \end{bmatrix} = \begin{bmatrix} \vec{q}_1^T & q_{14} \\ \vec{q}_2^T & q_{24} \\ \vec{q}_3^T & q_{34} \end{bmatrix} \tag{6}$$

Note that only 10 parameters in the matrix are independent: scaling in the image plane (2 parameters), translation in the image plane (2), rotation in the real world (3) and translation in the real world (3). So, a valid projection matrix must satisfy certain conditions:

$$||\vec{q}_3|| = 1 \tag{7}$$

$$(\vec{q}_1 \wedge \vec{q}_3) \cdot (\vec{q}_2 \wedge \vec{q}_3) = 0 \tag{8}$$

The estimation of the projection matrix P can be done on the basis of the original equation that relates the coordinates of a point in the real world and the coordinates of its projection in the image plane:

$$\begin{bmatrix} U \\ V \\ S \end{bmatrix} = P \begin{bmatrix} x \\ y \\ z \\ 1 \end{bmatrix} \tag{9}$$

with $u = \frac{U}{S}$ y $v = \frac{V}{S}$. Then, for each projected point two equation will be found (Faugeras, 1993, sec. 3.4.1.2):

$$\vec{q}_1^T \vec{C} - u \vec{q}_3^T \vec{C} + q_{14} - u q_{34} = 0 \tag{10}$$

$$\vec{q}_2^T \vec{C} - u \vec{q}_3^T \vec{C} + q_{24} - u q_{34} = 0 \tag{11}$$

where $\vec{C} = (x,y,z,1)^T$. So, if N point are used in the calibration process, then $2N$ equation will be found. The set of equation can be compactly written $A\vec{q} = \vec{0}$ and restrictions, (7) and (8), in order to find a proper solution.
It is possible to fix one of the parameters (i.e. $q_{34} = 1$) and then, the modified system, $A'\vec{q'} = \vec{b}$, can be solved in terms of the minimum square error, for example. Afterward, the condition in (7) can be applied. With this idea, the result will be a valid projection matrix in our context, although its structure will not follow the one in (6), so, extrinsic and intrinsic parameters cannot be properly extracted.
A different option is to impose the condition $||\vec{q}_3|| = 1$. Then it will be possible to perform a minimization of $||A\vec{q}||$ as described in (Faugeras, 1993, Appendix. A).

5.1 The epipolar constraint

The epipolar constraint helps to convert the 2D search for correspondences in a 1D search since this constraint establishes the following: the images of a stereo pair are formed by pairs of lines, called *epipolar lines*, such that points in a given epipolar line in one of the images will find their matching point in the corresponding epipolar line in the other image of the pair.

First, we define the *epipolar planes* as the planes that pass through the optical centers of the two cameras and any point in the space. The intersections of these planes with the image planes define the pairs of epipolar lines (Fig. 5).

Pairs of epipolar lines can be found using the projection matrices of a stereo camera system (Faugeras, 1993, cap. 6). To describe the process, we write, now, the projection matrices as: $T = \begin{bmatrix} T_1^T \\ T_2^T \\ T_3^T \end{bmatrix}$, and let $\vec{M}$ denote a point. Then $T_3^T \vec{M} = 0$ represents a plane that is parallel to the image plane that contains the optical center ($T_3^T \vec{M} = 0 \rightarrow p_w = 0 \rightarrow \frac{p_x}{p_w} = \infty$, $\frac{p_y}{p_w} = \infty$). if, in addition to this, $T_2^T \vec{M} = 0$ ($\rightarrow p_y = 0$) and $T_1^T \vec{M} = 0$ ($\rightarrow p_x = 0$), we find the equation of two other planes that contain the optical center. The intersection of these three planes is the center of projection in global coordinates:

$$T\vec{C} = \begin{bmatrix} \vec{T}_1^T \\ \vec{T}_2^T \\ \vec{T}_3^T \end{bmatrix} \vec{C} = \begin{bmatrix} \vec{q}_1^T & q_{14} \\ \vec{q}_2^T & q_{24} \\ \vec{q}_3^T & q_{34} \end{bmatrix} \vec{C} = \vec{0} \tag{12}$$

The projection equation can be written as:

$$\begin{bmatrix} \vec{q}_1^T \\ \vec{q}_2^T \\ \vec{q}_3^T \end{bmatrix} \vec{O} = - \begin{bmatrix} q_{14} \\ q_{24} \\ q_{34} \end{bmatrix}. \quad \rightarrow \quad \vec{O} = - \begin{bmatrix} \vec{q}_1^T \\ \vec{q}_2^T \\ \vec{q}_3^T \end{bmatrix}^{-1} \cdot \begin{bmatrix} q_{14} \\ q_{24} \\ q_{34} \end{bmatrix} \tag{13}$$

with $\vec{O} = (o_x, o_y, o_z)^T$.

Using the optical center, the *epipoles* E_1 y E_2 can be found. An epipole is the projection of and optical center in the opposite image plane. Then, the epipolar lines can be easily defined since

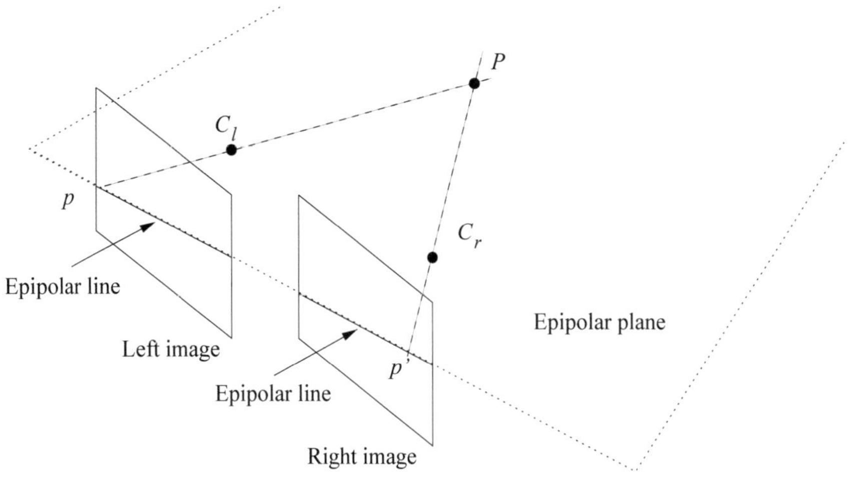

Fig. 5. Epipolar lines and planes.

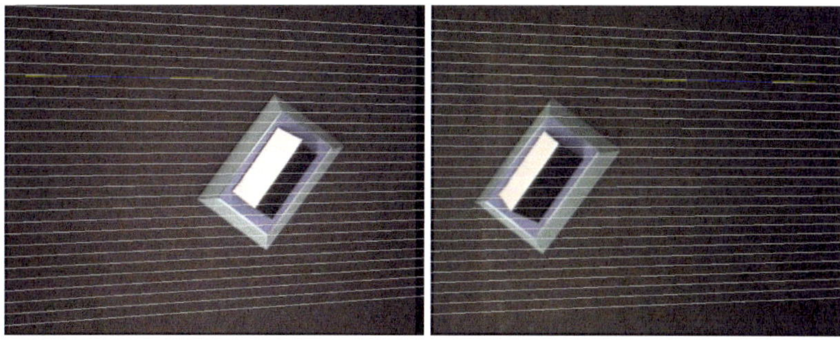

(a) (b)

Fig. 6. Left a) and right b) images of a stereo pair with superimposed epipolar lines obtained with the calibration matrices using homogeneous coordinates.

they all contain the respective epipole. Fig. 6 shows an example of application of the epipolar constraint derived from the calibration matrices of a binocular stereo setup.
Note that it is also possible to find the the relation that defines the epipolar constraint without the projection matrices (Trivedi, 1986). To this end, we will pay attention to the fundamental matrix.

5.1.1 The fundamental matrix

Since the epipolar lines are the projection of a single plane in the image planes, then there exists a projective transformation that transforms an epipolar line in an image of a stereo pair into the corresponding epipolar line in the other image of the pair. This transformation is defined by the *fundamental matrix*.
Let $\vec{l}$ and $\vec{l}'$ denote two corresponding epipolar lines in the two images of a stereo pair. The transformation between these two lines is a collineation: a projective transformation of the projective space that $\mathcal{P}^n$ into the same projective space (Mohr & Triggs, 1996). Collineations in the projective space are represented by 3×3 non-singular matrices. So, let A represent a collineation, then $l' = Al$.
Let $\vec{m} = [x,y,t]^t$ represent a point in the first image of the stereo pair and let $\vec{e} = [u,v,w]^t$ represent the epipole in the first image. Then, the epipolar line through $\vec{m}$ y $\vec{e}$ is given by $\vec{l} = [a,b,c]^t = \vec{m} \times \vec{e}$ (Mohr & Triggs, 1996, sec. 2.2.1). This is a linear transform that can be represented as:

$$\begin{bmatrix} a \\ b \\ c \end{bmatrix} = \begin{bmatrix} yw - tv \\ tu - xw \\ xv - yu \end{bmatrix} = \begin{bmatrix} 0 & w & -v \\ -w & 0 & u \\ v & -u & 0 \end{bmatrix} \begin{bmatrix} x \\ y \\ t \end{bmatrix}; \vec{l} = C\vec{m} \tag{14}$$

where C is a matrix with rank 2.
Then, we can write $\vec{l}' = AC\vec{m} = F\vec{m}$. Since this expression is accomplished by all the points in the line l', we can write:

$$\vec{m}'^t F \vec{m} = 0 \tag{15}$$

where F is 3×3 matrix with rank 2, called the fundamental matrix:

$$F = \begin{bmatrix} f_{11} & f_{12} & f_{13} \\ f_{21} & f_{22} & f_{23} \\ f_{31} & f_{32} & f_{33} \end{bmatrix} \tag{16}$$

Now, these relation must be estimated to simplify the correspondence problem. Linear and nonlinear techniques are available to this end (Luong & Faugeras, 1996). We will give a short discussion on the most frequently used procedures.

5.1.1.1 Estimation of the fundamental matrix

In the work by Xie and Yuan Li (Xie & Liu, 1995), it is considered that since the matrix F defines an application between projective spaces, than, any matrix $F' = kF$, where k is a scalar, defines the same transformation. Specifically, if an element F_{ij} of F is nonzero, say f_{33}, we can define $H = \frac{1}{f_{33}}F$, so that $\vec{m}'H\vec{m} = 0$, with

$$H = \begin{bmatrix} a & b & c \\ d & e & f \\ g & h & 1 \end{bmatrix} \tag{17}$$

The transformation represented by this equation is called generalized epipolar geometry and, since no additional constraints are imposed on the rank of F, the coefficients of the matrix can be easily estimated using sets of known matching point using a conventional least squares technique.

Mohr and Triggs (Mohr & Triggs, 1996) propose a more elaborate solution since the rank of the matrix is considered. Since, for each pair of matching points, we can write $\vec{m}'F\vec{m} = 0$, then for each pair, we can write the following equation:

$$xx'f_{1,1} + xy'f_{1,2} + xf_{1,3} + yx'f_{2,1} + yy'f_{2,2} + yf_{2,3} + x'f_{3,1} + y'f_{3,2} + f_{3,3} = 0 \tag{18}$$

The set of all the available equation can be written $D\vec{f} = 0$, where $\vec{f}$ is a vector that contains the 9 coefficients in F. The first constraint that can be imposed is that the solution have unity norm and, if more than 8 pairs of matching points are available, then, we can find the solution in the sense of minimum squares:

$$\min_{||\vec{f}||=1} ||D\vec{f}||^2 \tag{19}$$

which is equivalent to finding the eigenvector of the smallest eigenvalue in D^tD. The technique is similar to the one presented by Zhengyou Zhang in (Zhang, 1996, sec. 3.2). A different strategy is also shown in (Zhang, 1996, sec. 3.4), on the basis of the definition of proper error measures in the calculation of the fundamental matrix. Regardless of the technique employed, note that the process of estimation of the fundamental matrix is always very sensitive to noise

After the epipolar constraint is defined between the pairs of images, a geometrical transformation of the image is performed so that the corresponding epipolar lines will be horizontal and with the same vertical coordinate in both images.

Fig. 7 shows an example with selected epipolar lines, obtained using the fundamental matrix, superimposed on the images of a stereo pair.

Note that, in order to obtain reliable matching points to estimate the fundamental matrix, matching points should be well distributed over the entire image. In this example, we have

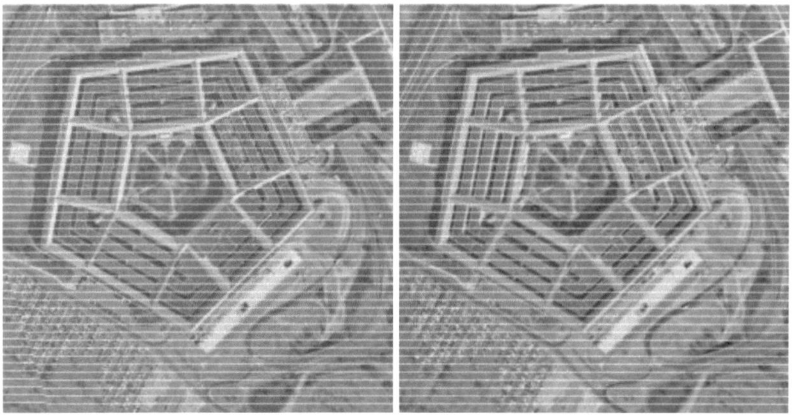

(a) (b)

Fig. 7. *Pentagon* stereo pair with superimposed epipolar lines. a) Left image. b) Right image.

used a set of the most probably correct matching points (about 200 points) obtained using the iterative Markovian algorithm that will be described.

5.2 Geometric correction of the images according to the epipolar constraint

Now, corrected pairs of images will be generated so that their corresponding epipolar lines will be horizontal and with the same vertical coordinate in both images to simplify the process of establishment of the correspondence. The process applied is the following:

- A list of vertical positions for the original images of the epipolar lines at the borders of the images will be generated.
- The epipolar lines will be redrawn in horizontal and the intensity values at the new pixel position of the rectified images will be obtained using a parametric bicubic model of the intensity surfaces (Foley et al., 1992), (Tardón, 1999).

6. Markov random fields

The formulation of MRFs in the context of stereo vision considers the existence of a set of irregularly distributed points or positions in an image, called (*nodes*) which are the image elements that will be matched. The set of possible correspondences of each node (*labels*) will be a discrete set selected from the image features extracted from the other image of the stereo pair, according to the disparity range allowed.

Our formulation of MRFs follows the one given by Besag (Besag, 1974). Note that the matching of a node will depend only on the matching of other nearby nodes called neighbors. The model will be supported by the Bayesian theory to incorporate levels of knowledge to the formulation:

- A priori knowledge: conditions that a set of related matchings must fulfill because of inherent restrictions that must be accomplished by the disparity maps.
- A posteriori knowledge: conditions imposed by the characterization of the matching of each node to each label.

Using this information in this context, restrictions are not imposed strictly, but in a probabilistic manner. So, correspondences will be characterized by a function that indicates a probability that each matching is correct or not. Then, the solution of the problem requires the maximization of a complex function defined in a finite but large space of solutions. The problem is faced by dividing it into smaller problems that can be more easily handled, the solutions of which can be mixed to give rise to the global solution, according to the MRF model.

6.1 Random fields

We will introduce in this section the concept of random field and some related notation. Let S denote all positions where data can be observed (Winkler, 1995). These positions define a graph in $\mathcal{R}^2$, where each position can be denoted $s \in S$. Each position can be in state x_s in a finite space of possible states X_s. We will call *node* each of the objects or primitives that occupy a position: a selected pixel to be matched will be a node. In the space of possible configurations of X ($\Pi_{s \in S} X_s$), we can consider the probabilities $P(x)$ con $x \in X$. Then, a strictly positive probability measure in X defines a *random field*.
Let A a subset in S ($A\ subsetS$) and X_A the set of possible configurations of the nodes that belong to A ($x_A\ inX_A$). Let $\bar{A}$ stand for the set of all nodes in S that do not belong to A. Then, it is possible to define the conditional probabilities $P(X_A = x_A / X_{\bar{A}} = x_{\bar{A}})$ that will be usually called *local characteristics*. These local characteristics can be handled with a reasonable computational burden, unlike the probability measures of the complete MRF.
The nodes that affect the definition of the local probabilities of another node s are called the neighborhood $\mathtt{V}(s)$. These are defined with the following condition: if node t is a neighbor of s, then s is a neighbor of t. *Clique* is another related and important concept: a set of nodes in S ($C \subset S$) is a clique in a MRF if all the possible pairs of nodes in a clique are neighbors.
With all this, we can define a Markov random field with respect to a neighborhood system $\mathtt{V}$ as a random field such that for each $A \subset S$:

$$P(X_A = x_A / X_{\bar{A}} = x_{\bar{A}}) = P(X_A = x_A / X_{\mathtt{V}(A)} = x_{\mathtt{V}(A)}) \tag{20}$$

Observe that any random field in which local characteristics can be defined in this way, is a random field and that positivity condition makes $P(X_A = x_A / X_{\bar{A}} = x_{\bar{A}})$ to be strictly positive.

6.2 Markov random fields and Markov chains

Now, more details on MRFs from a generic point of view will be given. Let $\Lambda = \{\lambda_\mathtt{p}, \lambda_\mathtt{q}, \ldots\}$ denote the set of nodes in which a MRF is defined. The set of locations in which the MRF is defined will be $\mathcal{P} = \{\mathtt{p}, \mathtt{q}, \mathtt{r}, \ldots\}$, which is very often related to rectangular structures, but this is not a requirement (Besag, 1974), (Kinderman & Snell, 1980). Let $\Delta = \{\delta_1, \delta_2, \ldots\}$ denote the set of possible labels, and $\Delta_\mathtt{p} = \{\delta_i, \delta_j, \ldots\}$, the set of possible labels for node $\lambda_\mathtt{p}$.
The matching of a node to a label will be $\lambda_\mathtt{i} = \delta_j$, and the probability of the assignation of a label to a node at position $\mathtt{p}$ will be $P(\lambda_\mathtt{p} = \delta_\mathtt{p})$. Since we are dealing with a MRF, then the following positivity condition is fulfilled:

$$P(\Lambda = \Xi) > 0 \tag{21}$$

where Ξ represents the set of all the possible assignments.
If the neighborhood $\mathtt{V}$ is the set of nodes with influence on the conditional probability of the assignation of a label to a node among the set of possible labels for that node:

$$P(\lambda_\mathtt{p} = \delta_\mathtt{p} | \lambda_\mathtt{q} = \delta_\mathtt{q}, \mathtt{q} \neq \mathtt{p}) = P(\lambda_\mathtt{p} = \delta_\mathtt{p} | \lambda_\mathtt{q} = \delta_\mathtt{q}, \mathtt{q} \in \mathtt{V}_\mathtt{p}) \tag{22}$$

where $\mathtt{V}_\mathtt{p}$ is the neighborhood of $\mathtt{p}$ in the random field, then:

- The process is completely defined upon the conditional probabilities: *local characteristics*.
- If $\mathtt{V_p}$ is the neighborhood of the node at $\mathtt{p}$, $\forall\, \mathtt{p} \in \mathcal{P}$, then Λ is a MRF with respect to $\mathtt{V}$ if and only if $P(\Lambda = \Xi)$ is a Gibbs distribution with respect to the defined neighborhood (Geman & Geman, 1984).

We can write the conditional probability as:

$$P(\lambda_A = \delta_A | \lambda_{\bar{A}} = \delta_{\bar{A}}) = \frac{e^{-\sum_{c \in C_1} \mathtt{U}_c(\delta_{A_v})}}{\sum_{\gamma_A \in \Delta_A} e^{-\sum_{c \in C_1} \mathtt{U}_c(\gamma_A, \delta_{V(A)})}} \tag{23}$$

This is a key result and some considerations must be done about it:

- Local and global Markovian properties are equivalent.
- Any MRF can be specified using the local characteristic. More specifically, these can be described using: $P(\lambda_{\mathtt{p}} = \delta_{\mathtt{p}} /\ \lambda_{\bar{\mathtt{p}}} = \delta_{\bar{\mathtt{p}}})$.
- $P(\lambda_{\mathtt{p}} = \delta_{\mathtt{p}} / \lambda_{\bar{\mathtt{p}}} = \delta_{\bar{\mathtt{p}}}) > 0, \forall\, \delta_{\mathtt{p}} \in \Delta_{\mathtt{p}}$, according to the positivity condition

Regarding neighborhoods, these are easily defined in regular lattices using the *order* of the field (Cohen & Cooper, 1987). In other structures, the concept of order can not be used, then the neighborhoods must be specially defined, for example, using a measure of the distance between the nodes.

The concept of clique is of main importance. According to its definition: if $C(\mathtt{t})$ is a clique in a certain neighborhood of $\lambda_{\mathtt{t}}$, $\mathtt{V_p}$, then if $\lambda_{\mathtt{o}}, \lambda_{\mathtt{p}}, \ldots, \lambda_{\mathtt{r}} \in C(\mathtt{t})$, then $\lambda_{\mathtt{o}}, \lambda_{\mathtt{p}}, \ldots, \lambda_{\mathtt{r}} \in \mathtt{V_s}$ $\forall\, \lambda_{\mathtt{s}} \in C(\mathtt{t})$. Note that a clique can contain zero nodes.

It is rather simple to define cliques in rectangular lattices (Cohen & Cooper, 1987), but is is a more complex task in arbitrary graphs and the condition of clique should be check for every clique defined. However, it can be easily observed that the cliques formed by up to two neighboring nodes are always correctly defined, so, since there is no reason that imposes us to define more complex cliques, we will use cliques with up to two nodes.

Regarding the local characteristic, it can be defined using information coming from two different sources: a priori knowledge about how the correspondence fields should be and a posteriori knowledge regarding the observations (characterization of the features to match). These two sources of information can be mixed up using the Bayes theorem which establishes the following relation:

$$P(x/\hat{y}) = \frac{P(x)P(\hat{y}/x)}{\sum_z P(z)P(\hat{y}/z)} \tag{24}$$

- $P(x)$: a priori probability of the correspondence fields.
- $P(\hat{y}/x)$ posterior probability of the observed data.
- $\sum_z P(z)P(\hat{y}/z) = P(\hat{y})$ represents the probability of the observed data. It is a constant.

6.2.1 A priori and posterior probabilities

The a priori probability density function (pdf) incorporates the knowledge of the field to estimate. This is a Gibbs function (Winkler, 1995) and, so, it is given by:

$$P(x) = \frac{e^{-H(x)}}{\sum_{x \in X} e^{-H(x)}} = \frac{1}{Z} e^{-H(x)} \tag{25}$$

where H is a real function:

$$\begin{array}{rccc} H: & X & \longrightarrow & \mathcal{R} \\ & x & \longrightarrow & H(x) \end{array} \tag{26}$$

Note that any strictly positive function in X can be written as a Gibbs function using:

$$H(x) = -\ln P(x) \tag{27}$$

The posterior probabilities must be strictly positive functions so that $P(\hat{y}/x)$ may follow the shape of a local characteristic of a MRF:

$$\exists\, G(\hat{y}/x) / G(\hat{y}/x) = -\ln P(\hat{y}/x) \tag{28}$$

6.3 Gibbs sampler and simulated annealing

Now, the problem that we must solve is that of generating Markov chains to update the configuration of the MRF in successive steps to estimate modes of the limit distributions (Winkler, 1995), (Tardón, 1999). This problem is addressed considering the *Gibbs sampler* with *simulated annealing* (Geman & Geman, 1984), (Winkler, 1995) to generate Markov chains defined by $P(y/x)$ using the local characteristic. The procedure is described in Table 1.

Note that there are no restrictions for the update strategy of the nodes, these can be chosen randomly. Also, the algorithm visits each node an infinite number of times. Note that the step Update Temperature T represents the modification of the original Gibbs sampler algorithm to give rise to the so-called *simulated annealing*. Recall that our objective is to estimate the modes of the limit distributions which are the *MAP* estimators of the MRF. Simulated annealing helps to find that state (Geman & Geman, 1984).

The main idea behind simulated annealing is now given. Consider a probability function $p(\psi) = \frac{1}{Z}e^{-H(\psi)}$ defined in $\psi \in \Psi$, where Ψ is a discrete and finite set of states. If the probability function is uniform, then any simulation of random variables that behaves according to that function will give any of the states, with the same probability as the other states. Instead, assume that $p(\psi)$ shows a maximum (mode). Then, the simulation will show that state with larger probability that the other states. Then, consider the following modification of the probability function in which the parameter *temperature* T is included:

$$p_T(\psi) = \frac{1}{Z_T}e^{-\frac{1}{T}H(\psi)} \tag{29}$$

This is the same function (a Gibbs function) as the original one when $T = 1$. If T is decreased towards zero, then $p_T(\psi)$ will have the same modes as the original one, but the difference in probability of the mode with respect to the other states will grow (see Fig. 8 as example).

A rigorous analysis of the behavior of the energy function H with T allows to determine the procedure to update the system temperature to guarantee the convergence, however, suboptimal simple temperature update procedures are often used (Winkler, 1995), (Tardón, 1999) (Sec. 9.2).

Now, simulated annealing can be applied to estimate the modes of the limit distributions of the Markov chains. According to our formulation, these modes will be to the MAP estimators of the correspondence map defined by the Markov random fields models we will describe.

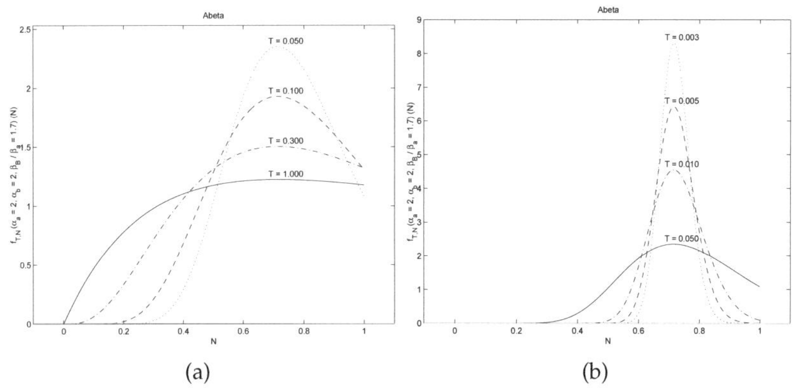

Fig. 8. Exaggeration of the modes of a probability function with decreasing temperature.

7. Using MRFs to find edges

Now, we are ready to consider the utilization of MRFs in a main stage of the stereo correspondence system. Since edges are known to constitute and important source of information for scene description, edges are used as feature to establish the correspondence. As described in Tardón et al. (2006), MRFs can be used for edge detection. The likelihood can be based on the Holladay's principle (Boussaid et al., 1996) to relate the detection process to the ability of the human visual system (HVS) to detect edges. This information can be written in the form of suitable energy functions, $H(y/x)$ (here, x denotes the underlying edge field and y denotes the observation), that can be used to define MRFs.
Also, a priori knowledge about the expected behavior of the edges can be incorporated and expressed as an energy function, $H(x)$.
Then, using the Bayes rule, the posterior distribution of the MRF can be found:

$$p(x/y) \propto p(x)p(y/x) \tag{30}$$

and it will have the form of a Gibbs function. So, it will be possible to write the energy of the MRF as follows (Tardón et al., 2006):

START: *Iteration*
    Update Temperature T
    $\forall s_i \in S$
        Select $s_i \in S_r$
        START: *Comment*
            s_i can be randomly selected from S_r.
            $S_r \subset S$ is the subset of nodes in S that have not been yet updated in the present iteration.
        END: *Comment*
        Determine the local characteristic $P_{T,A_{s_i}}$
        Randomly select the new state of s_i according to $P_{T,A_{s_i}}$
END: *Iteration*
GO TO: *Iteration*

Table 1. Gibbs sampler with simulated annealing.

(a) (b)

Fig. 9. a) Input image (*Lenna*). b) Edges detected using the MRF model in (Tardón et al., 2006).

$$H(x/y) = H(x) + H(y/x) \tag{31}$$

Fig. 9 shows an example of the performance of the algorithm. Simulated annealing is used (Sec. 6.3) with the following system temperature: $T = T_0 \cdot T_B^{k-1}$, where T_0 is the initial temperature, $T_B = 0.999$ and k stands for the iteration number. The number of iterations is 100. The parameter required by the algorithm is $C_w = 8$ (Tardón et al., 2006).
We have briefly introduced MRFS for the edge detection problem since MRFs are described in detail and they are used in the correspondence problem. However, the Nalwa-Binford edge detector Nalwa & Binford (1986) will be used in the stereo correspondence examples that will be shown in Sec. 10.

8. MRFs for stereo matching

In this section, we show how a Markovian model that makes use of an important psychovisual cue, the disparity gradient (*DG*) (Burt & Julesz, 1980), can be defined to help to solve the correspondence problem in stereo vision. We encode the behavior of the *DG* in a pdf to guide the definition of the energy function of the prior of a MRF for small baseline stereo. To complete the model based on a Bayesian approach, we also derive a likelihood function for the normalized cross-covariance (Kang et al., 1994) between any two matching points. Then, the correspondence problem is solved by finding the MAP solution using simulated annealing (Geman & Geman, 1984; Li et al., 1997) (Sec. 6.3).

8.1 Geometry of a stereo system for a MRF model of the correspondence problem

The setup of a stereo vision system is illustrated in Fig. 5. A point P in the space is projected onto the two image planes, giving rise to points p and p'. These two points are referred to as *matching* or *corresponding* points. Recall that these three points, together with the optical center of the two cameras, C_l and C_r, are constrained to lie on the same plane called the *epipolar* plane, and the line that joins p and p' is known as *epipolar* line.
As it has already been pointed, the *DG* is a main concept in stereo vision and for the correspondence problem (Burt & Julesz, 1980). Consider a pair of matching points $p \to p'$ and $q \to q'$. Their *DG* (δ) is defined by (Pollard et al., 1986):

$$\delta = \frac{\text{difference in disparity}}{\text{cyclopean separation}} = 2\frac{||(p' - q') - (p - q)||}{||(p' - q') + (p - q)||} \tag{32}$$

where the *cyclopean separation* represents the distance between the cyclopean image points ($\frac{p+p'}{2}$ and $\frac{q+q'}{2}$ as shown in figure 2) and the associated disparity vectors are $(p' - p)$ and $(q' - q)$.
Note that other constraints like surface continuity, figural continuity or uniqueness are subsumed by the DG (Faugeras, 1993), (Li & Hu, 1996).

8.2 Design of a MRF model for stereo matching

In this section, a methodology to design a MRF based on a Bayesian formulation on the basis of probabilistic analyses of the prior model of the expected correspondence maps and, also, on probabilistic analyses of the posterior information will be described (Tardón et al., 2006).

8.2.1 Neighborhood

The definition of the MRF requires the definition of the neighborhood system, so that each node, or feature for which a matching feature in the other image must be found, find some nearby nodes, neighbors, to define the local characteristic. In this case, a regular rectangular lattice can not be considered, and so, the concept of the order of the MRF can not be used to define neighbors or cliques.
We have decided to define a region around each node in which all the neighbors of the node can be found.
The neighborhood is defined upon the concept of superellipse (Fig. 10). This choice includes, in fact, different possibilities in the definition of the shape of the neighborhood. A superellipse with semi axes a and b and shape parameter p centered at the origin of the coordinate system is defined by:

$$\left(\frac{|x|}{a}\right)^p + \left(\frac{|y|}{b}\right)^p - 1 = 0 \tag{33}$$

with $a > 0$, $b > 0$ and $p > 0$.
Note that the structure of the neighborhood must be kept fixed along the image to guarantee the correct definition of the field in terms of neighbours and cliques.

8.2.2 Labels: sets of possible matchings

The region in which matching features for each node can be found is defined by superellipses, just like the neighborhoods. Labels are defined as the extracted features that can be found in the selected region of the other image of the stereo pair, plus the null-correspondence label (for the nodes that have no matching feature in the other image).
This search region is a superellipse (Fig. 10, eq. (33)) centered at the location point where we expect to find the correspondence of each node.
Note that if the images are correctly rectified, then the search region will become a segment in the corresponding epipolar line. This shape can, also, be easily described by the superellipse, with appropriate parameters.

8.3 A priori knowledge

Regarding a priori knowledge, the sources of information typically used in stereo matching are the maximum difference of disparity between two points (Barnard & Thompson, 1980),

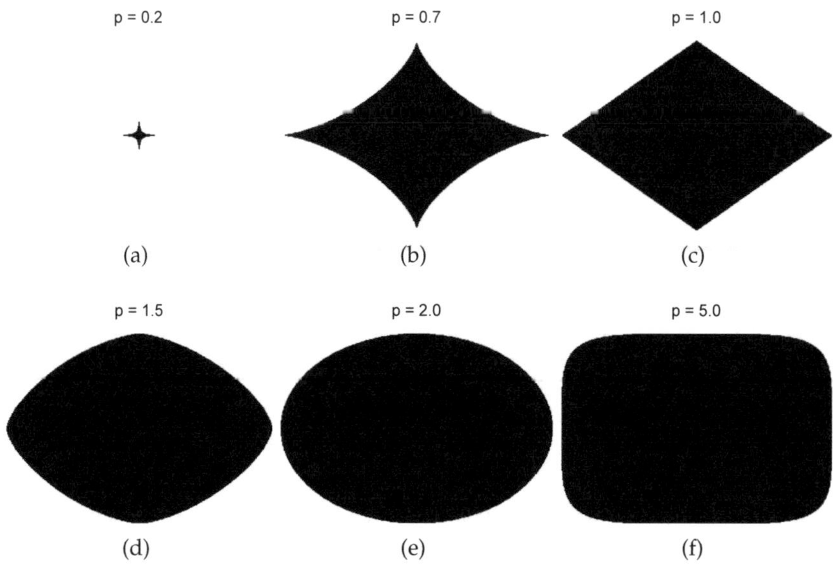

Fig. 10. Geometrical structures defined by the superellipse.

surface smoothness (Hoff & Ahuja, 1989), disparity continuity (Sherman & Peleg, 1990), ordering (Zhang & Gerbrands, 1995) and the disparity gradient DG (Olsen, 1990). However, the DG subsumes the rest of the constraints usually imposed for stereo matching (Li & Hu, 1996). Also, it is possible to obtain closed-from expressions of its probabilistic behavior under reasonable assumptions.

It has been demonstrated that the DG between two matching points should not be larger than 1 (Pollard et al., 1985), although this is a fuzzy limit, since it may vary slightly, depending on different factors (Wainman, 1997), (McKee & Verghese, 2002). Furthermore, in natural scenes, the DG between correct matches is usually small. We consider the limit of the DG as a soft threshold for the HVS, such that there should be a low probability that correct matches exceed this limit.

So, we define a MRF of matching points in which the information given by the DG is used to cope with the a priori knowledge (Tardón et al., 1999), (Tardón et al., 2004). To proceed with the design, notice that every match will be defined as the relationship between a selected feature in the left image (called *node*) and another feature in the right image (called *label*) (Fig. 11 and Sections 8.2.1 and 8.2.2).

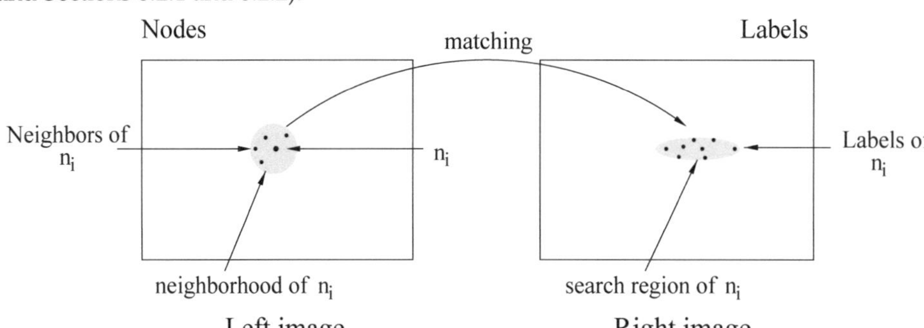

Fig. 11. Labels and nodes.

Consider a neighborhood system V for the set of sites S in the left image. Since the a priori knowledge will be based on the DG, which is defined for every pair of matching points, we will only use the set of binary cliques, $\mathcal{C}_b$, to build the a priori Gibbs function of the disparity map:

$$p_{S\Delta}(x) = \frac{1}{Z_x} e^{-H_{S\Delta}(x)} \tag{34}$$

where the energy function $H_{S\Delta}(x)$ consists of the potentials of the cliques in $\mathcal{C}_b$:

$$H_{S\Delta}(x) = \sum_{c \in \mathcal{C}_b} U_\Delta(\delta_c) \tag{35}$$

with δ_c the DG defined by the matches in the clique c. Note that when the DG is modeled as a random variable it will be denoted with the capital letter Δ, with δ a particular value of it. The same criterion will be used for other random variables in this section.

To derive the potential functions, consider, as an illustration, a node n_i that has a single neighbor n_j. Then a single clique $c_{i,j}$ contains the node n_i and the corresponding local characteristic will be (Winkler, 1995):

$$p(n_i = x_i / X_R = x_R, R = S - \{n_i\}) \propto p(n_i = x_i / X_{n_j} = x_{n_j}) \propto e^{-U_\Delta(\delta_{c_{i,j}})} \tag{36}$$

This function must be consistent with the behavior of the DG, so a natural choice for the potential functions is:

$$U_\Delta(\delta_c) \propto -\ln p(n_i = x_i / X_{n_j} = x_{n_j}) \propto -\ln f_\Delta(\delta) \tag{37}$$

In this way, the probabilistic behavior of the DG is easily accounted for in the prior. Recall that this is not an attempt to use the pdf of the DG to define the marginals of the MRF but to derive suitable potential functions using psycho-visual information. Now, we must derive the pdf the of the disparity gradient.

8.3.1 Pdf of the disparity gradient

Consider a simple geometry of parallel cameras of small aperture. Figure 12 shows a top view of the system with the Y axis protruding from the paper plane upwards; the terminology and the relationship between the parameters involved are described in figures 12 and 13.

The DG is defined upon the relationship between the projection of two points in 3D space, P and Q, the coordinates of which in the world reference system are given by the following relations:

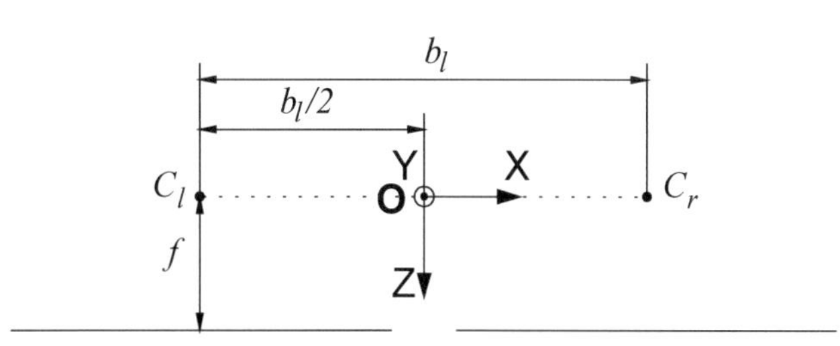

Fig. 12. Stereo system with parallel cameras of small aperture.

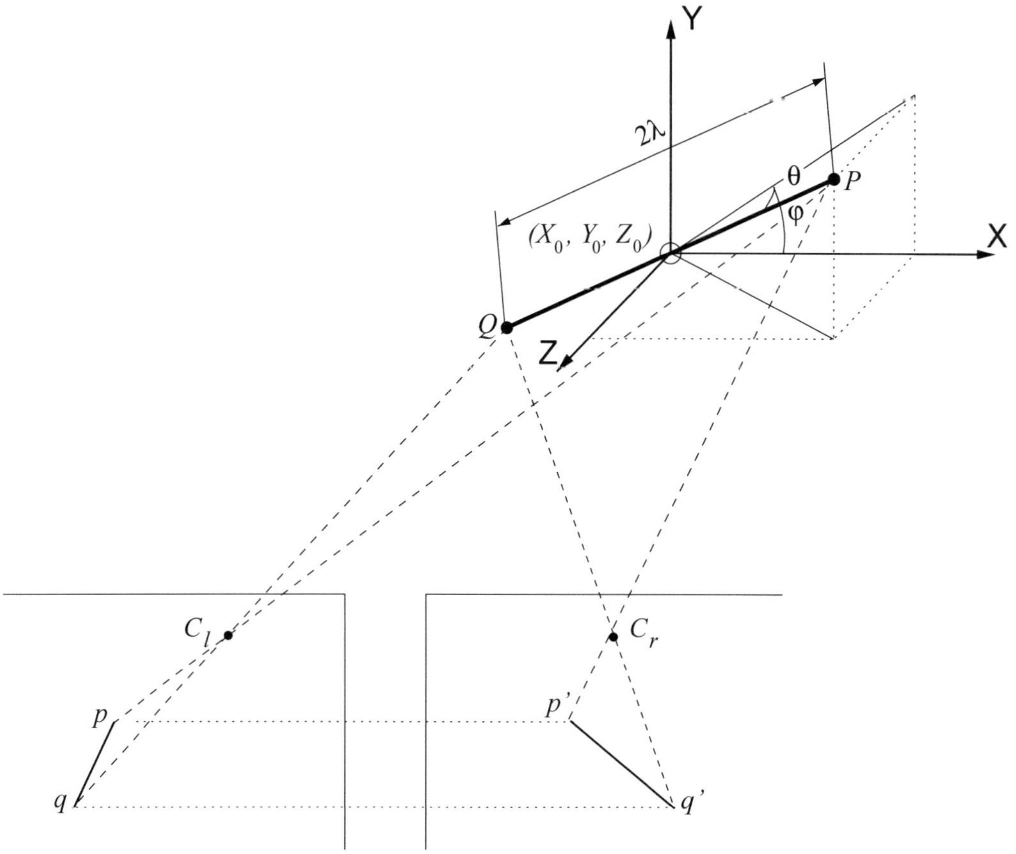

Fig. 13. Stereo system with parallel cameras of small aperture: projections and disparity gradient scenario.

$$P = (P_x, P_y, P_z) = (X_0 + \lambda \cos\theta \cos\psi, Y_0 + \lambda \cos\theta \sin\psi, Z_0 - \lambda \sin\theta) \tag{38}$$

$$Q = (Q_x, Q_y, Q_z) = (X_0 - \lambda \cos\theta \cos\psi, Y_0 - \lambda \cos\theta \sin\psi, Z_0 + \lambda \sin\theta) \tag{39}$$

where

- 2λ is an arbitrary distance that separates P and Q.
- (X_0, Y_0, Z_0) is a point which is equidistant between P and Q and belongs to the segment $\overline{PQ}$.
- ψ and θ are the angles that describe the orientation of $\overline{PQ}$.

  Note that it is reasonable to model these variables, in the absence of any other type of knowledge, as independent uniform random variables, Ψ and Θ, in the intervals $(-\pi, \pi)$ and $(0, \pi)$, respectively(Law & Kelton, 1991).

The projections of P and Q on the left and right image planes are given by:

$$p = \left(-\frac{f}{P_z}(P_x + \frac{b_l}{2}), -\frac{f}{P_z}P_y\right) \tag{40}$$

$$q = \left(-\frac{f}{Q_z}(Q_x + \frac{b_l}{2}), -\frac{f}{Q_z}Q_y\right) \tag{41}$$

$$p' = \left(-\frac{f}{P_z}(P_x - \frac{b_l}{2}), -\frac{f}{P_z}P_y\right) \tag{42}$$

$$q' = \left(-\frac{f}{Q_z}(Q_x - \frac{b_l}{2}), -\frac{f}{Q_z}Q_y\right) \tag{43}$$

where b_l and f represent the baseline and the focal distance, respectively (Fig. 12). Substituting equations (38)—(43) in equation (32) we obtain

$$\delta = \frac{||b_l \sin\theta||}{||(-X_0 \sin\theta - Z_0 \cos\theta \cos\psi, -Y_0 \sin\theta - Z_0 \cos\theta \sin\psi)||} \tag{44}$$

An approximated expression can be determined for the pdf of the DG for this general case (Tardón, 1999); however, a much more tractable and useful expression can be obtained if we assume that the primitives P and Q are approximately centered between the two cameras or if we use small aperture cameras. In this case, the conditions $Z_0 \gg X_0$, $Z_0 \gg Y_0$ and $\theta \neq \frac{\pi}{2}$ (not that in this case occlusions can not occur) are satisfied. Then, the DG can be expressed in the following simplified way:

$$\delta = \frac{b_l \sin\theta}{Z_0 |\cos\theta|} \tag{45}$$

and the pdf will be (Tardón, 1999), (Tardón et al., 2004):

$$f_\Delta(\delta) = \frac{\frac{2}{\pi}\frac{b_l}{Z_0}}{\delta^2 + \left(\frac{b_l}{Z_0}\right)^2} \tag{46}$$

This is a unilateral Cauchy pdf with parameters 0 and $\frac{b_l}{Z_0}$ ($UCau(0, \frac{b_l}{Z_0})$) (see figure 14). This pdf favors the label assignments with low DG values as required. This tendency to favor low DG matches increases when the ratio $\frac{b_l}{Z_0}$ decreases, as expected.

8.4 The likelihood function

Now, we consider the information that can be extracted form the observations that will be used for matching. In other words, we deal now with a measure of the probability of a certain observation y given an outcome of the MRF x. Observe that the intensity values of the pixels in the two images of the stereo pair located in a window centered at the matching primitives should be similar. So, a similarity measure defined taking into account this idea should be higher in windows centered about correct matching primitives than in windows centered at unrelated projections.

We will use a function, $\mathcal{V}$ (t.b.d.), of the normalized-cross-covariance $\mathcal{N}$ (Kang et al., 1994) to measure the similarity between every pair of corresponding primitives and to model $p(y/x)$ accordingly. Using the selected measure, the role played by the observation y will be played, here, by $\mathcal{V} = \mathcal{N}^2$, given the underlying disparity map x. Then, the likelihood function will be denoted by

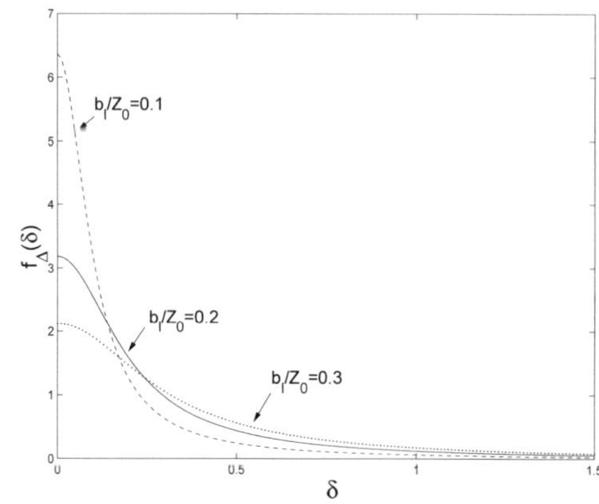

Fig. 14. Unilateral Cauchy pdf.

$$p_{S\mathcal{N}}(y/x) = \frac{1}{Z_{y/x}} e^{-H_{S\mathcal{N}}(y/x)} \tag{47}$$

And the energy of the system due to the similarity measures will be:

$$H_{S\mathcal{N}}(y/x) = \sum_{i=1}^{N} U_{\mathcal{N}}(n_i, l_{n_i}) \tag{48}$$

where the node n_i is matched to the label l_{n_i}. A natural choice for the potential functions is

$$U_{\mathcal{N}}(n_i, l_{n_i}) \propto -\ln f_{\mathcal{V}}(v) \tag{49}$$

where $f_{\mathcal{V}}(v)$ stands for the probability density function of the square of the normalized cross-covariance $\mathcal{V} = \mathcal{N}^2$. We use $f_{\mathcal{V}}(v)$ to derive a suitable form of the potential function as stated in (49) (Tardón, 1999),(Tardón et al., 2006).

8.4.1 Probabilistic analysis of the normalized cross-covariance

First of all, we recall the correlation coefficient (also called normalized cross-covariance (Kang et al., 1994)):

$$\mathcal{N}(N_i, L_j) = \frac{E\left[\{N_i - E[N_i]\} \cdot \left\{L_j - E[L_j]\right\}\right]}{\left(E\left[\{N_i - E[N_i]\}^2\right] \cdot E\left[\left\{L_j - E[L_j]\right\}^2\right]\right)^{\frac{1}{2}}} \tag{50}$$

where E represents the mathematical expectation operator and N_i and L_j, are the gray levels of the image windows considered, which will be treated as random variables, of node n_i, in the left image, and label l_j, in the right image, respectively. Needless to say, this coefficient must be replaced in practice by its estimation from the available data.
We assume that the image intensity can be considered Gaussian in each estimation window (Lim, 1990), with additive Gaussian noise. We will assume that only one of the image will corrupted by noise (Kanade & Okutomi, 1994). Specifically, let η denote a vector of independent and identically distributed Gaussian random variables, then $N_i = G + \eta$ and and $L_j = G$, where $G \sim N(\eta_l, \sigma_l)$ stands for the gray level in the absence of noise and $\eta \sim N(0, \sigma_\eta)$

represents the noise that corrupts the image with the labels. Using these conditions and operating in (50) we can find the following expression for the square of $\mathcal{N}$:

$$\mathcal{N}^2 = \frac{\sigma_l^2}{\sigma_l^2 + \sigma_\eta^2} \tag{51}$$

We will use the natural estimators of σ_n^2 and σ_l^2 and, so, we obtain the sample unbiased variances $\hat{\sigma}_n^2$ and $\hat{\sigma}_l^2$ using windows placed on both sides of each edge detected.
The noise η is obtained from the difference between the matched windows. The estimated unbiased variances $\hat{\sigma}_x^2 = \frac{1}{N-1}\sum_{i=1}^{N}(x_i - \hat{m}_x)^2$ will behave as gamma r.v.'s (Bain & Engelhardt, 1989) with parameters

$$\alpha = \frac{N-1}{2} \text{ and } \phi = \frac{2\sigma_x^2}{N-1} \tag{52}$$

For simplicity, for each window, let $\mathcal{V} = \hat{\mathcal{N}}^2$ and denote $a = \hat{\sigma}_l^2$ and $b = \hat{\sigma}_\eta^2$ which are two independent gamma r.v.'s: $A \sim \gamma(\alpha_a, \phi_a)$ and $B \sim \gamma(\alpha_b, \phi_b)$. Their joint pdf will be the product of the two gamma pdfs, and then, the pdf of

$$\mathcal{V} = \frac{A}{A+B} \tag{53}$$

is readily obtained (Tardón & Portillo, 1998). Using those results, one arrives at

$$f_{g\mathcal{V}}(v) = \begin{cases} \frac{(1-v)^{\alpha_b-1}v^{\alpha_a-1}}{B(\alpha_a,\alpha_b)} \cdot \frac{\phi_a^{\alpha_b}\phi_b^{\alpha_a}}{(\phi_b v - \phi_a v + \phi_a)^{\alpha_a+\alpha_b}} & , v \in [0,1] \\ 0 & , \text{otherwise} \end{cases} \tag{54}$$

with $B(\cdot,\cdot)$ the beta function. We call this pdf *generalized beta* and denote it by $Gbeta_{\mathcal{V},\left(\alpha_a,\alpha_b,\frac{\phi_b}{\phi_a}\right)}(v)$ (Tardón, 1999), (Tardón & Portillo, 1998) (Fig. 15). Observe that the *Gbeta* pdf is far more versatile that the *beta* pdf and the former naturally subsumes the behavior of the latter.
However, we have not finished with our model yet since a good estimate of the noise power will not be available at the early stages of the algorithm. In fact, the difference between the matched windows incorporates both actual noise and noise due to the incorrect matches. Then, the main idea, now is to consider the estimated noise power as an upper bound of the actual noise power.
Consider the same variables A and B, but assume, now, that ϕ_b is a uniform r.v. (Φ_b) (Law & Kelton, 1991) within the interval $[0, \phi_B]$, with ϕ_B the upper bound. Then, the conditional pdf of B given $\Phi_b = \phi_b$ is *gamma*, and the joint pdf of B and Φ_b is $f_{B,\Phi_b}(b,\phi_b) = f_{B/\Phi_b}(b/\phi_b) f_{\Phi_b}(\phi_b)$.
Then, it is possible to obtain the pdf of $\mathcal{V}$ defined by (53) ((Tardón & Portillo, 1998)):

$$f_{\mathcal{V}}(v) = \begin{cases} \frac{1}{v^2}\frac{\alpha_a}{\alpha_b-1}\frac{\phi_a}{\phi_B} I_{\frac{\phi_B v}{\phi_a - \phi_a v + \phi_B v}}(\alpha_a+1, \alpha_b-1) & , v \in [0,1] \\ 0 & , \text{otherwise} \end{cases} \tag{55}$$

where $I_*(\cdot)$ stands for the incomplete beta function (Abramowitz & Stegun, 1970) and α_* and ϕ_* are defined in (52).
We call this function *asymmetric beta* pdf and we will denote it by $Abeta_{\mathcal{V},\left(\alpha_a,\alpha_b,\frac{\phi_B}{\phi_a}\right)}(v)$. Figure 16 illustrates the behavior of this function.

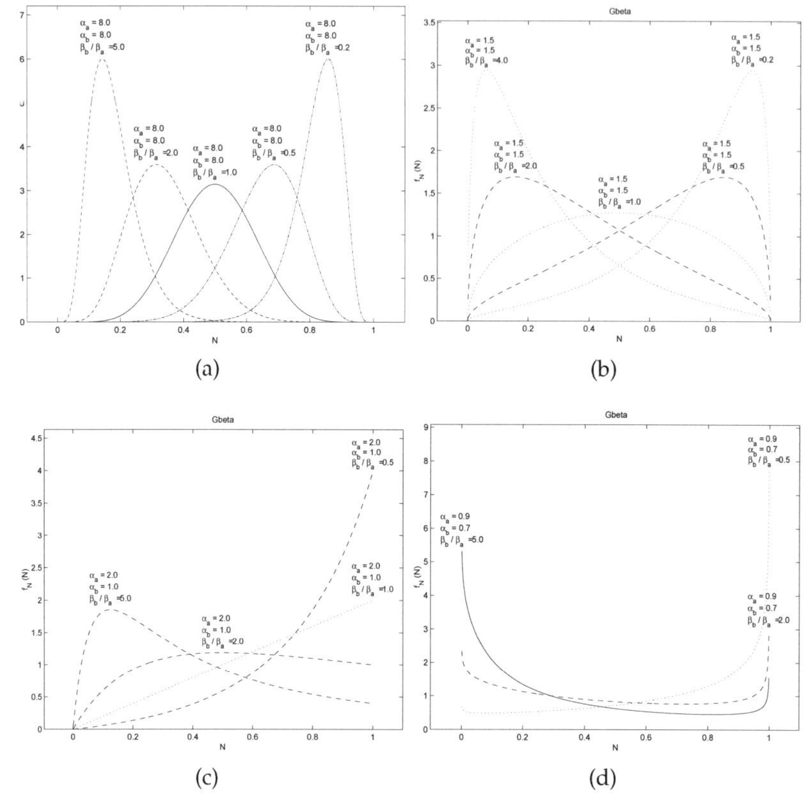

Fig. 15. $Gbeta_{\mathcal{V},\left(\alpha_a,\alpha_b,\frac{\phi_b}{\phi_a}\right)}(\nu)$.

Since $Abeta(\cdot) > 0$ for $\mathcal{N}^2 \in (0,1)$, reasoning as in section 8.3, we can use the derived *asymmetric beta* pdf for the normalized-cross-covariance to define the energy $H_{S\mathcal{N}}(y/x)$ (equation (48)), as stated in equation (49).

8.5 The posterior pdf

After all the pdfs are available, the posterior distribution will be found suing the Bayes rule:

$$p_S(x/y) \propto p_{S\Delta}(x) p_{S\mathcal{N}}(y/x) \tag{56}$$

Its energy can be written as follows:

$$H_S(x/y) = H_{S\Delta}(x) + H_{S\mathcal{N}}(y/x) \tag{57}$$

Since $p_{S\Delta}(x)$ and $p_{S\mathcal{N}}(y/x)$ are Gibbs functions, then $p_S(x/y)$ is also a Gibbs function and, consequently, it describes a MRF.

Once the posterior pdf has been defined, the MAP estimator of the disparity map can be obtained by well-known procedures (Winkler, 1995; Boykov et al., 2001; Geman & Geman, 1984) (Sec. 6.3).

Note that, after equation (57), it is clear that classical area correlation techniques only make use of the information that would be included in $H_{S\mathcal{N}}$.

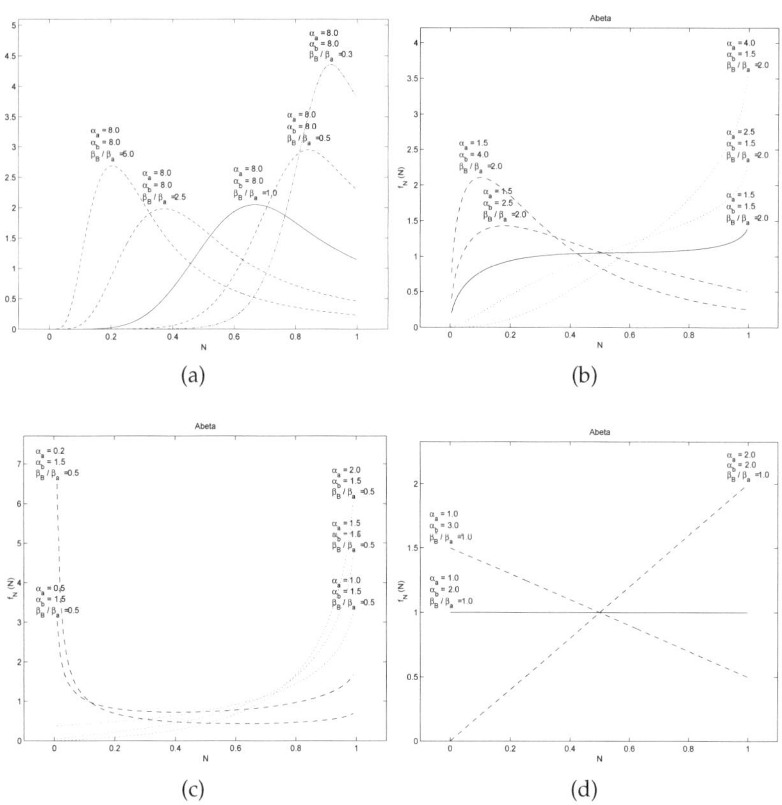

Fig. 16. $Abeta_{\mathcal{V},\left(\alpha_a,\alpha_b,\frac{\phi_B}{\phi_a}\right)}(\nu)$.

9. Implementation of a stereo correspondence system with a MRF model

In this section we include a number of notes about the model presented, the implementation and the technique used to solve the problem. Afterwards, we show some examples of the application of the algorithm to solve different stereo pairs.

9.1 Implementation details. Object model

The use of Markov fields allows not only to specify how the correspondence of each node with respect to each neighborhood and a similarity measure of the nodes must be established but also to define of a stereo correlation system intrinsically parallelizable (Geman & Geman, 1984). In fact, the system that implements the MRF based stereo matching algorithm is implemented according to an object-oriented paradigm. So, we briefly describe the implementation of the system using the Object Modeling Technique *OMT* (Rumbaugh, 1991). In accordance with the description of simulation algorithm of Markov chains (Gibbs sampler with simulated annealing, Table 1), the decision on the correspondence of each node is done at each node, according to a certain set of neighbors which are used to build the functions involved in the model. A set of labels (including the null-correspondence label) will be available to establish its correspondence according to the local characteristic. Specifically, each node at each iteration computes the prior and the likelihood pdfs, according to the neighborhood system defined, to solve its own correspondence.

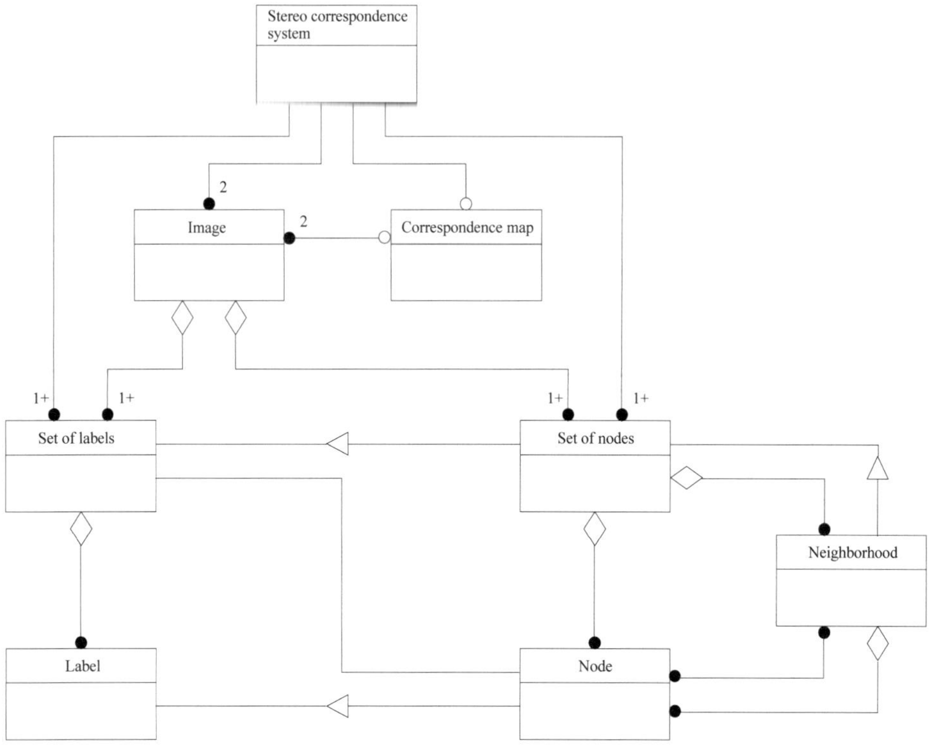

Fig. 17. MRF based stereo correspondence system. Object model (Rumbaugh, 1991).

Fig. 17 shows an object model that describes the relations between the main entities in the system.

The object that establishes the correspondence will be connected with at least other two that represent the real-world images and an initial correspondence map (if available). This object will contain a set of nodes and a set of labels (their roles are interchangeable: correspondence can be established from an image to another and vice versa), which are the features to match in both images of a stereo pair. Each of these sets is made up of many nodes or labels, respectively. Each node will be related to a neighborhood (a subset of the nodes in that image) and to a set of labels in the other image (plus the null correspondence label).

The sets of nodes and labels are identical, except for addition of some extra features in the set of nodes. So, the set of nodes and each particular node are derived from the set of labels and each particular label objects, respectively.

The main functionalities of the nodes, which constitute the main processing unit, are the following:

1. Define the set of possible labels to establish its own correspondence.
2. Define its neighborhood.
3. Determine an initial correspondence selecting a label from the available set for that node.
4. Establish its own correspondence using the local characteristic according to the information given by the neighborhood and using its particular set of possible labels.

The operation of the system is based on the activity of each node, which performs a relatively simple task at each stage: select randomly a label in accordance with the local characteristic to iteratively evolve toward the MAP estimator of the correspondence field.

9.2 Implementation details. Parameters and procedure

Correspondences are sought only within preselected features, instead of searching in the whole image, this helps to reduce computational burden. The features selected are edge pixels obtained by the Nalwa-Binford edge detector (Nalwa & Binford, 1986); specifically, the central pixel in the fitted surface is used. Other edge detectors could be used, including the MRF based edge detector described, however, the Nalwa-Binford edge detector has been selected because of its availability and because it extracts edge pixels with subpixel accuracy.

The matching procedure is performed solely from the left to the right image; uniqueness is imposed by the *DG* constraint itself (Li & Hu, 1996). The neighborhood system is defined by the nodes that lie inside a region defined around every node and a similar criterion is used to define the set of possible matches or labels for a node. The set of possible matches for a node will be defined by all the labels that lie inside the corresponding search window: a region centered at a likely match position. This selection is not critical since large windows will almost-surely contain the right label. Superellipses are used to define these regions in a compact widely usable form.

The null match, i.e., the label that leaves a node unmatched, must always belong to the set of possible matches, so its energy must be adequately defined. To this end, consider, separately, the a priori and likelihood information.

- Regarding the a priori information, and recalling how the HVS works, we define the energy of the null match as the energy of a *virtual match* in which all the neighbors have a *DG* equal to 0.8; this means that a null match is (probabilistically) preferred to other matches with a larger *DG*.
- With respect to the likelihood term, since the null match has obviously no data, we need to define it. We have implemented this choice as follows: recalling equation (54), for every node, obtain the energy of the current assignment (the one from the previous iteration) and pick the maximum of the *Gbeta* pdf under these working conditions. Let ν_{max} denote the mode of the *Gbeta* function. Then, find the argument ν_n of *Gbeta* (leftwards from the mode since no assignment tends to uncorrelation) such that $Gbeta_{\nu,\left(\alpha_a,\alpha_b,\frac{\phi_b}{\phi_a}\right)}(\nu_n)$ is half $Gbeta_{\nu,\left(\alpha_a,\alpha_b,\frac{\phi_b}{\phi_a}\right)}(\nu_{max})$. Finally, use this value, ν_n, as the argument to define the energy of the null match according to the likelihood information.

To evolve towards the MAP estimator we have resorted to a practical suboptimal cooling scheme (Winkler, 1995), defined by the following system temperature: $T = T_0 \cdot T_B^k$, where $T_0 = 1$, $T_B = 0.9998$ and k is the sweep number.

Different techniques to establish the initial matchings can be selected, however the initial state is significant only during the first stages of the algorithm, and after a number of iterations, the algorithm evolves to a solution independently of the initial state (Winkler, 1995).

The ratio $\frac{b_l}{Z_0}$ $\left(\frac{\text{baseline}}{\text{subject distance}}\right)$ modifies the sharpness of the a priori pdf (46) and so, the selection of this parameter has an influence on the system performance; if this parameter is too small, the algorithm could be easily trapped in local maxima. The ratio $\frac{b_l}{Z_0}$ has been manually tuned. However, note that it could be accurately estimated for every tentative matching using the calibration parameters.

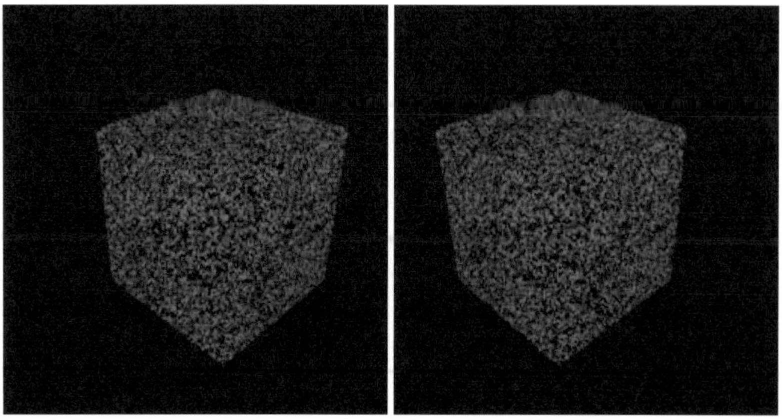

(a) (b)

Fig. 18. *Cube* stereo pair. a) Left image. b) Right image.

10. Experiments

We can observe the performance of the MRF based stereo matching system presented in this chapter in a number of experiments done with synthetic and real world stereo pairs (see Acknowledgments).

10.1 Synthetic images

Consider the synthesized random dot stereogram (RDS) (*cube*) shown in Fig. 18. The epipolar lines are horizontal so the search window becomes a segment of the corresponding epipolar line in the right image. We have used a horizontal disparity search within the interval $[-50, -20]$ pixels. The image size is 256×256 with 256 gray levels. Nodes and labels have been defined as those points that exceed an intensity threshold of 80, giving rise to the number of features shown in Table 2. The ratio $\frac{b_l}{Z_0}$ (recall figures 12 and 13) is approximately 0.3 and the cooling schedule is as described in section 9.2.

Note that, since there is no other information available, the neighborhood includes all the nodes in a circular region centered at each node. Regarding the size of the neighborhood, it should be large enough so that a sufficiently large set of nearby nodes can be employed to define the local interactions (Besag, 1974).

In this experiment, we have consciously ignored the brightness information of nodes and labels; this is equivalent to assuming that the likelihood pdf is non informative, i.e., the disparity map will only be a function of the *DG*.

Figure 19 shows a perspective view of the evolution of the disparity map with the number of iterations of the simulated annealing algorithm. The initial disparity map, shown in figure 19 a), is obtained randomly; it is just a random cloud of points. Also the final disparity

	Size		Selected features		
	Rows	Columns	# of nodes	# of labels	$\frac{b_l}{Z_0}$
Cube	256	256	6284	6332	0.3
rd1	250	250	8269	12834	0.3

Table 2. Synthetic images

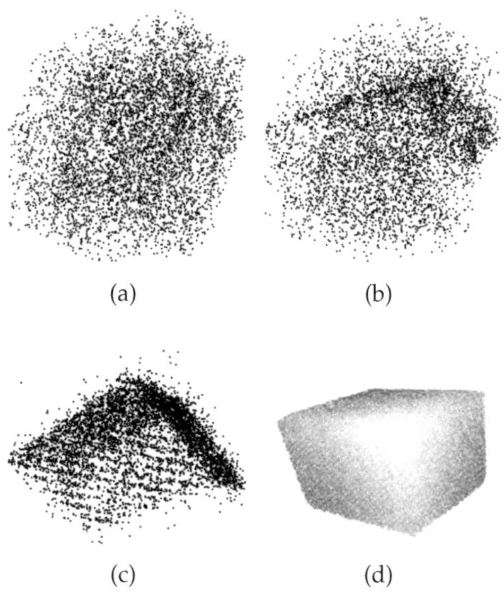

Fig. 19. *Cube* disparity map. a) Initial (random) configuration. b) After 500 iterations. c) After 5000 iterations. Three faces of the cube are clearly visible. d) After 10000 iterations. Interpolated disparity map of the stereo pair *cube*. Modified Hardy interpolation used with $b = 3$, radius= 15 and number of base functions= 15 (Vázquez, 1998).

map obtained after 10000 iterations, interpolated using a Hardy-like interpolation technique (Franke, 1982), (Bradley & Vickers, 1993), (Vázquez, 1998), is shown in Fig. 19 d).
We have also applied our stereo algorithm to the synthesized random dot stereogram *rd1* shown in Fig. 20.
Again, the epipolar lines are horizontal. The search region is a segment of the corresponding epipolar line in the right image defined by the following interval: $[-20, 20]$ pixels. The image size is 250×250 with 256 gray levels. Nodes and labels have been defined as those points that

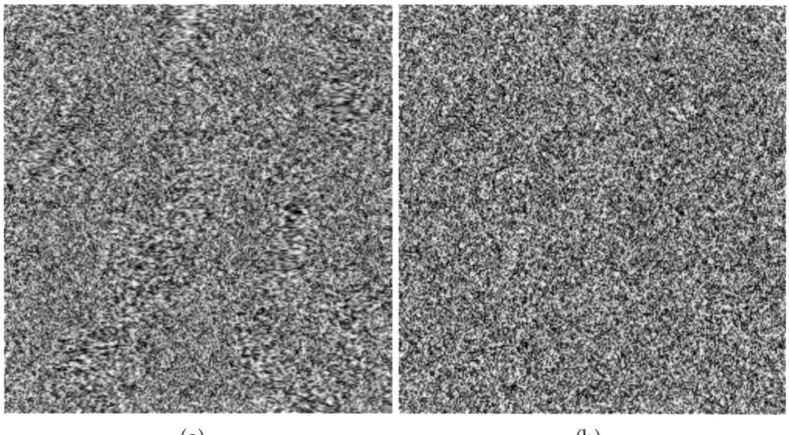

Fig. 20. *Rd1* stereo pair. a) Left image. b) Right image.

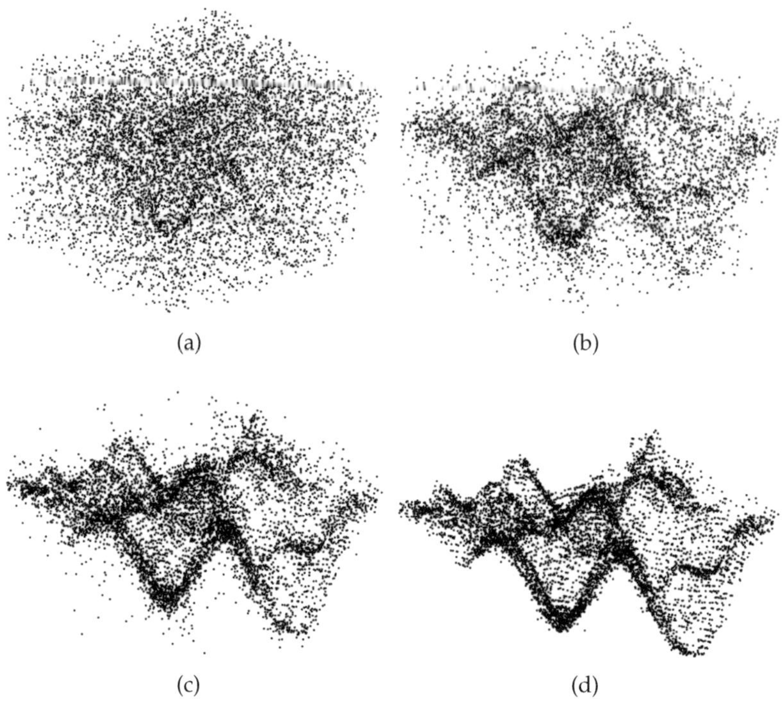

Fig. 21. Evolution of the correspondence map for the *rd1* stereo pair. a) Initial (random) configuration. b) After 1000 iterations. c) After 3000 iterations. d) After 7000 iterations.

exceed an intensity threshold of 80, giving rise to the number of features shown in Table 2. The ratio $\frac{b_l}{Z_0}$ (recall figures 12 and 13) is approximately 0.3. The cooling scenario is unchanged. Brightness information is ignored.
Fig. 21 shows the evolution of the correspondence map as the iteration number increases.

10.2 Real world images

In this section, we show the results found on some real world images. The images have been geometrically corrected to make the epipolar lines horizontal before performing the matching procedure. The rectification is done using the fundamental matrix (Sec. 5.1.1), which is estimated using a number of matches obtained carrying out a preliminary matching stage using the MRF based matching technique described. In this case, a smaller number of iterations are performed and the neighborhood and the search regions are defined by large superellipses with parameter $p = 2$. The search windows are, in this stage, circles (Sec. 8.2), centered at the expected matching label. The diameter of the window is large enough to capture the real matching, if any, even for high disparity values. Afterwards, only the matchings with highest probability are selected to estimate the fundamental matrix (usually between 100 and 200 matching points) (Tardón, 1999).
Nodes and labels (edges) are detected (see Sec. 9.2). Note that only the pixel that lays at the center of the edge detector window with a contrast larger than 70 is selected as node or label in the left and right images, respectively. The information of the node position and the edge orientation will be used to place the windows from which the normalized cross-covariance

(a) (b)

Fig. 22. *Pentagon* stereo pair. a) Left image. b) Right image.

will be calculated. A window at each side of the edge is considered to calculate the normalized cross-covariance. The outcomes of this measure, at each side of the edge, are considered to be independent.
Recall that we consider that the image intensity levels are of Gaussian nature and that these variables are affected by Gaussian noise in one of the images. Then, the asymmetric beta function can be used to model the behavior of the normalized-cross-covariance.
For the rectified stereo pair *pentagon*, shown in Fig. 7 c) and d), table 3 shows the size of the images, the number of features (nodes and labels) selected to establish correspondence (Fig. 23) and the approximate ratio $\frac{b_l}{Z_0}$.

	Size		Selected features		
	Rows	Columns	Left image	Right image	$\frac{b_l}{Z_0}$
Pentagon	512	512	26491	28551	0.01
Baseball	512	512	23762	24809	0.15

Table 3. Real world images

In order to establish the correspondence in the *pentagon* stereo pair, the horizontal search range is ± 15 pixels and the neighborhood of a node n_i is composed of the nodes ranging less than 25 pixels from n_i (the neighborhood area is a superellipse with $a = b = 25$ and $p = 2$).

(a) (b)

Fig. 23. Nodes and labels selected in the *pentagon* stereo pair to establish the correspondence. a) Left image (nodes). b) Right image (labels).

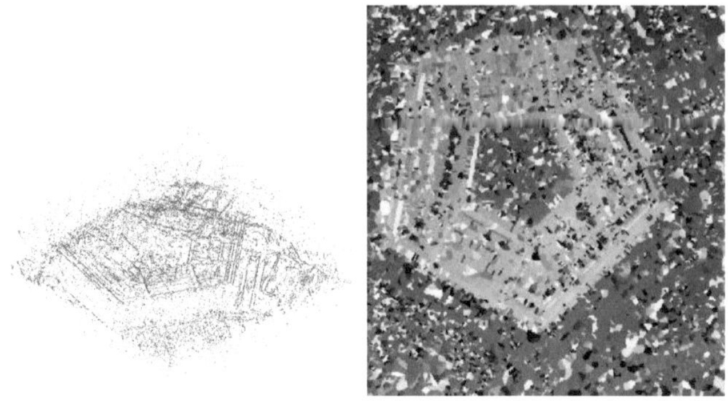

(a) (b)

Fig. 24. Disparity map for the *pentagon* stereo pair obtained using the normalized-cross-covariance. a) Matched points. b) Top view, with coded disparity, of the disparity map interpolated using planar patches (Bradley & Vickers, 1993).

Fig. 24 a) shows the disparity map obtained using only the likelihood information: the normalized cross-covariance. Fig. 24 b) shows a top view of the interpolated disparity map (Bradley & Vickers, 1993) (planar patches are grown around each matched node) with coded disparity (brighter color for larger disparity). Observe the noisy disparity map obtained.
Fig. 25 a) shows the disparity map obtained after 5000 iterations of the algorithm with simulated annealing using both a priori and likelihood. Fig. 25 b) shows the final disparity map interpolated using the Sheppard technique (Bradley & Vickers, 1993), the original gray levels where applied to the 3D representation.
The second example in this section is the baseball pair shown in Fig. 26. Table 3 shows the size of the *baseball* images, the number of nodes selected to establish correspondence and the approximate ratio $\frac{b_l}{Z_0}$. The search region ranges from -50 to -5 pixels and the neighborhood area is a circle of radius 15 pixels. Results are shown in figure 27 with an isometric plot of the matched nodes, a disparity coded view and the interpolated data with the same technique as before. Note that in this case, the lack of 3D information is evident in the reconstructed image.
An objective of the evaluation of the performance of a stereo correspondence system can be found in (Tardón et al., 2006).

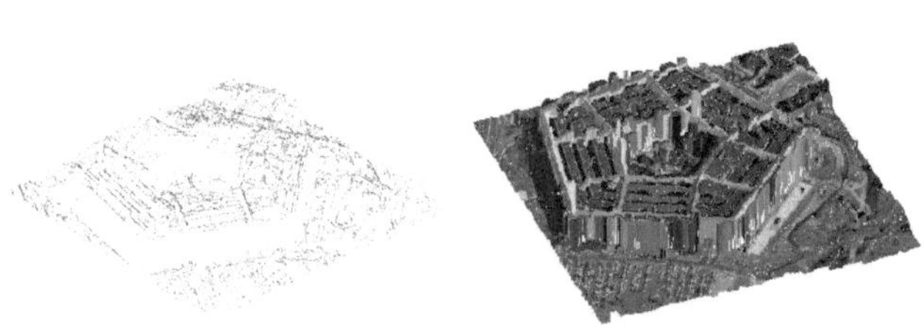

(a) (b)

Fig. 25. Disparity map for the *pentagon* stereo pair after 5000 iterations of the MRF based stereo correspondence algorithm. a) Matched points. b) 3D reconstruction. Surface interpolated using planar patches (Bradley & Vickers, 1993)

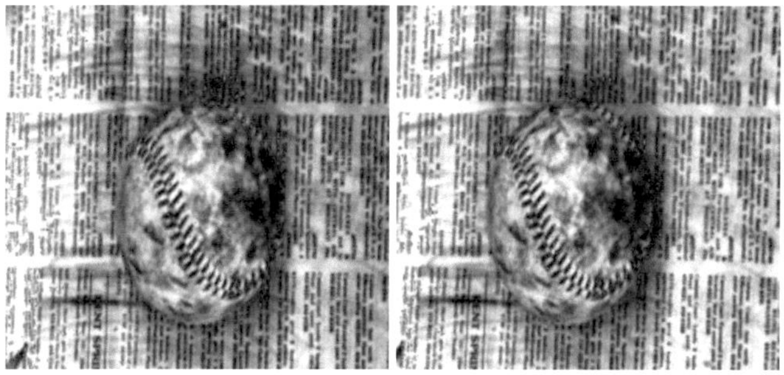

(a) (b)

Fig. 26. *Baseball* stereo pair. a) Left image. b) Right image.

11. Concluding remarks

In this chapter, we have shown how MRFs can be effectively used to solve the stereo correspondence problem and how the fields can be designed making use of the main concepts of cliques, energy and potentials that contribute to define the local characteristic of the MRF.
Local interactions between edge pixels and between matching points have been incorporated to a specific MRF model to solve the correspondence problem using a Markovian formulation. It has been shown how both a priori and a posteriori probabilities can be derived and incorporated in the MRF model. Probabilistic analyses have been described that lead to the definition of the functions that gave rise to the MRF model to solve the correspondence problem.
A Bayesian approach to edge detection based on MRFs has been briefly introduced because of its connection to the correspondence problem through MRF models.
Regarding the specific MRF model for stereo correspondence. We have described a complete Bayesian approach in which the a priori information is derived upon the probabilistic characterization of the disparity gradient obtained after a detailed analysis of its behavior under a specific camera model (the pinhole camera model). The likelihood term is derived upon the probabilistic characterization of the normalized-cross-covariance.
It is important to observe how MRFs can take into account psychovisual cues. Another main aspect of MRFs in the stereo vision context is that MRFs are able to cope, simultaneously, with both prior information extracted from the HVS (in our case related to the disparity gradient) and likelihood information (related to the normalized-cross-covariance in our model).
Note that in a stereo correspondence system, the null-correspondence must be taken into account since occlusions may happen and, then, some points in an image will not be able

(a) (b)

Fig. 27. *Baseball*.a) Disparity map after 5000 iterations. b) 3D reconstruction of the *baseball* scene.

to find their correspondence in the other image. This must be taken into account in any probabilistic correspondence method.

12. Acknowledgments

The image *Lenna* was obtained from the Electrical Engineering Department at the Signal & Image Processing Institute from the University of Southern California (USC).
The stereo pairs *cube*, *rd*, *pentagon* and *baseball* were obtained from the Vision and Autonomous Systems Center Database from the Carnegie Mellon University (CMU) (they were provided by Bill Hoff, University of Illinois).
This work has been partly funded by Junta de Andalucía under Project Number P07-TIC-02783, by the Spanish Ministerio de Ciencia e Innovación under Project Number TIN2010-21089-C03-02 and by the Spanish Ministerio de Industria Turismo y Comercio under Project Number TSI-020201-2008-0117.

13. References

Abramowitz, M. & Stegun, I. A. (1970). *Hanbook of Mathematical Functions*, Dover Publications Inc., New York.

Bain, L. J. & Engelhardt, M. (1989). *Introduction to Probability and Mathematical Statistics*, PWS-Kent Publishing Company.

Barnard, S. T. & Fischler, M. A. (1982). Computational stereo, *Computing Surveys* 14(4): 553 – 572.

Barnard, S. T. & Thompson, W. B. (1980). Disparity analysis of images, *IEEE Transactions on Pattern Analysis and Machine Intelligence* PAMI-2(4): 333 – 340.

Bensrhair, A., Miché, P. & Debrie, R. (1992). Binocular stereo matching algorithm using prediction and verification of hypotheses, *Proc. ISSPA 92, Signal Processing and Its Applications*, pp. 167 – 170.

Besag, J. (1974). Spatial interaction and the statistical analysis of lattice systems, *J. Royal Statistical Society* 34: 192 – 236. Series B.

Boussaid, K. B., Beghdadi, A. & Dupoisot, H. (1996). Edge detection using Holladay's principle, *Proc. ICIP'96, IEEE Int. Conference on Image Processing*, Vol. I, pp. 833 – 836.

Boykov, Y., Veksler, O. & Zabih, R. (2001). Fast approximate energy minimization via graphs cuts, *IEEE Transactions on Pattern Analysis and Machine Intelligence* 23(11): 1222 – 1239.

Bradley, C. & Vickers, G. W. (1993). Free-form surface reconstruction for machine vision rapid prototyping, *Optical Engineering* 32(9): 2191 – 2200.

Brown, M. Z., Burschka, D. & Hager, G. D. (2003). Advances in computational stereo, *IEEE Transactions on Pattern Analysis and Machine Intelligence* PAMI-25(8): 993 – 1008.

Burt, P. & Julesz, B. (1980). Modifications of the classical notion of Panum's fusional area, *Perception* 9: 671 – 682.

Cochran, S. D. & Medioni, G. (1992). 3-d surface description from binocular stereo, *IEEE Transactions on Pattern Analysis and Machine Intelligence* 14(10): 981 – 994.

Cohen, F. S. & Cooper, D. B. (1987). Simple parallel hierarchical and relaxation algorithms for segmenting noncausal markovian random fields, *IEEE Transactions on Pattern Analysis and Machine Intelligence* PAMI-9(2): 195 – 219.

Duda, R. O. & Hart, P. E. (1973). *Pattern Classification and Scene Analysis*, John Wiley & Sons, New York.

Faugeras, O. (1993). *Three-Dimensional Computer Vision. A Geometric Viewpoint*, The MIT Press, Cambridge.

Foley, vanDam, Feiner & Hughes (1992). *Computer Graphics. Principles and Practice*, second edn, Addison- Wesley, Reading, Massachusetts.

Franke, R. (1982). Scatterd data interpolation: Test of some methods, *Mathematics of Computation* 38(157): 181 – 200.

Geman, S. & Geman, D. (1984). Stochastic relaxation, Gibbs distributions and the bayesian restoration of images, *IEEE Transactions on Pattern Analysis and Machine Intelligence* PAMI-6(6): 721 – 741.

Grimson, W. E. L. (1985). Computational experiments with a feature based stereo algorithm, *IEEE Transactions on Pattern Analysis and Machine Intelligence* PAMI-7(1): 17 – 34.

Hoff, W. & Ahuja, N. (1989). Surfaces from stereo: Integrating feature matching, disparity estimation, and contour detection, *IEEE Transactions on Pattern Analysis and Machine Intelligence* 11(2): 121 – 136.

Kanade, T. & Okutomi, M. (1994). A stereo matching algorithm with an adaptive window: Theory and experiment, *IEEE Transactions on Pattern Analysis and Machine Intelligence* 16(9): 920 – 932.

Kang, M. S., Park, R.-H. & Lee, K.-H. (1994). Recovering an elevation map by using stereo modeling of the aerial image sequence, *Optical Engineering* 33(11): 3793 – 3802.

Kinderman, R. & Snell, J. L. (1980). *Markov Random Fields and Their Applications*, Providence RI, American Mathematical Society.

Lane, R. A., Thacker, N. A. & Seed, N. L. (1994). Stretch-correlation as a real-time alternative to feature-based stereo matching algorithms, *Image and Vision Computing* 12(4): 203 – 212.

Law, A. M. & Kelton, W. D. (1991). *Simulation Modeling & Analysis*, second edn, McGraw-Hill International Editions.

Li, S. Z. (2001). *Markov Random Field Modeling in Image Analysis*, Springer-Verlag.

Li, S. Z., Wang, H., Chan, K. L. & Petrou, M. (1997). Minimization of MRF energy with relaxation labeling, *Journal of Mathematical Imaging and Vision* 7: 149 – 161.

Li, Z.-N. & Hu, G. (1996). Analysis of disparity gradient based cooperative stereo, *IEEE Transactions on Image Processing* 5(11): 1493 – 1506.

Lim, J. S. (1990). *Two-Dimensional Signal and Image Processing*, Prentice Hall Inc., Englewood Cliffs, New Jersey.

Luong, Q.-T. & Faugeras, O. D. (1996). The fundamental matrix: Theory, algorithms and stability analysis, *Int. Journal of Computer Vision* 17: 43 – 75.

Marapane, S. B. & Trivedi, M. M. (1989). Region-based stereo analysis for robotic applications, *IEEE Transactions on Systems, Man and Cybernetics* 19: 1447–1464. Special issue on computer vision.

Marapane, S. B. & Trivedi, M. M. (1994). Multi-Primitive Hierarchical (MPH) stereo analysis, *IEEE Transactions on Pattern Analysis and Machine Intelligence* 16(3): 227 – 240.

McKee, S. P. & Verghese, P. (2002). Stereo transparency and the disparity gradient limit, *Vision Research* 42: 1963 – 1977.

Mohr, R. & Triggs, B. (1996). Projective geometry for image analysis. Tutorial given at ISPRS, Vienna.

Moravec, H. P. (1977). Towards automatic visual obstacle avoidance, *Proc. 5th Int. Joint Conf. Artificial Intell*, Cambridge, MA, p. 584.

Nalwa, V. S. & Binford, T. O. (1986). On detecting edges, *IEEE Transactions on Pattern Analysis and Machine Intelligence* PAMI-8(6): 699 – 714.

Ohta, Y. & Kanade, T. (1985). Stereo by intra- and inter-scanline search using dynamic progamming, *IEEE Transactions on Pattern Analysis and Machine Intelligence* PAMI-7(2): 139 – 154.

Olsen, S. I. (1990). Stereo correspondence by surface reconstruction, *IEEE Transactions on Pattern Analysis and Machine Intelligence* 12(3): 309 – 315.

Pollard, S. B., Mayhew, J. E. W. & Frisby, J. P. (1985). PMF: A stereo correspondence algorithm using a disparity gradient limit, *Perception* 14: 449 – 470.

Pollard, S. B., Porrill, J., Mayhew, J. E. W. & Frisby, J. P. (1986). Disparity gradient, Lipschitz continuity and computing binocular correspondences, *Robotics Research: The Third International Symposium* pp. 19 – 26.

Rumbaugh, J. (1991). *Object-Oriented Modelling and Design*, Prentice-Hall International Editions, London.

Sherman, D. & Peleg, S. (1990). Stereo by incremental matching of contours, *IEEE Transactions on Pattern Analysis and Machine Intelligence* 12(11): 1102 – 1106.

Tardón, L. J. (1999). *A robust method of 3D scene reconstruction using binocular information*, PhD thesis, E.T.S.I. Telecomunicación, Univ. Politécnica de Madrid. In spanish.

Tardón, L. J., Barbancho, I. & Marquez, F. (2006). A markov random field approach to edge detection, *Proceedings of the IEEE Mediterranean Electrotechnical Conference MELECON 2006*, pp. 482 – 485.

Tardón, L. J. & Portillo, J. (1998). Two new beta-related probability density functions, *IEE Electronics Letters* 34(24): 2347 – 2348.

Tardón, L. J., Portillo, J. & Alberola, C. (1999). Markov Random Fields and the disparity gradient applied to stereo correspondence, *Proc. of the IEEE International Conference on Image Processing, ICIP-99*, Vol. III, pp. 901 – 905.

Tardón, L. J., Portillo, J. & Alberola, C. (2004). A novel markovian formulation of the correspondence problem in stereo vision, *IEEE Transactions on Systems, Man and Cybernetics, Part A: Systems and Humans* 34(6): 779 – 788.

Trivedi, H. P. (1986). On the reconstruction of a scene from two unregistered images, *Proceedings of the AAAI*, pp. 652 – 656.

Trucco, E. & Verri, A. (1998). *Introductory Techniques for 3-D Computer Vision*, Prentice-Hall.

Vázquez, J. I. (1998). *Surface reconstruction from sparse data*, Master's thesis, E.T.S.I. Telecomunicación, Univ. Politécnica de Madrid, Madrid. In spanish.

Vince, J. A. (1995). *Virtual Reality Systems*, ACM Press Books, Siggraph Series, Addison-Wesley.

Wainman, G. (1997). *The effect of stimulus properties on the disparity gradient threshold for diplopia*, Master's thesis, York University.

Winkler, G. (1995). *Image Analysis, Random Fields and Dynamic Monte Carlo Methods*, Vol. 27 of *Applications of Mathematics*, Springer-Verlag.

Xie, M. & Liu, L. Y. (1995). Color stereo vision: Use of appearance constraint and epipolar geometry for feature matching, *in* S. Z. Li, D. P. Mital, E. K. Teoh & H. Wang (eds), *Recent Developments in Computer Vision*, Lecture Notes in Computer Science, Springer, pp. 255 – 264. Second Asian Conf. on Computer Vision, ACCV'95, Singapore, Invited Session Papers.

Zhang, Y. & Gerbrands, J. J. (1995). Method for matching general stereo planar curves, *Image and Vision Computing* 13(8): 645 – 655.

Zhang, Z. (1996). Determining the epipolar geometry and its uncertainty, *Technical Report 2927*, Institut National de Recherche en Informatique et en Automatique, INRIA. Rev. ver.

4

Type-2 Fuzzy Sets based Ego-Motion Compensation of a Humanoid Robot for Object Recognition

Tae-Koo Kang and Gwi-Tae Park
School of Electrical Engineering, Korea University
Korea

1. Introduction

Humanoid robots have the similar appearance to human being with a head, two arms and two legs, and has some intelligent abilities as human being, such as object recognition, tracking, voice identification, obstacle avoidance, and so on. Since they try to simulate the human structure and behavior and they are autonomous systems, most of the times humanoid robots are more complex than other kinds of robots. In the case of moving over an obstacle or detecting and localizing an object, it is critically important to attain as much precise information regarding obstacles/object as possible since the robot establishes contact with an obstacle/object by calculating the appropriate motion trajectories to the obstacle/object. Vision system supplies most of the information, but the image sequence from the vision system of a humanoid robot is not static when a humanoid robot is walking, so some problems occur due to the ego-motion. Therefore, the humanoid robots need the algorithms that can autonomously determine their action and paths in unknown environments and compensate the ego-motion using the vision system. The vision system is one of the most important sensors in the humanoid robot system, it can supply lots of information which a humanoid robot needs. However the vision system indispensably requires the stabilization module, which can compensate the ego-motion of itself for the more precise recognition.

Over the years, a number of researches have been achieved in motion compensation field on the vision system mounted in the robot. Some researches use single camera, but the stereovision, which can extract information regarding the depth of the environment, is commonly used. Robot motion from stereo-vision can be estimated by the 3D rigid transform, using the 2D multi-scale tracker, which projects 3D depth information on the 2D feature space. The scale invariant feature transform (SIFT) (Hu et al., 2007), which is a local feature based algorithms to extract features from images and estimate transformation using their location, and iterative closest point (ICP) (Milella & Siegwart, 2006), which is used for registration of digitized data from a rigid object with an idealized geometric model, have been used mainly for motion estimation using single camera or stereo camera for the video stabilization or autonomous navigation purposes, and have been widely used in wheeled robots (Lienhart & Maydt, 2002)(Beveridge et al., 2001)(Morency & Gupta, 2003). Moreover, the optical flow based method, which can estimate the motion by 3D normal flow constraint using gradient-based error function, is widely used, because of the simplicity of computation (Vedula et al., 1999). However, these are not appropriate methods for a biped humanoid robot, as walking motions of a humanoid robot simultaneously show the vertical and horizontal movement, unlike the motion of a mobile robot, as well as computation cost yielded by its point to point operation. Therefore, the more efficient stereo-vision based ego-motion estimation method, which is used for the ego-motion compensation, is proposed for a humanoid robot.

The proposed ego-motion compensation method using stereo camera consists of three parts - segmentation, feature extraction, and motion estimation. The stereo vision can obtain disparity images where objects are shown in different gray level according to the different distance between object and the humanoid robot itself. In the segmentation part, objects are extracts by the image analysis using our proposed fuzzy information theoretical approach based on type-2 fuzzy sets. Feature extraction part extracts the feature images using wavelet level set, which can obtain horizontal, vertical and diagonal information for each object. The results of feature extraction part are used as the input data of the estimation part. The position of each object can be calculated using least-square ellipse approximation. The differences of positions between two images are calculated as the compensation parameters. Moreover, a proposed type-2 fuzzy method is used to deal with the noise data to obtain a couple of precise rotation and translation date set.

This paper is organized as follows. In Chapter 2, the proposed the stereo-vision based motion stabilization of a humanoid robot by fuzzy sets is introduced specifically. In Chapter 3, the results of experiments focusing on verifying the performances of the proposed system is given. Chapter 4 concludes the paper by presenting the contributions.

2. Ego-motion compensation system

2.1 Architecture of the proposed ego-motion compensation system

In order to eliminate the error of the object recognition caused by the ego-motion of a humanoid robot when it is walking, we proposed a novel ego-motion compensation system based on fuzzy sets theory using stereo vision information. We also compare the performance using type-1 fuzzy sets and type-2 fuzzy sets, and the results show that the performance using type-2 fuzzy sets is better.

The vision system using SR4000 can supply stereo vision information. The stereo vision is generated based on the perspectives of our two eyes lead to slight relative displacements of objects (disparities) in the two monocular views of scene, then the disparities are used to calculate the distance between the object and the camera in a 3D scene to generate a depth image.

The overall ego-motion compensation system architecture of our proposed method is constructed as illustrated in Fig.1. The system largely consists of three parts: segmentation, feature extraction, and estimation. Finally, the estimation parameters obtained from depth image are used to compensate the ego-motion in gray image for object recognition.

In the segmentation process, the depth image is used as the input image, and the different objects show different depth information which is used to separate objects. Some image processing techniques are needed to preprocess the depth image to get rid of the information irrelative to the objects, such as ground and noise. A new fuzzy sets based segmentation method is proposed, and ype-2 fuzzy sets shows better performance than type-1 fuzzy sets. The number of object can be decided automatically, based on the number of local maximum. Then all objects shown in the image are extracted individually.

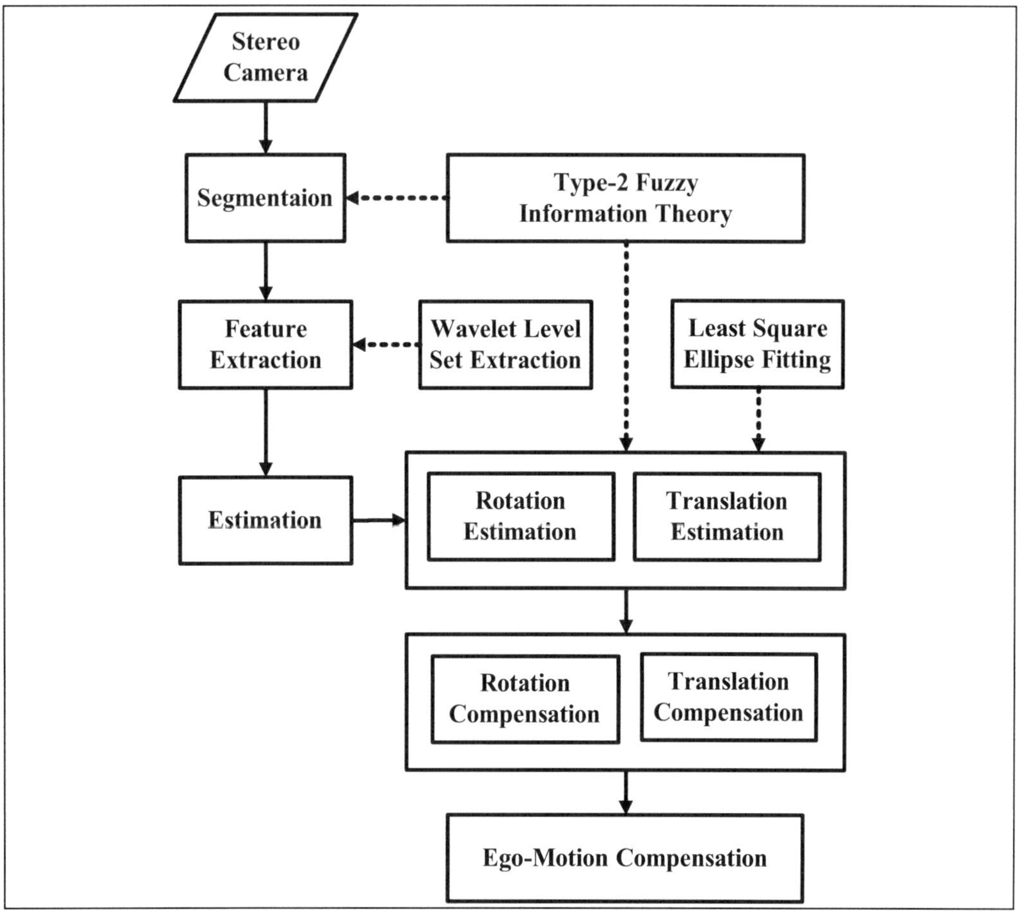

Fig. 1. Overall ego-motion compensation system architecture

In the feature extraction process, the feature data, such as the vertical, horizontal and diagonal coefficients of each segmented object are extracted using wavelet level-set transform.

In the estimation process, the extracted feature data of each object are used to fit an ellipse using the stable least square ellipse fitting method, the center and angle of the ellipse are obtained as the position and angle information of the object, and the difference of ellipse information of the same object in two images are calculated as the displacements for the angle and translation.

Consequently, the average angle and translation displacements of all objects are use as the compensation data in the final compensation process. The detailed explanations are given as follows.

2.2 Disparity image segmentation based on fuzzy information theory

From the depth image, objects can be segmented according to the different gray level. In this thesis, we proposed a novel fuzzy image segmentation method for depth image, which is based on fuzzy sets (Medel, 2001) and fuzzy information theoretical approach. Type-2 fuzzy set based method shows better performance than type-1 based method. The proposed method is fast and effective. The number of cluster seeds is determined automatically according to the number of local maximum, unlike other clustering method, such as FCM (Hwang & Phee, 2007), which needs to determine it ahead of time.

2.2.1 Fuzzy sets

Fuzzy techniques are suitable for development of new image processing algorithms because as nonlinear knowledge based methods, they are able to remove grayness ambiguities in a robust way.

A type-1 fuzzy set, A, which is in terms of a single variable, $x \in X$, is characterized by a membership function that takes values in the interval [0, 1], and can be defined as .

$$A = \{(x, \mu_A(x)) \mid \forall x \in X\} \\ \mu_A(x): \text{membership function} \tag{1}$$

Type 2 fuzzy sets was introduced first by Zadeh (1975) as an extension of the concept of an ordinary fuzzy set. Type-2 fuzzy sets are high level representation of vague data, and can handle the uncertainties in type-1 fuzzy sets, such as, the meaning of the word and noise measurements.

A type-2 fuzzy set, denoted $\tilde{A}$, is characterized by a type-2 membership function, $u_{\tilde{A}}(x,u)$, where X is the universal set, $x \in X$ and $u \in J_x \subseteq [0,1]$. That is,

$$\tilde{A} = \{((x,u), \mu_{\tilde{A}}(x,u)) \mid \forall x \in X, \forall u \in J_x \subseteq [0,1]\} \tag{2}$$

Where $0 \le u_{\tilde{A}}(x,u) \le 1$. Accordingly, at each value of x, say $x = x'$,

$$\mu_{\tilde{A}}(x') = \sum\nolimits_{u \in J_{x'}} f_{x'}(u)/u, \text{for } u \in J_{x'} \subseteq [0,1] \text{ and } x' \in X \tag{3}$$

where $u_{\tilde{A}}(x)$ represents the secondary membership function. When $f_x(u) = 1$, $\forall u \in J_x \subseteq [0,1]$, then the secondary membership functions are interval sets, and, if this is true for $\forall x \in X$, we have the case of an interval type-2 membership function. Interval secondary membership functions reflect a uniform uncertainty at the primary memberships of x.

Uncertainty in the primary memberships of a type-2 fuzzy set, $\tilde{A}$, consists of a bounded region that is called the footprint of uncertainty (FOU). It is the union of all primary memberships, i.e.,

$$FOU(\tilde{A}) = \cup_{X \in x} J_x \tag{4}$$

The FOU can be described in terms of upper and lower membership functions, denoted as $\bar{u}_{\tilde{A}}(x)$ *and* $\underline{u}_{\tilde{A}}(x)$, which are two type-1 membership functions that are bounds for the FOU of a type-2 fuzzy set. So a type-2 fuzzy set can also be given as follows:

$$\tilde{A} = \{(x, \underline{\mu}_{\tilde{A}}(x), \bar{\mu}_{\tilde{A}}(x)) \mid \forall x \in X, \underline{\mu}_{\tilde{A}}(x) \le \mu(x) \le \bar{\mu}_{\tilde{A}}(x) u \in [0,1]\} \tag{5}$$

The lower and upper membership can be defined by means of linguistic hedges like dilation and concentration:

$$\begin{cases} \underline{\mu}_{\tilde{A}}(x) = [\mu(x)]^{\alpha} \\ \overline{\mu}_{\tilde{A}}(x) = [\mu(x)]^{1/\alpha} \end{cases} \tag{6}$$

where $\alpha \in (1,\infty)$. Fig.2 shows an example of type 1 fuzzy set and FOU of type 2 fuzzy set for Gaussian primary membership function with uncertain mean. The uniform shading for the FOU denotes interval sets for the secondary membership functions and represents the entire interval type-2 fuzzy set.

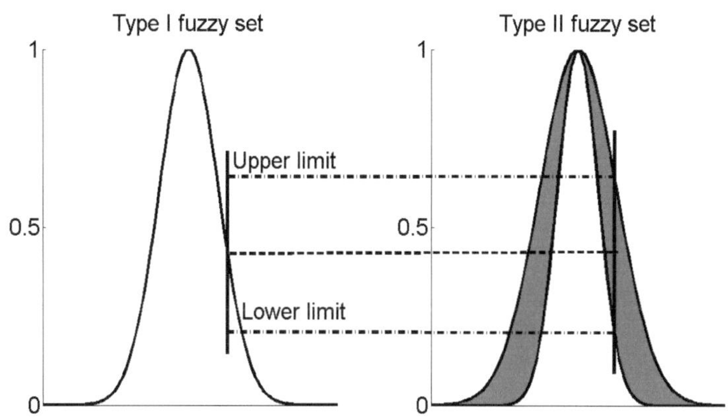

Fig. 2. Example of type-1 and type-2 membership functions.

2.2.2 Information-theoretical approach

Information-theoretical approach is the most used fuzzy technique because of its simplicity and high speed.

This approach minimizes or maximizes measures of fuzziness and image information such as index of fuzziness or crispness, fuzzy entropy, fuzzy divergence, etc. The most common measure of image fuzziness is the linear index of fuzziness. Tizhoosh (Tizhoosh, 2005) (Tizhoosh, 2008) has defined a linear index measure of fuzziness as follows.

$$Fuzziness: \gamma(\tilde{A}) = \frac{2}{MN} \sum_{g=0}^{L-1} h(g) \times \min[\mu_A(g), 1 - \mu_A(g)] \tag{7}$$

where A is an $M \times N$ image subset, and $A \subseteq X$ with L gray levels $g \in [0, L-1]$, $h(g)$ stands for the histogram, $u_A(g)$ stands for the membership function. Here fuzziness is calculated using type-1 fuzzy set $u_A(g)$.

Ultrafuzziness is an extension of fuzziness using type-2 fuzzy set.

$$Ultrafuzziness: \tilde{\gamma}(\tilde{A}) = \frac{2}{MN} \sum_{g=0}^{L-1} h(g) \times [\overline{\mu}_{\tilde{A}}(g) - \underline{\mu}_{\tilde{A}}(g)] \tag{8}$$

$\overline{u}_{\tilde{A}}(g)$ *and* $\underline{u}_{\tilde{A}}(g)$ stand for the upper and lower membership functions, which are calculated according to (6). Ultrafuzziness can not only remove the vagueness/imprecision in the data but also the uncertainty in assigning membership values to the data.

Tizhoosh (Tizhoosh, 1998) defined the suitable LR-type fuzzy number (9) for image thresholding, which is also suitable for segmentation, as shown in Fig.3, and the type-2 fuzzy membership function is generated using (6).

$$u(g)=\begin{cases}0, & g \le g_{\min} \ or \ g \ge g_{\max}, \\ L(g)=(\frac{g-g_{\min}}{T-g_{\min}})^{\alpha}, & g_{\min} \le g \le T, \\ R(g)=(\frac{g_{\max}-g}{g_{\max}-T})^{\beta}, & T \le g \le g_{\max} \end{cases} \quad (9)$$

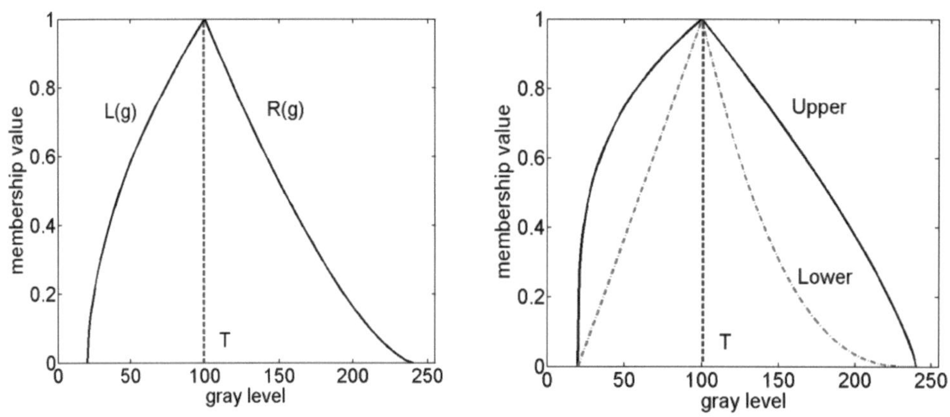

Fig. 3. LR type membership function. Left : type-1 LR type MF right : type-2 LR type MF

2.2.3 Segmentation algorithm

The general algorithm for our proposed image segmentation method based on type-2 fuzzy sets and fuzzy information theory can be summarized as following,

1. Use the LR shape membership function and initialize α.
2. Calculate the histogram of depth image.
3. Initialize the position of the membership function with minimum and maximum gray level of depth image.
4. Shift the membership function T along the gray-level range in histogram and calculate the amount of ultrafuzziness in each position (e.q. (8)).
5. Locate the segmentation point with local maximum ultrafuzziness.
6. Segment the image with all the segmentation points.

The segmentation algorithm based on type-1 fuzzy sets is almost the same with the algorithm based on type-2 fuzzy sets, except the calculation of fuzziness instead of ultrafuzziness and without initialization of α.

Fig.4 shows an example of the main segmentation process using type-2 fuzzy sets and fuzzy information theory. The begin and end point of gray level range are not considered as local maximum of ultrafuzziness, as shows in Fig.8, the local maximum are shown in red points.

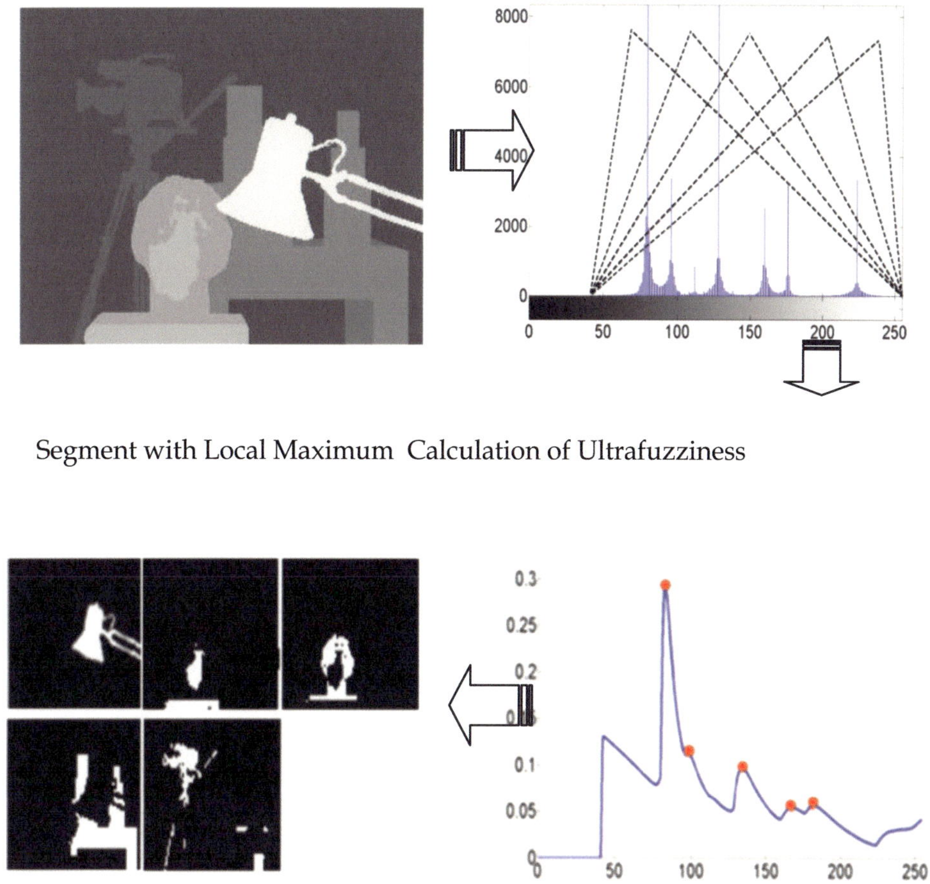

Fig. 4. Proposed segmentation process.

2.2.4 Comparison of type-1 and type-2 fuzzy sets

Fig.5 shows the different segmentation result using type-1 and type-2 fuzzy sets. The calculation results of fuzziness and ultrafuzziness are also showed. There are two local maximum points in fuzziness and five local maximum points in ultrafuzziness. So, only two objects are extracted using type-1 fuzzy sets, and 5 objects are extracted using type-2 fuzzy sets with the last part as the background, which has low gray level.

The difference of the results shows that type-2 fuzzy sets can handle the membership uncertainty and grayness difference to achieve a better segmentation performance than type-1 fuzzy sets. So, the type-2 fuzzy sets based method is proposed for segmentation in this thesis.

2.3 Feature extraction using wavelet transform

Wavelet transforms (Mallat, 1999) in two dimensions are multi-resolution decompositions that can be used to analyze images. The two dimensional DWT can be implemented using digital filters and down-samplers with separable two dimensional scaling and wavelet functions, which are one dimensional DWT of the rows and columns.

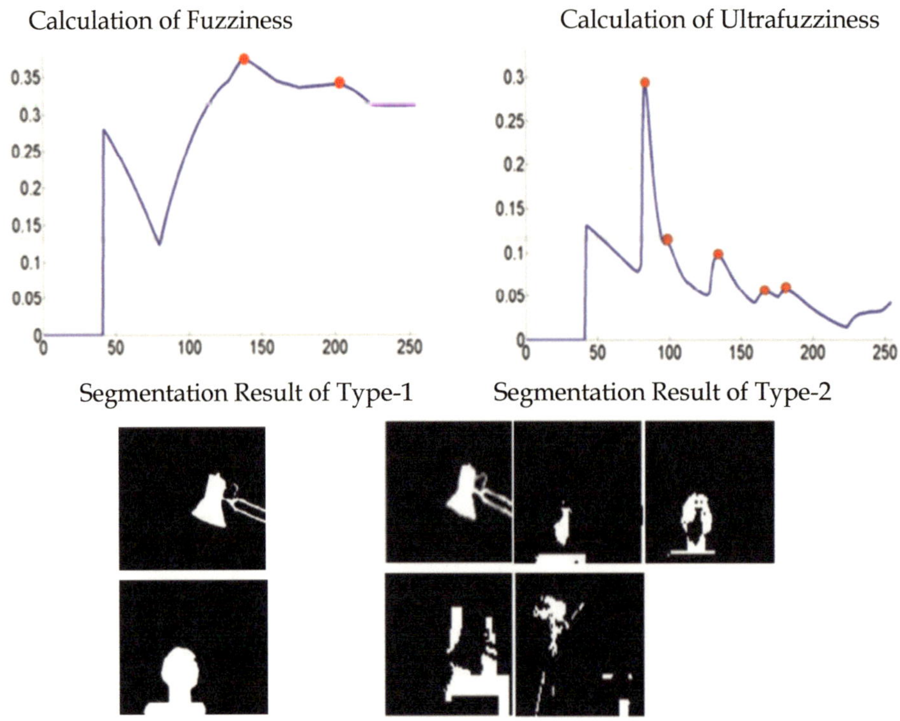

Fig. 5. Comparison of segmentation results based on type-1 and type-2 fuzzy sets.

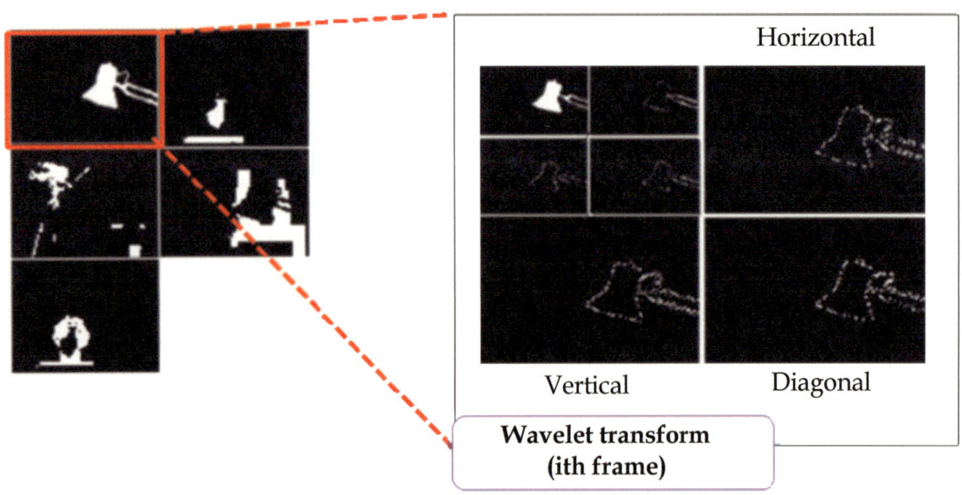

Fig. 6. Level-2 wavelet transform.

The single scale filter bank can be "iterated" to produce a P scale transform. After images are decomposed first, approximation components and detail coefficients (horizontal, vertical and diagonal coefficients) of the first level can be obtained. Then, decomposing directly the approximation components (by tying the approximation output to the input of another filter bank) to obtain approximation components and detail coefficients of the second level.

Repeatedly, multi-level detail coefficients can be found. As shown in Fig.6, the H, V, and D features of the lamp, which is one of the objects segmented, are obtained using level 2 wavelet transform method.

2.4 Rotation and translation estimation

A numerically stable least squares method fitting an ellipse(Radim & Jan, 1998) to a set of data points is proposed to calculate the rotation angle between the image sequences. This method is a simple, stable and robust non-iterative algorithm for fitting an ellipse to a set of data points. It is based on a least squares minimization and it guarantees an ellipse-specific solution even for scattered or noisy data.

This fitting method is robust for the localization of the optimal ellipse solution. The data sets which are used for fitting an ellipse are generated from the wavelet feature extraction process, such as the H, V, and D features. Every data set, the coordinate of the pixels of wavelet decomposed images, belongs to one ellipse, because it stands for one segmented object. The angles and centers of two ellipses from two sequences can be calculated, then the difference of rotation angle and the x, y axis transformation of centers between two sequences can be calculated. The center difference is not the real transformation data, before calculating the transformation $T(x_i, y_i)$, rotation angle should be compensated, and this can be done by a rotation matrix as follow, the center coordinates of ellipses in posterior sequence (C_{i+1}) are rotated around the image center (C_0) and then calculate the difference between the prior sequence (C_i).

$$R_\theta = \begin{pmatrix} \cos(\theta) & -\sin(\theta) \\ \sin(\theta) & \cos(\theta) \end{pmatrix}$$
$$T(x_i, y_i) = R_\theta(C_{i+1} - C_0) - (C_i - C_0) \tag{15}$$

Many rotation and translation values can be obtained according to the level of wavelet transform and the number n of objects segmented (3*level*n), including some big noise values that can occur in the case that the object partially disappears in the sequence image A type-2 fuzzy threshold method based on fuzzy information theory measures is used to get rid of such noise values. This method, which is similar with our segmentation method, selects two local maximum ultrafuziness as the optimal threshold to get rid of the left and right noise value, and then the average value can be calculated as the rotation or transformation values.

Finally, the estimated rotation and transformation information are used for ego-motion compensation in image sequence.

Fig.7 shows an example of rotation estimation and compensation, includes wavelet feature extraction, ellipse fitting, noise data deletion to get valid value, estimation and compensation.

3. Experimental results

The performance of the proposed motion compensation method of a humanoid robot is evaluated via experiments. Our experiments can be divided into two sub-experiments, one is estimation performance evaluation, and the other is processing time evaluation. The experiments are proceeded using URIA, SR4000 camera, and a computer with an AMD 2.3GHz CPU, 2.0GB RAM, and Matlab2008a.

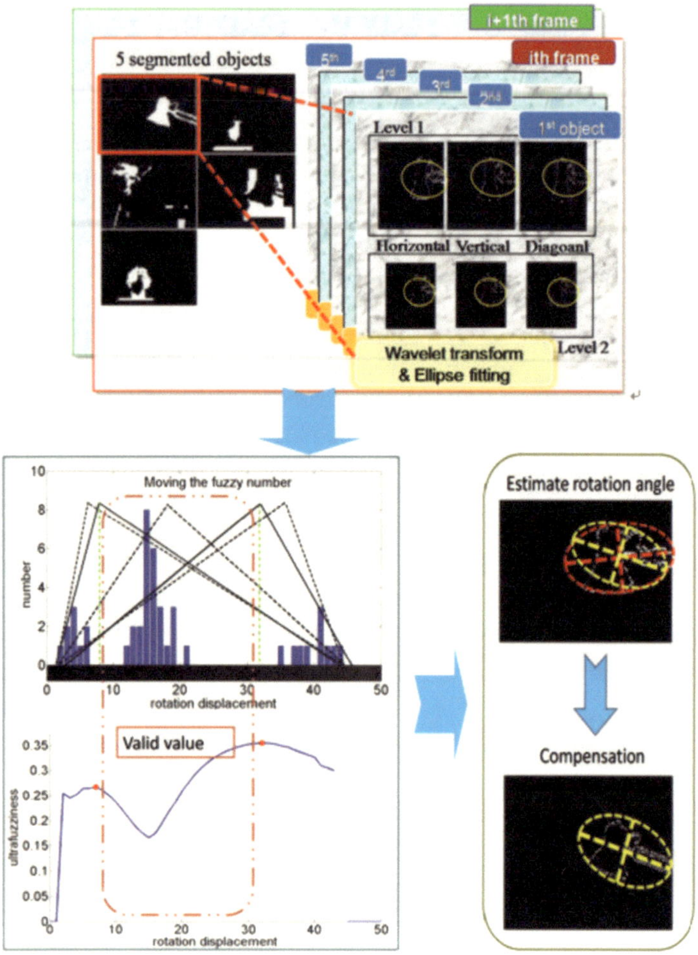

Fig. 7. Level-2 Example of rotation compensation.

3.1 Evaluation of the estimation performance

The proposed method regarding the motion stabilization is evaluated under the artificial ideal environment first. As such, the quantity of errors was determined by comparing the results of the test algorithms with the ideal data. The test algorithms, which are compared with the proposed method for the translation displacement and the rotation displacement, consist of SIFT, ICP. Performance evaluation measures the displacements of x axis, y axis, rotation angle and average error from the ideal case to results of each algorithm for one cycle respectively.

A standard set of stereo pairs with available ground truth (Scharstein, 2002) is used. Each depth values have 256 gray levels with brighter levels representing points closer to the camera and unmatched points depicted as white.

The results of estimation performance evaluation are presented in Fig.8. The origin of coordinate in Fig.8 is the center of the image. The left images in Fig.8 show the estimation performance and the right images in Fig.8 show the errors from the ideal case.

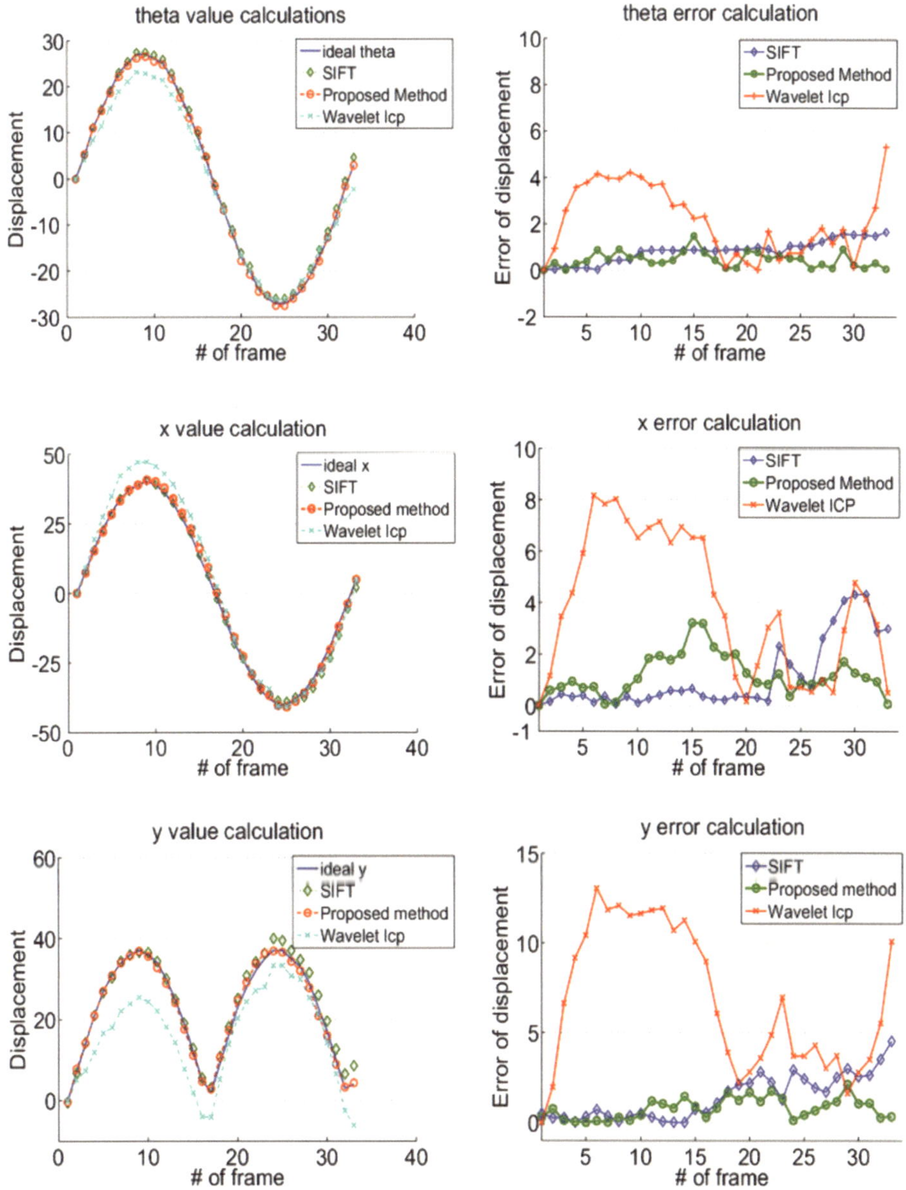

Fig. 8. Results of estimation performance.

Specific results for errors are shown in Table 1. As shown in table 1, proposed method demonstrates a better performance compared to the other algorithms. Especially, the proposed method shows good performance on same plane as SIFT or shows slightly better performance.

Method	Variable	Mean of Errors	Variance
Proposed Method	Rotation error	0.45	0.33
	X-axis error	1.18	0.79
	Y-axis error	0.79	0.59
SIFT	Rotation error	0.83	0.48
	X-axis error	1.12	0.37
	Y-axis error	1.40	1.23
ICP	Rotation error	2.14	1.52
	X-axis error	3.92	2.73
	Y-axis error	6.84	3.96

Table 1. Evaluation results of the estimation performance

3.2 Evaluation of the processing time

The second experiment is the processing time evaluation. The image sequence, which is made from a standard set of stereo pairs with available ground truth, is used. Each image sequence consists of 30, 35 frames and the test is performed 5 times per image sequence. The processing time was measured using the MATLAB and was compared with SIFT and ICP. Table.2 shows the experimental results regarding processing time. The proposed method is faster than the others.

Method	Processing Time(ms)		
	Minimum	Maximum	Average
Propose Method	151	160	156
SIFT	363	381	370
ICP	1472	1525	1490

Table 2. Evaluation results of the processing time

3.3 Evaluation of the processing time

We test the algorithms under the real image sequence obtained from SR4000 camera mounted on the humanoid robot URIA. Fig.9 shows the ego-motion estimation results which are executed in the real environment. In the Fig.9, X-axis displacements show the peak points around 40 and -40 and Y-axis show the peak points around 32 and 2. Rotation displacement shows the peak point around 12 and -12. Fig.10 shows the image sequence after ego-motion compensation. There are two steps in the compensation process, first is the rotation compensation and the second is transformation compensation.

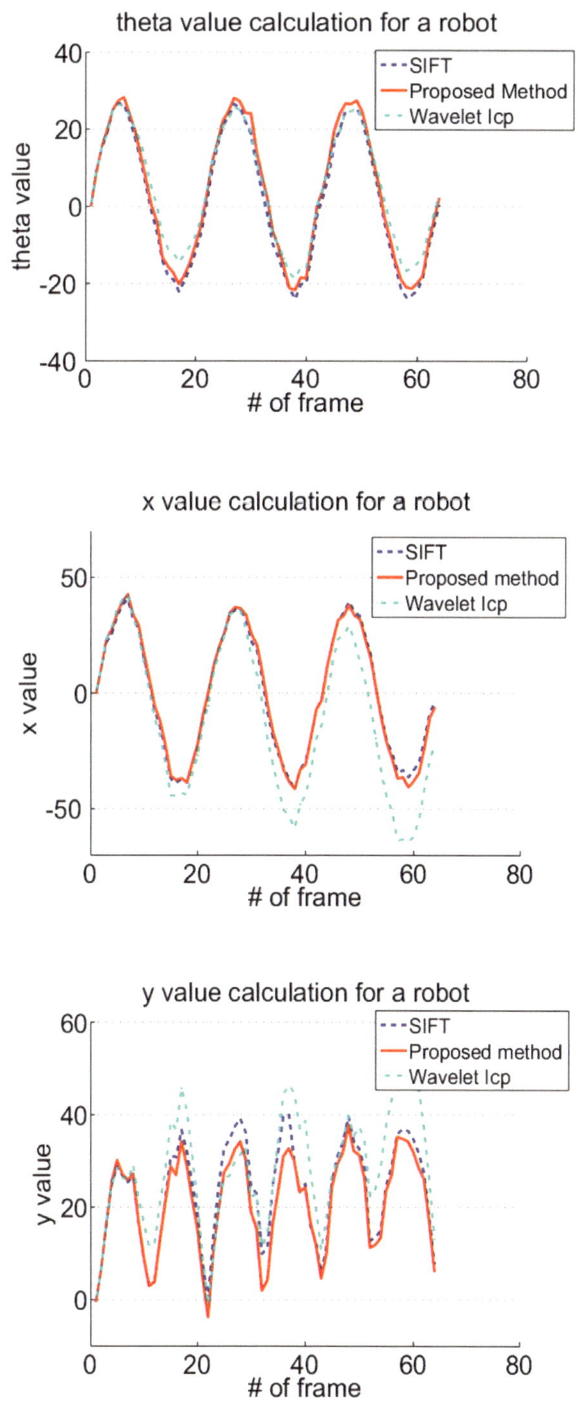

Fig. 9. Motion estimation results for a humanoid robot

Fig. 10. Image sequence after ego-motion compensation

3.4 Object recognition experiments

3.4.1 Training for HMAX model

The training process of object recognition experiments are performed over a set of classes provided by Caltech101(Caltech, 2003). CalTech101 database contains 101 object classes plus a background class collected by Fei-Fei. These datasets contain the target object embedded in a large amount of clutter in real environment. There are about 40 to 800 images per category and most categories have more than 50 images.

Some object categories and the background example images in the training process as shown in Fig. 11. For each object category, the system was trained with 50 positive examples from the target object class and 50 negative examples from the background class.

Fig. 11. Example images from CalTech101 database. The first and second rows show object, and the third row shows background

3.4.2 Object recognition after ego-motion compensation

The ego-motion of a humanoid robot causes the error of object recognition, the localization result changes according to the ego-motion, this generates errors. Ego-motion compensation system can cover this problem.

The notebook object from the real environment with ego-motion of URIA can be recognized in the image sequence, and can be localized with a more accurate position after ego-motion compensation as shown in Fig. 25. The biggest three response patches are showed in Fig.25 in red boxes.

4. Conclusion

Humanoid robot should have the ability to recognize and localize generic object in real world image obtained from its vision system. A number of object recognition algorithms have been developed in computer vision, but there are some problems in the platform of humanoid robot because of the ego-motion. Therefore, this paper has the meaning of developing an ego-motion compensation method used for precise object recognition technologies for humanoid robot.

Fig. 12. Recognition result after ego-motion compensation. First row is the notebook image (left) and depth image (right) for real environment test.

A humanoid robot simultaneously shows the vertical and horizontal movement when it is walking, therefore, the ego-motion estimation method is proposed using stereo vision to cover this problem. Through the compensation of ego-motion, the image sequences are stabilized to improve the recognition accuracy, which means the transformations generated when a humanoid is working are eliminated.

The object recognition system is realized by SR4000 camera mounted in its head. Among several object recognition algorithms, improved HMAX model is used to category and localize the object. HMAX has been demonstrated to be an efficient model in computer vision, and is proved to be appropriate for generic object recognition for our humanoid robot platform.

In conclusion, the systems proposed in this paper are significantly useful in the sense that they are the characterized systems highly focused on and applicable to real-world humanoid robot.

5. Acknowledgments

This work was supported by the Korean Institute of Construction & Transportation Technology Evaluation and Planning. (Program No.:06-United Advanced Construction Technology Program-D01)

6. References

Hu R., Shi R., Shen I. and Chen W. (2007). Video Stabilization Using Scale-Invariant Features, *Proceedings of IV2007*, pp. 871-876.

Milella, A., Siegwart R. (2006). Stereo-Based Ego-Motion Estimation Using Pixel Tracking and Iterative Closest Point, *Proceedings of International Conference on Computer Vision Systems*, pp.21-27.

Lienhart R. and Maydt J. (2002). An Extended Set of Haar-like Features for Rapid Object Detection, *Proceedings of IEEE International Conference on Image Processing*, Vol. 1, pp.900-903.

Beveridge J. R., She, K., Draper B. and Givens G. H. (2001). A nonparametric statistical comparison of principal component and linear discriminant subspaces for face recognition, *Proceedings of the IEEE Conference on Pattern Recognition and Machine Intelligence*, pp. 535-542, 2001.

Morency L. P., Gupta R. (2003). Robust real-time egomotion from stereo images, *Proceedings of Intl. Conference on Image Processing*, Vol. 2, pp.719-722.

Vedula S., Baker S., Rander P., Collins R. and Kanade T. (1999). Three-dimensional scene flow, *Proceedings of Intl. Conference on Computer Vision*, Vol. 2, pp.722-129, 1999.

Mendel, (2001). *Uncertain Rule-Based Fuzzy Logic Systems: Introduction and New Directions*, Prentice-Hall.

Hwang C., Rhee F. (2007). Uncertain Fuzzy Clustering: Interval Type-2 Fuzzy Approach to C-means, *IEEE Trans. on Fuzzy Systems*, vol.15 issue 1, pp. 107–120.

Tizhoosh H. R. (2005). Image Thresholding using Type II Fuzzy Sets, *Pattern Recognition*, vol.38 pp. 2363–2372.

Tizhoosh H. R. (2008) Type II Fuzzy Image Segmentation, *Fuzzy Sets and Their Extensions*, pp. 607-618.

Tizhoosh H.R. (1998). On Thresholding and Potentials of Fuzzy Techniques, *Informatik'98*,Berlin, pp. 97-106.

Mallat S. (1999). *A Wavelet Tour of Signal Processing*, Academic Press.

Radim H., Jan F.(1998). Nuberically Stable Direct Least Squares Fitting Ellipses, *Proceedings of Intl. Conf. on Computer Graphics and Visualization*, vol.1, pp. 125-132.

Scharstein D. and Szeliski R., Middlebury Stereo Vision Page. http://vision.middlebury.edu/stereo/.

Caltech , Caltech 101 image database(2003). http://www.vision.caltech.edu/archive.html

5

Combining Stereovision Matching Constraints for Solving the Correspondence Problem

Gonzalo Pajares, P. Javier Herrera and Jesús M. de la Cruz
University Complutense of Madrid
Spain

1. Introduction

A major portion of the research efforts of the computer vision community has been directed toward the study of the three-dimensional (3-D) structure of objects using machine analysis of images (Scharstein & Szeliski, 2002). We can view the problem of stereo analysis as consisting of the following steps: image acquisition, camera modelling, feature acquisition, image matching, depth determination and interpolation. The key step is that of image matching, that is, the process of identifying the corresponding points in two images that are cast by the same physical point in 3-D space (Barnard & Fishler, 1982). This chapter is devoted solely to this problem.

A correspondence needs to be established between features from two images that correspond to some physical feature in space. Then, provided that the position of centres of projection, the focal length, the orientation of the optical axes, and the sampling interval of each camera are known, the depth can be established by triangulation.

The stereo correspondence problem can be defined in terms of finding pairs of true matches, namely, pairs of features in two images that are generated by the same physical entity in space. These true matches generally satisfy some constraints (Tang et al., 2002):

1. *Epipolar*, given two features, one in an image and a second in the other one in the stereoscopic pair, if we follow a given line, established by the system geometry, these two features must lie on this line, which is the epipolar.
2. *Similarity*, matched features have similar local properties or attributes.
3. *Smoothness*, disparity values in a given neighbourhood change smoothly, except at a few depth discontinuities.
4. *Ordering*, the relative position among two features in an image is preserved in the other one for the corresponding matches.
5. *Uniqueness*, each feature in one image should be matched to a unique feature in the other image.

A review of the state-of-art in stereovision matching allows us to distinguish two sorts of techniques broadly used in this discipline: area-based and feature-based. Area-based stereo techniques use correlation between brightness (intensity) patterns in the local neighbourhood of a pixel in one image with brightness patterns in the local neighbourhood of the other image (Scharstein & Szeliski, 2002; Herrera et al., 2009*a,b,c*; Herrera, 2010; Klaus et al., 2006). Feature-based methods use sets of pixels with similar attributes, normally, either pixels belonging to edges (Grimson, 1985; Ruichek & Postaire, 1996; Tang et al., 2002), the corresponding edges themselves (Medioni & Nevatia, 1985; Pajares & Cruz, 2006; Ruichek et al., 2007; Scaramuzza et al., 2008), regions (Marapane & Trivedi, 1989; Lopez-Malo & Pla, 2000; McKinnon & Baltes, 2004; Herrera et al., 2009*d*; Herrera, 2010) or hierarchical approaches (Wei & Quan, 2004) where firstly edges or corners are matched and afterwards the regions.

The stereovision system geometry is another issue concerning the application of methods and constraints. Conventional stereovision systems consist of two cameras under perspective projection with the optical axes in parallel (Scharstein & Szeliski, 2002) or in convergence (Krotkov, 1990); they have a limited field of view. In opposite, the omni-directional stereovision systems allow enhancing the field of view, under this category fall the systems in which the optics and consequently the image projection is based on fish-eye lenses (Abraham & Förstner, 2005; Schwalbe, 2005; Herrera et al., 2009*a,b,c,d*; Herrera, 2010).

Depending on the application for which the stereovision system is to be designed one must choose either area-based or feature-based, the system geometry and also the strategy for combining the different constraints. In this chapter we focus the attention on the combination of the matching constraints. As features we use area-based when the pixels are the basic elements to be matched and also feature-based with straight line segments and regions. Moreover, both area-based and feature-based are used in conventional and omni-directional stereovision systems with parallel optical axes.

The main contribution of this work is the design of a general scheme with three approaches for combining the matching constraints. The aim is to solve different stereovision correspondence problems.

The chapter is organised as follows. In section 2 we give details about the three approaches for combining the matching constraints. In sections 3, 4 and 5 these approaches are explained giving details about their application with different features and optical projections. Finally, in section 6 some conclusions are provided.

2. Matching constraints combination

The matching constraints can be combined under different strategies, figure 1 displays a tree with three branches (A,B and C). Each branch represents a path where the matching constraints are applied in a different way.

As one can see, given a pair of stereoscopic images the epipolar and similarity constraints are always applied and then depending on some factors, explained below, one can choose one of the three alternatives, i.e. branch A, B or C. All paths end with the computation of a disparity map, in the path A this map is a refined version of the one previously obtained after the application of the smoothness constraint. This combination is more suitable if an area-based strategy is being used because pixels are the most flexible features for smoothness. Nevertheless, following the path A, we could use feature-based approaches, such as edge-segments or regions, for computing the first disparity map. On the contrary, branch B is more suitable when regions are used as features because it does not include the smoothness constraint. Indeed, this constraint assumes similar disparities for entities which are spatially near among them, but the regions could belong to different objects in the scene and these objects do not necessarily present similar disparities. Finally, branch C could be considered as a mixed approach where area-based or feature-based could be used, although in this last case perhaps excluding regions. The system's geometry which is determinant for defining the epipolar constraint does not affect the choice of a given branch.

In summary, following the branch A in section 3, we describe a first procedure based on edge-segments as features under a conventional stereovision system and compute the first disparity map. A second procedure is described for an omni-directional stereovision system under an area-based approach (pixels) where a refined disparity map is finally obtained. Following the branch B, section 4, we describe a procedure for matching regions as features from an omni-directional stereovision system. Finally, following the branch C, section 5, the procedure described uses again edge-segments as features in a conventional stereovision system.

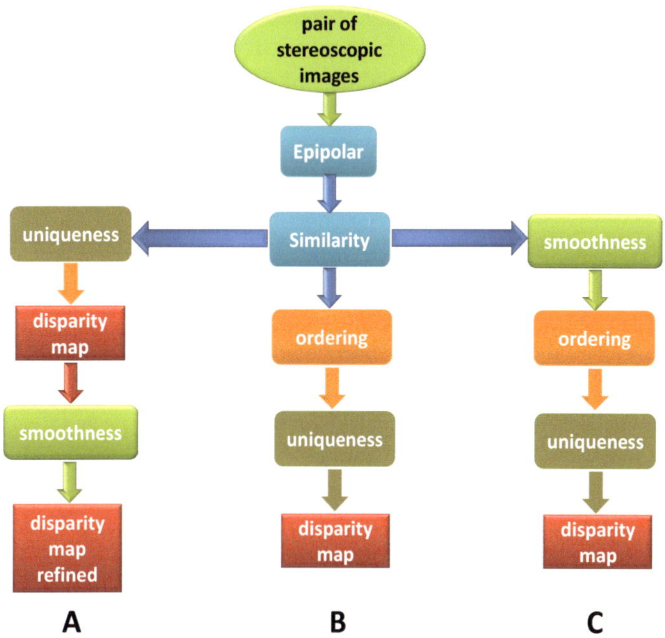

Fig. 1. Three different strategies for combining the stereovision matching constraints

3. Branch A: edge-segment based and pixel-based approaches

As mentioned before, under the combination scheme displayed in branch A, we describe two procedures for computing the disparity map. The first is based on edge-segments as features under a conventional stereovision system with parallel optical axes, where only the first disparity map is obtained. The second uses pixels as features under a fish-eye lens based optical system, also with parallel optical axes, where the first map is later filtered and refined by removing errors and spurious disparity values.

3.1 Edge-segments as features: conventional stereovision systems

Under this approach the stereo matching system is designed with a parallel optical axis geometry working in the following three stages:

1. Extracting edge-segments and their attributes from the images;
2. Performing a *training process*, with the samples (true and false matches) which are supplied to a classifier based on the Support Vector Machines (SVM) framework, where an output function is estimated through a set of attributes extracted from the edge-segments;

3. Performing a *matching process* for each new incoming pair of features. According to the value of the estimated output function provided by the SVM, each pair of edge-segments is classified as a true or false match.

The first segmentation stage is common for both training and matching processes. This scheme follows the well-known SVM learning based strategy. It has been described in Pajares & Cruz (2003). Other learning-based methods with a similar approach, but different learning strategies can be found in Pajares & Cruz (2002) which applies the Parzen´s window, Pajares & Cruz (2001) which uses the ADALINE neural network, Pajares & Cruz (2000) based on a fuzzy clustering strategy, Pajares & Cruz (1999) where the Hebbian learning is applied and the Self-organizing framework in Pajares et al. (1998*a*).

Figure 2 dispalys a mapping of edge segments (*u,v,h,i,c,z,k,j,s,q*) as features for matching under a conventional stereovision system with parallel optical axes and the cameras horizontally aligned. With this geometry, the epipolar lines are horizontal crossing the left (*LI*) and right (*RI*) images. This figure contains details about the overlapping concept firstly introduced in Medioni & Nevatia (1985). Two segments, one in *LI* and the second in *RI*, overlap if by sliding one of them following the epipolar line they intersect. By example, *u* overlaps with *c, z, s* and *q*, but segment *v* does not overlap with *s*. Moreover, Figure 2 contains two windows, *w*(*i*) and *w*(*j*) for applying a neighbourhood criterion, described in section 5.2.1, for mapping the smootheness constraint.

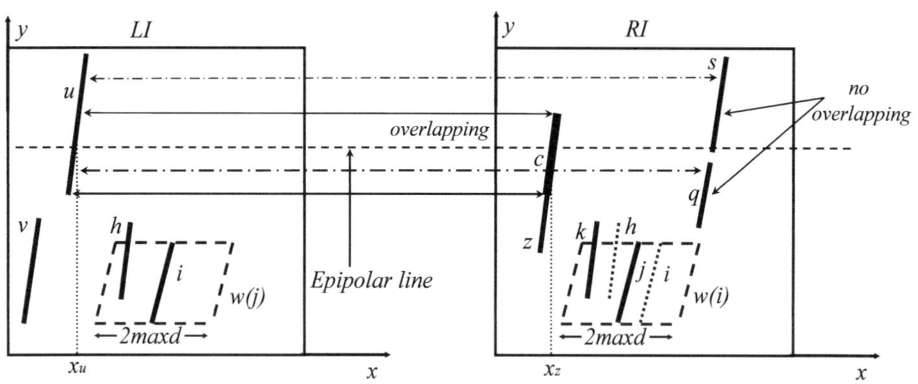

Fig. 2. Left (*LI*) and right (*RI*) images based on a conventional stereovision system with parallel optical axes geometry and perspective projection with edge-segments as features.

3.1.1 Feature and attribute extraction

This is the first stage of the proposed approach. The contour edge pixels in both images are extracted using the Laplacian of the Gaussian filter in accordance with the zero-crossing criterion (Huertas & Medioni, 1986). At each zero-crossing in a given image we compute the magnitude and the direction of the gradient vector as in Leu and Yau (1991), the Laplacian as in Lew et al. (1994) and the variance as in Krotkov (1989). These four attributes are computed from the gray levels of a central pixel and its eight immediate neighbors. The gradient magnitude is obtained by taking the largest difference in gray levels of two opposite pixels in the corresponding eight-neighbourhood of a central pixel. The gradient direction points from the central pixel towards the pixel with the maximum absolute value of the two opposite pixels with the largest difference. It is measured in degrees, quantified by multiples of 45. The normalization of the gradient direction is achieved by assigning a digit from 0 to 7 to each principal direction. The Laplacian is computed by using the corresponding Laplacian operator over the eight neighbors of the central pixel. The variance indicates the dispersion of the nine gray level values in the eight-neighborhood of the same central pixel. In order to avoid noise effects during edge-detection that can lead to later mismatches in realistic images, the following two globally consistent methods are used: 1) the edges are obtained by joining adjacent zero-crossings following the algorithm in Tanaka & Kak (1990), in which a margin of deviation of ± 20% and ±45° is tolerated in magnitude and direction respectively; 2) then each detected contour is approximated by a series of line segments as in Nevatia & Babu (1980); finally, for each segment an average value for the four attributes is obtained from all computed values of its zero-crossings. All average attribute values are scaled, so that they fall within the same range. Each segment is identified by its initial and final pixel coordinates, its length and its label.

Therefore, each stereo-pair of edge-segments has two associated four-dimensional vectors $\mathbf{x}_l$ and $\mathbf{x}_r$, where the components are the attribute values and the sub-indices l and r denote features belonging to the left and right images respectively. A four-dimensional difference vector of the attributes $\mathbf{x} = \{x_m, x_d, x_p, x_v\}$ is obtained from $\mathbf{x}_l$ and $\mathbf{x}_r$, whose components are the corresponding differences for the module of the gradient vector, the direction of the gradient vector, the Laplacian and the variance respectively.

3.1.2 Training process: the support vector machines classifier

The SVM classifier is based on the observation of a set X of n pattern samples to classify them as true or false matches, i.e. the stereovision matching is mapped as the well-known two classification problem. The outputs of the system are two symbolic values $y \in \{+1,-1\}$ corresponding each to one of the classes. So, $y = +1$ and $y = -1$ are with the class of true and false matches respectively.

The finite sample (training) set is denoted by: $(\mathbf{x}_i, y_i)$, $i = 1,\ldots,n$, where each $\mathbf{x}_i$ vector denotes a training element and $y_i \in \{+1,-1\}$ the class it belongs to. In our problem $\mathbf{x}_i$ is as before the 4-dimensional difference vector.

The goal of SVM is to find, from the information stored in the training sample set, a decision function capable of separating the data into two groups. The technique is based on the idea of mapping the input vectors into a high-dimensional feature space using nonlinear transformation functions. In the feature space a separating hyperplane (a linear function of the attribute variables) is constructed (Vapnik 2000; Cherkassky & Mulier 1998). The SVM decision function has the following general form

$$f(\mathbf{x}) = \sum_{i=1}^{n} a_i y_i H(\mathbf{x}_i, \mathbf{x}) \qquad (1)$$

The equation (1) establishes a representation of the decision function $f(\mathbf{x})$ as a linear combination of kernels centred in each data point. A common kernel is the Gaussian Radial Basis $H(\mathbf{x},\mathbf{y}) = \exp\left\{-\left|\mathbf{x}-\mathbf{y}\right|^2 / \sigma\right\}$ which is used in Pajares & Cruz (2003) where σ defines the width of the kernel and was set to 3.0 after different experiments.

The parameters α_i, $i = 1,\ldots n$, in equation (1) are the solution for the following quadratic optimisation problem consisting in the maximization of the functional in equation (2)

$$Q(a) = \sum_{i=1}^{n} \alpha_i - \frac{1}{2} \sum_{i,j=1}^{n} \alpha_i \alpha_j y_i y_j H\left(\mathbf{x}_i, \mathbf{x}_j\right)$$
$$\text{subject to } \sum_{i=1}^{n} y_i \alpha_i = 0, \qquad 0 \le \alpha_i \le \frac{c}{n}, \; i = 1,\ldots,n \tag{2}$$

and given the training data $(\mathbf{x}_i, y_i)$, $i = 1,\ldots,n$, the inner product kernel *H*, and the regularization parameter *c*. As stated in Cherkassky & Mulier (1998), at present, there is not a well-developed theory on how to select the best *c*, although in several applications it is set to a large fixed constant value, such as 2000, which is used in Pajares & Cruz (2003).
The data points $\mathbf{x}_i$ associated with the nonzero α_i are called *support vectors*. Once the support vectors have been determined, the SVM decision function has the form,

$$f(\mathbf{x}) = \sum_{\text{support vectors}} \alpha_i y_i H(\mathbf{x}_i, \mathbf{y}_i) \tag{3}$$

3.1.3 Matching process: epipolar, similarity and uniqueness constraints

Now, given a new pair of edge-segments the goal is to determine if they represent a true or false match. Only those pairs fulfilling the overlapping concept, section 3.1, are considered. This represents the mapping of the *epipolar* constraint. The pair of segments is represented by its attribute vector **x**, therefore through the function estimated in equation (3), we compute the scalar output $f(\mathbf{x})$ whose polarity, sign of $f(\mathbf{x})$, determines the class membership, i.e. if **x** represents a true or false match for the incoming pair of edge segments. This is the mapping of the *similarity* constraint.
During the decision process there are unambiguous and ambiguous pairs of features, depending on whether a given left image segment corresponds to one and only one, or several right image segments, respectively based only on the polarity of $f(\mathbf{x})$. In any case, the decision about the correct match is made by choosing the pair with the greater magnitude $f(\mathbf{x})$ when ambiguity. Because, $f(\mathbf{x})$ ranges in [-1, +1] we only consider pairs with a certain guarantee of correspondence, this means that only pairs with positive values of $f(\mathbf{x})$ are potential candidates. Therefore, the *uniqueness* constraint is formulated based on the following decision rule: if the sign of $f(\mathbf{x})$ is positive and its value is the greatest among the ambiguous pairs, it is chosen as a correct match, otherwise it is a false correspondence.
Figure 3 displays a pair of stereo images, which is a representative pair of the 70 pairs used for testing in Pajares & Cruz (2003), where (*a*) and (*b*) are respectively the left and right

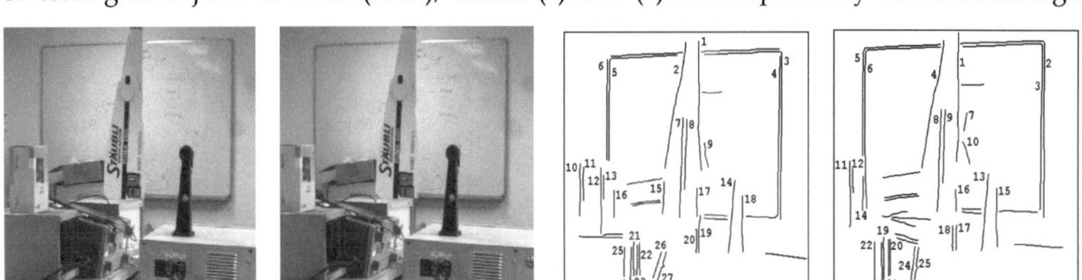

(*a*) (*b*) (*c*) (*d*)

Fig. 3. (*a*)-(*b*) original left and right stereo images acquired in an indoor environment; (*c*)-(*d*) labeled left and right edge-segments extracted from the original images.

images of the stereo pair. In (*c*) and (*d*) are represented the edge segments extracted following the procedure described in section 3.1.1. Details about the experiments are provided in Pajares & Cruz (2003), where on average the percentage of successes overpasses the 94%. The matching between these edge segments determines the disparity map, as one can see this map is sparse because only edges are considered.

3.2 Pixels as features: fish-eye based systems

Following the branch A, Figure 1, we again combine the epipolar, similarity and uniqueness constraints obtaining a first disparity map. The difference with respect the method described in section 3.1 is twofold: (*a*) here the pixels are used as features, instead of edge segments; (*b*) the disparity map is later refined by applying the smoothness constraint.
Additionally, the stereovision is based on cameras equipped with fish eye lenses. This affects mainly the epipolar constraint, which is considered in section 3.2.1. Following the full branch in figure 1, we give details about how the stereovision matching constraints are applied under this approach. This method is described in Herrera (2010). Figure 4 displays a pair of stereovision images captured with fish eye lenses. The method proposed here is based on the work of Herrera et al. (2009*a*) and was intended as a previous stage for forest inventories, where the estimation of wood or the growth are some of the inventory variables to be computed.

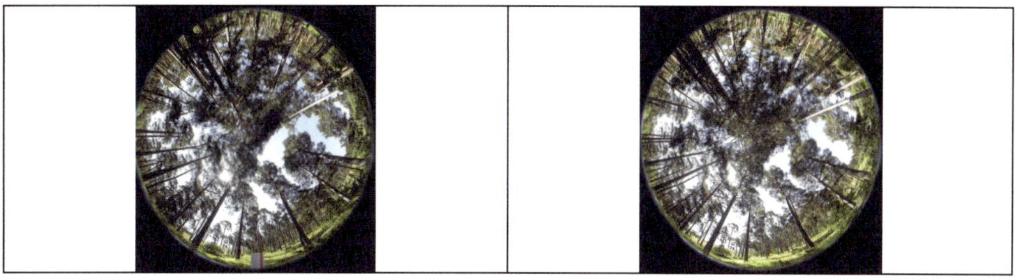

Fig. 4. Original stereovision images acquired with fish-eye lenses from a forest environment.

3.2.1 Epipolar constraint: system geometry

Figure 5 displays the stereo vision system geometry (Abraham & Förstner, 2005). The 3D object point *P* with world coordinates with respect to the systems (X_1, Y_1, Z_1) and (X_2, Y_2, Z_2) is imaged as (x_{i1}, y_{i1}) and (x_{i2}, y_{i2}) in image-1 (left) and image-2 (right) respectively in coordinates of the image system; a_1 and a_2 are the angles of incidence of the rays from *P*; y_{12} is the baseline measuring the distance between the optical axes in both cameras along the *y*-axes; *r* is the distance between an image point and the optical axis; *R* is the image radius, identical in both images.
According to Schwalbe (2005), the following geometrical relations can be established,

$$r = \sqrt{x_{i1}^2 + y_{i1}^2}\ ;\ \ a_1 = \frac{r\pi}{2R};\ \ \beta = tg^{-1}\left(y_{i1}/x_{i1}\right) \tag{4}$$

Now the problem is that the 3D world coordinates (X_1, Y_1, Z_1) are unknown. They can be estimated by varying the distance *d* as follows,

$$X_1 = d\cos\beta;\quad Y_1 = d\sin\beta;\quad Z_1 = \sqrt{X_1^2 + Y_1^2}\Big/\tan\alpha_1 \tag{5}$$

From (4) we transform the world coordinates in the system $O_1X_1Y_1Z_1$ to the world coordinates in the system $O_2X_2Y_2Z_2$ taking into account the baseline as follows,

$$X_2 = X_1; \quad Y_2 = Y_1 + y_{12}; \quad Z_2 = Z_1 \tag{6}$$

Assuming no lenses radial distortion, we can find the imaged coordinates of the 3D point in image-2 as in Schwalbe (2005),

$$x_{i2} = \frac{2R\arctan\left(\sqrt{X^2+Y^2}/Z_2\right)}{\pi\sqrt{\left(Y_2/X_2\right)^2+1}}; \quad y_{i2} = \frac{2R\arctan\left(\sqrt{X^2+Y^2}/Z_2\right)}{\pi\sqrt{\left(X_2/Y_2\right)^2+1}} \tag{7}$$

Because of the system geometry, the epipolar lines are not concentric circumferences and this fact is considered for matching. Figure 6 displays four epipolar lines, in the third quadrant of the right image, they have been generated by the four pixels located at the positions marked with the squares, which are their equivalent locations in the left image.

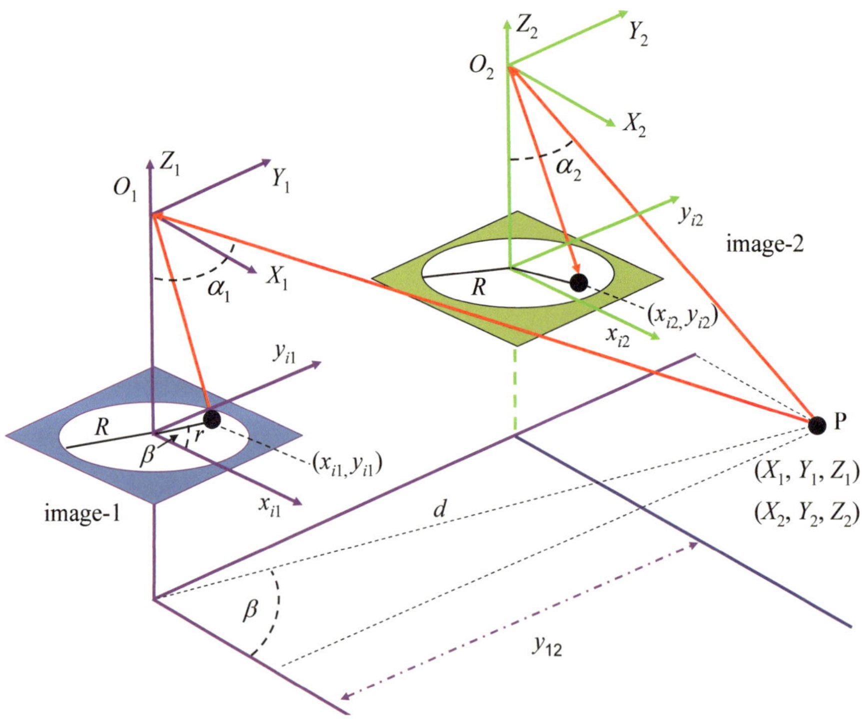

Fig. 5. Geometric projections and relations for the fish-eye based stereo vision system.

Using only a camera, we capture a unique image and each 3D point belonging to the line $\overline{O_1P}$, is imaged in (x_{i1}, y_{i1}). So, the 3D coordinates with a unique camera cannot be obtained. When we try to match the imaged point (x_{i1}, y_{i1}) into the image-2 we follow the epipolar line, i.e. the projection of $\overline{O_1P}$ over the image-2. This is equivalent to vary the parameter d in the 3-D space. So, given the imaged point (x_{i1}, y_{i1}) in the image-1 and following the epipolar line, we obtain a list of m potential corresponding candidates represented by (x_{i2}, y_{i2}) in the image-2. The best match is associated to a distance d for the 3D point in the scene, which is computed from the stereo vision system. Hence, for each d we obtain a specific (x_{i2}, y_{i2}), so that when it is matched with (x_{i1}, y_{i1}) d is the distance for the point P. Different measures of distances during different time intervals (years) for specific points in the trunks, such as the ends or the width of the trunk measured at the same height, allow determining the evolution of the tree and consequently its state of growth and also the volume of wood, which are as mentioned before inventory variables. This requires that the stereovision system is placed at the same position in the 3D scene and also with the same camera orientation (left camera North and right camera South).

Fig. 6. Epipolar lines in the right image generated from the locations in the left image.

3.2.2 Similarity constraint: attributes or properties

Each pixel l in the left image is characterized by its attributes; one of such attributes is denoted as A_l. In the same way, each candidate i in the list of m candidates is described by identical attributes, A_i. So, we can compute differences between attributes of the same type A, obtaining a similarity measure for each one as follows,

$$s_{iA} = \left(1 + |A_l - A_i|\right)^{-1}; \quad \mathrm{i} = 1, \ldots, m \tag{8}$$

$s_{iA} \in [0,1]$, $s_{iA} = 0$ if the difference between attributes is large enough (minimum similarity), otherwise if they are equal, $s_{iA} = 1$ and maximum similarity is obtained.

We use the following six attributes for describing each pixel: *a*) correlation; *b*) texture; *c*) colour; *d*) gradient magnitude; *e*) gradient direction and *f*) Laplacian. Both first ones are area-based computed on a 3×3 neighbourhood around each pixel through the correlation coefficient (Barnea & Silverman, 1972; Koschan & Abidi, 2008; Klaus et al., 2006) and standard deviation (Pajares & Cruz, 2007) respectively. The four remaining ones are considered as feature-based (Lew et al., 1994). The colour involves the three red-green-blue spectral components (R,G,B) and the absolute value in the equation (8) is extended as the sum of absolute differences as $|A_l - A_i| = \sum_H |H_l - H_i|$, H = R,G,B. It is a similarity measurement for colour images (Koschan & Abidi, 2008), used satisfactorily in Klaus et al. (2006) for stereovision matching. Gradient (magnitude and direction) and Laplacian are computed by applying the first and second derivatives respectively (Pajares & Cruz, 2007) over the intensity image after its transformation from the RGB plane to the HSI (hue, saturation, intensity) one. The gradient magnitude has been used in Lew et al. (1994) and Klaus et al. (2006) and the direction in Lew et al. (1994). Both, colour and gradient magnitude have been linearly combined in Klaus et al. (2006) producing satisfactory results as compared with the Middlebury test bed (Scharstein & Szeliski, 2002). The coefficients involved in the linear combination are computed by testing reliable correspondences in a set of experiments carried out during a previous stage.

Given a pixel in the left image and the set of m candidates in the right one, we compute the following similarity measures for each attribute A: s_{ia} (correlation), s_{ib} (colour), s_{ic} (texture), s_{id} (gradient magnitude), s_{ie} (gradient direction) and s_{if} (Laplacian). The identifiers in the sub-indices identify the attributes according to these assignments. The attributes are the six ones described above, i.e. $\Omega \equiv \{a,b,c,d,e,f\}$ associated to correlation, texture, colour, gradient magnitude, gradient direction and Laplacian.

3.2.3 Uniqueness constraint: Dempster-Shafer theory

Based on the conclusions reported in Klaus et al. (2006), the combination of attributes appears as a suitable approach. The Dempster-Shafer theory owes its name to the works by the both authors in Dempster (1968) and Shafer (1976) and can cope specifically with the combination of attributes because they are specifically designed for classifier combination Kuncheva (2004). With a little adjusting they can be used for combining attributes in stereovision matching. They allow making a decision about a unique candidate (uniqueness constraint). Now we must match each pixel l in the left image with the best of the m potential candidates.

The Dempster-Shafer theory as it is applied in our stereovision matching approach is as follows (Kuncheva, 2004):

1. A pixel l is to be matched either correctly or incorrectly. Hence, we identify two classes, which are the class of true matches, w_1, and the class of false matches, w_2. Given a set of samples from both classes, we compute the similarities of the matches belonging to each class according to (8) and build a 6-dimensional mean vector, where its components are the mean values of their similarities, i.e. $\bar{\boldsymbol{v}}_j = \left[\bar{s}_{ja}, \bar{s}_{jb}, \bar{s}_{jc}, \bar{s}_{jd}, \bar{s}_{je}, \bar{s}_{jf}\right]^{\mathrm{T}}$; $\bar{\boldsymbol{v}}_1$ and $\bar{\boldsymbol{v}}_2$ are the mean for w_1 and w_2 respectively; T denotes transpose. This is carried out during a previous phase, equivalent to the training one in classification problems and the one in section 3.1.2.
2. Given a candidate i from the list of m candidates for l, we compute the 6-dimensional vector $\boldsymbol{x}_i$, where its components are the similarity values obtained according to (8) between l and i, i.e. $\boldsymbol{x}_i = \left[s_{ia}, s_{ib}, s_{ic}, s_{id}, s_{ie}, s_{if}\right]^{\mathrm{T}}$. Then we calculate the proximity Φ between each component in $\boldsymbol{x}_i$ and each component in $\bar{\boldsymbol{v}}_j$ based on the Euclidean norm $\|\cdot\|$, equation (9).

$$\Phi_{jA}(\boldsymbol{x}_i) = \frac{\left(1 + \left\|s_{iA} - \bar{s}_{jA}\right\|^2\right)^{-1}}{\sum_{k=1}^{2}\left(1 + \left\|s_{iA} - \bar{s}_{kA}\right\|^2\right)^{-1}} \quad \text{where } A \in \Omega \tag{9}$$

3. For every class w_j and for every candidate i, we calculate the belief degrees,

$$b_j^i(A) = \frac{\Phi_{jA}(\boldsymbol{x}_i)\prod_{k \neq j}\left(1 - \Phi_{kA}(\boldsymbol{x}_i)\right)}{1 - \Phi_{jA}(\boldsymbol{x}_i)\left[1 - \prod_{k \neq j}\left(1 - \Phi_{kA}(\boldsymbol{x}_i)\right)\right]}; \quad j = 1,2 \tag{10}$$

4. The final degree of support that candidate i, represented by $\boldsymbol{x}_i$, receives for each class w_j taking into account that its match is l is given in equation (11)

$$\mu_j(\boldsymbol{x}_i) = \prod_{A \in \Omega} b_j^i(A) \tag{11}$$

5. We chose as the best match for l, the candidate i with the maximum support received for the class of true matches (w_1), i.e. $\max_i \{\mu_1(\boldsymbol{x}_i)\}$ but only if it is greater than a threshold, which can be fixed to 0.5, as in Herrera et al. (2009*a*).

Other approaches based on the combination of attributes have been applied in Herrera et al., (2009*b*,*c*) where the Choquet, Sugeno and a Fuzzy multicriteria decision making methods are respectively used for applying the uniqueness constraint.

3.2.4 Smoothness constraint: mean filtering

We have available a first disparity map after applying the above three constraints: epipolar, similarity and uniqueness.

The disparity map contains pixels which have been erroneously classified either as true or false matches. Based on the obvious assumption that the structures in the 3-D scene are spatially preserved in the 2-D images we consider that if a pixel with a disparity value different from those values on its neighbourhood, such value must be changed toward the disparities of the pixels which are surrounding it. This is an obvious interpretation of the smoothness constraint. Indeed, if a point and its neighbours belong to a region in the 3-D space, all are probably placed at a given distance from the stereovision system, this spatial region is mapped as a 2-D region in the images and the disparities still preserve similar values. A simple statistical averaging filter has the ability for changing erroneous or spurious disparity values of a pixel with respect its neighbours. This technique is used in Lankton (2010) which implements the method described in Klaus et al. (2006). Other statistical filters could be used such as the median or the mode.

In Herrera (2010) is reported that the errors obtained without smoothing are about the 11% and after the filtering the error decreases until the 8% on average. Figure 7 displays the disparity maps obtained without and with smoothing. The colour bar represents the disparity levels in sexagesimal degrees considering a circumference of 360°. The maximum disparity value found in the twenty pairs of stereovision images used is 8°, therefore the colour bar ranges from 0° to 8°.

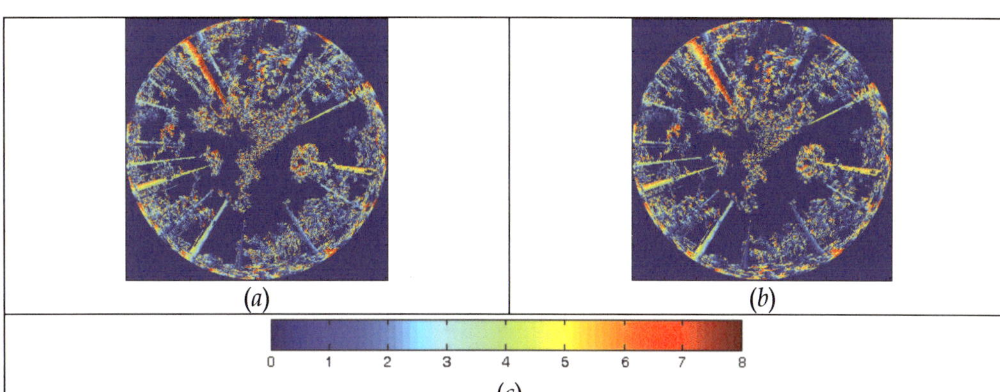

Fig. 7. Disparity maps (*a*) without smoothing and (*b*) with smoothing; (c) colour bar representing the disparity levels in sexagesimal degrees.

4. Branch B: regions based

Now we describe the mapping of the matching constraints in the branch B, figure 1, i.e. epipolar, similarity, ordering and uniqueness. Under this feature-based approach, the features are regions. The stereovision system is also equipped with fish eye lenses obtaining omnidirectional images, as the ones in figure 4. Figure 8 displays a pair of such stereo images. As we can see, the images display similar geometry but different types of forest environments, i.e. pines and oaks respectively. The main goal on the images in figure 8 is the correspondence between the trunks of the trees for forest inventories because they concentrate the greatest volume of wood and determines the growth stage of the trees, which are important variables for inventories, as mentioned before. Therefore, this is a clear example where the type of scene is decisive for choosing one or another strategy. So, the strategy here differs from the one described in section 3.2, although the same final goal (inventories) is pursued. The trunks are the regions to be matched due to its appearance. Therefore, under this approach, an important issue concerning the stereovision matching is the regions *segmentation*, including the identification and extraction of properties, which are used for matching. In section 4.1 we describe the segmentation process and in section 4.2 the *correspondence* process, describing how the matching constraints are applied during the correspondence process. This procedure can be found exhaustively described in Herrera et al. (2009*d*).

(*a*) (*b*)

Fig. 8. Original stereo images captured in an outdoor forest environment.

4.1 Segmentation process

This process is focused on the isolation of the trunks. As we can see from figure 8, the trunks (dark) and the sky (clear) display high contrast in a broad area in the inner part of the image, but in the outer part they get confused with the grass in the soil. The procedure exploits the high contrast and takes into account the last observation. By applying the following steps in a sequential order the trunks are conveniently extrated:

1. *Valid image:* the central part of the image is the one to be processed, the Charge Coupled Device of the cameras has 1616×1616 pixels in width and height dimensions respectively. The centre is located in the coordinates (808, 808). The radius R of the valid image is 808 pixels.
2. *Detecting thin branches:* thin branches are not significant for forest inventories, but they are highly harmful from the point of view of segmentation; this is because most of these thin branches belonging to different trees appear overlapped among them. With such purpose we compute the standard deviation at pixel-level (Pajares & Cruz, 2007) with a

window of size 5x5. Considering this window, a pixel belonging to a thin branch fullfills the following conditions: a) displays a low intensity value, as it belongs to the tree; b) must be surrounded by pixels with high intensity values, belonging to the sky, this means that in the window appear pixels of this class at least in two opposite sides, i.e. left and right or up and bottom; c) the standard deviation computed through this window is greater than a threshold set to a value of twenty five in our experiments after several trial and error tests, which verifies the high variability in the contrast.

3. *Concentric circumferences*: we draw concentric circumferences starting with a radius r of 250 pixels from the centre, with increases of 50 pixels until r = R. We trace the intensity profile for each circunference until a profile displays large dark areas. This means that we have already reached the area where the trunks and soil get confused. The other circunferences display alternative dark and clear levels, these last circumferences are identified as type 1 and the remainder ones as type 2.
4. *Putting seeds in the trunks*: given a profile of type 1, we consider a pixel in each dark region as a seed and compute the average intensity value and standard deviation of the dark region associated to the seed. Only dark regions with more than T_1=10 pixels in the profile and with intensity values below T_2=75 are retained. Considering the outer circumference of type 1, identified as c_i we select only dark regions whose intersection with this circumference gives a line with a number of pixels lower than T_3=120. The maximum value of all lines of intersection is $t^i_{\max} < T_3$. Then for the next circumference towards the centre of the image, c_{i+1}, T_3 is now set to $t^i_{\max}$, which is the value used when the next circumference is processed and so on until the inner circumference of type 1 is reached. This is justified because the thickness of the trunks always diminishes towards the centre.
5. *Region growing*: this process is based on the procedure described in Gonzalez & Woods (2008), we start in the outer circumference of type 1 by selecting the seed pixels obtained in this circumference. From these seed points we append to each seed those neighbouring pixels that have a similar intensity value than the seed. The similarity is measured as the difference between the intensity value of the pixel under consideration and the mean value in the zone where the seed belongs to, they do not differ more than the standard deviation for each zone. The region growing ends when no more similar neighbouring pixels are found for that seed between this circumference and the centre of the image. The regions obtained are labelled following the procedure described in Haralick & Shapiro (1992).
6. *Estimation*: for each labelled region we have available its orientation towards the centre of the image and also its decreasing ratio. This allows to estimate the part of the trunk confused with the soil. So, after this operation we obtain new enlarged regions representing the full trunks. These regions are finally re-labelled and for each region we extract the following attributes: area (number of pixels), centroid (xy-averaged pixel positions in the region), angles in degrees of each centroid and the seven Hu invariant moments (Pajares & Cruz, 2007; Gonzalez and Woods, 2008).

4.2 Matching process

Once the regions and their attributes are extracted according to the above procedure, we are ready to apply the stereovision matching constraints in figure 1, branch B, i.e. epipolar, similarity, ordering and uniqueness.

4.2.1 Epipolar constraint

As mentioned before, the images in figure 9 are captured with fish eye lenses, therefore the epipolar lines are defined according to equations (4) to (7). So, given a region in an image with its centroid, we search for its potential matched region following the epipolar lines and looking for regions whose centroids fall in or near the corresponding epipolar line generated by the first centroid in the other image of the stereoscopic pair. This idea is illustrated in figure 9, given a red square in the image (a), following the epipolar line towards the south direction we will find the corresponding matching, Figure 9(b). This implies that given a centroid of a region in the left image its corresponding matching in the right image will be probably in the epipolar line.

Because the sensor could introduce errors due to wrong calibration of the cameras, we have considered an offset out of the epipolar lines quantified as 10 pixels in distance. Moreover, in the epipolar line, the corresponding centroids are separated a certain angle, as we can see in Figure 9(b) expressed by the red and blue squares. After experimentation with the set of images tested, the maximum separation found in degrees has been quantified in 22°, i.e. this determines the limit on the disparity.

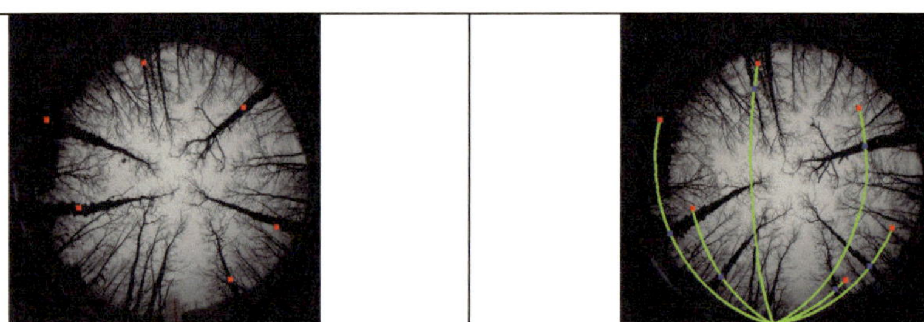

(a) (b)

Fig. 9. Original stereo images captured with a fish eye lens in an outdoor forest environment.

4.2.2 Similarity constraint

All regions with centroids fulfilling the similarity constraint are considered as candidates for matching. We build a list of such candidate regions according to the similarities based on their areas and the seven Hu's invariant moments. So, we have eight similarity measurements, which are mapped to range in the interval [0,1]. The similarities are stablished as differences in the absolute value between attributes. All regions with a number of similarities greater than four and each one less than a threshold of 0.2, are considered as candidates for matching. This threshold is fixed to this relative low value in order to guarantee a strong similarity, taking into account that the most favourable value is zero and the most unfavourable is +1.

4.2.3 Ordering and uniqueness constraints

The ordering constraint assumes that the relative position between two regions in an image is preserved in the other one for the corresponding matches. The application of this constraint is limited to regions with similar heights and areas in the same image and also if the areas overpass a threshold T_4 set to 6400 in this work. This tries to avoid violations of this constraint based on closeness and remoteness relations of the trunks with respect the sensor in the 3D scene.

If after applying the similarity constraint still remain ambiguities because different pairs of regions still involve the same region, the application of the ordering constraint could remove these possible ambiguities. This implies the implicit application of the uniqueness constraint. Nevertheless, if still ambiguities persist, we strictly select the most similar pairs in application of the similarity constraint until all ambiguities are resolved.

Figure 10 displays the regions extracted by the segmentation process. Each region appears with a unique label. The number near of the regions identifies each label. This number is represented as a color in a scale ranging from 1 to 14, where 1 is blue and 14 orange. This representation is only for a best visualization of the regions.

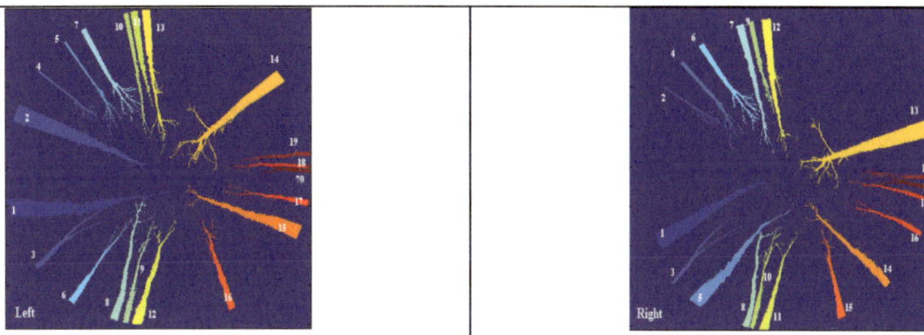

(*a*) (*b*)

Fig. 10. Labelled regions: (*a*) left image, (*b*) right image. Each region appears identified by a unique number.

From Figure 10, we can see how the segmented regions come from the trunks in Figure 4, even trunks displaying small areas. The proposed approach over the set of 20 stereo pairs of images analyzed has achieved a performance of 88.4% of successes.

5. Branch C: edge segments based

This approach follows the branch C in figure 1, i. e. here epipolar, similarity, smoothness ordering and uniqueness are the constraints to be applied. The features are edge segments as the ones used in section 3.1. We extract these features and apply the two first constraints exactly as described in such section. The full procedure is described in Pajares & Cruz (2004). Other similar global stratetigies can be found in Pajares et al. (2000) where a Hopfield neural network is the chosen global matching approach selected or in Pajares et al., (1998*b*) where a relaxation approach is applied. Also global strategies are applied in Ishikawa & Geiger (2007) where an energy minimization is defined with such purpose or in Pajares & Cruz (2006), where the fuzzy cognitive map framework is the method selected for achieving the proposed globality.

5.1 Epipolar and similarity constraints

Consequently, after applying the training process described in section 3.1.2, we obtain the decision function in equation (3). Given a pair of stereo images as those displayed in figure 3(*a*) and (*b*) we obtain for each pair of edge segments the corresponding attribute difference vector, $\boldsymbol{x}$, as described in section 3.1.1. Once this vector is computed, we could take a decision about tha matching of the pair of edge segments that it represents as in section

3.1.3. Nevertheless, in order to embed the similarity in the global matching process described later, we map the value provided by the decision function to range in the continuous interval [-1,+1] as a similarity measurement between features as follows,

$$s_{ij}(x) = \frac{2}{1+\exp(-af(x))} - 1 \tag{12}$$

where, in order to avoid severe bias, the parameter a is estimated experimentally, verifying that a value of 0.2 suffices for the type of images analysed. Implicitly, at this stage we have already applied the epipolar and similarity constraints.

5.2 Simulated annealing: a global matching strategy

In order to formulate the Simulated Annealing (SA) we build a network of nodes, where each pair of edge-segments to be matched creates a node with its own state, which determines the strength of the correspondence. Through the equation (12), the nodes are loaded with an initial state, which is updated through the SA optimization process. The correspondences are established based on the final values of the states.
The goal of the optimization process is to increase the consistency of a given pair of edge segments among three constraints (smoothness, ordering and epipolar) so that the state of a node representing a correct match can be increased and the state of any incorrect match can be decreased during the optimization process. Suppose the network with N nodes. The simulated annealing optimization problem is: modify the state values s_{ij} so as to minimize the energy,

$$E = -\frac{1}{2}\sum_{ij=1}^{N}\sum_{hk=1}^{N} w_{(ij)(hk)} s_{ij} s_{hk} \tag{13}$$

where $w_{(ij)(hk)}$ is a symmetric weight interconnecting two nodes (i,j) and (h,k). We require the self-feedback terms to vanish (i.e. $w_{(ij)(ij)} = 0$) because the nonzero merely add an unimportant constant to E, independent of the s_{ij}. The optimization task is to find the network with the most stable configuration, the one with lowest energy. The energy function is built so that it embeds three stereovision constraints: *smoothness*, *ordering* and *epipolar*, this last once again considered. Therefore, we look for a compatibility coefficient, which must be able to represent the consistency between the current pair of edge segments under correspondence and the pairs of edge segments in a given neighborhood. The compatibility coefficient makes global consistency between neighbors pairs of edge segments based on such constraints.

5.2.1 Mapping the smoothness constraint

The smoothness constraint assumes that neighboring edge segments have similar disparities, except at a few depth discontinuities (Medioni & Nevatia, 1985). Generally, when the smoothness constraint is applied, it is assumed there is a bound on the disparity range allowed for any given segment. We denote this limit as *maxd*, in the set of images tested, a value of 15 suffices, (see figure 2). According to the procedure described in Medioni & Nevatia (1985), for each edge segment "*i*" in the left image we define a window $w(i)$ in the right image in which corresponding segments from the right image must lie and, similarly, for each segment "*j*" in the right image, we define a window $w(j)$ in the left image in which

corresponding edge segments from the left image must lie. It is said that "a segment h must lie" if at least the 30% of the length of the segment "h" is contained in the corresponding window. The shape of this window is a parallelogram, one side is "i", for left to right match, and the other a horizontal vector of length *2.maxd*. The smoothness constraint implies that "i" in $w(j)$ assumes "j" in $w(i)$.
Now, given "i" and "h" in $w(j)$ and "j" and "k" in $w(i)$ where "i" matches with "j" and "h" with "k" the differential disparity $|d_{ij} - d_{hk}|$, measures how close the disparity between edge segments "i" and "j" denoted as d_{ij} is to the disparity d_{hk} between edge segments "h" and "k". The disparity between edge segments is the average of the disparity between the two edge segments along the length they overlap. This differential disparity criterion is used in Medioni & Nevatia (1985), Ruichek & Postaire (1996), Pajares et al., (1998*b*, 2000), Pajares & Cruz (2004) or Nasrabadi & Choo (1992) among others. We define a compatibility coefficient derived from Ruichek & Postaire (1996) and Nasrabadi & Choo (1992) given by the following expression,

$$c_{(ij)(hk)}(D) = \frac{2}{1 + \exp\left[\gamma\left(D/m(D) - 1\right)\right]} - 1 \tag{14}$$

where $D = \left|d_{ij} - d_{hk}\right|$, $m(D)$ denotes the average of all values D in the pair of stereo images (*LI* and *LR*, see figure 2) under processing. The slope of the compatibility coefficient in (14) is expressed by γ and varies for each pair of stereo images. To determine γ, it is assumed that the probability distribution function of D is Gaussian with average $m(D)$ and standard deviation $\sigma(D)$, i.e. $p(D) = \left[1 + \exp\left[\gamma\left(D_{(ij)(hk)}/m(D) - 1\right)\right]\right]^{-1}$.
Under this assumption and following Kim et al. (1997) and Kreszig (1983), to set the possibility value to 0.1 when the value of cumulative distribution function is 0.9, γ value is calculated by $\gamma = \ln 9\left((m(D))/(1.282\sigma(D))\right)$. In our experiments, typical values of γ, $m(D)$ and $\sigma(D)$ are about 6, 9 and 2 respectively. So, values of D near 0 should give high values in the compatibility coefficient $c_{(ij)(hk)}(\cdot) \approx +1$, but near 25 they give low values, $c_{(ij)(hk)}(\cdot) \approx -1$ and intermediate values should give values near zero, as expected. Note that $c_{(ij)(hk)}(\cdot)$ ranges in (–1,1). This means that a compatibility coefficient of +1 is obtained for a good consistency between two nodes (i,j) and (h,k) (i.e. D = 0) and a compatibility of –1 for a bad consistency between these nodes (i.e. $D >> 0$).
The energy function embedding the smoothness constraint must be minimum when D = 0 (i.e. corresponding to a high compatibility coefficient value) and high states values. We define an energy function assuming the above as follows,

$$E_S = -\frac{A}{2}\sum_{ij=1}^{N}\sum_{hk=1}^{N} c_{(ij)(hk)} s_{ij} s_{hk} \tag{15}$$

where A is a positive constant to be defined later.

5.2.2 Mapping the ordering constraint

We define the ordering coefficient $\bar{O}_{(ij)(hk)}$ for the edge-segments according to (16), which measures the relative average position of edge segments "i" and "h" in the left image with respect to "j" and "k" in the right image, it ranges from 0 to 1.

$$\bar{O}_{(ij)(hk)} = \frac{1}{N}\sum_{N} o_{(ij)(hk)} \quad where \quad o_{(ij)(hk)} = \left|S(x_i x_h) - S(x_j - x_k)\right| \quad and \quad S(r) = \begin{cases} 1 & if \quad r > 0 \\ 0 & otherwise \end{cases} \tag{16}$$

We trace S scanlines (in our experiments four are sufficient) along the common overlapping length, each scanline produces a set of four intersection points (i_S and h_S in LI and j_S and k_S in the RI) with the four edge-segments. Hence, the lower-case o_{ijhk} can be computed as in Ruichek & Postaire (1996) considering the above four edge points, and it takes 0 and 1 as two discrete values.
As $c_{(ij)(hk)}(\cdot)$ ranges in [–1,+1], in order to achieve similar contributions, we re-scale the $\bar{O}_{(ij)(hk)}$ values to [–1,+1] as follows: $O_{(ij)(hk)} = 2\bar{O}_{(ij)(hk)} - 1$.
To satisfy the ordering constraint, the energy function should have its minimum value when the nodes constituting each pair of nodes, for which the corresponding edges do not satisfy the ordering constraint, have high states values simultaneously. The energy function could be written as follows,

$$E_o = \frac{B}{2}\sum_{ij=1}^{N}\sum_{hk=1}^{N} O_{(ij)(hk)} s_{ij} s_{hk} \tag{17}$$

where B is a positive constant to be defined later.

5.2.3 Mapping the epipolar constraint

Although this constraint has been applied previously during the matching based on the similarity, now it is again mapped under the global point of view based on the overlapping concept, section 3.1. Based on the Figure 2, the overlap rate between edge segments (u,z), a_{uz} is defined as the percentage of coincidence, ranging in [0,1], when two segments u and z overlap, and it is computed taken into account the common overlap length l_c defined by c and the two lengths for the involved edge segments l_u and l_z respectively. All lengths are measured in pixels.

$$a_{uz} = 2l_c / (l_u + l_z) \tag{18}$$

Based on the overlapping concept, we compute the overlapping coefficient as follows,

$$\bar{\lambda}_{(ij)(hk)} = 0.5\left(a_{ij} + a_{hk}\right) \tag{19}$$

Under the epipolar constraint we can assume that correct matches should have high overlap rates and $\bar{\lambda}_{(ij)(hk)}$ for neighborhoods should be high, increasing the consistency. The overlapping criterion is justified by the fact that the edge segments are reconstructed by piecewise linear line segments as described in section 3.1.1. As before, we re-scale the $\bar{\lambda}_{(ij)(hk)}$ values to the interval [–1,+1] as follows: $\lambda_{(ij)(hk)} = 2\bar{\lambda}_{(ij)(hk)} - 1$. The energy function should have its minimum value when the nodes constituting each pair of nodes, for which the corresponding edges satisfy the overlapping concept, have high $\lambda_{(ij)(hk)}$ (≈ 1) and high states values simultaneously. The energy could be written as

$$E_e = -\frac{C}{2}\sum_{ij=1}^{N}\sum_{hk=1}^{N} \lambda_{(ij)(hk)} s_{ij} s_{hk} \tag{20}$$

5.2.4 Deterministic simulated annealing

The total energy function can be obtained as $E = E_s + E_o + E_e$. By comparison of expressions (15), (17) and (20) and (13), by multiplying the constant term by -1, it is easy to derive the connection weights,

$$w_{(ij)(hk)} = \left(Ac_{(ij)(hk)} - BO_{(ij)(hk)} + C\lambda_{(ij)(hk)} - \delta_{(ij)(hk)} \right) \tag{21}$$

where the delta function $\delta_{(ij)(hk)} = 1$ for (i,j) = (h,k) and 0 otherwise. To ensure the convergence to stable state, symmetrical inter-connection weights and no self-feedback are required, i.e. we see that by setting A = B = C = 1 both conditions are fulfilled.

The simulated annealing process, was originally developed in Kirkpatrick et al. (1983) and Kirkpatrick (1984), in this chapter we have implemented the approach described in Duda et al. (2001) and Haykin (1994). According to Duda et al. (2001), we have chosen deterministic simulated annealing because the stochastic one is slow. Nevertheless, the deterministic version has been faster than the stochastic, by exactly two orders of magnitude, this agrees with Duda et al. (2001).

In the original SA algorithm, the forces exerted by the other nodes are summed to find an analogue value s_{ij} without the intervention of the state of the node which is being updated. We modify this in order to include the contribution of its own state, so that the power of the similarity constraint is considered. The temperature (T) also plays a very important role in the optimization process.

Let $F_{(ij)} = \sum_{(hk)} w_{(ij)(hk)} s_{hk}$ be the force exerted on node (i,j) by the other nodes (h,k), then the new state $s_{ij}(t)$ is obtained by adding the fraction $f(\cdot,\cdot)$ to the previous one,

$$s_{ij}(t) = f(F_{(ij)}(t), T(t)) + s_{ij}(t-1) = tanh\left(F_{(ij)}(t) / T(t) \right) + s_{ij}(t-1) \tag{22}$$

where t represents the iteration index. The fraction $f(\cdot,\cdot)$ depends upon the temperature. At high T, the value of $f(\cdot,\cdot)$ is lower for a given value of the forces F. Details about the behavior of T are given in Duda et al. (2001). We have verified that this fraction must be small as compared to $s_{ij}(t-1)$ in order to avoid that the updating is controlled by this fraction exclusively and that the similarity constraint is cancelled. Under the above considerations and based on Starink & Backer (1995) and Hajek (1988), the following annealing schedule suffices to obtain a global minimum: $T(t) = T_0 / log(t+1)$, with T_0 being a sufficiently high initial temperature. We have computed T_0 as follows (Laarhoven & Aarts, 1989): 1) we select four stereo images, previously the Support Vector Machines has been trained and the support vectors obtained; now we compute the initial energy; 2) we choose an initial temperature that permits about 80% of all transitions to be accepted (i.e. transitions that decrease the energy function), and this value is changed until such percentage is achieved; 3) we compute the M transitions ΔE_i and we look for a value for T for which $\frac{1}{M} \sum_{i=1}^{M} \exp\left(-\frac{\Delta E_i}{T} \right) = 0.8$, after rejecting the higher order terms of the Taylor expansion of the exponential, $T = 5\langle \Delta E_i \rangle$, where $\langle \cdot \rangle$ is the mean value. In our experiments, we have obtained $\langle \Delta E_i \rangle = 6.10$, giving $T_0 = 30.5$ (with a similar order of magnitude as that reported in Starink & Backer (1995) and Hajek (1988)). We have also verified that a value of t_{max} = 100 suffices,

although the expected condition $T(t)=0,\ t\to+\infty$ in the original algorithm is not fully fulfilled. But this last requirement and a possible overly rapid cooling only occur when simulated annealing is applied for achieving the solid thermal equilibrium but not in our approach in which there is not a solid. Moreover, the above cooling scheduling is justified by the fact that our initial state has reached a certain equilibrium as a result of the Support Vector Machines local matching process and it is unnecessary to heat at high temperature, hence we have a prior knowledge about the system before it is relaxed by SA.
The proposed deterministic SA algorithm derived from Duda et al. (2001) including the modifications mentioned is summarized as follows:

1. *Initialization*: t = 0, $T(0)=T_0$, $w_{(ij)(hk)}$ as given by equation (21), s_{ij} ij = 1,...,N the state values received from the Support Vector Machines
2. *Simulated Annealing process*: set $t = t + 1$ and $np = 0$
   for each node (*i,j*) update $s_{ij}(t)$ according to (22) and *if* $|s_{ij}(t)-s_{ij}(t-1)|>\varepsilon$ *then* $np = np +$ 1 when all (*i,j*) nodes are updated, *if* $np \neq 0$ or $t<t_{\max}$ then go to step 2, *else* stop.
3. *Output*: s_{ij} updated

np is the number of nodes for which the matching states are modified by the updating procedure, N is the number of nodes, $T(t)$ is the annealing schedule, ε is a constant to accelerate the convergence, set to 0.01.

5.2.5 Mapping the uniqueness constraint

This stage represents the mapping of the *uniqueness* constraint, which completes the set of matching constraints used for solving our stereovision matching problem.
A left edge segment can be assigned to a unique right edge segment (unambiguous pair) or several right edge segments (ambiguous pairs).
The decision about whether a match is correct is made by choosing the greater state value in the network of nodes (in the unambiguous case there is only one) whenever it surpasses a previous fixed threshold U_1 (= 0), intermediate value for s_{ij} ranging in [–1,+1]. A true match should have s_{ij} = +1.
The ambiguities produced by broken edge segments are allowed. Therefore, we make a provision for broken segments resulting in possible multiple correct matches. The following pedagogical example from figure 2 clarifies this. The edge segment u in *LI* matches with the broken segment represented by s and q in *RI*, but under the condition that s and q do not overlap, that the s and q orientations do not differ by more than U_2 (±10°) and both s_{us}, s_{ut} are greater than U_1.

6. Conclusion

This chapter presents a survey about the application of several stereovision matching approaches which are applied under different strategies. Three main features are used: pixels, edge-segments and regions. The mapping of the constraints differs depending on these features that in turn are determined depending on the type of scene. Also, a general review is made about different strategies in conventional and fish eye based systems. These last producing omni-directional images.
We have established the bases for extending the scheme in figure 1, if required, by introducing more matching constraints, such as the optical flow (Kim & Yi, 2008).

7. Acknowledgments

We would like to thank Dr. Fernando Montes and Isabel Cañellas from the Forest Research Centre (CIFOR) in the National Institute for Agriculture and Food Research and Technology (INIA) for the omnidirectional images supplied and acquired by the measurement device with number of patent MU-200501738. The authors wish to acknowledge to the Council of Education of the Autonomous Community of Madrid and the Social European Fund for the research contract with the second author.

Authors thank the European Union, the European Commission and CONACYT by the economical support received from the European Commission under grant FONCICYT 93829 and grant 245986 in the Theme NMP-2009-3.4-1 (Automation and robotics for sustainable crop and forestry management). The content of this chapter is an exclusive responsibility of the University Complutense and it cannot be considered that it reflects the position of the European Union.

Finally, partial funding has also been received from DPI2009-14552-C02-01 project, supported by the Ministry of Spain Science and Technology within the Plan Nacional de I+D+i.

8. References

Abraham, S. & Förstner, W. (2005). Fish-eye-stereo calibration and epipolar rectification. *Photogrammetry and Remote Sensing*, vol. 59, pp. 278–288.

Barnard, S. & Fishler, M. (1982). Computational Stereo. *ACM Computing Surveys*, vol. 14, pp. 553-572.

Barnea, D.I. & Silverman, H.F. (1972). A class of algorithms for fast digital image registration. *IEEE Trans. Computers*, 21, 179-186.

Cherkassky, V. and Mulier, F. 1998. *Learning from Data: Concepts, Theory and Methods*. Wiley, New York.

Dempster, A.P. (1968). A generalization of Bayesian inference, *Journal of the Royal Statistical Society*, vol. B 30, pp. 205-247.

Duda, R.O.; Hart, P.E. & Stork, D.G. (2001). *Pattern Classification*, Wiley, New York.

Gonzalez, R.C. & Woods, R.E. (2008). *Digital Image Processing*, Prentice-Hall: Bergen County, NJ, USA.

Grimson, W.E.L. (1985). Computational experiments with a feature-based stereo algorithm. *IEEE Transactions on Pattern Analysis and Machine Intelligence*, vol. 7, pp. 17-34.

Haralick, R.M. & Shapiro, L.G. (1992). *Computer and Robot Vision, Vols. I–II*, Addison-Wesley: Reading, MA, USA.

Hajek, B. (1988). Cooling schedules for optimal annealing. *Mathematical Operation Research*, vol. 13, pp. 311-329.

Haykin, S. (1994). Neural Networks: *A Comprehensive Foundation*, Macmillan College Publishing Company, New York.

Herrera, P.J.; Pajares, G.; Guijarro, M.; Ruz, J.J. & Cruz, J.M. (2009*a*). Choquet Fuzzy Integral applied to stereovision matching for fish-eye lenses in forest analysis, in: W. Yu and E.N. Sanchez (Eds.), *Advances in Computational Intell.*, AISC 61, Springer-Verlag Berlin Heidelberg, pp. 179–187.

Herrera, P.J.; Pajares, G.; Guijarro, M.; Ruz, J.J. & Cruz, J.M. (2009*b*). Combination of attributes in stereovision matching for fish-eye lenses in forest analysis, in: J. Blanc-

Talon et al. (Eds.), *Advanced Concepts for Intelligent Vision Systems* (ACIVS 2009), LNCS 5807, Springer-Verlag Berlin Heidelberg, pp. 277-287.
Herrera, P.J.; Pajares, G.; Guijarro, M.; Ruz, J.J. & Cruz, J.M. (2009*c*). Fuzzy Multi-Criteria Decision Making in Stereovision Matching for Fish-Eye Lenses in Forest Analysis, in: H. Yin and E. Corchado (Eds.), *Intelligent Data Engineering and Automated Learning* (IDEAL 2009), Lecture Notes Computer Science vol. 5788, pp. 325-332, Springer-Verlag Berlin Heidelberg, .
Herrera, P.J.; Pajares, G.; Guijarro; M., Ruz, J.J.; Cruz, J.M. & Montes, F., (2009*d*). A Featured-Based Strategy for Stereovision Matching in Sensors with Fish-Eye Lenses for Forest Environments, *Sensors*, vol. 9, no. 12, pp. 9468-9492.
Herrera, P.J. (2010). Correspondencia estereoscópica en imágenes obtenidas con proyección omnidireccional para entornos forestales. PhD Dissertation (in spanish), Facultad of Informatics. University Complutense.
Huertas, A. & Medioni, G. (1986). Detection of Intensity Changes with Subpixel Accuracy Using Laplacian-Gaussian Masks. *IEEE Trans. Pattern Anal. Machine Intelligence*, vol. 8, no. 5, pp. 651-664.
Ishikawa, H. & Geiger, D. (2007). Local Feature Selection and Global Energy Optimization in Stereo. In : *Scene Reconstruction, Pose Estimation and Tracking*, R. Stolkin (Ed.), pp. 411-429, I-Tech, ISBN: 978-3-902613-06-6, Vienna, Austria.
Kim, Y.S.; Lee, J.J. & Ha, Y.H. (1997). Stereo matching algorithm based on modified Wavelet decomposition process. *Pattern Recognition*, vol. 30, no. 6, pp. 929-952.
Kim, Y.H. & Yi, S.Y. (2008). Using Optical Flow as an Additional Constraint for Solving the Correspondence Problem in Binocular Stereopsis. In : *Stereo Vision*, Asim Bhatti (Ed.), pp. 335-348, I-Tech, ISBN: 978-953-7619-22-0, Vienna, Austria.
Kirkpatrick, S.; Gelatt, C.D. & Vecchi, M.P. (1983). Optimization by simulated annealing, *Science*, vol. 220, pp. 671-680.
Kirkpatrick, S. (1984). Optimization by simulated annealing: quantitative studies. J. Statistical Physics, vol. 34, pp. 975-984.
Klaus, A.; Sormann, M. & Karner, K. (2006). Segmented-Based Stereo Matching Using Belief Propagation and Self-Adapting Dissimilarity Measure, In: *Proc. of 18th Int. Conference on Pattern Recognition*, vol. 3, pp. 15-18.
Koschan, A. & Abidi, M. (2008). *Digital Color Image Processing*, Wiley.
Kreszig, E. (1983). *Advanced Engineering Mathematics*, Wiley, New York.
Krotkov, E.; Henriksen, K., & Kories, R. (1990). Stereo Ranging with Verging Cameras. *IEEE Trans. on Pattern Analysis and Machine Intelligence*, vol. 12, no. 12, pp. 1200-1205.
Kuncheva, L. (2004). *Combining Pattern Classifiers: Methods and Algorithms*, Wiley.
Laarhoven, P.M.J. & Aarts, E.H.L. (1989). *Simulated Annealing: Theory and Applications*, Kluwer Academic, Holland.
Lankton, S. (2010). http://www.shawnlankton.com/2007/12/3d-vision-with-stereo-disparity/ (available on-line).
Leu, J.G. & Yau, H.L. (1991). Detecting the Dislocations in Metal Crystals from Microscopic Images. *Pattern Recognition*, vol. 24, no. 1, pp. 41-56.
Lew, M.S., Huang, T.S. & Wong, K. (1994). Learning and Feature Selection in Stereo Matching. *IEEE Trans. Pattern Anal. Machine Intell.* vol. 16, no. 9, pp. 869-881.
Lopez-Malo, M.A. & Pla, F. (2000). Dealing with Segmentation Errors in Region-based Stereo Matching, *Pattern Recognition*, vol. 8, no. 33, pp. 1325-1338.

McKinnon, B. & Baltes, J. (2004). Practical Region-Based Matching for Stereo Vision. In: *10th International Workshop on Combinatinal Image Analysis* (IWCIA'04), Klette, R., Zunic, J., (Eds.), vol. 3322, pp. 726–738, *Lecture Notes Computer Science*, Springer, Berlin.

Marapane, S.B. & Trivedi, M.M. (1989). Region-based stereo analysis for robotic applications. *IEEE Transactions on Systems, Man and Cybernetics* vol. 19(6), pp. 1447-1464.

Medioni, G. & Nevatia, R. (1985). Segment Based Stereo Matching. *Computer Vision, Graphics and Image Processing*, vol. 31, pp. 2-18.

Nasrabadi, N.M. & Choo, C.Y. (1992). Hopfield network for stereovision correspondence. *IEEE Transactions on Neural Networks*, vol. 3, pp. 123-135.

Nevatia, R. & Babu, K.R. (1980). Linear Feature Extraction and Description. *Computer Vision, Graphics, and Image Processing*, vol. 13, pp. 257-26.

Pajares, G. & Cruz, J. M. & Aranda, J. (1998*a*). Stereo Matching based on the Self-Organizing Feature-Mapping algorithm, *Pattern Recognition Letters* , vol. 19, pp. 319-330.

Pajares, G. ; Cruz, J.M. & Aranda, J. (1998*b*). Relaxation by Hopfield Network in Stereo Image Matching, Pattern Recognition, vol. 31(5), pp. 561-574.

Pajares, G. & Cruz, J. M. (1999). Stereo Matching using Hebbian learning, *IEEE Transactions on Systems Man and Cybernetics, Part B: Cybernetics*, vol. 29, no. 4, pp. 553-559.

Pajares, G. & Cruz, J.M. (2000). A new learning strategy for stereo matching derived from a fuzzy clustering method, *Fuzzy Sets and Systems*, vol. 110, no. 3, pp. 413-427.

Pajares, G. ; Cruz, J.M. & López-Orozco, J.A. (2000). Relaxation labeling in stereo image matching, *Pattern Recognition*, vol. 33, pp. 53-68.

Pajares, G. & Cruz, J. M. (2001). Local stereovision matching through the ADALINE neural network, *Pattern Recognition Letters*, vol. 22, no. 14, pp. 1457-1473.

Pajares, G. & Cruz, J. M. (2002). The non-Parametric Parzen's window in stereovision matching, *IEEE Transactions on Systems Man and Cybernetics*, Part B: Cybernetics, vol. 32, no. 2, pp. 225-230.

Pajares, G. & Cruz, J.M. (2003). Stereovision matching through Support Vector Machines, *Pattern Recognition Letters*, vol. 24, no. 15, pp. 2575-2583.

Pajares, G. & Cruz, J. M. (2004). On combining support vector machines and simulated annealing in stereovision matching. *IEEE Trans. Systems Man and Cybernetics, Part B*, vol. 34, no. 4, pp. 1646-1657.

Pajares, G & Cruz, J.M. (2006). Fuzzy cognitive Maps for Stereo Matching. *Pattern Recognition*, vol 39, pp. 2101-2114.

Pajares, G. & de la Cruz, J.M. (2007). *Visión por Computador: Imágenes digitales y aplicaciones*, RA-MA.

Ruichek, Y. & Postaire, J.G. (1996). A neural network algorithm for 3-D reconstruction from stereo pairs of linear images. *Pattern Recognition Letters*, vol. 17, pp. 387-398.

Ruichek, Y.; Hariti, M. & Issa, H. (2007). Global Techniques for Edge based Stereo Matching. In : *Scene Reconstruction, Pose Estimation and Tracking*, R. Stolkin (Ed.), pp. 383-410, I-Tech, ISBN: 978-3-902613-06-6, Vienna, Austria.

Scaramuzza, D.; Criblez, N.; Martinelli, A. & Siegwart, R. (2008). Robust Feature Extraction and Matching for Omnidirectional Images. In: *Field and Service Robotics*, Laugier, C., Siegwart, R., (Eds.), vol. 42, pp. 71–81, Springer, Berlin, Germany.

Scharstein, D. & Szeliski, R. (2002). A taxonomy and avaluation of dense two-frame stereo correspondence algorithms, *Int. J. Computer Vision*, vol. 47, no. 1-3, pp. 7–42, (2002). http://vision.middlebury.edu/stereo/

Schwalbe, E. (2005). Geometric modelling and calibration of fisheye lens camera systems. In *Proc. 2nd Panoramic Photogrammetry Workshop*, Int. Archives of Photogrammetry and Remote Sensing, vol. 36, Part 5/W8.

Shafer, G. (1976). *A Mathematical Theory of Evidence*. Princeton University Press.

Starink, J. P. & Backer, E. (1995). Finding Point Correspondences Using Simulated Annealing, *Pattern Recognition*, vol. 28, no. 2, pp. 231-240.

Tanaka, S. & Kak, A.C. 1990. A Rule-Based Approach to Binocular Stereopsis. In: *Analysis and Interpretation of Range Images,* Jain, R.C. Jain, A.K. (Eds.), Chapter 2, Springer-Verlag, Berlin.

Tang, L. ; Wu, C. & Chen, Z. (2002). Image dense matching based on region growth with adaptive window. *Pattern Recognition Letters*, vol. 23, pp. 1169-1178.

Vapnik, V.N. 2000. *The nature of Statistical Learning Theory*. Springer-Verlag, New York.

Wei, Y. & Quan, L. (2004). Region-Based Progressive Stereo Matching. In: *Proc. of the IEEE Computer Society Conference on Computer Vision and Pattern Recognition* (CVPR'04), vol. 1. pp. 106-113.

A High-Precision Calibration Method for Stereo Vision System

Chuan Zhou, Yingkui Du and Yandong Tang
State Key Laboratory of Robotics
Shenyang Institute of Automation
Chinese Academy of Sciences
P.R. China

1. Introduction

Stereo vision plays an important role in planetary exploration, for it can percept and measure the 3-D information of the unstructured environment in a passive manner (Goldberg et al., 2002; Olson et al., 2003; Xiong et al., 2001). It can provide consultant support for robotics control and decision-making. So it is applied in the field of rover navigation, real-time hazard avoidance, path programming and terrain modelling. In some cases, one stereo-vision system must accomplish both hazard detection and accurate localization with short baseline, i.e. 100-200mm in length. This seems to be a little ambivalent, for hazard detection needs wide view field, while accurate localization is on the contrary. Reconstruction precision is inverse proportion to focal length if the baseline is fixed. So researchers have to first select a compatible view angle, which guarantees the task workspace is within the view field. Then they must refine their camera calibration method in order to satisfy the accuracy requirement of rover localization, navigation and task operation.

In order to satisfy these requirements, wide angle lens is usually used. Lens distortion may reduce the precision of localization. So distortion parameter calibration plays an important part in such case. Moreover, calibration accuracy may also affect the complexity of the matching process. Tsai (R, Y, Tsai, 1987) proposed a method, in which a distorted parameter is used to describe the radial distortion of the lens. A five-parameter model is exploited to characterize several kinds of lens distortion (Yunde et al., 2000). A more complicated model, CAHVORE, is introduced (Gennery, 2001). Calibration becomes a nonlinear process if lens distortion is introduced. Usually camera calibration needs two steps. The first step generates an approximate solution using a linear technique, while the second step refines the linear solution using a nonlinear iterative procedure. The approximate solutions provided by the linear techniques must be good enough for the subsequent nonlinear technique to correctly converge. After the initial value has been obtained, the precision of the final result and convergence speed depends closely on optimization algorithm. Most of existing nonlinear methods minimize the geometric cost function using variants of conventional optimization techniques like gradient-descent, conjugate gradient descent Newton or Levenberg-Marquardt (LM) method. Therefore there are some problems in these circumstances. First, it is the commonly used cost function, reprojection error, which minimizes the distance between the measured image points and estimated image points. The points in each image are subject to noise, while the refined solution is only optimal to measured 2D image points, not to the real 3D points. So the final solution can inevitably be contaminated with large error, especially in depth direction when this refined solution is used for 3D reconstruction. Secondly, not all the parameters are optimized simultaneously. In most cases only part of the parameters are assumed to need refining while others are assumed to be correct and keep constant in optimization process, just like Tsai (R, Y, Tsai, 1987), which may result in the parameter not globally optimized. The third is the above techniques inherit well-known problems plaguing these differential-based methods, i.e. poor convergence and susceptibility to be trapped in local minimum. This is especially true for the objective function of camera calibration involves too many camera parameters and leads to a complex error surface. So the risk of local rather than global optimization might be severe with conventional methods. To alleviate the problems in the existing calibration techniques, we develop an alternative paradigm based on a new cost function to conventional reprojection error cost function. And we try Genetic Algorithms (GA) in the searching process instead of differential method in order to get globally optimal solution in high-dimension parameter space and avoid trapping in local minimum.

This chapter is organized as follow. In section 2, the space rover simulation system is introduced. In section 3, the camera model of stereo-vision system is proposed. Section 4 introduces the calibration method, which is based on planar homography constraint to get the initial solution. Section 5 gives the optimization strategy, including Reconstruction Error Sum, a new cost function, and GA searching process. Simulation images, real images and real environment experiment results are given in section 6. The article is concluded in section 7.

2. Space rover simulation system

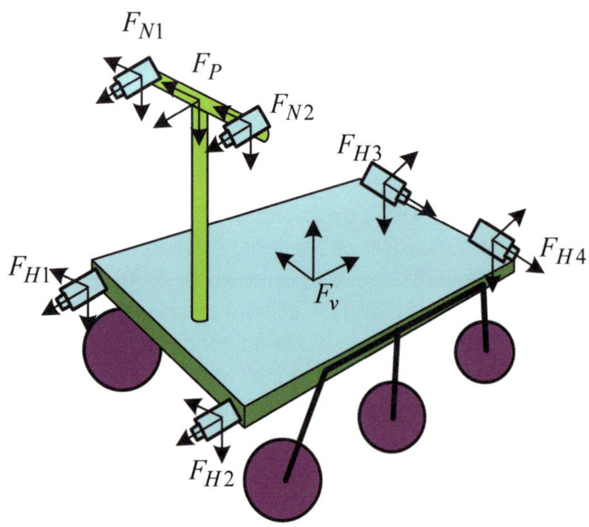

Fig. 1. Space rover cameras system.

In our space rover, we fix 3 pairs of cameras, i.e. navigation cameras on mast, 2 pairs of hazard detection cameras in front of the rover and at the back of the rover, as Fig.1 shows.

The hazard detection cameras are used to real-time obstacle detection and arm operation observation. The navigation cameras can pan and tilt together with the mast to capture environmental images all round the rover, then these images are matched and reconstructed to create Digital Elevation Map (DEM). Simulation environment can be built, including camera images, DEM, visulization interface and simulation space rover, as Fig.2 indicates. In real application, rover sends back images and status data. Operators can plan the rover path or arm motion trajectory in this tele-operation system (Backes & Tso, 1999). The simulation rover moves in the virtual environment to see if collision occurs. The simulation arm moves in order to find whether the operation point is within or out of the arm work space. This process repeats until the path or the operation point is guaranted to be safe. After these validations, instructions are sent to remote space rover to execute.

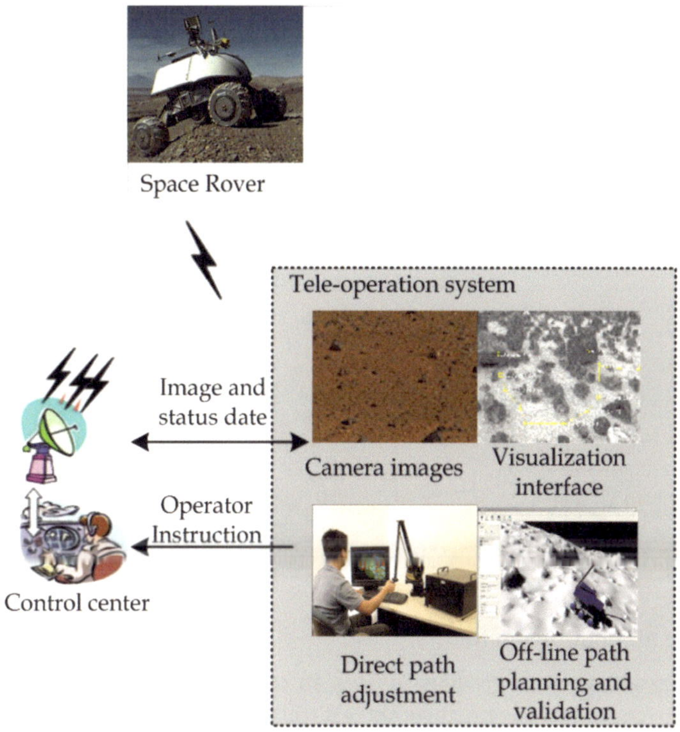

Fig. 2. Space rover simulation system.

3. Camera model

The finite projective camera, which often has pinhole model, is used in this chapter just like Faugeras suggested (Faugeras and Lustman, 1988). As Fig.3 shows, left and right cameras have intrinsic parameter matrixes K_q:

$$K_q = \begin{bmatrix} k_{uq} & s_q & u_{0q} \\ 0 & k_{vq} & v_{0q} \\ 0 & 0 & 1 \end{bmatrix}, q = 1,2 \quad (1)$$

The subscript q=1,2 denotes left and right camera respectively. If the number of pixels per unit distance in the image coordinates are m_x and m_y in the x and y directions, f is the focal of length, $k_{uq}=fm_x$ and $k_{vq}=fm_y$ represent the focal length of camera in terms of pixel dimensions in the x and y directions respectively. S_q is skew parameter, which is zero for most normal cameras. However, it is not in some instances like x and y axes is not perpendicular in the CCD array. u_{0q} and v_{0q} are the pixel coordinates of image center. The rotation matrix and translation vector between camera frame F_{cq} and world frame F_w are R_q and t_q respectively. A 3D point P projects on image plane. The coordinate transformation from world reference frame to camera reference frame can be denoted:

$$\mathrm{P_{cq}} = \mathrm{R_q P_w} + \mathrm{t_q}, q = 1,2 \tag{2}$$

The suffix indicates the reference frame, c is camera frame and w is world frame. The undistorted normalized image projection of P is:

$$n_{uq} = \begin{bmatrix} x_q \\ y_q \end{bmatrix} = \begin{bmatrix} X_{cq} / Z_{cq} \\ Y_{cq} / Z_{cq} \end{bmatrix} \tag{3}$$

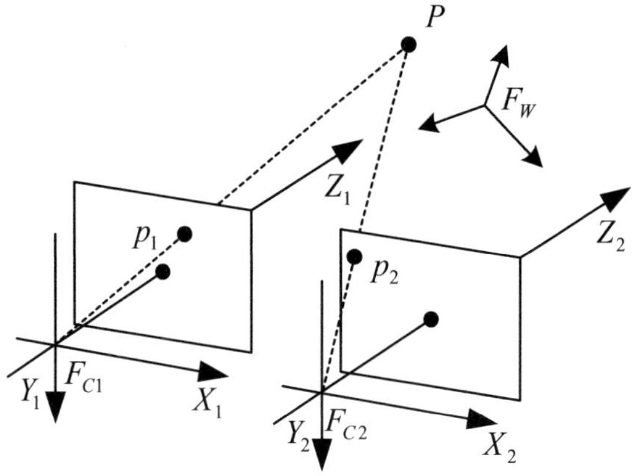

Fig. 3. World frame and camera frames.

As 4mm-focal-length wide angle lens is used in our stereo-vision system, the view angle approaches 80°. In order to improve reconstruction precision, lens distortion must be considered. Image distortion coefficients are represented by k_{1q}, k_{2q}, k_{3q}, k_{4q} and k_{5q}. k_{1q}, k_{2q} and k_{5q} denote radial distortion component, and k_{3q}, k_{4q} denote tangential distortion component. The distorted image projection n_{dq} is the function of the radial distance from the image center:

$$n_d^2 = (1 + k_{1q} r_q^2 + k_{2q} r_q^4 + k_{5q} r_q^6) n_{uq} + dn_q \tag{4}$$

With $r_q^2 = x_q^2 + y_q^2$. dn_q represents tangential distortion in x and y direction:

$$dn_q = \begin{bmatrix} dx_q \\ dy_q \end{bmatrix} = \begin{bmatrix} 2k_{3q} x_q y_q + k_{4q}(r_q^2 + 2x_q^2) \\ k_{3q}(r_q^2 + 2y_q^2) + 2k_4 x_q y_q \end{bmatrix} \tag{5}$$

From (1)(2) and (3), the final distorted pixel coordinate is:

$$\tilde{p}_q \cong K_q \cdot \tilde{n}_{dq}, q = 1,2 \tag{6}$$

Where $\cong$ means equal up to a scale factor.

4. Calibration method

The calibration method we use is on the basis of planar homography constraint between the model plane and its image. The model plane is observed in several positions, just like Zhang (Z, Z, Zhang, 2000) introduced. At the beginning of calibration, image distortion is not considered. And the relationship between the 3D point P and its pixel projection p_q is:

$$\lambda_q \tilde{p}_q = K_q \begin{bmatrix} R_q & t_q \end{bmatrix} \tilde{P}, q = 1,2 \tag{7}$$

Where λ_q is an arbitrary factor. We assume the model plane is on Z=0 of the world coordinate system. Then (6) can be changed into:

$$\lambda_q \tilde{p}_q = H_q P \text{ with } H_q = K_q \begin{bmatrix} r_{1q} & r_{2q} & t_q \end{bmatrix} \tag{8}$$

Here r_{1q}, r_{2q} are the first two columns of rotation matrix of two cameras, and H_q is the planar homography between two planes. If more than four pairs of corresponding points are known, H_q can be computed. Then we can use orthonormal constraint of r_{1q} and r_{2q} to get the closed-form solution of intrinsic matrix. Once K_q is estimated, the extrinsic parameters R_q, t_q and the scale factor λ_q for each image plane can be easily computed, as Zhang (Z, Z, Zhang, 2000) indicated.

5. Optimization scheme

As image quantification error exists, the estimated point position and the true value don't coincide correctly, especially in z direction. Experiment shows if quantification error reaches 1/4 pixel, the error in z direction may be beyond 1%. Fig.4 shows the observation model geometrically. Gray ellipses represent uncertainty of 2D image points while the ellipsoids represent the uncertainty of 3D points. Constant probability contours of the density describe ellipsoids that approximate the true error density. For nearby points the contours will be close to spherical; the further the points the more eccentric the coutours become. This illustrates the importance of modelling the uncertainty by a full 3D Gaussian density, rather than by a single scalar uncertainty factor. Scalar error models are equivalent to diagonal convariance matrics. This model is appropriate when 3D points are very close to the camera, but it breaks down rapidly with increasing distance. Ever though Gaussian error model and uncertainty regions don't coincide completely, we still have the opinion Gaussian model will be useful when quantization error is a significant component of the uncertainty in measured image coordinates. This uncertainty model is very important in space rover ego-mtion estimation in space environment when there is no Global Position System(Z, Chuan.& Y, K, Du. 2007).

The above solution in (8) is obtained through minimizing the algebraic distance, which is not physically meaningful. The commonly used optimization scheme is based on maximum likelihood estimation:

$$\sum_{i=1}^{n}\sum_{j=1}^{m}\sum_{q=1}^{2}\left\|p_{ijq}-\hat{p}(K_q,k_{1q},\cdots,k_{5q},R_{iq},t_{iq},P_j)\right\|^2 \quad (9)$$

Where $\hat{p}(K_q,k_{1q},\cdots,k_{5q},R_{iq},t_{iq},P_j)$ is the estimated projection of point P_j in image i, followed by distortion according to (3) and (4). The minimizing process is often solved with LM Algorithm. However, (8) is not accurate enough if it is used for localization and 3D reconstruction. The reason is just like section 1 described. Moreover, there are too many parameters to be estimated, namely, five intrinsic parameters, and five distorted parameters plus 6n extrinsic parameters for each camera. Each group of extrinsic parameter might be only optimized for the points on the current plane, while it maybe deviate too much from its real value. So a new cost function is explored here, which is on the basis of Reconstruction Error Sum (RES).

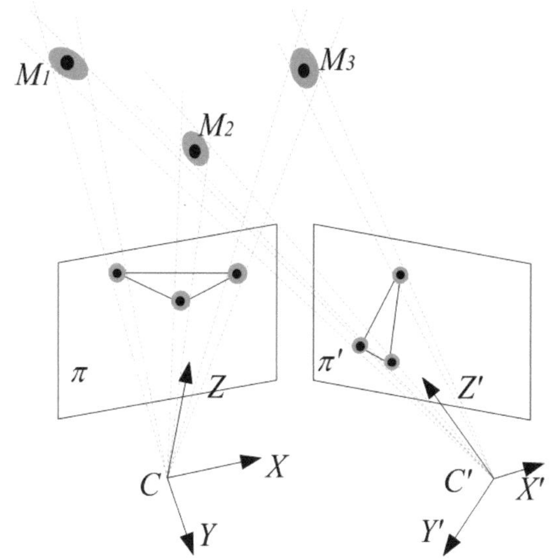

Fig. 4. Binocular uncertainty analysis.

5.1 Cost function

Although the cost function using reprojection error is equivalent to maximum likelihood estimation, it has defect in recovering depth information, for it iteratively adjusts the estimated parameters to make the estimated image point approach the measured point as closely as possible. While for 3D points, it may be not. We use Reconstruction Error Sum (RES) as cost function (Chuan, Long and Gao, 2006):

$$RES(b)=\sum_{i=1}^{n}\sum_{j=1}^{m}\left\|P_j-\prod(p_{ij1},p_{ij2},b_1,b_2)\right\|^2 \quad (10)$$

Where P_j is a 3D point in the world frame. Its estimated 3D coordinate can be denoted as: $\prod(p_{ij1},p_{ij2},b_1,b_2)$, which is reconstructed through triangulation method with given camera parameters b_1, b_2 and image projections p_{ij1}, p_{ij2}. b is a vector consisting 32 calibration parameters of both left and right cameras, including extrinsic, intrinsic and lens distortion described in (1), (2), (4), (5):

$$b=\{b_1,b_2\} \tag{11}$$

$b_q=\{k_{uq}, k_{vq}, s_q, u_{0q}, v_{0q}, k_{1q}, k_{2q}, k_{3q}, k_{4q}, k_{5q}, \alpha_q, \beta_q, \gamma_q, t_{xq}, t_{yq}, t_{zq}\}$, q=1,2. And α_q, β_q, γ_q, t_{xq}, t_{yq}, t_{zq} are rotation angle and translation component between the world frame and camera frame. So (10) minimizes the sum of all distance between the real 3D points and their estimated points. This cost function might be better than (9), because (10) is a much stricter constraint. It exploits the 3D constraint in world frame, while (9) is just a kind of 2D constraint on image plane. The optimization target P_j is no bias, because it is assumed to have no error in 3D space, while p_{ijq} in (9) is subject to image quantification error. Even though (10) still has image quanti-fication error in the image projections, which might propagate itself to calibration parameter and propagate calibration error to reconstructed 3D points, the calibration error and the reconstruction error can be reduced by comparing the 3D reconstructed points with their no-bias optimization target P_j iteratively.

5.2 Searching process

Finding solution b in (11) is a searching process in 32- dimension space. Common optimization methods like Gauss Newton and LM method might be trapped in local minimum. Here we use Genetic Algorithms (GA) to search the optimal solution (Gong and Yang, 2002). GA has been employed with success in variety of problems and it is robust to local minima and very easy to implement.

The chromosome we construct is b in (11), which has 32 genes. We use real coding because problems exists in binary encoding, like Hamming Cilff, computing precision and decoding complexity. The initial parameters of camera calibration are obtained from the methods introduced in section 3. At the beginning of GA, searching scope must be determined. It is very important because appropriate searching scope can reduce computational complexity. The chromosome is generated randomly in the region near the initial value. The fitness function we chose here is (10). The whole population consists of M individuals, where M=200. The full description of GA is below:

- Initialization: Generate M individuals randomly. Suppose the generation number t=0, i.e.:

  $$G^0=\{b_1^0,\cdots,b_j^0,\cdots,b_M^0\}$$

  Where b is chromosome. Superscript is generation number. And subscript denotes individual number.
- Fitness Computation: Compute fitness value of each chromosome according to (9) and they are sorted by ascent order, i.e.

  $$G^t=\{b_1^t,\cdots,b_j^t,\cdots,b_M^t\} \ \ and \ \ F(b_j^t)\le F(b_{j+1}^t)$$

- Selection operation: Select k individuals according to optimal selection and random selection.

  $$G^{t+1}=\{b_1^{t+1},\cdots,b_k^{t+1}\}$$

- Mutation operation: Select p individuals from the new k individuals, and mutate part of genes randomly.

$$G^{t+1} = \{b_1^{t+1},\cdots,b_k^{t+1},b_{k+1}^{t+1},\cdots,b_{k+p}^{t+1}\}$$

- Crossover operation: Perform crossover operation. Select l genes for crossover randomly. Repeat it M-k-p times.

$$G_i^{t+1} = \{b_1^{t+1},\cdots,b_k^{t+1},\cdots,b_{k+p}^{t+1},\cdots,b_M^{t+1}\}$$

- Let t=t+1. Select the best chromosome as current solution:

$$b_{best} = \{b_i^t \mid F(b_i^t) = \min_{j=1}^{M}(F(b_j^t))\}$$

If termination conditions are satisfied, i.e. t is bigger than a predefined number or $F(b_{best}) < \varepsilon$, search process will end. Otherwise, goto step 2.

6. Experiment result

6.1 Simulation experiment result

Both simulation and real image experiments have been done to verify the proposed method. Both left and right simulated cameras have the following parameter: $k_{uq}=k_{vq}=540$, $s_q=0$, $u_{0q}=400$, $v_{0q}=300$, q=1,2. The length of the baseline is 200mm. World frame is bound at the midpoint on the line connecting the two optic centers. Rotation and translation between two frames are pre-defined. The distortion parameters of the two cameras are given. Some emulated points in 3D world, whose distances to the image center are about 1m, project on the image planes. These image points are added with Gauss noise of different level. With these image projections and 3D points, we calibrate both emulation cameras with three different methods, Tsai method, Matlab method (Camera calibration toolbox for matlab), and our scheme. A normalized error function is defined as:

$$E(b) = \sqrt{\sum_{i=1}^{n} \frac{(1-\hat{b}_i / \bar{b}_i)^2}{n}} \tag{12}$$

It is used to measure the distance between estimated cameras parameters and true cameras parameters so as to compare the performance of each method. Where $\hat{b}_i, \bar{b}_i$ are the ith element estimated and real values of (11) respectively, and n is the parameter number of each method. The performances of three methods are compared, and the results are shown in table 1, where RES is our method. 1/8, 1/4, and 1/2 pixel noise is added in image points to verify the robustness of each method. From table 1, it can be seen our method has higher precision and better robustness than Tsai and Matlab methods.

Scheme / Error	Tsai	Matlab	RES
1/8 pixel	1.092	1.245	0.7094
1/4 pixel	1.319	1.597	0.9420
1/2 pixel	2.543	3.001	1.416

Table 1. Normalized error comparison

6.2 Real image experiment result

Real image experiment is also performed on the 3D platform, which can translate in X, Y, Z direction with 1mm precision. The cameras used are IMPERX 2M30, which are working in the binning mode with 800×600 resolution, together with 4mm-focal-length lens. The length of baseline is 200mm. A calibration chessboard is fixed rigidly on this platform about 1m away from the camera. About 40 images, which are shown in Fig.5, are taken every ten-centimeter on left, middle and right side of view field along depth direction. The configuration between the camers and chessboard is shown in Fig.6. First we use all the corner points as control points for coarse calibration. Then 4 points of each image, altogether about 160 points are selected for optimization with (10). The rest 7000 points are used for verification. We use Pentium 1.7GHz CPU, and VC++ 6.0 developing environment, calibration process needs about 30 minutes. Calibration result obtained from Tsai method, Matlab toolbox and our scheme, are used to reconstruct these points. Error distribution histogram is shown in Fig.7, in which (a) is Tsai method, (b) is Matlab scheme, and (c) is our RES method. The unit of horizontal axis is millimeter. Table 2 shows statistic reconstruction errors along X, Y, Z direction, including mean error A(X), A(Y), A(Z), maximal error M(X),

Fig. 5. All calibration images of left camera.

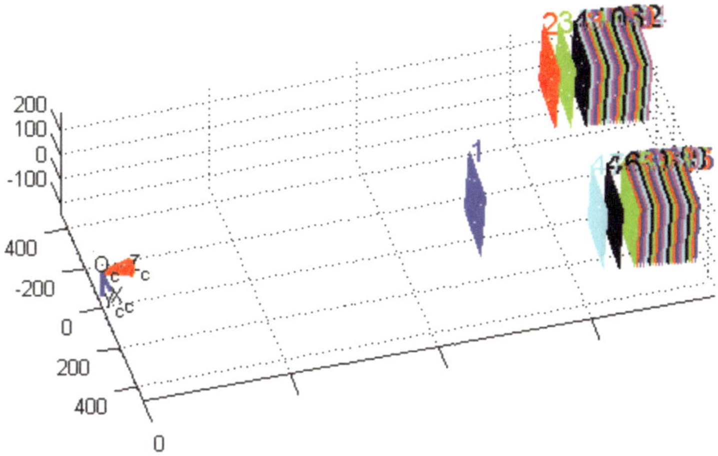

Fig. 6. Chessboard and cameras configration.

M(Y), M(Z), and variance $\sigma_x, \sigma_y, \sigma_z$. From these figures and table, it can be seen our scheme can have much higher precision than other method, especially in depth direction.

Error \ Scheme	**Tsai**	**Matlab**	**RES**
A(X)	2.3966	3.4453	1.7356
A(Y)	2.1967	2.2144	1.6104
A(Z)	4.2987	5.2509	2.3022
M(X)	9.5756	13.6049	5.7339
M(Y)	9.8872	12.5877	7.3762
M(Z)	15.1088	19.1929	7.3939
σ_x	2.4499	2.7604	1.7741
σ_y	2.3873	3.0375	1.8755
σ_z	4.7211	4.8903	2.4063

Table 2. Statistic error comparison

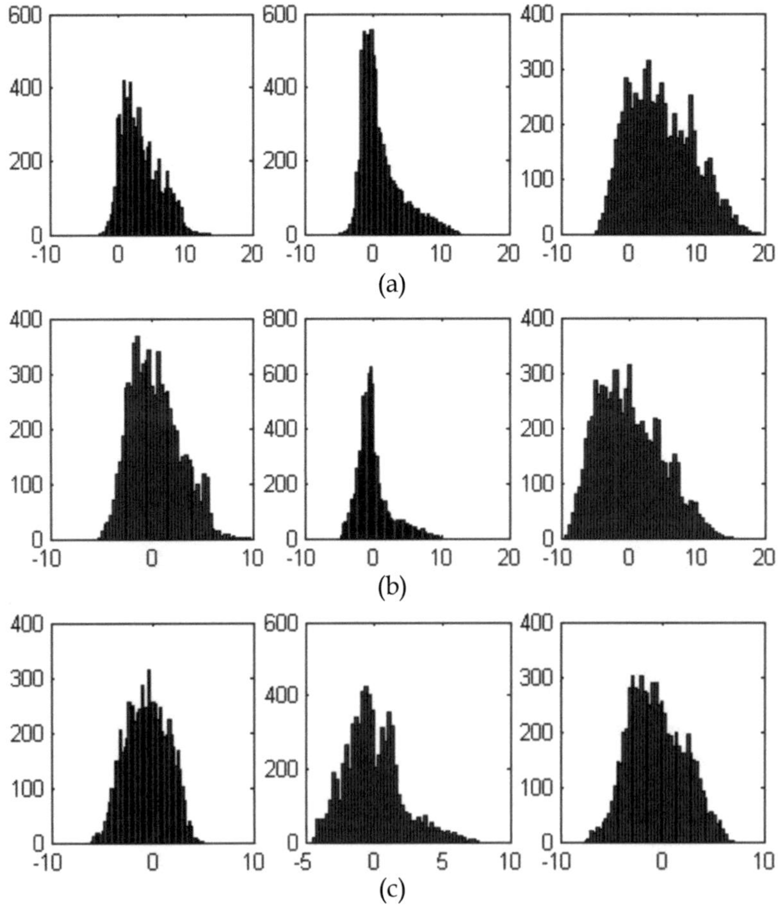

Fig. 7. Reconstruction error distribution comparison. (a) Tsai method. (b) Matlab method. (c) RES method.

6.3 Real environment experiment result

In order to validate the calibration precision in real application, we set up a 15×20m indoor environment, and a 6×3m slope made up of sand and rock. We calibrate the navigation cameras, which have 8mm-focal-length lens, in the way introduced above. After the images are captured, as Fig.8 shows, we perform character extraction, point match, 3D point-cloud creation. DEM and triangle grids are generated using these 3D points. Then the gray levels of the images are mapped to the virtual environment graphics. Finally, we have the virtual simulational environment, as Fig.9 indicates, which is highly consistent with the real environment. The virtual space rover is put into this environment for path planning and validation. In Fig.10, the blue line, which is the planned path, is generated by operator. The simulation rover follows this path to detect if there is any collision. If not, the operator transmitts this instruction to space rover to execute.

In order to validate the calibration precision for arm operation in real environment, we set up a board in front of the rover arm. The task of the rover arm is to drill the board, collect sample and analyse its component. We calibrate the hazard detection cameras, which have 4mm-focal-length lens, in the way introduced above too. After the images are captured, as Fig.11 shows, we perform character extraction, point match, 3D point-cloud creation. DEM and triangle grids are generated using these 3D points. The virtual simulation environment, as Fig.12 indicates, can be generated in the same way as mentioned above. The virtual space rover together with its arm, which has 5 degree of freedom, are put into this environment for trajectory planning and validation. After the opertor interactively gives a drill point on the board, the simalation system calculates whether point is within or out of the arm work space. Or there is any collision and singularity configuration on the trajectory. This process repeats until it proves to be safe. Then the operator transmitts this instruction to the rover arm to execute. Both of the experients prove the calibration precision is accurate enough for rover navigation and arm operation.

Fig. 8. Image captured by navigation camera.

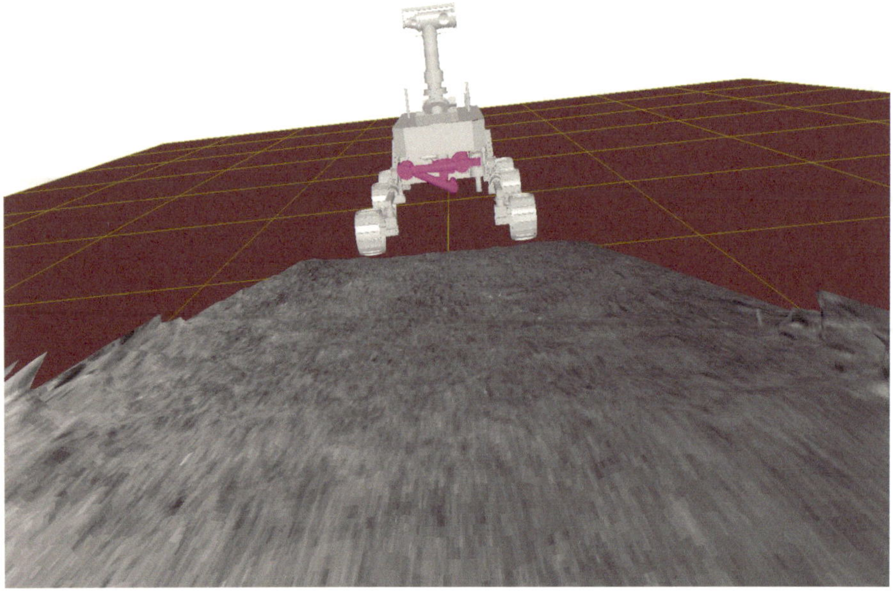

(a)

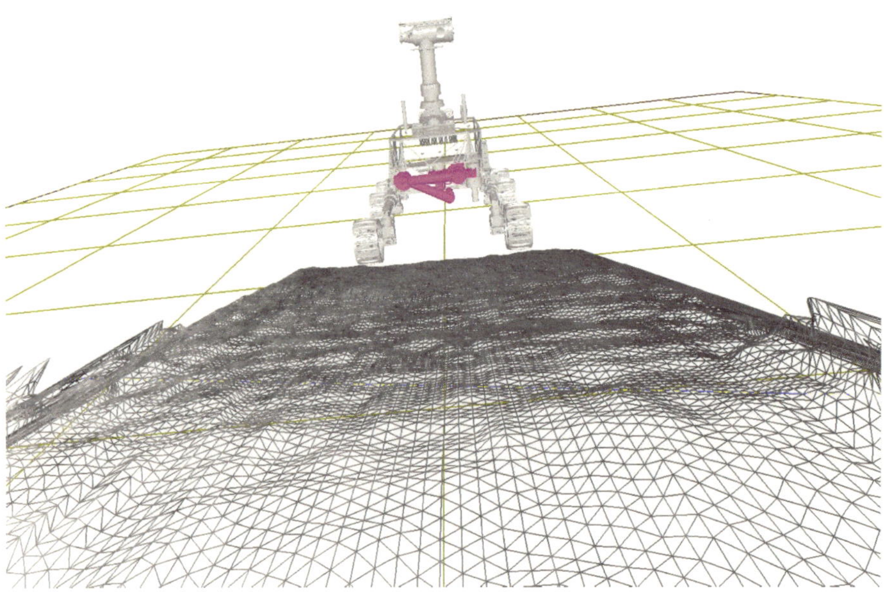

(b)

Fig. 9. Virtual simulation environment. (a) Gray mapping frame. (b) Grid frame.

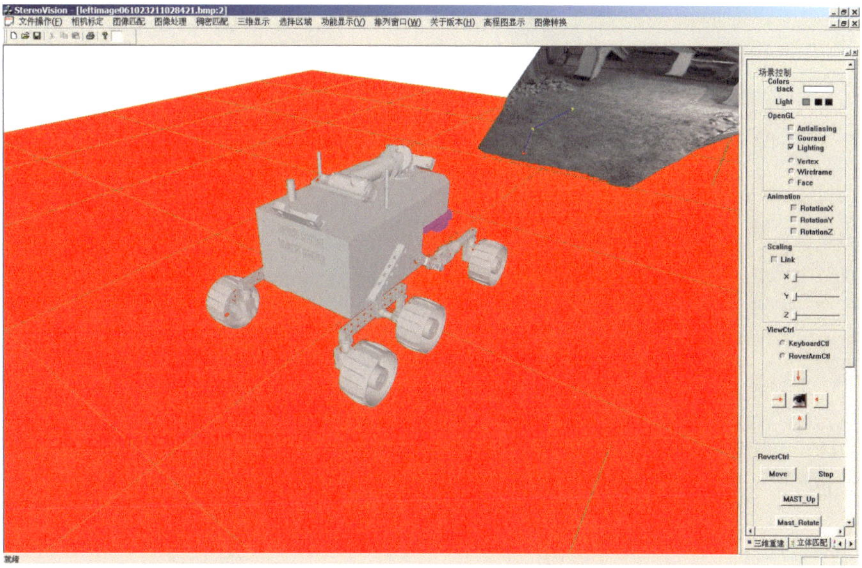

Fig. 10. Path planning for simulation rover.

Fig. 11. Image captured by hazard detection camera.

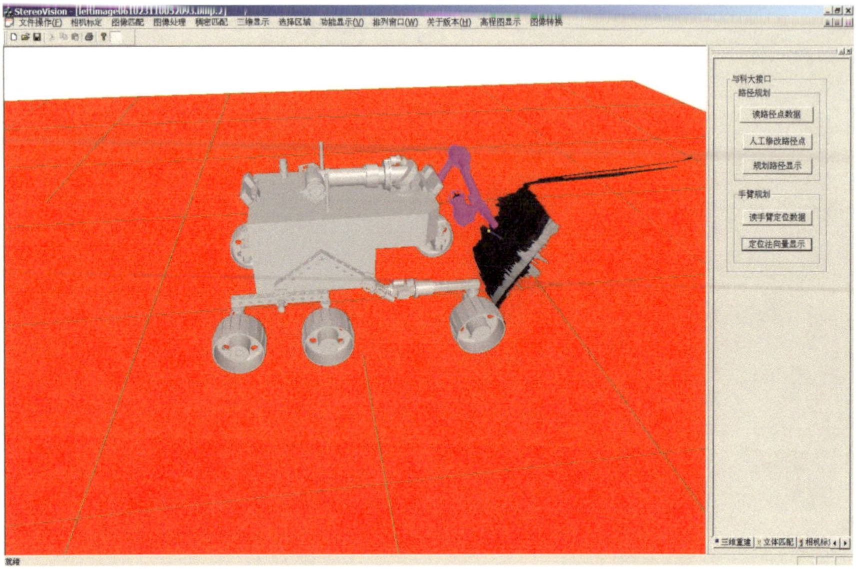

Fig. 12. Drill operation simulation for rover arm

7. Conclusion

Stereo vision can percept and measure the 3-D information of the unstructured environment in a passive manner. It provides consultant support for robotics control and decision-making, and it can be applied in the field of rover navigation, real-time hazard avoidance, path programming and terrain modelling. In this chapter, a high precision camera calibration method is proposed for stereo vision system in space rover using wide angle lens. It exploits 5 parameters to describe lens distortion. To alleviate the problems in the existing calibration techniques, we develop an alternative paradigm based on a new cost function to conventional reprojection error cost function. Genetic algorithm is used in searching process in order to get globally optimal solution in high-dimension parameter space and avoid trapping in local minimum instead of differential method. Simulation and real images experiments show that this scheme has higher precision and better robustness than traditional method for space localization. In real envrionment experiment, both Digital Elevation Map and virtual simulation environment can be generated accurately for rover path planning, validation and arm operation. It can be successfully used in space rover simulation system.

8. Acknowledgement

This research is supported by the National High-Technology 863 Program (Grant No. 2004AA420090).

9. References

Murry, D.& Jennings C. (1997). "Stereo vision based mapping and navigation for mobile robots", In: *Proceedings of IEEE Conference on Robotics and Automation*, pp.1694- 1699.

R, Y, Tsai. (1987). "A versatile camera calibration technique for high-accuracy 3d machine vision metrology using off-the shelf tv cameras and lenses," *IEEE Journal of Robotics and Automation*, vol.3, no.4, pp.323-344.

J, Yunde.; L. Hongjing,; X. An,& L. Wanchun. (2000). "Fish-Eye Lens Camera Calibration for Stereo Vision System", *Chinese Journal of Computers*, vol.23, no.11, pp.1215-1219.

Camera calibration toolbox for matlab, web site: http://www.vision.cal-tech.edu/bouguetj /calib_doc/.

D, B, Gennery. (2001). "Least-squares camera calibration includeing lens distortion and automatic editing of calibration points", *Calibration and Orien-tation of Cameras in Computer Vision*, T. Huang, Springer-Verlag, New York.

Z, Z, Zhang. (2000). "A flexible new technique for camera calibration," *IEEE Transactions on Pattern Analysis and Machine Intelligence*, vol.22, no. 11, pp. 1330- 1334.

M, L, Gong.& Y. H. Yang. (2002). "Genetic-based stereo algorithm and disparity map evaluation," *International Journal of Computer Vision*, vol.47, no.1, pp.63-77.

Z, Chuan.; T, D, Long.& Z, Feng. (2004). "A High- Precision Calibration Method for Distorted Camera." *IROS*, Sep 28-Oct 2, Sendai, Japan, pp.2618- 2623.

T. S. Huang, A. N. Arun, "Motion and structure from feature correspondences: a review," *Proceedings of the IEEE*, vol.82, no.2, 1994, pp.252-268.

J. Weng, P. Cohen, and M. Herniou, "Camera calibration with distortion models and accuracy evaluation," *IEEE Transaction on Pattern Analysis and Machine Intelligence*, vol.14, no.10, 1992, pp. 965-980.

Z, Chuan.; T, D, Long. & H, W, Gao. (2006). "A High-Precision Calibration and Optimization Method for Stereo Vision System." *International Conference on Control, Automation, Robotics and Vision*, Singapore, 5-8th December, pp.1158-1162.

Z, Chuan.; T, D, Long.& Z. Feng. (2004). "A High-Precision Binocular Method for Model-Based Pose Estimation", *International Conference on Control, Automation, Robotics and Vision*, Kunming, China, 6-9th December, pp.1067-1071.

Z, Chuan.& Y, K, Du. (2007). "A motion estimation method based on binocular reconstruction uncertainty analysis. " *Chinese Journal of Science Instrument (in Chinese)*. Vol.4, pp.15-17.

Z, Chuan.; T, D, Long.; Z, F,& D, Z, Li. (2003). "A Planar Homography Estimation Method for Camera Calibration." *IEEE International Symposium on Computational Intelligence in Robotics and Automation*, Kobe, Japan, pp.424-429.

C, F, Olson.; L, H, Matthies.; M, Schoppers.& M, W, Maimone. (2003). "Rover navigation using stereo ego-motion". *Robotics and Autonomous Systems*, 2003, vol.43, pp.215-229.

R, Hartley.& A, Zisserman. (2001). "Multiple View Geometry in Computer Vision." Cambridge University Press.

Y. L. Xiong.; C, F, Olson.& L, H, Matthies. (2001). "Computing Depth Maps From Descent Imagery." *Proceedings of the IEEE Computer Society Conference on Computer Vision and Pattern Recongnition*, Kauai, Hawaii, Dec, Vol.1, pp. 392-397.

P, G, Backes.& K, S, Tso. (1999). "The Web Interface for Telescience." *Presence*, vol.8, No.5, pp.531-529.

M, A, Vona.& P, G, Backes.; J, S, Norris.& M, W, Powell. "Challenges in 3D Visualization for Mars Exploration Rover Mission Science Planning."

S, B, Goldberg.; M, W, Maimone.& L, Matthies. (2002). "Stereo Vision and Rover Navigation Software for Planetary Exploration." *IEEE Aerospace Conference Proceedings*, March, Big Sky, Montana, USA, pp.

O, Faugeras.& F, Lustman. (1988). "Motion and structure from motion in a piecewise planar environment". *International Journal of Pattern Recognition and Artificial Intelligence.* 2(3), pp.485-508.

E, Malis.& R, Cipolla. (2000). "Multi-view constraints between collineations: application to self-calibration from unknown planar structures". *European Conference on Computer Vision,* vol.2, Dublin, Ireland, pp.610-624.

M, Muhlich.& R, Mester. (1998). "The role of total least squares in motion analysis". *European Conference on Computer Vision,* pp. 305-321.

M, Muhlich.& R, Mester. "The subspace method and equilibration in computer vision". *Technical report XP-TR-C-21*

7

Stereo Correspondence with Local Descriptors for Object Recognition

Gee-Sern Jison Hsu
National Taiwan University of Science and Technology
Taiwan

1. Introduction

Stereo correspondence refers to the matches between two images with different viewpoints looking at the same object or scene. It is one of the most active research topics in computer vision as it plays a central role in 3D object recognition, object categorization, view synthesis, scene reconstruction, and many other applications. The image pair with different viewpoints is known as stereo images when the baseline and camera parameters are given. Given stereo images, the approaches for finding stereo correspondences are generally split into two categories: one based on sparse local features found matched between the images, and the other based on dense pixel-to-pixel matched regions found between the images. The former is proven effective for 3D object recognition and categorization, while the latter is better for view synthesis and scene reconstruction. This chapter focuses on the former because of the increasing interests in 3D object recognition in recent years, also because the feature-based methods have recently made a substantial progress by several state-of-the-art local (feature) descriptors.

The study of object recognition using stereo vision often requires a training set which offers stereo images for developing the model for each object considered, and a test set which offers images with variations in viewpoint, scale, illumination, and occlusion conditions for evaluating the model. Many methods on local descriptors consider each image from stereo or multiple views a single instance without exploring much of the relationship between these instances, ending up with models of multiple independent instances. Using such a model for object recognition is like matching between a training image and a test image. It is, however, especially interested in this chapter that models are developed *integrating* the information across multiple training images. The central concern is how to extract local features from stereo or multiple images so that the information from different views can be integrated in the modeling phase, and applied in the recognition phase. This chapter is composed of the following contents:

1. Affine invariant region detection in Section 2: Many invariant image features are proposed in the last decade. Because these features are invariant to image variations in viewpoint, scale, illumination, and other variables, they serve well for establishing stereo correspondences across images. Those with better invariance to viewpoint changes are of special interest as they can be of direct use in the development of object models from stereo or multi-view.

2. Local region descriptors in Section 3: These descriptors transform affine invariant regions into vectors or distributions so that some distance measure can be applied to discern the similarity or difference between features. Again, those with better invariance to viewpoint changes are especially interested.
3. Object modeling and recognition using local region descriptors from multi-view in Section 4: A couple methods are reviewed that develop models by combining the information from local descriptors extracted across multiple views. These methods offer good examples on how to integrate local invariant features across different views.
4. A case study on performance evaluation and benchmark databases in Section 5: Implementation of others' methods for performance comparison with one's own proposed method takes a tremendous amount of time and efforts. Therefore, a database commonly accepted for performance benchmark is needed, and different methods can be evaluated on the same testbed. A performance evaluation example is reviewed with an introduction on its database, followed by a snapshot on other databases also good for study on 3D object recognition using stereo correspondences.

2. Affine regions for stereo correspondence

Affine-invariant region detectors can identify the affine-invariant regions on multiple images which are the projections of the same 3D surface patches. The regions are also considered as *covariant* with geometric and photometric transformations, as the regions detected in one image can be mapped onto those detected in the other using these transformations. Different affine detectors give different local regions in terms of different locations, sizes, orientations and the numbers of detected regions.

Mikolajczyk et al. (2005) have evaluated six affine region detectors, including Harris-affine, Hessian-affine, edge-based region, intensity extrema-based region, salient region and maximally stable extremal region (MSER). This evaluation focuses on the performance of matching between two images with variations caused by viewpoint, scale, illumination, blur and JPEG compression. The detectors for regions only covariant to similarity transform are excluded in their evaluation, for example the interest regions extracted to develop the Scale-Invariant Feature Transform (SIFT) by Lowe (1999; 2004) and the scale invariant features by Mikolajczyk & Schmid (2001). However, the SIFT descriptor (Lowe, 1999; 2004) is used in this evaluation to characterize the intensity patterns of the regions detected by the above six detectors.

The scope of this chapter is on finding stereo correspondences for object recognition, subject to the requirement that the object's model is built on at least a pair of stereo images with different viewpoints. In certain cases, the objects in stereo or multiple images may appear slightly different in scale. Therefore the detectors that perform better than others in rendering correct matches under viewpoint and scale changes are of special interest in this chapter. This performance can be justified by the *repeatability* and *matching score* from the evaluation in Mikolajczyk et al. (2005). It is shown that the Harris-affine detector, Hessian-affine detector and the maximally stable extremal region (MSER) detector are three promising ones in offering reliable stereo correspondences under viewpoint and scale changes. Note that illumination changes, blur and JPEG compression are among the major challenging parameters when recognizing a test image, the three aforementioned detectors also perform well when testing against these parameters, as revealed by Mikolajczyk et al. (2005).

2.1 Harris and hessian affine detectors

Harris affine region detector exploits a combination of Harris corner detector, Gaussian scale-space and affine shape adaptation. The core part is based on the following second moment matrix,

$$M(\mathbf{x},\sigma_D,\sigma_I) = \sigma_D^2 G(\sigma_I) * \begin{bmatrix} L_x^2(\mathbf{x},\sigma_D) & L_x L_y(\mathbf{x},\sigma_D) \\ L_x L_y(\mathbf{x},\sigma_D) & L_y^2(\mathbf{x},\sigma_D) \end{bmatrix} \quad (1)$$

where $L(\cdot;\sigma_D)$ is the image smoothed by a Gaussian kernel with differentiation scale σ_D; $L_x(\mathbf{x},\sigma_D)$ and $L_y(\mathbf{x},\sigma_D)$ are the first derivatives of the image along $x-$ and $y-$ directions, respectively, at point $\mathbf{x}$. The derivatives are then averaged in a neighborhood of $\mathbf{x}$ by convolving with $G(\sigma_I)$, a Gaussian filter with integration scale σ_I. The eigenvalues of $M(\mathbf{x},\sigma_D,\sigma_I)$ measure the changes of the gradients along two orthogonal directions in that neighborhood region. When the change is larger than a threshold, the region is considered a corner-like feature in the image.

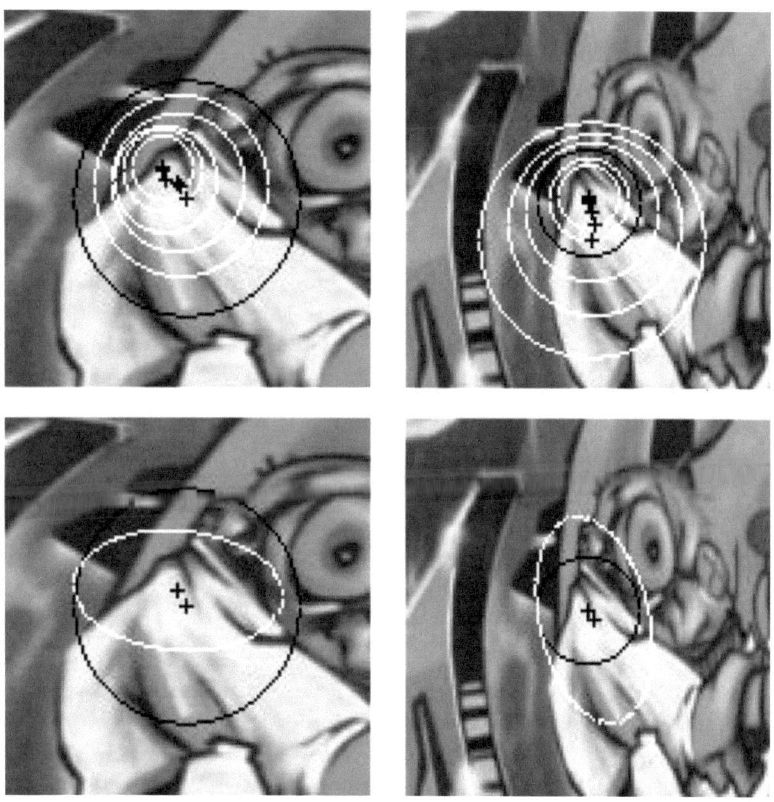

Fig. 1. Scale invariant interest point detection in affine transformed images: (Top) Initial interest points detected by multi-scale Harris detector with characteristic scales selected by Laplacian scale peak (in black–Harris-Laplace). (Bottom) Characteristic point detected with Harris-Laplace (in black) and the corresponding point from the other image projected with the affine transformation (in white). Reproduced from Mikolajczyk & Schmid (2004).

Given an image, the algorithm for detecting Harris affine regions consists of the following steps (Mikolajczyk & Schmid, 2002; 2004; Mikolajczyk et al., 2005):

1. *Detection of scale-invariant interest regions using the Harris-Laplace detector and a characteristic scale selection scheme*: Given σ_I and σ_D, the scale-adapted Harris corner detector using the second moment matrix M in (1) can be used to estimate corner-like features. To determine the characteristic scale, σ_I^*, the scale-adapted Harris corner is first applied with a number of preselected scales, resulting in corners in multiple scales. Given these corners, the algorithm given by Lindeberg (1998) can be applied, which iteratively searches for both the characteristic scale σ_I^* and the spatial location $\mathbf{x}^*$ that maximize the Laplacian-of-Gaussians (LoG) over the preselected scales.
2. *Normalization of the scale-invariant interest regions obtained in Step 1 using Affine Shape Adaptation*: The obtained scale-invariant interest regions are normalized using affine shape adaptation (Lindeberg & Gårding, 1997), which again uses the second moment matrix M in (1) but generalized with non-uniform Gaussian kernels for anisotropic regions (versus the uniform Gaussian kernels in (1) for isotropic regions). It is an extension of the regular scale-space obtained by convolution with *rotationally symmetric* Gaussian kernels to an affine Gaussian scale-space obtained by *shape-adapted* Gaussian kernels. This step results in initial estimates on the affine regions.
3. *Iterative estimation of the affine region*: The step in each iterative loop are composed of the generation of a reference frame using a shape adaptation matrix $U^{(k-1)}$, the selection of an appropriate integration scale $\sigma_I^{(k)}$ and differentiation scale $\sigma_D^{(k)}$, and the spatial localization of an interest point $\mathbf{x}^{(k)}$, where $\cdot^{(k)}$ denotes for the k-th iteration. The shape adaptation matrix is the concatenation of square roots of the second moment matrices and is often initialized by the identity matrix. The integration scale is selected at the maximum over a predefined range of scales of the normalized Laplacian, and the differentiation scale is selected at the maximum of normalized isotropy. To reduce complexity, Mikolajczyk & Schmid (2002; 2004) make $\sigma_D = s\sigma_I$, where s is a constant factor between 0.5 to 0.75.
4. Affine region update using the updated scales, $\sigma_I^{(k)}$ and $\sigma_I^{(k)}$, and spatial localizations $\mathbf{x}^{(k)}$. This allows the second moment matrix $M^{(k)}$ renewed, and the shape adaptation matrix $U^{(k)}$ updated.
5. Return to Step 3 if the stopping criterion on the isotropy measure is not met. Because the above algorithm in each iterative loop searches for the shape adaptation matrix $U^{(k)}$ that transforms an anisotropic region into an isotropic region, the iteration terminates when the ratio between the minimum and maximum eigenvalues of $M^{(k)}$ becomes sufficiently close to 1.

Fig. 1, reproduced from Mikolajczyk & Schmid (2004), shows an example from initial estimates of the regions using multi-scale Harris detector to the final affine invariant regions. In addition to the above Harris-Affine region detector based on the Harris-Laplace detector in (1), a similar alternative is Hessian-Affine region detector based on the Hessian matrix (Mikolajczyk et al., 2005),

$$H(\mathbf{x},\sigma_D) = \begin{bmatrix} L_{xx}(\mathbf{x},\sigma_D) & L_{xy}(\mathbf{x},\sigma_D) \\ L_{xy}(\mathbf{x},\sigma_D) & L_{xx}(\mathbf{x},\sigma_D) \end{bmatrix} \tag{2}$$

According to Mikolajczyk et al. (2005), the second derivatives, L_{xx}, L_{xy} and L_{xy} give strong responses on blobs and ridges. The scheme is similar to the blob detection given by Lindeberg (1998). The points maximizing the determinant of the Hessian matrix will penalize long structures with small second derivatives in one particular orientation. A local maximum of the determinant indicates the presence of a blob. The detection of Hessian-Affine regions is almost the same as the iterative algorithm for Harris-Affine regions, but with the second moment matrix in (1) replaced by the Hessian matrix in (2). Fig. 2, given in Mikolajczyk et al. (2005), shows examples of Harris-Affine and Hessian-Affine regions.

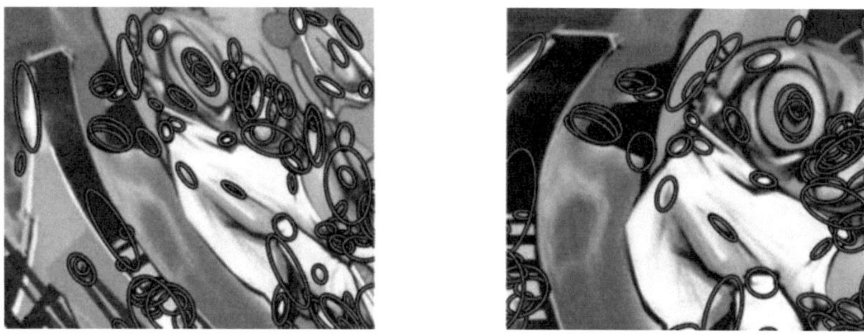

(a) Harris-Affine

(b) Hessian-Affine

Fig. 2. Examples of regions detected by Harris-Affine and Hessian-Affine detectors; reproduced from Mikolajczyk et al. (2005)

3.3 Maximally stable extremal region (MSER)

MSER is proposed by Matas et al. (2002) to find correspondences between two images of different viewpoints. The extraction of MSER considers the set of all possible thresholds able to binarize an intensity image $I(\mathbf{x})$ into a binary image $E_{t_M}(\mathbf{x})$,

$$E_{t_M}(\mathbf{x}) = \begin{cases} 1 & if I(\mathbf{x}) \leq t_M \\ 0 & otherwise. \end{cases} \quad (3)$$

where t_M is the threshold. A MSER is a connected region in $E_{t_M}(\mathbf{x})$ with little change in its size for a range of thresholds. The number of thresholds that maintain the connected region similar in size is known as the *margin* of the region. One can successively increase the threshold t_M in (3) to detect dark regions, denoted as MSER+; or invert the intensity image first and then increase the threshold to detect bright regions, denoted as MSER-. An example given by Forssén & Lowe (2007) with margin larger than 7 is shown in Fig. 3.

Because it is defined exclusively by the intensity function in the region and the outer border, and the local binarization is stable over a large range of thresholds, the MSER possesses the following characteristics which make it favorable in many cases (Matas et al., 2002; Nistér & Stewénius, 2008):

Fig. 3. Regions detected by a MSER with margin 7, reproduced from Forssén & Lowe (2007).

- The regions are closed under continuous (and thus projective) transformation of image coordinates, indicating that they are affine invariant regardless if the image is warped or skewed.
- The regions are closed under monotonic transformation of image intensities, reflecting that photometric changes have no effect on these regions, so they are robust to illumination variations.
- The regions are stable because their support is virtually unchanged over a range of thresholds.
- The detection performs across multiple scales without any smoothing involved, so both fine and large structures are discovered. If it operates with a scale pyramid, the repeatability and the number of correspondences across scales can be further improved.
- The set of all extremal regions can be enumerated in worst-case $O(n)$, where n is the number of pixels in the image.

Besides, the extensive performance evaluation by Mikolajczyk et al. (2005) shows the following characteristics of MSER:

- Viewpoint change: MSER outperforms other detectors in both the original images and those with repeated texture motifs.
- Scale change: MSER is outperformed by the Hessian-Affine detector only, in the repeatability percentage and matching score when the scale factor is large than 2.
- Illumination change: MSER gives the highest repeatability percentage.
- Region size - MSER appears to render more small regions than many others do, and small interest regions can be better in recognizing objects with occlusion.
- Blur - The performance of MSER degrades substantially when blur increases, and therefore, other detectors should be considered when recognizing objects in blur images. This might be the only variable that MSER cannot handle well.

MSER has been extended to color images by Forssén & Lowe 2007. This extension studies successive time-steps of an agglomerative clustering of color pixels. The selection of time-steps is stabilized against intensity scalings and image blur by modeling the distribution of edge magnitudes. The algorithm contains an edge significance measure based on a Poisson image noise model, yielding a better performance than the original MSER from Matas et al. (2002), especially when extracting such interest regions from color images.

3. Local region descriptors

Local region descriptors are mostly in vector forms that can characterize the pattern of an interest point with its neighboring region. Ten different descriptors are reviewed and evaluated by Mikolajczyk & Schmid (2005), including the scale invariant feature transform (SIFT) by Lowe (2004), gradient location and orientation histogram (GLOH) by Mikolajczyk & Schmid (2005), shape context (Belongie et al., 2002), PCA-SIFT (Ke & Sukthankar, 2004), spin images (Lazebnik et al., 2003), steerable filters (Freeman & Adelson, 1991), differential invariants (Koenderink & van Doom, 1987), complex filters (Schaffalitzky & Zisserman, 2002), moment invariants (Gool et al., 1996) , and cross-correlation of sampled pixel values (Mikolajczyk & Schmid, 2005). Five region detectors are used to offer interest regions in this evaluation study: Harris corners, Harris-Laplace regions, Hessian-Laplace regions, Harris-Affine regions and Hessian-Affine regions. Given an image, these detectors are first applied to identify interest regions, which are used to compute the descriptors.
Similar to the previous section that selects the affine invariant regions good for handling viewpoint and scale variations, this section focuses on the region descriptors good for the same variables. Fig. 4, reproduced from Mikolajczyk & Schmid (2005), shows a few comparisons on viewpoint and scale changes in terms of $1-$*precision* versus *recall*. $1-$precision and recall are defined as follows:

$$1 - precision = \frac{N_f}{N_c + N_f} \tag{4}$$

$$recall = \frac{N_c}{N_{cr}} \tag{5}$$

where N_c and N_f are the numbers of correct and false matches, respectively, and both change with the threshold that measures the distance between descriptors. N_{cr} is the number of correspondences. N_c and N_{cr} depend on the overlap error, which measures how well the corresponding regions fit each other under homography transformation. A perfect descriptor would give a unity recall for any precision. In practice, recall increases with decreasing precision (and thus increasing $1-$precision). For any fixed precision, the descriptors that yield higher recalls are more desirable.
It can be seen that GLOH (Mikolajczyk & Schmid, 2005) performs the best, closely followed by SIFT (Lowe, 2004) and shape context (Belongie et al. 2002) in generating more correct matches under viewpoint and scale changes. Actually, as revealed by the extensive experimental study in Mikolajczyk & Schmid (2005), these three descriptors also outperform the others in most tests with other variables.

3.1 SIFT and GLOH descriptors

SIFT (Scale-Invariant Feature Transform) descriptor, proposed by Lowe (2004), is derived from a 3D histogram of gradient location and orientation. GLOH (Gradient Location and

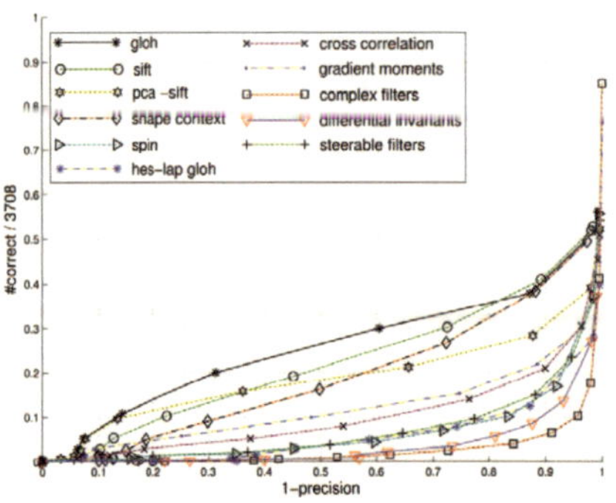

(a) Viewpoint change with structured scene and Hessian-Affine regions

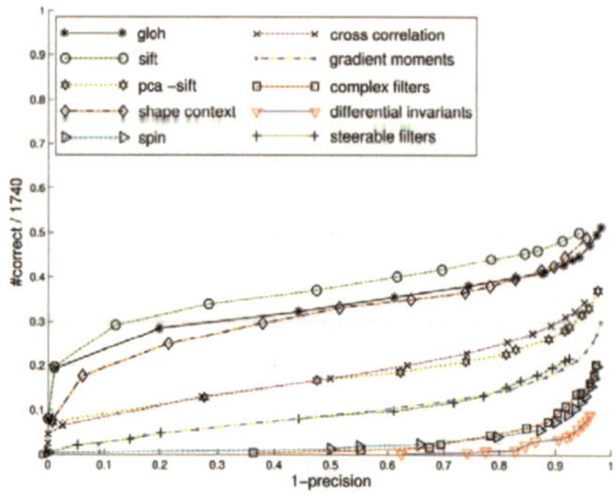

(b) Viewpoint change with textured scene and Hessian-Affine regions

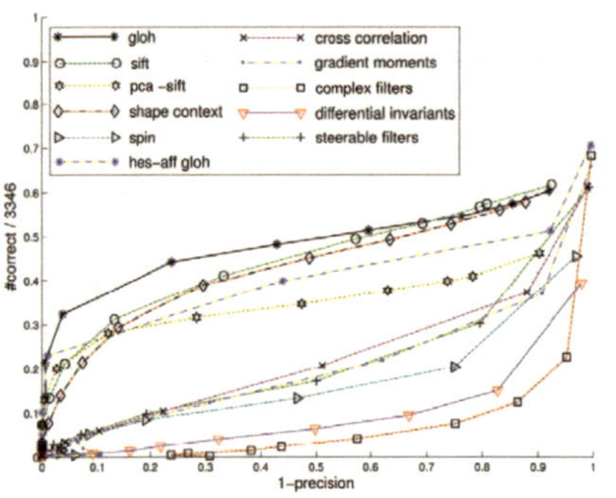

(c) Scale change with structured scene and Hessian-Laplace regions

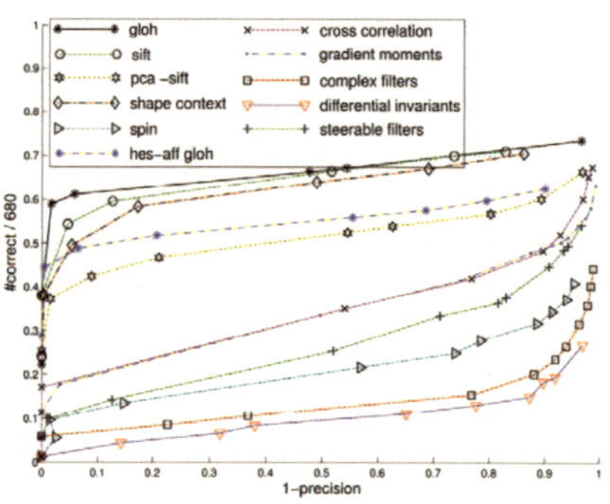

(d) Scale change with textured scene and Hessian-Laplace regions

Fig. 4. Performance comparison of region descriptors for viewpoint and scale changes, reproduced from Mikolajczyk & Schmid (2005).

Orientation Histogram) is a modified version of SIFT, given by Mikolajczyk & Schmid (2005), which computes a SIFT descriptor for a log-polar location grid with bins in both radial and angular directions.

Figs. 5a and 5b summarizes the computation of a SIFT descriptor. The gradient magnitudes and orientations are first computed at each sample point in a region around an interest point (or *keypoint* as called in Lowe, 2004), as the arrows shown in Fig. 5a. Each arrow shows the magnitude of the gradient by its length, and the orientation by its arrowhead. A Gaussian blur window, shown by the blue circle in Fig. 5a, is imposed on the interest region with σ equal to one half the width of the region's scale, assigning a weight to the magnitude of each sample point. This Gaussian window can avoid sudden changes in the descriptor with small perturbations on the position of the region, and weaken the contribution from the gradients far from the center of the region. Fig. 5a shows a 2×2 descriptor array with 4 subregions inside, and each subregion is formed by 4×4 elements. The gradients in each subregion can be segmented according to the eight major orientations, and summed up in magnitude for each orientation, transforming the 8×8 gradient patterns to the 2×2 descriptor patterns, as shown in Fig. 5b. This 2×2 descriptor pattern gives a vector of $2 \times 2 \times 8 = 32$ in dimension. However,

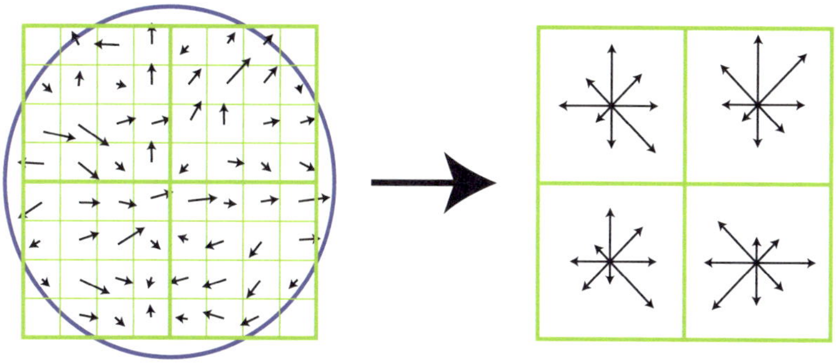

Fig. 5. (a) 2×2 descriptor array with 4 subregions inside, and each subregion is formed by 4×4 elements. The gradients are smoothed by a Gaussian window shown in blue circle. (b) The 8 orientation bins in each subregion can be combined with bins from other subregions, leading to a vector descriptor for this interest region.

based on the experiments by Lowe (2004), the best descriptor that has been exhaustively tested is with 4×4 array, leading to a descriptor vector of $4 \times 4 \times 8 = 128$ in dimension. To obtain illumination invariance, this descriptor is normalized by the square root of the sum of squared components.

GLOH is SIFT descriptor computed for a log-polar location grid with three spatial elements in radial direction (with radius 6, 11, and 15) and eight orientations. Only the subregion with smallest radius is not segmented to orientations, and this gives $2 \times 8 + 1 = 17$ subregion in total. The gradient orientations in each subregion are quantized into 16 bins, and this gives to the interest region a vector of 272 in dimension. PCA (Principal Component Analysis) is then applied to downsize its dimension to 128 using the principal components extracted from 47,000 patches collected from various images. The experiments in Mikolajczyk & Schmid (2005) reveal that GLOH performs slightly better than SIFT in many tests.

3.2 Shape context descriptor

Shape context, proposed by Belongie et al. (2002), is a descriptor that characterize the shape of an object. Given a shape, which can be obtained by an edge detector, one can pick a point p_i out of the n points on the shape and compute the histogram h_i of the relative coordinates of the remaining $n-1$ points,

$$h_i(k) = \#\{q \neq p_i : (q - p_i) \in bin(k)\} \tag{6}$$

where k denotes for the k-th bin of the histogram, q denotes a point on the shape. This histogram, measured in a log-polar space, defines the shape context descriptor of p_i. It reveals the distribution of the shape relative to p_i in terms of $\log(r)$ and θ, where r measures the distance and θ measures the orientation. This design makes the descriptor more sensitive to the locations of nearby shape points than to those farther apart. Belongie et al. (2002), use 5 bins for $\log(r)$ and 12 bins for θ, giving a descriptor of dimension 60; while in Mikolajczyk & Schmid (2005), r is split into 9 bins with θ in 4 bins, resulting in a descriptor of dimension 36. Fig.6, from Belongie et al. (2002), shows an example of shape context computation and matching.

Given a point p_i on the first shape and a point q_i on the second shape, C_{ij}, which denotes the cost of matching these two points, can be computed using their shape context descriptors as

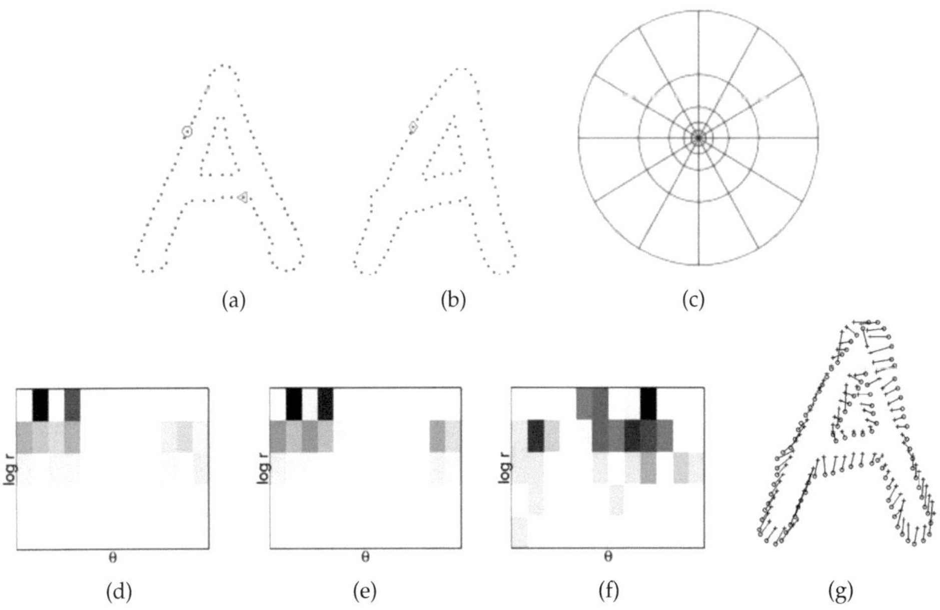

Fig. 6. Shape context computation and matching, (a) and (b) are the sampled edge points of two "A" shapes. (c) Diagram of log-polar histogram bins used for computing shape contexts, 5 bins for $\log r$ and 12 for θ. (d), (e) and (f) are the shape contexts obtained for the reference points marked by $\circ$, $\diamond$, and $\triangleleft$, respectively. Similar patterns between $\circ$ and $\diamond$, and a different one at $\triangleleft$ can be observed. (g) Correspondences found by bipartite matching. All are reproduced from Belongie et al. 2002.

follows,

$$C_{ij} \equiv C(p_i, q_j) = \frac{1}{2} \sum_{k=1}^{K} \frac{|h_i(k) - h_j(k)|^2}{h_i(k) + h_j(k)} \tag{7}$$

where $h_i(k)$ and $h_j(k)$ denote the K-bin normalized histogram at p_i and q_j, respectively. (7) applies the χ^2 test for measuring the difference between distributions. The total cost of matching all point pairs can then be written as

$$H(\pi) = \sum_i C(p_i, q_{\pi(i)}) \tag{8}$$

where π is a permutation to be determined to minimize $H(\pi)$. This is a typical case in weighted bipartite matching problem, which can be solved in $O(N^3)$ time using the Hungarian algorithm (Papadimitriou and Stieglitz, 1982).

Minimization of $H(\pi)$ over π gives the correspondences at the sample points. The correspondence is extended to the complete shape using the regularized thin plate splines as the aligning transform. Aligning shapes leads to a general measure of shape similarity. The dissimilarity between two shapes can thus be computed as the sum of matching errors between corresponding points. Given this dissimilarity measure, Belongie et al. (2002), apply nearest-neighbor algorithms for object recognition.

4. Integration of local descriptors from multiple views

Depending on how the model of a given object is built, the approaches of using local invariant regions for object recognition can be split into two categories. One takes a single view of the object for developing the model, while the other uses multiple views. Both recognize the object in different views along with occlusions and different geometric and photometric conditions. Because of multiple views of the object considered in the modeling phase, the multi-view based methods can recognize the object in a much broader range of conditions. As far as stereo vision for 3D object recognition is concerned, only the methods using multi-views are considered in this section. Two methods are reviewed, one is given by Lowe (2001) that fuses the SIFT features from multiple views of an object into a single model with view-dependent clusters, and the other, proposed by Rothganger et al. ((2006), builds a patch-based 3D model using affine region descriptors and multi-view spatial constraints.

4.1 Fusion of SIFT features from multiple views

Lowe (2001) proposes a method that combines SIFT features from multiple views to model the appearance of an object for full 3D object recognition. The feature combinations are performed according to the closeness of the geometric fit to existing views, and similar views are fused into view clusters. For nearby views that are not combined, matching features are linked across the views so that a match in one view is automatically propagated as a potential match in neighboring views. Therefore additional training images continue to contribute to the robustness of the model by capturing more feature variation without leading to a continuous increase in the number of view clusters.

Assuming a model of an object built on the SIFT features extracted from a given view of the object, the determination on whether to cluster a new view with the existing model depends on e, which is an error between the model-based projected features and the image features in the new view (Lowe, 2001).

$$e = \sqrt{\frac{2||\mathbf{Ax} - \mathbf{b}||}{r - 4}} \tag{9}$$

where $\mathbf{A}$ is a matrix formed by the coordinates of model-based projected features, r is the number of rows in $\mathbf{A}$, $\mathbf{x}$ is the parameters of the similarity transform (Lowe, 2001), and $\mathbf{b}$ is the the coordinates of image features. Lowe chooses a threshold, T_e, as 0.05 times the maximum dimension of the training image, which results in clustering views that differ by less than roughly 20 degrees rotation in depth. As each new training image arrives, it is matched to the existing model views. Three possible cases can occur:

1. The training image does not match any existing model. In this case, the image is used to form a new model.
2. The training image matches an existing model view, and $e > T_e$. In this case, a new model view is formed from this training image. This is similar to forming a new object model, except that all matching features are linked between the current view and the three closest matching model views.
3. The training image matches an existing model view, and $e \leq T_e$, which means the new training image is to be combined with the existing model view. All features from the new training image are transformed into the coordinates of the model-based view using the similarity transform. The new features are added to those of the existing model view and

linked to any matching features. Any features that are very similar to existing ones (have a distance that is less than a third that of the closest non-matching feature) will be removed, as they do not add significant new information.

The result is that training images that are closely matched by the similarity transform are clustered into model views that combine their features for improved robustness. Otherwise, the training images form new views in which features are linked to their neighbors.

Although Lowe (2001) shows an examples in which a few objects are successfully identified in a cluttered scene, no results are reported on recognizing objects with large viewpoint variations, significant occlusions and illumination variations.

4.2 Patch-based 3D model with affine detector and spatial constraint

Generic 3D objects often have non-flat surfaces. To model and recognize a 3D object given a pair of stereo images, Rothganger et al. (2006 proposes a method for capturing the non-flat surfaces of the 3D object by a large set of sufficiently small patches, their geometric and photometric invariants, and their 3D spatial constraints. Different views of the object can be matched by checking whether groups of potential correspondences found by correlation are geometrically consistent. This strategy is used in the object modeling phase, where matches found in pairs of successive images of the object are used to create a 3D affine model. Given such a model consisting of a large set of affine patches, the object in a test image can be claimed recognized if the matches between the affine regions on the model and those found in the test image are consistent with *local appearance models* and *geometric constraints*. Their approach consists of three major modules:

1. Appearance-based selection of possible matches: Using the Harris affine detector (Section 2) and a DoG-based (Difference-of-Gaussians) interest point detector, corner-like and blob-like affine regions can be detected. Each detected affine region has an elliptical shape. The dominant gradient orientation of the region (Lowe, 2004) can transform an ellipse into a parallelogram and a unit circle into a square. Therefore, the output of this detection process is a set of image regions in the shape of parallelograms. The affine rectifying transformations can map each parallelogram onto a "unit" square centered at the origin, known as a rectified affine region. Each rectified affine region is a normalized representation of the local surface appearance, invariant to planar affine transformations. The rectified affine regions are matched across images of different views, and those with high similarity in appearance are selected as an initial match set to reduce the cost of latter constrained search. An example of the matched patch pairs on a teddy bear, reproduced from Rothganger et al. (2006, is shown in Fig. 7

2. Refine selection using geometrical constraints: RANSAC (RANdom SAmple Consensus, Fischler & Bolles 1981) is applied to the initial appearance-based matched set to find a geometrically consistent subset. This is an iterative process that keeps on until a sufficiently large geometrically consistent set is found, and the geometric parameters are finally renewed. The patch pairs which appear to be similar in Step 1 but fail to be geometrically consistent are removed in this step.

3. Addition of geometrically consistent matches: Explore the remainder of the space of all matches, and search for other matches which are consistent with the established geometric relationship between the two sets of patches. Obtaining a nearly maximal set of matches can improve recognition, where the number of matches acts as a confidence measure, and object modeling, where they cover more surface of the object.

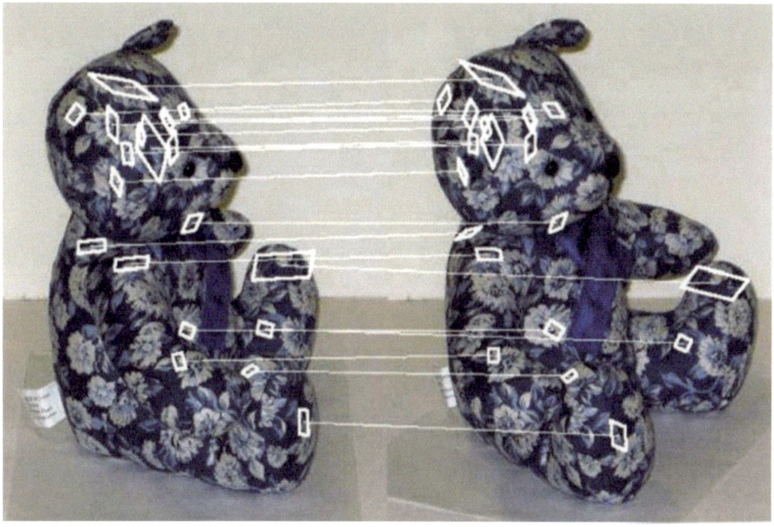

Fig. 7. An example of the matched patches between two images, reproduced from Rothganger et al. ((2006).

To verify their proposed approach, Rothganger et al. (2006) design an experiment that allows an object's model built on tens of images taken from cameras roughly placed in an equatorial ring centered at the object. Fig. 8 shows one such training set, composed of images used in building the model for the object "teddy bear". Fig. 9 shows all the objects with models built from the patches extracted from the training sets. Table 1 summarizes the number of images in the training set of each object, along with the number of patches extracted from each training set for forming the object's model. The model is evaluated in recognizing the object in cluttered scenes with it placed in arbitrary poses and, in some cases, partial occlusions. Fig. 10 shows most test images for performance evaluation. The outcomes of this performance evaluation, among others, will be presented in the next section.

	Apple	Bear	Rubble	Salt	Shoe	Spidey	Truck	Vase
Training images	29	20	16	16	16	16	16	20
Model patches	759	4014	737	866	488	526	518	1085

Table 1. Numbers of training images and patches used in the model for each object in the object gallery shown in Fig. 9

5. Performance evaluation and benchmark databases

As reviewed in Section 4, only few methods develop object recognition models on interest points with information integrated across stereo or multiple views; however, many build their models with one single image or a set of images without considering the 3D geometry of the objects. The view-clustering method by Lowe (2001), reviewed in Section 4.1, can be considered in between of these two categories. Probably because few works of the same category are available, Lowe (2001) does not present any comparison with other methods using multiple views. Nevertheless, Rothganger et al. ((2006) report a performance comparison of their method with a few state-of-the-art algorithms using the training and test images as shown in Fig.10. This comparison study is briefly reviewed below, followed by an introduction to the databases that offer samples taken in stereo or multiple views.

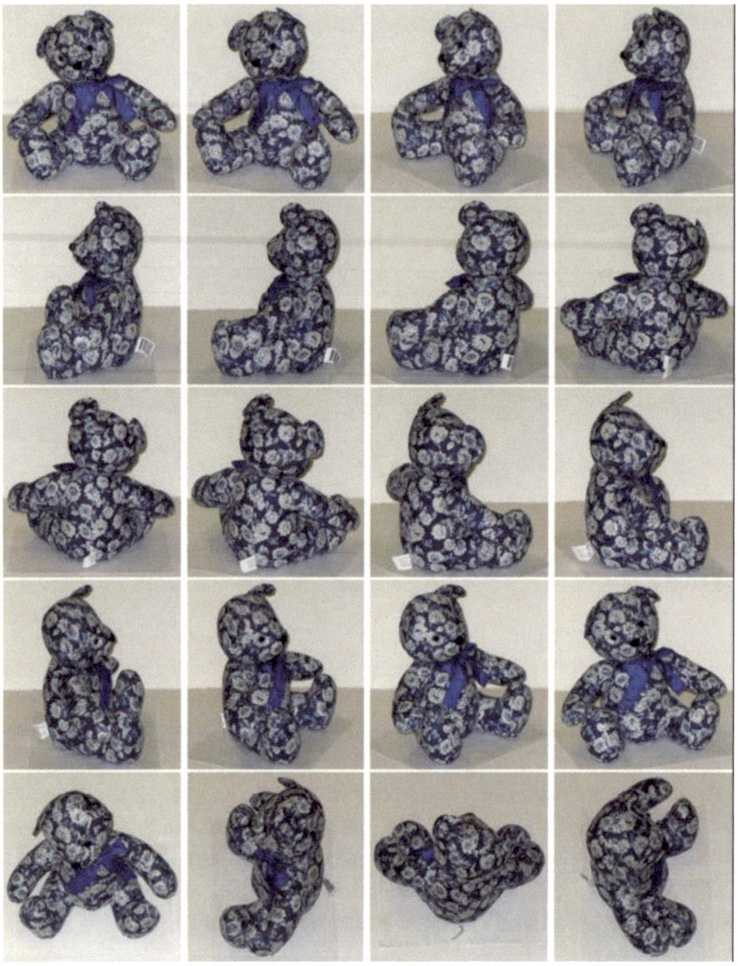

Fig. 8. The training set used in building the model for "teddy bear", reproduced from Rothganger et al. ((2006).

5.1 Performance comparison in a case study

This section summarizes the performance comparison conducted by Rothganger et al. ((2006), which include the algorithms given by Ferrari et al. (2004), Lowe (2004), Mahamud & Hebert (2003), and Moreels et al. (2004). The method by Lowe (2004) has been presented in Section 3, and the rest are addressed below.

Mahamud & Hebert (2003) develop a multi-class object detection framework with a nearest neighbor (NN) classifier as its core. They derive the optimal distance measure that minimizes a nearest neighbor mis-classification risk, and present a simple linear logistic model which measures the optimal distance in terms of simple features like histograms of color, shape and texture. In order to perform search over large training sets efficiently, their framework is extended to finding the Hamming distance measures associated with simple discriminators. By combining different distance measures, a hierarchical distance model is constructed, and their complete object detection system is an integration of the NN search over object part classes.

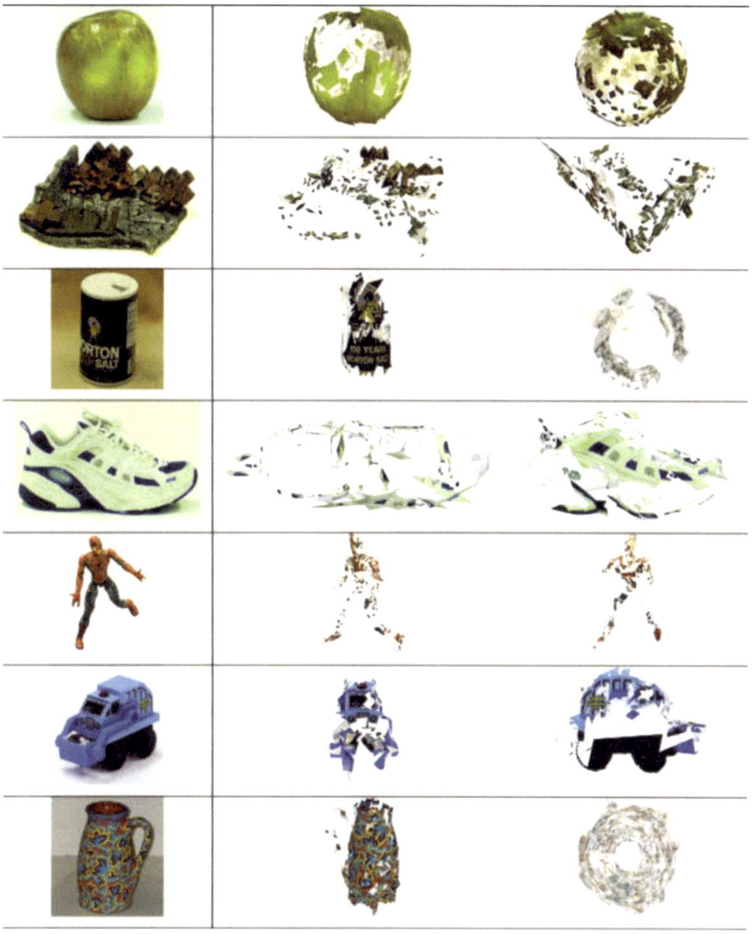

Fig. 9. Object gallery. Left column. One of several input pictures for each object. Right column: Renderings of each model, not necessarily in same pose as input picture, reproduced from Rothganger et al. ((2006).

The method proposed by Ferrari et al. (2004) is initialized by a large set of unreliable region correspondences generated purposely to maximize the amount of correct matches, at the cost of producing many mismatches. A grid of circular regions is generated for covering the modeling image[1]. The method then iteratively alternates between expansion and contraction phases. The former aims at constructing correspondences for the coverage regions, while the latter attempts to remove mismatches. At each iteration, the newly constructed matches between the modeling and test images help a filter to take better mismatch removal decisions. In turn, the new set of supporting regions makes the next expansion more effective. As a result, the amount, and the percentage, of correct matches grows every iteration.
Moreels et al. (2004) proposes a probabilistic framework for recognizing objects in images of cluttered scenes. Each object is modeled by the appearance of a set of features extracted from a single training image, along with the position of the feature set with respect to a common

[1] *Modeling* images or *training* images refer to the image samples used in building an object's model.

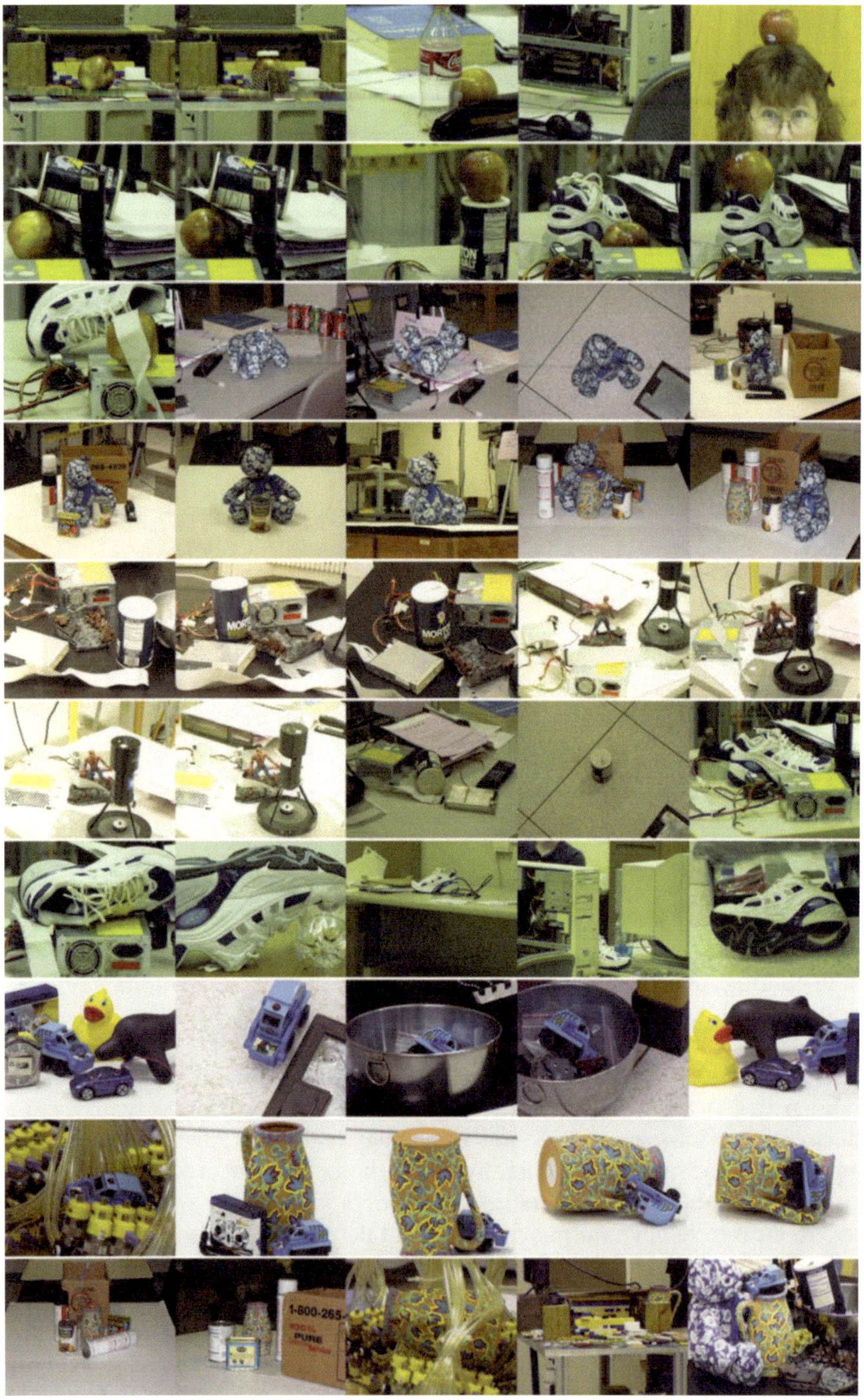

Fig. 10. The test set for performance evaluation, the objects shown in Fig. 1 are placed in arbitrary poses in cluttered scenes and, in some cases, with partial occlusions; reproduced from Rothganger et al. ((2006).

reference frame. In the recognition phase, the object and its position is estimated by finding the best interpretation of the scene in terms of object models. Features detected in a test image are hypothesized as features from either the database or clutters. Each hypothesis is scored using a generative model of the image which is defined using the object models and a model for clutter. Heuristics are explored to find the best from a large hypothesis space, improving the performance of this framework.

As shown in Fig. 11, Rothganger et al.'s and Lowe's algorithms perform best with true positive rates over 93% at false positive rate 1%. The algorithm by Ferrari et al. keeps improving its performance as the false positive rate is allowed to increase, and can reach > 95% in true positive rate if the false positive rate increases to 7.5%. It is interesting to see that two of Rothganger et al.'s methods (color and black-and-while) and Lowe's method perform almost equally well across for all false positive rates shown. This can be caused by the fact that their models can fit to the objects in most views, but fail in a few specific views because of the lack of samples from these views used in building the model. Although all tested

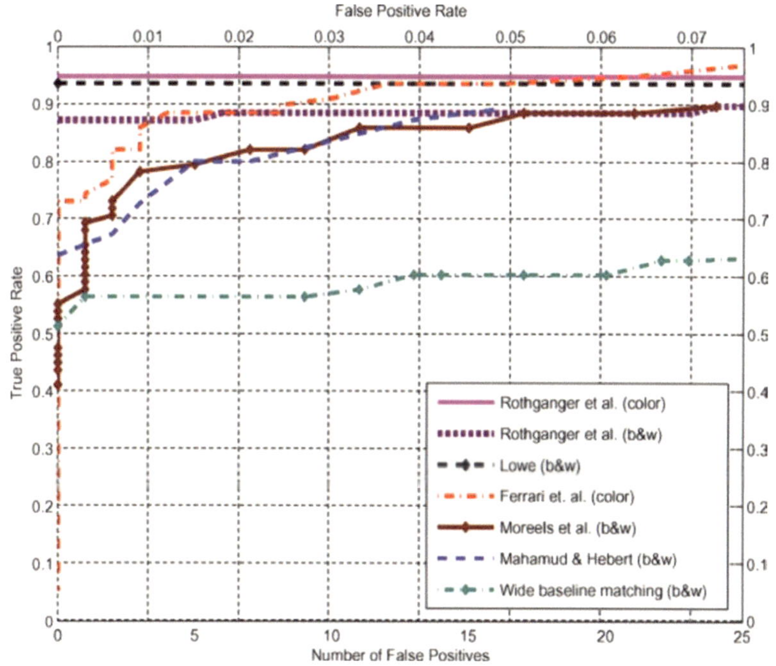

Fig. 11. Performance comparison reported in Rothganger et al. ((2006).

algorithms use multiple views to build object models, only Lowe's and Rothganger et al.'s algorithms combine the information from across multiple views for recognition. The rest consider all modeling images independently, without looking into geometric relationships between these images, and tackle object recognition as an image match problem. To evaluate the contribution made from geometric relationships, Rothganger et al. ((2006) have studied a base line recognition method where the pairwise image matching part of their modeling algorithm is used as the recognition kernel. An object is considered recognized when a sufficient percentage of the patches found in a training image are matched to the test image. The result is shown in Fig. 11 in the green doted line, it performs worst in all range of false positive rates.

5.2 Databases for 3D object recognition

The database used in Rothganger et al. ((2006) consists of 9 objects and 80 test images. The training images are stereo views for each of the 9 objects that are roughly equally spaced around the equatorial ring for each of them, as an example "teddy bear" shown in Fig. 8. The number of stereo views ranges from 7 to 12 for different objects. The test images, shown in Fig. 10, are monocular images of objects under varying amounts of clutter and occlusion and different lighting conditions. It can be downloaded at `http://www-cvr.ai.uiuc.edu/~kushal/Projects/StereoRecogDataset/`. In addition, several other databases can also be considered for benchmarking stereo vision algorithms for object recognition. The ideal databases must offer stereo images for training, and test images collected with variations in viewpoint, scale, illumination, and partial occlusion.

Columbia Object Image Library (COIL-100) database offers 7,200 images of 100 objects (72 images per object). The objects have a wide variety of complex geometric and reflectance characteristics. The images were taken under well-controlled conditions. Each object was placed on a turntable, and an image was taken by a fixed camera when the turntable made a 5^0 rotation. Most studies take a subset of images with viewing angles equally apart for training, and the rest for testing. A few samples are shown in Fig. 12. It serves as a good database for evaluating object recognition with viewpoint variation, but is inappropriate for testing against other variables. COIL-100 can be downloaded via `http://www1.cs.columbia.edu/CAVE/software/softlib/coil-100.php`.

Fig. 12. Samples from COIL-100.

The Amsterdam Library of Object Images (ALOI), made by Geusebroek et al. (2005), offers 1,000 objects with images taken under various imaging conditions. The primary variables considered include 72 different viewing angles with 5^0 apart, 24 different illumination conditions, and 12 different illumination colors in terms of color temperatures. 750 out of the 1,000 objects were also captured with wide baseline stereo images. Figs. 13, 14, and 15 give samples in viewpoint change, illumination variation, and stereo, respectively. The stereo images can be used for training, and the rest can be used for testing. This dataset appears better than COIL-100 in terms of offering samples of a large amount of objects with a broader scope of variables. ALOI can be downloaded via `http://staff.science.uva.nl/~aloi/`.

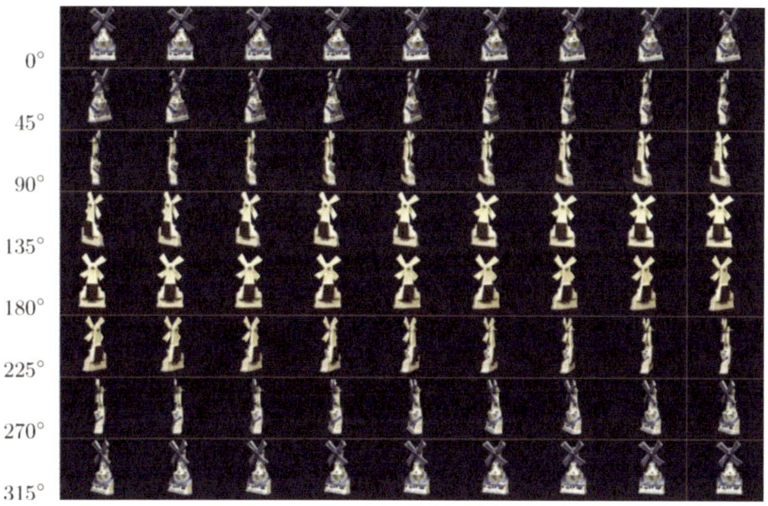

Fig. 13. A example viewpoint subset from ALOI database, reproduced from Geusebroek et al. (2005).

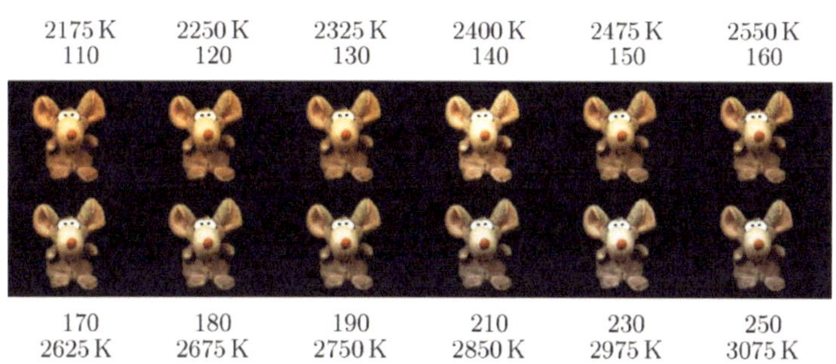

Fig. 14. A example of illumination subset from ALOI database, reproduced from Geusebroek et al. (2005).

The ETHZ Toy database offers 9 objects with single or multiple views for modeling, and 23 test images with different viewpoints, scales, and occlusions in cluttered backgrounds. Fig. 16 shows 2 sample objects and each with 5 training images, and Fig. 17 shows 15 out of the 23 test images. It can be downloaded via `http://www.vision.ee.ethz.ch/~calvin/datasets.html`.

6. Conclusion

This chapter discusses methods using affine invariant descriptors extracted from stereo or multiple training images for object recognition. It focuses on the few that integrate information from multiple views in the model development phase. Although the objects in single test images can appear in different viewpoint, scale, illumination, blur, occlusion, and image quality, the training images must be taken from multiple views, and thus can only have different viewpoints and probably a little scale variation.

Because of their superb invariance to viewpoint and scale changes, Hessian-Affine, Harris-Affine, and MSER detectors are introduced as the most appropriate ones for extracting

Fig. 15. A sample stereo subset from ALOI database, reproduced from Geusebroek et al. (2005).

Fig. 16. Sample training images of 2 objects from the ETHZ Toys database.

Fig. 17. 15 sample test images from the ETHZ Toys database.

interest regions from the training set. SIFT and shape context are selected as two promising descriptors for representing the extracted interest regions. Methods that combine the aforementioned affine detectors and descriptors for 3D object recognition are yet to develop, but the view-clustering in Lowe (2001) and the modeling with geometric consistency in Rothganger et al. ((2006) serve as good references for integrating information from multiple views. A sample performance evaluation study is introduced along with several benchmark databases that offer stereo or multiple views for training. This chapter is expected to offer some perspectives toward potential research directions in the stereo correspondence with local descriptors for 3D object recognition.

7. Acknowledgement

This research is supported by Taiwan National Science Council (NSC) under grant 99-2221-E-011-098.

8. References

Belongie, S., Malik, J. & Puzicha, J. (2002). Shape matching and object recognition using shape contexts, 24(4): 509–522.

Ferrari, V., Tuytelaars, T. & Gool, L. J. V. (2004). Simultaneous object recognition and segmentation by image exploration, *ECCV (1)*, pp. 40–54.

Fischler, M. A. & Bolles, R. C. (1981). Random sample consensus: A paradigm for model fitting with applications to image analysis and automated cartography, *Commun. ACM* 24(6): 381–395.

Forssén, P.-E. & Lowe, D. G. (2007). Shape descriptors for maximally stable extremal regions, *ICCV*, pp. 1–8.

Freeman, W. T. & Adelson, E. H. (1991). The design and use of steerable filters, *IEEE Trans. Pattern Anal. Mach. Intell.* 13(9): 891–906.

Geusebroek, J.-M., Burghouts, G. J. & Smeulders, A. W. M. (2005). The amsterdam library of object images, *International Journal of Computer Vision* 61(1): 103–112.

Gool, L. J. V., Moons, T. & Ungureanu, D. (1996). Affine/ photometric invariants for planar intensity patterns, *ECCV (1)*, pp. 642–651.

Ke, Y. & Sukthankar, R. (2004). Pca-sift: a more distinctive representation for local image descriptors, *CVPR*, pp. 506–513.

Koenderink, J. J. & van Doom, A. J. (1987). Representation of local geometry in the visual system, *Biol. Cybern.* 55(6): 367–375.

Lazebnik, S., Schmid, C. & Ponce, J. (2003). A sparse texture representation using affine-invariant regions, *CVPR (2)*, pp. 319–326.

Lindeberg, T. (1998). Feature detection with automatic scale selection, *International Journal of Computer Vision* 30(2): 79–116.

Lindeberg, T. & Gårding, J. (1997). Shape-adapted smoothing in estimation of 3-d shape cues from affine deformations of local 2-d brightness structure, *Image Vision Comput.* 15(6): 415–434.

Lowe, D. G. (1999). Object recognition from local scale-invariant features, *ICCV*, pp. 1150–1157.

Lowe, D. G. (2001). Local feature view clustering for 3d object recognition, *CVPR (1)*, pp. 682–688.

Lowe, D. G. (2004). Distinctive image features from scale-invariant keypoints, *International Journal of Computer Vision* 60(2): 91–110.

Mahamud, S. & Hebert, M. (2003). The optimal distance measure for object detection, *CVPR (1)*, pp. 248–258.

Matas, J., Chum, O., Urban, M. & Pajdla, T. (2002). Robust wide baseline stereo from maximally stable extremal, *In British Machine Vision Conference*, pp. 384–393.

Mikolajczyk, K. & Schmid, C. (2001). Indexing based on scale invariant interest points, *ICCV*, pp. 525–531.

Mikolajczyk, K. & Schmid, C. (2002). An affine invariant interest point detector, *ECCV (1)*, pp. 128–142.

Mikolajczyk, K. & Schmid, C. (2004). Scale & affine invariant interest point detectors,

International Journal of Computer Vision 60(1): 63–86.

Mikolajczyk, K. & Schmid, C. (2005). A performance evaluation of local descriptors, *IEEE Trans. Pattern Anal. Mach. Intell.* 27(10): 1615–1630.

Mikolajczyk, K., Tuytelaars, T., Schmid, C., Zisserman, A., Matas, J., Schaffalitzky, F., Kadir, T. & Gool, L. J. V. (2005). A comparison of affine region detectors, *International Journal of Computer Vision* 65(1-2): 43–72.

Moreels, P., Maire, M. & Perona, P. (2004). Recognition by probabilistic hypothesis construction, *ECCV (1)*, pp. 55–68.

Nistér, D. & Stewénius, H. (2008). Linear time maximally stable extremal regions, *ECCV (2)*, pp. 183–196.

Rothganger, F., Lazebnik, S., Schmid, C. & Ponce, J. ((2006)). 3d object modeling and recognition using local affine-invariant image descriptors and multi-view spatial constraints, *International Journal of Computer Vision* 66(3): 231–259.

Schaffalitzky, F. & Zisserman, A. (2002). Multi-view matching for unordered image sets, or "how do i organize my holiday snaps?", *ECCV (1)*, pp. 414–431.

8

Three Dimensional Measurement Using Fisheye Stereo Vision

Jun'ichi Yamaguchi
Kagawa University
Japan

1. Introduction

Studies on omni-directional vision sensor with a large field of view have shown a superiority in sensing of surrounding and scene analysis. For omni-directional view, mainly a hyperboloid mirror or a conic mirror is installed in front of the camera lens, and application equipments are used in robot, car, etc. (Yamazawa et al., 1997; Torii & Imiya, 2004; Kawanishi et al., 2008; Kawanishi et al., 2009). Recently, in accordance with an experience in such applications, the study on omni-directional three dimensional (3D) recognition is increasing (Kubo & Yamaguchi, 2007; Nishimoto & Yamaguchi, 2008). This chapter describes 3D measurement using fish-eye lens as omni-directional optical device.

Fish-eye lens provides a remarkable large field of view compared with a standard lens. Field of view (FOV) is nearly 180°. Concerning FOV, there are some FOVs (170°, 180°, 185°, etc.) by lens. Fish-eye camera is simple and compact compared with mirror mounting camera above. Difference from mirror mounting camera is as follows: no optical device in front of camera, and no blind spot in center of the image (mirror system captures the camera). 3D measurement by fish-eye stereo vision is one of evolution for wide range measuring. Fish-eye image has a peculiar distortion. But, handling of it is not hard, by using an established process to the distortion.

Methods of 3D measurement using fish-eye camera have been proposed until now (Shah & Aggarwal, 1997; Oizumi et al., 2003; Hrabar et al., 2004; Gehrig et al., 2008). Necessary images for making a range data are acquired by binocular stereo or motion stereo. Range data is obtained by 3D equation which is decided by optical system, using a parallax quantity which is given by detection of a correspondence between two image pixels. Therefore, correctness of the correspondence is important. In correspondence process, an undistorted image, which is obtained by correcting an inherent distortion of the fish-eye image, is generally used. Correction of the distortion is performed by calibration methods as follows: method using the radial and tangential offset components by Nth-order polynomial, method of non-linear least mean squares fit, Bundle adjustment method, method by inverse model of fish-eye projection, etc. Using the undistorted image, the correspondence between two image pixels is decided by image matching (for example template matching). As such, the corrected image has an important role and is generally used for obtaining the range data. On the other hand, the method without the corrected image has been proposed. In such method, corresponding pixel is searched following an epipolar line at every coordinate. The epipolar line draws a complicated locus and the shape of the locus is different every coordinate due to inherent distortion of fish-eye image. Therefore, it is generally hard to apply the epipolar geometry to fish-eye image. But, that method shows the applicability of the epipolar geometry using an invariance feature on translation, rotation and scale change in the image. Consequently, such method has the advantage that correspondence can be decided directly from the fish-eye image, though the measuring object is restricted because of a fixed shooting condition.

For defining the region which is composed of homogeneous pixels, segmentation is performed using the result of the correspondence process. Namely, segmentation process is needed for region classification and region extraction. For example, it can be used for recognizing the objects individually in moving objects measurement. Thus, this process has important role for scene analysis. In case of using corrected image, the conventional segmentation method which is used to the image from normal lens camera can be applied. Segmentation based on feature extraction is one of well known methods. If a specified shape (for example, pillar, door, ...) is stably shot, scene can be analyzed by depth information of vertical lines and/or horizontal lines. But, in case of a general scene and overlapping objects, it is considered that the method based on feature extraction is not enough accuracy. In such case, clustering based on 3D position data is useful. Namely, the pixels which close each other within a threshold of 3D distance are clustered. According to it, the region can be decided regardless shape and feature of the object. On the other hand, a direct segmentation to fish-eye image is proposed. Such method is based on homogeneity of pixels on concentric circumference. It has the advantage that the pixels are classified directly in the fish-eye image. However, application of the method is restricted because objects must be always shot from a particular angle. In 3D measurement using fish-eye images, correspondence process and 3D segmentation process have important role. Therefore, the process should be designed appropriately to a purpose of application.

In this chapter, section 2 describes fish-eye lens and construction of fish-eye vision, section 3 describes correspondence process and section 4 describes 3D segmentation. Section 5 explains an example of the experimental result in study of 3D measurement using fish-eye stereo vision. Result shows the measurement accuracy on 3D structure of scene and moving objects. Finally, section 6 concludes the chapter.

2. Fish-eye stereo vision

2.1 Fish-eye camera

Fish-eye lens provides a remarkable large FOV (nearly 180°) compared with a standard lens. Lineup of FOV which depends upon lens are 170°, 180°, 185°, etc. Using the fish-eye lens mounting camera (fish-eye camera), all-direction space in front of the lens is projected onto an image plane. Namely, by the projection image (fish-eye image), it is possible to handle a semispherical space in front of the fish-eye camera. As such, an extreme wide measurable space is an advantage of the fish-eye camera. So it is expected that the fish-eye camera produces a novel and creative possibilities of image application. As fish-eye transform, some methods (logarithmic mapping, log-polar mapping, polynomial transform, etc.) had been proposed. Recently, the equidistance projection model, the orthogonal projection model, etc. are used well. It is considered that these models are easily accepted because of popular first-order approximation and enough accuracy. Fig.1 shows the projection model of fish-eye lens. Fish-eye mapping is expressed by some of following (1)-(4):

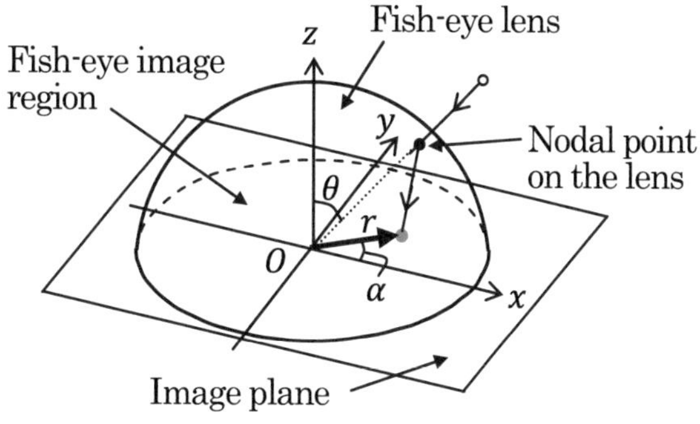

Fig. 1. Fish-eye mapping model

$$r = f\theta \quad \text{(equidistance projection)}, \tag{1}$$

$$r = f\sin\theta \quad \text{(orthogonal projection)}, \tag{2}$$

$$r = 2f\tan(\theta/2) \quad \text{(stereographic projection)}, \tag{3}$$

$$r = 2f\sin(\theta/2) \quad \text{(equisolid angle projection)}. \tag{4}$$

Where, r is the distance of the point from the fish-eye image center, f is the focal length of the fish-eye lens and θ is the zenith angle. Mechanism of the mapping is that a 3D ray from the nodal point on the lens is projected onto an image position which is specified by r using θ and α. According to the mapping, as θ is larger, the extension rate of r is reduced. Namely, space resolution towards periphery of image is decreased. Fig.2 shows sample of fish-eye images. Caption of each figure mean as follows: Object, Direction of camera, Height above the ground. Inside of circle area is the fish-eye image region. According to it, decrease of space resolution towards periphery and large observable area can be confirmed. Decrease of resolution causes an image distortion. As seen in the sample, object bends in an arc by coordinate. That is there are different degrees of the distortion on different coordinates. Therefore, it is generally hard to apply the epipolar analysis to fish-eye image because of complicated epipolar lines. The sample also expresses a possibility of various shooting and measurement. For example, as seen in fig.2(c) and (d), omni-directional 3D recognition by looking up and overall observation of a passing object are interesting subjects. As such, though we need to note fish-eye image in handling, it is considered that the fish-eye camera has the potential on novel and creative image application.

2.2 Stereo vision

As a fish-eye vision system for 3D measurement, a binocular stereo or a motion stereo is generally used. In case of binocular stereo, matters to be attended to construct a stereo vision system are as follows: (1)Simultaneous capturing of two images, (2)Parallel two camera axes, (3)Center of each fish-eye image region, (4)Space resolution, etc. (1) is especially important in case of capturing moving object. Capturing equipments of two channels are used in many case. In case of using 1-ch capturing equipment, two images mixing device is useful. The device can be easily made by low cost relatively. It has an advantage that simultaneous capturing of two images and stereo image transmission by

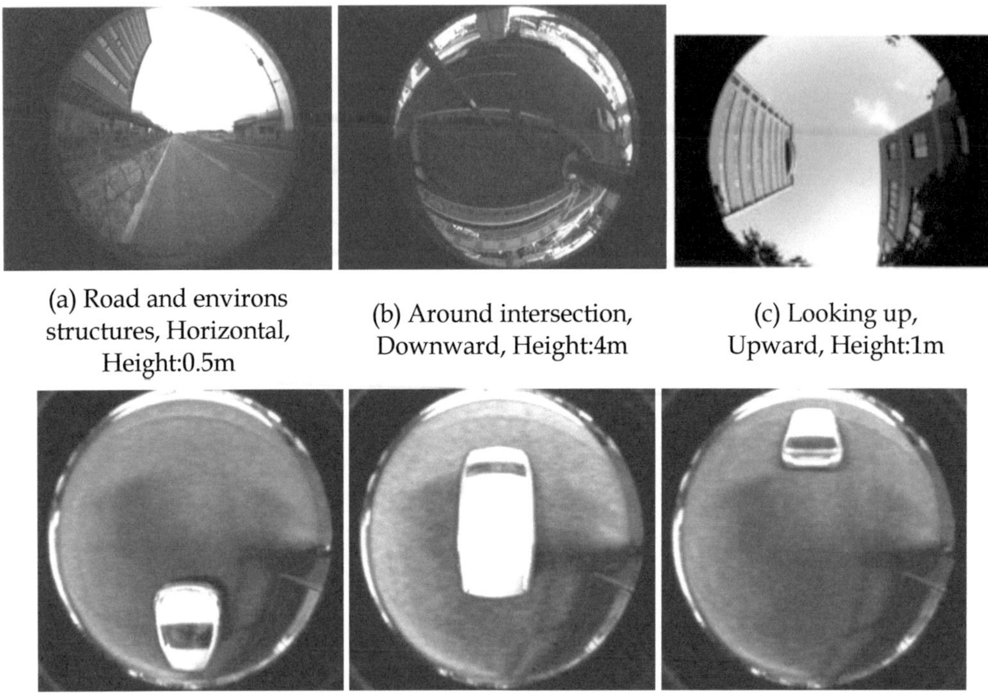

(a) Road and environs structures, Horizontal, Height:0.5m

(b) Around intersection, Downward, Height:4m

(c) Looking up, Upward, Height:1m

(d) Passing vehicle, Downward, Height:3.5m

Fig. 2. Samples of fish-eye image

1-ch are compensated. Fig.3 shows a sample of a mixed fish-eye image. It is a frame image composed of even field image of a picture from left camera and odd field image of a picture from right camera. Also, in the sample image, an image shift is seen. The shift quantity means parallax. It is different from the parallax of standard lens camera image. In fish-eye image, the quantity and the direction of shift are changed by coordinate. Then, it is hard to apply epipola geometry to fish-eye image directly, because epipola line is very complicated. Epipola geometry is important approach to 3D measurement and is described in section 3. (2) affects 3D measurement accuracy directly. Therefore, both of camera axes must be adjusted precisely on parallel. (3) means that fish-eye image is not always projected at same coordinate of different image plane. Projection shift is caused by lens attachment structure and is a few pixels in general. Therefore, for appropriate image processing, the coordinate of center of fish-eye image region must be reflected. Concerning (4), the number of pixel (m×n) of image plane should be decided with a mind to object image size. On the other hand, in case of motion stereo, matters to be attended to construction are as follows: (5)Correctability of camera moving, (6)Non-simultaneous of two images capturing. In motion stereo, two images are captured by position change of one camera. Therefore, (1) in binocular stereo is not probable. Concerning (2) and (3), problem for binocular stereo is not connected with motion stereo. Concerning (4), motion stereo and binocular stereo are the same. (5) means a high accurate moving system which is equivalent to a base-line in binocular stereo. Namely, correctness on a position and a direction in camera movement is required. (6) means second image is captured late because it takes time for position change of camera. Therefore, basically, moving object is not measurable in motion stereo.

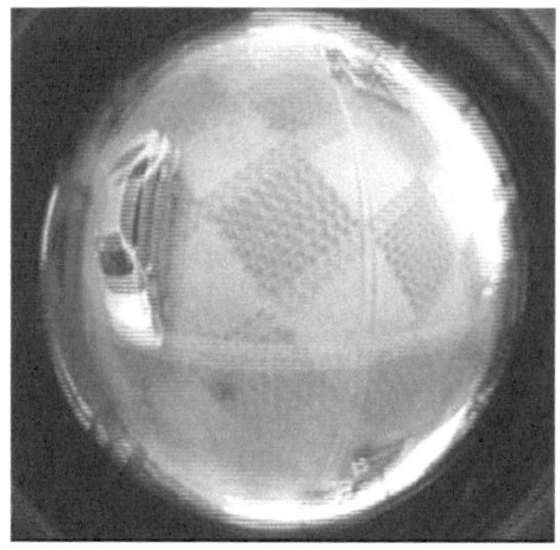

Fig. 3. Sample of a mixed image

3. Correspondence process

3.1 Correction of image

In case of normal camera, correspondence pixel is easily detected by template matching method because epipolar line is simple. But, in case of fish-eye stereo, the shape and the direction of the epipolar line are different at different coordinate, due to an inherent distortion of the image. Then, it is generally impossible to apply the simple method to detection of correspondence pixel. So, an undistorted image is usually made by correction of the fish-eye image. For image correction, some calibration methods have been proposed. A method using fifth-order polynomial is described in (Shah & Aggarwal, 1996). According to it, the correction of the radial and tangential offset components is performed. Also there is the method of non-linear least mean squares fit (Madsen et al., 1999). It is based on a physically motivated corner model with better sub-pixel accuracy and performs non-linear minimization of least mean squares error. For estimation of better extrinsic parameter accuracy, Bundle adjustment method is described in (Triggs et al., 2000; Mitsumoto et al., 2008). It performs the minimization of inverse projection error. In addition, the method using an inverse model of fish-eye projection, the method using an panoramic image, etc. are mentioned. As such, some calibration is performed in general for better image correction accuracy. Using the undistorted image, it is easy to search correspondence pixel and then the parallax can be detected. In figure 4, an example of the correction image is shown.

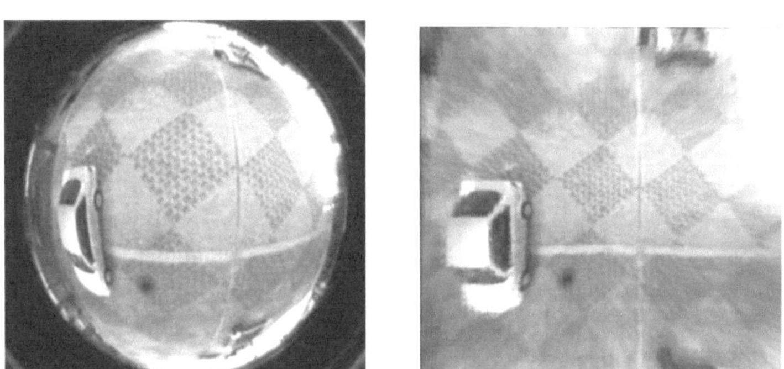

Fish-eye image Correction image

Fig. 4. Example of the correction image

On the other hand, there is the case that correspondence can be decided directly from the fish-eye image. Such correspondence is possible in case of a scene which is composed of an invariance feature on translation, rotation and scale change. For example, as seen in (Herrera et al., 2009), objects which grow straightly toward zenith is mentioned. In the case, correspondent point is searched in limited region in fish-eye image. As such, there is an advantage that correspondent point can be decided directly without image correction, though application is restricted because of a fixed shooting condition.

In order to apply fish-eye stereo to 3D measurement of various scene, correction of image is useful and then calibration has an important role for better correction accuracy. Using the correction image, it is easy to detect the parallax in various applications.

3.2 Stereo matching

The analysis of stereo images is a well-established method for 3D structure extracting from 2D projection images. For 3D structure expression, 3D position data is needed. And parallax data obtained by image matching is needed for 3D position detection. In case of using the undistorted image obtained by correction, template matching which is well known in pattern matching can be applied to parallax detection. Actually template matching is well used in normal FOV stereo. But it is needed to notice to uniform region and only horizontal line region, because right correlation result is not obtained in such region. When characteristic texture is detected stably in the images, a feature-based method can be applied. For example, parallax detection on vertical line is well known as described in (Shah & Aggarwal, 1997). If object is rigid body and its shape is unique, image matching is easier.

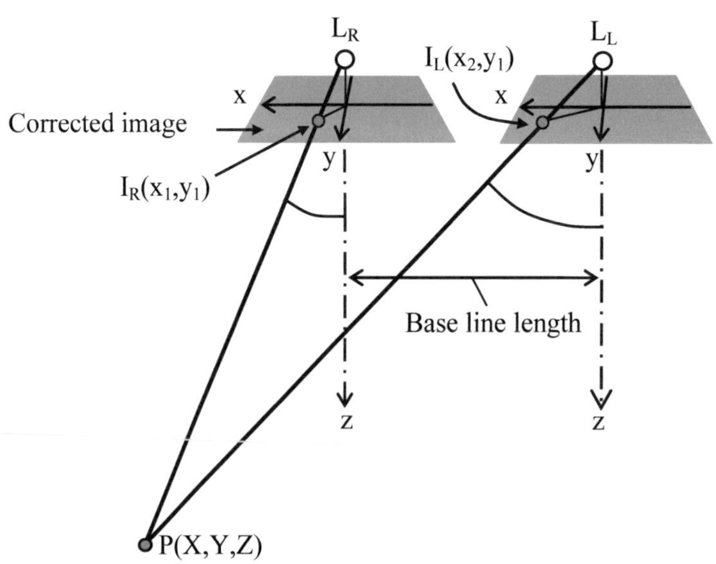

Fig. 5. Stereo system

3D position of a point on the corrected image is calculated by the geometry as shown in figure 5, using the parallax as a shift quantity between left and right images (Schwalbe, 2005). In figure 5, P(X,Y,Z) is 3D position, and parallax is the difference between (x_2,y_1) and (x_1,y_1). L_R and L_L are imaginary lenses and are origins of camera system respectively. Applying 3D calculation to all points in image, it is possible to recognize 3D structure of scene.

4. Segmentation process

4.1 Clustering

In image recognition and image analysis, detection and distinction of region are important. Then, clustering which connects neighboring homogeneous pixels has an important role. Concerning such pixels, there is the case that homogeneity accuracy is lowered by brightness change, low contrast or 3D objects overlapping. Especially, such lowering occurs frequently in outdoor scene. So, in general, clustering is performed using 3D position data obtained by correspondence process. 3D distance between two points in space is used for judgment whether points are homogeneous or not. In clustering, two points in fish-eye image are combined if 3D distance is smaller than a threshold value. In case that 3D distance is larger than the threshold, two points in fish-eye image are separated. This operation is applied to all points in fish-eye image and labeling (for example numbering) is performed to neighboring points as homogeneous pixels. Then, combining points with same label, a cluster is expressed by a label and shows the region. According to this method, it is possible to analysis scene. On the other hand, clustering method without 3D position data is proposed as described in (Herrera et al., 2009). In that method, clustering is performed using the position of points on concentric circumferences in fish-eye image. Purpose is to analyze trunks grow toward zenith, and shooting condition is that trunks are not cross each other in the image. In case of using such uncrossed objects image, there is an advantage that clustering is performed directly in fish-eye image. But, handleable scene is restricted because of a fixed shooting condition and an assumption of uncrossed objects. In addition to this, as data for clustering, flow data from moving object, color information, etc. are mentioned. By using these data with 3D position above, it is expected to obtain better clustering accuracy.

4.2 Extraction

Correctness of 3D object extraction is important. When an appearance of the object is invariant, the extraction method based on shape feature verification can be applied. Then, using the extraction result, the object is analyzed on pose, situation, etc. If invariance of the object is not compensated, it is hard to apply such extraction method. Also, if background change is not dealt with, extraction error occurs frequently. For example, in case of response to a shadow above the ground, a false object is extracted in error. On the basis of such circumstance, it is needed to estimate the difference obtained by comparing background structure data with acquired 3D data. Figure 6 shows an example of car extraction. Shadow of the car is not extracted. After extraction process, in many cases, extraction data is translated to a geometry model, an approximation value, and so on. Figure 7 shows an example of translation. Figure 7(a) shows a cylindroid which is expressed by an ellipse (center of gravity, inclination of a principal axis, length of principal axis and length of minor axis) and a height (maximum value above ground). Figure 7(b) shows an ellipse which height is expressed by gray level of inner part. Both models are expressed by five parameters above and are easy understandable and handleable.

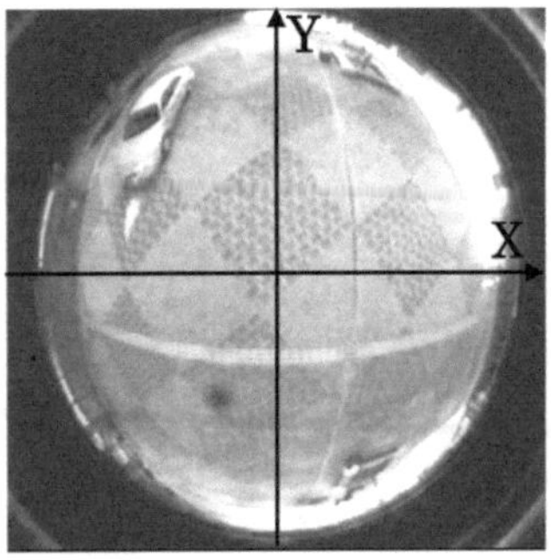

(a) fish-eye image

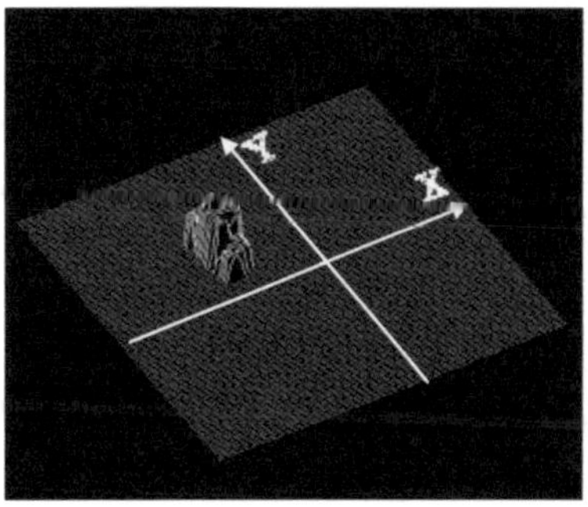

(b) 3D data

Fig. 6. Example of image extraction

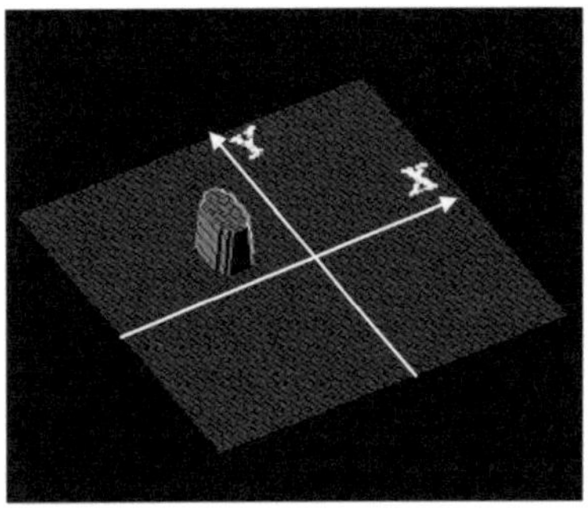

(a) Cylindroid. By ellipse and maximum Z value as height.

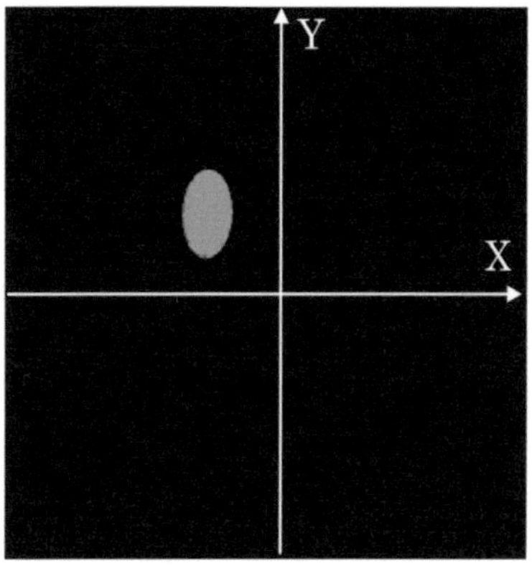

(b) Ellipse. Gray level in ellipse corresponds to height.

Fig. 7. Example of translation result.

5. Experiment of 3D measurement

5.1 Experimental system

Figure 8 shows an exterior of our experimental binocular stereo equipment (that is detached from a tripod in experiment) (Nishimoto & Yamaguchi, 2007). The binocular stereo is composed of two CCD cameras which mount fish-eye lens of 170° FOV. Fish-eye transform is the equidistance projection model ($r = f\theta$). Length of base line is 50cm. In the experiment, this equipment was installed at 4m above the ground and was downward look. When a person was standing at about 30m distance from center of observation area, his image was very small at near edge of fish-eye image and was visible limit. Background structure data (that is 3D shape data of road surface) was measured beforehand. Deducting it from measured 3D structure data, object data was extracted. In correspondence process, correction image as seen in figure 4 was made using inverse model of fish-eye projection and correction of lens aberration. For parallax detection, template matching was applied using left and right correction images. In segmentation process, clustering was performed using 3D position data and object region was extracted as seen in figure 6. In clustering process, an isolated point and a minute particle lump were excluded. Geometry models as seen in figure 7 were shown as object measurement result.

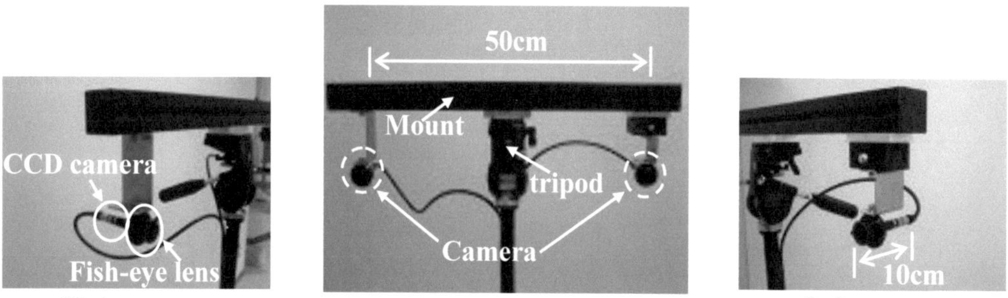

Right camera | Front view | Left camera

Fig. 8. Experimental binocular stereo equipment

5.2 Result

Figure 9 shows an example of 3D measurement in case of car and motorcycle. Also the result in case of pedestrians and bicycle is shown in figure 10. Car and motorcycle ran abreast by keeping about 1m distance. Pedestrians walked keeping rough distance and bicycle wove through them. According to these results, it seems that 2D region, volume and position of each object are detected in good accuracy. This means that correspondence process and segmentation process functioned appropriately. But it seems that the inclination of ellipse lacks stability a bit. It is considered that lack of object extraction accuracy affected the inclination of ellipse sensitively.

Measurement results of the object height above the road are shown in table 1 and table 2. These show the measurement accuracy on Z value. Measured height data of car (correct height: 120cm) changed within ±10cm and measured height data of motorcycle driver with helmet (correct height: 140cm) changed within ±15 cm. Concerning pedestrians and bicycle driver, measured height data changed within ±20cm and within ±15cm respectively. In case of human, there had been shown to be a tendency to be smaller value. Concerning measurement accuracy and object position, the further from center, the larger error caused. Namely, by one pixel error on parallax, larger 3D position error was caused. In case of condition that measurement error is within table 1 and table 2, the measurable observation area was the radius of about 15m on the road. In order to improve 3D measurement accuracy, a high resolution image device should be used. Equipment install accuracy is also important. That is parallel precision of two camera axes and perpendicular precision of camera axis to the ground. Reexamination of base line length is also necessary. Improvement of background structure accuracy is important, too. The improvement above is needed for better measurement accuracy and extension of measurable area.

This experiment was performed to study one application of 3D measurement using fish-eye stereo vision. The results showed a possibility of application, though improvement on measurement accuracy is needed.

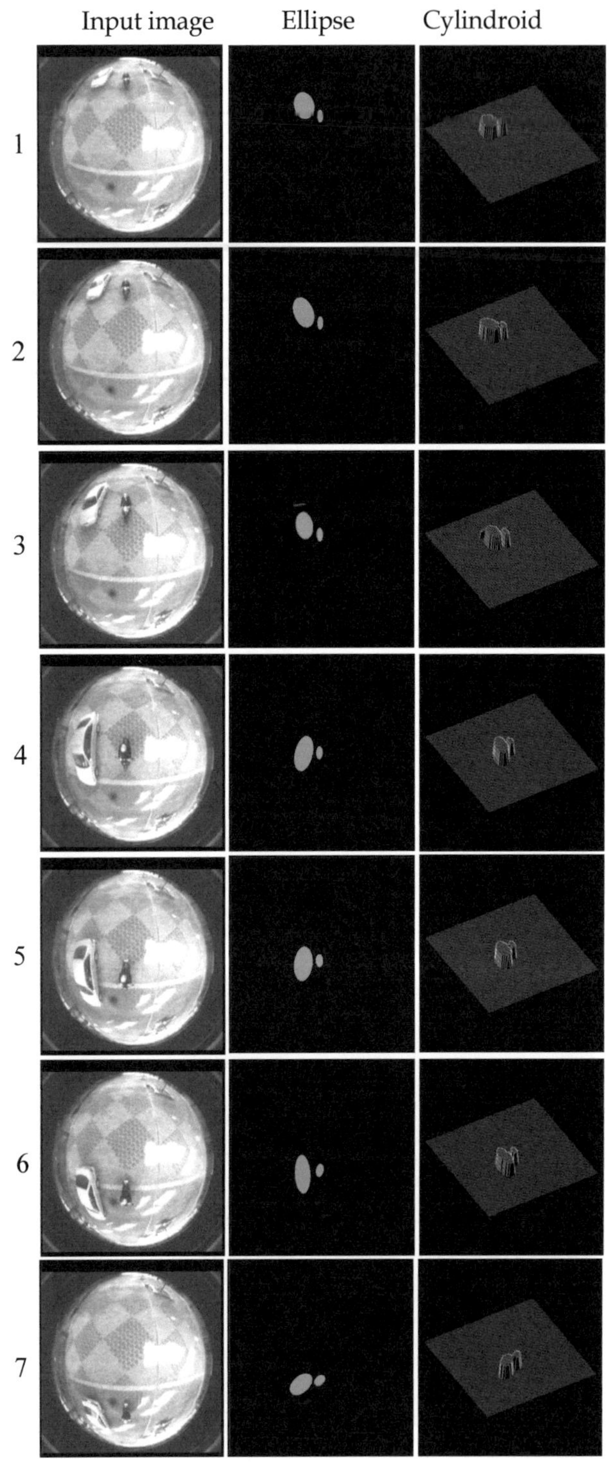

Fig. 9. Experimental result 1 (car and motorcycle)

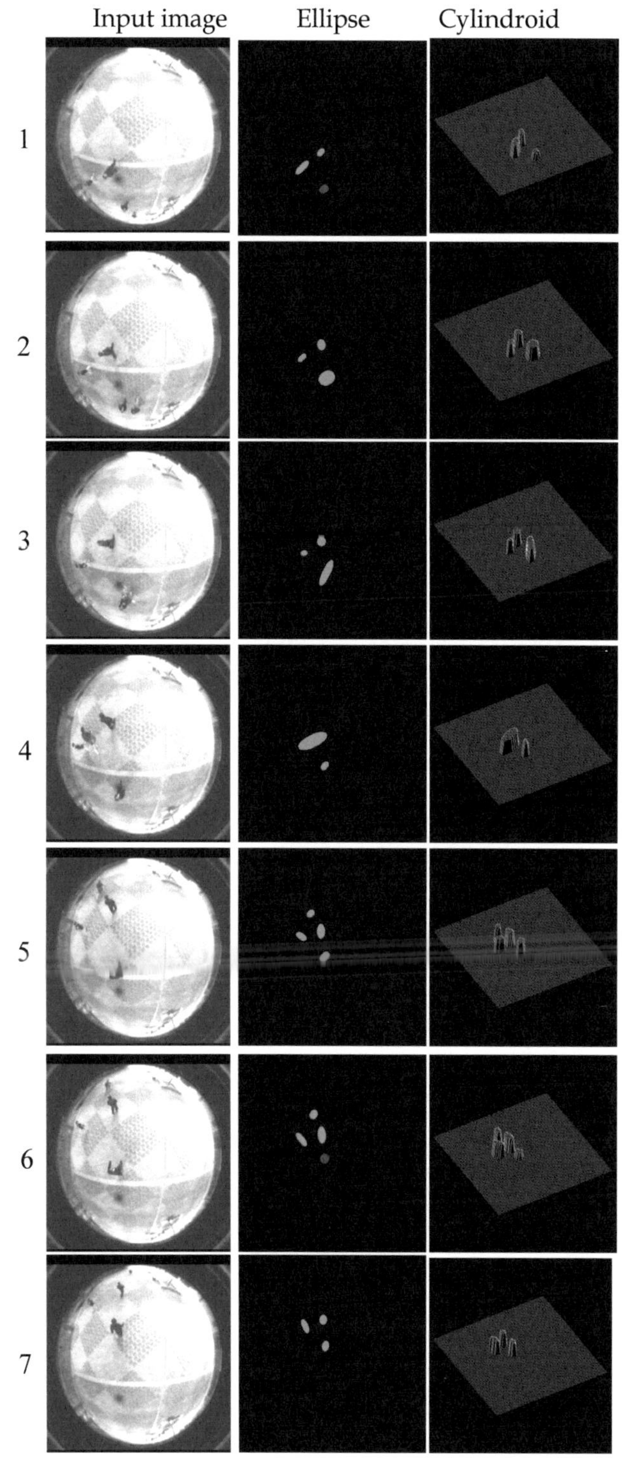

Fig. 10. Experimental result 2 (pedestrians and bicycle)

	Measurement	Correct
Car	110 ~ 130	120
Motorcycle	120 ~ 150	140

(cm)

Table 1. Measurement accuracy on height in figure 9

	Measurement	Correct
Pedestrian	130 ~ 170	170, 167, 161
Bicycle	140 ~ 170	170

(cm)

Table 2. Measurement accuracy on height in figure 10

6. Conclusion

This chapter described on 3D measurement using fish-eye stereo vision. Section 2 explained a feature of fish-eye lens and construction of fish-eye vision. Section 3 described correspondence process which is needed for image matching. For better stereo matching accuracy and application to various scene, correction of the fish-eye image is important. In section 3, some calibration methods for image correction were explained. Section 4 described segmentation process which is needed for region detection and object extraction. Combining the neighboring homogeneous points by clustering and labeling, the region is decided. 3D structure of the scene is recognized using 3D information of the regions. In 3D measurement using fish-eye stereo vision, the processes in section 3 and 4 should be designed appropriately to scene and object. Section 5 explained our experimental system. It is binocular stereo which is composed of two CCD cameras with fish-eye lens. The experiment was performed to study one application of fish-eye stereo vision and the measurement accuracy on moving objects was confirmed. The results showed a possibility of application, though improvement on measurement accuracy is needed.

Fish-eye stereo vision can measure 3D objects in relatively large space, using only a pair of images (left image and right image). Recently, fish-eye stereo is studied as a vision sensor mounted on a car, a robot vision system, etc. It is considered that the studies of application which make the most of the advantage of the fish-eye vision will increase.

7. References

Kazumasa Yamazawa, Yasushi Yagi, and Masahiko Yachida (1997). HyperOmni Vision: Visual Navigation with an Omnidirectional Image Sensor, Systems and Computers in Japan, Vol.28, No.4, pp.36-46.

Akihiko Torii, Atsushi Imiya (2004). Panoramic Image Transform of Omnidirectional Images Using Discrete Geometry Techniques, Proceedings of the 2nd International Symposium on 3D Data Processing, Visualization, and Transmission (3DPVT'04), pp.608-615.

Ryosuke Kawanishi, Atsushi Yamashita and Toru Kaneko (2008). Construction of 3D Environment Model from an Omni-Directional Image Sequence, Asia International Symposium on Mechatronics, pp.1-6.

Ryosuke Kawanishi, Atsushi Yamashita, and Toru Kaneko (2009). Three-Dimensional Environment Model Construction from an Omnidirectional Image Sequence, Journal of Robotics and Mechatronics, Vol.21, No.5, pp.574-579,

Yohei Kubo and Jun'ichi Yamaguchi (2007). Human Tracking Using Fisheye Images, Proceedings of SICE Annual Conference 2007, pp.2013-2017.

Takeshi Nishimoto and Jun'ichi Yamaguchi (2008). A Vehicle Identification Using Fisheye Camera, Proceedings of Asia International Symposium on Mechatronics (AISM2008), TA1-1(1), pp.5-8.

Shishir Shah, J. K. Aggarwal (1997). Mobile robot navigation and scene modeling using stereo fish-eye lens system, Machine Vision and Applications (ISSN:0932-8092), Vol.10, No.4, pp.159-173.

Oizumi Ken, Yamamoto Yasuhide, Sakata Masao, Inoue Masato (2003). Development of "All-Around View" system, Nissan Technical Review, Vol.53, pp.52-56.

Stefan Hrabar, Gaurav S. Sukhatme, Peter Corke, Kane Usher and Jonathan Roberts (2004). Combined Optic-Flow and Stereo-Based Navigation of Urban Canyons for a UAV, proceedings of IEEE International Conference on Intelligent Robots and Systems, pp.3609-3615.

Stefan Gehrig, Clemens Rabe, Lars Krüger (2008). 6D Vision Goes Fisheye for Intersection Assistance, Proceeding of Canadian Conference on Computer and Robot Vision, pp.34-41.

Shah S, Aggarwal J. K. (1996). Intrinsic parameter calibration procedure for (high-distortion) fish-eye lens Camera with distortion model and accuracy estimation, Pattern Recognition, 29(11), pp.1775-1788.

K. Madsen, H. B. Nielsen, and O. Tingleff (1999). Methods for non-linear least squares problems, IMM, pp.1-29.

Bill Triggs, Philip F. McLauchlan, Richard I. Hartley, and Andrew W. Fitzgibbon (2000). Bundle Adjustment – A Modern Synthesis, Vision Algorithms'99, LNCS 1883, pp. 298-372.

Hisanori Mitsumoto, Yohei Aragaki, Noriko Shimomura, Kenji Terabayashi and Kazunori Umeda (2008). Basic Examination on Motion Stereo Vision Using a Fish Eye Camera, Proceeding of the 26th Annual Conference of the Robotics Society of Japan, Vol.26, pp.1L1-07.

P. Javier Herrera, Gonzalo Pajares, Maria Guijarro, Jose J. Ruz, and Jesus M. Cruz (2009). Choquet Fuzzy Integral Applied to Stereovision Matching for Fish-Eye Lenses in Forest Analysis, Advances in Soft Computing (ISSN:1615-3871), Vol.116, pp.179-187.

Pedro Javier Herrera, Gonzalo Pajares, Maria Guijarro, Jose J. Ruz, Jesus M. Cruz and Fernando Montes (2009). A Featured-Based Strategy for Stereovision Matching in Sensors with Fish-Eye Lenses for Forest Environments, Sensors (ISSN 1424-8220), 9, pp.9468-9492.

Schwalbe (2005). Geometric modeling and calibration of fisheye lens camera systems, Proceedings of the 2nd

Panoramic Photogrammetry Workshop, International Archives of Photogrammetry and Remote Sensing, Vol.36, Part5/W8.

Pedro Javier Herrera, Gonzalo Pajares, Maria Guijarro, Jose J. Ruz, and Jesus M. Cruz (2009). Combination of attributes in stereovision matching for fish-eye lenses in forest analysis, In ACIVS 2009, Springer-Verlag, LNCS 5807, pp.277-287.

Takeshi Nishimoto and Jun'ichi Yamaguchi (2007). Three-dimensional measurement using fisheye stereo vision, Proceedings of SICE Annual Conference 2007, pp.2008-2012.

9

Address-Event based Stereo Vision with Bio-inspired Silicon Retina Imagers

Jürgen Kogler[1], Christoph Sulzbachner[1], Martin Humenberger[1] and Florian Eibensteiner[2]
[1]*AIT Austrian Institute of Technology*
[2]*Upper Austria University of Applied Sciences*
Austria

1. Introduction

Several industry, home, or automotive applications need 3D or at least range data of the observed environment to operate. Such applications are, e.g., driver assistance systems, home care systems, or 3D sensing and measurement for industrial production. State-of-the-art range sensors are laser range finders or laser scanners (LIDAR, light detection and ranging), time-of-flight (TOF) cameras, and ultrasonic sound sensors. All of them are embedded, which means that the sensors operate independently and have an integrated processing unit. This is advantageous because the processing power in the mentioned applications is limited and they are computationally intensive anyway. Another benefits of embedded systems are a low power consumption and a small form factor. Furthermore, embedded systems are full customizable by the developer and can be adapted to the specific application in an optimal way.

A promising alternative to the mentioned sensors is stereo vision. Classic stereo vision uses a stereo camera setup, which is built up of two cameras (stereo camera head), mounted in parallel and separated by the baseline. It captures a synchronized stereo pair consisting of the left camera's image and the right camera's image. The main challenge of stereo vision is the reconstruction of 3D information of a scene captured from two different points of view. Each visible scene point is projected on the image planes of the cameras. Pixels which represent the same scene points on different image planes correspond to each other. These correspondences can then be used to determine the three dimensional position of the projected scene point in a defined coordinate system. In more detail, the horizontal displacement, called the disparity, is inverse proportional to the scene point's depth. With this information and the camera's intrinsic parameters (principal point and focal length), the 3D position can be reconstructed. Fig. 1 shows a typical stereo camera setup. The projections of scene point P are p_l and p_r. Once the correspondences are found, the disparity is calculated with

$$d = u_2 - u_1. \tag{1}$$

Furthermore, the depth of P is determined with

$$z = \frac{b \cdot f}{d}, \tag{2}$$

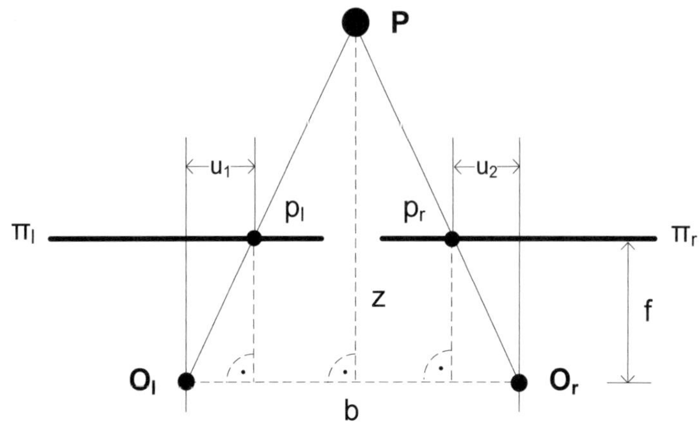

Fig. 1. Stereo vision setup; two cameras capture a scene point

where z is the distance between the camera's optical centers and the projected scene point P, b is the length of the baseline, d the disparity, and f is the focal length of the camera.
All stereo matching algorithms available for the mentioned 3D reconstruction are expecting images as captured from conventional camera sensors (Belbachir, 2010). The output of conventional cameras is organized as a matrix and copies slightly the function of the human eye. Thus, all pixels are addressed by coordinates, and the images are sent to an interface as a whole, e.g., over Cameralink. Monochrome cameras deliver grayscale images where each pixel value represents the intensity within a defined range. Color sensors additionally deliver the information of the red, green, and blue spectral range for each pixel of a camera sensor matrix.
A different approach to conventional digital cameras and stereo vision is to use bio-inspired transient senors. These sensors, called *Silicon Retina*, are developed to benefit from certain characteristics of the human eye such as reaction on movement and high dynamic range. Instead of digital images, these sensors deliver on and off events which represent the brightness changes of the captured scene. Due to that, new approaches of stereo matching are needed to exploit these sensor data because no conventional images can be used.

2. Silicon retina sensor

The silicon retina sensor differs from monochrome/color sensors in the case of chip construction and functionality. These differences of the retina imager can be compared with the principle operation of the human eye.

2.1 Sensor design

In contrast to conventional *Charge-coupled-Device* (CCD) or *Complementary Metal Oxide Semiconductor* (CMOS) imagers, which that encode irradiance of the image and produce constant amount of data at a fixed frame rate, irrespective of scene activity, the silicon retina sensor contains a pixel array of autonomous, self-signaling pixels which individually respond in real-time to relative changes in light intensity (temporal contrast) by placing their address on an asynchronously arbitrated bus. Pixels which are not stimulated by a change in illumination are not triggered; hence static scenes produce no output. In Fig. 2 an enhanced detail of the silicon retina chip is shown. The chip is equipped with the photo cells and the analogue circuits which emulate the function of the human eye.

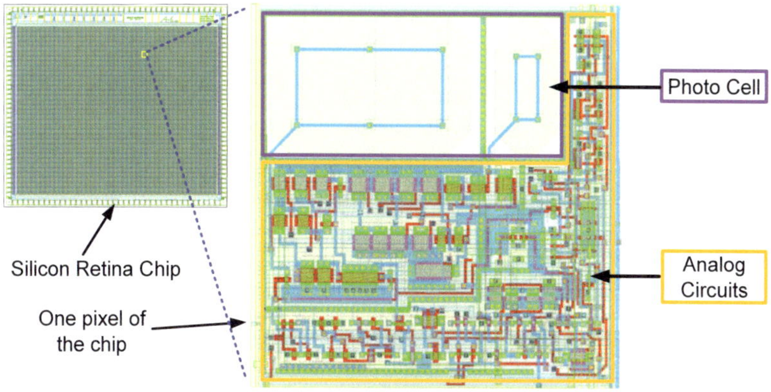

Fig. 2. Enhanced photo cell with analogue circuits of the silicon retina chip

Each pixel is connected via analog circuits with its neighbors. Due to these additional circuits on the sensor area, the density of the pixels is not as high as on conventional monochrome/color sensors, which results in a lower fill factor.

The research of this sensor type goes back to Fukushima et al. (Fukushima et al., 1970) who made a first implementation of an artificial retina in 1970. In this first realization, electronic standard components, which emulate the photo receptors and ganglion cells of the eyes, were used. A lamp array provided the visualization of the transmitted picture of the artificial retina. In 1988 Mead and Mahowald (Mead & Mahowald, 1988) developed a silicon model of the early steps in human visual processing. One year later, Mahowald and Mead (Mahowald & Mead, 1989) implemented the first retina sensor based on silicon and established the name *Silicon Retina*. The optical transient sensor (Häflinger & Bergh, 2002), (Lichtsteiner et al., 2004) used for the stereo matching algorithms described in this work, is a sensor developed at the AIT[1] and ETH[2] and is described in the work of Lichtsteiner et al. (Lichtsteiner et al., 2006).

The silicon retina sensor operates quite independently of scene illumination and greatly reduces redundancy while preserving precise timing information. Because output bandwidth is automatically determined by the dynamic parts of the scene, a robust detection of fast moving objects at variable lighting conditions is achieved. The scene information is transmitted event-by-event via an asynchronous bus. The pixel location in the pixel array is encoded in the event data using the *Address-Event-Representation* (AER) (see section 2.2) protocol.

The silicon retina sensor has three main advantages in comparison to conventional CCD/CMOS camera sensors. First, the high temporal resolution allows quick reactions on fast motion in the visual field. Due to the low resolution (128×128 with 40μm pixel pitch) and the asynchronous transmission of address-events (AEs) from pixels where an intensity change has been occurred, a temporal resolution of up to $1ms$ is achieved. In Fig. 3 (1) the speed of a silicon retina imager compared to a monochrome camera (Basler A601f@60fps) is shown.

The top image in column (1) of Fig. 3 shows a running LED pattern with a frequency of $450Hz$. The silicon retina can capture the LED changing sequence, but the monochrome camera can not capture the fast moving pattern and therefore, more than one LED column is visible in a single image.

[1]AIT Austrian Institute of Technology GmbH (`http://www.ait.ac.at`)

[2]Eidgenössische Technische Hochschule Zürich (`http://www.ethz.ch`)

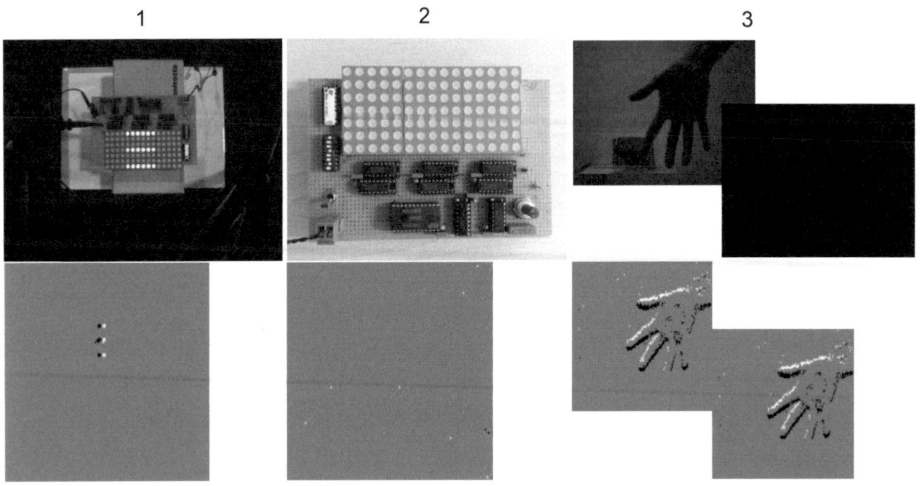

Fig. 3. Advantages of the silicon retina sensor technology, (1) high temporal resolution, (2) data transmission efficiency, (3) wide dynamic range

In Fig. 3 (2) the efficiency of the transmission is illustrated. The monochrome camera at the top of in the column (2) has no new information over time, nevertheless the unchanged image has to be transferred in any case. In case of silicon retina imagers, shown underneath, no information has to be transferred with exception of a few noise events which are visible in the field of view. Therefore, the second advantage is the on-sensor pre-processing because it reduces significantly both, memory requirements and processing power.
The third benefit of the silicon retina is the wide dynamic range of up to $120dB$, which helps to handle difficult lighting situations, encountered in real-world traffic and is demonstrated in Fig. 3 (3). The left image of the top pair shows a moving hand in an average illuminated room with an illumination of $\sim$1000 lm/m^2 and captured with a conventional monochrome camera. The second image of this pair on the right shows also a moved hand captured with a monochrome camera at an illumination of $\sim$5 lm/m^2. In case of the monochrome sensors only the hand in the well illuminated environment is visible, but the silicon retina sensor covers both situations, what is depicted in the image pair below in Fig. 3 (3).
The next generation of silicon retina sensors is a custom 304$\times$240 pixel (near QVGA) vision sensor *Application-Specific Integrated Circuit* (ASIC) also based on a bio-inspired analog pixel circuit. The sensor encodes, as well as the described 128$\times$128 sensor, relative changes of light intensity with low latentency, wide dynamic range, and communicates the information with a sparse, event based communication concept. The new sensor has not only a higher spatial resolution, the sensor has also a higher temporal resolution of up to $10ns$ and a decreased pixel pitch of 30μm. This kind of sensor is used for further research, but for the considerations in this work the 128$\times$128 pixel sensor is used.

2.2 Address-event data representation

The silicon retina uses the so-called *Address-Event-Representation* (AER) as output format which was proposed by Sivilotti (Sivilotti, 1991) and Mahowald (Mahowald, 1992) in order to model the transmission of neural information within biological systems. It is a digital asynchronous multiplexing protocol and the idea is that the bandwidth is only used if it is necessary. The protocol is event-driven what means that only active pixels transmit their

output, and in contrast, the bus is unused if the pixels of the sensor cannot detect any changes. Different AER implementations have been presented in the work of Mortara (Mortara, 1998) and the work of Boahen (Boahen, 2000). In the work of Häflinger and Bergh (Häflinger & Bergh, 2002) an one-dimensional correspondence search takes place and the underlying data protocol is AER.
The protocol consists of the timestamp *TS* which describes the time when an event has occurred, the coordinates (x,y) define where the event has occurred, and the polarity p of the contrast change (event) which is encoded as an extra bit and can be ON or OFF, representing a fractional change from dark to bright or vice-versa. In the current version the timestamp is transmitted in absolut time which means it increases continuously from the start of the camera. The new protocol version sends a relative timestamp which saves transmission bandwidth.

3. Stereo processing with silicon retina cameras

The stereo matching is the elementary algorithm of each stereo vision application. Two cameras are placed in a certain distance (baseline) to observe the same scene from two different point views. Existing stereo matching algorithms deal with data from conventional monochrome/color cameras and cannot be applied directly to silicon retina data.
Existing methods for adjustment of the cameras, as well as calibration and rectification methods have to be extended and changed for the event-based stereo processing.
Also, for algorithm verification, existing data-sets could not be used, as these are based on frame-based representation of a scene. Thus, an event-based stereo verification method was implemented that describes a scene using geometric primitives. For verification purpose, ground truth information is essential, which could also be generated based on this scene description.

3.1 Stereo sensor setup

The goal of the stereo vision sensor described in this chapter is to detect fast approaching objects to forecast side impacts. For this reason, two silicon retina sensors are placed on a baseline to build up a stereo system. This stereo system is designed for pre crash warning and consists of the stereo head and an embedded system for data acquisition and processing. The stereo vision sensor must fulfill requirements given by the traffic environment. In Fig. 4 a sketch of the side impact scenario including some key parameters is shown.
In the mentioned application, the stereo vision system has to detect closer coming objects and activates pre-safe mechanisms of the car. The speed of the approaching vehicle is defined with $60km/h$ and a minimal width of an object of $0.5m$. For activating the corresponding safety mechanisms of the car, we assume that the vehicle needs about $300ms$ which defines the detection duration of the camera system. A vehicle with a speed of $60km/h$ passes a distance of $5m$ in $300ms$, therefore the decision if an impact will occur or not has to be made $5m$ before the vehicle will impact. In Fig. 4 the detection distance and the critical distance, where a decision has to be made, are shown. These requirements define the key parameters of the optical system and the following embedded processing units.

3.2 Adjustment of the stereo sensor

Before the silicon retina stereo vision system can be used, a configuration has to be made. The focus of the lenses has to be set, the calculation of the calibration parameters has to be computed and for stereo matching the rectification parameters has to be extracted. In contrast

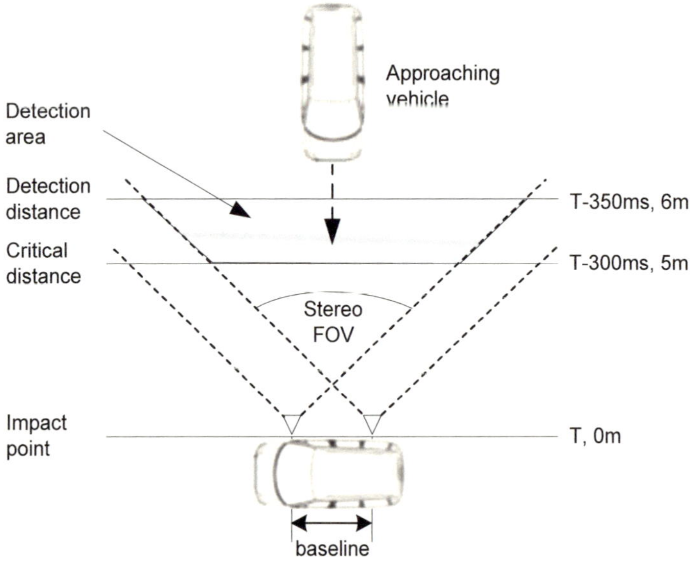

Fig. 4. Stereo vision setup for the use in a pre-crash warning side impact detection application

to conventional camera sensors, the silicon retina has no stable image which can be used for configuration and calibration purposes. Therefore, new methods for lens adjustment, calibration and rectification were implemented.

3.2.1 Lens configuration

Before the camera system can be used, the lenses must be brought in-focus with respect to the desired sensing range. The silicon retina sensor delivers image information only when changes in intensity happen. Therefore, an object must be moved in front of the camera, so that address-events will be generated. For this reason, a hardware which helps to adjust the lenses of silicon retina cameras was built. It allows the definition of thick or thin lines, which are moving in front of the camera to generate a stimulus. The hardware was built on a breadboard shown in Fig. 5. The board consists of a 15×5 LED matrix which is used

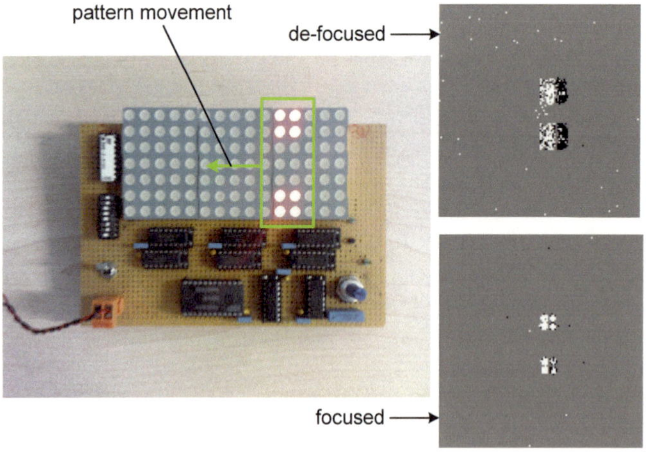

Fig. 5. Hardware for the adjustment of silicon retina camera lenses

to generate the stimuli for the silicon retina cameras. With the potentiometer the frequency (speed) of LED changes can be configured. After each cycle the pattern of highlighted LEDs is moved leftwards by one column. There is a software tool available, which allows a live view of the silicon retina output. This software transforms the address-events to an image frame and displays this stream on the screen. Using this tool, the impact of the lens adjustment can be directly observed on the screen. The images on the right side show the de-focused silicon retina image on the top and the correctly focused lens on the bottom. After the adjustment of the lenses, the data of the stereo vision system can be used.

3.2.2 Calibration and rectification

The acquired data from the cameras are not prepared for line-by-line matching, respectively event-by-event matching, because the epipolar lines (Schreer, 2005) are not in parallel. Therefore, a rectification of the camera data is carried out. Before this rectification can be done, the cameras have to be calibrated. With conventional cameras, the calibration pattern (Fig. 6 on the top) is captured in different views from the right and left camera. Then the

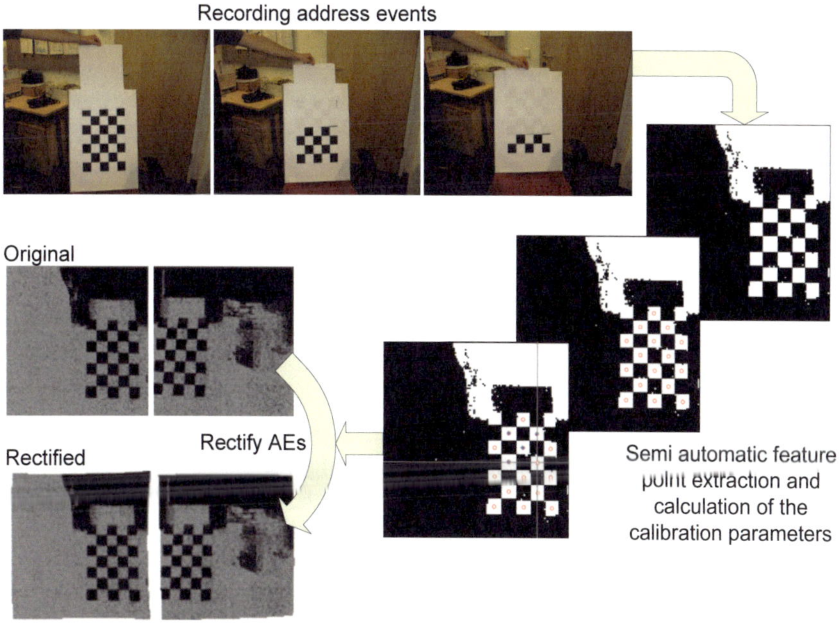

Fig. 6. Calibration and rectification of silicon retina cameras

corners of the pattern are used for calculation of the camera parameters. For silicon retina imagers, it is not possible to capture a static calibration pattern if there is no movement, more precisely no change in the intensity. Thus, an alternative approach is necessary. In Fig. 6 on the top, the calibration pattern is shown in a stable position and a white paper is moved up and down in front of the calibration pattern. During a period of time all address-events are collected and stored in an output file. The collected address-event data are converted into a binary image, which is used for the extraction of feature points. Instead of the corners from the calibration pattern, the center of gravity of the squares for extraction of corresponding features are used. The right side in Fig. 6 shows the semi-automatic extraction of the feature points, because not all centers are feasible for the calibration step. That means, the algorithm extracts more points but not all of them are supporting the calibration process and therefore, the user has to choose manually which points should be used for the calibration step. For the calibration itself the method from (Zhang, 2002) in combination with the calibration toolbox from Caltech for Matlab (Bouguet, 2008) is used. All data extracted from the binary images are loaded via the external interface into the calibration engine and the results are applied on silicon retina data for the calibration and rectification step.

The left side of Fig. 6 shows an example of rectified silicon retina data from the left and right camera. In a next generation of calibration and rectification of silicon retina cameras LCD screens will be used where a pattern changes in a defined way in order to excite events.

3.3 Frame-based stereo matching

In the field of stereo matching exists different approaches for solving the stereo correspondence problem, but these approaches are developed for frame-based data from stereo vision systems based on conventional monochchrome/color cameras. If existing frame-based stereo matching algorithms shall be used with silicon retina cameras, the data of the silicon retina stereo vision system has to be converted into framed image/data streams before the frame-based stereo matching approaches can be applied.

3.3.1 Address-event to frame converter

Before the AE data can be used with full frame image processing algorithms, the data structure is changed into a frame format. For this reason an address-event-to-frame converter has been implemented.

The silicon retina sensor delivers permanently ON- and OFF-events, which are marked with a timestamp t_{ev}. The frame converter collects the address-events over a defined time period $\Delta t = [t_{start} : t_{end}]$ and inserts these events into a frame. After the time period the frame is closed and the generation of the next frame begins. The definition of an event frame is

$$AE_{frame} = \int_{t_{start}}^{t_{end}} AE_{xy}(t_{ev})dt_{ev}. \tag{3}$$

Different algorithm approaches need a different frame format. The silicon retina stereo camera system used within this work is evaluated with two algorithms derived from two different categories. The first algorithm is an area-based approach, which works with the comparison of frame windows. The second algorithm is a feature-based variant which matches identified features. Both categories need differently constructed frames from the converter. Due to this reason, the converter offers configurations to fulfil these requirements. Fig. 7 shows on the left side the output frame of the converter with the collected ON- and OFF-events. The resolution

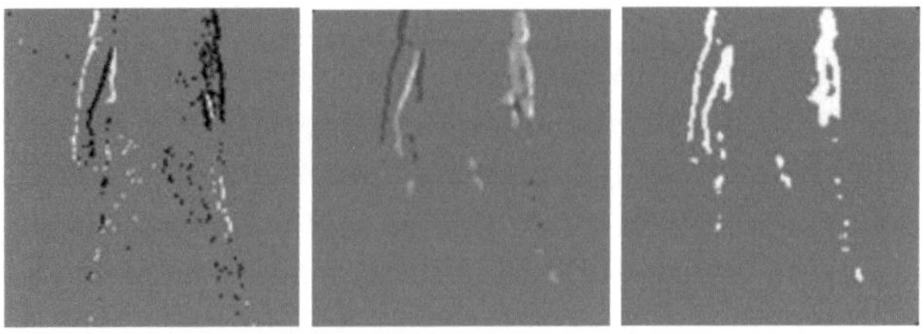

Fig. 7. Different results of AE to frame converter

of the timestamp mechanism of the silicon retina is $1ms$, but for the algorithm evaluated in this work a Δt of $10ms$ and $20ms$ is used. The Δt is changed for different conditions, which produce a different number of events.

The image in the middle of Fig. 7 shows a frame built for an area-based matching algorithm. For this reason each event received in the defined time period is interpreted as a gray value, with

$$AE_{frame} = \int_{t_{start}}^{t_{end}} graystep(AE_{xy}(t_{ev}))dt_{ev}. \tag{4}$$

The background of the frame is initialized with 128 (based on a 8 bit grayscale model) and each ON-event adds a gray value, and an OFF-event subtracts one. In Equation 5, the function for generating a gray value frame is shown. The 8 bit grayscale model limits the additions and subtractions of the $\Delta_{grayvalue}$ and saturates if an overflow occurs.

$$graystep(AE_{xy}(t_{ev})) = \begin{cases} AE_{frame_{xy}} + \Delta_{grayvalue} & AE_{xy}(t_{ev}) = ON_{event} \\ AE_{frame_{xy}} - \Delta_{grayvalue} & AE_{xy}(t_{ev}) = OFF_{event} \end{cases} \tag{5}$$

The right image in Fig. 7 shows a frame built for a feature-based image processing algorithm. In this case, multiple events received within the defined period of time will be overwritten instead of accumulated. Equation 6 shows the frame building and the used simplify function is illustrated in Equation 7.

$$AE_{frame} = \int_{t_{start}}^{t_{end}} simplify(AE_{xy}(t_{ev}), conv_{on})dt_{ev} \tag{6}$$

The simplify function gets a second parameter ($conv_{on}$) to decide the event variant (only ON or OFF). This frame is prepared for different kind of feature-based algorithms and also for algorithms based on segmentation.

$$simplify(AE_{xy}(t_{ev}), conv_{on}) = \begin{cases} ON_{ev} & AE_{xy}(t_{ev}) = ON_{ev} \wedge conv_{on} = 1 \\ OFF_{ev} & AE_{xy}(t_{ev}) = ON_{ev} \wedge conv_{on} = 0 \\ ON_{ev} & AE_{xy}(t_{ev}) = OFF_{ev} \wedge conv_{on} = 1 \\ OFF_{ev} & AE_{xy}(t_{ev}) = OFF_{ev} \wedge conv_{on} = 0 \end{cases} \tag{7}$$

Both specialized generated frames (middle and right in Fig. 7) can optionally be filtered with a median filter to reduce noise and small artifacts. With those settings every Δt, a new frame from the left and right address-event-stream is generated. These frames are now handled as images for the stereo matching algorithms described in the next section.

3.3.2 Area-based frame stereo matching

The area-based approach uses the neighborhood (block) of the considered pixel for the matching of each pixel and tries to match this with a corresponding block from the other camera image. These kind of algorithms are used if rectified stereo image pairs are available and if the output shall be a dense disparity map. Some algorithms using block-based techniques are shown in ((Banks et al., 1997), (Banks et al., 1999), (Zabih & Woodfill, 1994)). For the demonstration of area-based processing with silicon retina data a *Sum of Absolute Differences* (SAD) correlation algorithm (Schreer, 2005) was chosen. A block matching, based on ON and OFF events, produces a lot of similar blocks and a lot of mismatches will appear. The grayscale images have more then two values and therefore, the statistical significance of a block is larger. Also in the work from Milosevic et al. (Milosevic et al., 2007) a silicon retina stereo matching algorithm based on SAD is shown. This algorithm uses an address-event-to-frame conversion to get grayscale images, which can be matched with the SAD technique. Milosevic et al. use in their work correlation windows of up to

15×15 without a proper rectification step to find the matches, perhaps this window size leads to a low processing performance. Therefore, the approach in our work uses different conversion outputs (see 3.3.1) and an adequate rectification step to enable smaller window sizes for the SAD and increase the performance of the computation. For the processing of the SAD algorithm the grayscale frames, as shown in Fig. 8 on the left side, are used. These

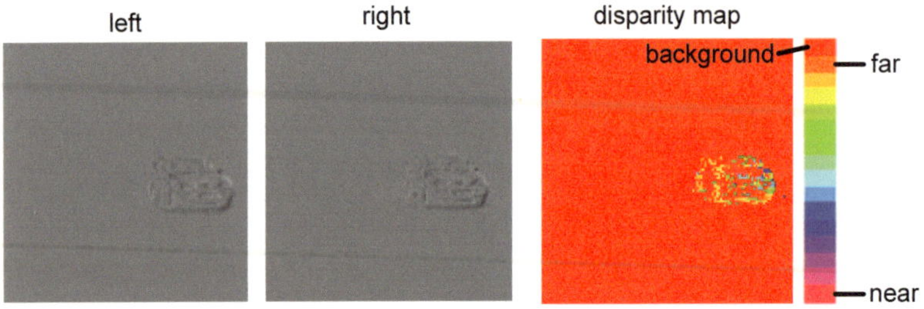

Fig. 8. Input stereo images for the SAD algorithm (left two images) and result of the matching process (right image)

input images consist of pixels with different grayscale values (accumulated address-events), therefore the matching results of the correlation are more confident. The found matches are used for the calculation of the disparity value, whereby the absolute value of the difference of both x-coordinates is taken (x-coordinate of the left and right image). In Fig. 8 on the right side the disparity image of the stereo pair on the left side is shown.
The disparity values are visualized in a color-coded manner according to the legend at the bottom of Fig. 8 on the right side. Due to the large amount of background pixels, the result is not a dense disparity map. The disparity map shall have the same or equal outlines as the original silicon retina input image.

3.3.3 Feature-based frame stereo matching

For feature-based stereo matching with silicon retina data, the address-event-data must be converted again, as described in section 3.3.1, before the features can be extracted from the image. Shi and Tomasi (Shi & Tomasi, 1994) give more details about features in their work and describe which features are good for tracking. Within their work they discuss e.g. the texturedness, dissimilarity and convergence of features. For the evaluation of the feature-based stereo matching with silicon retina cameras, a segment center matching approach is chosen. Tang et al. (Tang et al., 2006) describe in their work an approach for matching feature points. In Fig. 9, the left stereo pair shows the address-event-data converted into images feasible for the feature-based algorithm approach. If the image was not filtered

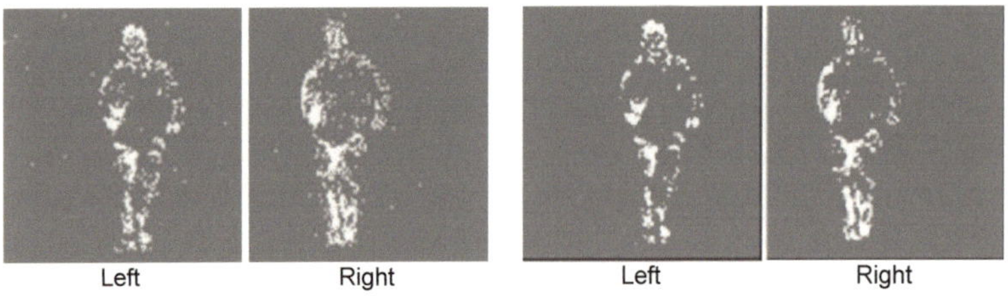

Fig. 9. Left: Input stereo images for the feature matching algorithm, Right: Input images filtered with a 3×3 median filter

during the conversion step, the image must be filtered now in order to remove noise in the

image. The right image pair in Fig. 9 shows the data after a 3×3 median filter has been applied.
In the next step some morphological operators are used to get linked regions of pixels which can be labeled as one connected area. The images are treated with some morphological operations (Gonzales & Woods, 2002) for the enhancement of features, which are required by the next step of the center matching algorithm. In the algorithm for the silicon retina images a square shape structuring element was used. The structuring element for the erosion has a size of 4×4 and the square for the dilation a size of 7×7. In the first row of Fig. 10, the silicon retina images after the dilation (left image pair) operation are shown and the results after the erosion (right image pair) are depicted. The images are now prepared for the segmentation

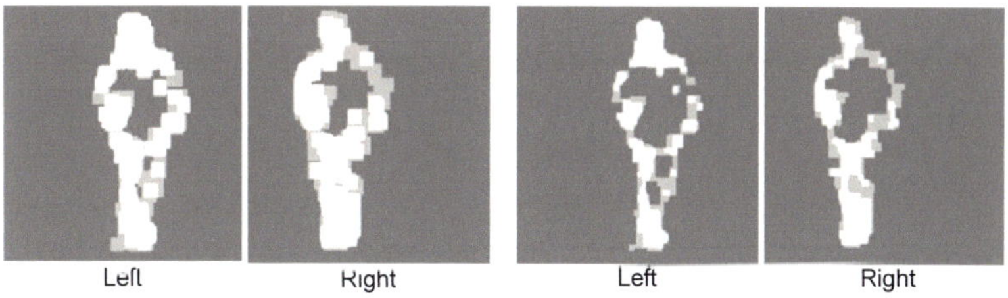

Fig. 10. Stereo images after the morphological operation dilation and erosion

and labeling step. For the region labeling a flood fill (Burger & Burge, 2005) algorithm is used. This algorithm labels all linked areas with a number in a way that the regions can be identified. The result of region labeling is shown in Fig. 11 in the left image pair. After region labeling, a

Fig. 11. Left: all found regions, Right: all found segments and the corresponding center of each segment (red dot)

few segments should be available which are used for matching. Before the matching can start, all segments with less than a defined amount of pixels, are removed. A region is a collection of more than one pixel and has a defined shape. A pixel-by-pixel matching is not possible and therefore, it must be defined how the whole feature (region) shall be matched. In a first step, the features are ordered downwards according to their area pixel count. This method is only useful if the found regions in the left and right image are nearly the same (also the same area pixel count). As representative point of the feature the center of the feature was chosen. The so called *center-of-gravity* must be searched for each feature. All found centers are marked with a red dot as shown in the right image pair in Fig. 11.
The center of the corresponding segment in the left and right frame can differ. Due to this reason the confidence of the found centers are checked. This mechanism checks the differences of center points, if they are too large, the center points are ignored for the matching. If the center points lie within the predefined tolerances, the disparity is calculated which represents the disparity of the whole object.

3.4 Event-based stereo matching

The usage of conventional block-based and feature-based stereo algorithms has shown a reduction of the advantage of the asynchronous data interface and throttle the performance of the silicon retina cameras. Due to this fact, a frame-less and therefore event-based stereo matching approach, which exploits the characteristics of the silicon retina technology, has to be developed. For this reason, a time-correlation algorithm for the correspondence search is used. This algorithm uses the time difference between events as the primary matching costs. In Fig. 12, the whole workflow of the event-based algorithm approach is shown.

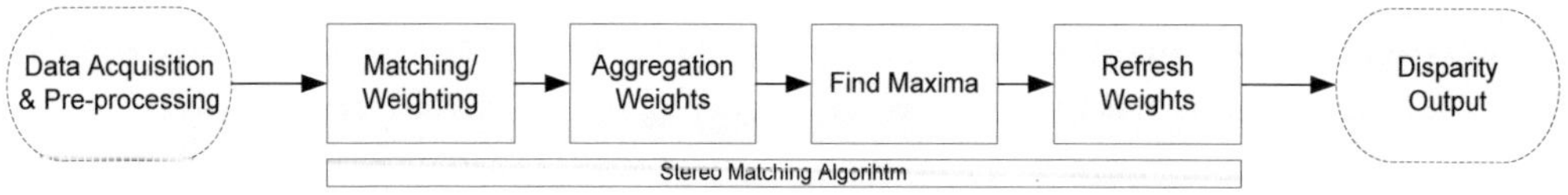

Fig. 12. Workflow of the event-based time correlation stereo matching algorithm

Data Acquisition and Pre-processing

Before the stereo matching workflow starts, the data from the silicon retina sensors are acquired, which means the data are read from the adapter board buffers and given to the rectification unit. For the rectification step, all needed parameters were calculated in a previous calibration step. The calibration determines the intrinsic camera parameters plus the rectification matrices for both sensors. For the calibration of silicon retina cameras the method described in section 3.2.2 is used and it is part of the pre-processing step.

Matching and Weighting

After the pre-processing, the stereo algorithm starts and uses the rectified data stream from silicon retina cameras. In the first step, the matching of the events is carried out where for each oncoming event a corresponding event on the opposite side is searched. For this search, all events of the current timestamp, as well as events from the past are used. This means also previous events are considered during the correspondence search. Due to the previous rectification, the search is carried out in a horizontal line within the disparity range.

In Fig. 13, on the top left side the event buffers are shown which store the current and the historical events. If there are possible matching candidates within the disparity range of actual and historical events, which have the same polarity, the timestamps are used for calculating the matching costs. In Fig. 13, the matching of an event at the x-coordinate 40 is illustrated. The left event is the reference event and the search takes place on the right side where three candidates with the same polarity and within the considered history are found. Now, the time difference between the timestamp of the left camera and the three found events of the right camera is calculated.

For determination of the costs of a found matched event pair, different weighting functions were used. In Fig. 14, all used weighting functions are depicted. On the abscissa of the diagrams the weighting costs which may achieve a maximum of 10 (derived from the maximal considered historical events) are plotted and on the ordinate of the diagrams the time difference is shown. In the example, the considered history is 10, which means from the current timestamp of an event 10 timestamps of the past are regarded for the current calculations. The left function shows a simple inverse linear relation between the time difference Δt and the weight. In the middle chart an inverse quadratic function is depicted which is faster declining and matches more current events and does not consider older events in the same amount. The Gaussian function shown in the right diagram of Fig. 14 increases,

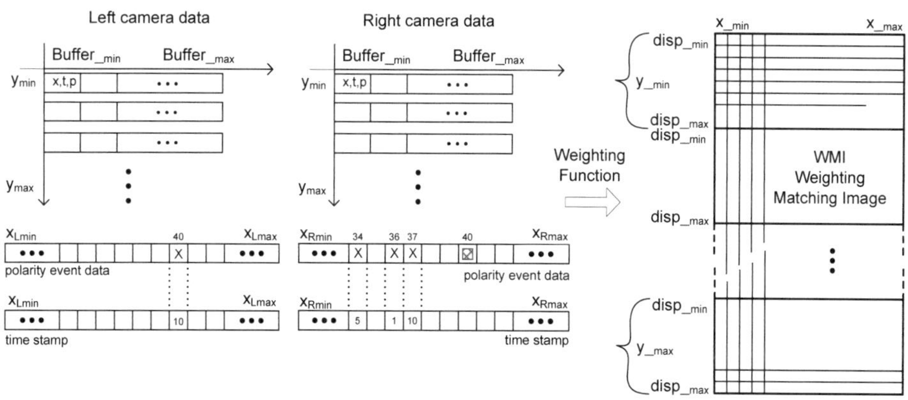

Fig. 13. Matching and weighting of corresponding address-events and writing of calculated costs into the WMI

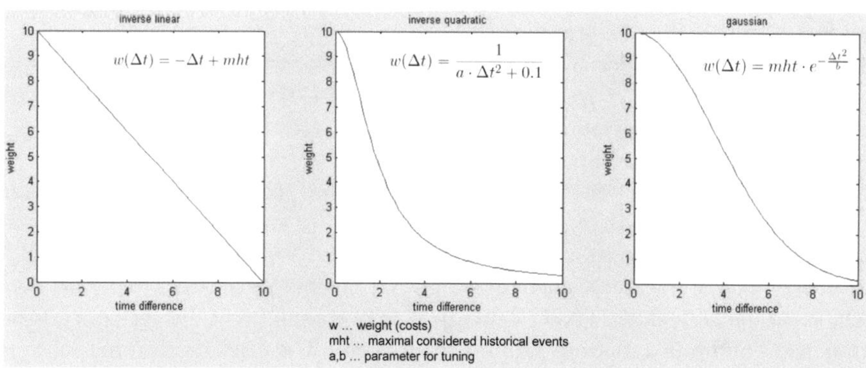

Fig. 14. Weighting function for calculating the costs of matched address -events

In comparison to the inverse linear function, the weights of current timestamps and decreases the older timestamps. Both functions on the right side, the inverse quadratic and the Gaussian can be tuned with a parameter for the adaption to different weighting needs. All the matched and weighted events are written into the *Weighted Matching Image* (WMI) shown in Fig. 13. This data storage is a two dimensional representation of a three dimensional space, where a place for each pixel coordinate and disparity level is reserved. The WMI is a dynamic data storage which is updated each processing cycle and only deleted if a reset takes place. That means all costs entered, stay in the WMI for a defined time till they are removed and so the matched costs from previous steps contribute to the results of the current calculations.

Aggregation Weights

The next step of the algorithm is the aggregation of the weights in the WMI. Therefore, the WMI structure is transformed logically and a filter kernel works on the weights with the same disparity. In the current algorithm, an average filter kernel with a variable window size is used.

Find Maxima
After the aggregation step, the maximum costs for each coordinate which represents the best matching disparity are searched.

Refresh Weights
In consideration that the WMI is a refreshing data structure, after the maximum search all weights are checked if they have to be deleted from the WMI, and therefore the weight itself is a lifetime counter. In each round, the weight is reduced with a defined value till the weight is zero and then deleted from the WMI or refreshed by a new match as well as a new weight.

Write Disparity Output
The results are written into the disparity map, which can be used from the application for further processing.

3.5 Verification of event-based stereo matching algorithms

Existing performance and quality metrics cannot be used within event-based data processing, thus a new approach has been implemented that redefines existing metrics for the event-based approach and describes the performance.
Early verification and validation approaches used in real-world environments were justified with a measuring tape. This was sufficient for some estimations whether an algorithm approach was generally computing or not. Predictions and declarations of the achieved quality of an algorithm were not possible.
A method for visualizing the performance of classifiers are receiver operating characteristics (ROC). Fawcett (Fawcett, 2004), (Fawcett, 2006) and Provost and Fawcett (Provost & Fawcett, 2001) give an introduction and practical considerations for ROC analysis in their work. Within verification of silicon retina stereo matching algorithms, we also address two-class problems. Each instance of the *ground truth* (**GT**) is mapped to one element of the set $\{p, n\}$, where p is an existing event and n is a missing ground truth event. The classification model represents the mapping from **GT** to a predictable class, the *disparity map* (**DM**) is mapped to the set $\{y, n\}$, where y is an existing and n is a missing disparity event. Based on these combinations, a two-by-two confusion matrix can be build. Metrics evaluation is based on comparing the disparity to the ground truth data set. Equation 8 defines both, the disparity and the ground truth set for metrics evaluation, where t_h defines the propagation delay of a set.

$$\begin{aligned} dm(x,y,t) &:= \int_{t-t_h}^{t} DM(x,y,t)dt \\ gt(x,y,t) &:= \int_{t-t_h}^{t} GT(x,y,t)dt \end{aligned} \tag{8}$$

- A *true positive* is defined by Equation 9 for both existing disparity and ground truth data with an error tolerance δ_d.

$$tp(t) := \sum_{x \in X, y \in Y} [|dm(x,y,t) - gt(x,y,t)| < \delta_d] \tag{9}$$

- A *false positive* is defined in Equation 10 for the same restrictions as *true positives*, though the error tolerance δ_d is exceed.

$$fp(t) := \sum_{x \in X, y \in Y} [|dm(x,y,t) - gt(x,y,t)| \geq \delta_d] \tag{10}$$

- A *false negative* $fn(t)$ is defined by an existing ground truth and a missing disparity value.
- A *true negative* $tn(t)$ is defined by both, a missing ground truth and a missing disparity value.

Based on these performance primitives, further performance metrics such as true positive rate or false positive rate of a time-slot can be computed.

4. Implementation

Due to the special characteristics of this novel sensor technology and the asynchronously data processing algorithm approach, existing data acquisition and processing techniques are not adequate. The high temporal resolution of the sensor results in data peaks up to $10Meps$ (Mega events per second).
Within the project, two system demonstrators were implemented. The PC based demonstrator is used for low-speed data processing and algorithm verification. The DSP demonstrator is intended to be used for high-speed real-time data processing. A third FPGA based demonstrator is outlined and represents the next step after the DSP implementation and gives and overview how the performance of event-based stereo matching can be increased.

4.1 PC demonstrator

The PC demonstrator is used for low-speed data processing, coupling the Ethernet interface of the imagers which offers AE without time-information. The timing information, which is essential for event based stereo matching, is assigned when acquiring the data.
The implemented tool is shown in Fig. 15. The tool consists of an viewer optimized for AE data and an embedded interpreter language, including the data objects for scene generation and verification. Scene generation contains geometric primitives that can be used for scene description. Also, recorded scenes can be used as objects for scene description. All geometric objects are inhered from a base object, afford generating ground truth information that is essential for verification. Using these base objects, also complex objects e.g. vehicles, can be compound.

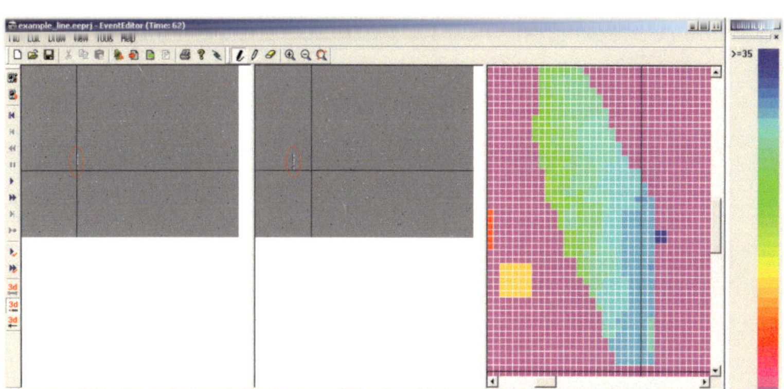

Fig. 15. Verification Tool; scenario shows a moving line from the upper left to the bottom right corner of the visualized time-slot. left window: left imager; middle window: right imager; right window: processed disparity map by the stereo matching algorithm

The tool handles and processes the address-event represented data asynchronously similar to the real environment. For data visualization, visualized time-slots are used, as shown in section 3.3.1. The internal data management is realized using data containers enclosing timestamp-sorted AEs, the identifier, and the coordinates. For advanced visualizing of the data, the virtual reality modeling language (VMRL) (World Wide Web Consortium (W3C), 1995) is used. Fig. 16 shows a processed disparity map of a recorded scene of a pedestrian.

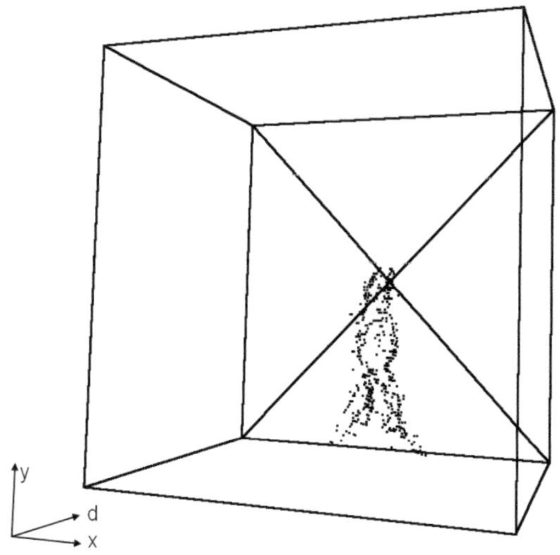

Fig. 16. Disparity map of scene with a pedestrian processed with an area-based stereo matching algorithm and visualized in VRML.

4.2 DSP demonstrator

The embedded system used for data acquisition and data processing is based on a distributed digital signal processing solution. Fig. 17 shows a schematic diagram of this demonstrator consisting of two silicon retina imagers connected to an adapter-board, that implements a memory mapped interface to the TMS320C6455. Both imagers stream data to the first in first out (FIFO) devices on this board. Once enough data are acquired, an interrupt is triggered and the direct memory access (DMA) controller flushes the FIFOs and transfers the data to the DSP, where it is available for further processing.

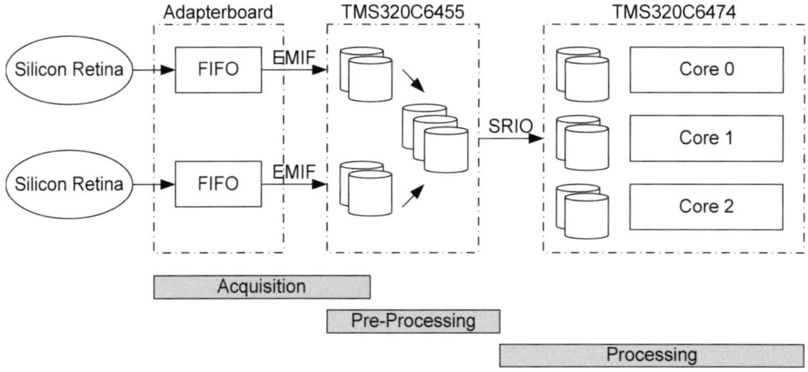

Fig. 17. Schematic diagram of the DSP-based demonstrator.

Further processing on the data acquisition processor includes noise filtering of events and a load balancer for partitioning the acquired amount of data on the multi-core processor that is responsible for processing the stereo matching algorithm. Equation 11 shows the balancing criteria of the load balancer, where $\mathbf{E}(\mathcal{Y})$ is the y-coordinate of the event, N is the number of parallel units, H is the height of the sensor, and n is the processor identifier.

$$n = \frac{\mathbf{E}(\mathcal{Y})N}{H} \tag{11}$$

For data exchange between the single-core to the multi-core processor, a serial high performance interface is used which is intended for interconnecting distributed processing systems on chip-to-chip and board-to-board level. The data transfer is completely handled in hardware using a processor peripheral module. After transferring a burst of data, an interrupt is triggered on the specific core to initiate the stereo matching process.

4.3 FPGA demonstrator

The introduced DSP-based platform generally enables parallel computation of the proposed stereo vision algorithm by using multi-core processors. Additionally, the behavior of the used silicon retina sensors leads, in contrast to frame-based imagers, not only to less redundancy but also to a reduced amount of data because the retina only delivers data on intensity changes of the ambient light. Therefore, the underlying vision system usually have not to cope with a huge amount of data and so have to provide less memory bandwidth, which usually is the bottleneck in embedded vision systems. Unfortunately, the asynchronous characteristics of the silicon retina yields to a non-constant data rate, but any data peaks can be caught with a simple FIFO at the intput-stage.

Due to the computationally sophisticated and expensive nature of the presented event-based stereo matching algorithm, a more parallelized data processing would be obvious, and effectively necessary to fulfill the timing constraints of real-time applications and fully exploiting the high temporal resolution of the silicon retina sensors. This algorithms however, can significantly benefit from application depended customizations of the underlying system architecture: hence optimized memory access patterns, fast on-chip buffers or line-caches, and special computation units for data correlation are preferred. ASICs or even more FPGAs, can be used to put such customized architectures into practice and thus to exploit the immanent parallelism of stereo-vision algorithms (Porter & Bergmann, 1997).

However, an FPGA-based implementation will decrease the overall complexity of the embedded system because, e.g., in our case, as it is shown in Fig. 18, the data acquisition unit, the rectification module, the computation units, and finally the transmission of the disparity map can be integrated into one single chip, which obviously leads to a smart stereo vision systems (Belbachir, 2010). Nevertheless, by adapting the memory interfaces and access patterns, and the data path of the processing units to the asynchronous behavior of the silicon retina and the address-event format, the latency of the system would be reduced.

Furthermore, by using massively parallel hardware architectures the throughput of the system would be increased. The integration of all functional blocks into one customized FPGA or ASIC yields not only to a simplification but also to an improvement of the scalability and the overall energy efficiency of the system.

Fig. 18 shows a recommendation of a hardware-based implementation of the event-based stereo matching algorithm. First of all, data from the sensor must be gathered within the acquisition unit by a FIFO, which could be either on-chip if there is sufficient memory and the succeeding units are fast enough or even off-chip. In this case, the FIFO itself could be bigger and therefore the following processing units can operate at lower speed. After this, the events must be rectified, done by a pipelined online rectification unit. Unfortunately, this step is

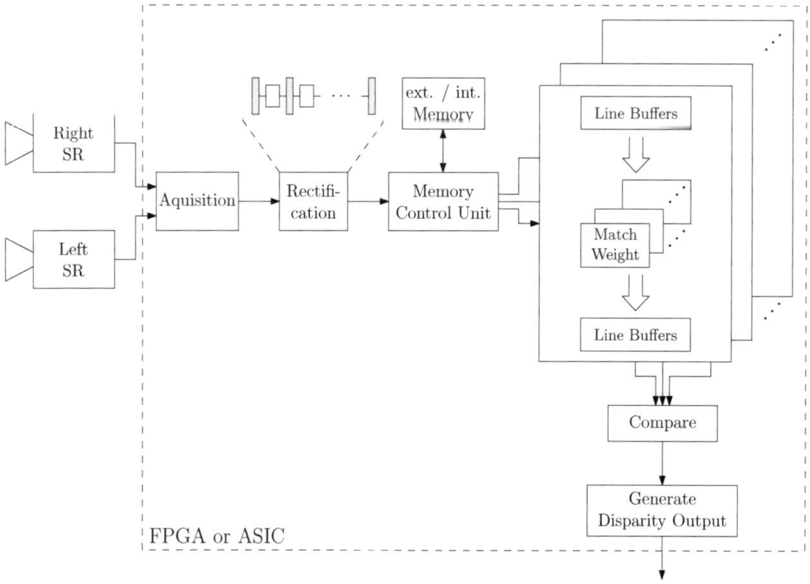

Fig. 18. Possible architecture of a hardware-based implementation

computationally very intensive even if tight tolerances should be attained, but this approach is very memory-efficient and, compared to the current used look-up table-based approach, can be parallelized as well. This processing step is one of the main challenges of the whole algorithm because it must entirely be accomplished before proceeding with the subsequent calculation.

An other key point of the system will be the memory control unit, because here all data accesses must be merged and a high bandwidth will be required. Here are also on- or off-chip memories possible, since the resources which are provided by up-to-date high-end FPGAs and the reduced amount of data supplied by silicon retina sensors, on-chip memory would be preferred. Additionally, the on-chip variant allows the usage of several dual-ported memories enabling the parallelization of the accesses and therefore a very high bandwidth. On the other side, using an off-chip memory leads to a simpler memory architecture and facilitates the deployment of a mid-end FPGA which yields also to a simplification of the overall system. In order to overcome this bottleneck, a further reduction of the address-event data should be done in any cases, e.g., using not the whole timestamp for an event, but only differences of timestamps corresponding to the depth of the considered history. Thus, memory accesses and space can be optimized even if off-chip memory with limited bandwidth will be used.

The matching and weighting of the address-events can be done in a parallel manner by selective pre-fetching of the events, although one match and weight unit processes one single line of pixels from the left and right sensor. If a block-based approach is used, the line buffers on the input side must be interconnected according to the block size. The criterion for matching and the weighting function are not important for the architecture as far as they can be mapped onto hardware. In the end, the results will be brought together and the disparity output will be generated.

5. Results

The different stereo matching approaches for address-event-data have been tested with a variety of parameters. This section compares the results of frame-based stereo matching divided into area-based approaches and feature-based approaches, as well as an event-based stereo matching approach. Each of the algorithm has defined parameters which can be used for the tuning of the algorithm results.

5.1 Results of frame-based address-event stereo matching

This section shows the results of frame-based stereo matching with silicon retina data. For this tests, the silicon retina data streams were converted into frames which can be used from stereo matching algorithms developed for conventional frame-based cameras.

5.1.1 Area-based address-event stereo matching

The algorithm parameter of the SAD is the size of the correlation window. We tested the algorithm with an object at three different distances ($2m$, $4m$, $6m$) and different settings of the address-event converter. In Fig. 19, the results of the SAD algorithm processing AE frames are given. On the x-axis the different converter settings at three different distances are shown. The first number represents the object distance in meters, the second value describes the time

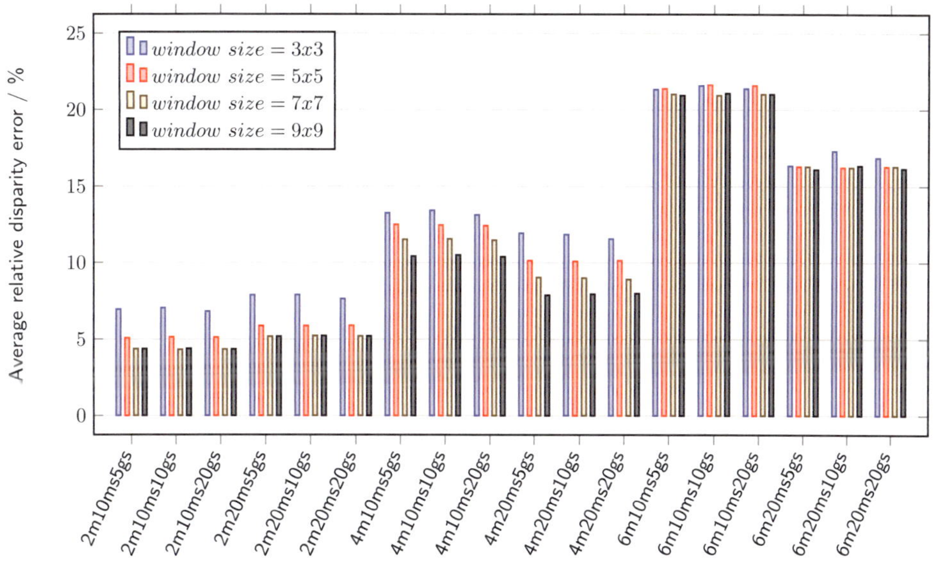

Fig. 19. Results of the area-based stereo matching algorithm on address-event frames

period for collecting address-events, and the last value represents the grayvalue stepsize for the accumulation function described in section 3.3.1. For each distance, all four converter settings with four different SAD correlation window sizes are evaluated. The output on the y-axis is the average relative error of the distance estimation based on 500 image pairs. The results in Fig. 19 show that the average relative disparity error increases with the distance of the object. In near distances, the results are influenced by the correlation window size, especially there is a significant difference between the usage of a 3×3 window and a 9×9 window. In the distance of $4m$ and $6m$, the results with a timestamp collection time Δt of 20ms are better. The third parameter of the generated input AE frame is the grayscale step size which has no influence at any distance. Generally, we achieve with the SAD stereo matching approach used for AE frames in the main operating distance of 4m a minimal error of 8%. That is equivalent to an estimated distance range of $3.68m$-$4.32m$.

5.1.2 Feature-based address-event stereo matching

This section shows results of the feature-based stereo matching algorithm using AE frames. The parameters of the segment center matching are the morphological erosion and dilation function at the beginning of the algorithm. In Fig. 20, the results of the feature-based algorithm processing AE frames are given. For center matching only the collecting time period

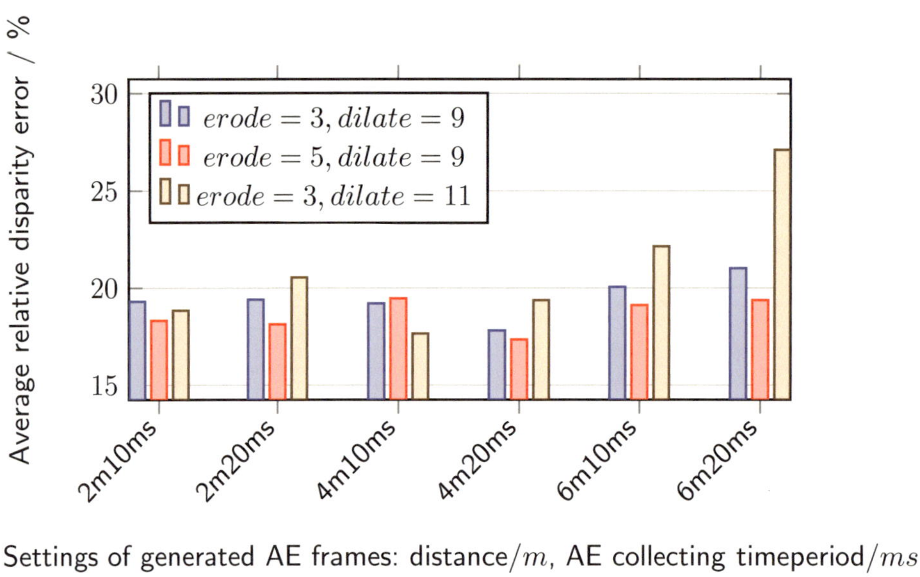

Fig. 20. Results of the feature-based stereo matching algorithm on address-event frames

Δt of the address-events is varied, which is shown with the second value from the descriptors on the x-axis. All converter settings with three different morphological erosion and dilation settings are evaluated. The structuring element is always a square. The results on the y-axis shows the average relative disparity error of the feature center matching at three different distances with two different address converter settings and with three different morphological function combinations. The results are based on 500 image pair samples. The achievements in Fig. 20 show that the average relative disparity error depends on the sizes of the structuring elements. At all distances, the morphological combination erosion=3 and dilation=5 produces the best results. The timestamp collection time Δt has only a significant influence at the distance of $6m$. In the main operating distance of 4m, the minimal error is 17%, which is equivalent to an estimated distance range of $3.32m$-$4.68m$.

5.2 Results of event-based address-event stereo matching

For the evaluation of the event-based stereo vision algorithm, a specific tool was used which is shown in Fig. 15. It is called Event-Editor and gives the opportunity to generate synthetic stereo data which allows a verification of the algorithm because of available ground truth information.

Before the evaluation, the parameters for the synthetic data have to be set. The detection range is between $6m$ and $5m$ what gives, considering the system configuration, a disparity range of 15 to 20. In the evaluation phase we considered a higher range of 35, which evaluates the capability of the algorithm to detect closer objects as well. The simplified model of the silicon retina used for the generation of synthetic silicon retina data is a suitable approximation of the real silicon retina sensor for the algorithm evaluation.
In Fig.21, the evaluation results of the algorithm are shown. Different aggregation window

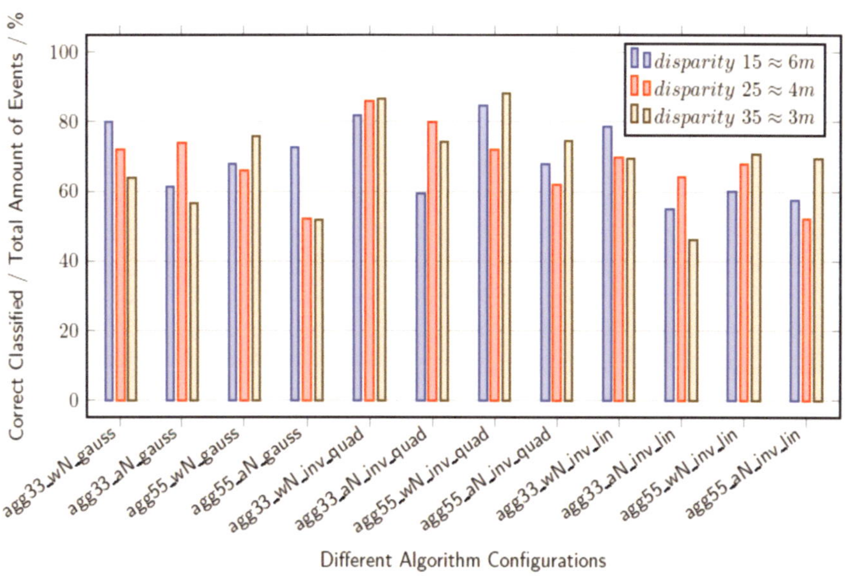

Fig. 21. Experimental results of the event-based stereo matching algorithm with different evaluation and algorithm settings

sizes, noise amounts, and weighting functions are compared. The value, in percent, plotted on the y-axis, gives the information of how many disparities were calculated correctly in relation to the total amount of events in the current matching step. The evaluation was carried out in three different disparity distances, depicted with the three colors in Fig. 21. The three parts of the values, plotted on the x-axis and divided by an underscore describe the algorithm evaluation settings. The first part shows the aggregation window size (3×3 or 5×5), the second part shows if there was a noise signal added (aN) or not (wN), and the last part describes the weighting function used. The results show that the quality of disparity calculation is independent of the evaluated distances. As expected, added noise effects the rate of correct classified disparity values in comparison to noise free data. The aggregation window size has only a small impact but especially when noise is added, the amount of correct classified disparities increase if the window size is enlarged. The highest influence has the weighting function (Gaussian function, an inverse quadratic function or an inverse linear function). In case of a linear quadratic function, the best results of more than 80% correct classified disparities could be achieved.

6. Conclusion and future work

The silicon retina is a new type of image sensor which opens up a new kind of sensor field next to conventional monochrome/color sensors and emulates, in terms of principle of operation,

the human eye better than the other sensors. This new type of sensor used in a stereo setup can be used for extracting depth information.
To do this, the correspondence problem has to be solved, but the silicon retina has a new data interface and therefore, novel approaches of stereo matching are needed. In a first step, the data of the silicon retina were adapted for stereo matching algorithms built for conventional image data. This method was not accurate enough and does not use the full potential of the silicon retina technology. Due to this fact, a new algorithm approach was implemented which uses the data of the silicon retina directly without conversion and exploits the novelty of the sensor.
In this approach, the time was used as the primary matching criterion to find corresponding events from the left and right camera. The results showed that the event-based stereo matching exploits the advantages of the silicon retina in comparison to the frame-based approaches. Even so, the results of the event-based approach needs an improvement in accuracy and confidence, which means that the event-based approach has to be enhanced. For this reason, new algorithm approaches which improve, in combination with the existing algorithms, the results of the stereo matching are implemented, or novel new algorithm approaches will be designed which achieve better results and significantly better accuracy.
The algorithm improvements may increase the accuracy and quality of the results, but for extensive algorithmic calculations also an adequate hardware performance is necessary. Therefore, new ways of hardware implementations are considered which can handle the amount of data and process the results in real-time. After the implementation of algorithms into a PC-based solution and migration to a optimized DSP-multicore solution, the event-based matching approach will be integrated into a FPGA, expecting not only a reduction of the latency and an improvement of the throughput of the system, but also an enhancement of the scalability and the overall energy efficiency of the system. A further advantage is that a FPGA-based platform facilitates fast prototyping and a high degree of flexibility because of reconfigurability. Hence the system can easily be adapted to changes in requirements, e.g. sensor size, timing constraints and communication interfaces.

7. Acknowledgments

The research leading to these results has received funding from the European Community's Seventh Framework Program (FP7/2007-2013) under grant agreement n° ICT-216049 (ADOSE).

8. References

Banks, J., Bennamoun, M. & Corke, P. (1997). Non-parametric techniques for fast and robust stereo matching, *Proceedings of the IEEE Region 10th Annual Conference on Speech and Image Technologies for Computing and Telecommunications*, Brisbane/Australia, pp. 365–368.

Banks, J., Bennamoun, M., Kubik, K. & Corke, P. (1999). A constraint to improve the reliability of stereo matching using the rank transform, *Proceedings of the International Conference on Acoustics, Speech, and Signal Processing*, Phoenix/USA, pp. 3321–3324.

Belbachir, A. (2010). *Smart Cameras*, Springer New York Dordrecht Heidelberg London.

Boahen, K. (2000). Point-to-point connectivity between neuromorphic chips using address events, *In IEEE Trans. on Circuits and Systems II* 47(5): 416–433.

Bouguet, J. (2008). Camera calibration toolbox for matlab, Publised in the Internet.

Computer Vision Research Group/Department of Electrical Engineering/California Institute of Technology - www.vision.caltech.edu/bouguetj/calib_doc/index.html.

Burger, W. & Burge, M. (2005). *Digital Image Processing An Algorithmic Introduction using JAVA - First Edition*, Springer-Science/Business Media LLC.

Fawcett, T. (2004). Roc graphs : Notes and practical considerations for researchers, *Technical Report HP Labratories* .

Fawcett, T. (2006). An introduction to roc analysis, *Pattern Recognition Letters* 27(8): 861–874.

Fukushima, K., Yamaguchi, Y., Yasuda, M. & Nagata, S. (1970). An electronic model of the retina, *Proceedings of the IEEE* 58(12): 1950–1951.

Gonzales, R. & Woods, R. (2002). *Digital Image Processing - Second Edition*, Prentice Hall/Pearson Education International.

Häflinger, P. & Bergh, F. (2002). An integrated circuit computing shift in stereo pictures using time domain spike signals, *Proceedings of the Conferenece NORCHIP*, Kopenhagen/Denmark.

Lichtsteiner, P., Kramer, J. & Delbruck, T. (2004). Improved on/off temporally differetiating address-event imager, *Proceedings of the 11th IEEE International on Electronics, Circuits and Systems*, TelAviv/Israel.

Lichtsteiner, P., Posch, C. & Delbruck, T. (2006). A 128×128 120db 30mw asynchronous vision sensor that responds to relative intensity change, *Proceedings of the IEEE International Solid-State Circuits Conference*, SanFrancisco/USA.

Mahowald, M. (1992). *VLSI analogs of neuronal visual processing: a synthesis of form and function*, Phd-thesis, California Institute of Technology.

Mahowald, M. & Mead, C. (1989). Silicon retina, *Analog VLSI and Neural Systems* pp. 257–278.

Mead, C. & Mahowald, M. (1988). A silicon model of early visual processing, *Neural Networks Journal* 1(1): 91–97.

Milosevic, N., Schraml, S. & Schön, P. (2007). Smartcam for real-time stereo vision - address-event based stereo vision, *Proceedings of Image Understanding / Motion, Tracking and Stereo Vision; INSTICC Inst. f. systems and technologies of information, control and communication; INSTICC Press*, Barcelona/Spain, pp. 466–471.

Mortara, A. (1998). A pulsed communication / computation framework for analog vlsi perceptive systems, *Neuromorphic Systems Engineering* 447(3): 201–215.

Porter, R. & Bergmann, N. (1997). A generic implementation framework for fpga based stereo matching, *Proceedings of the IEEE Region 10th Annual Conference on Speech and Image Technologies for Computer and Telecommunications*, Brisbane/Australia, pp. 461–464.

Provost, F. & Fawcett, T. (2001). Robust classification for imprecise environments, *Machine Learning* 42(3): 203–231.

Schreer, O. (2005). *Stereoanalyse und Bildsynthese*, Springer Verlag Berlin Heidelberg.

Shi, J. & Tomasi, C. (1994). Good features to track, *Proceedings of the IEEE Computer Vision and Pattern Recognition Conference*, Seattle/USA, pp. 593–600.

Sivilotti, M. (1991). *Wiring consideration in analog vlsi systems with application to field programmable networks*, Phd-thesis, California Institute of Technology.

Tang, B., AitBoudaoud, D., Matuszewski, B. & Shark, L. (2006). An efficient feature based matching algorithm for stereo images, *roceedings of the IEEE Geometric Modeling and Imaging Conference*, London/UK, pp. 195–202.

World Wide Web Consortium (W3C) (1995). Vrml virtual reality modeling language, http://www.w3.org/MarkUp/VRML.

Zabih, R. & Woodfill, J. (1994). Non-parametic local transforms for computing visual correspondence, *Proceedings of the third European conference on Computer Vision*, Stockholm/Sweden, pp. 151–158.

Zhang, Z. (2002). A flexible new technique for camera calibration, *Technical Report MSRTR9-71*, Microsoft Research.

10

Stereo Measurement of Objects in Liquid and Estimation of Refractive Index of Liquid by Using Images of Water Surface

Atsushi Yamashita, Akira Fujii and Toru Kaneko
Shizuoka University
Japan

1. Introduction

In this paper, we propose a new stereo measurement method of objects in liquid whose refractive index is unknown.

In recent years, demands for underwater tasks, such as digging of ocean bottom resources, exploration of aquatic environments, rescues, and salvages, have increased. Therefore, underwater robots or underwater sensing systems that work instead of human become important, and technologies for observing underwater situations correctly and robustly from cameras of these systems are needed (Yuh, 2001). However, it is very difficult to observe underwater environments with cameras (Hulburt, 1945; Stewart, 1991; Caimi, 1996), because of the following three big problems.

1. View-disturbing noise (Fig. 1(a))
2. Light attenuation effect (Fig. 1(b))
3. Light refraction effect (Fig. 1(c))

The first problem is about suspended matters, such as bubble noises, small fishes, small creatures, and so on. They may disturb camera's field of view (Fig. 1(a)).

(a) View-disturbing noise.

(b) Light attenuation effect.

(c) Light refraction effect.

Fig. 1. Examples of aquatic images.

The second problem is about the attenuation effects of light. The light intensity decreases with the distance from objects in water by light attenuation depending on the wavelength of light. Red light decreases easier than blue light in water (Hulburt, 1945). In this way, colors of objects observed in underwater environments are different from those in air (Fig. 1(b)).

Those two problems make it very difficult to detect or to recognize objects in water by observing their textures and colors.

As to these two problems, theories or methods for aerial environments can be expanded for underwater sensing. Several image processing techniques can be effective for removing adherent noises. Color information can be also restored by considering reflection, absorption, and scattering phenomena of light in theory (Hulburt, 1945). Indeed, we have already proposed underwater sensing methods for the view-disturbing noise problem (Yamashita et al., 2006) and the light attenuation problem (Yamashita et al., 2007).

The third problem is about the refraction effects of light. If cameras and objects are in the different condition where the refraction index differs from each other, several problems occur and a precise measurement cannot be achieved.

For example, Fig. 1(c) shows an image of a duck model when water is filled to the middle. In this case, contour positions of the duck model above and below the water surface looks discontinuous and disconnected, and its size and the shape look different between above and below the water surface. This problem occurs not only when a vision sensor is set outside the liquid but also when it is set inside, because in the latter case we should usually place a protecting glass plate in front of viewing lens.

As to the light refraction problem, three-dimensional (3-D) measurement methods in aquatic environments are also proposed (Coles, 1988; Tusting & Davis, 1992; Pessel et al., 2003; Li et al., 1997; Yamashita et al., 2010). However, techniques that do not consider the influence of the refraction effects (Coles, 1988; Tusting & Davis, 1992; Pessel et al., 2003) may have the problems of accuracy.

Accurate 3-D measurement methods of objects in liquid with a laser range finder (Yamashita et al., 2003; Yamashita et al., 2004; Kondo et al., 2004; Yamashita et al., 2005) and with a light projection method (Kawai et al., 2009) by considering the refraction effects are also proposed. However, it is difficult to measure moving objects with these methods.

A stereo camera system is suitable for measuring moving objects, though the methods by using a stereo camera system (Li et al., 1997) have the problem that the corresponding points are difficult to detect when the texture of the object's surface is simple in particular when there is the refraction on the boundary between the air and the liquid. The method by the use of motion stereo images obtained with a moving camera (Saito et al., 1995) also has the problem that the relationship between the camera and the object is difficult to estimate because the camera moves. The surface shape reconstruction method of objects by using an optical flow (Murase, 1992) is not suitable for the accurate measurement, too.

By using properly calibrated stereo systems, underwater measurements can be achieved without knowing the refraction index of the liquid. For example, we can make a calibration table of relations between distances and pixel positions in advance and utilize this table for 3-D measurement (Kondo et al., 2004). However, the calibration table is useless when the refractive index of liquid changes.

Therefore, the most critical problem in aquatic environments is that previous studies cannot execute the 3-D measurement without the information of the refractive index of liquid (Li et al., 1997; Yamashita et al., 2006). It becomes difficult to measure precise positions and shapes of objects when unknown liquid exists because of the image distortion by the light refraction.

Accordingly, it is very important to estimate the refractive index for underwater sensing tasks.

In this paper, we propose a new 3-D measurement method of objects in unknown liquid with a stereo vision system. The refractive index of unknown liquid is estimated by using images of water surface (Fig. 2). Discontinuous and disconnected edges of the object in the image of the water surface can be utilized for estimating the refractive index. A 3-D shape of the object in liquid is measured by using the estimated refractive index in consideration of refractive effects. In addition, images that are free from refractive effects of the light are restored from distorted images.

Our proposed method is easy to apply to underwater robots. If there is no information about refractive index of work space of an underwater robot, the robot can know the refractive index and then measure underwater objects only by broaching and acquiring an image of water surface.

The composition of this paper is detailed below. In Section 2, an estimation method of the refractive index is explained. In Sections 3 and 4 describe a 3-D measurement and image restoration method that are based on the ray tracing technique, respectively. Sections 5 and 6 mention about experiments and discussion. Section 7 describes conclusions.

2. Estimation of refractive index

There is the influence of the light refraction in liquid below the water surface, while there is no influence above the water surface. An image below the water surface is distorted in consequence of the light refraction effect in liquid, and that above the water surface is not distorted (Fig. 2). Therefore, such discontinuous contour indicates the refraction information. We utilize the difference between edges in air and those in liquid to estimate the refractive index of the liquid.

Figure 3 shows the top view of the situation around the water surface region when the left edge of the object is observed from the right camera.

Here, let u_1 be a horizontal distance in image coordinate between image center and the object edge in air, and u_2 be that in liquid. Note that u_1 is influenced only by the refraction effect in glass (i.e. camera protection glass), and u_2 is influenced by the refraction effects both in glass and in liquid (Lower figure in Fig. 3).

Angles of incidence from air to glass in these situations (θ_1 and θ_4) are expressed as follows:

$$\theta_1 = \phi + \tan^{-1}\frac{u_2}{f} \tag{1}$$

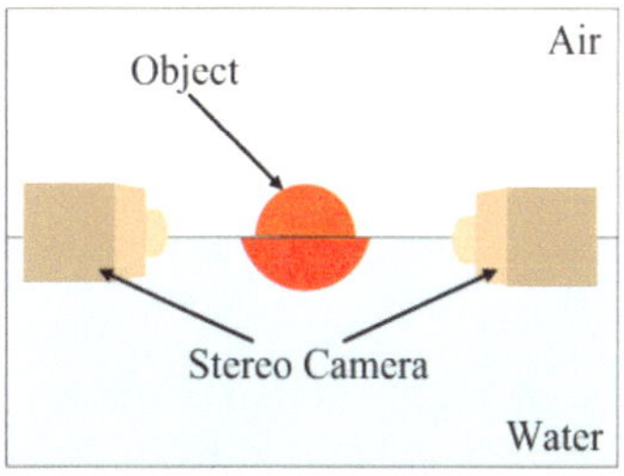

Fig. 2. Stereo measurement of objects in liquid by using images of water surface. An image below the water surface is distorted in consequence of the light refraction effect in liquid, and that above the water surface is not distorted.

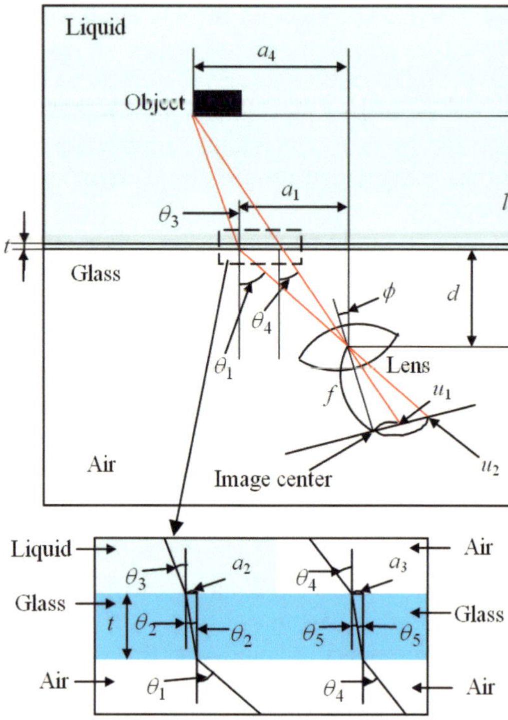

Fig. 3. Estimation of refractive index.

$$\theta_4 = \phi + \tan^{-1}\frac{u_1}{f} \tag{2}$$

where ϕ is the angle between the optical axis of the camera and the normal vector of the glass, and f is the image distance (the distance between the lens center and the image plane), respectively.

Parameters f and ϕ can be calibrated easily in advance of the measurement, and coordinate values u_1 and u_2 can be obtained from the acquired image of the water surface. Therefore, we can calculate θ_1 and θ_4 from these known parameters.

By using Snell's law of refraction, angles of refraction (θ_2 and θ_5) are expressed as follows:

$$\frac{n_1}{n_2} = \frac{\sin\theta_2}{\sin\theta_1} \tag{3}$$

$$\frac{n_1}{n_2} = \frac{\sin\theta_5}{\sin\theta_4} \tag{4}$$

where n_1 is the refractive index of air, and n_2 is that of glass, respectively.

On the other hand, we can obtain a_1, a_2, a_3, and a_4 from the geometrical relationship among the lens, the glass, and the object.

$$a_1 = d\tan\theta_1 \tag{5}$$

$$a_2 = t \tan \theta_2 \tag{6}$$

$$a_3 = t \tan \theta_5 \tag{7}$$

$$a_4 = (l - t) \tan \theta_4 + a_3 \tag{8}$$

where d is the distance between the lens center and the glass surface, t is the thickness of the glass, and l is the distance between the lens center and the object.
Refractive indices n_1 and n_2 can be calibrated beforehand because they are fixed parameters. Parameters d and t can be calibrated in advance of the measurement, too. This is because we usually placed a protecting glass in front of the lens when we use a camera in liquid, and the relationship between the glass and the lens never changes. Parameter l can be gained from the stereo measurement result of the edge in air.
By using these parameters, angle of refraction from glass to liquid θ_3 can be calculated as follow:

$$\theta_3 = \tan^{-1} \frac{a_4 - a_2 - a_1}{l - t - d} \tag{9}$$

Consequently, refractive index of liquid n_3 can be obtained by using Snell's law.

$$n_3 = n_1 \frac{\sin \theta_1}{\sin \theta_3} \tag{10}$$

In this way, we can estimate refractive index of unknown liquid n_3 from the image of water surface, and measure objects in liquid by using n_3.

3. 3-D measurement

It is necessary to search for corresponding points from right and left images to measure the object by using the stereo vision system. In our method, corresponding points are searched for with template matching by using the normalized cross correlation (NCC) method.
After detecting corresponding points, an accurate 3-D measurement can be executed by considering the refraction effects of light in aquatic environments.
Refractive angles at the boundary surfaces among air, glass and liquid can be determined by using Snell's law (Fig. 4).
We assume the refractive index of air and the glass to be n_1 and n_2, respectively, and the incidence angle from air to the glass to be θ_1. A unit ray vector $\vec{d_2} = (\alpha_2, \beta_2, \gamma_2)^T$ (T denotes transposition) travelling in the glass is shown by (11).

$$\begin{pmatrix} \alpha_2 \\ \beta_2 \\ \gamma_2 \end{pmatrix} = \frac{n_1}{n_2} \begin{pmatrix} \alpha_1 \\ \beta_1 \\ \gamma_1 \end{pmatrix} + \left(\sqrt{1 - \frac{n_1^2}{n_2^2} \sin^2 \theta_1} - \frac{n_1}{n_2} \cos \theta_1 \right) \begin{pmatrix} \lambda \\ \mu \\ \nu \end{pmatrix} \tag{11}$$

where $\vec{d_1} = (\alpha_1, \beta_1, \gamma_1)^T$ is the unit ray vector of the camera in air and $\vec{N} = (\lambda, \mu, \nu)^T$ is a normal vector of the glass plane. Vector $\vec{d_1}$ can be easily calculated from the coordinate value of the corresponding point, and vector $\vec{N}$ can be calibrated in advance of the measurement as described above.

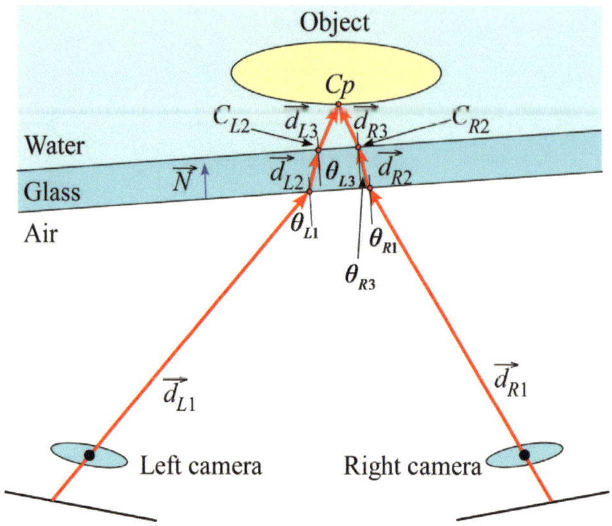

Fig. 4. 3-D measurement.

A unit ray vector $\vec{d}_3 = (\alpha_3, \beta_3, \gamma_3)^T$ travelling in liquid is shown by (12).

$$\begin{pmatrix} \alpha_3 \\ \beta_3 \\ \gamma_3 \end{pmatrix} = \frac{n_2}{n_3} \begin{pmatrix} \alpha_2 \\ \beta_2 \\ \gamma_2 \end{pmatrix} + \left(\sqrt{1 - \frac{n_2^2}{n_3^2} \sin^2 \theta_3} - \frac{n_2}{n_3} \cos \theta_3 \right) \begin{pmatrix} \lambda \\ \mu \\ \nu \end{pmatrix} \tag{12}$$

where n_3 is the refractive index of liquid that is estimated in Section 2, and θ_3 is the angle of incidence from the glass to liquid, respectively.

An arbitrary point $\vec{C}_p = (x_p, y_p, z_p)^T$ on the ray vector is shown by (13).

$$\begin{pmatrix} x_p \\ y_p \\ z_p \end{pmatrix} = c \begin{pmatrix} \alpha_3 \\ \beta_3 \\ \gamma_3 \end{pmatrix} + \begin{pmatrix} x_2 \\ y_2 \\ z_2 \end{pmatrix} \tag{13}$$

where $\vec{C}_2 = (x_2, y_2, z_2)^T$ is the point on the glass and c is a constant.

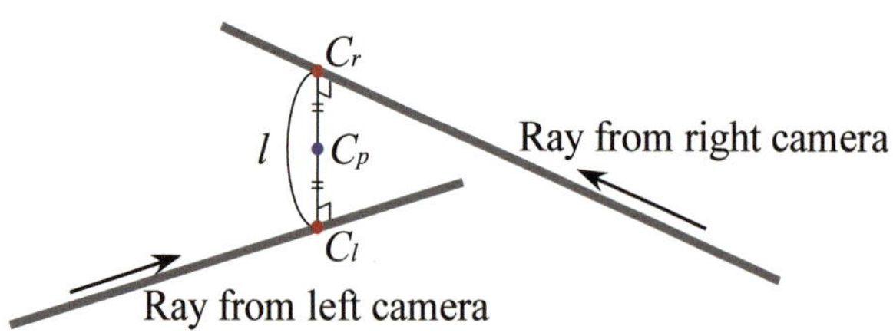

Fig. 5. Ray tracing from two cameras.

Two rays are calculated by ray tracing from the left and the right cameras, and the intersection of the two rays gives the 3-D coordinates of the target point in liquid. Theoretically, the two rays intersect at one point on the object surface, however, practically it is not always true

because of noises and quantization artifacts. Consequently, we select the midpoint of the shortest line connecting two points each of which belongs to each ray (Fig. 5).
Note that the detail of the solution is explained in (Yamashita et al., 2003).

4. Image restoration

Images that are free from the refraction effects can be generated from distorted images by using 3-D information acquired in Section 3.
Figure 6 shows the top view of the situation around the water surface region. Here, let e_2 be the image coordinate value that is influenced by the refraction effect in liquid, and e_1 be the image coordinate value that is rectified (in other word, free from the refraction effect of liquid). The purpose is to reconstruct a new image by obtaining e_1 from the observed value e_2.
In Fig. 6, the image distance (f), the angle between the optical axis of the camera and the normal vector of the glass (ϕ), the distance between the lens center and the glass (d), the thickness of the glass (t), the distance between the image center and e_2 (g_{2x}), and the distance between the lens and the object (z_i) is known parameters.
We can restore the image if g_{1x} (the distance between the image center and e_1) is obtained.
At first, angle of incidence θ_{1x} is expressed as follows:

$$\theta_{1x} = \phi + \tan^{-1}\frac{g_{2x}}{f} \tag{14}$$

Angle of refraction from air to glass θ_{2x} and that from glass to liquid θ_{3x} is obtained by using Snell's law.

$$\theta_{2x} = \sin^{-1}\frac{n_1 \sin\theta_{1x}}{n_2} \tag{15}$$

$$\theta_{3x} = \sin^{-1}\frac{n_1 \sin\theta_{1x}}{n_3} \tag{16}$$

On the other hand, parameters a_{1x}, a_{2x}, and a_{3x} are obtained from the geometrical relationship in Fig. 6.

$$a_{1x} = d\tan\theta_{1x} \tag{17}$$

$$a_{2x} = t\tan\theta_{2x} \tag{18}$$

$$a_{3x} = (z_i - t - d)\tan\theta_{3x} + a_{1x} + a_{2x} \tag{19}$$

At the same time, a_{3x} can be expressed as follows:

$$a_{3x} = (z_i - t)\tan\theta_{4x} + t\tan\theta_{5x} \tag{20}$$

Finally, we can obtain the following equation.

$$a_{3x} = (z_i - t)\tan\theta_{4x} + t\tan\left(\sin^{-1}\frac{n_1 \sin\theta_{4x}}{n_2}\right) \tag{21}$$

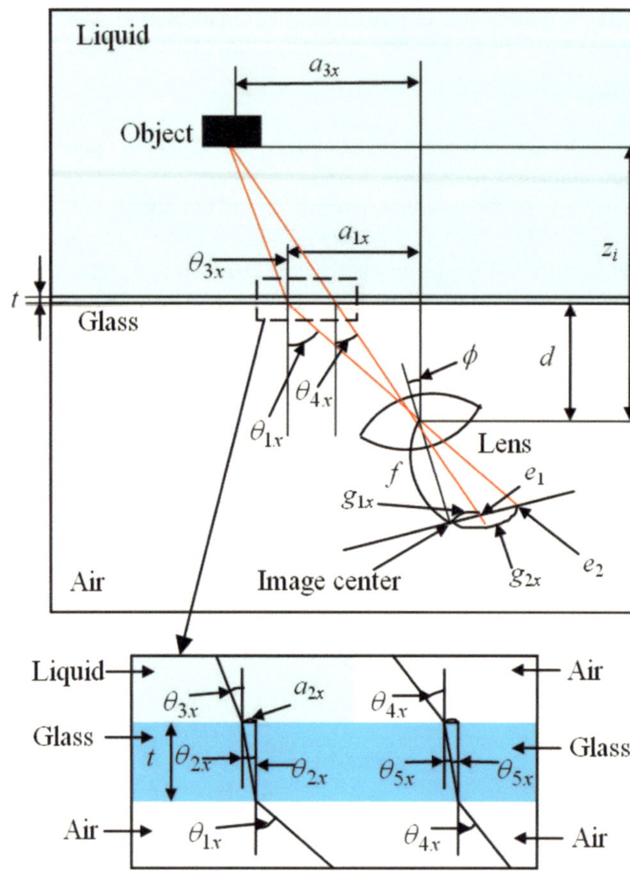

Fig. 6. Image restoration.

From (21), we can calculate θ_{4x} by numerical way. Therefore, parameter g_{1x} is gained by using obtained θ_{4x} and f.

$$g_{1x} = f \tan \theta_{4x} \tag{22}$$

By using g_{1x}, the image that is free from the refraction effect can be restored.
The vertical coordinate value after the restoration is also calculated in the same way. In this way, the image restoration is executed.
However, there may be no texture information around or on the water surface because a dark line appears on the water surface in images.
Therefore, textures of these regions are interpolated by image inpainting algorithm (Bertalmio et al., 2000). This method can correct the noise of an image in consideration of slopes of image intensities, and the merit of this algorithm is the fine reproducibility for edges.
Finally, we can obtain the restored image both below and around the water surface.

5. Experiment

We constructed an underwater environment by using a water tank (Fig. 7). It is an equivalent optical system to sinking the waterproof camera in underwater. We used two digital video cameras for taking images whose sizes are 720x480pixels. We set the optical axis parallel to the plane of the water surface.

In the experiment, the geometrical relationship between two cameras and the glass, the thickness of the glass, and intrinsic camera parameters (Tsai, 1987) were calibrated before the 3-D measurement in air. These parameters never change regardless of whether there is water or not.

To evaluate the validity of the proposed method, two objects are measured in liquid whose refractive index is unknown. Object 1 is a duck model and Object 2 is a cube.

Object 1 (duck model) floated on the water surface, and Object 2 (cube) was put inside the liquid (Fig. 7).

Figures 8(a) and (b) show acquired left and right images of the water surface, respectively.

At first, the refractive index of unknown liquid (n_3) is estimated from four edge positions inside red circles. Table 1 shows the result of estimation. The variation of the results is small enough to trust, and the average of four results is 1.333, while the ground truth is 1.33 because we used water as unknown liquid.

From this result, it is verified that our method can estimate the refractive index precisely.

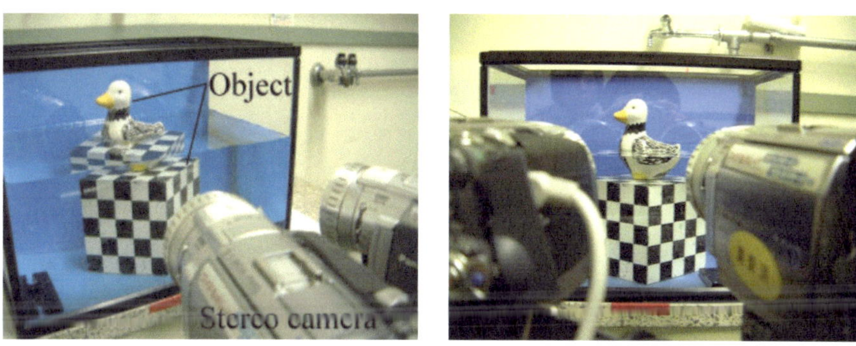

(a) Birds-eye view. (b) Front view.

Fig. 7. Overview of experiments.

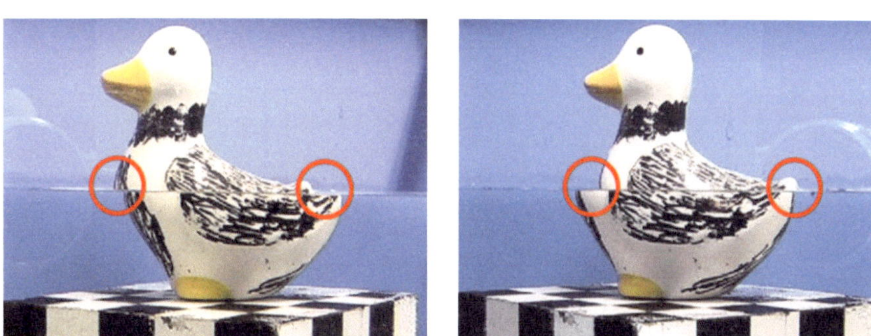

(a) Left image. (b) Right image.

Fig. 8. Stereo image pair.

Left camera		Right camera		Average
Left edge	Right edge	Left edge	Right edge	
1.363	1.335	1.334	1.300	1.333

Table 1. Estimation result of refractive index.

Figure 9 shows the 3-D shape measurement result of Object 1. Figure 9(a) shows the result without consideration of light refraction effect. There is the disconnection of 3-D shape between above and below the water surface. Figure 9(b) shows the result by our method. Continuous shape can be acquired, although the acquired images have discontinuous contours (Fig. 8).

By using the estimated refractive index, the shape of Object 2 (cube) was measured quantitatively. When the refractive index was unknown (n_3 = 1.000) and the refraction effect was not considered, the vertex angle was measured as 111.1deg, while the ground truth was 90.0deg. On the other hand, the result was 90.9deg when the refraction effect was considered by using the estimated refractive index.

From these results, it is verified that our method can measure accurate shape of underwater objects.

Figure 10 shows the result of the image restoration. Figure 10(a) shows the original image, Fig. 10(b) shows extracted result of the object by using color extraction method (Smith et al., 1996), and Fig. 10(c) shows the restoration result, respectively.

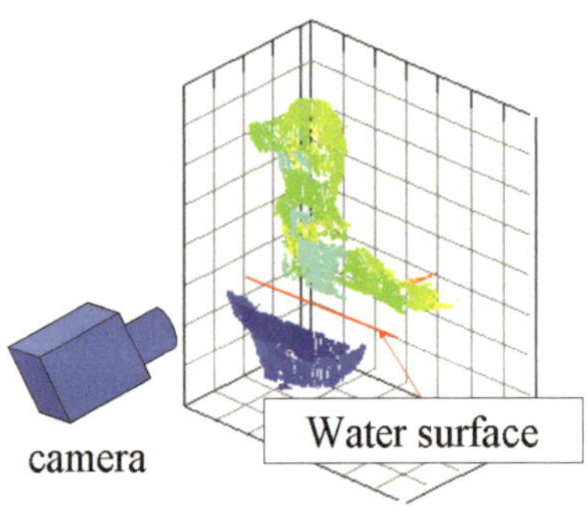

(a) Without consideration.

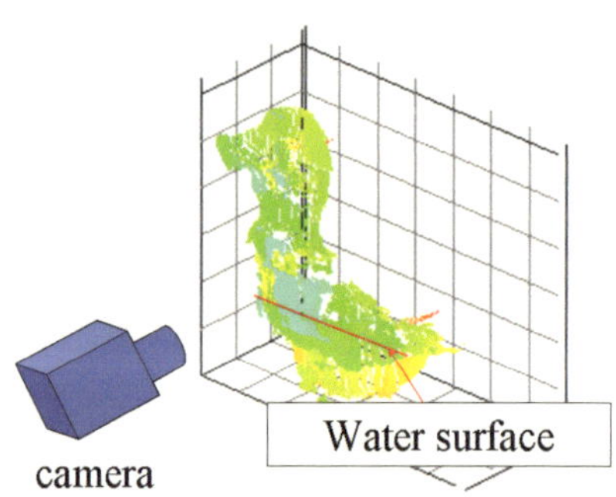

(b) With consideration.

Fig. 9. 3-D measurement results.

(a) Original image.

(b) Extraction result.

(c) Image restoration result.

Fig. 10. Image restoration results.

These results show that our method can work well without failure regardless of the existence of unknown liquid by estimating the refractive index of liquid and considering the light refraction.

6. Discussion

As to the estimation of the refractive index, the error of the estimation is within 1% through all experiments.

The accuracy and the stability is very high, however, the proposed method needs image pairs of the water surface. Therefore, this method may not be applicable directly for deep water applications, because the refractive index changes little by little when water pressure and temperature change. On the other hand, we can use the distance between two rays (l in Fig. 5) for the estimation when water surface images are difficult to obtain. The value of the refractive index in case that the distance between two rays becomes the smallest is a correct one. Therefore, the refractive index n_{est} can be estimated by using following optimization.

$$n_{est} = \arg\min_{n} \sum_{i} l_i(n) \tag{23}$$

where $l_i(n)$ is the calculated distance between two rays at i-th measurement point when the refractive index is presumed as n. However, this method is not robust because it is very sensitive to an initial value of the estimation. Therefore, it is better to use both two approaches for deep water applications; at first in shallow water the refractive index is estimated by using water surface images, then in deep water by using the distance between two rays.

As to the refraction effects, they may be reduced by using an individual spherical protective dome for each camera. However, it is impossible to eliminate the refraction effects. Therefore, our method is essential to the precise measurement in underwater environments.

As to the image restoration, near the water surface appears an area without information in form of a black strip. We cannot have information about this area. Therefore, textures of these regions are interpolated for visibility. Note that 3-D measurement explained in Section 3 can be achieved without the image restoration. Therefore, 3-D measurement results do not include interpolated results. This means that the proposed method shows both reliable results that is suitable for underwater recognition and images that have good visibility for the sake of human operators.

	With consideration	Without consideration
Average	2.0mm	36.1mm
Standard deviation	0.4mm	1.1mm

Table 2. Accuracy of measurement (position error).

To evaluate the proposed method quantitatively, another well-calibrated objects whose shapes are known and whose positions were measured precisely in air in advance were measured in water. Table 2 shows the measurement result. In this experiment, mis-corresponding points were rejected by a human operator. Position error with consideration of the refraction effects is 2.0mm on an average when the distance between the stereo camera system and the object is 250mm, while the error without consideration of the refraction effects is 36.1mm. The error in the depth direction was dominant in all cases.

From these results, it is verified that our method can measure accurate positions of objects in water.

7. Conclusion

We propose a 3-D measurement method of objects in unknown liquid with a stereo vision system. We estimate refractive index of unknown liquid by using images of water surface, restore images that are free from refractive effects of the light, and measure 3-D shapes of objects in liquids in consideration of refractive effects. The effectiveness of the proposed method is verified through experiments.

It is expected that underwater robots acquire the refractive index and then measure underwater objects only by broaching and acquiring an image of water surface in the case of unknown refractive index by using our method.

8. Acknowledgement

This research was in part supported by MEXT KAKENHI, Grant-in-Aid for Young Scientist (A), 22680017.

9. References

Yuh, J. & West, M. (2001). Underwater Robotics, *Advanced Robotics*, Vol.15, No.5, pp.609-639

Hulburt, E. O. (1945). Optics of Distilled and Natural Water, *Journal of the Optical Society of America*, Vol.35, pp.689-705

Stewart, W. K. (1991). Remote-Sensing Issues for Intelligent Underwater Systems, *Proceedings of the 1991 IEEE Computer Society Conference on Computer Vision and Pattern Recognition (CVPR1991)*, pp.230-235

Caimi, F. M. (1996). Selected Papers on Underwater Optics, *SIPE Milestone Series*, Caimi, F. M. (Ed.), Vol.MS118

Yamashita, A.; Kato, S. & Kaneko, T. (2006). Robust Sensing against Bubble Noises in Aquatic Environments with a Stereo Vision System, *Proceedings of the 2006 IEEE International Conference on Robotics and Automation (ICRA2006)*, pp. 928-933

Yamashita, A.; Fujii, M. & Kaneko, T. (2007). Color Registration of Underwater Images for Underwater Sensing with Consideration of Light Attenuation, *Proceedings of the 2007 IEEE International Conference on Robotics and Automation (ICRA2007)*, pp.4570-4575

Coles, B. W. (1988). Recent Developments in Underwater Laser Scanning Systems, *SPIE Vol.980 Underwater Imaging*, pp.42-52

Tusting, R. F. & Davis, D. L. (1992). Laser Systems and Structured Illumination for Quantitative Undersea Imaging, *Marine Technology Society Journal*, Vol.26, No.4, pp.5-12

Pessel, N.; Opderbecke, J. & Aldon, M.-J. (2003). Camera Self-Calibration in Underwater Environment, *Proceedings of the 11th International Conference in Central Europe on Computer Graphics, Visualization and Computer Vision (WSCG2003)*, pp.104-110

Li, R.; Li, H.; Zou, W.; Smith, R. G. & Curran, T. A. (1997). Quantitive Photogrammetric Analysis of Digital Underwater Video Imagery, *IEEE Journal of Oceanic Engineering*, Vol.22, No.2, pp.364-375

Yamashita, A.; Shirane, Y. & Kaneko, T. (2010). Monocular Underwater Stereo - 3D Measurement Using Difference of Appearance Depending on Optical Paths -, *Proceedings of the 2010 IEEE/RSJ International Conference on Intelligent Robots and Systems (IROS2010)*

Yamashita, A.; Hayashimoto, E.; Kaneko, T. & Kawata, Y. (2003). 3-D Measurement of Objects in a Cylindrical Glass Water Tank with a Laser Range Finder, *Proceedings of the 2003 IEEE/RSJ International Conference on Intelligent Robots and Systems (IROS2003)*, pp.1578-1583

Yamashita, A.; Higuchi, H.; Kaneko, T. & Kawata, Y. (2004). Three Dimensional Measurement of Object's Surface in Water Using the Light Stripe Projection Method, *Proceedings of the 2004 IEEE International Conference on Robotics and Automation} (ICRA2004)*, pp.2736-2741

Kondo, H.; Maki, T.; Ura, T.; Nose, Y.; Sakamaki, T. & Inaishi, M. (2004). Relative Navigation of an Autonomous Underwater Vehicle Using a Light-Section Profiling System, *Proceedings of the 2004 IEEE/RSJ International Conference on Intelligent Robots and Systems (IROS2004)*, pp.1103-1108

Yamashita, A.; Ikeda, S. & Kaneko, T. (2005). 3-D Measurement of Objects in Unknown Aquatic Environments with a Laser Range Finder, *Proceedings of the 2005 IEEE International Conference on Robotics and Automation (ICRA2005)*, pp. 3923-3928

Kawai, R.; Yamashita, A. & Kaneko, T. (2009). Three-Dimensional Measurement of Objects in Water by Using Space Encoding Method, *Proceedings of the 2009 IEEE International Conference on Robotics and Automation (ICRA2009)*, pp.2830-2835

Saito, H.; Kawamura, H. & Nakajima, M. (1995). 3D Shape Measurement of Underwater Objects Using Motion Stereo, *Proceedings of 21th International Conference on Industrial Electronics, Control, and Instrumentation*, pp.1231-1235

Murase, H. (1992). Surface Shape Reconstruction of a Nonrigid Transparent Object Using Refraction and Motion, *IEEE Transactions on Pattern Analysis and Machine Intelligence*, Vol.14, No.10, pp.1045-1052

Bertalmio, M.; Sapiro, G.; Caselles, V. & Ballester, C. (2000). Image Inpainting, *ACM Transactions on Computer Graphics (Proceedings of SIGGRAPH2000)*, pp.417-424

Tsai, R. Y. (1987). A Versatile Camera Calibration Technique for High-Accuracy 3D Machine Vision Metrology Using Off-the-Shelf TV Cameras and Lenses, *IEEE Journal of Robotics and Automation*, Vol.RA-3, No.4, pp.323-344

Smith, A. R. & Blinn, J. F. (1996). Blue Screen Matting, *ACM Transactions on Computer Graphics (Proceedings of SIGGRAPH1996)*, pp.259-268

11

Detecting Human Activity by Location System and Stereo Vision

Yoshifumi Nishida, Koji Kitamura
National Institute of Advanced Industrial Science and Technology
Japan

1. Introduction

Information processing services centered around human activity in the real world has attracted increased attention recently (1). Human-centered applications require the facility to observe and recognize activities as a basis, and the present paper describes a method for quickly realizing a function for robustly detecting daily human activity events in the real world.

Generally, the problem of human activity recognition can be formulated as a kind of pattern recognition problem as follows.

$$P(\hat{W}|Y) = \max_{W_i} \frac{P(Y|W_i)P(W_i)}{P(Y)}, \tag{1}$$

where $P(W_i|Y)$ denotes the posterior probability that the meaning of an observed behavior pattern Y is W_i, $P(Y)$ denotes the probability that a behavior pattern Y will be observed, $P(W_i)$ denotes the probability that the behavior meaning W_i will occur, and $P(Y|W_i)$ denotes the conditional probability. Thus, the problem of human activity recognition becomes that of searching for the maximum posterior probability $P(\hat{W}|Y)$.

There are three problems in realizing and utilizing a function for recognizing human activity in the real world: the robust observation of a activity pattern Y, the efficient recognition of meaning W from the observed pattern, and quick implementation of a function for robustly observing and efficiently recognizing human activity. Without solving the first problem, equation (1) cannot be formed. Without tackling the second problem, guaranteeing a solution to the equation within the time frame demanded by the application is impossible. Without dealing with the third problem, it is difficult to utilize a funtion for observing and recognizing human activity for a basis of a real world application or various field researches.

As a method for efficient recognition of activites, the idea of object-based activity recognition has been proposed (2). In theory, the behavior of handling objects in an environment such as an office or home can be recognized based on the motion of the objects. However, when applying the method to real environments, it is difficult to even achieve an adequate level of object recognition, which is the basis of the method.

Separating the problems of object recognition and activity recognition is becoming increasingly realistic with the progress in pervasive computing technology such as microcomputers, sensor, and wireless networks technology. It has now become possible to resolve object recognition into the problems of sensorizing objects and tagging the objects with identification codes (IDs), and to address activity recognition separately through the development of applied technology.

The present authors have developed a three-dimensional ultrasonic location and tagging system for the fundamental function of robustly tracking objects(3). This system enables a new approach of tag-based activity recognition. In terms of cost and robustness against environmental noise, the ultrasonic system is superior to other location techniques such as visual, tactile, and magnetic systems. Several types of ultrasonic location systems have been proposed. The Bat Ultrasonic Location System (4; 5; 6; 7) developed by AT&T, and the MIT Cricket Indoor Location System (8) are well known. Although a calibration method using a robot (9) has been proposed, the required calibration device is too large for use in a number of environments. An auto calibration method was considered in the DOLPHIN system (10), which can calibrate the positions of receivers/transmitters using a small number of reference receivers/transmitters having known positions. However, the system has only been tested in narrow areas having dimensions of approximately 2.5 m $\times$ 2 m. Bristol University proposed another auto calibration method, in which the positions of n transmitters and m receivers can be calculated given n$\times$m distance data among the transmitters and receivers and that the condition, $3(n+m)-6 < n \cdot m$, is satisfied(11). However, the scalability of this method is limited. In contrast, the present study proposes and examines a new calibration method, "global calibration based on local calibration," that requires a relatively small number of transmitters and is independent of room size. Using the proposed method, the calibration problem becomes a similar to a fitting problem in object modeling with multiple range images(12; 13) after local calibration. The present paper describes the method for global calibration based on local calibration and the constraints that are used in conjunction with the method for reducing the error of the calibrated receiver positions.

This paper focuses on a system for quickly realizing a function for robustly detecting daily human activity events in handling objects in the real world. This paper deals with a method for robustly measuring 3D positions of the objects handled by a person, a quick calibrating method for constructing a measuring system for 3D positions of the objects, and a quick registering method for target activity events. The next section describes the system for quick realization of the function for detecting human activity events. Section 3 shows algorithms for robustly measuring 3D positions of the objects handled by a person, and evaluates the algorithms. Section 4 describes a quick calibrating method, and Section 5 describes quick registration of human activity by a stereoscopic camera with ultrasonic 3D tags and interactive software for registering human activity events.

2. Quick realization of function for detecting human activity events

This section describes a system for quickly realizing a function for robustly observing and efficiently recognizing daily human activities.

2.1 System for quick realization for function of detecting human activity events

The configuration of the proposed system is shown in Fig. 1. The system consists of an ultrasonic 3D tag system, a calibrating device, a stereoscopic camera with ultrasonic 3D tags, and a host computer. The system has three functions: 1) robustly measuring 3D positions of the objects (Fig. 1(A)), 2) quickly calibrating a system for measuring 3D positions of the objects (Fig. 1(B)), 3) quickly registering target activity events (Fig. 1(C)), and 4) robustly detecting the registered events in real time (Fig. 1(D)).

As for 1), the system realizes robust measurement of 3D positions of the objects using an ultrasonic 3D tag system and robust estimation algorithm known as random sample consensus (RANSAC). As for 2), the system realizes quick calibration by a calibrating device having three or more ultrasonic transmitters. Quick calibration enables the system to be portable. As for 3), quick registration of target activity events is realized by a stereoscopic camera with ultrasonic 3D tags and interactive software for creating 3D shape model, creating virtual sensors based on the 3D shape model, and associating the virtual sensors with the target events.

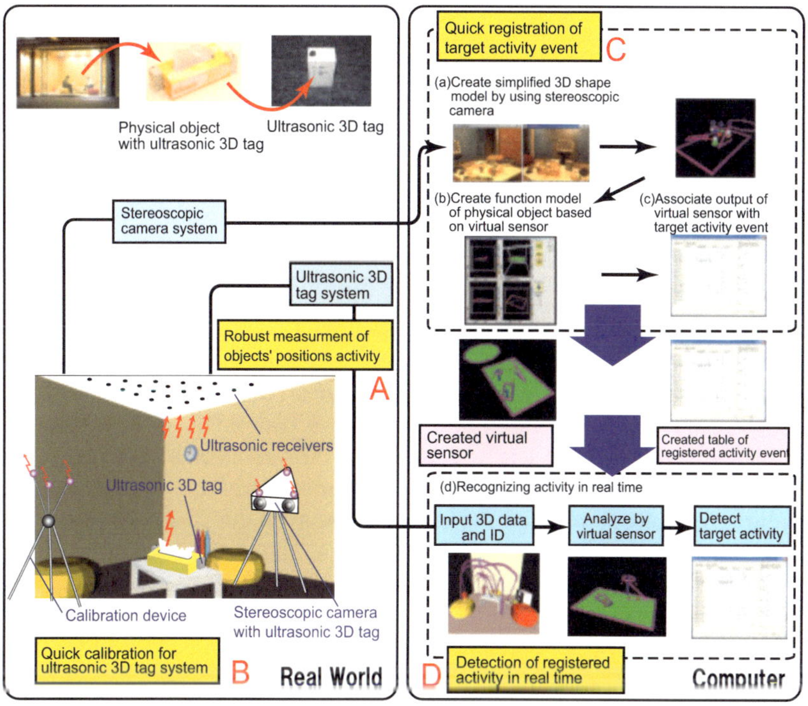

Fig. 1. Configuration of system for quick realization for function for detecting human activity events

2.2 Steps for quick realization for function of detecting human activity events

1. Install ultrasonic receivers in a target environment.
2. Calculate 3D positions of installed ultrasonic receivers using a calibration device. The details of a calibration method and a calibrating system are described in Section 4.
3. Register target activity events using a stereoscopic camera with ultrasonic 3D tags and interactive software. The details are described in Section 5.
4. Detect the registered target events using the ultrasonic 3D tags and the created virtual sensors.

2.3 Advantage of proposed system

Advantages of the proposed system are following points.

- **Utilization of user's knowledge** Since users know target activity to be detected, the system can make full use of knowledge of users familiar with target area by interactively registering target events.
- **Efficient processing** It is possible to create the minimum system by determining the number of ultrasonic receivers and the number of target events depending on the place where the users want to install and the activity events which the users want to target.
- **Inexpensive system** It is possible to utilize inexpensive sensors such as the ultrasonic 3D tag system (about $45 for a sensor and $200 for a tag), and the stereoscopic camera (about $200 in our system) to create the proposed system.
- **Robust system** It is easy to increase the number of ultrasonic receivers for robust estimation because they are inexpensive sensors. The details of an algorithm for robust estimation are described in Section 3.
- **Easy to improve** The function for quickly registration of target events enables to improve the constructed system by trial and error.

3. Robust observation of human activity in handling objects

3.1 System configuration of ultrasonic 3D tag system

Figure 2 shows the system configuration for the ultrasonic 3D tag system. The system consists of an ultrasonic receiving section, an ultrasonic transmitting section, a time-of-flight measuring section, a network section, and a personal computer. The ultrasonic receiving section receives ultrasonic pulses emitted from the ultrasonic transmitter and amplifies the received signal. The time-of-flight measuring section records the travel time of the signal from transmission to reception. The network section synchronizes the system and collects time-of-flight data from the ultrasonic receiving section. The positions of objects are calculated based on more than three time-of-flight results. The sampling frequency of the proposed system is 50 Hz.

The ultrasonic tag system calculates the 3D position of an object by trilateration using three distance measurements. Two methods of multilateration are investigated for use with the proposed system: multilateration based on a least-squares method using redundant distance data, and multilateration based on robust estimation.

The room used to conduct the experiments is shown in Fig. 3. The room was 3.5 × 3.5 × 2.7 m in size, and was fitted with 307 ultrasonic receivers embedded in the wall and ceiling. Tags were attached to various objects, including a cup and a stapler as shown in and Fig. refsensor-room. Some objects were fitted with two transmitters. The purpose of the experimental room is to clarify the effect of the use of redundant sensors. More than 300 receivers do not mean that the algorithms described in the next section need such a large number of sensors. In actual usage, a smaller number of receivers can be used.

3.2 Multilateration method 1: linearization of the minimization problem

The receiver position (x,y,z) is calculated by a multilateration algorithm, such as that used in the Global Positioning System(14). Trilateration or multilateration algorithms have been proposed in the field of aerospace(15; 16). This paper presents the multilateration algorithms applicable to a more general case that multiple ultrasonic receivers are put on arbitrary positions. Using distance data l_i, l_j and the receiver positions $(x_i, y_i, z_i), (x_j, y_j, z_j)$, we obtain the following spherical equations for the possible position of the target.

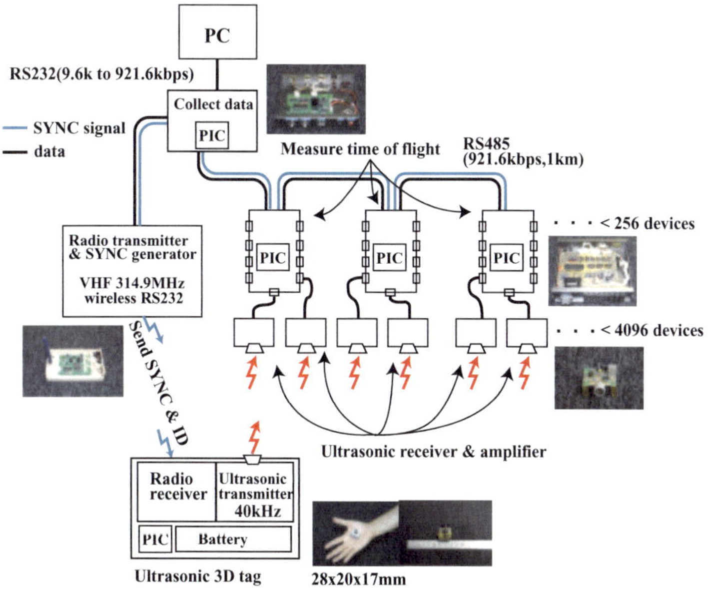

Fig. 2. System configuration of ultrasonic 3D tag system

$$(x_i - x)^2 + (y_i - y)^2 + (z_i - z)^2 = l_i^2, \tag{2}$$

$$(x_j - x)^2 + (y_j - y)^2 + (z_j - z)^2 = l_j^2. \tag{3}$$

By subtracting Eq. (3) from Eq. (2), we obtain an equation for intersecting planes between the spheres, as shown in Fig. 5.

$$2(x_j - x_i)x + 2(y_j - y_i)y + 2(z_j - z_i)z = l_i^2 - l_j^2 - x_i^2 - y_i^2 - z_i^2 + x_j^2 + y_j^2 + z_j^2 \tag{4}$$

By inputting pairs of (i, j) into the above equation, we obtain simultaneous linear equations, as expressed by

$$\mathbf{AP} = \mathbf{B}, \tag{5}$$

$$\text{where} \quad \mathbf{P} = \begin{pmatrix} x \\ y \\ z \end{pmatrix}, \tag{6}$$

$$\mathbf{A} = \begin{pmatrix} 2(x_0 - x_1) & 2(y_0 - y_1) & 2(z_0 - z_1) \\ 2(x_0 - x_2) & 2(y_0 - y_2) & 2(z_0 - z_2) \\ 2(x_0 - x_3) & 2(y_0 - y_3) & 2(z_0 - z_3) \end{pmatrix}, \tag{7}$$

Fig. 3. Experimental daily living space

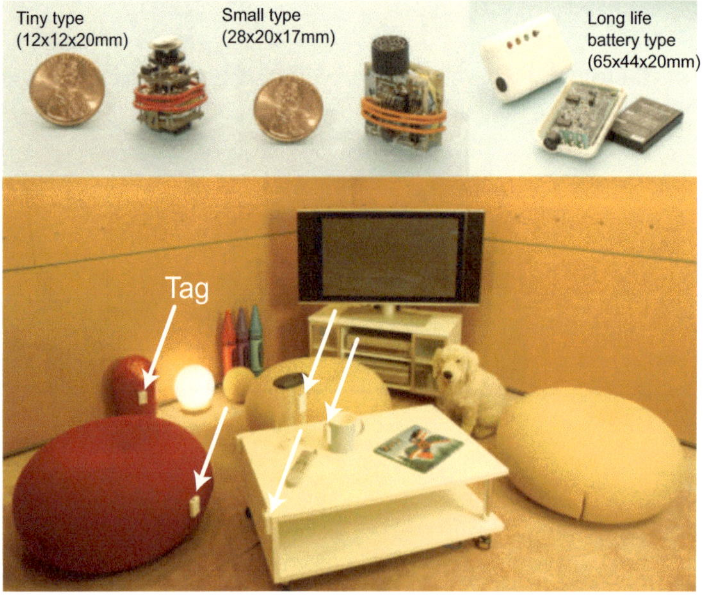

Fig. 4. Developed ultrasonic 3D tags and example of attaching tags to objects

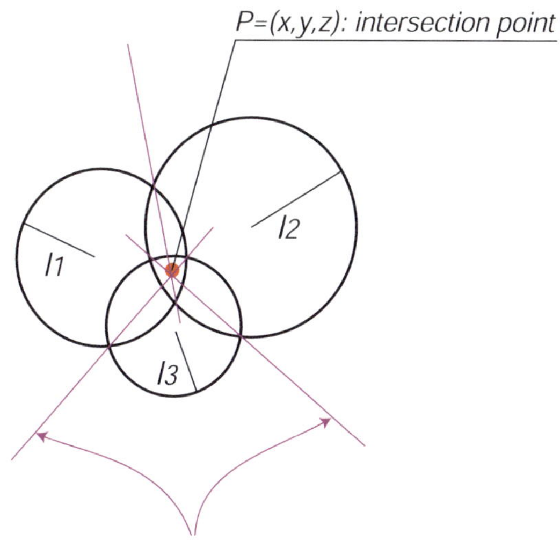

Fig. 5. Planes of intersection between spheres used to give the estimated position

$$\mathbf{B} = \begin{pmatrix} l_1^2 - l_0^2 - x_1^2 - y_1^2 - z_1^2 + x_0^2 + y_0^2 + z_0^2 \\ l_2^2 - l_0^2 - x_2^2 - y_2^2 - z_2^2 + x_0^2 + y_0^2 + z_0^2 \\ l_3^2 - l_0^2 - x_3^2 - y_3^2 - z_3^2 + x_0^2 + y_0^2 + z_0^2 \\ \vdots \end{pmatrix}. \quad (8)$$

The position $(\hat{x}, \hat{y}, \hat{z})$ can then be calculated by a least-squares method as follows.

$$\mathbf{P} = (\mathbf{A}^{\mathbf{T}}\mathbf{A})^{-1}\mathbf{A}^{\mathbf{T}}\mathbf{B}. \quad (9)$$

This method minimizes the square of the distance between the planes expressed by Eq. (4) and the estimated position. The algorithm is described in detail in Fig. 6. In actual usage, the rank of matrix **A** must be considered.

3.3 Multilateration method 2: robust estimation by RANSAC

Data sampled by the ultrasonic tagging system is easily contaminated by outliers due to reflections. Method 1 above is unable to estimate the 3D position with high accuracy if sampled data includes outliers deviating from a normal distribution. In the field of computer vision, robust estimation methods that are effective for sampled data including outliers have already been developed. In this work, the random sample consensus (RANSAC) (17; 18) estimator is adopted to eliminate the undesirable effects of outliers. The procedure is as follows.

1. Randomly select three distances measured by three receivers (jth trial).
2. Calculate the position (x_{cj}, y_{cj}, z_{cj}) by trilateration.
3. Calculate the error ε_{cji} for all receivers ($i = 0, 1, ..., n$) by Eq. (10), and find the median ε_{mj} of ε_{cji}.

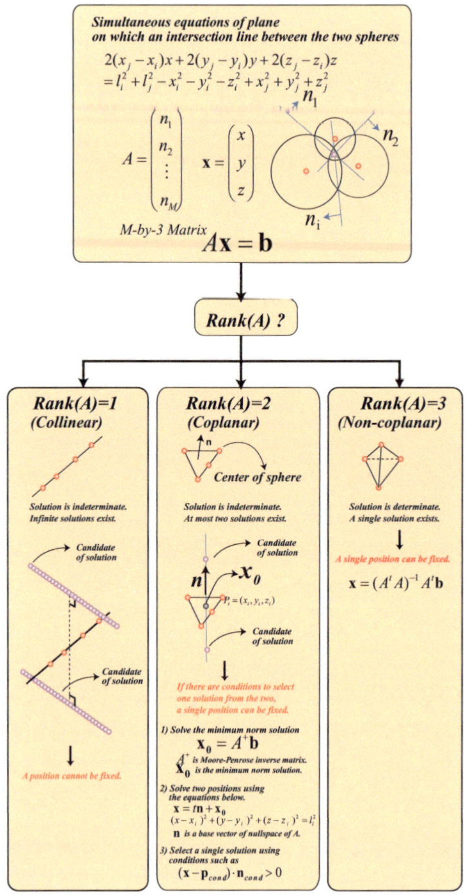

Fig. 6. Algorithm for estimating 3D position by a least-squares method considering the rank of **A**

4. Repeat steps 1 to 3 as necessary to find the combination of measurements giving the minimum error, and adopt the corresponding 3D position.

$$\varepsilon_{cji} = \left| l_i - \sqrt{(x_i - x_{mj})^2 + (y_i - y_{mj})^2 + (z_i - z_{mj})^2} \right| \tag{10}$$

$$\varepsilon_{mj} = med_j \, |\varepsilon_{cji}| \tag{11}$$

$$(\hat{x}, \hat{y}, \hat{z}) = min \, \varepsilon_{mj} \tag{12}$$

3.4 Resolution

Figure 7 shows the relationship between the number of receivers and the deviation of the estimated position for 4, 6, 9, 24, and 48 receivers in the ceiling. To compare the effect of the RANSAC method and that of the least-squares method, one receiver is selected randomly and 500[mm] is added to the distance data of the selected receiver as outlier. Each point was derived from 30 estimations of the position. The 5 lines in the figures represent estimation for 5 different locations of the transmitter. The resolution increases with the number of receivers,

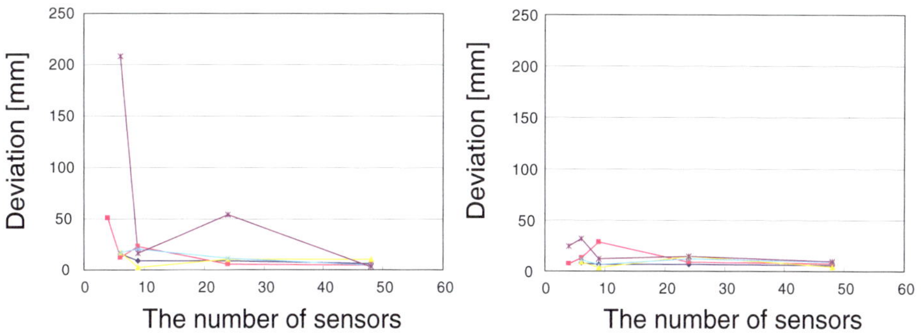

Fig. 7. Relationship between resolution and the number of sensors for the least-squares method (upper) and RANSAC (lower)

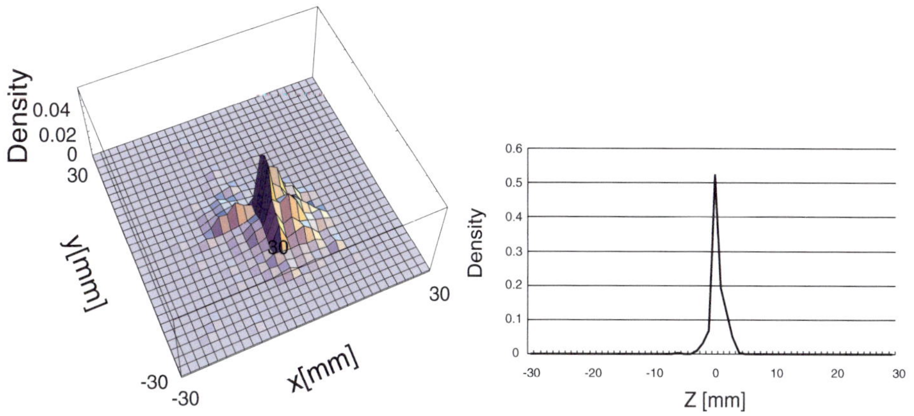

Fig. 8. Resolution in the x and y directions (upper) and z direction (lower) (grid size: 2 x 2 mm)

and the RANSAC method provides a more stable estimation with higher resolution compared to the least-squares method.

The resolution in the x, y, and z directions is illustrated in Fig. 8, which shows the probability density distribution for 1000 estimations using RANSAC. The resolution in x and y directions is about 15 mm, while that in the z direction is about 5 mm.

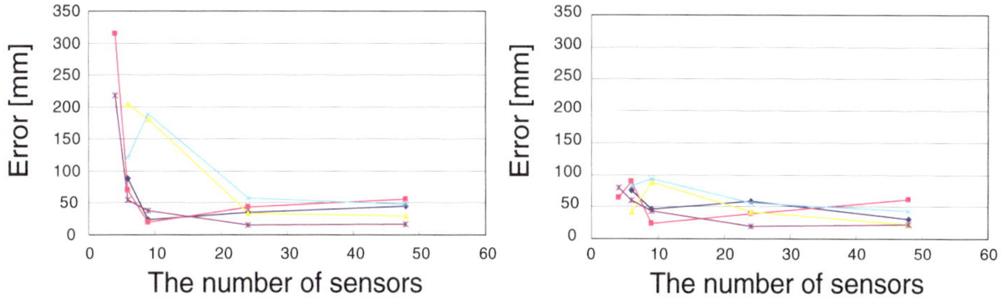

Fig. 9. Relationship between positioning accuracy and the number of receivers for the least-squares method (upper) and RANSAC (lower)

3.5 Positioning accuracy

Figure 9 shows the relationship between the number of receivers and the error of the estimated position for 4, 6, 9, 24, and 48 receivers. The error is taken as the distance from the position measured by a visual motion capture system. One receiver is selected randomly and 500[mm] is added to the distance data of the selected receiver as outlier. Each point was derived from 30 estimations of the position. The 5 lines in the figures represent estimation for 5 different locations of the transmitter. The error decreases as the number of receivers is increased, and the RANSAC method is appreciably more accurate with fewer receivers. It is considered that the least-squares method is easily affected by outliers, whereas the RANSAC method is not.
Figure 10 shows the 3D distribution of error for 1400 measured positions in the room. The figures show that the error is lowest (20–80 mm) immediately below the 48 receivers in the ceiling, increasing toward the edges of the room.
The results of experiments for evaluating accuracy and resolution demonstrate that it is possible to improve accuracy and resolution by increasing the number of receivers, and that the undesirable effect of outliers can be mitigated through the use of RANSAC estimation.

3.6 Robustness to occlusion

As in other measuring techniques such as vision-based methods, it is necessary to increase the number of sensors to solve the problem of sensor occlusion, where the line of sight to the target object is obstructed by other objects such as walls or room occupants. In the present tagging system, the problem of occlusion occurs often when a person moves or operates an object. These situations give rise to two separate problems; a decrease in the number of usable sensors for the target, and an increase in reflections due to obstruction and movement. As one of the most typical situations where occlusion occurs, this section focuses on occlusion due to a hand.
Figure 11 shows how the error increases and the number of usable sensor decreases as a hand approaches an object fitted with an ultrasonic transmitter for the least-squares and RANSAC methods. Although the error increases significantly by both methods when the hand approaches the object, the RANSAC method is much less affected than the least-squares method. This demonstrates that the proportion of outliers increases when occlusion occurs, and that RANSAC is more robust in this situation because it can mitigate the effect of such outliers.

3.7 Real-time position measurement

Figure 12 shows the measured trajectory for a person moving a cup to a chair, the floor, and a desk. The figure demonstrates that the system can robustly measure the positions of the objects in most places of the room regardless of occlusion by a hand or body.
In the current system, the sampling frequency is about 50 Hz. This frequency decreases to $50/n$ Hz when n objects are being monitored. However, it is possible to maintain a high sampling frequency by selecting which transmitters to track dynamically. For example, a transmitter can be attached to a person's wrist, and the system can select transmitters in the vicinity of the wrist to be tracked, thereby reducing the number of transmitters that need to be tracked at one time and maintaining the highest sampling frequency possible. Figure 13 shows the measured trajectory in a dynamic selection mode. The red sphere in the figure shows the position of the hand.

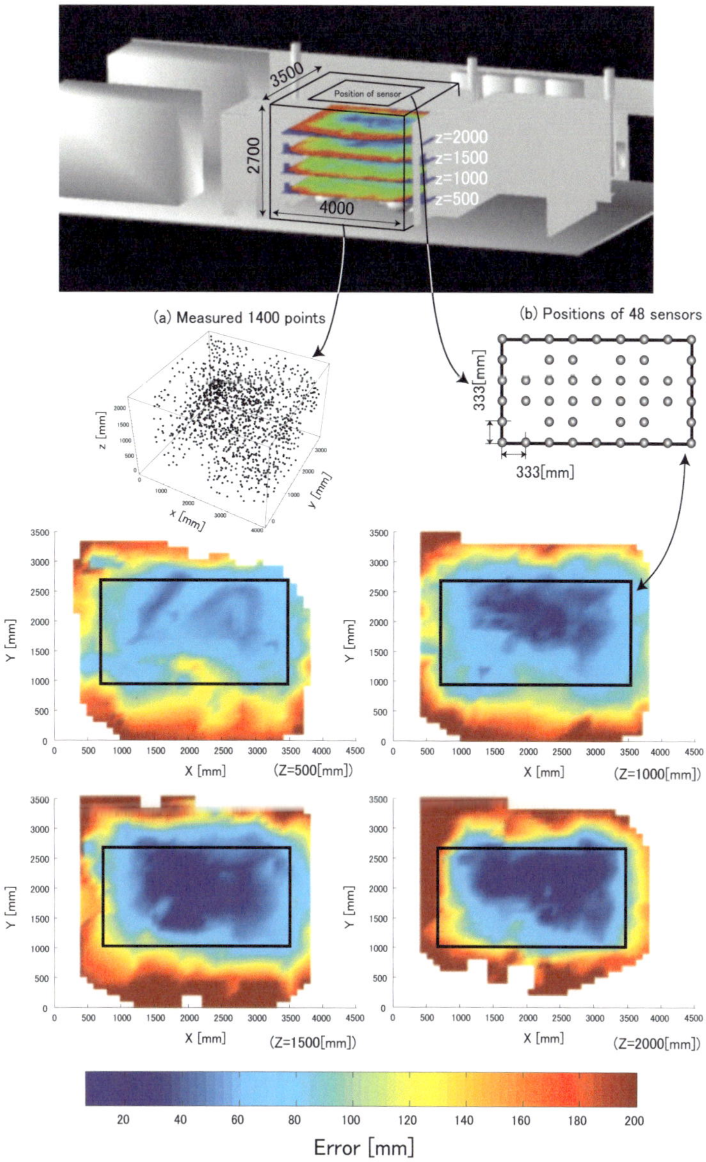

Fig. 10. 3D distribution of error in the experimental room

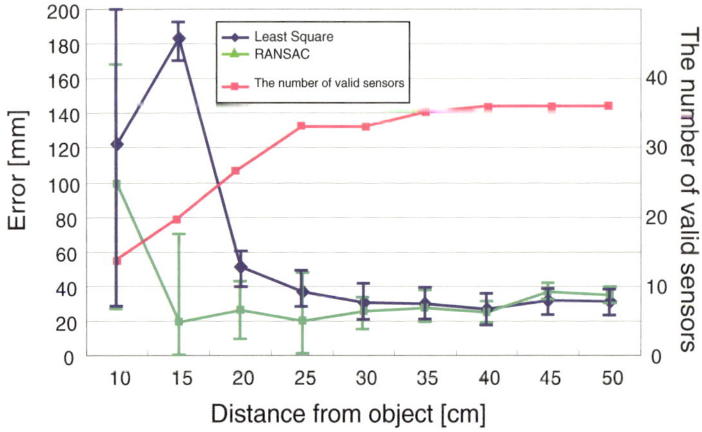

Fig. 11. Accuracy of the ultrasonic tagging system when occlusion due to a hand occurs

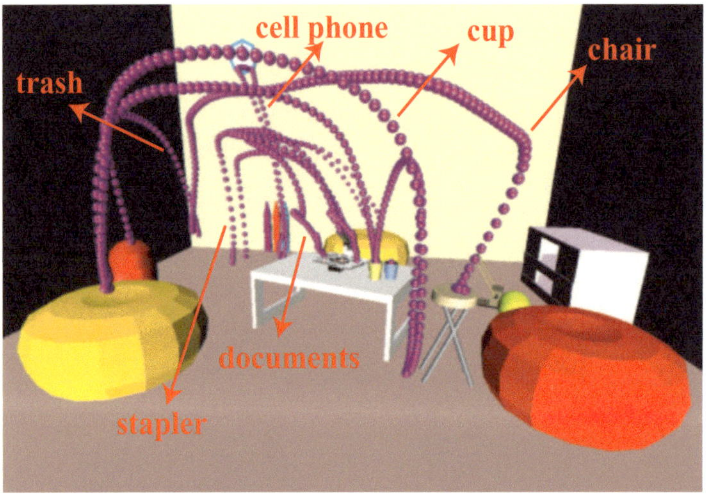

Fig. 12. Measured trajectory for movement of several objects one after another

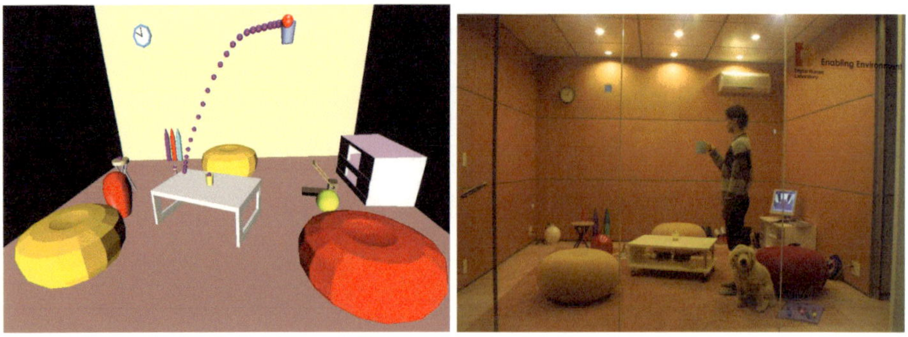

Fig. 13. Dynamic selection of transmitters

4. Quick calibration method for ultrasonic 3D tag system

4.1 Measurement and calibration

In the ultrasonic 3D tag system that the authors have developed, calibration means calculation of receivers' positions and measurement means calculation of transmitters' positions as shown in Fig. 14. Essentially, both problems are the same. As described in the previous section, the robustness of the ultrasonic 3D tag system can be improved by increasing the number of ultrasonic receivers. However, as the space where the receivers exist widens, it becomes more difficult to calibrate receivers' positions because a simple calibration method requires almost the same size of a calibration device which has multiple transmitters. This paper describes a calibration method which requires relatively small number of transmitters such as three or more and therefore doesn't require the same size of the calibration system as that of the space where the receivers exist.

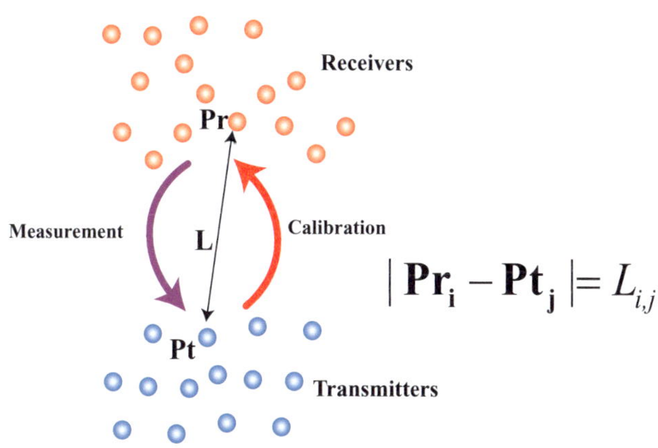

Fig. 14. Calibration and measurement

4.2 Quick calibration method

In the present paper, we describes "a global calibration based on local calibration (GCLC)" method and two constraints that can be used in conjunction with the GCLC method.

The procedure for GCLC is described below.

1. Move the calibration device arbitrarily to multiple positions (A, B, and C in Fig. 15).

2. Calculate the positions of the receivers in a local coordinate system, with the local origin set at the position of the calibration system. The calculation method was described in the previous section.

3. Select receivers for which the positions can be calculated from more than two calibration system positions.

4. Select a global coordinate system from among the local coordinate systems and calculate the positions of the calibration device in the global coordinate system using the receivers selected in Step 3. Then, calculate transformation matrices ($\mathbf{M_1}$ and $\mathbf{M_2}$ in Fig. 15).

5. Calculate the receiver positions using the receiver positions calculated in Step 2 and the transformation matrices calculated in Step 4.

Steps 4 are described in detail in the following.

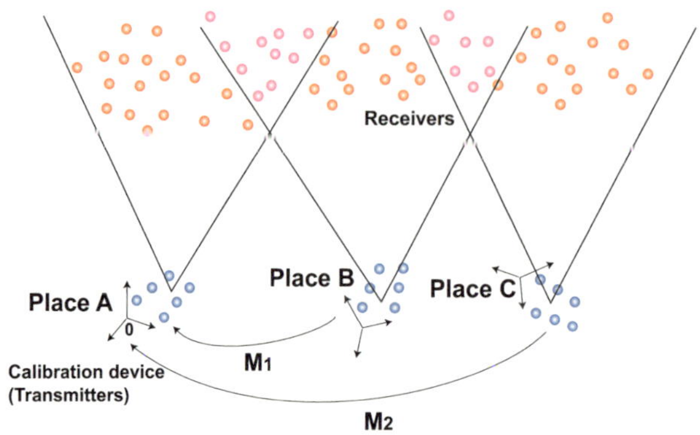

Fig. 15. Quick calibration method

4.3 Details of quick calibration

4.3.1 Calculating the positions of the calibration device in the global coordinate system (Step 4)

The error function E can be defined as follows:

$$E = \sum_{i=0}^{n} \sum_{j=i+1}^{n} ||\mathbf{M}_i \mathbf{P}_i^{(i,j)} - \mathbf{M}_j \mathbf{P}_j^{(i,j)}||^2, \tag{13}$$

where $\mathbf{M_i}$ is the transformation matrix from the local coordination system i to the global coordination system, and $\mathbf{P}_j^{(i,j)}$ denotes points in the local coordination system j for the case in which the points can be calculated in both local coordination systems i and j.

$$\begin{aligned}
&\frac{\partial E}{\partial \mathbf{M_i}} \\
&= \frac{\partial}{\partial \mathbf{M_i}} \sum_{\substack{j=0 \\ (i \neq j)}}^{n} Tr\left\{\left(\mathbf{M}_i\mathbf{P}_i^{(i,j)} - \mathbf{M}_j\mathbf{P}_j^{(i,j)}\right)^T \left(\mathbf{M}_i\mathbf{P}_i^{(i,j)} - \mathbf{M}_j\mathbf{P}_j^{(i,j)}\right)\right\} \\
&= \frac{\partial}{\partial \mathbf{M_i}} \sum_{\substack{j=0 \\ (i \neq j)}}^{n} Tr\left\{-(\mathbf{M}_j\mathbf{P}_j^{(i,j)})^T\mathbf{M}_i\mathbf{P}_i^{(i,j)} - (\mathbf{M}_i\mathbf{P}_i^{(i,j)})^T\mathbf{M}_j\mathbf{P}_j^{(i,j)}\right. \\
&\qquad \left. +(\mathbf{M}_i\mathbf{P}_i^{(i,j)})^T\mathbf{M}_i\mathbf{P}_i^{(i,j)} + (\mathbf{M}_j\mathbf{P}_j^{(i,j)})^T\mathbf{M}_j\mathbf{P}_j^{(i,j)}\right\} \\
&= -2\mathbf{M}_0\mathbf{P}_0^{(i,n)}(\mathbf{P}_i^{(i,n)})^T - \cdots - 2\mathbf{M}_{i-1}\mathbf{P}_{i-1}^{(i,i-1)}(\mathbf{P}_{i-1}^{(i,i-1)})^T \\
&\qquad +2\mathbf{M}_i \sum_{\substack{j=0 \\ (i \neq j)}}^{n} \mathbf{P}_i^{(i,j)}(\mathbf{P}_i^{(i,j)})^T \\
&\qquad -2\mathbf{M}_{i+1}\mathbf{P}_{i+1}^{(i,i+1)}(\mathbf{P}_i^{(i,i+1)})^T - \cdots - 2\mathbf{M}_n\mathbf{P}_n^{(i,n)}(\mathbf{P}_i^{(i,n)})^T.
\end{aligned} \tag{14}$$

If we select the local coordinate system 0 as the global coordinate system, $\mathbf{M_0}$ becomes an identity matrix. From Eq. (14), we can obtain simultaneous linear equations and calculate $\mathbf{M_i}$ using Eq. (15),

$$\begin{aligned}
&\begin{pmatrix} \mathbf{M_1} & \mathbf{M_2} & \cdots & \mathbf{M}_n \end{pmatrix} = \\
&\begin{pmatrix} \mathbf{P}_0^{(0,1)}(\mathbf{P}_1^{(0,1)})^T & \mathbf{P}_0^{(0,2)}(\mathbf{P}_2^{(0,2)})^T & \cdots & \mathbf{P}_0^{(0,n)}(\mathbf{P}_n^{(0,n)})^T \end{pmatrix} \times \\
&\begin{pmatrix}
\sum_{i=0}^{n} \mathbf{P}_1^{(1,i)}(\mathbf{P}_1^{(1,i)})^T & -\mathbf{P}_1^{(1,2)}(\mathbf{P}_2^{(1,2)})^T & \cdots & -\mathbf{P}_1^{(1,n)}(\mathbf{P}_n^{(1,n)})^T \\
-\mathbf{P}_2^{(1,2)}(\mathbf{P}_1^{(1,2)})^T & \sum_{i=0}^{n} \mathbf{P}_2^{(2,i)}(\mathbf{P}_2^{(2,i)})^T & \cdots & -\mathbf{P}_2^{(2,n)}(\mathbf{P}_n^{(2,n)})^T \\
\vdots & \vdots & \ddots & \vdots \\
-\mathbf{P}_n^{(1,n)}(\mathbf{P}_1^{(1,n)})^T & -\mathbf{P}_n^{(2,n)}(\mathbf{P}_2^{(2,n)})^T & \cdots & \sum_{i=0}^{n} \mathbf{P}_n^{(n,i)}(\mathbf{P}_n^{(n,i)})^T
\end{pmatrix}^{-1}.
\end{aligned} \tag{15}$$

4.4 Considering the environment boundary condition

Regarding the GCLC method as presented above, the error of calibration will accumulate as the space in which the ultrasonic receivers are placed becomes larger. Therefore, the number of moving calibrating devices becomes larger. For example, if we place receivers on the ceiling of a corridor of size 2 x 30 m, the accumulated error may be large. This section describes the boundary constraint with which we can reduce the error accumulation.

In most cases, the ultrasonic location system will be placed in a building or on the components of a building, such as on a wall or ceiling. If we can obtain CAD data of the building or its components or if we can measure the size of a room inside the building to a high degree of accuracy, then we can use the size data as a boundary condition for calibrating the receiver positions.

Here, let us consider the boundary constraint shown in Fig. 16. We can formulate this problem using the Lagrange's undecided multiplier method as follows:

$$E' = \sum_{i=0}^{3}\sum_{j=i+1}^{3} \left\| M_i P_i^{(i,j)} - M_j P_j^{(i,j)} \right\|^2 + \lambda F(M_3), \tag{16}$$

$$F(M_3) = (M_3 P_{b1} - P_{b0}) \cdot n + l_0 - l_1 = 0 \tag{17}$$

where λ denotes a Lagrange's undecided multiplier. By solving this equation, we can obtain the following equations:

$$\begin{pmatrix} \mathbf{M}_1 & \mathbf{M}_2 & \mathbf{M}_3 \end{pmatrix} = \begin{pmatrix} \mathbf{P}_0^{(0,1)}(\mathbf{P}_1^{(0,1)})^T & 0 & -1/2\lambda\mathbf{n}\mathbf{P}_{b1}^T \end{pmatrix} \times \begin{pmatrix} \begin{matrix}\mathbf{P}_1^{(0,1)}(\mathbf{P}_1^{(0,1)})^T \\ +\mathbf{P}_1^{(1,2)}(\mathbf{P}_1^{(1,2)})^T\end{matrix} & -\mathbf{P}_1^{(1,2)}(\mathbf{P}_2^{(1,2)})^T & 0 \\ -\mathbf{P}_2^{(1,2)}(\mathbf{P}_1^{(2,1)})^T & \begin{matrix}\mathbf{P}_2^{(1,2)}(\mathbf{P}_2^{(1,2)})^T \\ +\mathbf{P}_2^{(2,3)}(\mathbf{P}_2^{(2,3)})^T\end{matrix} & -\mathbf{P}_2^{(2,3)}(\mathbf{P}_3^{(2,3)})^T \\ 0 & -\mathbf{P}_3^{(2,3)}(\mathbf{P}_2^{(2,3)})^T & \mathbf{P}_3^{(2,3)}(\mathbf{P}_3^{(2,3)})^T \end{pmatrix}^{-1}. \tag{18}$$

By substituting $\mathbf{M_3}$ into Eq. (17), we can solve λ and eliminate it from Eq. (18).

The general case of the GCLC method with multiple boundary constraints is as follows:

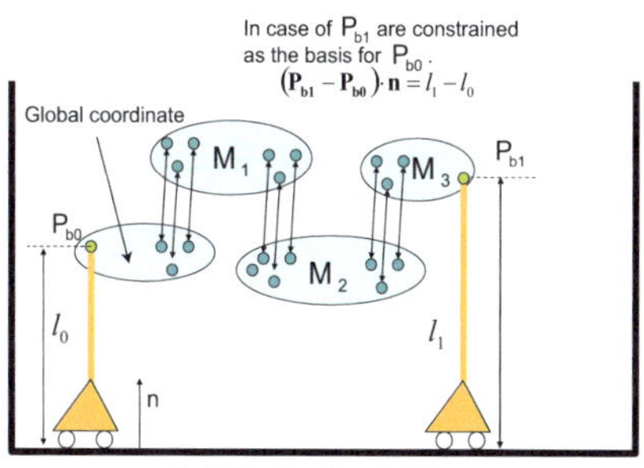

Fig. 16. Example of a boundary condition as the basis for the building

$$\begin{pmatrix} \mathbf{M}_1 & \mathbf{M}_2 & \cdots & \mathbf{M}_n \end{pmatrix} = \begin{pmatrix} \mathbf{P}_0^{(0,1)}(\mathbf{P}_1^{(0,1)})^T \\ -1/2\sum_{i=0}^{n_i}\lambda_{1,i}\mathbf{n}_{1,i}\mathbf{P}_{1,i}^T & \cdots & \cdots & \mathbf{P}_0^{(0,n)}(\mathbf{P}_n^{(0,n)})^T \\ & & & -1/2\sum_{i=0}^{n_n}\lambda_{n,i}\mathbf{n}_{n,i}\mathbf{P}_{n,i}^T \end{pmatrix} \times \begin{pmatrix} \sum_{\substack{i=0\\i\neq 1}}^{n}\mathbf{P}_1^{(1,i)}(\mathbf{P}_1^{(1,i)})^T & -\mathbf{P}_1^{(1,2)}(\mathbf{P}_2^{(1,2)})^T & \cdots & -\mathbf{P}_1^{(1,n)}(\mathbf{P}_n^{(1,n)})^T \\ -\mathbf{P}_2^{(1,2)}(\mathbf{P}_1^{(1,2)})^T & \sum_{\substack{i=0\\i\neq 2}}^{n}\mathbf{P}_2^{(2,i)}(\mathbf{P}_2^{(2,i)})^T & \cdots & -\mathbf{P}_2^{(2,n)}(\mathbf{P}_n^{(2,n)})^T \\ \vdots & \vdots & \ddots & \vdots \\ -\mathbf{P}_n^{(1,n)}(\mathbf{P}_1^{(1,n)})^T & -\mathbf{P}_n^{(2,n)}(\mathbf{P}_2^{(2,n)})^T & \cdots & \sum_{\substack{i=0\\i\neq n}}^{n}\mathbf{P}_n^{(n,i)}(\mathbf{P}_n^{(n,i)})^T \end{pmatrix}^{1}, \quad (19)$$

where $\lambda_{i,j}, \mathbf{n_{i,j}}$, and $\mathbf{P_{i,j}}$ denote the j-th undecided multiplier, the j-th constraint vector, and the j-th constrained point in the i-th local coordinate system, respectively. In this case, the boundary constraints are as follows:

$$F_{i,j} = \left(\mathbf{M_i P_{i,j}} - \mathbf{P_{b0}}\right) \cdot \mathbf{n_{i,j}} - \Delta l_{i,j} = 0, \quad (20)$$

where $\Delta l_{i,j}$ denotes a distance constraint. The above GCLC method with boundary constraints is applicable to, for example, the case in which more complex boundary conditions exist, as shown in Fig. 17.

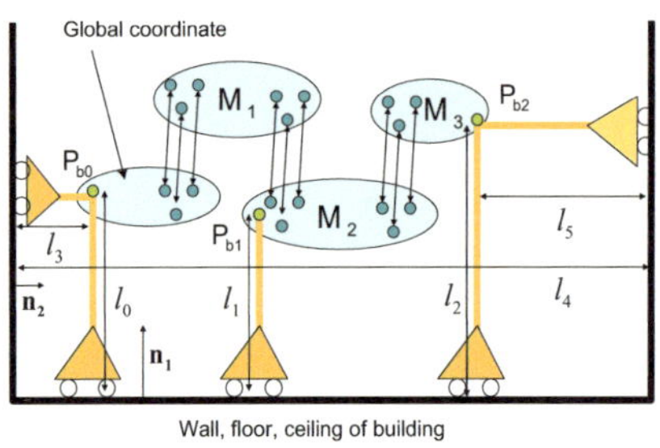

Fig. 17. Example of a greater number of boundary conditions as the basis of the building

4.5 Experimental results of GCLC

4.5.1 Method for error evaluation

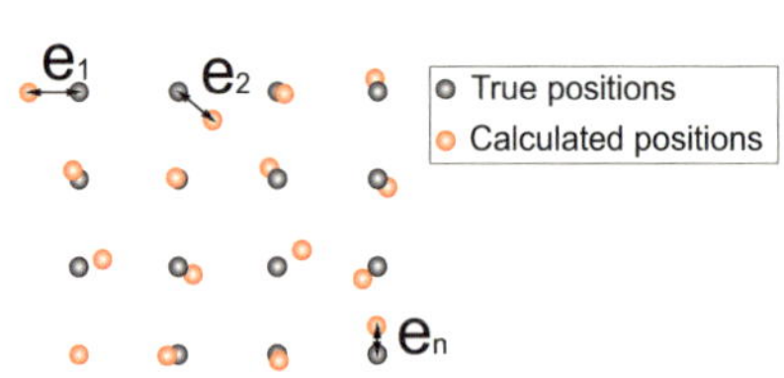

Fig. 18. Method for calculating error

Figure 18 shows the method used to calculate error. The distances between the calculated receiver positions and the true receiver positions are denoted by $e_1, e_2, \cdots, e_n$. The average error is defined by

$$E = \frac{1}{n}\sum_{i=1}^{n} e_i. \quad (21)$$

4.5.2 Accuracy evaluation

Calibration was performed in a room (4.0×4.0×2.5 m) having 80 ultrasonic receivers embedded in the ceiling. Figure 19 shows the experimental results obtained using the GCLC method without any constraints. The authors performed calibration at 16 points in the room. Seventy-six receivers were calculated. In the figure, the red spheres indicate calculated receiver positions, the black crosses indicate the true receiver positions, and the blue spheres indicate the positions of the calibration device. Figure 20 shows the experimental results for the GCLC method considering directivities. Seventy-six receivers were calculated. Table 1 shows the average error E, maximum error, and minimum error for these methods. The above results show that using the GCLC method we can calibrate the position of receivers placed in a space of average room size and that the error can be reduced significantly by considering directivity.

Another calibration was performed in a rectangular space (1.0×4.5) having a longitudinal length that is much longer than its lateral length. Seventy-six ultrasonic receivers are embedded in the space. Figure 21 shows the experimental results obtained using the GCLC method without any constraints. Seventy-five receivers were calculated. Figure 22 shows the experimental results obtained using the GCLC method with directivity consideration and a boundary constraint. Table 2 shows the average error E, maximum error, and minimum error for these methods. The above results show that with the GCLC method with directivity consideration and boundary constraint has a significantly reduced error.

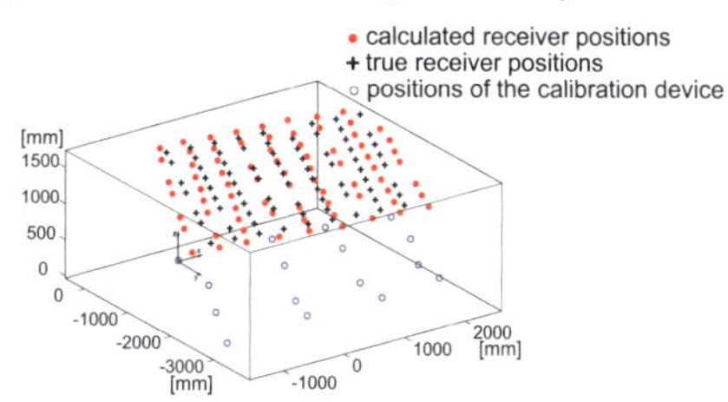

Fig. 19. Experimental result obtained by the GCLC method

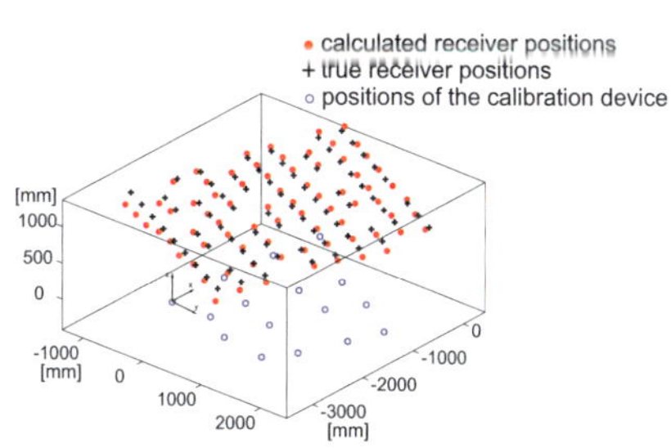

Fig. 20. Experimental result obtained by the GCLC method considering directivity

4.6 Advantages of the GCLC method

The advantages of the GCLC method are listed below.

- The method requires a relatively small number of transmitters, at least three transmitters, so that the user can calibrate the ultrasonic location system using a small calibrating device having at least three transmitters.
- The method can calibrate the positions of the receivers independent of room size.

	Ave. error	Max. error	Min. error
GCLC	195 mm	399 mm	66 mm
GCLC with directivity consideration	75 mm	276 mm	9 mm

Table 1. Errors (mm) of the proposed method for the case of a square-like space

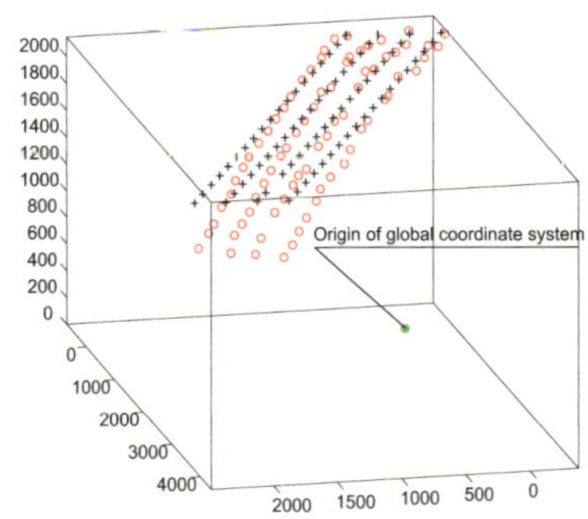

Fig. 21. Experimental results obtained by the GCLC method

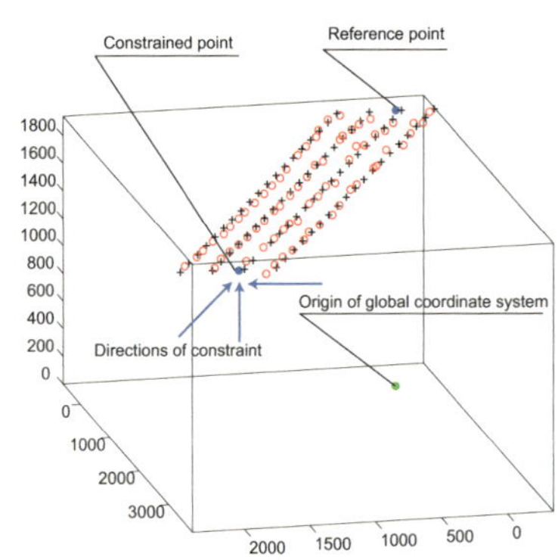

Fig. 22. Experimental results obtained by the GCLC method with directivity consideration and a boundary constraint

	Ave. error	Max. error	Min. error
GCLC	236 mm	689 mm	17 mm
GCLC with directivity consideration and boundary constraint	51 mm	121 mm	10 mm

Table 2. Errors (mm) of the proposed method for the case of a rectangular space having a longitudinal length that is much longer than its lateral length

- The error can be reduced by considering the directivity constraint. The constraint is useful for cases in which the ultrasonic location system adopts a method in which the time-of-fight is detected by thresholding ultrasonic pulse.
- The error can be reduced by considering the boundary constraint. The constraint is useful for cases in which the receivers to be calibrated are placed in a rectangular space having a longitudinal length that is much greater than the lateral length, such as a long corridor.

4.7 Development of Ultrasonic Portable 3D Tag System

The GCLC method enables a portable ultrasonic 3D tag system. Figure 23 shows a portable ultrasonic 3D tag system, which consists of a case, tags, receivers, and a calibration device. The portable system enables measurement of human activities by quickly installing and calibrating the system on-site, at the location where the activities actually occur.

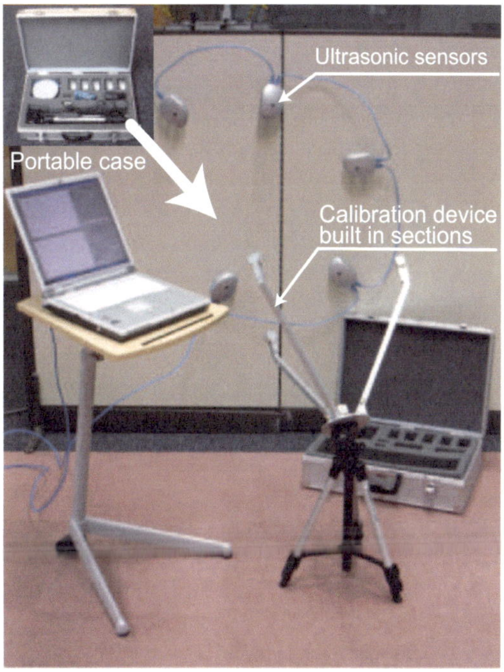

Fig. 23. Developed portable ultrasonic 3D tag system

5. Quick registration of human activity events to be detected

This section describes quick registration of target human activity events. Quick registration is performed using a stereoscopic camera with ultrasonic 3D tags as shown in Fig. 24 and interactive software. The features of this function lie in simplification of 3D shape, and simplification of physical phenomena relating to target events. The software abstracts the shapes of objects in real world as simple 3D shape such as lines, circles, or polygons. In order to describe the real world events when a person handles the objects, the software abstracts the function of objects as simple phenomena such as touch, detouch, or rotation. The software adopts the concept of virtual sensors and effectors to enable for a user to define the function of the objects easily by mouse operations.

For example, if a person wants to define the activity of "put a cup on the desk", firstly, the person simplifies the cup and the desk as a circle and a rectangle respectively using a photo-modeling function of the software. Second, using a function for editting virtual sensors, the person adds a touch type virtual sensor to the rectangle model of the desk, and adds a bar type effector to the circle model of the cup.

5.1 Software for quick registration of human activity events to be detected

5.1.1 Creating simplified 3D shape model

Figure 26 shows examples of simplified 3D shape models of objects such as a Kleenex, a cup, a desk and stapler. The cup is expressed as a circle and the desk is a rectangle. The simplification is performed using a stereoscopic camera with the ultrasonic 3D tags and a photo-modeling function of the software. Since the camera has multiple ultrasonic 3D tags, the system can track its position and posture. Therefore, it is possible to move the camera freely when the user creates simplified 3D shape models and the system can integrate the created 3D shape models in a world coordinate system.

5.1.2 Creating model of physical object's function using virtual sensors/effectors

The software creates the model of a object's function by attaching virtual sensors/effectors which are prepared in advance in the software to the 3D shape model created in step (a). Virtual sensors and effectors work as sensors and ones affecting the sensors on computer. The current system has "angle sensor" for detecting rotation, "bar effector" for causing phenomenon of touch, "touch sensor" for detecting phenomenon of touch. In the right part of Fig. 27, red bars indicate a virtual bar effector, and green area indicates a virtual touch sensor. By mouse operations, it is possible to add virtual sensors/effectors to the created 3D shape model.

5.1.3 Associating output of model of physical object's function with activity event

Human activity can be described using output of the virtual sensors which are created in Step (b). In Fig. 28, red bar indicates that the cup touches with the desk and blue bar indicates that the cup doesn't touch with the desk. By creating the table describing relation between the output of the virtual sensors and the target events, the system can output symbolic information such as "put a cup on the desk" when the states of virtual sensors change.

5.1.4 Detecting human activity event in real time

When the software inputs position data of ultrasonic 3D tag, the software can detect the target events using the virtual sensors and the table defined in Step (a) to (c) as shown in Fig. 29

6. Conclusion

This paper described a system for quickly realizing a function for robustly detecting daily human activity events in handling objects in the real world. The system has three functions: 1) robustly measuring 3D positions of the objects, 2) quickly calibrating a system for measuring 3D positions of the objects, 3) quickly registering target activity events, and 4) robustly detecting the registered events in real time.
As for 1), In order to estimate the 3D position with high accuracy, high resolution, and robustness to occlusion, the authors propose two estimation methods, one based on a least-squares approach and one based on RANSAC.

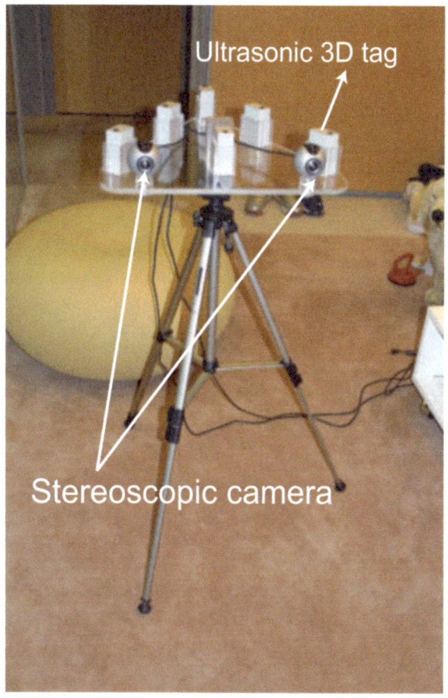

Fig. 24. UltraVision (a stereoscopic camera with the ultrasonic 3D tags) for creating simplified 3D shape model

Fig. 25. Photo-modeling by stereoscopic camera system

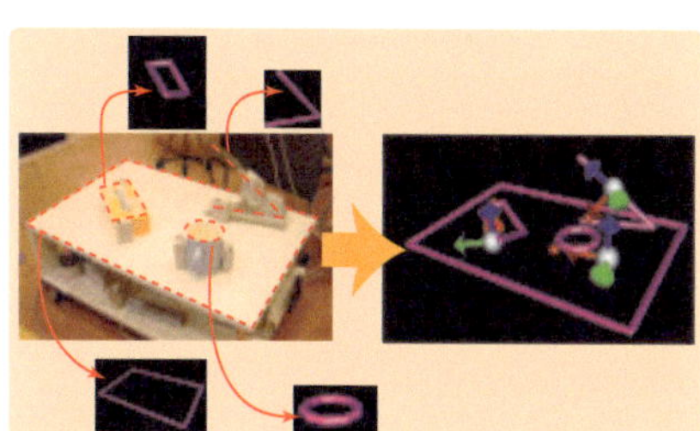

Fig. 26. Create simplified shape model

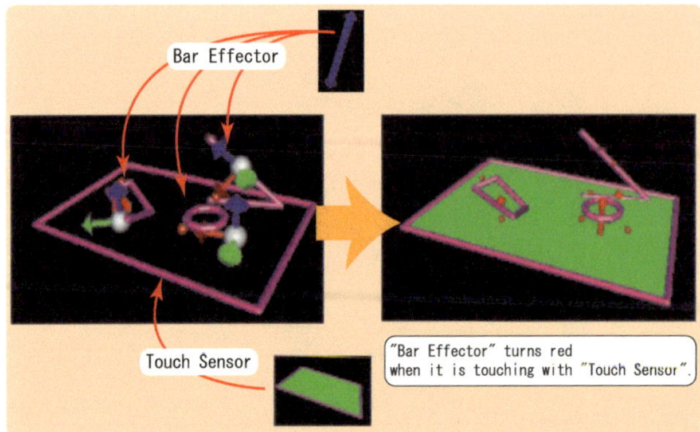

Fig. 27. Create model of physical object's function using virtual sensors/effectors

The system was tested in an experimental room fitted with 307 ultrasonic receivers; 209 in the walls and 98 in the ceiling. The results of experiments conducted using 48 receivers in the ceiling for a room with dimensions of 3.5 × 3.5 × 2.7 m show that it is possible to improve the accuracy, resolution, and robustness to occlusion by increasing the number of ultrasonic receivers and adopting a robust estimator such as RANSAC to estimate the 3D position based on redundant distance data. The resolution of the system is 15 mm horizontally and 5 mm vertically using sensors in the ceiling, and the total spatially varying position error is 20–80 mm. It was also confirmed that the system can track moving objects in real time, regardless of obstructions.

As for 2), this paper described a new method for quick calibration. The method uses a calibration device with three or more ultrasonic transmitters. By arbitrarily placing the device at multiple positions and measuring distance data at their positions, the positions of receivers can be calculated. The experimental results showed that with the method, the positions of 80 receivers were calculated by 4 transmitters of the calibration device and the position error is 103 mm.

As for 3), this paper described a quick registration of target human activity events in handling objects. To verify the effectiveness of the function, using a stereoscopic camera with ultrasonic 3D tags and interactive software, the authors registered activities such as "put a cup on the

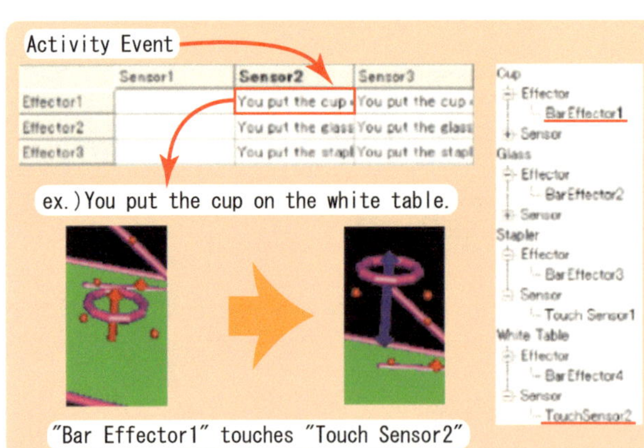

Fig. 28. Associate output of virtual sensors with target activity event

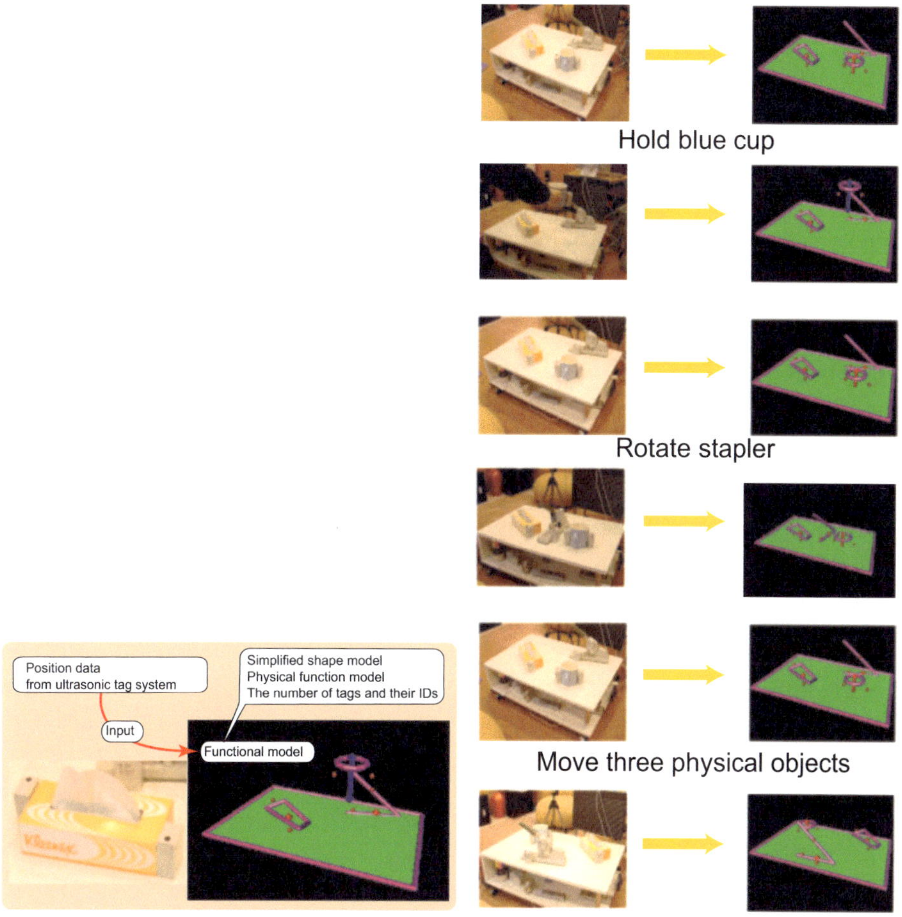

Fig. 29. Recognize human activity in real time by function's model

desk" and "staple document" through creating the simplified 3D shape models of ten objects such as a TV, a desk, a cup, a chair, a box, and a stapler.
Further development of the system will include refinement of the method for measuring the 3D position with higher accuracy and resolution, miniaturization of the ultrasonic transmitters, development of a systematic method for defining and recognizing human activities based on the tagging data and data from other sensor systems, and development of new applications based on human activity data.

7. References

[1] T. Hori. Overview of Digital Human Modeling. *Proceedings of 2000 IEEE/RSJ International Conference on Intelligent Robots and Systems (IROS2000), Workshop Tutorial Note*, pp. 1–14, 2000
[2] H. Mizoguchi, T. Sato, and T. Ishikawa. Robotic Office Room to Support Office Work by Human Behavior Understanding Function with Networked Machines. *IEEE/ASME Transactions on Mechatronics*, Vol. 1, No. 3, pp. 237–244, September 1996
[3] Y. Nishida, H. Aizawa, T. Hori, N.H. Hoffman, T. Kanade, M. Kakikura, "3D Ultrasonic

Tagging System for Observing Human Activity, " in *Proceedings of IEEE International Conference on Intelligent Robots and Systems (IROS2003)*, pp. 785-791, October 2003.

[4] A. Ward, A. Jones, A. Hopper, "A New Location Technique for the Active Office, " *IEEE Personal Communications*, Vol. 4, No. 5, pp. 42-47, October 1997.

[5] A. Harter, A. Hopper, P. Steggles, A. Ward, P. Webster, "The Anatomy of a Context-Aware Application, " in *Proceedings of the ACM/IEEE MobiCom*, August 1999.

[6] M. Addlesee, R. Curwen, S. Hodges, J. Newman, P. Steggles, A. Ward, A. Hopper, "Implementing a sentient computing system, " *IEEE Computer*, Vol. 34, No. 8, pp. 50-56, August 2001.

[7] M. Hazas and A. Ward, "A Novel Broadband Ultrasonic Location System, " in *Proceedings of UbiComp 2002*, pp. 264-280, September 2002.

[8] N.B. Priyantha, A. Chakraborty, H. Balakrishnan, "The Cricket Location-Support system, " in *Proceedings of the 6th International Conference on Mobile Computing and Networking (ACM MobiCom2000)*, pp. 32-43, August 2000

[9] A. Mahajan and F. Figueroa, "An Automatic Self Installation and Calibration Method for a 3D Position Sensing System using Ultrasonics," *Robotics and Autonomous Systems*, Vol. 28, No. 4, pp. 281-294, September 1999.

[10] Y. Fukuju, M. Minami, H. Morikawa, and T. Aoyama, "DOLPHIN: An Autonomous Indoor Positioning System in Ubiquitous Computing Environment, " in *Proceedings of IEEE Workshop on Software Technologies for Future Embedded Systems (WSTFES2003)*, pp. 53-56, May 2003.

[11] P. Duff, H. Muller, "Autocalibration Algorithm for Ultrasonic Location Systems," in *Proceedings of 7th IEEE International Symposium on Wearable Computer*, pp. 62-68, October 2003.

[12] Y. Chen, G. Medioni, "Object Modeling by registration of multiple range images," *Image and Vision Computing*, Vol. 10, No. 3, pp. 145-155, April 1992.

[13] P.J. Neugebauer, "Geometrical Cloning of 3D Objects via Simultaneous Registration of Multiple Range Images," in *Proceedings of the 1997 International Conference on Shape Modeling and Application (SMA'97)*, pp. 130-139, 1997.

[14] B.W. Parkinson, J.J. Spilker, P. Axelrad, P. Enge, *The Global Positioning System: Theory and Applications*, American Institute of Aeronautics and Astronautics, 1996.

[15] K.C. Ho. Solution and Performance Analysis of Geolocation by TDOA. *IEEE Transaction on Aerospace and Electronic Systems*, Vol. 29, No. 4, pp. 1311–1322, October 1993.

[16] D.E. Manolakis, "Efficient Solution and Performance Analysis of 3-D Position Estimation by Trilateration, " *IEEE Trans. on Aerospace and Electronic Systems*, Vol. 32, No. 4, pp. 1239–1248, October 1996

[17] P. J. Rousseeuw, and A. M. Leroy. *Robust Regression and Outlier Detection*. Wiley, New York, 1987.

[18] M.A. Fishler, and R.C. Bolles. Random Sample Consensus: A Paradigm for Model Fitting with Application to Image Analysis and Automated Cartography. *Communication of the ACM*, Vol. 24, No. 6, pp. 381–395, June 1981.

12

Global 3D Terrain Maps for Agricultural Applications

Francisco Rovira-Más
Polytechnic University of Valencia
Spain

1. Introduction

At some point in life, everyone needs to use a map. Maps tell us where we are, what is around us, and what route needs to be taken to reach a desired location. Until very recently, maps were printed in paper and provided a two-dimensional representation of reality. However, most of the maps consulted at present are in electronic format with useful features for customizing trips or recalculating routes. Yet, they are still two-dimensional representations, although sometimes enriched with real photographs. A further stage in mapping techniques will be, therefore, the addition of the third dimension that provides a sense of depth and volume. While this excess of information may seem somewhat capricious for people, it may be critical for autonomous vehicles and mobile robots. Intelligent agents demand high levels of perception and thus greatly profit from three-dimensional vision. The widespread availability of global positioning information in the last decade has induced the development of multiple applications within the framework of precision agriculture. The main idea beyond this concept is to supply the right amount of input at the appropriate time for precise field locations, which obviously require the knowledge of field coordinates for site-specific applications. The practical implementation of precision farming is, consequently, tied to geographical references. However, prescription and information maps are typically displayed in two dimensions and generated with the level of resolution normally achieved with satellite-based imagery. The generation of *global three-dimensional (3D) terrain maps* offers all the advantages of *global localization* with the extra benefits of *high-resolution local perception* enriched with three dimensions plus color information acquired in real time.

Different kinds of three-dimensional maps have been reported according to the specific needs of each application developed, as the singular nature of every situation determines the basic characteristics of its corresponding 3D map. Planetary exploration, for example, benefits from virtual representations of unstructured and unknown environments that help scouting rovers to navigate (Olson et al., 2003; Wang et al., 2009); and the military forces, the other large group of users of 3D maps for recreating off-road terrains (Schultz et al., 1999), rely on stereo-based three-dimensional reconstructions of the world for a multiplicity of purposes. From the agricultural point of view, several attempts have been made to apply the mapping qualities of compact binocular cameras to production fields. Preceding the advent of compact cameras with real-time capabilities, something that took place at the turn of this century, airborne laser rangefinders allowed the monitoring of soil loss from gully erosion by sensing surface topography (Ritchie & Jackson, 1989). The same idea of a laser map generator, but this time from a ground vehicle, was explored to generate elevation maps of a field scene (Yokota et al., 2004), after the fusion of several local maps with an RTK-GPS. Due to the fact that large extensions of agricultural fields require an efficient and fast way for mapping, unmanned aircrafts have offered a trade-off between low-resolution non-controllable remote sensing maps from satellite imagery and high-resolution ground-based robotic scouting. MacArthur et al. (2005), mounted a binocular stereo camera on a miniature helicopter with the purpose of monitoring health and yield in a citrus grove, and Rovira-Más et al. (2005) integrated a binocular camera in a remote controlled medium-size helicopter for general 3D global mapping of agricultural scenes. A more interesting and convenient solution for the average producer, however, consists of placing the stereo mapping engine on conventional farming equipment, allowing farmers to map while performing other agronomical tasks. This initiative was conceived by Rovira-Más (2003) – later implemented in Rovira-Más et al. (2008)–, and is the foundation for the following sections. This chapter explains how to create 3D terrain maps for agricultural applications, describes the main issues involved with this technique while providing solutions to cope with them, and presents several examples of 3D globally referenced maps.

2. Stereo principles and compact cameras

The geometrical principles of stereoscopy were set more than a century ago, but their effective implementation on compact off-the-shelf cameras with the potential to correlate stereo-based image pairs in real time, and therefore obtain 3D images, barely covers a decade. Present day compact cameras offer the best solution for assembling the mapping engine of an intelligent vehicle: favorable cost-performance ratio, portability, availability, optimized and accessible software, standard hardware, and continuously updated technology. The perception needs of today's 3D maps are mostly covered by commercial cameras, and very rarely will be necessary to construct a customized sensor. However, the fact that off-the-shelf solutions exist and are the preferred option does not mean that they can be simply approached as "plug and play." On the contrary, the hardest problems appear after the images have been taken. Furthermore, the configuration of the camera is a crucial step for developing quality 3D maps, either with retail products or customized prototypes. One of the early decisions to be made with regards to the camera configuration is whether using fixed baseline and permanent optics or, on the contrary, variable baselines and interchangeable lenses. The final choice is a trade-off between the high flexibility of the latter and the compactness of the former. A compact solution where imagers and lenses are totally fixed, not only offers the comfort of not needing to operate the camera after its installation but adds the reliability of precalibrated cameras. Camera calibration is a delicate stage for cameras that are set to work outdoors and onboard off-road vehicles. Every time the baseline is modified or a lens changed, the camera has to be calibrated with a calibration panel similar to a chessboard. This situation is aggravated by the fact that cameras on board farm equipment are subjected to tough environmental and physical conditions, and the slightest bang on the sensor is sufficient to invalid the calibration file comprising the key transformation parameters. The mere vibration induced by the diesel engines that power off-road agricultural vehicles is enough to unscrew lenses during field duties, overthrowing the entire calibration routine. A key matter is, therefore, finding out what is the best camera configuration complying with the expected needs in the field, such that a precalibrated rig can be ordered with no risk of losing optimum capabilities. Of course, there is always a risk of dropping the precalibrated camera and altering the relative position between imagers, but this situation is remote. Nevertheless, if this unfortunate accident ever happened, the camera would have to be sent back to the original manufacturer for the alignment of both imaging sensors and, subsequently, a new calibration test. When the calibration procedure is carried out by sensor manufacturers, it is typically conducted under optimum conditions and the controlled environment of a laboratory; when it is performed *in-situ*, however, a number of difficulties may complicate the generation of a reliable calibration file. The accessibility of the camera, for example, can cause difficulties for setting the right diaphragm or getting a sharp focus. A strong sun or unexpected rains may also ruin the calculation of accurate parameters. At least two people are required to conduct a calibration procedure, not always available when the necessity arises. Another important decision to be made related to the calibration of the stereo camera is the size of the chessboard panel. Ideally, the panel should have a size such that when located at the targeted ranges, the majority of the panel corners are found by the calibration software. However, very often this results in boards that are too large to be practical in the field, and a compromise has to be found. Figure 1 shows the process of calibrating a stereo camera installed on top of the cabin of a tractor. Since the camera features variable baseline and removable lenses (Fig. 5b), it had to be calibrated after the lenses were screwed and the separation between imagers secured. Notice that the A-4 size of the calibration panel forces the board holder to be quite close to the camera; a larger panel would allow the holder to separate more from the vehicle, and consequently get a calibration file better adjusted to those ranges that are more interesting for field mapping. Section 4 provides some recommendations to find a favorable camera configuration as it represents the preliminary step to design a compact mapping system independent of weak components such as screwed parts and in-field calibrations.

Fig. 1. Calibration procedure for non-precalibrated stereo cameras

The position of the camera is, as illustrated in Fig. 1, a fundamental decision when designing the system as a whole. The next section classifies images according to the relative position between the camera and the ground, and the system architectures discussed in Section 5 rely on the exact position of the sensor, as individual images need to be fused at the correct position and orientation. It constitutes a good practice to integrate a mapping system in a generic vehicle that can perform other tasks without any interference caused by the camera or related hardware. Apart from the two basic configuration parameters —i. e. baseline and optics—, the last choice to make is the image resolution. It is obvious that the higher resolution of the image the richer the map; however, each pair of stereo images leads to 3D clouds of several thousand points. While a single stereo pair will cause no trouble for its virtual representation, merging the 3D information of many images as individual building blocks will result in massive and unmanageable point clouds. In addition, the vehicle needs to save the information in real time and, when possible, generate the map "on the fly." For this reason, high resolution images are discouraged for the practical implementation of 3D global mapping unless a high-end computer is available onboard. In summary, the robust solutions that best adapt to off-road environments incorporate precalibrated cameras with an optimized baseline-lenses combination and moderate resolutions as, for instance, 320 x 240 or 400 x 300.

3. Mapping platforms, image types, and coordinate transformations

The final 3D maps should be independent of the type of stereo images used for their construction. Moreover, images taken under different conditions should all contribute to a unique globally-referenced final map. Yet, the position of the camera in the vehicle strengthens the acquisition of some features and reduces the perception of others. Airborne images, for instance, will give little detail on the position of tree trunks but, on the other hand, will cover the top of canopies quite richly. Different camera positions will lead to different kind of raw images; however, two general types can be highlighted: ground images and aerial images. The essential difference between them is the absence of perspective —and consequently, a vanishing point— in the latter. *Aerial images* are taken when the image plane is approximately parallel to the ground; and *ground images* are those acquired under any other relative position between imager and ground. There is a binding relationship between the vehicle chosen for mapping, the selected position of the camera, and the resulting image type. Nevertheless, this relationship is not exclusive, and aerial images may be grabbed from an aerial vehicle or from a ground platform, according to the specific position and orientation of the camera. Figure 2 shows an aerial image of corn taken from a remote-controlled helicopter (a), an aerial image of potatoes acquired from a conventional small tractor (b), and a ground image of grapevines obtained from a stereo camera mounted on top of the cabin of a medium-size tractor (c). Notice the sense of perspective and lack of parallelism in the rows portrayed in the ground-type image.

a b c

Fig. 2. Image types for 3D mapping: aerial (a and b), and ground (c)

The acquisition of the raw images (left-right stereo pairs) is an intermediate step in the process of generating a 3D field map, and therefore the final map must have the same quality and properties regardless of the type of raw images used, although as we mentioned above, the important features being tracked might recommend one type of images over the other. What is significantly different, though, is the coordinate transformation applied to each image type. This transformation converts initial camera coordinates into practical ground coordinates. The camera coordinates (x_c, y_c, z_c) are exclusively related to the stereo camera and initially defined by its manufacturer. The origin is typically set at the optical center of one of the lenses, and the plane X_cY_c coincides with the image plane, following the traditional definition of axes in the image domain. The third coordinate, Z_c, gives the depth of the image, i. e. the ranges directly calculated from the disparity images. The camera coordinates represent a generic frame for multiple applications, but in order to compose a useful terrain map, coordinates have to meet two conditions: first, they need to be tied to the ground rather than to the mobile camera; and second, they have to be globally referenced such that field features will be independent from the situation of the vehicle. In other words, our map coordinates need to be *global* and *grounded*. This need is actually accomplished through two consecutive steps: first from local camera coordinates (x_c, y_c, z_c) to local ground coordinates (x, y, z); and second, from local ground coordinates to global ground coordinates (e, n, z_g). The first step depends on the image type. Figure 3a depicts the transformation from camera to ground coordinates for aerial images. Notice that ground coordinates keep their origin at ground level and the z coordinate always represents the height of objects (point P in the figure). This conversion is quite straightforward and can be mathematically expressed through Equation 1, where D represents the distance from the camera to the ground. Given that ground images are acquired when the imagers plane of the stereo camera is inclined with respect to the ground, the coordinate transformation from camera coordinates to ground coordinates is more involving, as graphically represented in Figure 3b for a generic point P. Equation 2 provides the mathematical expression that allows this coordinate conversion, where h_c is the height of the camera with respect to the ground and ϕ is the inclination angle of the camera as defined in Figure 3b.

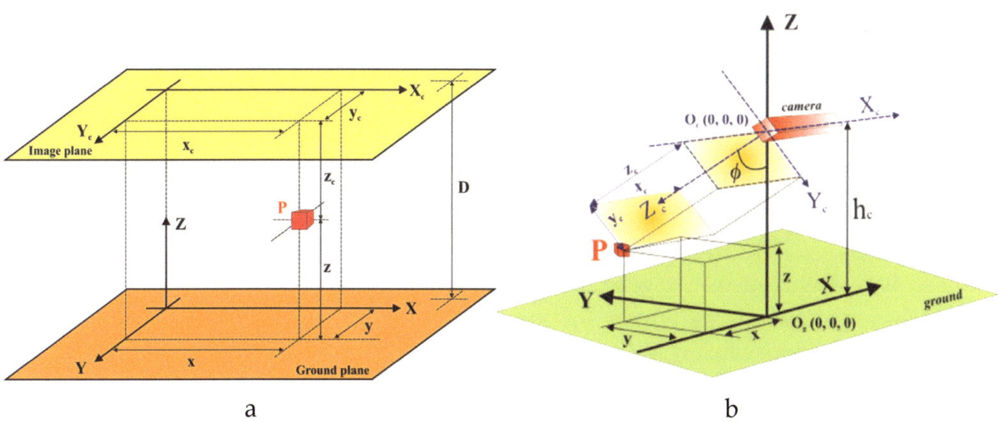

Fig. 3. Coordinate transformations from camera to ground coordinates for aerial images (a) and ground images (b)

$$\begin{bmatrix} x \\ y \\ z \end{bmatrix} = \begin{bmatrix} 1 & 0 & 0 \\ 0 & 1 & 0 \\ 0 & 0 & 1 \end{bmatrix} \times \begin{bmatrix} x_c \\ y_c \\ z_c \end{bmatrix} + D \begin{bmatrix} 0 \\ 0 \\ 1 \end{bmatrix} \tag{1}$$

$$\begin{bmatrix} x \\ y \\ z \end{bmatrix} = \begin{bmatrix} 1 & 0 & 0 \\ 0 & -\cos\varnothing & \sin\varnothing \\ 0 & -\sin\varnothing & -\cos\varnothing \end{bmatrix} \times \begin{bmatrix} x_c \\ y_c \\ z_c \end{bmatrix} + h_c \times \begin{bmatrix} 0 \\ 0 \\ 1 \end{bmatrix} \tag{2}$$

The transformation of equation 2 neglects roll and pitch angles of the camera, but in a general formulation of the complete coordinate conversion to a global frame, any potential orientation of the stereo camera needs to be taken into account. This need results in the augmentation of the mapping system with two additional sensors: an inertial measurement unit (IMU) for estimating the pose of the vehicle in real time, and a global positioning satellite system to know the global coordinates of the camera at any given time. The first transformation from camera coordinates to ground coordinates occurs at a local level, that is, the origin of ground coordinates after the application of Equations 1 and 2 is fixed to the vehicle, and therefore travels with it. The second stage in the coordinate transformation establishes a static common origin whose position depends on the global coordinate system employed. GPS receivers are the universal global localization sensors until the upcoming completion of Galileo or the full restoration of GLONASS. Standard GPS messages follow the NMEA code and provide the global reference of the receiver antenna in geodetic coordinates latitude, longitude, and altitude. However, having remote origins results in large and inconvenient coordinates that complicate the use of terrain maps. Given that agricultural fields do not cover huge pieces of land, the sphericity of the earth can be obviated, and a flat reference (ground) plane with a user-set origin results more convenient. These advantages are met by the *Local Tangent Plane* (ENZ) model which considers a flat surface containing the plane coordinates *east* and *north*, with the third coordinate (*height*) z_g perpendicular to the reference plane, as schematized in Figure 4a. Equation 3 gives the general expression that finalizes the transformation to global coordinates represented in the Local Tangent Plane. This conversion is applied to every single point of the local map —3D point cloud— already expressed in ground coordinates (x, y, z). The final coordinates for each transformed point in the ENZ frame will be (e, n, z_g). Notice that Equation 3 relies on the global coordinates of the camera's instantaneous position—center of the camera coordinate system—given by (e^c, n^c, $z^c{}_g$), as well as the height h_{GPS} at which the GPS antenna is mounted, and the distance along the Y axis between the GPS antenna and the camera reference lens d_{GPS}. The attitude of the vehicle given by the pitch (α), roll (β), and yaw (φ), has also been included in the general transformation equation (3) for those applications where elevation differences within the mapped field cannot be disregarded. Figure 4b provides a simplified version of the *coordinate globalization* for a given point P, where the vehicle's yaw angle is φ and the global position of the camera when the image was taken is determined by the point O_{LOCAL}. A detailed step-by-step explanation of the procedure to transform geodetic coordinates to Local Tangent Plane coordinates can be followed in Rovira-Más et al. (2010).

$$\begin{bmatrix} e \\ n \\ z_g \end{bmatrix} = \begin{bmatrix} e^c \\ n^c \\ z_g^c\text{-}h_{GPS}\cdot\cos\beta\cdot\cos\alpha \end{bmatrix} + \begin{bmatrix} \cos\varphi\cdot\cos\beta & \cos\varphi\cdot\sin\beta\cdot\sin\alpha\text{-}\sin\varphi\cdot\cos\alpha & \cos\varphi\cdot\sin\beta\cdot\cos\alpha+\sin\varphi\cdot\sin\alpha \\ \sin\varphi\cdot\cos\beta & \sin\varphi\cdot\sin\beta\cdot\sin\alpha+\cos\varphi\cdot\cos\alpha & \sin\varphi\cdot\sin\beta\cdot\cos\alpha\text{-}\cos\varphi\cdot\sin\alpha \\ \text{-}\sin\beta & \cos\beta\cdot\sin\alpha & \cos\beta\cdot\cos\alpha \end{bmatrix} \times \begin{bmatrix} x \\ y+d_{GPS} \\ z \end{bmatrix} \quad (3)$$

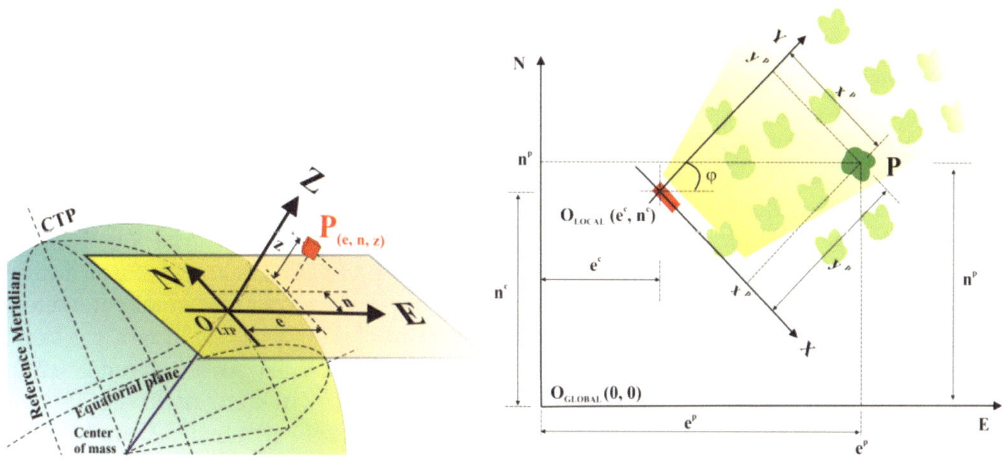

a b

Fig. 4. Local Tangent Plane coordinate system (a), and transformation from local vehicle-fixed ground frame XYZ to global reference frame ENZ (b)

4. Configuration of 3D stereo cameras: choosing baselines and lenses

It was stated in Section 2 that precalibrated cameras with fixed baselines and lenses provide the most reliable approach when selecting an onboard stereo camera, as there is no need to perform further calibration tests. The quality of a 3D image mostly depends on the quality of its corresponding depth map (disparity image) as well as its further conversion to three-dimensional information. This operation is highly sensitive to the accuracy of the calibration parameters, hence the better calibration files the higher precision achieved with the maps. However, the choice of a precalibrated stereo rig forces us to permanently decide two capital configuration parameters which directly impact the results: *baseline* and *focal length* of the lenses. In purity, stereoscopic vision can be achieved with binocular, trinocular, and even higher order of multi-ocular sensors, but binocular cameras have demonstrated to perform excellently for terrain mapping of agricultural fields. Consequently, for the rest of the chapter we will always consider binocular cameras unless noted otherwise.
Binocular cameras are actually composed of two equal monocular cameras especially positioned to comply with the stereoscopic effect and epipolar constriction. This particular disposition entails a common plane for both imagers (arrays of photosensitive cells) and the (theoretically) perfect alignment of the horizontal axes of the images (usually x). In practice, it is physically achieved by placing both lenses at the same height and one besides the other

at a certain distance, very much as human eyes are located in our heads. This inter-lenses separation is technically denominated the *baseline* (B) of the stereo camera. Human baselines, understood as inter-pupil separation distances, are typically around 60 - 70 mm. Figure 5 shows two stereo cameras: a precalibrated camera (a), and a camera with interchangeable lenses and variable baseline (b). Any camera representing an intermediate situation, for instance, when the lenses are removable but the baseline fixed, cannot be precalibrated by the manufacturer as every time a lens is changed, a new calibration file has to be immediately generated. The longer the baseline the further ranges will be acceptably perceived, and vice versa, short baselines offer good perceptual quality for near distances. Recall that 3D information comes directly from the disparity images, and no correlation can be established if a certain point only appears in one of the two images forming the stereo pair; in other words, enlarging the baseline increases the minimum distance at which the camera can perceive, as objects will not be captured by both images, and therefore pixel matching will be physically impossible. The effect of the *focal length* (f) of the lenses on the perceived scene is mainly related to the field of view covered by the camera. Reduced focal lengths (below 6 mm) acquire a wide field of view but possess lower resolution to perceive the background. Large focal lengths, say over 12 mm, are acute sensing the background but completely miss the foreground. The nature and purpose of each application must dictate the baseline and focal length of the definite camera, but these two fundamental parameters are coupled and should not be considered independently but as a whole. In fact, the same level of perception can be attained with different B-f combinations; so, for instance, 12 m ranges have been optimally perceived with a baseline of 15 cm combined with 16 mm lenses, or alternatively, with a baseline of 20 cm and either lenses of 8 mm or 12 mm (Rovira-Más et al., 2009). Needless to say that both lenses in the camera have to be identical, and the resolution of both imagers has to be equally set.

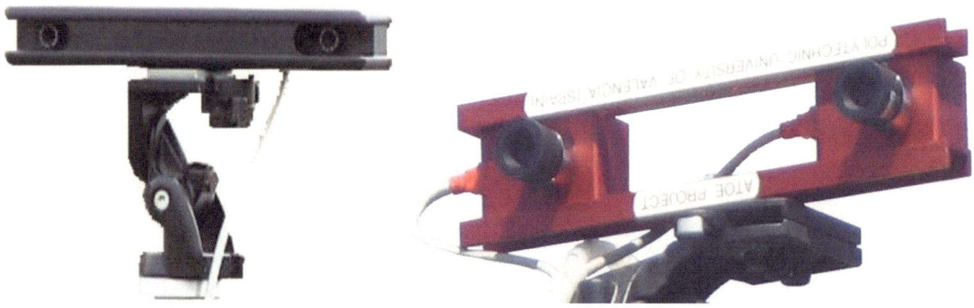

a b

Fig. 5. Binocular stereoscopic cameras: precalibrated (a), and featuring variable baselines and interchangeable lenses (b)

5. System architecture for data fusion

The coordinate transformation of Equation 3 demands the real time acquisition of the vehicle pose (roll, pitch, and yaw) together with the instantaneous global position of the camera for each image taken. If this information is not available for a certain stereo pair, the resulting 3D point cloud will not be added to the final global map because such cloud will lack a global reference to the common user-defined origin. The process of building a global

3D map from a set of stereo images can be schematized in the pictorial of Figure 6. As represented below, the vehicle follows a —not always straight— course while grabbing stereo images that are immediately converted to 3D point clouds. These clouds of points are referenced to the mapping vehicle by means of the ground coordinates of each point as defined in Figure 3. As shown in the left side of Figure 6, every stereo image constitutes a local map with a vehicle-fixed ground coordinate system whose pose with relation to the global frame is estimated by an inertial sensor, and whose origin's global position is given by a GPS receiver. After all the points in the 3D cloud have been expressed in vehicle-fixed ground coordinates (Equations 1 and 2), the objective is to merge the local maps in a unique global map by reorienting and patching the local maps together according to their global coordinates (Equation 3). The final result should be coherent, and if for example the features perceived in the scene are straight rows spaced 5 m, the virtual global map should reproduce the rows with the same spacing and orientation, as schematically represented in the right side of Figure 6.

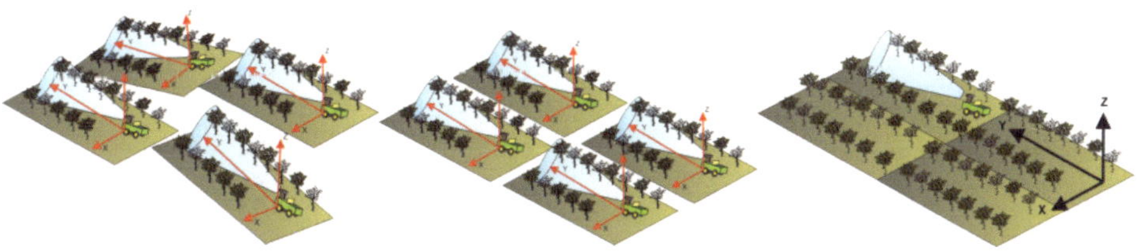

Fig. 6. Assembly of a global map from individual stereo-based local maps

The synchronization of the local sensor —stereo camera— with the attitude and positioning sensors has to be such that for every stereo image taken, both inertial measurements (α, β, φ) and geodetic coordinates are available. Attitude sensors often run at high frequencies and represent no limitations for the camera, which typically captures less than 30 frames per second. The GPS receiver, on the contrary, usually works at 5 Hz, which can easily lead to the storage of several stereo images (3D point clouds) with exactly the same global coordinates. This fact requests certain control in the incorporation of data to the global map, not only adjusting the processing rate of stereo images to the input of GPS messages, but considering as well the forward speed of the mapping vehicle and the field of view covered by the camera. Long and narrow fields of view (large B and large f) can afford longer sampling rates by the camera as a way to reduce computational costs at the same time overlapping is avoided. In addition to the misuse of computing resources incurred when overlapping occurs, any inaccuracy in either GPS or IMU will result in the appearance of artifacts generated when the same object is perceived in various consecutive images poorly transformed to global coordinates. That phenomenon can cause, for example, the representation of a tree with a double trunk. This issue can only be overcome if the mapping engine assures that all the essential information inserted in the global map has been acquired with acceptable quality levels. As soon as one of the three key sensors produces unreliable data, the assembly of the general map must remain suspended until proper data reception is resumed. Sensor noise has been a common problem in the practical generation of field maps, although the temporal suspension of incoming data results in incomplete, but correct, maps, which can be concluded in future missions of the vehicle. There are many ways to be aware of, and ultimately palliate, sensor inaccuracies. IMU drift can be assessed with the yaw estimation calculated from GPS coordinates. GPS errors can be reduced with the subscription to differential signals, and by monitoring quality indices such as dilution of precision or the number of satellites in solution. Image noise is extremely important for this application as perception data constitute the primary source of information for the map; therefore, it will be separately covered in the next section. The 3D representation of the scene, composed of discrete points forming a cloud determined by stereo perception, can be rendered in false colors, indicating for example the height of crops or isolating the objects located at a certain placement. However, given that many stereo cameras feature color (normally RGB) sensors, each point P can be associated with its three global coordinates plus its three color components, resulting in the six-dimensional vector $(e, n, z_g, r, g, b)_P$. This 3D representation maintains the original color of the scene, and besides providing the most realistic representation of that scene, also allows the identification of objects according to their true color. Figure 7 depicts, in a conceptual diagram, the basic components of the architecture needed for building 3D terrain maps of agricultural scenes.

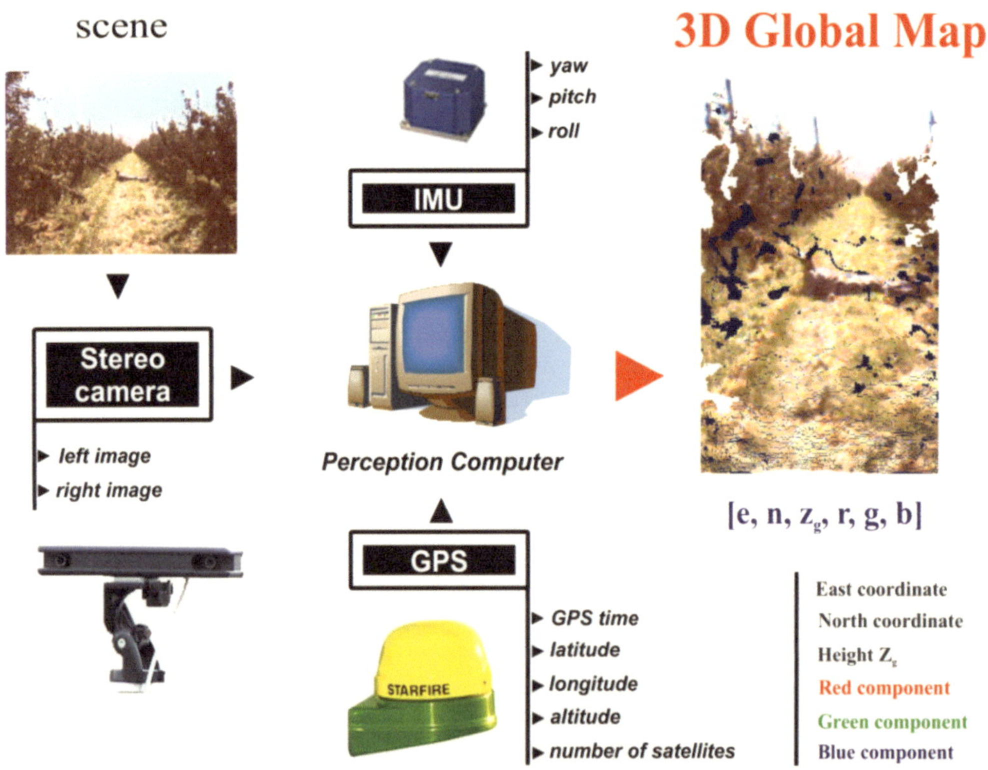

Fig. 7. System architecture for a stereo-based 3D terrain mapping system

6. Image noise and filters

Errors can be introduced in 3D maps at different stages according to the particular sensor yielding spurious data, but while incorrect position or orientation of the camera may be detected and thus prevented from being added to the global map, image noise is more difficult to handle. To begin with, the perception of the scene totally relies on the stereo camera and its capability to reproduce the reality enclosed in the field of view. When correlating the left and right images of each stereo pair, mismatches are always present. Fortunately, the majority of miscorrelated pixels are eliminated by the own filters embedded in the camera software. These unreliable pixels do not carry any information in the disparity image, and typically represent void patches as the pixels mapped in black in the central image of Fig. 8. However, some mismatches remain undetected by the primary filters and result in disparity values that, when transformed to 3D locations, point at unrealistic positions. Figure 8 shows a disparity image (center) that includes the depth information of some clouds in the sky over an orchard scene (left). When the clouds were transformed to 3D points (right), the height of the clouds was obviously wrong, as they were place below 5 m. The occurrence of outliers in the disparity image is strongly dependent on the quality of the calibration file, therefore precalibrated cameras present an advantage in terms of noise. Notice that a wrong GPS message or yaw estimation automatically discards the entire image, but erroneously correlated pixels usually represent an insignificant percentage of the point cloud and it is neither logical nor feasible to reject the whole image (local map). A practical way to avoid the presence of obvious outliers in the 3D map is by defining a *validity box* of logical placement of 3D information. So, when mapping an orchard, for instance, negative heights make no sense (underground objects) and heights over the size of the trees do not need to be integrated in the global map, as they very likely will be wrong. In reality, field images are rich in texture and disparity mismatches represent a low percentage over the entire image. Yet, the information they add is so wrong that it is worth removing them before composing the global map, and the definition of a validity box has been effective to do so.

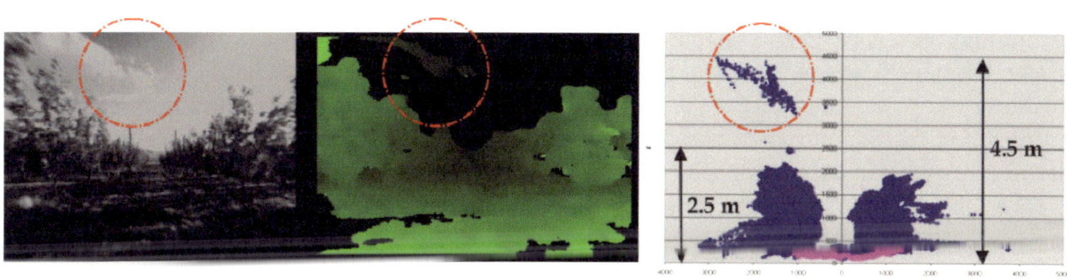

Fig. 8. Correlation errors in stereo images

7. Real-time 3D data processing

The architecture outlined in Figure 7 is designed to construct 3D terrain maps "on the fly", that is, while the vehicle is traversing the field, the stereo camera takes images that are converted to 3D locally-referenced point clouds, and in turns added to a global map after transforming local ground coordinates to global coordinates by applying Equation 3. The result is a large text file with all the points retrieved from the scene. This file, accessible after the mapping mission is over, is ready for its virtual representation. This *online* procedure of building a 3D map strongly relies on the appropriate performance of localization and attitude sensors. An alternative method to generate a 3D field map is when its construction is carried out *off-line*. This option is adequate when the computational power onboard is not sufficient, if memory resources are scarce, or if some of the data need preprocessing before the integration in the general map. The latter has been useful when the attitude sensor has been inaccurate or not available. To work offline, the onboard computer needs to register a series of stereo images and the global coordinates at which each stereo image was acquired. A software application executed in the office transforms all the points in the individual images to global coordinates and appends the converted points to the general global map. The advantage of working off-line is the possibility of removing corrupted data that passed the initial filters. The benefit of working on-line is the availability of the map right after the end of the mapping mission.

8. Handling and rendering massive amounts of 3D Data

The reason behind the recommendation of using moderate resolutions for the stereo images is based on the tremendous amount of data that gets stored in 3D field maps. A typical 320 x 240 image can easily yield 50000 points per image. If a mapping vehicle travels at 2 m/s (7 km/h), it will take 50 s to map a 100 m row of trees. Let us suppose that images are acquired every 5 s, or the equivalent distance of 10 m; then the complete row will require 10 stereo images which will add up to half million points. If the entire field comprises 20 rows, the whole 3D terrain map will have *10 million points*. Such a large amount of data poses serious problems when handling critical visual information and for efficiently rendering the map. *Three-dimensional virtual reality chambers* are ideal to render 3D terrain maps. Inside them, viewers wear special goggles which adapt the 3D represented environment to the movement of the head, so that viewers feel like they were actually immersed in the scene and walking along the terrain. Some of the examples described in the following section were run in the John Deere Immersive Visualization Laboratory (Moline, IL, USA). However, this technology is not easily accessible and a more affordable alternative is necessary to make use of 3D maps with conventional home computers. Different approaches can be followed to facilitate the management and visualization of 3D maps. Many times the camera captures information that is not essential for the application pursued. For example, if the objective is to monitor the growth of canopies or provide an estimate of navigation obstacles, the points in the cloud that belong to the ground are not necessary and may occupy an important part of the resources. A simple redefinition of the validity box will only transfer those points that carry useful information, reducing considerably the total amount of points while maintaining the basic information. Another way of decreasing the size of file maps is by enlarging the spacing between images. This solution requires an optimal configuration of the camera to prevent the presence of gaps lacking 3D information. When all the information in the scene is necessary, memory can be saved by condensing the point cloud in regular grids. In any case, a mapping project needs to be well thought in advance because not only difficulties can arise in the process of map construction but also in the management and use that comes afterwards. There is no point in building a high-accuracy map if no computer can ever handle it at the right pace. More than being precise, 3D maps need to fulfill the purpose for which they were originally created.

9. Examples

The following examples provide general-purpose agricultural 3D maps generated by following the methodology developed along the chapter. In order to understand the essence of the process, it is important to pay attention to the architecture of the system on one hand, and to the data fusion on the other. No quality 3D global map can be attained unless both local and global sensors perform acceptably. When the assembly of the map is carried out off-line, it is helpful to plot first the positions of the stereo camera where images were taken to make sure that global coordinates are correct. Only when this happens, we can proceed with the integration of the independent images into the global map by performing all the coordinate transformations given before. The scene portrayed in Figure 9 represents a series of wooden posts used as supporting structures for growing hops. Posts were either straight up or inclined, but they were equally spaced, which gave us a good opportunity to test if the transformation from local to global provided coherent results. The images were taken with two commercial stereo cameras; one with a (9 cm) fixed baseline but removable 4.8 mm lenses, and the other with fixed lenses and (22 cm) baseline, both mounted on the front of a utility off-road vehicle. A GPS receiver provided global references and no attitude sensor was integrated in the vehicle, which forced the map construction to be off-line. The field was flat and both roll and pitch were negligible. The yaw angle was directly estimated from the GPS-determined trajectory followed by the vehicle (Fig. 9, top-center). This map was created without including the true color code of each correlated point, and as a result its 3D representation is only available in false colors. It proved that 3D terrain mapping with the degree of detail given by an in-field stereo camera plus the benefits of global references is feasible as long as the architecture of the system is properly designed.

The perceptual data of the second map, given in Figure 10, was acquired with a precalibrated camera, with a fixed baseline of 22 cm and integrated miniature lenses. The presence of a fiber optic gyroscope (FOG) and an RTK-GPS in the vehicle allowed for on-line map construction, following the architecture schematized in Figure 7. As color images were saved and decoded, true color was incorporated to the final global map as rendered in the multiple views included in Figure 10. This scene represents a turf lane bounded by two rows of trees, although the map mostly includes the right row. On the whole, 12 images were acquired to cover the approximately 30 m of the row, summing up a total of 379,517 points. The GPS-based camera positions show that the vehicle basically moved straight in the direction W-E. The top view demonstrates an adequate performance of the IMU when measuring yaw angles. The side view shows that the terrain was fairly even, as corroborated by the pitch angles estimated with the FOG, always below 3°. The availability of true color helps to discriminate the yellowish turf from the darker hues of the trees. However, note that the color of the pixels corresponding to the top of the trees got confused with that of the pixels representing the sky, and consequently they display a false white color.

10. Conclusion

The adoption of new technologies by agricultural producers is a matter of time. Thirty years ago the GPS was a military device; today, it is offered by all major manufacturers of farm equipment. Social and economic problems in the production of competitive agricultural goods are pushing these technologies even further, especially precision farming and agricultural robotics. GPS-based automatic guidance solutions are being implemented in the field, and precision agriculture applications are successfully combined with conventional production systems. However, most of the maps utilized so far are two-dimensional and lack the level of detail that can be reached with a stereoscopic camera. These cameras have been successfully used in other robotic applications, but the ever growing need of handling richer and more updated information for better and faster decision making in the competitive agriculture of the future makes them a favorite resource.

Fig. 9. Three-dimensional terrain map of a barren field with crop-supporting structures

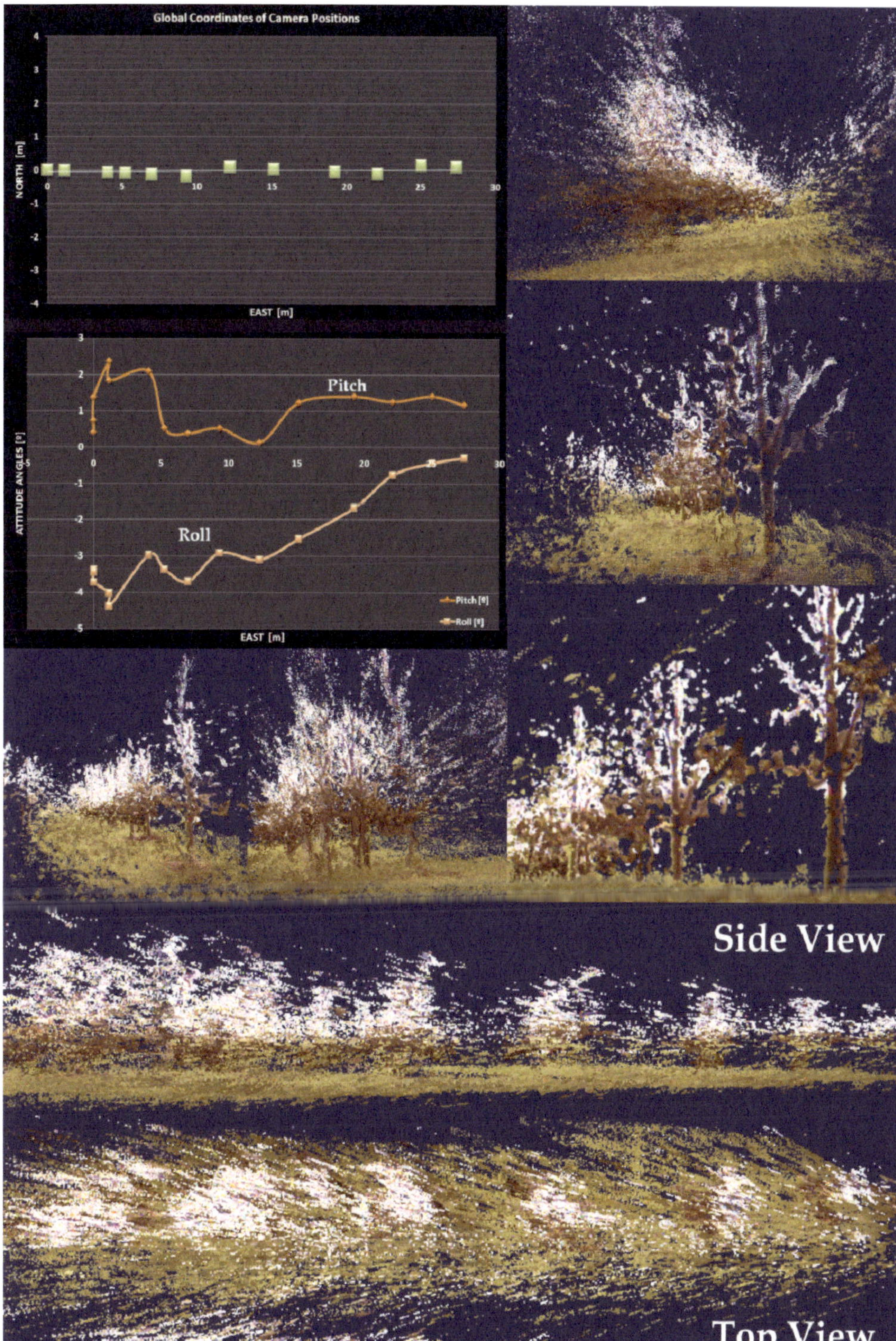

Fig. 10. True color three-dimensional terrain map

Yet, three-dimensional field information without a general frame capable of providing global references is not very practical. For that reason, the methodology elaborated along the chapter provides a way to build globally-referenced maps with the highest degree of visual perception, that in which human vision is based on. This theoretical framework, dressed with numerous practical recommendations, facilitates the physical deployment of real 3D mapping systems. Although not in production yet, the information attained with these systems will certainly help to the development and progress of future generations of intelligent agricultural vehicles.

11. References

MacArthur, D. K.; Schueller, J. K. & Crane, C. D. (2005). Remotely-piloted mini-helicopter imaging of citrus. ASAE Publication 051055, ASABE, St. Joseph, MI

Olson, C. F.; Abi-Rached, H.; Ye, M. & Hendrich, J. P. (2003). Wide-baseline stereo vision for Mars rovers, *Proceedings of the International Conference on Intelligent Robots and Systems*, pp. 1302-1307, IEEE

Ritchie, J. C. & Jackson T. J. (1989). Airborne laser measurements of the surface topography, *Transactions of the ASAE*, Vol. 32(2), pp. 645-658

Rovira-Más, F. (2003). *Applications of stereoscopic vision to agriculture*. Unpublished doctoral dissertation, University of Illinois at Urbana-Champaign

Rovira-Más, F.; Zhang, Q. & Reid, J. F. (2005). Creation of three-dimensional crop maps based on aerial stereoimages, *Biosystems Engineering*, Vol. 90(3), pp. 251-259

Rovira-Más, F.; Zhang, Q. & Reid, J. F. (2008). Stereo vision three-dimensional terrain maps for precision agriculture, *Computers and Electronics in Agriculture*, Vol. 60, pp. 133-143

Rovira-Más, F.; Wang, Q. & Zhang, Q. (2009). Design parameters for adjusting the visual field of binocular stereo cameras, *Biosystems Engineering*, Vol. 105, pp. 59-70

Rovira-Más, F.; Zhang, Q. & Hansen A. C. (2010). *Mechatronics and intelligent systems for off-road vehicles*, Springer, UK, Chapter 3

Schultz, H.; Riseman, E. M.; Stolle, F. R. & Woo, D. (1999). Error detection and DEM fusion using self-consistency, *Proceedings of the Seventh IEEE International Conference on Computer Vision*, pp. 1174-1181, Vol. 2, IEEE

Wang, W.; Shen, M.; Xu, J.; Zhou, W. & Liu, J. (2009). Visual traversability analysis for micro planetary rover, *Proceedings of the International Conference on Robotics and Biomimetics*, pp. 907-912, Guilin, China, December 2009, IEEE

Yokota, M.; Mizushima, A.; Ishii, K. & Noguchi, N. (2004). 3-D map generation by a robot tractor equipped with a laser range finder. *Proceedings of the Automatic Technology for Off-road Equipment Conference*, pp. 374-379, Kyoto, Japan, October 2004, ASAE Publication 701P1004, ASABE, St. Joseph, MI

13

Construction Tele-Robotic System with Virtual Reality (CG Presentation of Virtual Robot and Task Object Using Stereo Vision System)

Hironao Yamada, Takuya Kawamura and Takayoshi Muto
Department of Human and Information Systems, Gifu University
Japan

1. Introduction

A remote-control robotic system using bilateral control is useful for performing restoration in damaged areas, and also in extreme environments such as space, the seabed, and deep underground.

In this study, we investigated a tele-robotics system for a construction machine. The system consists of a servo-controlled construction robot, two joysticks for operating the robot from a remote place, and a 3-degrees-of-freedom motion base. The operator of the robot sits on the motion base and controls the robot bilaterally from a remote place. The role of the motion base is to realistically simulate the motion of the robot.

In order to improve the controllability of the system, we examined (1) the master and slave control method between joysticks and robot arms (Yamada et al., 1999, 2003a), (2) a presentation method for the motion base (Zhao et al., 2002, 2003), and (3) the visual presentation of the task field for an operator (Yamada et al., 2003b). Because the visual presentation is the information most essential to the operator, in this study we focused on the presentation method of the operation field of a remote place.

The world's first remote control system was a mechanical master-slave manipulator called ANL Model M1 developed by Goertz (Goertz, 1952). Since its introduction, the field of tele-operation has expanded its scope. For example, tele-operation has been used in the handling of radioactive materials, sub-sea exploration, and servicing. Its use has also been demonstrated in space, construction, forestry, and mining. As an advanced form of tele-operation, the concept of "telepresence" was proposed by Minsky (Minsky, 1980). Telepresence enables a human operator to remotely perform tasks with dexterity, providing the user with the feeling that she/he is present in the remote location. About the same time, "telexistence", a similar concept, was proposed by Tachi (Tachi et al., 1996).

Incidentally, practical restoration systems using tele-operation have been tested in Japan, because volcanic or earthquake disasters occur frequently. For example, unmanned construction was introduced in recovery work after the disastrous eruption of Mount Unzen Fugen Dake in 1994 and was used in a disastrous eruption on Miyakejima, which was made uninhabitable due to lava flows and toxic volcanic gas. In these tele-operation systems, however, simple stereo video image feedback was adopted; there remains some room for improvement in the details of telepresence.

As an application for excavator control, bilateral matched-impedance tele-operation was developed at the University of British Columbia (Tafazoli et al. 1999; Salcudean et al., 1999). They have also developed a virtual excavator simulator suitable for experimentation with user interfaces, control strategies, and operator training (DiMaio et al., 1998). This simulator comprises machine dynamics as an impedance model, a ground-bucket interaction model, and a graphical display sub-system. In their experiment, an actual excavator is operated by a bilateral control method. However, they did not evaluate the effectiveness of the visual display system with the computer graphics image for real time teleoperation.

With regard to the method of visual presentation for tele-operation, augmented reality (AR) has lately become of major interest (Azuma, 1997). AR enhances a user's perception of and interaction with the real world. For example, stereoscopic AR, which is called "ARGOS", was adopted for robot path planning by Milgram (Milgram et al., 1993). Others have used registered overlays with telepresence systems (Kim et al. 1996; Tharp et al., 1994). It is expected that effectiveness of display method can be improved by using an AR system. However, registration and sensing errors are serious problems in building practical AR systems, and these errors may make the working efficiency lower.

In our previous paper, we proposed a presentation method that used a mixed image of stereo video and the CG image of the robot, and clarified that the task efficiency was improved (Yamada et al., 2003b). At this stage, however, because the position and the shape of the task object have not been presented to the operator, the operator cannot help feeling inconvenienced. In this study, therefore, a full CG presentation system, which enables presentation not only of the robot but also of the position and the shape of a task object, was newly developed. The proposed display method enables the operator to choose the view point of the camera freely and thereby presumably improve the task efficiency. This "virtualized reality" system, proposed by Kanade (Kanade et al., 1997)., is perhaps similar in spirit to the CG presentation system that we proposed, although it is not currently a real-time system. They use many cameras in order to extract models of dynamic scenes. Our system uses a single stereo vision camera for practical tele-operation. Another CG presentation system, "Networked Telexistence" has been proposed by Tachi (Tachi, 1998), but the task efficiency was not evaluated in the proposal. Utsumi developed a CG display method for an underwater teleoperation system (Utsumi et al., 2002). He clarified that the visualization of the haptic image is effective for the grasping operation under conditions of poor visibility. However, the CG image is generated based on a force sensor attached to a slave manipulator, and thus no detailed CG image of task objects can be presented. In our system, the CG image is generated based on a stereo vision camera, so it is possible to display task objects clearly.

In this study, a full CG presentation system, which enables presentation not only of the robot but also of the position and the shape of a task object, was newly developed. Application of the method was expected to increase the task efficiency. To confirm this, a CG of a virtual robot was created, and its effectiveness for the task of carrying an object was determined. The results of the experiment clarified that tasking time was shortened effectively even for amateur operators. Thus, the usefulness of the developed CG system was confirmed.

2. Tele-robotic system using CG presentation

Fig. 1 shows a schematic diagram of the tele-robotic system that was developed in the course of this research (Yamada et al., 2003a). The system is of a bilateral type and is thus divided into two parts; the master system and the slave system. Here, the slave system is a construction robot equipped with a pair of stereo CCD cameras. The master system is controlled by an operator and consists mainly of a manipulator and a screen. The robot has four hydraulic actuators controlled by four servo valves through a computer (PC). Acceleration sensors were attached to the robot for feeding back the robot's movement to the operator.

The manipulator controlled by the operator consists of two joysticks and a motion base on which a seat is set for the operator. The motion base provides 3 degrees of freedom and can move in accordance with the motion of the robot. This means that the operator is able to feel the movement of the robot as if she/he were sitting on the seat of the robot.

The joysticks can be operated in two directions; along the X- and Y-axes. The displacements of the joysticks are detected by position sensors, while the displacements of the actuators are detected by magnetic stroke sensors embedded in the pistons.

A stereo video image captured by the CCD cameras is transmitted to a 3D converter then projected onto the screen by a projector. Simultaneously, a signal synchronized with the video image is generated by the 3D converter and transmitted to an infrared unit. This signal enables the liquid crystal shutter glasses to alternately block out light coming toward the left and right eyes. Thus, the operator's remote vision is stereoscopic.

In the previous paper (Yamada et al., 2003b), a CG image of robot motion (without a CG image of the task object) was additionally presented; i.e., with the video image from the CCD cameras. In that case, the operator had to watch both the CG and the video image at the same time, which was tiring.

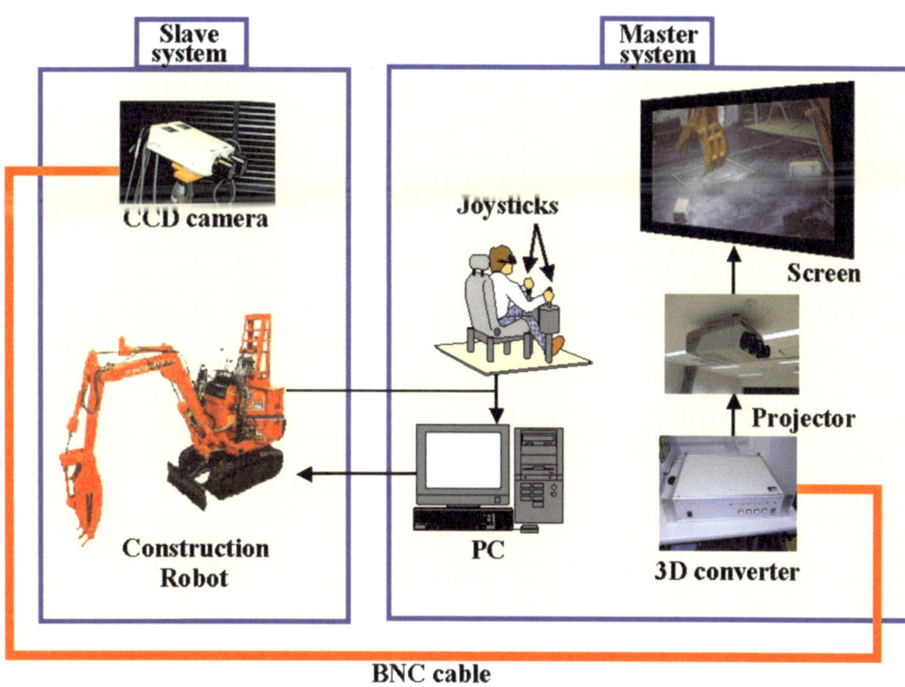

Fig. 1. Construction Tele-Robot System using CCD camera

In this study, we developed a visual presentation system for producing two CG images; one is the robot, the other the task object. As a tool for making a CG image of the task object, we adopted a stereo vision camera named "Digiclops" (Fig.2), a product of Point Grey Research, Inc.

Digiclops is a color-stereo-vision system that provides real-time range images using stereo-computer vision technology. The system consists of a three-calibrated-colors camera module, which is connected to a Pentium PC. Digiclops is accurately able to measure the distance to a task object in its field of view at a speed of up to 30 frames/second. In the developed presentation system, the operator can view CG images of the remote robot and

Fig. 2. Stereo vision camera "Digiclops"

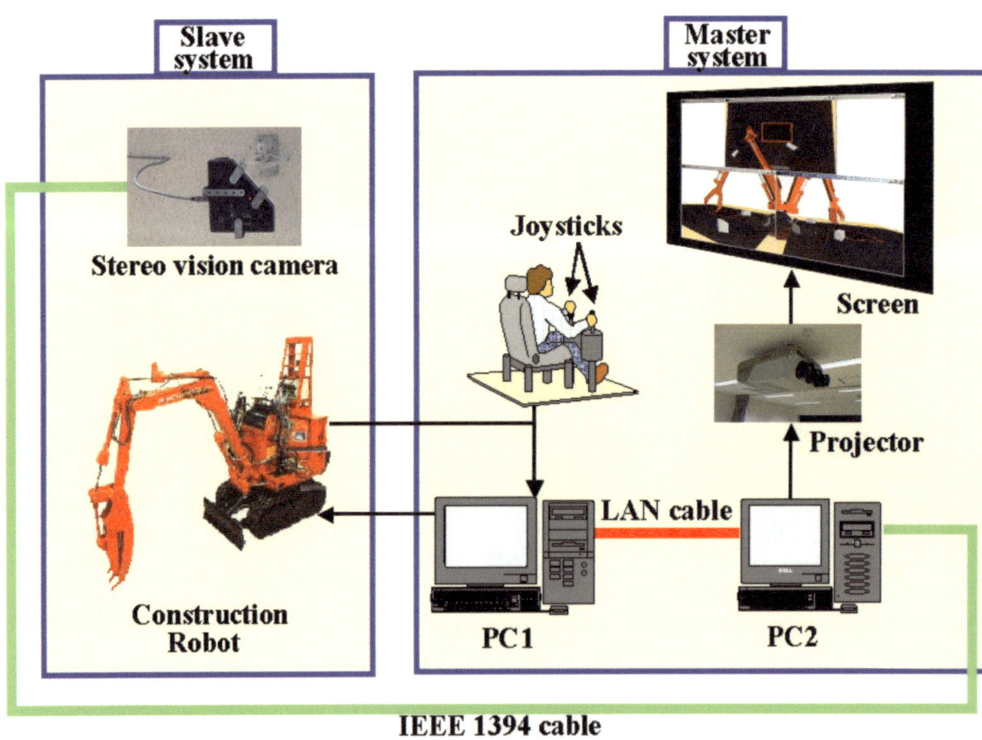

Fig. 3. Construction Tele-Robot System using stereo vision camera

the task object from all directions. Fig. 3 shows a schematic diagram of the developed tele-robotic system with CG presentation. In the figure., PC1 has the same role as the PC in Fig.1. The CG images of the robot and the task object are generated by a graphics computer (PC2) according to the signals received from the joysticks and the stereo vision camera "Digiclops".
Fig.s 4 and 5 show the arrangement of the experimental setup and a top view of the tele-robotic system, respectively. The robot is set on the left-hand side of the operation site. The operator controls the joysticks, watching the screen in front of him/her. The stereo CCD video cameras are arranged at the back left side of the robot; thus, the operator observes the operation field from a back oblique angle through the screen. When the operator looks directly at the robot, he/she is actually looking from the right-hand side.
In this study, the video image of the virtual robot was produced using a graphics library called Open-GL. The produced virtual robot is 1/200th the size of the real one; is composed of ca. 350 polygons; and is able to move in real time.
Details about the implementation of CG images generated from stereo images are as follows. The CG image of the robot is generated according to the displacements, which are detected from sensors attached to the hydraulic cylinders. On the other hand, the CG images of the objects are generated using the Digiclops. In this experiment, it is assumed that the robot handles only several concrete blocks as work objects and the other objects are neglected because of the limitation of the computer processing power. The shape of these objects is represented by a convex polygon element. The Digiclops is set up just above the robot as shown in Fig.4. The optical axis of the Digiclops is made to intersect the floor perpendicularly. The stereo algorithm, which is installed in the Digiclops, is reliable enough for this application. Thus, the CG images of the objects are generated according to the following procedure.

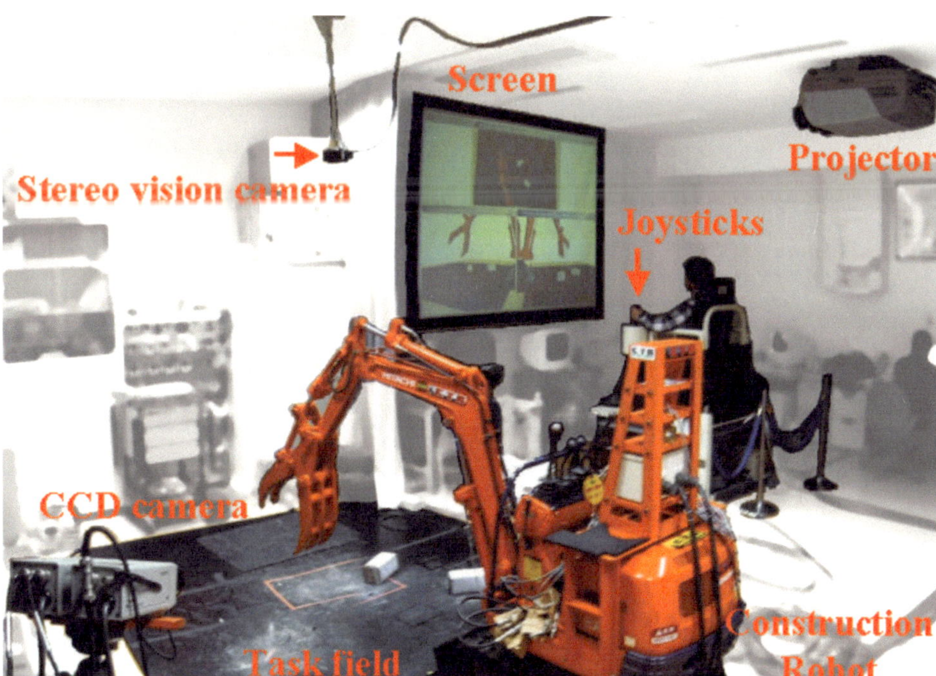

Fig. 4. Arrangement of system

1. Digiclops measures the distance to a task object and also captures a video image in its field of view
2. The image of the robot arm is eliminated by using color data on the video image.
3. After the image of the objects has been extracted from the distance data, a binary image of the objects is generated and labeling is executed.
4. Small objects with a size less than 10x10 cm are eliminated.
5. The shape of the objects is obtained by computing the convex hull.

The animated CG image of the objects is generated by repeating above (1)-(4). The moment at which an object is grasped by the robot is detected from the relationship between the measured displacements of the robot arm and the size of the object. While the robot is holding the object, a CG image of the robot and the held object are generated by using the information on the moment at which it was grasped. After the robot releases the object, the object is recognized again by using the above process. The experiment was conducted in an indoor environment. As to the generation algorithm of the CG image of the objects, the elimination of the robot from the camera image is robust enough to conduct the experiment under various interior lighting conditions. (We have not yet executed the outdoor experiment. The outdoor experiment is planned as future work.)

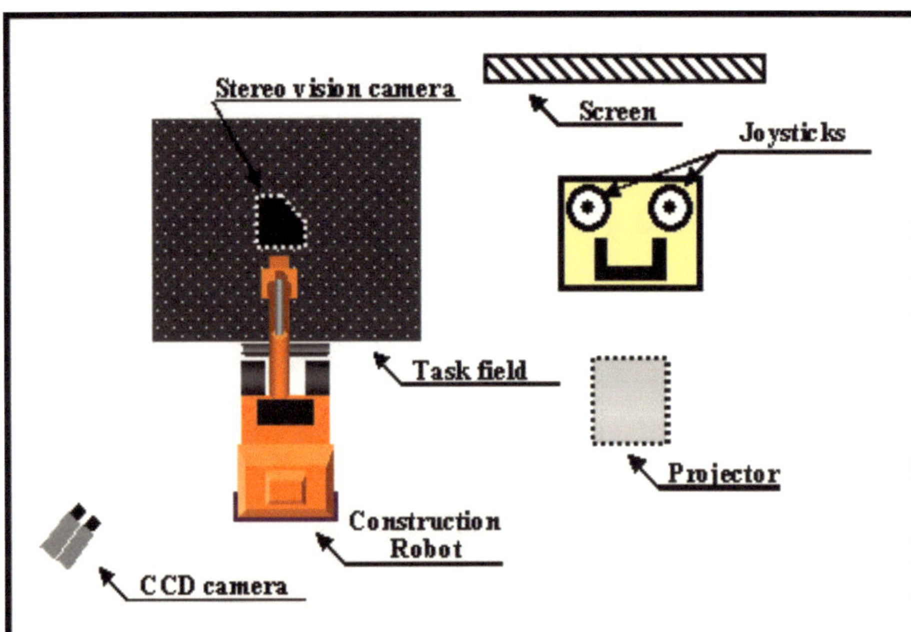

Fig. 5. Arrangement of the system (top view)

3. Experimental results

In the experiment, the operator controls the robot by using the joysticks according to predetermined tasks. In the beginning, the robot is set at the neutral position (Fig.6), and two concrete blocks are placed on a pair of the marked places each other (Fig.7). The operator grasps one of the concrete blocks set in a marked place, then carries it to the center marked place and releases it. Subsequently, and in a similar fashion, the operator grasps and carries the other block.

As control conditions for the operator, three types of visual presentation, shown in Table 1, are set. That is, "Stereo Video" corresponds to the stereo vision presentation given by stereo CCD cameras. In this case, the operator observes the operation field from a back oblique angle through the screen because the stereo CCD video cameras are arranged to the back left side of the robot. (In the case in which the stereo CCD cameras are arranged on the construction robot, the visibility is poor because the operation field is hidden by the robot arm. Therefore, the best viewpoint is found by trial and error.) "CG" corresponds to the presentation of the virtual robot and task objects by Computer Graphics, and "Direct" corresponds to watching the task field directly. In this case, the operator is actually looking from the right-hand side because the operation platform is set up to the right of the robot as shown in Fig.5.

In the experiments, three kinds of CG video images of the virtual robot are simultaneously presented to the operator. The first is a lateral view from the left-hand side; the second a lateral view from the right-hand side; and the third a top view. These view angles were selected so that the operator could effectively confirm the position of two concrete blocks. Fig. 8 shows a projected image presented to the operator.

Fig. 6. Task field

Fig. 7. Image from CCD camera

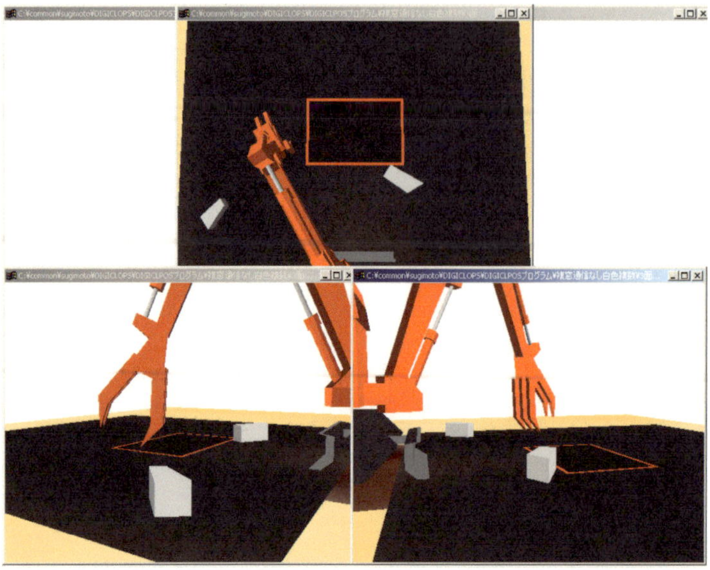

Fig. 8. CG image

Thirty-three subjects served as respective operators of the robot, and we measured the time it took each subject to complete the task. Moreover, we counted the number of failed attempts—that is, when a subject could not succeed in completing a task.

Abbreviation	Conditions
Stereo Video	Operator observes in stereo vision provided by stereo CCD cameras.
CG	Virtual robot and task object are presented solely by Computer Graphics.
Direct	Operator controls the robot while watching the task field directly.

Table 1. Control conditions for the operator

Fig. 9 shows the average values of the tasking times it took the 33 subjects to complete the assigned tasks. The average tasking time in "Stereo Video" was longer than that in "CG" or "Direct". This is thought to be due to the difficulty the operator has in observing the operation field only from a back oblique angle through the screen in the case of "Stereo Video". In the case of "CG", however, the operator has access to a VR image of the robot, even when the robot is at a dead angle; thus, the tasking times in this case is considered to nearly coincide with those in "Direct".

Fig. 10 shows the ratio of tasking time of direct control to that of each experiment. Based on this result, the efficiency in "Stereo Video" is approximately 40%. To date, several types of telerobotic construction systems have been tested by construction companies in Japan, and it was reported that their working efficiency of remote operation by using stereo video was from 30% to 50% of that in direct operation. Therefore, our result is quite similar to the efficiency of 'Stereo Video' illustrated in Fig.10. On the other hand, the efficiency in "CG" amounts to nearly 80%. These results confirm the usefulness of the VR image.

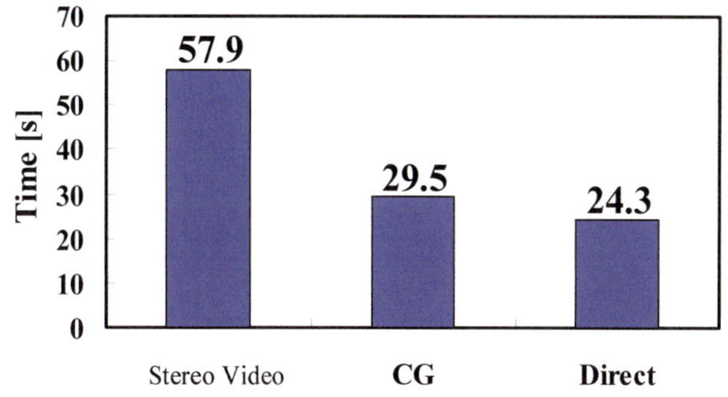

Fig. 9. Average values of tasking times

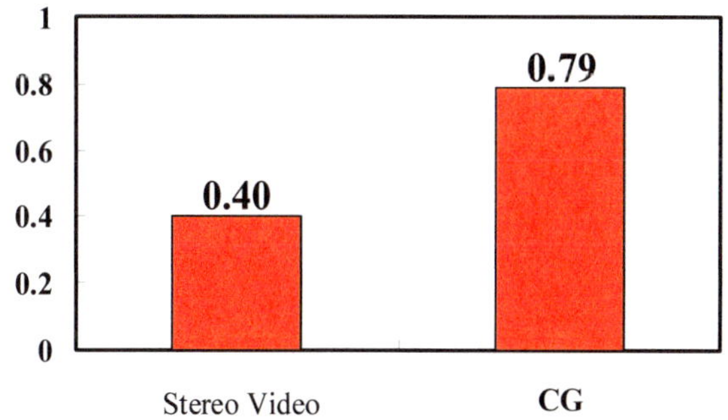

Fig. 10. The ratio of tasking time of direct control to that of each experiment

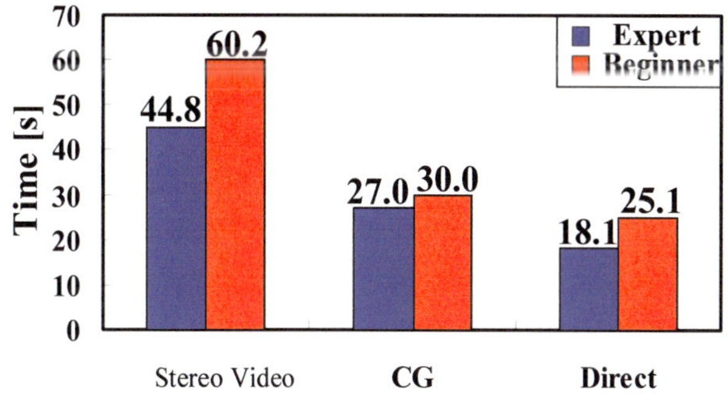

Fig. 11. The time required by an expert and that by a beginner

Fig. 11 shows the time required by experts (operators who had operated the tele-robot system several times before) and that by beginners (operators operating the tele-robot system for the first time). In our study, there were 5 experts and 26 beginners. In this figure, it can be seen that the graphs of experts and beginners show nearly the same shape. However, the tasking time of the beginners is longer than that of the experts. The difference in tasking time between the beginners and the experts is the smallest in the case of "CG", indicating that CG presentation is most effective for beginners.

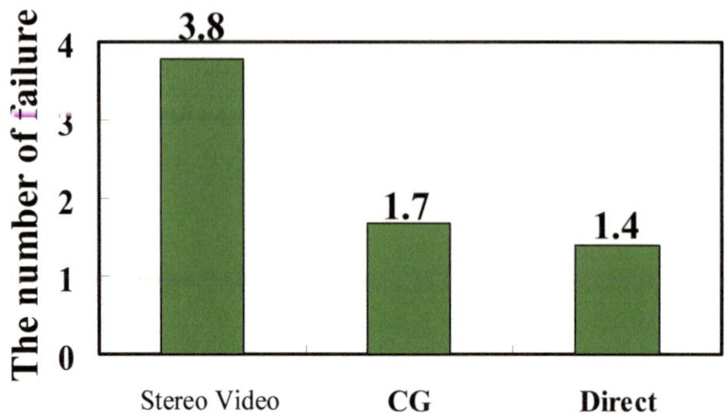

Fig. 12. The average of the number of failed attempts

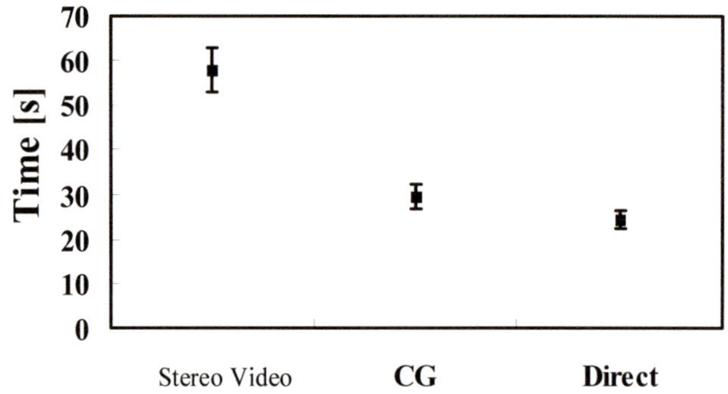

Fig. 13. Standard deviation

Fig. 12 shows the average number of failed attempts. We can see in the figure that the number of failed attempts in "CG" is less than half that in "Stereo Video". This is because in the former, the operators could recognize the end position of the robot arm accurately, via the CG image. We will add the function of "zoom-in with CG and view only the interesting parts" in future work. Use of that function is expected to reduce the number of failed attempts.

Fig. 13 shows the dispersion of the tasking times with standard deviation. From the figure, it can be seen that the tasking times in "Stereo Video" vary relatively widely. In the case of "CG" or "Direct", on the other hand, the dispersion is small, as a result of the stability of the tasks.

Another task, one in which the robot piles up blocks, was also executed. The efficiency results obtained were similar to those outlined above. Therefore, a similar result is expected for other tasks. However, we did not execute experiments on tasks such as excavating the ground because that kind of work is impracticable for the system. Investigation of such tasks will be undertaken in future work.

4. Conclusion

In this research, we investigated a tele-robotic construction system developed by us. In our previous study, we developed a system that presents video images transmitted from an operation field. This image was generated by a pair of stereo CCD cameras, allowing a real stereo video image to be observed through 3D glasses. However, this system was difficult in that the operator observed the operation field only from a back oblique angle through the screen. We considered that if, instead of the video, CG of the robot were presented to the operator, the task efficiency would be expected to increase because the operator would have a multi-angle view of the operation field.

In the present study, we investigated the application of a method that allows the operator to obtain a better sense of the operation field, in order to confirm that this method allowed the operator to control the robot more effectively and stably. To this end, CG images of a virtual robot were generated. It was expected that watching a thus obtained VR robot image in addition to viewing the task object would increase the task efficiency. In the experiments, the task of carrying a concrete block was performed by 33 operators, some of whom were amateurs. The results confirmed statistically that the tasking time was shortened by introduction of the VR images. Considering that the 3D glasses are tiring to wear, the overall usefulness of the developed system remains to be assessed.

5. References

Azuma, R.T. (1997). A Survey of Augmented Reality in Presence, *Teleoperators and Virtual Environments*, Vol. 6, No. 4, pp. 355-385.

DiMaio, S.P.; Salcudean, S.E.; Reboulet, C.; Tafazoli, S. & Hashtrudi-Zaad, K. (1998). A Virtual Excavator for Controller Development and Evaluation, *Proceedings of IEEE International Conference on Robotics and Automation*, pp. 52-58.

Goertz, R.C. (1952). Fundamentals of General-Purpose Remote Manipulators, *Nucleonics*, Vol. 10, No. 11, pp. 36-42.

Kanade, T.; Rander, P. & Narayanan, P. (1997). Virtualized Reality: Constructing Virtual Worlds from Real Scenes, *IEEE Multimedia Magazine*, Vol. 1, pp. 34-47.

Kim, W.S. (1996). Virtual Reality Calibration and Preview / Predictive Displays for Telerobotics, *Presence: Teleoperators and Virtual Environments*, Vol. 5, No. 2, pp. 173-190.

Milgram, P.; Zhai, S.; Drascic, D. & Grodski, J.J. (1993). Applications of Augmented Reality for Human-Robot Communication, *Proceedings of International Conference on Intelligent Robotics and Systems*, pp. 1467-1472.

Minsky, M. (1980). Telepresence, Omni Publications International Ltd., New York.

Salcudean, S.E.; Hashtrudi-Zaad, K.; Tafazoli, S.; DiMaio, S.P. & Reboulet, C. (1999). Bilateral Matched-Impedance Teleoperation with Applications to Excavator Control, *Control Systems Magazine*, Vol. 19, No. 6, pp. 29-37.

Tachi, S.; Maeda, T.; Yanagida, Y.; Koyanagi, M. & Yokoyama, Y. (1996). A Method of Mutual Tele-existence in a Virtual Environment, *Proceedings of the ICAT*, pp. 9-18.

Tachi, S. (1998). Real-time Remote Robotics - Toward Networked Telexistence, *IEEE Computer Graphics and Applications*, pp. 6-9.

Tafazoli, S.; Lawrence, P.D. & Salcudean, S. E. (1999). Identification of Inertial and Friction Parameters for Excavator Arms, *IEEE Transactions on Robotics and Automation*, Vol. 15, No. 5, pp. 966-971.

Tharp, G.; Hayati, S. & Phan, L. (1994). Virtual Window Telepresence System for Telerobotic Inspection, *SPIE Proceedings* Vol. 2351, Telemanipulator and Telepresence Technologies, pp. 366-373.

Utsumi, M.; Hirabayashi, T. & Yoshie, M. (2002). Development for Teleoperation Underwater Grasping System in Unclear Environment, *IEEE Proceedings of the 2002 Int. Symp. on Underwater Technology*, pp.349-353.

Yamada, H.; Muto, T. & Ohashi, G. (1999). Development of a Telerobotics System for Construction Robot Using Virtual Reality, *Proceedings-of European Control Conference ECC'99*, F1000-6.

Yamada, H.; Kato, H. & Muto, T. (2003a). Master-Slave Control for Construction Robot Teleoperation, *Journal of Robotics and Mechatronics*, Vol. 15, No. 1, pp. 54-60.

Yamada, H. & Muto, T. (2003b). Development of a Hydraulic Tele-operated Construction Robot using Virtual Reality - New Master-Slave Control Method and an Evaluation of a Visual Feedback System -, *International Journal of Fluid Power*, Vol. 4, No. 2, pp. 35-42.

Zhao, D.; Xia, Y.; Yamada, H. & Muto, T. (2002). Presentation of Realistic Motion to the Operator in Operating a Tele-operated Construction Robot, *Journal of Robotics and Mechatronics*, Vol. 14, No. 2, pp. 98-104.

Zhao, D.; Xia, Y.; Yamada, H. & Muto, T. (2003). Control Method for Realistic Motions in a Construction Tele-robotic System with a 3-DOF Parallel Mechanism, *Journal of Robotics and Mechatronics*, Vol. 15, No. 4, pp.361-368.

14

Navigation in a Box Stereovision for Industry Automation

Giacomo Spampinato, Jörgen Lidholm, Fredrik Ekstrand, Carl Ahlberg, Lars Asplund and Mikael Ekström
School of innovation, design and technology, Mälardalen University
Sweden

1. Introduction

The research presented addresses the emerging topic of AGVs (Automated Guided Vehicles) specifically related to industrial sites. The work presented has been carried out in the frame of the MALTA project (Multiple Autonomous forklifts for Loading and Transportation Applications), a joint research project between industry and university, funded by the European Regional Development and Robotdalen, in partnership with the Swedish Knowledge Foundation. The project objective is to create fully autonomous forklift trucks for paper reel handling. The result is expected to be of general benefit for industries that use forklift trucks in their material handling through higher operating efficiency and better flexibility with reduced risk for accidents and handling damages than if only manual forklift trucks are used.

A brief overview of the state of the art in AGVs will be reported in order to better understand the new challenges and technologies. Among the emerging technologies used for vehicle automation, vision is one of the most promising in terms of versatility and efficiency, with a high potential to drastically reduce the costs.

2. AGVs for industry, new challenges and technologies

Commonly known as AGVs, automatic vehicles able to drive autonomously while transporting materials and goods are present on the market since the middle of the 20th century. They are both used in indoor and outdoor environments for industrial as well as for service applications for improving the production efficiency and reducing the staff costs.

In field robotics, fully autonomous vehicles are of great interest and still a challenge for researchers and industrial entrepreneurs. The concepts of mobile robotics in indoor and outdoor environment has already exploded on the market in the recent years with a large amount of "intelligent" products like autonomous lawn mower, vacuum cleaner robots, and ATS (Automatic Transportation Systems) in public services. Although the huge amount of automatic moving platforms already present on the market, almost no one is able to perform automatic navigation in dynamic environments without predefined information. In indoor environments, traditional AGVs typically rely on magnetic wires placed on the ground or other kind of additional infrastructures, like active inductive elements and reflective bars, located in strategic positions of the working area. Such techniques are mostly used by AGVs

to provide autonomous transportations in industrial sites, (Danaher Motion, Corecon, Omnitech robotic, Egemin Automation), and in service environments like hospitals (TransCar AGV by Swisslog, ALTIS by FMC and MLR). These systems mainly rely on bi-dimensional views from conventional laser based sensors and need pre-defined maps of the environment. As a consequence they show very low flexibility to environment changes.
On the other hand, in outdoor environments, AGVs mainly rely on high-precision global positioning systems (GPS) and predefined maps. One classical example is represented by the construction vehicles field. The current generation of autonomous hauler trucks (the Front Runner system from Komatsu shown in Fig. 1), consists of a vehicle controller over a wireless network, operated via a supervisory computer. Information on target course and speed is sent wirelessly from the supervisory computer, while the GPS is used to obtain the position. The architecture is rather classical for outdoor robotics navigation, and makes use of conventional sensors that are costly and do not provide complete 3D information about shapes and obstacles. Moreover, the navigation quality is strongly dependent on the GPS precision, and cannot be used in indoor environments or near buildings. There exist also several mining loaders on the market, from different manufacturers, like Atlas Copco, Sandvik, and Caterpillar that are semiautonomous with very simple trajectory following techniques, and normally remote controlled while loading and unloading.

Fig. 1. Two examples of ATS: the automatic hauler track Front Runner from Kumatsu operating in outdoor, and the autonomous trailer drive from Swisslog operating indoor.

Fully autonomous navigation is still on the research level and rare examples are present on the market as a commercial product. It requires autonomous self localization and simultaneous map building of unknown environments, with additional capabilities of unforeseen obstacles detection and avoidance. Dynamic path planning and online trajectory generation is also essential to guarantee an acceptable trade-off between efficiency and safety. A recent overview of the challenges in dynamic environments can be found in [Laugier & Chatilla, 2007].
On the other hand, vision is broadly recognized as the most versatile sensor for recognition and surveillance in non controlled situations, where the conventional laser based solutions are not suitable without using costly and complex equipments. Typically, 2D environmental representations provided by laser scanners cannot capture the complexity of the unstructured dynamic environments, especially in outdoor scenarios.
At present, industrial vision systems are equipped with fast image processing algorithms and highly descriptive feature detectors that provide impressive performances in highly

controlled situations. However it is not always possible to achieve an adequate level of control of the environmental settings.
Autonomous vehicle navigation is often achieved by using specific infrastructures, which are seen by the system as artificial landmarks. Some examples available on the market are given through video based solutions that use image processing for recognizing different unique patterns spread in strategic positions of the environment (like Sky-trax).
The obvious drawback with this approach is the additional effort required to "dress" the working space with external material not related to the production lines. Sometimes it is also impossible to modify the environmental setting due to the highly dynamic conditions in the production operations.
To overcome these drawbacks, a more versatile and robust vision system is required, which allows automatic vehicle navigation using only pre-existing information from the working setting that is seen by the system as "natural landmarks". This concept requires a new paradigm for the traditional image processing approach that shifts the attention from the two dimensions to the more complete and emerging 3D vision. A three dimensional representation of the operational space is necessary, and modern cameras are able to provide high resolution images with high frame rates. Stereovision is one of the most advanced methodologies today established in the field of 3D vision and utilize the sense of depth and the possibility to build a 3D map of the explored environment by the use of multiple views of the scene. We propose high speed stereo vision to achieve unmanned transportation in structured dynamic environments.

3. Description of the system

The stereo vision system is made of two 5-megapixel CMOS digital image sensors from Micron (MT9P031) and a Xilinx Virtex II XC2V8000 eight million gates equivalent FPGA .

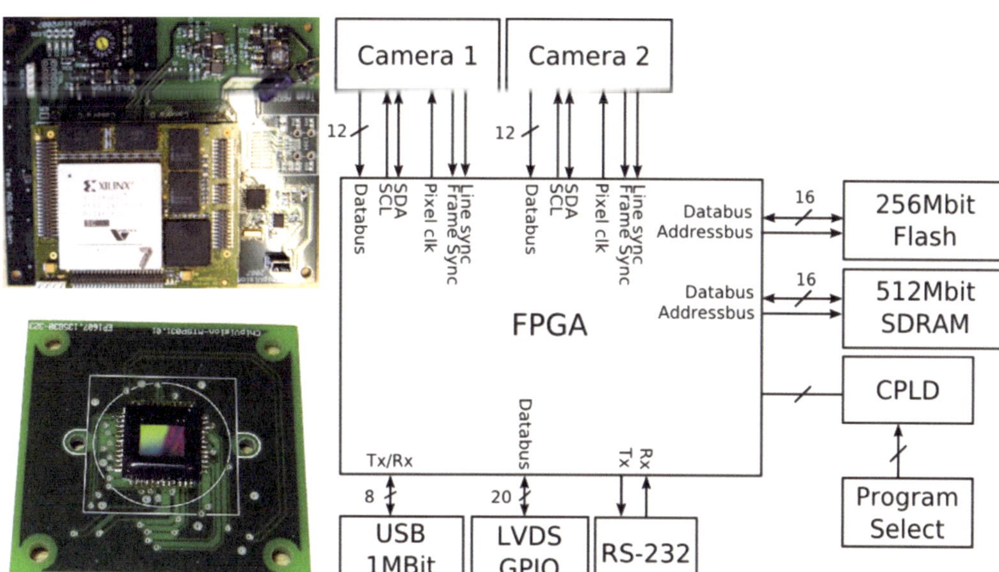

Fig. 2. The HW platform block diagram

On the board there is also 512 MB SDRAM and 256 MB Flash EPROM. The board can hold up to seven different configurations for the FPGA stored in Flash, thus seven different algorithms can be selected during run-time. The FPGA can communicate with the external systems over USB at 1 MBit/s. The system architecture is shown in Fig. 2.
The final configuration of the stereo system includes the camera sensors, two optical lenses, camera board, FPGA, the power supply and USB interface. All is packed in a compact aluminium box (19x12x4cm3) easy to install and configure through the USB connection. Fig. 3 shows the box and the optics adopted. The lenses adopted are two fisheye lenses with 2,1mm focal length from Mini-Objektiv, with F2.0 aperture and 100 degrees field of view. The system also includes additional lighting through ten power LEDs mounted on the chassis but not used for the specific application reported.

Fig. 3. The HW platform block diagram

3.1 Stereo camera calibration

The first procedure always needed to start working with a vision system is to perform the calibration in order to identity both the intrinsic and the extrinsic parameters. The calibration procedure has been performed using the Matlab® camera calibration toolbox. The intrinsic parameters identified include the lens distortion map, the principle points coordinates (*C*) for the two sensors and the focal lengths (*f*) in pixel units [Heikkilä & Silvén, 1997], [Zhang, 1999]. For simplicity, the lens distortion function has been assumed to be radial, identified by a sixth order polynomial coefficients (k_i) containing only even exponential terms. As shown by the relation (1), the normalized point (p_n) in image space is required to find the corresponding distorted points (p_d) in the distortion map.

$$p_d = p_n \cdot \left(1 + k_1 \cdot r^2 + k_2 \cdot r^4 + k_3 \cdot r^6\right) + C \tag{1}$$

in which

$$p_n = \begin{bmatrix} p_x - C_x \\ \\ p_y - C_y \end{bmatrix}, \quad r = |p_n| \tag{2}$$

Typically, one or two coefficients are enough to compensate for the lens distortion, but in the actual case of the fisheye lenses adopted, all three coefficients have been used. The comparison between the use of two (fourth order distortion model) instead of three (sixth order distortion model) terms in the polynomial map (1), is shown in Fig. 4. The fourth order model is unable to compensate for the strong distortion introduced by the fisheye lens (Fig. 4 - c), which is correctly compensated by the sixth order model (Fig. 4 - d).

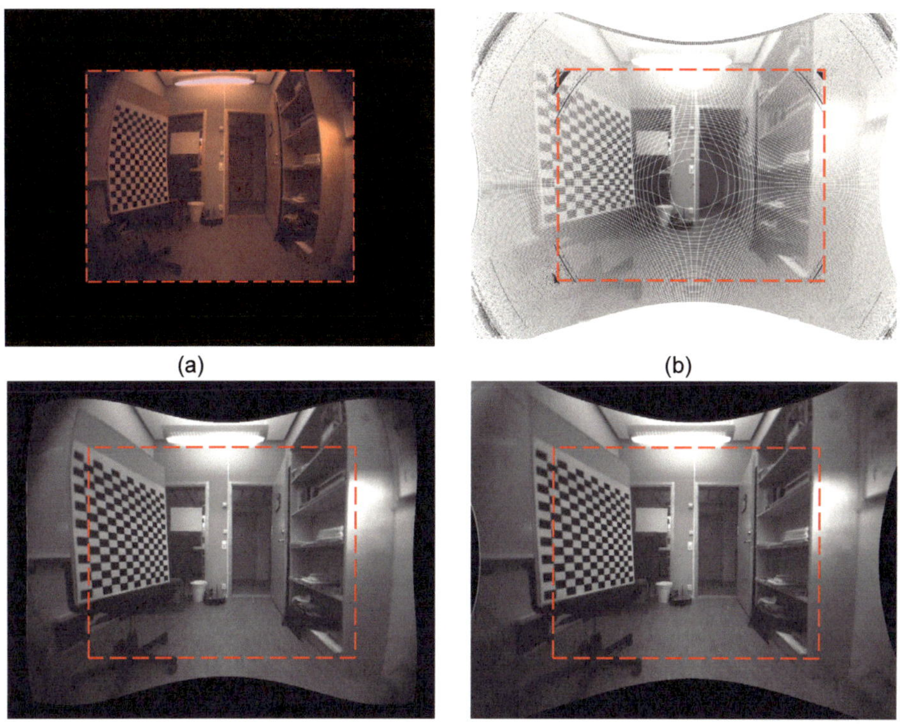

Fig. 4. Original image (a), fourth order distortion compensation (c), sixth order distortion compensation (d). The red squares indicate the original image size. (b) shows the undistorted image without bilinear interpolation.

It is worth to note that the original image size has been expanded by a factor of 1.6 (1024x768) in order to use all the visual information acquired. The principle point has been rescaled according to the new image resolution. The red square in Fig. 4, shows the original image size 640x480.

The undistortion procedure is applied online through an undistortion look up table pre-computed offline using the iterative algorithm described in [Heikkilä & Silvén, 1997] reversing the relation (1). Once the lens distortion has been correctly identified and compensated, the camera system can be used as a standard projective camera, and the pin-hole camera model has been adopted. According to the projective geometry, the 3x4 camera matrix $\boldsymbol{P}$ relates the point $\boldsymbol{p}$ in the image space with the feature $\boldsymbol{F}$ in the 3D space both in homogenous coordinates [Kannala et al., 2009]. Such a matrix is calculated according to the equations (3), where $\boldsymbol{R}$ and $\boldsymbol{T}$ represent the camera pose in terms of rotation and translation with respect to the global reference frame, also known as the extrinsic parameters identified by the calibration procedure.

$$K=\begin{bmatrix} f_x & 0 & C_x \\ 0 & f_y & C_y \\ 0 & 0 & 1 \end{bmatrix} \text{ and } P=K\cdot\begin{bmatrix} R & T \end{bmatrix} \tag{3}$$

$$p=\begin{bmatrix} p_x \\ p_y \\ 1 \end{bmatrix}=\tilde{F}/\tilde{F}_z=\begin{bmatrix} \tilde{F}_x/\tilde{F}_z \\ \tilde{F}_y/\tilde{F}_z \\ 1 \end{bmatrix} \text{ in which } \tilde{F}=\begin{bmatrix} \tilde{F}_x \\ \tilde{F}_y \\ \tilde{F}_z \end{bmatrix}=K\cdot\begin{bmatrix} R & T \end{bmatrix}\cdot\begin{bmatrix} F_x \\ F_y \\ F_z \\ 1 \end{bmatrix}=P\cdot F \tag{4}$$

In the simple case of $R=I$ and $T=[0\ 0\ 0]^T$ the relation (4) yields

$$p=\begin{bmatrix} p_x \\ p_y \\ 1 \end{bmatrix}=\begin{bmatrix} f_x\cdot\dfrac{F_x}{F_z}+C_x \\ f_y\cdot\dfrac{F_y}{F_z}+C_y \\ 1 \end{bmatrix} \tag{5}$$

According to the stereo vision conventions, the translation and rotation matrices ***R*** and ***T*** represent the position and orientation of the right camera with respect the left one, whereas the global reference frame is placed on the center of the left camera image sensor, giving $R=I$ and $T=[0\ 0\ 0]^T$ as left extrinsic parameters. Extending the relations (3) to the stereo system, the left and right camera matrices can be expressed as $P_R=K_R\cdot\begin{bmatrix} R & T \end{bmatrix}$ and $P_L=K_L\cdot\begin{bmatrix} I & 0 \end{bmatrix}$.

4. Feature extraction

The Harris and Stephens combined corner and edge detection algorithm [Harris & Stephens, 1988] has been implemented in hardware on the FPGA working in real-time. The purpose is to extract the image features in a sequence of images taken by the two cameras for subsequent stereo matching and triangulation. The algorithm is based on a local autocorrelation window and performs very well on natural images. The window traverses the image with small shifts and tests each pixel by comparing it to neighbouring pixels. A Gaussian filter returns the most distinct corners within a projected 5x5 pixels window sliding over the final feature set. Pixels whose strength is above an experimental threshold are chosen as visual features.

To gain real-time speed of the system, the algorithm is designed as a pipeline, so each step executes in parallel. (Three different window generators are used for the derivative, factorization, and comparison masks).

The resulting corner detector algorithm is powerful and produces repeatable features extraction. Fig. 5, shows the block diagram of the feature extractor.

The core of the algorithm is based on the autocorrelation window ***M*** that makes use of the horizontal (along the rows: $\partial I/\partial X$) and vertical (along the columns $\partial I/\partial Y$) partial derivatives as shown in Fig. 6.

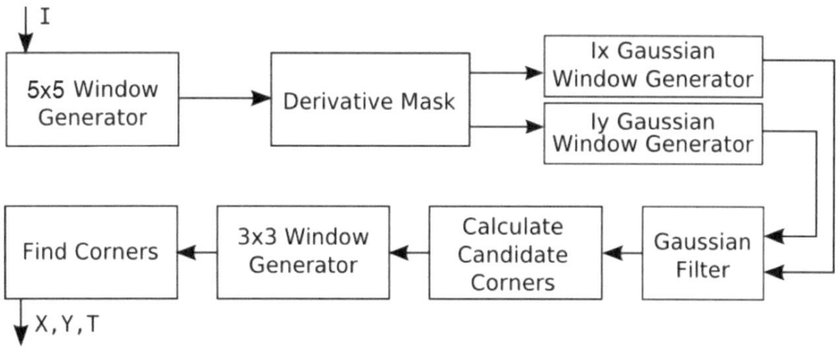

Fig. 5. Stephens-Harris features extractor block diagram

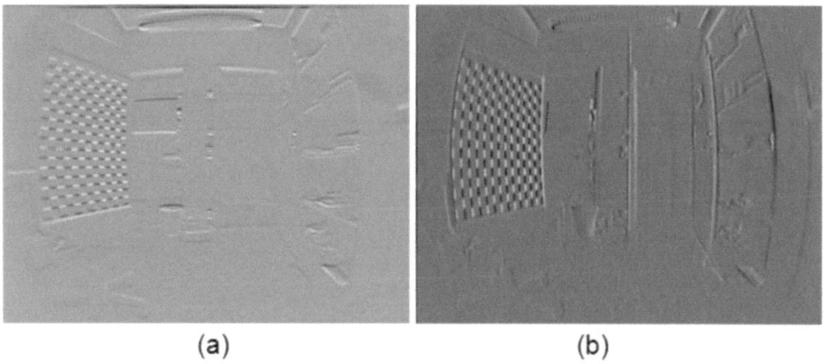

Fig. 6. Image partial derivatives: horizontal image gradient (a), vertical image gradient (b)

From the autocorrelation mask ***M*** and its convolution with the Gaussian kernel ***G*** (6) two methods for extracting the "*cornerness*" value ***R*** against a fixed threshold are universally accepted by the research community: the original method from Harris and Stephens [Harris & Stephens, 1988] (7) and the variation proposed by Noble [Noble 1989] (8) in order to avoid the heuristic choice of the ***k*** value (commonly fixed to 0.04 as suggested in [Harris & Stephens, 1988]).

$$M = \begin{bmatrix} \left(\frac{\partial I}{\partial X}\right)^2 & \left(\frac{\partial I}{\partial X}\cdot\frac{\partial I}{\partial Y}\right) \\ \left(\frac{\partial I}{\partial X}\cdot\frac{\partial I}{\partial Y}\right) & \left(\frac{\partial I}{\partial Y}\right)^2 \end{bmatrix} \bullet G \tag{6}$$

$$R = det(M) - k \cdot \left[Tr(M)\right]^2 \tag{7}$$

$$R = \frac{det(M)}{Tr(M) + \varepsilon} \tag{8}$$

As shown if Fig. 7, the choice of the two methods for extracting the "*cornerness*" value are rather equivalent and both effective for the case analyzed in our proposed applications. The main difference is the dynamic threshold that has to be three magnitude orders more in case (7) than (8). This is due to the division that keeps the "*cornerness*" lower.

In Fig. 7 the original Harris is reported in (a) and (b) whereas the Noble case in (c) and (d). On the left side the result of the processing after the autocorrelation M is shown, whereas on the right side, the Harris corners extraction after the thresholding is reported. In the Harris case, a threshold around 10^6 has been applied, whereas 10^3 has been used in the Noble case.

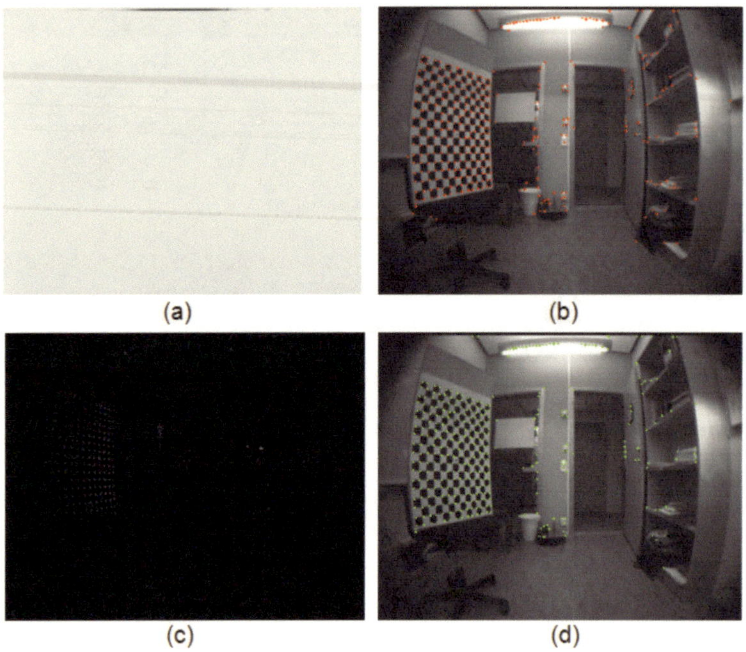

Fig. 7. Comparison between the two methods for corner extraction : Original Harris (a,b), and the Noble variant (c,d).

In our implementation we decided to implement the original method (7) by Harris and Stephens since the division implementation of (8) in the FPGA would have required a lot more resources more.

5. Stereo matching

After the features extraction, the matching of the interest points in the different cameras has to be performed. This phase is essential in stereo and in multiple views based vision, and represents an overhead with respect to a monocular solutions. On the other hand, the matching process acts as a filter removing the most of the noise produced from the feature extraction, since only the strongest features are matched. Although increasing the computational load, the stereo matching increases the process robustness as well.
Two different techniques have been implemented and tested to perform the stereo matching between the left and right images from the stereo rig. Once the features have been extracted from the images, the ICP (Iterative Closest Point) algorithm has been applied to the feature points in order to overlap the two point constellations and find a rigid transformation (rotation and translation) between the images. Since the images are just undistorted but not rectified, a fully rigid transformation (rotation and translation) is needed. The resulting disparity between the two images is considerably reduced, as the example shown in Fig. 8,

so that the correlation based matching on the transformed feature points results in a reduced number of outliers, since the maximum search distance for matching is reduced. A typical reduction in the search distance using this technique is about 70%. Fig. 8 shows sequentially the undistorted stereo images, their overlap from the ICP, and the final features correspondences.

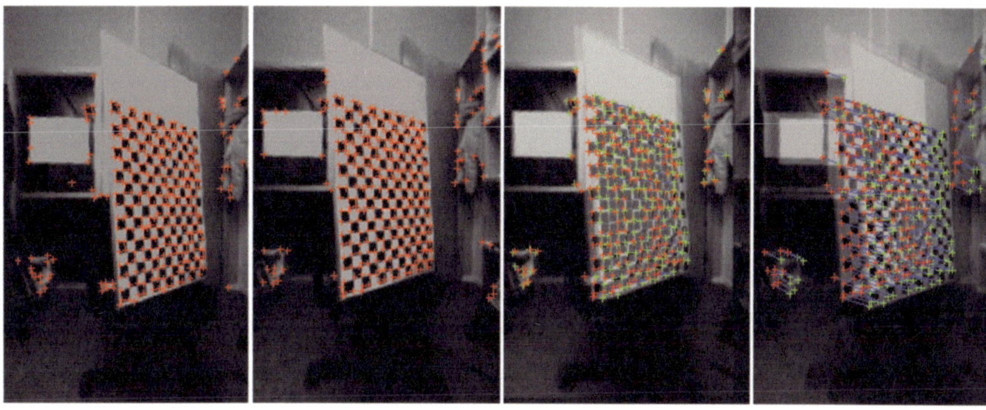

Fig. 8. Stereo matching using the ICP algorithm and correlation

The matching of the feature points is based on the normalized cross correlation (9) computed over an 11x11 window that yields the number of rows ***R*** and columns ***C*** in (9). About 80% of the corresponding features are correctly matched.

$$Corr = \sum_{r=1}^{R}\sum_{c=1}^{C} \frac{IL(p_{rc}) \cdot IR(p_{rc})}{\sqrt{\sum_{r=1}^{R}\sum_{c=1}^{C} IL(p_{rc})} \cdot \sqrt{\sum_{r=1}^{R}\sum_{c=1}^{C} IR(p_{rc})}} \qquad (9)$$

To reduce the computational load, the matching algorithm has been implemented to work directly within the feature space using binary images. The advantage of using this approach is to simplify the cross correlation implementation in the FPGA by reducing the amount of information. The binary images are compared with the XOR bitwise operator instead of the binary multiplication, as shown in (10).

$$Corr = \sum_{r=1}^{R}\sum_{c=1}^{C} \frac{not\left\{XOR\left[IL(p_{rc}), IR(p_{rc})\right]\right\}}{R \cdot C} \qquad (10)$$

One example of this technique is shown in Fig. 9, where the ICP is applied to edge reference points and matched with an 11x11 correlation window according to (10). In this case, only 60 % of the corresponding features are correctly matched.

Although the ICP algorithm performs quite robustly, due to its iterative nature, it is time consuming and it is difficult to be parallelized for the implementation into the FPGA.

Another option is to use the epipolar constraint on the undistorted images, using the intrinsic and extrinsic parameters obtained from the calibration. The essential and the fundamental matrices are computed according to (11) and (12) respectively.

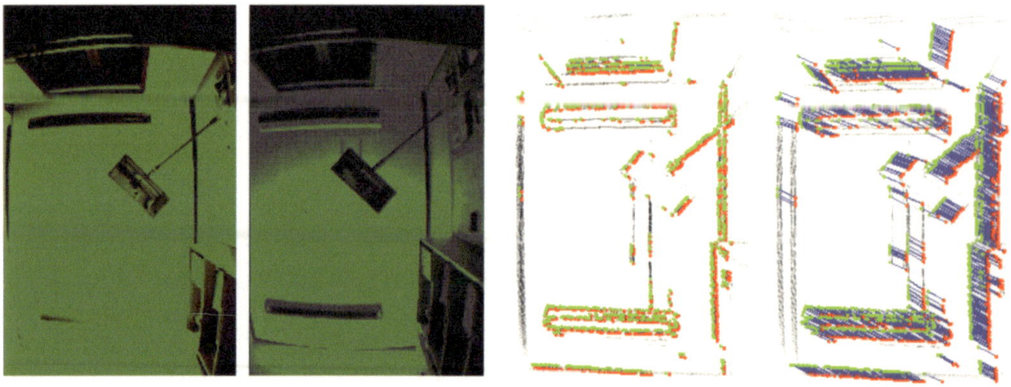

Fig. 9. Stereo matching through ICP and correlation using binary images.

$$E = S(T) \cdot R \tag{11}$$

$$F = K_R^{-T} \cdot E \cdot K_L^{-1} \tag{12}$$

As well known from the multiple view projective geometry theory [Hardley & Zisserman, 2000], for each feature extracted from the left image, the corresponding point in the right image lies on the corresponding epipolar line on the right image whose analytical coefficients are easily extracted from the fundamental matrix ***F***. Instead of using the ICP algorithm, a proper search window has to be defined in order to apply the correlation function (10) to the possible corresponding candidates along the epipolar line. The search window is defined to be large enough to cover the maximum disparity at the investigated depth of view. The search window is heuristically defined and strongly depends on the interested depth and the camera vergence. The proposed system has theoretically zero

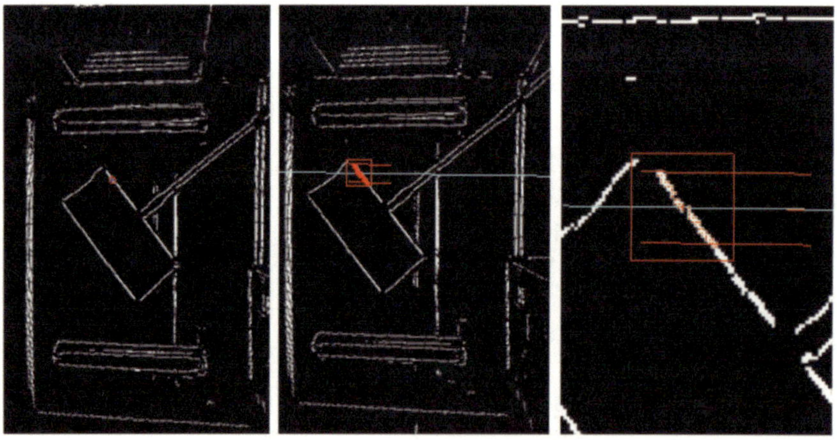

Fig. 10. Stereo matching using the epipolar constraint and the correlation on candidate matches. The search window is represented by the two lines (red) under and above the epipolar line (blue), and the contained candidates within the window are marked in red. Also the correlation window is shown around the correspondent feature indicated by the red square.

vergence due to calibration so that the corresponding feature in the right camera always lies on the left side along the epipolar line with respect to the left feature coordinates (this is not the case of stereo cameras with non zero vergence). In Fig. 10 an example of the described technique is shown. The left feature in the image defines the epipolar line in the right image, as well as the related search window along the epipolar line.

6. Stereo triangulation and depth error modelling

After the corresponding features in the two images are correctly matched, the stereo triangulation can be used to project the interest points in the 3D space. Unfortunately the triangulation procedure is affected by an heteroscedastic error [Matei & Meer, 2006], [Dubbelman & Groen, 2009] (non homogeneous and non isotropic) as shown in Fig.11. An accurate error analysis has been performed in order to provide an uncertainty modelling of the stereo system to the subsequent mapping algorithms that are based on probabilistic estimations. Both 2D and 3D modelling has been investigated.
Knowing the feature projections in the left and right images x_L and x_R, the two dimensional triangulated point $\boldsymbol{P}$ can be found by the well known relations (13), as a function of the baseline $\boldsymbol{b}$ and the focal length $\boldsymbol{f}$.

$$P_X = \frac{x_L + x_R}{x_L - x_R} \cdot \frac{b}{2} \qquad P_Z = \frac{b \cdot f}{x_L - x_R} \tag{13}$$

$$P_X(s) = \frac{x_L \pm s + x_R \pm s}{x_L \pm s - x_R \mp s} \cdot \frac{b}{2} \qquad P_Z(s) = \frac{b \cdot f}{x_L \pm s - x_R \mp s} \tag{14}$$

A noise error ±$\boldsymbol{s}$ has been added to the features coordinates in both images, and the resulting noise in the triangulation is represented by a rhomboid whose shape is analytically described by eight points obtained appropriately adding and subtracting the noise $\boldsymbol{s}$ to the nominal image coordinates through (14). The diagonals $\boldsymbol{D}$ and $\boldsymbol{d}$ in Fig.11 represent the corresponding uncertainty in the space reconstruction. The vertical and horizontal displacements $\boldsymbol{H}$ and $\boldsymbol{W}$ in Fig.11 show the heteroscedastic nature of the reconstruction noise since they have different analytical behaviours (non isotropic in the two dimensions) and non linear variations for each point along the two axis (non homogeneous).

$$\begin{gathered} d(s) = 2\frac{s}{f} \cdot P_Z \qquad D(s) = \sqrt{H^2 + W^2} \\ H(s) = \frac{4 \cdot b \cdot f \cdot s \cdot P_Z^{\,2}}{b^2 \cdot f^2 - 4 \cdot s^2 \cdot P_Z^{\,2}} \qquad W(s) = \left| P_X \cdot \frac{2 \cdot s}{x_L - x_R - 2 \cdot s} \right| + \left| P_X \cdot \frac{2 \cdot s}{x_L - x_R + 2 \cdot s} \right| \end{gathered} \tag{15}$$

It is worth to note that the error along the horizontal axis is the maximum between $\boldsymbol{d}$ and $\boldsymbol{W}$ and coincides with $\boldsymbol{d}$ in all the points that are triangulated between the two cameras (with an horizontal coordinate within the baseline).
To better analyse the heteroscedastic behaviour of the stereo system adopted, the rhomboid descriptive parameters (***H,W,D***), are presented in Fig. 12 as a function of the reconstructed point $\boldsymbol{P}$ in the plane in front of the cameras for an error of three pixels.

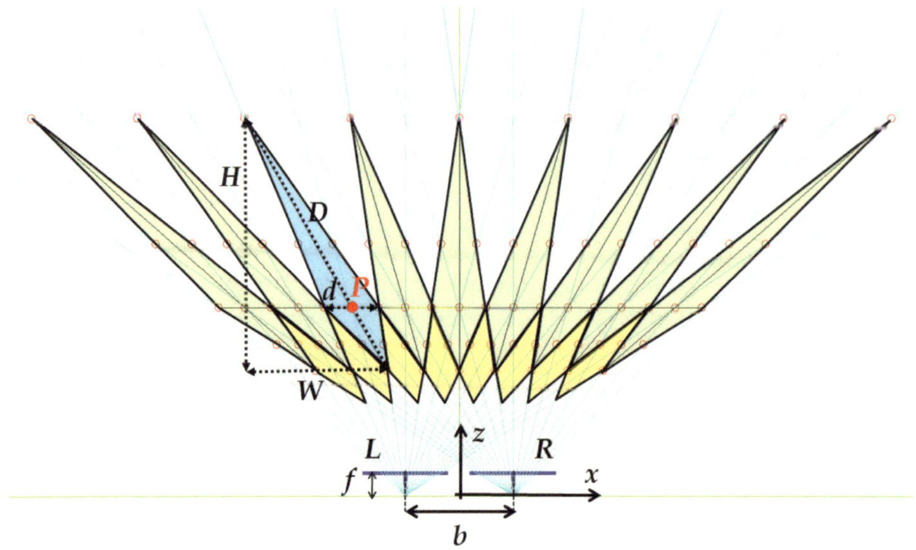

Fig. 11. 2D depth error in stereo triangulation. Two depths of view are reported.

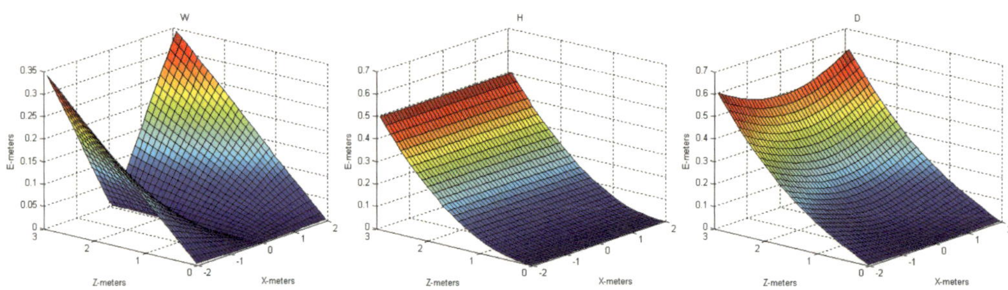

Fig. 12. The descriptive parameters of the rhomboid. From left to right: the horizontal, vertical, and diagonal errors. As expected, only the vertical error remains constant along the horizontal axis while growing non linearly along the vertical axis.

Fig. 13. 3D uncertainty model due to a circular uncertainty in the left and the right images. Matching the feature point in one camera with the circle in the other camera results in the projected ellipse reported inside the 3D intersection region.

Leaving the epipolar plane, the stereo triangulation in 3D space requires a more complex solution in the triangulation procedure since the projective lines could be skew lines in absence of epipolar constraints. Also a more complex 3D error modelling is derived in the

3D space. The feature points affected by a circular noise of certain radius produces two uncertainty circles in the left and in the right images. The corresponding 3D uncertainty is a solid intersection of the two cones obtained projecting the two circles. As direct extension of the two dimensional rhomboid, the solid shape reported in Fig. 13 represents the triangulation uncertainty in 3D space.
The triangulation procedure makes use of a least square solution to minimize reprojection error in both images. The initial hypothesis comes from the extrinsic parameters **R** and **T** that relates the two image planes $P_R = R \cdot P_L + T$, that can be rewritten as $P_{ZR} \cdot F_R = R \cdot P_{ZL} \cdot F_L + T$ using the projective transformations for each image plane.

$$F = \begin{bmatrix} F_x & F_y & 1 \end{bmatrix}^T = \begin{bmatrix} \frac{x}{f} & \frac{y}{f} & 1 \end{bmatrix}^T = \begin{bmatrix} \frac{P_x}{P_z} & \frac{P_y}{P_z} & 1 \end{bmatrix}^T \quad (16)$$

Using the matrix formulation the problem can be rewritten.

$$\begin{bmatrix} F_R & -R \cdot F_L \end{bmatrix} \cdot \begin{bmatrix} P_{ZR} \\ P_{ZL} \end{bmatrix} = T \quad (17)$$

Posing $A = \begin{bmatrix} F_R & -R \cdot F_L \end{bmatrix}$ and solving using the LSM, the 3D point **P** can be computed both in the left and right reference frames.

$$\begin{bmatrix} P_{ZR} \\ P_{ZL} \end{bmatrix} = \left(A^T \cdot A\right)^{-1} \cdot A^T \cdot T \qquad \begin{matrix} P_R = F_R \cdot P_{ZR} \\ P_L = F_L \cdot P_{ZL} \end{matrix} \quad (18)$$

To make a systematic analysis of the triangulation accuracy, analytical relations between the uncertainty in the image space and the related uncertainty in 3D space can be computed through the partial derivatives of the stereo triangulation procedure with respect to the feature points in the two images. Through the jacobian matrix J_{PS} (19) computation, it is easy to find the related 3D uncertainty ΔP under a given uncertainty in **X** and **Y** coordinates in both images.

$$J_{PS} = \frac{\partial P}{\partial S} = \begin{bmatrix} \frac{\partial P_X}{\partial L_X} & \frac{\partial P_X}{\partial L_Y} & \frac{\partial P_X}{\partial R_X} & \frac{\partial P_X}{\partial R_Y} \\ \frac{\partial P_Y}{\partial L_X} & \frac{\partial P_Y}{\partial L_Y} & \frac{\partial P_Y}{\partial R_X} & \frac{\partial P_Y}{\partial R_Y} \\ \frac{\partial P_Z}{\partial L_X} & \frac{\partial P_Z}{\partial L_Y} & \frac{\partial P_Z}{\partial R_X} & \frac{\partial P_Z}{\partial R_Y} \end{bmatrix} \qquad \Delta P = \begin{bmatrix} \Delta P_X \\ \Delta P_Y \\ \Delta P_Z \end{bmatrix} = J_{PS} \cdot \begin{bmatrix} \Delta R_X \\ \Delta R_Y \\ \Delta L_X \\ \Delta L_Y \end{bmatrix} \quad (19)$$

In Fig. 14 the 3D distribution of the uncertainty along the long diagonal (equivalent to **D** in the two dimensional case) is reported, showing the heteroscedastic behaviour.
A known grid pattern, shown in Fig. 15, has been used to measure the triangulation error under the hypothesis of three pixels uncertainty in the image space re-projection. For the stereo system adopted, the 3D reconstruction mostly suffers of uncertainty along the long diagonal (equivalent to **D** in the two dimensional case) of the 3D rhomboid, that is, along the line connecting the centre of the stereo rig and the landmark observed in 3D.

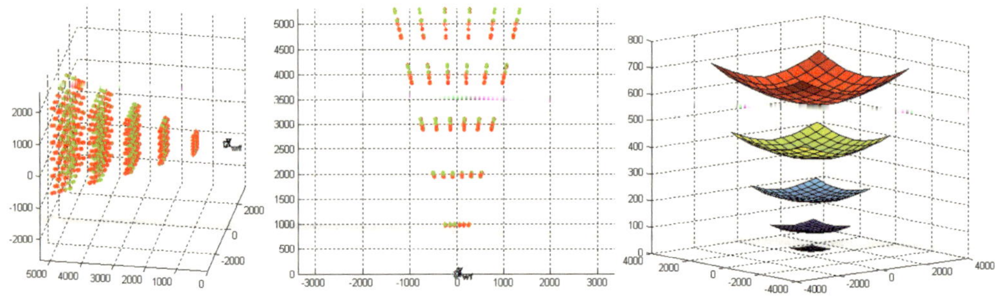

Fig. 14. The 3D uncertainty of the major axis of the ellipsoid related to a grid pattern analyzed at different depths from the cameras.

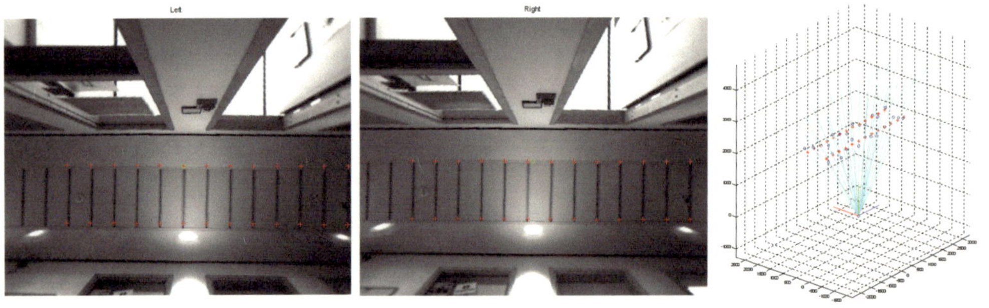

Fig. 15. The reference pattern used to analyse the triangulation error at a 3 m distance from the ceiling.

Extending the reference plane from the ceiling height to arbitrary heights, so that the image projections remain unchanged, the average uncertainty in the three dimensions has been reported in Fig. 16 for distances to the stereo rig from 1 to 30 meters, showing the non linear behaviour as expected. The distribution of the error in the three directions is also presented in the left-most picture for the specific depth of 3 meters.

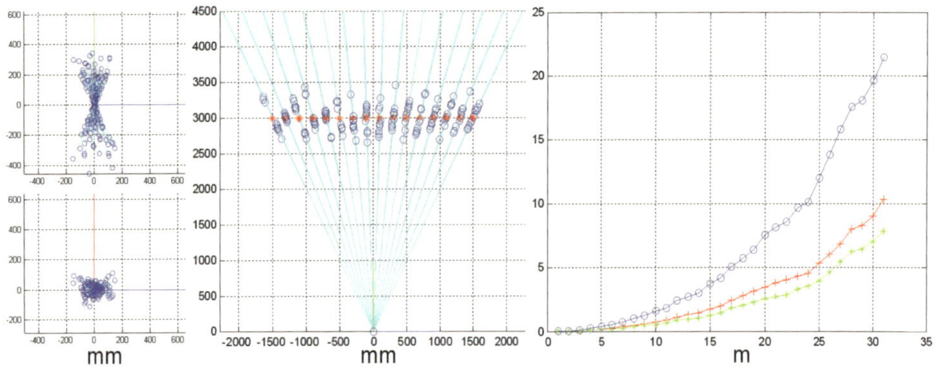

Fig. 16. Distribution of the error along the three dimensions for a fixed depth of view of 3 m; non linear behaviour of the average errors increasing the depth from 1 to 30 m.

7. Visual SLAM

The Simultaneous Localization And Mapping (SLAM) is an acronym often used in robotics to indicate the process through which an automatic controller onboard a vehicle is able to build a map while driving the vehicle in an unknown map or environment and simultaneously localize the robot in the environment.

7.1 Odometry based auto calibration

The SLAM algorithm has been implemented using an Extended Kalman Filter (EKF) based on the visual information coming from the stereo-camera, and using the odometry information coming from the vehicle for simultaneously estimating the camera parameters and the robot landmarks respective positions [Spampinato et al., 2009]. The state variables to be estimated are ***3+3N+C***, corresponding to the robot position and orientation (3 dofs), three dimensional coordinates of ***N*** landmarks in the environment, and camera parameters C, constituting the state vector ***x(k)*** as shown in (20).

$$
\begin{aligned}
x(k) &= [X, Y, \vartheta, X_{L1}, Y_{L1}, Z_{L1} \cdots, X_{LN}, Y_{LN}, Z_{LN}, S, \cdots, f] \\
u(k) &= [V_X, V_Y, V_\vartheta] \\
y(k) &= \left[F_{R1}, F_{L1}, \cdots, F_{RN}, F_{LN}\right]^T
\end{aligned}
\tag{20}
$$

The inputs to the system are the robot velocities for both the position and orientation, whereas the outputs are ***4N*** feature coordinates on the right and left camera sensors. The model of the system is computed as shown in the relations (21), constituting the *predict phase* of the algorithm.

$$
\begin{aligned}
x(k+1) &= f(x(k), u(k), k) + v(k) = F(k) \cdot x(k) + G(x, u, k) + v(k) \\
y(k) &= h(x(k), k) + w(k)
\end{aligned}
\tag{21}
$$

The state equations are not linear and generic with respect to the inputs ***u(k)*** representing the robot generalized velocities. The kinematic model related to the specific vehicle considered is solved a part. The output model is also non linear, and represents the core of the estimator. The state matrix ***F(k)*** provides the robot position and orientation, computing the corresponding state variables form the input velocities. On the other hand, the landmarks positions and the camera parameters have a zero dynamic behavior.

$$
F(k) = \begin{bmatrix} \overset{3\times 3}{I} & 0 & 0 \\ 0 & \overset{3N\times 3N}{I} & 0 \\ 0 & 0 & \overset{C\times C}{I} \end{bmatrix} \qquad G(x, u, k) = \begin{bmatrix} R(x_3(k)) & 0 \\ 0 & 1 \end{bmatrix} \cdot u(k)
\tag{22}
$$

The predicted state covariance ***P*** is a block diagonal matrix, symmetric and positive definite, containing the predicted variances of the state elements.

$$P(k+1) = G_v(k)\cdot P(k)\cdot G_v(k)^T + G_u(k)\cdot v(k)\cdot G_u(k)^T \quad G_v(k) = \left.\frac{\partial f}{dx}\right|_{x=\hat{x}(k)} \quad G_u(k) = \left.\frac{\partial f}{du}\right|_{x=\hat{x}(k)} \tag{23}$$

The system model and the system measurements uncertainties are respectively indicated by the 3x3 diagonal matrix v and the 4x4 diagonal matrix w containing the variances terms. In particular, the model uncertainty are computed basing on the specific kinematics involved, whereas the measurements uncertainty are computed basing on the considerations reported in the previous section regarding the 3D reconstruction accuracy.
During the *update phase* of the EKF, the state variables, and the related covariance matrix $\boldsymbol{P}$, are updated by the correction from the Kalman gain R and the innovation vector e, as reported by the relations (24).

$$\begin{aligned} \hat{x}(k+1\,|\,k+1) &= \hat{x}(k+1\,|\,k) + R\cdot e \\ P(k+1\,|\,k+1) &= P(k+1\,|\,k) - RH(k+1)P(k+1\,|\,k) \\ H(k+1) &= \left.\frac{\partial h}{dx}\right|_{x=\hat{x}(k+1|k)} \end{aligned} \tag{24}$$

The innovation vector represents the difference between the estimated model output $\boldsymbol{h}$ and the real measurements from the stereo camera sensors.

$$\begin{aligned} e &= y(k+1) - h(x(k+1\,|\,k), k+1) \\ R &= P(k+1\,|\,k)H(k+1)^T S^{-1} \\ S &= H(k+1)P(k+1\,|\,k)H(k+1)^T + w(k+1) \end{aligned} \tag{25}$$

The computation of the Kalman gain $\boldsymbol{R}$, comes from the linearization of the output model around the current state estimation, through the corresponding jacobian matrix $\boldsymbol{H}$, as presented in (26).

H: 4N x (3+3N+C)   **dx** (3+3N+C)x1   **dy** 4Nx1

$$\underbrace{\begin{bmatrix} \frac{\partial F_1}{\partial X_R} & \frac{\partial F_1}{\partial Y_R} & \frac{\partial F_1}{\partial \vartheta_R} & \frac{\partial F_1}{\partial L_1} & 0 & 0 & 0 & \frac{\partial F_1}{\partial f} & \cdots & \frac{\partial F_1}{\partial S} \\ \frac{\partial F_2}{\partial X_R} & \frac{\partial F_2}{\partial Y_R} & \frac{\partial F_2}{\partial \vartheta_R} & 0 & \frac{\partial F_2}{\partial L_2} & 0 & 0 & \frac{\partial F_2}{\partial f} & \cdots & \frac{\partial F_2}{\partial S} \\ \vdots & \vdots & \vdots & 0 & 0 & \ddots & 0 & \vdots & \cdots & \vdots \\ \frac{\partial F_N}{\partial X_R} & \frac{\partial F_N}{\partial Y_R} & \frac{\partial F_N}{\partial \vartheta_R} & 0 & 0 & 0 & \frac{\partial F_N}{\partial L_N} & \frac{\partial F_N}{\partial f} & \cdots & \frac{\partial F_N}{\partial S} \end{bmatrix}}_{1\ \ 1\ \ 1\ \ 3\ \ 3\ \cdots\ 3\ \ 1\ \cdots\ 1} \cdot \begin{bmatrix} dX \\ dY \\ d\vartheta \\ dL_1 \\ dL_2 \\ \vdots \\ dL_N \\ df \\ \vdots \\ dS \end{bmatrix} = \begin{bmatrix} dF_1 \\ dF_2 \\ \vdots \\ dF_N \end{bmatrix} \tag{26}$$

(row blocks of the H matrix: 4, 4, ⋮, 4)

The three groups of parameters to be estimated are quite evident by the structure of the $\boldsymbol{H}$ matrix, where the central part is block diagonal indicating the feature-landmark correspondences.

The camera calibration has been tested on the camera separation estimation using a five LEDs unknown pattern shown in Fig. 17. The camera motion with respect to the landmarks has been performed in a straight path along the *X* axis.

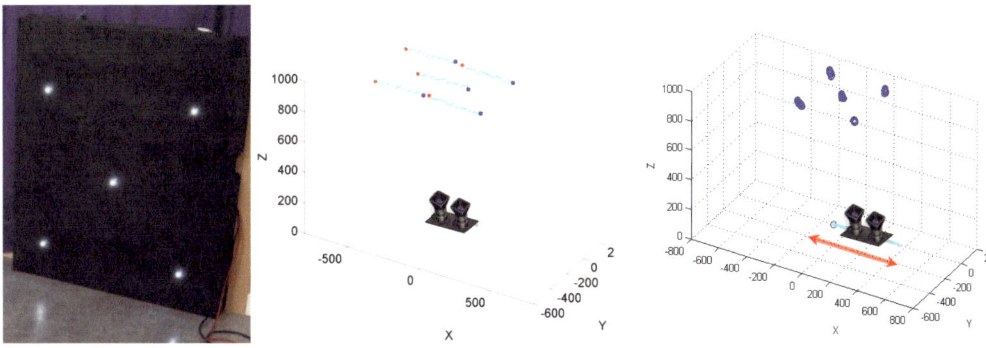

Fig. 17. Landmarks 3D reconstruction with respect to the robot (left) and to the world reference frame (right).

The localization and mapping algorithm has been implemented using the odometry data for the *predict* phase, and the stereo vision feedback for the *update* phase. The state vector is made out of 19 elements, (having one camera parameters *C=1*, and five landmarks *N=5*), representing the three robot DoFs, the 5 three dimensional coordinates of the landmarks, and the camera separation *S*. Some experimental results are shown in Fig. 17 in which the five landmarks locations are estimated simultaneously with the robot motion back and forth along the *X* axis, and the camera separation. The position estimation of the central landmark is presented in the upper part of Fig. 18 together with the error with respect to the real three dimensional coordinates. The algorithm errors with respect to the sensor feedback (representing the innovation vector ***e*** as described in (25)), are also reported in both the three dimensional space and in the pixels space.

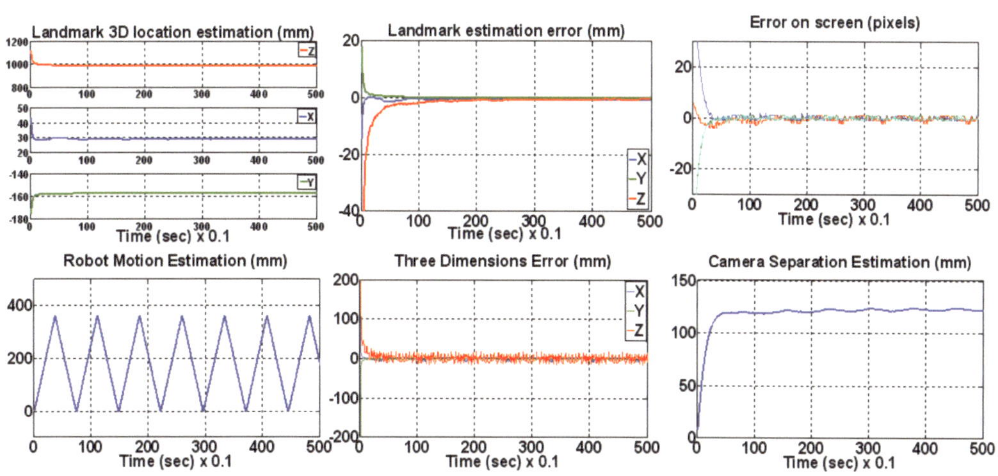

Fig. 18. Experimental results related to the landmarks, robot motion, and camera separation estimation.

7.2 Visual odometry

To keep the whole system simple to use and easy to maintain, more effort has been devoted to avoid to read the odometry data from the vehicle. At the same time, the localization algorithm become more robust to uncertainties that easily arise in the vehicle kinematic model. After the calibration phase, the calibrated stereo rig can be used to estimate the vehicle motion data using solely visual information. The technique, known in literature as *visual odometry* [Nistér et al., 2004], is summarized in Fig. 19 in which the apparent motion of the feature points $\boldsymbol{F}$ in the image space (corresponding to the landmarks $\boldsymbol{P}$ in the 3D space with respect to the vehicle) in two subsequent instants of time, are used to estimate the vehicle motion $\Delta\boldsymbol{T}$ and $\Delta\boldsymbol{R}$, in both translation and rotation terms.

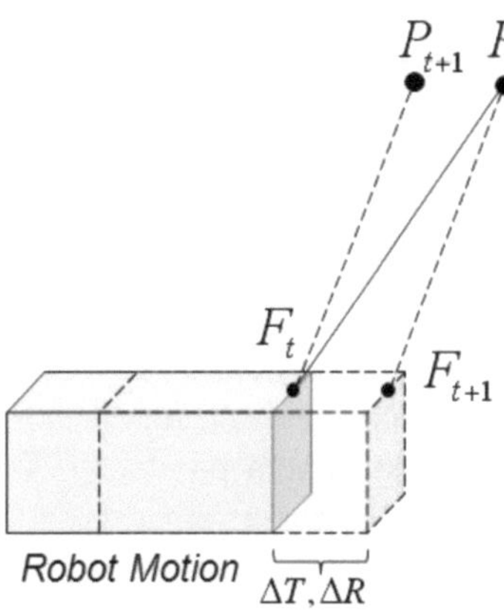

Fig. 19. The visual odometry concept. The vehicle ego-motion is estimated from the apparent motion of the features in the image space.

Back-projecting the features coordinates in the image space to the 3D space using the triangulation described in the previous section, the problem is formalized in estimating the rotation and translation terms that minimize the functional (27).

$$\sum_{i=1}^{n} \left\| P_{t,i} - T - R \cdot P_{t,i+1} \right\|^2 \tag{27}$$

The translation vector is easily computed once the rotation matrix is known, by the distance between the centroids of the two point clouds generated by the triangulated feature points in the subsequent instants of time: $T = \overline{P}_t - R \cdot \overline{P}_{t+1}$, in which the two centroids can be computed as in (28).

$$\overline{P}_{t+1} = \frac{1}{n}\sum_{i=1}^{n} P_{t+1,i} \quad \overline{P}_t = \frac{1}{n}\sum_{i=1}^{n} P_{t,i} \tag{28}$$

The rotation matrix minimizes the functional (29) representing the Frobenius norm of the residual of the landmarks distance with respect to the centroids in the two subsequent instants.

$$\sum_{i=1}^{n} \left\| \overline{P}_{t,i} - R \cdot \overline{P}_{t,i+1} \right\|^2 \tag{29}$$

in which $\overline{P}_{t,i} = P_{t,i} - \overline{P}_t$ and $\overline{P}_{t+1,i} = P_{t+1,i} - \overline{P}_{t+1}$. The rotation term minimizing (29) minimizes also the trace of the matrix $R^T \cdot K$, with $K = \sum_{i=1}^{n} \left(\overline{P}_{t,i}\right)^T \cdot \left(\overline{P}_{t+1,i}\right)$ [Siciliano et al., 2009].

The rotation matrix ***R*** is computed through the right and left eigenvector matrices from the SVD of the matrix ***K***, $svd(K) = U \cdot \Sigma \cdot V^T$.

$$R = U \cdot \begin{bmatrix} 1 & 0 \\ 0 & \sigma \end{bmatrix} \cdot V^T \text{ in which } \sigma = \det\left(U \cdot V^T\right). \tag{30}$$

The visual odometry strategy, as described above, is computed within the *predict* phase of the Kalman filter in place of the traditional odometry readings and processing from the vehicle, resulting in a reduced communication overhead, during the motion. An increased robustness to polarized errors, coming from the vehicle kinematic model uncertainties, is also gained.

8. Experimental results

In the current version of the platform, the localization system has been implemented on a standard PC, communicating with the stereo camera through USB. The system has been mounted on three different platforms and tested both within university buildings as well as in industrial sites. The system has been tested at Mälardalen University (MDH), Örebro University (ORU) and in Stora Enso paper mill in Skoghall (Karlstad, Sweden).

The localization in unknown environments and the simultaneous map building solely use visual landmarks (mostly using light sources coming from the lamps in the ceiling), and operate without reading the odometry information from the vehicle.

In the working demonstrator at Mälardalen University, the stereo system has been placed on a wheeled table. The vision system looks upwards, extracts information from the lamps in the ceiling, builds a map of the environment and localizes itself inside the map with a precision within the range of 1-3 cms depending on the height of the ceiling. Two different test cases have been provided for small and large environments as shown, in Fig. 20 and Fig. 21. The system is also able to recover its correct position within the map after a severe disturbance like, for example, a long period of "blind" motion as known as kidnapping.

Fig. 20. Simultaneous localization and map building using only visual information at MDH. The table was moved at about 1m/s producing the map of the room with 9 landmarks on a surface of about 50 m^2

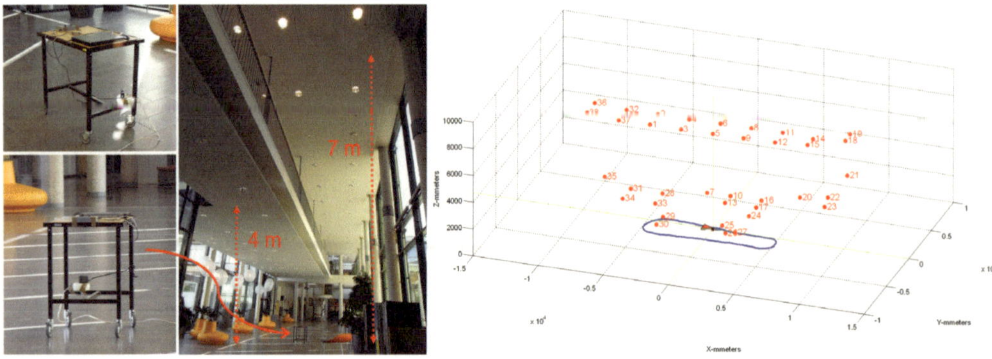

Fig. 21. Simultaneous localization and map building using only visual information at MDH. The table was moved at about 1m/s producing the map of the university hall with 40 landmarks on a surface of about 600 m^2. The landmarks are mainly grouped in two layers, at respectively 4 and 7 meters from the cameras.

In the frame of the MALTA project, some experiments have been performed at Örebro university, to test the system when mounted on a small scale version of the industrial vehicle controller used in the project. The robot is equipped with the same navigation system installed by Danaher Motion (industrial partner in the project) in the "official industrial truck", used in the project (the H50 forklift by Linde, also industrial partner in the project).

The system has been tested to verify the vSLAM algorithm to localize and build the map on an unknown environment, and to feed the estimated position to the Danaher Motion system installed in the vehicle as an "epm" (external positioning measurement), and let the robot be controlled by the Danaher system using our localization information, as proof of the reliability of our estimation.

The complete map of two rooms employed a total of 26 landmarks on a surface of about 80 m^2. The precision of the localization system has been proved marking specific positions in the room and using the map built to verify the correspondence. The precision of the localization was about 1 cm. The three dimensional representation of the robot path and the created map during the experiments is shown in Fig 22. The robot was run for about 10

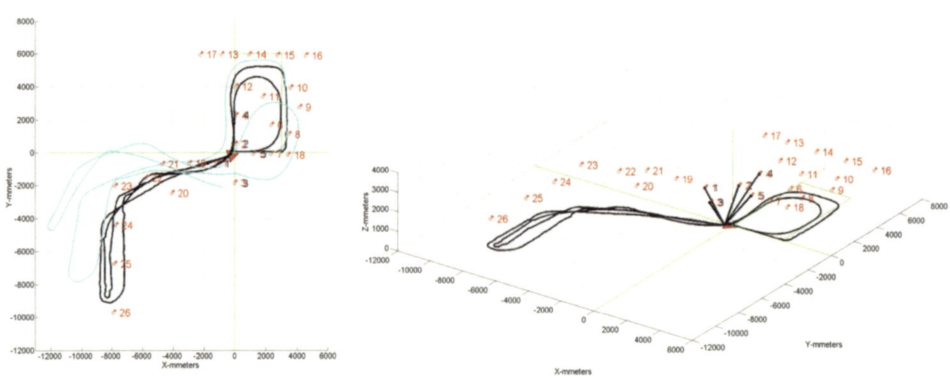

Fig. 22. Three dimensional representations of the robot path and the related map built during the experiments at ORU.

minutes at a speed of 0.3 m/s. The visual odometry estimated path is also reported to show the drift of the odometry only based estimation with respect to the whole localization algorithm.
Two cubic b-splines trajectories are shown in Fig. 23, while driving the robot using the Danaher Motion navigation system using the proposed position estimation provided as "epm" (external positioning measurement) to the Danaher system. The precision of the localization is within 1 cm.

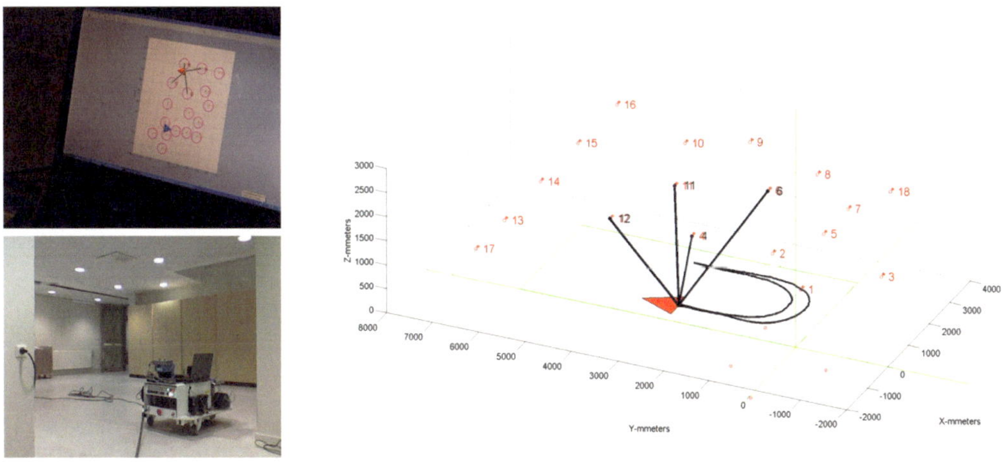

Fig. 23. Three dimensional representations of the robot path and the related map built during two splines based trajectories control executed through the Danaher navigation system and the MDH position estimation provided as "epm".

During the frame of the MALTA project, some tests have been organized in Skoghall, inside the Stora Enso (industrial partner in the project) paper mill to test different localization systems proposed inside the project and also to avoid adding additional infrastructure to the environment.
The vehicle used during the experiments is the H50 forklift provided by Linde Material Handling, and properly modified by Danaher Motion. The tests site, as well as the industrial vehicle used during the demo are shown in Fig. 24. The stereovision navigation system has been placed on top of the vehicle, like shown in the picture, making the system integration extremely easy.
The environmental conditions are completely different from the labs at the universities, and the demo surface was about 2800 m^2. The height of the ceiling, and so the distance of the lamps from the vehicle (used as natural landmarks by our navigation system), is about 20m. The experiments have been performed, like in the previous cases, estimating the position of the robot and building the map of the environment simultaneously. The estimated position and orientation of the vehicle were provided to the Danaher Motion navigation system as "epm". In Fig. 25 the path estimation is reported while the vehicle was performing a cubic b-spline driving with a speed of 0.5 m/s. In Fig. 26, a longer path was performed with the purpose to collect as many landmarks as possible and build a more complete map. In this case the complete map employed a total of 14 landmarks on a surface of about 2800 m2 with a precision of about 10 cm.

Fig. 24. The demo industrial site in the Stora Enso paper mill in Skoghall (Karlstad, Sweden). The integration of the proposed visual localization system is extremely fast since it is enough to place the stereocamera on top of the vehicle.

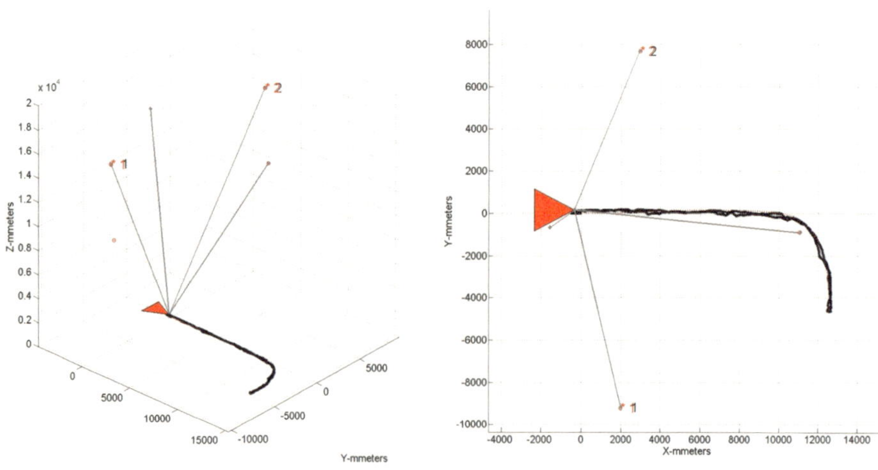

Fig. 25. The planar and three dimensional representation of the vehicle path estimation while performing a b-spline trajectory at 0.5 m/s inside the Stora Enso industrial site in Skoghall.

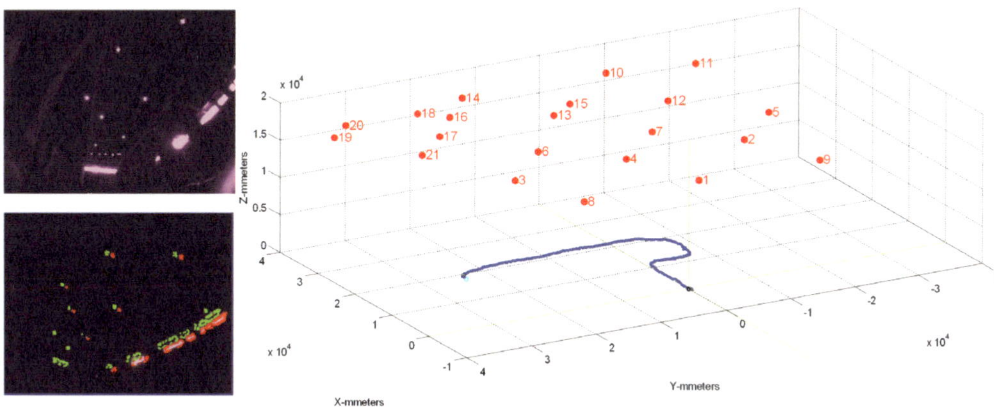

Fig. 26. The three dimensional representation of the vehicle path estimation and map built inside the Stora Enso industrial site in Skoghall. On the left side is shown one screenshot of the feature extraction process.

9. Conclusion

The proposed solution makes use of stereo vision to realize localization and map building of unknown environments without adding any additional infrastructure. The system has been tested in three different environments, two universities and one industrial site. The great advantage for a potential user is the simple installation and integration with the vehicle, since it is enough to place the camera box on the vehicle ad connect via USB to a standard PC to localize the vehicle inside a generated map.
From the industrial point of view, the overall impression is that the precision of the system is good even if the conditions are very different form the lab. The distance from the landmarks is bigger than in the lab, and so the accuracy errors registered. Increasing the speed of the vehicle to 1-1.5 m/s, the performances of the system severely decrease, resulting in accuracy errors of 30-40 cm from the desired path in the worst cases, that is unacceptable in normal industrial operating conditions.
In order to address the target of autonomous navigation at full speed (30 Km/h), the core of the vSLAM system needs to be updated to run at a higher frequency (from 3 Hz of the current implementation to 30 Hz), so to speed up also the performances of the "epm" driving mode. Moreover, the USB communication will be substituted with the Ethernet running at 100 Mb/s, in a closer future. However, in the final version, it is foreseen that the whole system should be implemented in hardware, living the PC as a configuration terminal.
From the algorithmic point of view the next step will update the EKF from 3 DoF to full 6 DoF vehicle position and orientation modeling, in order to compensate for non flat ground and slopes often present in industrial sites.

10. References

Dubbelman, G. & Groen, F.(2009), Bias reduction for stereo based motion estimation with applications to large scale visual odometry. *Proc. Of IEEE Computer Society*

Conference on Computer Vision and Pattern Recognition, pp. 2222–2229, ISBN 978-1-4244-3991-1, Miami, Florida, June, 2009.

Heikkilä J, & Silven O, (1997), A four-step camera calibration procedure with implicit image correction. *Proc. of IEEE Conference on Computer Vision and Pattern Recognition,* pp. 1106-1112, Puerto Rico, San Juan, June, 1997.

Harris, C. & Stephens, M. (1988). A combined corner and edge detection. *In Proceedings of The Fourth Alvey Vision Conference,* pp 147-151, Manchester, UK, 1988.

Hartley, R. & Zisserman, A. (2000). *Multiple View Geometry in Computer Vision.* Cambridge University Press,. ISBN: 0521540518.

Kannala J; Heikkilä J & Brandt S, (2009) Geometric camera calibration. In: *Encyclopedia of Computer Science and Engineering,* Wah BW, Wiley, Hoboken, NJ, 3:1389-1400.

Laugier, C. & Chatila R. (2007), *Autonomous Navigation in Dynamic Environments.* Springer Verlag, ISBN-13 978-3-540-73421-5.

Matei, B. & Meer, P. (2006) Estimation of Nonlinear Errors-in-Variables Models for Computer Vision Applications. *IEEE Transactions On Pattern Analysis And Machine Intelligence,* Vol. 28, No. 10, (October 2006), pp. 1537-1552, ISSN 0162-8828.

Nistér, D.; Naroditsky,O., & Bergen,J. (2004) Visual Odometry. *Proceedings of the 2004 IEEE Computer Society Conference on Computer Vision and Pattern Recognition (CVPR 2004),* 0-7695-2158-4, Washington DC, USA, June, 2004.

Noble, A. (1989), *Descriptions of Image Surfaces,* PhD thesis, Department of Engineering Science, Oxford University.

Siciliano, B.; Sciavicco, L., Villani,L. & Oriolo,G. (2008) *Robotics: modelling, planning and control. Advanced textbooks in control and signal processing.* Springer, ISBN 1846286417.

Spampinato, G; Lidholm, J; Asplund, L; & Ekstrand,F. (2009) Stereo Vision Based Navigation for Automated Vehicles in Industry. *Proceedings of the 14th IEEE International Conference on emerging Technologies and Factory Automation (ETFA 2009),* ISBN: 978-1-4244-2728-4, Mallorca, Spain, September, 2009.

15

New Robust Obstacle Detection System using Color Stereo Vision

Iyadh Cabani, Gwenaëlle Toulminet and Abdelaziz Bensrhair
Laboratoire d'Informatique, de Traitement de l'Information et des Systèmes - EA 4051, INSA de Rouen
Campus du Madrillet, Avenue de l'Université
76801 Saint-Etienne-du-Rouvray Cedex
France

1. Introduction

Intelligent transportation systems (ITS) are divided into intelligent infrastructure systems and intelligent vehicle systems. Intelligent vehicle systems are typically classified in three categories, namely 1) Collision Avoidance Systems; 2) Driver Assistance Systems and 3) Collision Notification Systems. Obstacle detection is one of crucial tasks for Collision Avoidance Systems and Driver Assistance Systems. Obstacle detection systems use vehicle-mounted sensors to detect obstuctions, such as other vehicles, bicyclists, pedestrians, road debris, or animals, in a vehicle's path and alert the driver.

Obstacle detection systems are proposed to help drivers see farther and therefore have more time to react to road hazards. These systems also help drivers to get a large visibility area when the visibility conditions is reduced such as night, fog, snow, rain, ...

Obstacle detection systems process data acquired from one or several sensors: radar Kruse et al. (2004), lidar Gao & Coifman (2006), monocular vision Lombardi & Zavidovique (2004), stereo vision Franke (2000) Bensrhair et al. (2002) Cabani et al. (2006b) Kogler et al. (2006) Woodfill et al. (2007), vision fused with active sensors Gern et al. (2000) Steux et al. (2002) Möbus & Kolbe (2004)Zhu et al. (2006) Alessandretti et al. (2007)Cheng et al. (2007). It is clear now that most obstacle detection systems cannot work without vision. Typically, vision-based systems consist of cameras that provide gray level images. When visibility conditions are reduced (night, fog, twilight, tunnel, snow, rain), vision systems are almost blind. Obstacle detection systems are less robust and reliable. To deal with the problem of reduced visibility conditions, infrared or color cameras can be used.

Thermal imaging cameras are initially used by militaries. Over the last few years, these systems became accessible to the commercial market, and can be found in select 2006 BMW cars. For example, vehicle headlight systems provide between 75 to 140 meters of moderate illumination; at 90 K meters per hour this means less than 4 seconds to react to hazards. When with PathFindIR *PathFindIR* (n.d.) (a commercial system), a driver can have more than 15 seconds. Other systems still in the research stage assist drivers to detect pedestrians Xu & Fujimura (2002) Broggi et al. (2004) Bertozzi et al. (2007).

Color is appropriate to various visibility conditions and various environments. In Betke et al. (2000) and Betke & Nguyen (1998), *Betke et al.* have demonstrated that the tracking of vehicles by night, in tunnels, in rainy and snowy weather in various environment is possible with color. Recently, *Jia* Jia et al. (2007) fuses information captured by color cameras and inertial motion sensors for tracking objects. *Steux et al.* use color to recognize vehicles on highways, roads and in an urban environment Steux et al. (2002). The same approach has been used to recognize vehicles: rear lights are extracted in the RGB color space. *Daimler Chrysler* Franke et al. (1999) and *Maldonado-Bascon et al.* Maldonado-Bascon et al. (2007) use color to detect road, traffic signs and traffic signals in urban traffic environment. Recently, we have proposed a color based method to detect vehicle lights Cabani et al. (2005). The vision system detects three kinds of vehicle lights: rear lights and rear-brake-lights; flashing and warning lights; reverse lights and headlights. *Cheng et al.* Cheng et al. (2006) use color to detect lane with moving vehicles.

Initially, our laboratory has conceived a gray level stereo vision system for obstacle detection Toulminet et al. (2004) Toulminet et al. (2006) based on declivity for edges extraction Miché & Debrie (1995) and dynamic programming approach for matching Bensrhair et al. (1996). In order to improve its robustness and reliability, we currently work on the conception of a color stereo vision system for obstacle detection. The color-based approach is achieved in three main steps. In the first step, vertical edge points are extracted using the color-declivity operator. It is self-adaptive in order to face different conditions of illumination (sun; twilight; rain; fog; transition between sun and shadow; entrance or exit from a tunnel). In the second step, stereoscopic vertical edge points are matched self-adaptively using a dynamic programming algorithm. Finally, 3D edges of obstacles are detected.

The paper is organized as follows. Section 2 presents the first step of the proposed method together with color based edges segmentation methods. In section 3, the second step of our method is detailed. The state of the art of color matching is given in the first subsection. Color-based obstacle detection is depicted in section 4. Performance of each step is discussed and experimental results are shown.

2. Edge-based color image segmentation

2.1 State of the art

A lot of research has been done recently to tackle the color edge detection problem can be divided into three parts as follows Ruzon & Tomasi (2001):

- output fusion methods
- multidimensional gradient methods
- vector methods

Recently, *Macaire* Macaire (2004) takes back this classification and enriched it by a new category. This new category regroups methods based on vector gradient computed on single channel image called single channel methods.

2.1.1 Single channel methods

These methods perform the grayscale edge detection (Sobel, Prewitt, Kirsch, Robinson, etc.) on single channel. Often, luminance channel is used. These methods prove to be efficient when the levels of luminance of the pixels representing objects are enough to differentiate them.

2.1.2 Output fusion methods

Output fusion appears to be the most popular. These methods perform the grayscale edge detection on each channel and then the results are combined to produce the final edge map using simple logical/arithmetical operations (i.e. OR Fan, Yau, Elmagarmid & Aref (2001)Fan, Aref, Hacid & Elmagarmid (2001), AND, majority-voting, a summation Heddley & Yan (1992), a weighted sum Nevatia (1977)Carron & Lambert (1994)Carron & Lambert (1995)). *Nevatia* Nevatia (1977) developed the first output fusion method, in which he extended the Hueckel operator Hueckel (1971) to color edges. *Shiozaki* Shiozaki (1986) weighted the results of his entropy operator by the relative amounts of each channel at a pixel. *Malowany* and *Malowany* Malowany & Malowany (1989) added absolute values of Laplacien outputs. *Carron* and *Lambert* computed edge strength using a weighted sum over each component in Carron & Lambert (1994) and extension using fuzzy sets in Carron & Lambert (1995) on HSI color space. *Weeks et al.* Weeks et al. (1995) combined edges found in the H, S and I components of a color image. *Alberto-Salinas et al.* Salinas et al. (1996) have proposed a more sophisticated approach. The Canny operator Canny (1986) is applied to each channel then regularization is used as a way to fuse the outputs.

2.1.3 Multidimensional gradient methods

Multidimensional gradient methods are characterized by a single estimate of the orientation and strength of an edge at a point. *Robinson* suggest to compute 24 directional derivatives (8 neighbors × 3 components) and chose the one with the highest magnitude as the gradient. The most known multidimensional gradient method have been defined by *Di Zenzo* Di-Zenzo (1986). Di Zenzo gives formulas for computing the magnitude and direction of the gradient (which, for color images, is a tensor) given the directional derivatives in each channel. A 2 × 2 matrix is formed from the outer product of the gradient vector in each component. These matrices are summed together, noted S. The square root of the principal eigenvalue represents the magnitude of the gradient. The corresponding eigenvector yields the gradient direction. Di Zenzo showed howto compute this gradient using the Sobel operator, but he did not detect edges directly. Cumani Cumani (1991) is the first to have use multidimensional gradients for detecting edges. *Chapron* Chapron (1992)Chapron (1997) used the Canny-Deriche gradient in each component. The DempsterShafer theory is used in Chapron (2000) for fusing the gradients. Others have developed distinctly different approaches. *Moghaddemzadeh* and *Bourbakis* Moghaddamzadeh & Bourbakis (1995) Moghaddamzadeh et al. (1998) used a normalized hue contrast in the HSI color space to compensate for low saturations. *Tsang* and *Tsang* Tsang & Tsang (1996) Tsang & Tsang (1997) used a heuristic choice of component gradients in HSV color space. *Macaire et al.* Macaire et al. (1996) used relaxation on the normalized Sobel gradient to classify pixels. Finally, *Scharcanski* and *Venetsanopoulos* Scharcanski & Venetsanopoulos (1997) averaged color vectors together before computing directional derivatives and a gradiant.

2.1.4 Vector methods

The first research works into vector methods has used differential geometry to determine the rate of change and corresponding direction at each pixel Chapron (1997)Zugaj & Lattuati (1998). Other research has considered the use of probability distributions. In Machuca & Phillips (1983), *Machuca* and *Phillips* defined the first vector method for color edge detection. They created onedimensional vectors, as they felt that color was useful only where grayscale edge detection failed. *Huntsberger* and *Descalzi* Huntsberger & Descalzi (1985) used fuzzy membership values. *Pietikainen* and *Harwood* Pietikainen & Harwood (1986) used histograms of vector differences. *Yang* and *Tsai* Yang & Tsai (1996) and *Tao* and *Huang* Tao & Huang

(1997) used vector projections. *Trahanias* and *Venetsanopoulos* Trahanias & Venetsanopoulos (1996) used the median of a set of vectors. *Djuric* and *Fwu* Djuric & Fwu (1997) found edges using the MAP (maximum a posteriori) rule. *Fotinos et al.* suggest the use of relative entropy as a dissimilarity measure between a local probability distribution and that of a homogenous region. *Ruzon* and *Tomasi* Ruzon & Tomasi (2001) suggest the use of color signatures generated using vector quantization. *Wen et al.* Wen et al. (2002) used a vector difference.

- Simplicity: OR operation can be easily implemented on dedicated architecture
- Real time constraint: OR operation is a fast solution which enables color-declivity to be fast also
- Binary output of declivity operation: as a logical operator, OR operator is more appropriate than arithmetic ones; note that AND operator is not appropriate for segmentation of real road scenes

Declivity is defined as a set of consecutive pixels in an image line whose amplitudes are a strictly monotonous function of their positions Miché & Debrie (1995). Let d a declivity denoted $d(x_i, x_{i+1}, w_i, A_i, X_i)$ where (see Fig. 1):

- x_i represents the coordinate of its first pixel in the image line
- x_{i+1} represents the coordinate of its last pixel in the image line
- $w_i = x_{i+1} - x_i$ represents its width
- $A_i = |I(x_{i+1}) - I(x_i)|$ represents its amplitude
- X_i represents its position in the image line and defined by:

$$X_i = \frac{\sum_{x=x_i}^{x_{i+1}-1} \left[I(x+1) - I(x)\right]^2 (x+0.5)}{\sum_{x=x_i}^{x_{i+1}-1} \left[I(x+1) - I(x)\right]^2} \tag{1}$$

where $I(x)$ indicates the gray level value of the pixel at position x.

In order to have an accurate disparity map, efficient locations of declivities are essential. The position of a declivity is calculated using the mean position of the declivity points weighted by the gradients squared. This quadratic form is well suited to irregular extended edges, i.e. spread over several pixels with a variable slope as it may result from the effect of non-filtered noise, and it enables the real position of edges to be computed with sub-pixel precision.

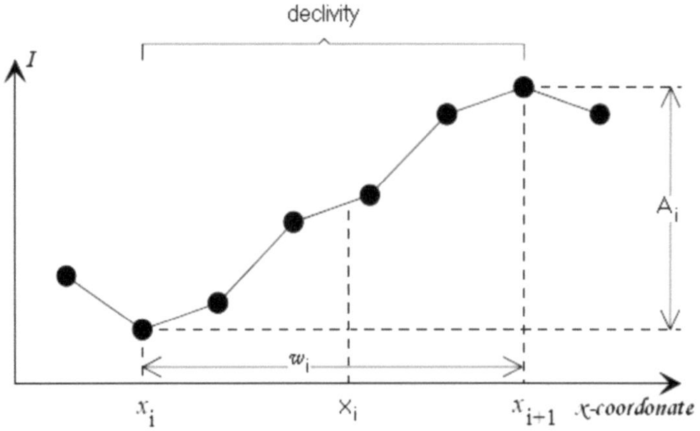

Fig. 1. Characteristics parameters of a declivity.

Declivities are independently constructed in each line of the three channels of color image. Let $D_{c\in 1,2,3}$ the set of declivities of channel c in an image line. For $d \in D_c$, the position of the declivity is noted $d(X_i)$ and its amplitude is noted $d(A_i)$. Relevant declivities (i.e. edge points) are extracted by thresholding their amplitude. Given an optimal threshold for channel c, say T_c, the E_c function, below, classifies the pixels on channel c into two opposite classes: *edge* versus *non-edge*.

$$\forall d \in D_c,\quad E_c\left(d(X_i)\right) = \begin{cases} 1, \text{ edge pixel} & \text{if } d(A_i)^2 \geq T_c^{\,2} \\ 0, \text{ non-edge pixel} & \text{if } d(A_i)^2 < T_c^{\,2} \end{cases} \tag{2}$$

E_c is the set of relevant declivities of channel c in an image line.
In this proposed edge detection technique, the optimal threshold T_c is self-adaptive as described in subsection 2.3. Edge results for the three color components are integrated throught the following fusion rule:

$$\forall rd \in \bigcup_{c\in[1,3]} E_c,\quad E\left(rd(X_i)\right) = \begin{cases} 1, \text{ edge pixel} & \text{if } E_1(rd(X_i)) = 1 \\ & \text{or } E_2(rd(X_i)) = 1 \\ & \text{or } E_3(rd(X_i)) = 1 \\ 0, \text{ non-edge pixel} & \text{otherwise.} \end{cases} \tag{3}$$

The pixel is classified as the edge pixel if and only if at least one of its three color components is detected as an edge and $E(rd(X_i))$ is set to 1, otherwise, it is classified as a non-edge pixel and $E(rd(X_i))$ is set to 0. These obtained color edges can provide a simplified image that preserves the domain geometric structures and spatial relationships found in the original image.
Finally, each color-declivity is characterized by the following attributes:

- its set Ω_i which contains the numbers of channels in which declivities have been extracted. There are 8 possible sets Ω for color image. For example, $\Omega = \{1, 2,3\}$, or $\Omega = \{1,3\}$, or $\Omega = \{2\}$, ...
- the coordinate of its first pixel u_i in the color image line.

$$u_i = \max_{\forall c\in\Omega_i} \{x_{j_c}\}$$

- the coordinate of its last pixel u_{i+1} in the color image line.

$$u_{i+1} = \min_{\forall c\in\Omega_i} \{x_{j+1_c}\}$$

- its width equal to $W_i = u_{i+1} - u_i$
- its position.

The computation of u_i and u_{i+1} are obtained by maximizing, respectively minimizing the position of the first, respectively the last, pixels of relevant declivities extracted in the set of channel Ω_i. As a result monotony is observed in each channel of Ω_i.

The proposed structure of color declivity has the following advantages. It can be used for any color spaces and for any hybrid color spaces. It can also be extended to multi-spectral images.

2.3 Self-adaptive thresholding

Based on both the taxonomy of thresholding algorithms presented in Sankur & Sezgin (2004) and our previous works Miché & Debrie (1995), a self-adaptive thresholding is defined as follows:

$$T_c = \alpha \times \sigma_c \tag{4}$$

where σ_c is the standard deviation of the component of a white noise which is supposed to be Gaussian. It is deduced from the histogram of amplitude variations of pixels in an image line on channel c. In Miché & Debrie (1995), α is fixed to 5.6 for gray level image line in order to reject 99.5% of increments due to noise.

α equal to 5.6 is not appropriate for color edges segmentation, because over segmentation is observed. In Peli & Malah (1982), Pratt's figure-of-merit (FOM) is computed in order to set threshold value for edge segmentation. FOM measurement Pratt (1977) is widely used to estimate performance of edge segmentation. It is defined by:

$$FOM = \frac{1}{\max(N_I, N_D)} \sum_{i=1}^{N_D} \frac{1}{1 + ad_i^2} \tag{5}$$

where N_D is the number of detected edge points, N_I is the number of ideal edge points (ground truth), d_i is the edge deviation or error distance for the ith detected edge pixel and a is a scaling factor chosen to be $a = \frac{1}{9}$ to provide a relative penalty between smeared edges and isolated, but offset, edges. A larger value of FOM corresponds to better performance, with 1 being a perfect result.

In order to evaluate color edges segmentation and to estimate α, FOM was computed based on original Lena image (see Fig. 2) and its ideal edge map provided by experts. The best segmentation of Lena image according to FOM definition is obtained for α equal to 8 (FOM = 0.88) (see Fig. 3).

Fig. 2. Original Lena image.

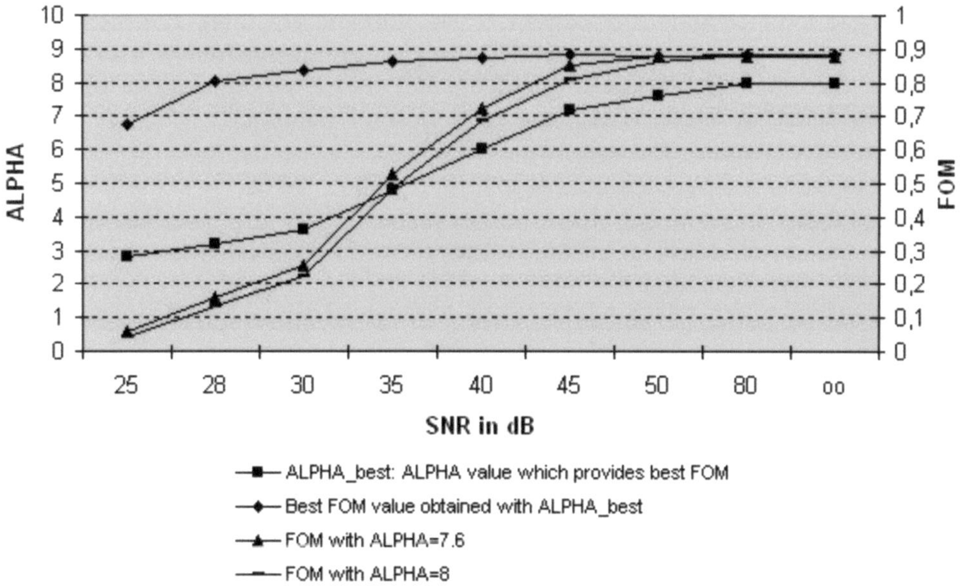

Fig. 3. Three Pratt's figures-of-merit (FOM) computed with different value of α; and obtained from Lena image in which gaussian noise of different amplitude has been added $SNR \in [25,\infty[\ dB$.

Values of $\alpha \in [6.4, 9.2]$ ($FOM > 0.8$) have been studied for edge segmentation of real color images of road scenes. After many tests α was fixed to 7.6. It corresponds to rejection of 99.98% increments due to noise supposed to be gaussian in color image. In order to evaluate its noise sensitivity, color edges segmentation has been performed using Lena image in which gaussian noise of different amplitude has been added ($SNR \in [25,\infty[\ dB$). Figure 2 shows that if $SNR > 40dB$, the edges segmentation obtained with α equal to 7.6 is almost as good as the best segmentation according to definition of Pratt's figure-of-merit. Consequently, α equal to 7.6 is appropriate to standard color camera: as an example, color camera JAI CV-M91 features $SNR > 54\ dB$.

2.4 Experimental results and discussion

For evaluating the real performance of the proposed color edge detector. It has been tested on synthetic and real road scenes. A comparison is accomplished between our color operator and the declivity operator to estimate the color improvment. For providing more convincing performance, the proposed color edge detector has been compared to variant of color Canny operator.

Fig. 4(a) shows a synthetic image consisting of three different color squares of similar intensity in a grid pattern and Fig. 5(a) shows a synthetic road scene. When a color version of the Canny operator and color-declivity operator are able to detect the borders between the squares (see Fig. 4(b) and Fig. 4(d), respectively), the declivity operator is not able to detect any edges (see Fig. 4(c)). We remark that all edges are not detected by declivity operator (Especially, border between both vehicles on Fig. 5(c)) while with color variant of Canny operator, we succeed in detecting these edges (see Fig. 5(b)). On the other hand, positions of edges detected with color variant of Canny operator are less accurate particularly in the intersections of edges (see Fig. 4(b) and Fig. 5(b)). The color declivity succeeds in extracting edges correctly with a very good precision particularly in the case of the intersections of edges (see Fig. 4(d) and Fig. 5(d)). So we proposed a new operator for color edges detection which takes advantage of color information and advantages of declivity operator (accuracy and auto-adaptivity).

To be able to estimate the contribution of color information, we decide to push comparison between declivity operator and color-declivity operator. For this purpose, we use the Middlebury database Scharstein & Szeliski (2002). Table 1 shows that the novel approach extracts more edge points than the former one. In Fig. 7(f), edge points extracted in gray level Cones image but not in color Cones image are superimposed in color Cones image. These results can be justified by:

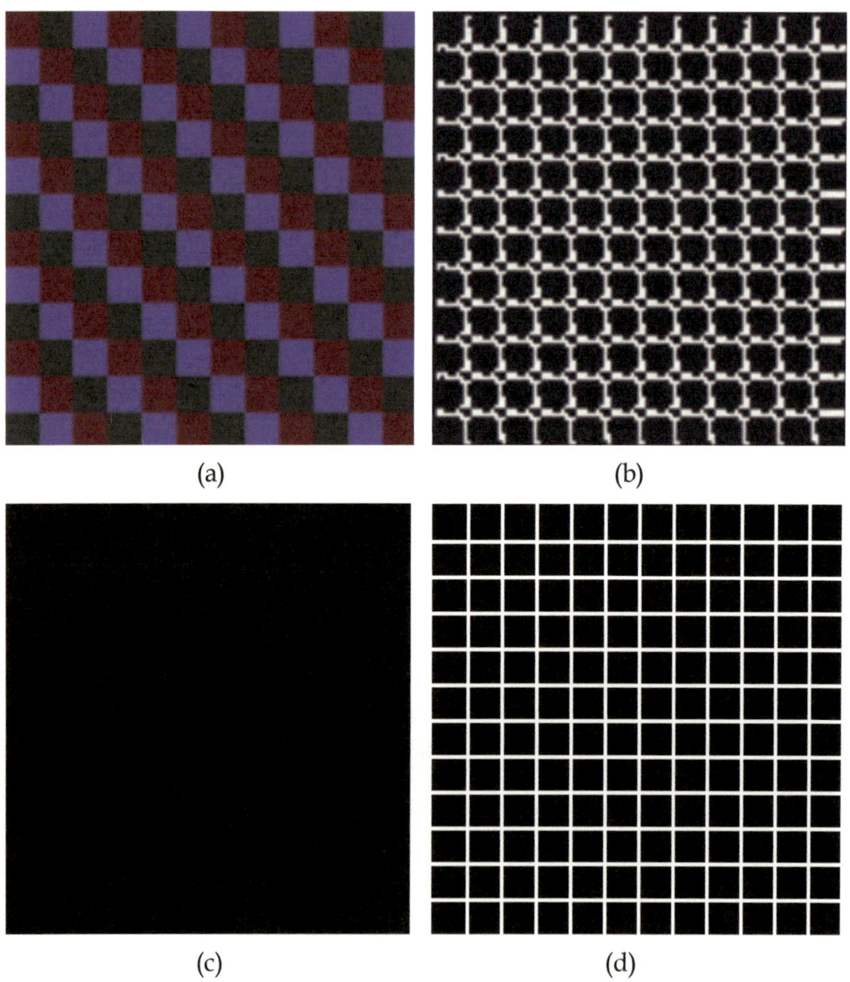

Fig. 4. Experimental results of edge detection (a) Original color image consisting of three different color squares of similar intensity in a grid pattern. (b) Results for a color variant of the Canny operator applied to the color image. (c) Results of declivity operator applied to the gray level image. (d) Results of color-declivity operator applied to the color image.

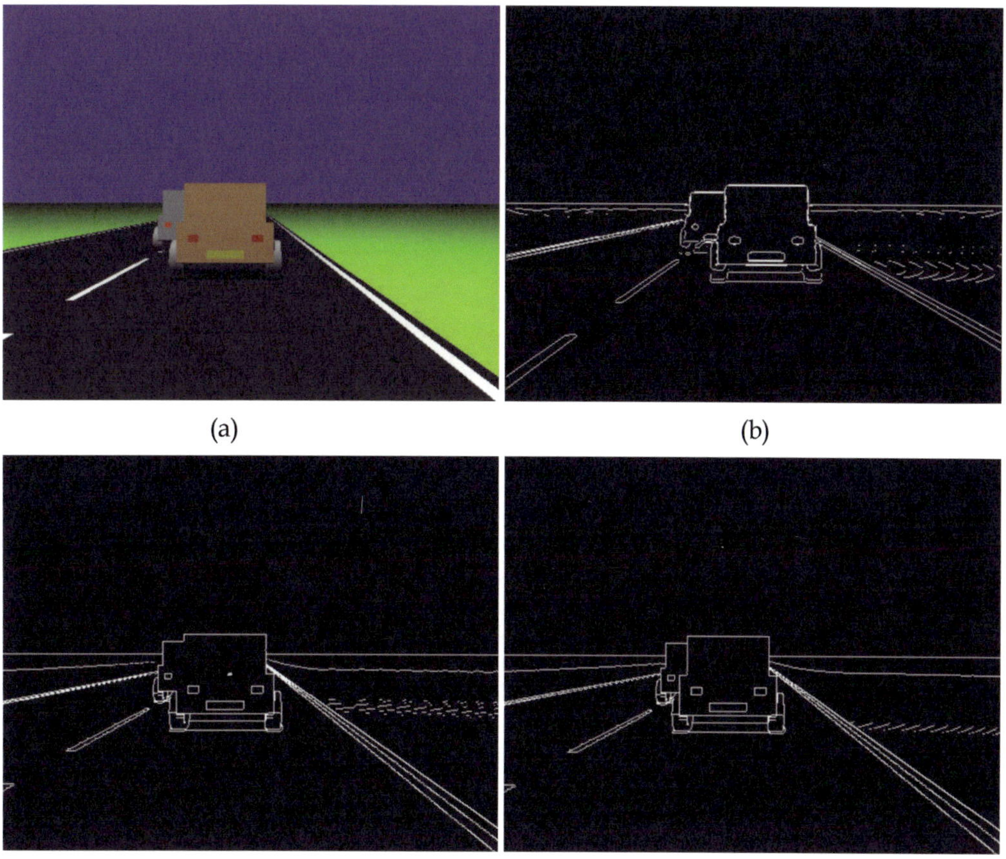

(a) (b) (c) (d)

Fig. 5. Results of edge detection (a) Original color image consisting of three different color squares of similar intensity in a grid pattern. (b) Results for a color variant of the Canny operator applied to the color image. (c) Results of declivity operator applied to the gray level image. (d) Results of color-declivity operator applied to the color image.

1. Edge positions have not been correctly computed. This is due to pixels of adjacent different colored objects which feature strictly monotonous gray level values. Fig. 8 illustrates this phenomenon. In this case, two edge segments are correctly extracted using color declivity, whereas only one edge segment is extracted in gray level image. As a consequence, the position of the extracted edge segment does not correspond to position of actual edge.
2. Amplitudes of color declivity and its correspond on gray level are not the same. α is equal to 7.6 for color image and 5.6 for gray level image. The edge points extracted in gray level image but not in color image correspond to edges which have an amplitude between 5.6× σ and 7.6× σ. Infact, lower value of α for gray level image is a compromise which enables not to reject too much gray level edges and not to extract too much noise.

In Fig. 7(e), edge points extracted in color Cones image but not in gray level Cones image are superimposed in color Cones image. These edge points extracted by color-declivity are

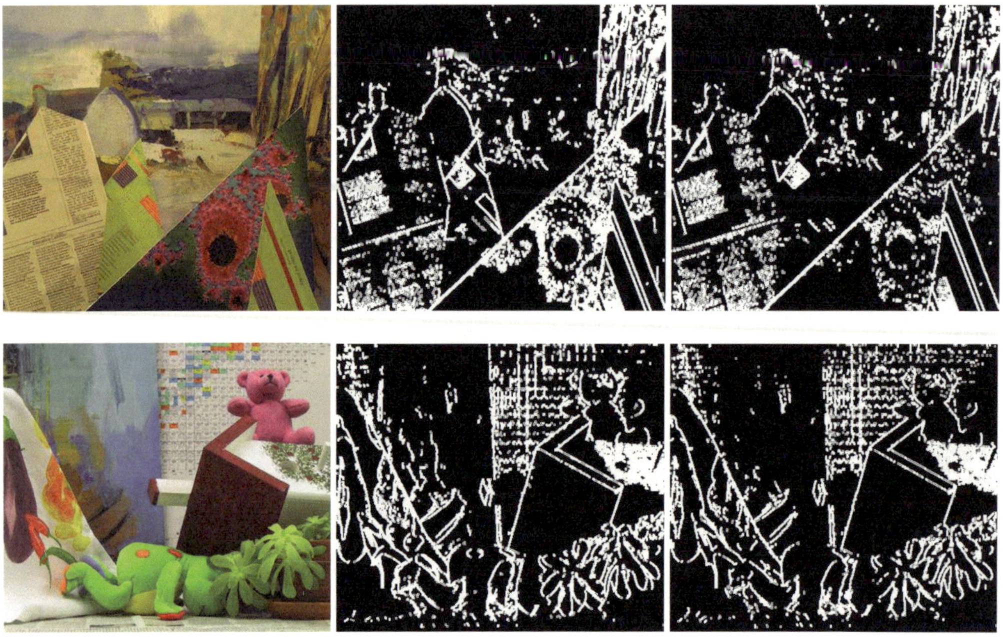

(a) (b) (c)

Fig. 6. Experimental results of edge extraction: (a) color image (Barn 1 and Teddy). (b) color declivity image. (c) declivity image.

relevant for scene understanding. In addition to better positioning of color declivity for particular case explained in point 1., color enables to face problems of:

3. Metamerism: metamerism is observed if different colored objects reflect the same amount of light. Examples of colors which have the same gray level value in gray level image are presented in Fig. 9. Edges of adjacent different colored objects which reflect the same intensity are robustly extracted in color image, while they are not extracted in gray level image. Gray level edges segmentation problem due to metamerism is illustrated in Fig. 4. The case of the Fig. 9(b) is very interesting. We see that a shade of the red, the green and the blue be able to have an intensity in gray level equal to 127. So, the edges point separating both vehicles on the road having these colors will not be discerned by the declivity (see Fig. 5(c))
4. Adjacent different colored objects which reflect almost the same intensity: using color process, the amplitude of relevant color declivity is greater than $7.6 \times \sigma$. In this particular case, its corresponding in graylevel process have an amplitude smaller than $5.6 \times \sigma$.

As a conclusion, color edges segmentation based on color-declivity is more robust and reliable than gray level edges segmentation based on declivity. Note also that the proposed definition of color declivity can be used for any color spaces and for any hybrid color spaces. We can also extend color-declivity to multi-spectral images.

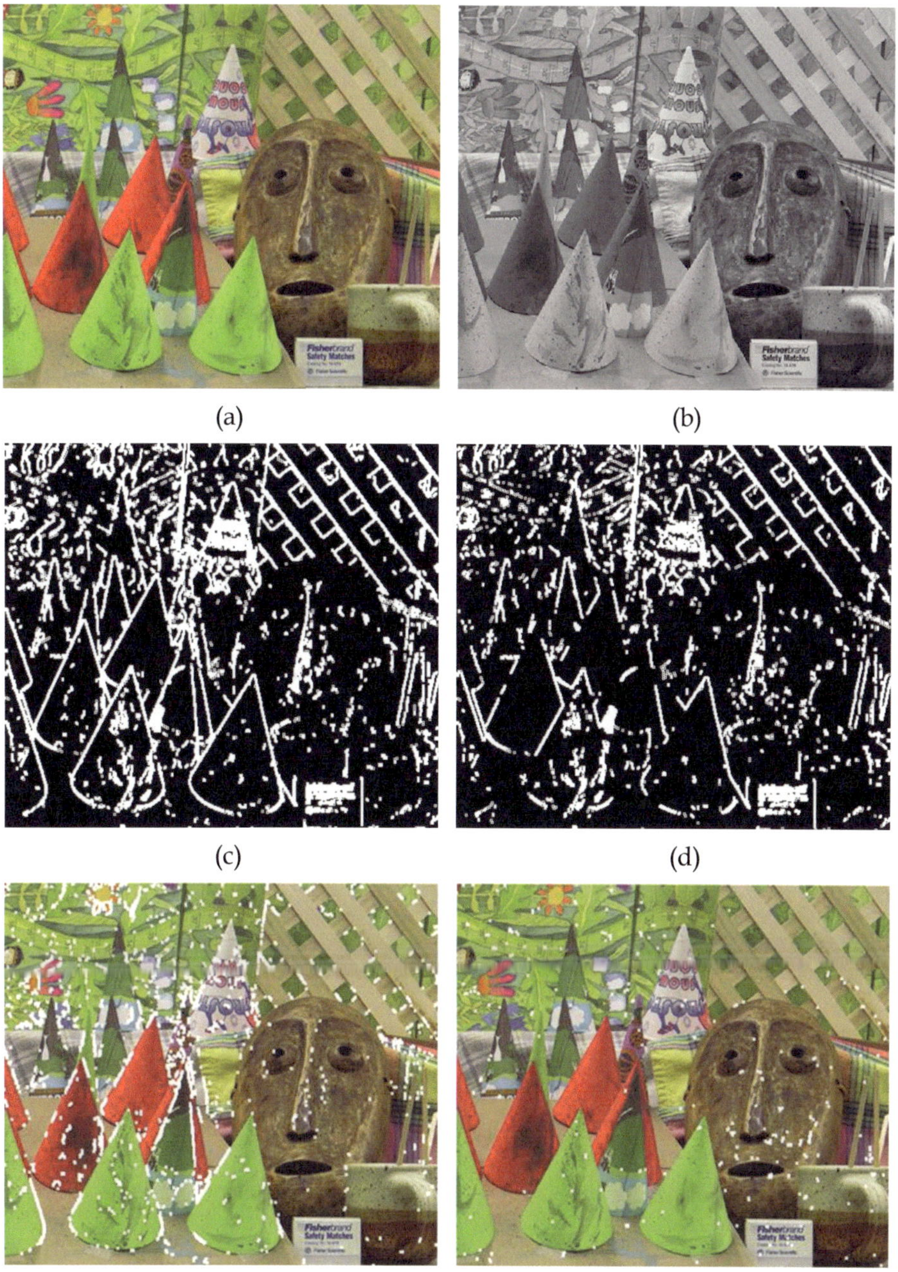

(a) (b) (c) (d) (e) (f)

Fig. 7. Experimental results of color edges segmentation and gray level segmentation of Cones image of Middlebury database Scharstein & Szeliski (2002). (a) Color image. (b) The corresponding gray level image of (a). (c) Color-declivity image. (d) Declivity image. (e) Edge points extracted in color image but not in gray level image superimposed in white on color images. (f) Edge points extracted in gray level image but not in color image superimposed in white on color images.

	Number of	
Image name	declivities	color declivities
Barn 1	8446	12177
Cones	8538	12880
Teddy	8710	11733
Tsukuba	7216	10214

Table 1. Number of color declivities extracted in color images compared to number declivities extracted in corresponding gray level image

Fig. 8. Pixels of adjacent different colored objects with strictly monotonous gray level values. (a) color image. (b) color declivity image. (c) the corresponding gray level image of (a). (d) declivity image.

Fig. 9. Metamerism phenomena. Colors which reflect the same amount of light. Colors for gray level values equal to (a) 200, (b) 127 and (c) 50.

3. Color matching

3.1 State of the art

Introduction of different stereo correspondence algorithms can be found in the survey by *Scharstern* and *Szeliski* Scharstein & Szeliski (2002) and the one by *Brown et al.* Brown & Hager (2003). Matching approaches can be divided into *local* and *global* methods depending on their optimization strategy Brown & Hager (2003).

3.1.1 Local methods

Local methods can be very efficient but they are sensitive to locally ambiguous regions in images. They fall into three categories:

- Block matching Banks & Corke (2001): Search for maximum match score or minimum error over small region, typically using variants of cross-correlation or robust rank metrics. These methods are very suitable for dense matching and conceivable in real-time. We have a correct matching in the case of a light vertical displacement between stereoscopic pair. These algorithms always provide a matching result even in the case of an occlusion which implicates a false matching. They are also little accurate on zones with not enough textures and sensitive to depth discontinuity.

- Gradient methods Twardowski et al. (2004): Minimize a functional, typically the sum of squared differences, over a small region. These methods has a correct matching in the case of a light vertical displacement between stereoscopic pair. They are little accurate on zones with few texture or too texture and sensitive to depth discontinuity. They give a poor results with scenes which have a large disparity.
- Feature matching Shen (2004): Match dependable features rather than intensities themselves. The quality of matching and the computation time depends on quality and computation time of detection algorithms of features.

3.1.2 Global methods

Global methods can be less sensitive to locally ambiguous regions in images, since global constraints provide additional support for regions difficult to match locally. They fall into six categories:

- Dynamic programming Bensrhair et al. (1996)Deng & Lin (2006): Determine the disparity surface for a scanline as the best path between two sequences of ordered primitives. Typically, order is defined by the epipolar ordering constraint. These methods have a good matching in the case of zones with not enough textures. They resolve the problems of the matching in the case of occlusions. Nevertheless, a light vertical displacement between stereoscopic pair misleads the matching. In the case of a local error of matching, this error is spread throughout the research line.
- Graph cuts Veksler (2007): Determine the disparity surface as the minimum cut of the maximum flow in a graph. The disparity map obtained with these methods is more accurate than that obtained by the dynamic programming. These methods have tendency to flatten objects on the disparity map. They consume too much computation time and as a result it is not possible to use them for real-time application.
- Intrinsic curves: Map epipolar scanlines to intrinsic curve space to convert the search problem to a nearest-neighbors lookup problem. Ambiguities are resolved using dynamic programming.
- Nonlinear diffusion: Agregate support by applying a local diffusion process.
- Belief propagation: Solve for disparities via message passing in a belief network.
- Correspondenceless methods: Deform a model of the scene based on an objective function.

3.2 Color matching based on dynamic programming

The matching problem based on dynamic programming can be summarized as finding an optimal path on a two-dimensional graph whose vertical and horizontal axes respectively represent the color declivities of a left line and the color declivities of the stereo-corresponding right line. Axes intersections are nodes that represent hypothetical color-declivity associations. Optimal matches are obtained by the selection of the path which corresponds to a maximum value of a global gain. The matching algorithm consists of three steps:

Step 1. Taking into account a geometric constraint, all possible color-declivity associations $(R(i, l); L(j, l))$ are constructed. Let X_{cRi} be the position of the right color-declivity $R(i,$

l) in the line l of right image. Let X_{cLj} be the position of the left color-declivity $L(j, l)$ in the line l of left image. ($R(i, l)$; $L(j, l)$) satisfies the geometric constraint if $0 < X_{cRi} - X_{cLj} < disp_{max}$. $disp_{max}$ is the maximum possible disparity value; it is adjusted according to the length of the baseline and the focal length of the cameras.

Step 2. Hypothetical color-declivity associations (constructed in step 1) which validate non-reversal constraint in color-declivity correspondence are positioned on the 2D graph. Each node in the graph (i.e. hypothetical color-declivity association) is associated to a local gain (see subsection 3.3) which represents the quality of the declivity association. As a result, we obtain several paths from an initial node to a final node in the graph. The gain of the path, i.e., the global gain, is the sum of the gains of its primitive paths. This gain is defined as follows. Let $G(e, f)$ be the maximum gain of the partial path from an initial node to node (e, f), and let $g(e, f, q, r)$ be the gain corresponding to the primitive path from node (e, f) to node (q, r), which in fact, only depends on node (q, r). Finally, $G(q, r)$ is computed as follows:

$$G(q,r) = \max_{(e,f)} [G(e,f) + g(e,f,q,r)] \tag{6}$$

Step 3. The optimal path in the graph is selected. It corresponds to the maximum value of the global gain. The best color-declivity associations are the nodes of the optimal path taking the uniqueness constraint into account. A disparity value $\delta(i, j, l)$ is computed for each color-declivity association ($R(i, l)$; $L(j, l)$) of the optimal path of line l. $\delta(i, j, l)$ is equal to $X_{cLj} - X_{cRi}$, where X_{cRi} and X_{cLj} are the respective positions of $R(i, l)$ and $L(j, l)$ in the l right and l left epipolar lines. The result of color matching based on dynamic programming is a sparse disparity map.

3.3 Computation of local gain function

Computation of local gain associated to node in the 2D graph is based on photometric distance between two color declivities. Let X_{cRi} and X_{cLj} be the positions of two color declivities $R(i, l)$ and $L(j, l)$ respectively. Let $I_{R_c}(u_i - k)$ and $I_{L_c}(u_j - k)$ be the intensity of left neighbors of $R(i, l)$ and $L(j, l)$ respectively in color channel c, with k = 0,1 and 2 and c = 1,2 and 3. And, let $I_{R_c}(u_{i+1} + k)$ and $I_{L_c}(u_{j+1} + k)$ be the intensity of right neighbors of $R(i, l)$ and $L(j, l)$ respectively in color channel c with k = 0,1 and 2. Left and right photometric distances between $R(i, l)$ and $L(j, l)$ in channel c of color image are computed based on SAD (Sum of Absolute Differences):

$$l_{phdist_c} = \sum_{k=0}^{2} | I_{R_c}(u_i - k) - I_{L_c}(u_j - k) | \tag{7}$$

$$r_{phdist_c} = \sum_{k=0}^{2} | I_{R_c}(u_{i+1} + k) - I_{L_c}(u_{j+1} + k) | \tag{8}$$

Based on (7) and (8), local gain is computed. Classic methods tend to minimize a cost function. The main difficulty with this approach is that the cost value can increase indefinitely, which affects the computation time of the algorithm. Contrary to classic methods, the gain function is a non-linear function which varies between 0 and a maximum self-adaptive value equal to:

$$3 \times \max_{\forall m \in \Omega_{i,j}} (g_{max_c}) \tag{9}$$

with

$$g_{max_c} = 3 \times (d_{tR_c} + d_{tL_c}) \tag{10}$$

d_{tRc} and d_{tLc} are respectively the self-adaptive threshold value for the detection of relevant color declivities in right and left corresponding scan lines for channel number c. $\Omega_{i,j} = \Omega_i \cup \Omega_j$, where Ω_i and Ω_j are the sets (see subsection 2.2) associated respectively to color declivities $R(i, l)$ and $L(i, l)$. The gain function is calculated as follow:

Case 1.
if $\forall c \in \{1, 2,3\}$ ($l_{phdist_c} < g_{max_c}$ and $r_{phdist_c} < g_{max_c}$) then

$$gain = \frac{1}{Card(\Omega_{i,j})} \sum_{c \in \Omega_{i,j}} (3 \times g_{max_c} - l_{phdist_c} - r_{phdist_c}) \tag{11}$$

Case 2.
if $\forall c \in \{1, 2,3\}$ ($l_{phdist_c} < g_{max_c}$ and $r_{phdist_c} \geq g_{max_c}$) then

$$gain = \frac{1}{Card(\Omega_{i,j})} \sum_{c \in \Omega_{i,j}} (g_{max_c} - l_{phdist_c}) \tag{12}$$

Case 3.
if $\forall c \in \{1, 2,3\}$ (l_{phdist_c} _ g_{max_c} and $r_{phdist_c} < g_{max_c}$) then

$$gain = \frac{1}{Card(\Omega_{i,j})} \sum_{c \in \Omega_{i,j}} (g_{max_c} - r_{phdist_c}) \tag{13}$$

The gain function is computed

1. If there is a global (case 1), a left (case 2) or a right (case 3) color photometric similarity (i.e. a photometric similarity in each channel of color image). The gain function is computed to advantage global color photometric similarity compared to left or right similarity.
2. If monotonies of considered left and right color declivities are the same in each channel of $\Omega_{i,j}$. Due to different view of stereoscopic cameras, occlusions may occur. For example, background of left side of an object in left image may be occluded in right image. As a consequence, projections of a 3D point in color planes of the two cameras (declivities to be matched) may not be extracted in same channels. Then, $\Omega_{i,j}$ is equal to $\Omega_i \cup \Omega_j$. In the case of the example of occlusion, declivities to be matched have the same right photometric neighborhood. As a consequence, declivities in order to be matched must have the same monotony, otherwise it means that one of the edge point has not been extracted.

3.4 Experimental results and discussion

In Fig. 11, Fig. 12 and table 1 color matching is compared to gray level matching. The MARS/PRESCAN database van der Mark & Gavrila (2006) is used. It is composed of 326 pairs of synthetic color stereo images and ground truth data. Resolution of image is 256 x 256 pixels.

Image size	MARS/PRESCAN database 256 × 256 × 24 (color)	256 × 256 × 8 (gray level)
Number of frames	326	326
Mean of number of declivity associations	4503	3470
Mean computation time of edge extraction in a line of image (in ms)	0.12	0.04
Mean computation time of matching in a line of image (in ms)	0.12	0.12
Processor	Centrino 1.73 GHz	Centrino 1.73 GHz

Table 2. Computation time of color and gray level matching based on dynamic programming obtained from MARS/PRESCAN database which is composed of 326 stereo images.

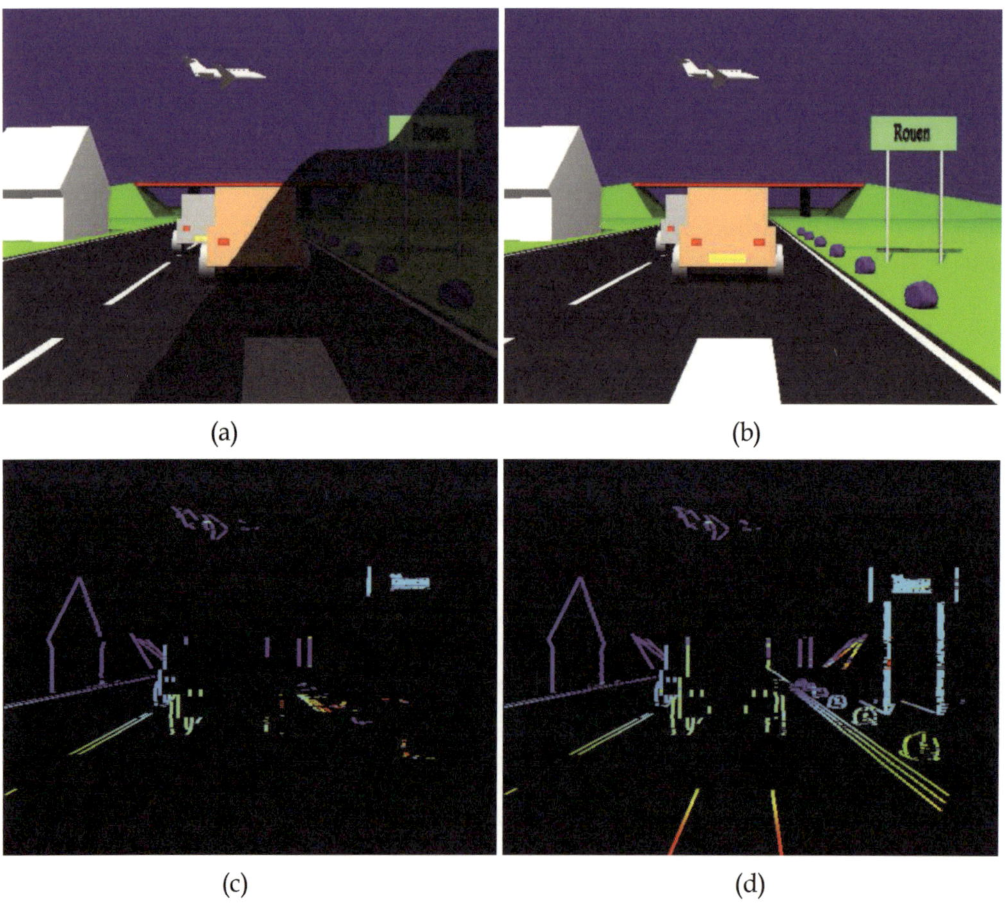

Fig. 10. Experimental results of disparity map construction. Disparity is coded with false color: hot color corresponds to close objects; cold color corresponds to far objects. (a) Left color syhntetic image with different contrast in the bottom-right region. (b) Right color syhntetic image. (c) Gray level matching. (d) Color matching.

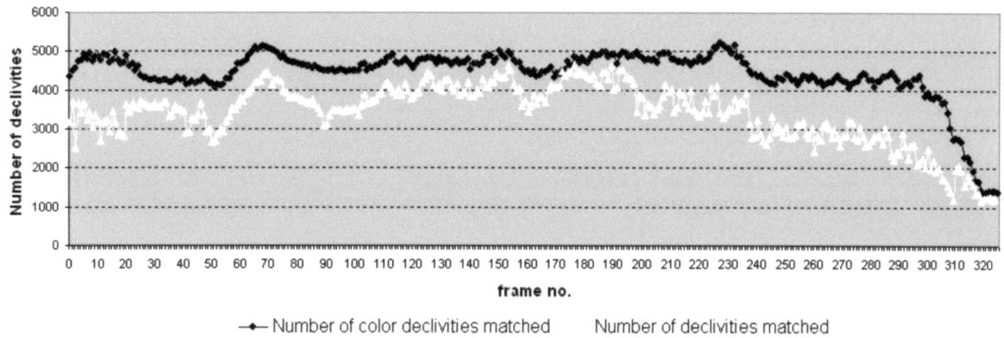

Fig. 11. Number of color declivity associations compared to gray level declivity associations obtained from MARS/PRESCAN database which is composed of 326 stereo images.

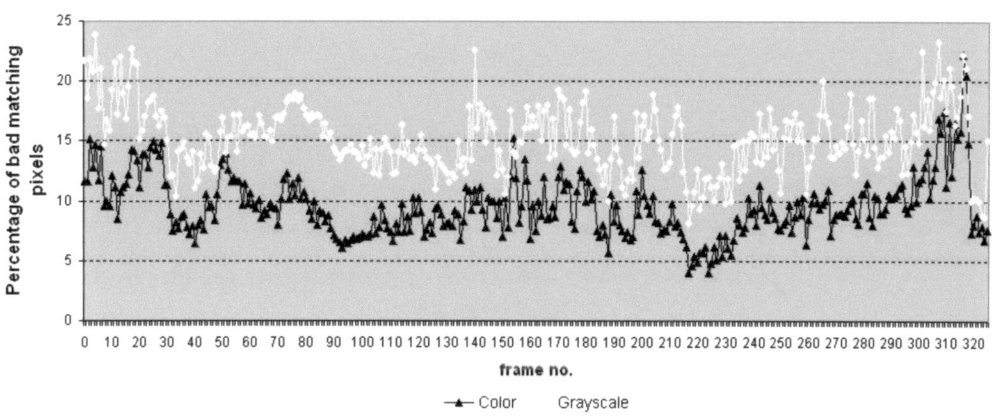

Fig. 12. Percentage of bad color matching compared to percentage of bad gray level matching obtained from MARS/PRESCAN database which is composed of 326 stereo images. These percentages have been computed based on (14).

Fig. 11 shows that the number of color association obtained from MARS/PRESCAN database is higher than the number of gray level association obtained from the gray level version of MARS/PRESCAN database. For this sequence, contribution of color corresponds to a 33% mean increase in the number of association with respect to the number of gray level association. The mean number of color declivities is 5700 for color image. The mean number of declivities is 5200 for gray level image. It corresponds to a 10% mean increase in the number

$$B = \frac{1}{100} \times \frac{1}{Card(\Lambda)} \sum_{k=1}^{Card(\Lambda)} \left(\left| \delta(x(k), y(k)) - \delta_{gt}(x(k), y(k)) \right| > \Delta \right) \tag{14}$$

4. Obstacle detection

4.1 Ground plane estimation

In the previous sections we proved that color matching is more reliable than gray level matching in associating edge points. In this section we will show some of the consequences for a typical application of stereo vision in intelligent vehicles: ground plane estimation. Often, the v-disparity Labayrade et al. (2002) is used to estimate ground plane that allows to distinguish obstacles. The road surface of the synthetic images from MARS/PRESCAN database is flat van der Mark & Gavrila (2006). They, to detect road surface, the Hough transformation is used to detect only a single dominant line feature. This line is then compared to the line found by the same method in the ground truth disparity image. The difference in angle between the two lines shows how ground plane estimation is affected by the quality of the disparity image. For all images from test sequence, the differences in ground plane angle is shown on Fig. 13(a) for color process and on Fig. 13(b) for grayscale process. With the first third of the stereo pairs of database, the ground plane is detected without error. From frame number 188, we diagnose errors in the detection of the angle of ground plane. Using sparse 3D map computed with color process, We improve the perfect detection of ground plane of 10%.

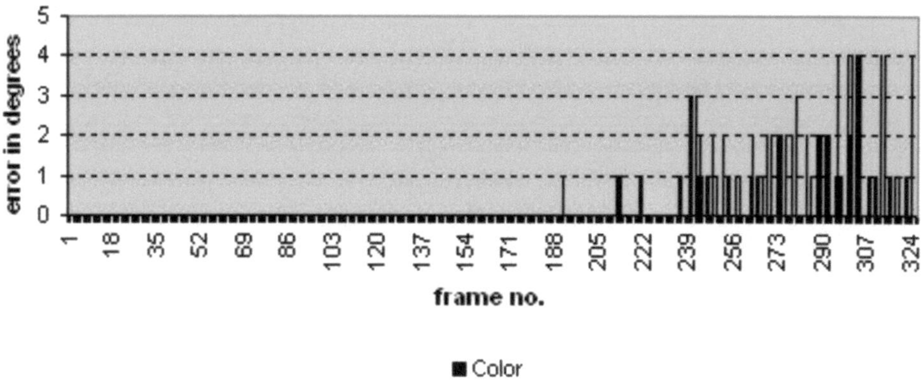

(a)

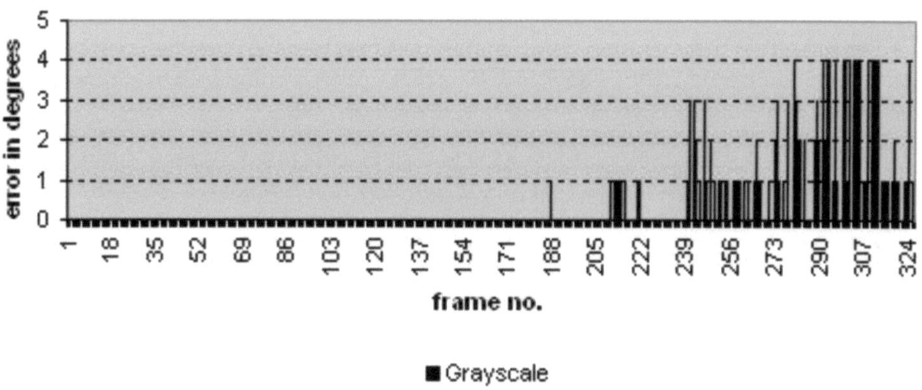

(b)

Fig. 13. Error in ground plane angle estimation based on V-disparity using (a) color matching process, (b) graylevel process to compute 3D Sparse Map

4.2 Extraction of 3D edges of obstacle

Within the framework of road obstacle detection, road features can be classified into two classes: *Non-obstacle* and *Obstacle*. An obstacle is defined as something that obstructs or may obstruct the intelligent vehicle driving path. Vehicles, pedestrians, animals, security guardrails are examples of Obstacles. Lane markings, artifacts are examples of Non-obstacles. In order to detect obstacles, our laboratory has conceived an operator which extracts 3D edges of obstacle from disparity map Toulminet et al. (2004) Cabani et al. (2006b) Cabani et al. (2006a) Toulminet et al. (2006). The extraction of the 3D edges of obstacles has been conceived as a cooperation of two methods:

- Method 1: this method selects 3D edges of obstacle by thresholding their disparity value; the threshold values are computed based on the detection of the road modeled by a plane. This method is sensitive to modeling and method used to detect the road (the v-disparity is used to detect road plane).
- Method 2: this method selects 3D straight segments by thresholding their inclination angle with respect to the road plane; 3D straight segments are constructed based on disparity map. This method does not suffer from approximate modeling and detection of the road. But, the extraction of 3D edges of obstacle is sensitive to noise in disparity measurement.

The cooperation of the two methods takes advantage of different sensitivity of the two methods in order to optimize robustness and reliability of the extraction of 3D edges of obstacle.

The output of the cooperation is a set of 3D points labeled as

- Edge of obstacle: extracted by the cooperation process or extracted by one of the two methods.
- Edge of non obstacle: not extracted.

4.3 Experimental results and discussion

In Fig. 14, the number of point of 3D edges of obstacle using color process is compared to number of point of 3D edges of obstacle using grayscale process obtained from MARS/PRESCAN database which is composed of 326 stereo images. Using color process, we succeed in extracting on average 20% of more points of 3D edges of obstacle. This contribution is very significant and is very important for a possible classification of obstacles in future works. The mean computation time for obstacle detection step is 31 ms. This important number of point of 3D edges of obstacle is owed in most cases in:

- Color declivity operator extract more relevant declivities (See subsection 2.4)
- Color matching is more robust in associating edge points (See subsection 3.4).
- For obstacle detection, method 1 depend on precision of plane road detection. In subsection 4.1, we prove that using 3D sparse map obtained with color process, the ground plane is detected more precisely.

Finally, we present in Fig. 15 an example of experimental results obtained on urban images acquired by our color stereo vision system Cabani et al. (2006a)Cabani et al. (2006b). The stereo vision system features 52 cm between the two optical centers and 8 mm of focal length of the lenses. Stereoscopic images have been acquired and registered on disc at the format of 768×574×24 bits at the rate of 5Hz (10 images per second). They have been processed at the format of 384×287×24 bits using a Pentium Centrino 1.73 GHz with 1 GByte memory using Windows XP. For sequences of Fig. 15, the stereo vision system was static.

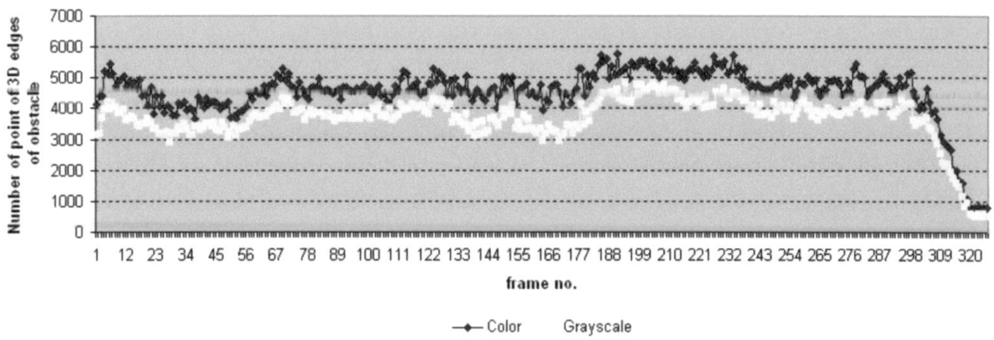

Fig. 14. Number of point of 3D edges of obstacle using color process compared to number of point of 3D edges of obstacle using grayscale process obtained from MARS/PRESCAN database which is composed of 326 stereo images.

edge extraction of both left and right images*	48 ms
color matching based on dynamic programming*	90 ms
obstacle detection	32 ms
Total computation time of extraction of 3D edges of obstacle	170 ms

*: these processes can be parallelized because the treatment is realized independently line by line.

Table 3. Computation time of obstacle detection on real road scene acquired by our color stereo vision system.

These stages have been acquired during daylight; they represent walking pedestrians and cars driving at low speed. In table 3, the mean computation time for each step of obstacle detection is presented. The total computation time of extraction of 3D edges of obstacle is equal to 170 ms. Therefore, our color stereo vision system works on quasi-real time (6 Hz).

5. Conclusion

In this paper, we have presented a color stereo vision-based approach for road obstacle detection. A self-adaptive color operator called color-declivity is presented. It extracts relevant edges in stereoscopic images. Edges are self-adaptively matched based on dynamic programming algorithm. Then, 3D edges of obstacle are extracted from constructed disparity map. These processes have been tested using Middlebury and MARS/PRESCAN databases. To test performance of the proposed approaches they have been compared to gray level-based ones and the improvement is highlighted.

Comparing the result obtained from the color stereo vision system to gray level stereo visions system initially conceived Bensrhair et al. (2002)Toulminet et al. (2006), we verified that more declivities are extracted and matched; and percentage of correct color matching is higher than the corresponding gray-level based matching. In addition, color matching is little sensitive to the intensity variation. Consequently, it is not necessary to obtain and maintain precise online color calibration.

Within the Driving Assistance Domain, color information presents an very important advantage. The extraction of ground plane is more accurate and the number of 3D edges of obstacles is more important.

(a) (b) (c) (d)

Fig. 15. Experimental results: (a) Leftt image. (b) Right image. (c) 3D sparse map obtained after the matching of color declivities using dynamic programming (d) 3D edges of obstacle superimposed in red on the right image.

Finally, color-based extraction of 3D edges of obstacle has been tested on real road scenes. It works on quasi-real time (6 Hz). The future work will focus to optimize computation time. In fact, extraction edges based on color declivity and color matching based on dynamic programming can be parallelized because these processes are executed line by line.

6. References

Alessandretti, G., Broggi, A. & Cerri, P. (2007). Vehicle and guard rail detection using radar and vision data fusion, *IEEE Transactions on Intelligent Transportation Systems* 8(1): 95- 105.

Banks, J. & Corke, P. (2001). Quantitative evaluation of matching methods and validity measures for stereo vision, *The International Journal of Robotics Research* 20(7): 512–532. URL: *http://ijr.sagepub.com/cgi/content/abstract/20/7/512*

Bensrhair, A., Bertozzi, M., Broggi, A., Fascioli, A., Mousset, S. & Toulminet, G. (2002). Stereo vision-based feature extraction for vehicle detection, *Proceedings of the IEEE Intelligent Vehicles Symposium, Versailles, France.*

Bensrhair, A., Miché, P. & Debrie, R. (1996). Fast and automatic stereo vision matching algorithm based on dynamic programming method, *Pattern Recognition Letters* 17: 457- 466.

Bertozzi, M., Broggi, A., Caraffi, C., Del Rose, M., Felisa, M. & Vezzoni, G. (2007). Pedestrian detection by means of far-infrared stereo vision, *Computer Vision and Image Understanding* 106(2-3): 194–204.

Betke, M., Haritaoglu, E. & Davis, L. (2000). Real-time multiple vehicle detection and tracking from a moving vehicle, *Machine Vision and Applications* 12(2): 69–83.

Betke, M. & Nguyen, H. (1998). Highway scene analysis from a moving vehicle under reduced visibility conditions, *Proceedings of the IEEE Intelligent Vehicles Symposium, Stuttgart, Allemagne.*

Broggi, A., Fascioli, A., Carletti, M., Graf, T. & Meinecke, M. (2004). A multi-resolution approach for infrared vision-based pedestrian detection, *Proceedings of the IEEE Intelligent Vehicles Symposium, Parma, Italy.*

Brown, M. & Hager, G. (2003). Advances in computational stereo, *IEEE Transactions on Pattern Analysis and Machine Intelligence* 25(8): 993–1008.

Cabani, I., Toulminet, G. & Bensrhair, A. (2005). Color-based detection of vehicle lights, *Proceedings of IEEE intelligent Vehicle Symposium, Las Vegas, USA.*

Cabani, I., Toulminet, G. & Bensrhair, A. (2006a). A color stereo vision system for extraction of 3d edges of obstacle, *Proceedings of the IEEE International Conference on Intelligent Transportation Systems*, Toronto, Canada.

Cabani, I., Toulminet, G. & Bensrhair, A. (2006b). Color stereoscopic steps for road obstacle detection, *The 32nd Annual Conference of the IEEE Industrial Electronics Society, IECON'06*, Paris, France.

Canny, J. (1986). A computational approach to edge detection, *IEEE Transactions on Pattern Analysis and Machine Intelligence* 8(6): 679–698.

Carron, T. & Lambert, P. (1994). Color edge detector using jointly hue, saturation and intensity, *Proceedings of the IEEE International Conference on Image Processing*, Vol. 3, pp. 977–981.

Carron, T. & Lambert, P. (1995). Fuzzy color edge extraction by inference rules quantitative study and evaluation of performances, *Proceedings of the IEEE International Conference on Image Processing*, Vol. 2, pp. 181–184.

Chapron, M. (1992). A new chromatic edge detector used for color image segmentation, *Proceedings of the IEEE International Conference on Pattern Recognition*, Vol. 3, pp. 311–314.

Chapron, M. (1997). A chromatic contour detector based on abrupt change techniques, *Proceedings of the IEEE International Conference on Image Processing*, Vol. 3, Santa Barbara, CA, pp. 18–21.

Chapron, M. (2000). A color edge detector based on dempster-shafer theory, *Proceedings of the IEEE International Conference on Image Processing*, Vol. 2, pp. 812–815.

Cheng, H.-Y., Jeng, B.-S., Tseng, P.-T. & Fan, K.-C. (2006). Lane detection with moving vehicles in the traffic scenes, *IEEE Transactions on Intelligent Transportation Systems* 7(4): 571- 582.

Cheng, H., Zheng, N., Zhang, X. & van deWetering, H. (2007). Interactive road situation analysis for driver assistance and safety warning systems: Framework and algorithms, *IEEE Transactions on Intelligent Transportation Systems* 8(1): 157–167.

Cumani, A. (1991). *Edge detection in multispectral images, Comput. Vis. Graph. Image Process.: Graphical Models Image Processing* 53(1): 40–51.

Deng, Y. & Lin, X. (2006). A fast line segment based dense stereo algorithm using tree dynamic programming, *Proceedings of the European Conference on Computer Vision*, Vol. 3953/2006, Springer Berlin / Heidelberg, pp. 201–212.

Di-Zenzo, S. (1986). A note on the gradient of a multi-image, *Computer Vision, Graphics and Image Processing* 33(1): 116–125.

Djuric, P. & Fwu, J. (1997). On the detection of edges in vector images, *IEEE Transactions on Image Processing* 6(11): 1595–1601.

Fan, J., Aref,W. G., Hacid, M.-S. & Elmagarmid, A. K. (2001). An improved automatic isotropic color edge detection technique, *Pattern Recognition Letters* 22(13): 1419–1429.

Fan, J., Yau, D., Elmagarmid, A. & Aref, W. (2001). Automatic image segmentation by integrating color-edge extraction and seeded region growing, *IEEE Transactions on Image Processing* 10(10): 1454–1466.

Franke, U. (2000). Real-time stereo vision for urban traffic scene understanding, *Proc. of the IEEE Intelligent Vehicles Symp., Dearborn, USA*.

Franke, U., Gavrila, D., Gorzig, S., Lindner, F., Paetzold, F. & Wohler, C. (1999). Autonomous driving goes downtown, *IEEE Intelligent Systems* 13(6): 40–48.

Gao, B. & Coifman, B. (2006). Vehicle identification and gps error detection from a lidar equipped probe vehicle, *Proceedings of the IEEE International Conference on Intelligent Transportation Systems*, pp. 1537–1542.

Gern, A., Franke, U. & Levi, P. (2000). Advanced lane recognition - fusing vision and radar, *Proc. of the IEEE Intelligent Vehicles Symp., Dearborn, USA*.

Heddley, M. & Yan, H. (1992). Segmentation of color images using spatial and color space information, *Journal Electron. Imag.* 1(4): 374–380.

Hueckel, M. H. (1971). An operator which locates edges in digitized pictures, *J. ACM* 18(1): 113–125.

Huntsberger, T. & Descalzi, M. (1985). Color edge detection, *Pattern Recognition Letters* 3(3): 205–209.

Jia, Z., Balasuriya, A. & Challa, S. (2007). Vision based data fusion for autonomous vehicles target tracking using interacting multiple dynamic models, *Computer Vision and Image Understanding, In Press, Corrected Proof*.

Kogler, J., Hemetsberger, H., Alefs, B., Kubinger, W. & Travis, W. (2006). Embedded stereo vision system for intelligent autonomous vehicles, *Proceedings of the IEEE Intelligent Vehicles Symposium*, pp. 64–69.

Kruse, F., Follster, F. & Ahrholdt, M. (2004). Target classification based on near-distance radar sensor, *Proc. of the IEEE Intelligent Vehicles Symp., Parma, Italy*.

Labayrade, R., Aubert, D. & Tarel, J. (2002). Real time obstacle detection in stereovision on non flat road geometry through v-disparity representation, *Proc. of the IEEE Intelligent Vehicles Symp., Versailles, France*.

Lombardi, P. & Zavidovique, B. (2004). A context-dependent vision system for pedestrian detection, *Proceedings of the IEEE Intelligent Vehicles Symposium, Parma, Italy*.

Macaire, L. (2004). *Exploitation de la couleur pour la segmentation et l'analyse d'images*, PhD thesis, (HDR), Universit´e des Sciences et Technologies de Lille.

Macaire, L., Ultre, V. & Postaire, J. (1996). Determination of compatibility coefficients for color edge detection by relaxation, *Proceedings of the IEEE International Conference on Image Processing*, Vol. 3, pp. 1045–1048.

Machuca, R. & Phillips, K. (1983). Applications of vector fields to image processing, *IEEE Transactions on Pattern Analysis and Machine Intelligence* 5(3): 316–329.

Maldonado-Bascon, S., Lafuente-Arroyo, S., Gil-Jimenez, P., Gomez-Moreno, H. & Lopez-Ferreras, F. (2007). Road-sign detection and recognition based on support vector machines, *IEEE Transactions on Intelligent Transportation Systems* 8(2): 264–278.

Malowany, M. & Malowany, A. (1989). Color edge detectors for a vlsi convolver, *in* W. Pearlman (ed.), *Proc. SPIE Vol. 1199, p. 1116-1126, Visual Communications and Image Processing IV, William A. Pearlman; Ed.*, Vol. 1199 of *Presented at the Society of Photo-Optical Instrumentation Engineers (SPIE) Conference*, pp. 1116–1126.

Miché, P. & Debrie, R. (1995). Fast and self-adaptive image segmentation using extended declivity, *Annals of telecommunication* 50(3-4): 401–410.

Möbus, R. & Kolbe, U. (2004). Multi-target multi-object tracking, sensor fusion of radar and infrared, *Proceedings of the IEEE Intelligent Vehicles Symposium, Parma, Italy.*

Moghaddamzadeh, A. & Bourbakis, N. (1995). A fuzzy approach for smoothing and edge detection in color images, *In Proceedings of the SPIE*, Vol. 2421, pp. 90–102.

Moghaddamzadeh, A., Goldman, D. & Bourbakis, N. (1998). Fuzzy-like approach for smoothing and edge detection in color images, *International Journal of Pattern Recognition and Artificial Intelligence* 12(6): 801–816.

Nevatia, R. (1977). A color edge detector and its use in scene segmentation, *IEEE Trans. Syst., Man, Cybern.* 7: 820–826. *PathFindIR* (n.d.). URL: *www.flir.com*

Peli, T. & Malah, D. (1982). A study of edge detection algorithms, *Computer Graphics and Image Processing* 20: 1–21.

Pietikainen, M. & Harwood, D. (1986). Edge information in color images based on histograms of differences, *Proceedings of the IEEE International Conference on Pattern Recognition*, Paris, France, pp. 594–596.

Pratt,W. (1977). *Digital Image Processing*,Wiley, New York.

Ruzon, M. & Tomasi, C. (2001). Edge, junction, and corner detection using color distributions, *IEEE Transactions on Pattern Analysis and Machine Intelligence* 23(11): 1281–1295.

Salinas, R., Richardson, C., Abidi, M. & Gonzalez, R. (1996). Data fusion: color edge detection and surface reconstruction through regularization, *IEEE Transactions on Industrial Electronics* 43(3): 355–363.

Sankur, B. & Sezgin, M. (2004). Survey Over Image Thresholding Techniques and Quantitative Performance Evaluation, *Journal of Electronic Imaging* 13(1): 146–165.

Scharcanski, J. & Venetsanopoulos, A. (1997). Edge detection of color images using directional operators, *IEEE Transactions on Circuits and Systems for Video Technology* 7(2): 397–401.

Scharstein, D. & Szeliski, R. (2002). A taxonomy and evaluation of dense twoframe stereo correspondence algorithms, *International Journal of Computer Vision, www.middlebury.edu/stereo/* 47: 7–42.

Shen, D. (2004). Image registration by hierarchical matching of local spatial intensity histograms., *Medical Image Computing and Computer-Assisted Intervention*, Vol. 3216/2004, Springer Berlin/Heidelberg, pp. 582–590.

Shiozaki, A. (1986). Edge extraction using entropy operator, *Computer Vision, Graphics and Image Processing* 36(1): 1–9.

Steux, B., Laurgeau, C., Salesse, L. & Wautier, D. (2002). Fade : A vehicle detection and tracking system featuring monocular color vision and radar data fusion, *Proceedings of the IEEE Intelligent Vehicles Symposium, Versailles, France.*

Tao, H.&Huang, T. (1997). Color image edge detection using cluster analysis, *Proceedings of the IEEE International Conference on Image Processing*, Vol. 1, Washington, D.C., pp. 834– 837.

Toulminet, G., Bertozzi, M., Mousset, S., Bensrhair, A. & Broggi, A. (2006). Vehicle detection by means of stereo vision-based obstacles features extraction and monocular pattern analysis, *IEEE Transactions on Image Processing* 15(8): 2364–2375.

Toulminet, G., Mousset, S. & Bensrhair, A. (2004). Fast and accurate stereo vision-based estimation of 3-d position and axial motion of road obstacles, *International Journal of Image and Graphics, Special Issue on 3D Object Recognition* 4(1): 99–126.

Trahanias, P. & Venetsanopoulos, A. (1996). Vector order statistics operators as color edge detectors, *IEEE Transactions on Systems, Man, and Cybernetics* 26(1): 135–143.

Tsang, P. & Tsang,W. (1996). Edge detection on object color, *Proceedings of the IEEE International Conference on Image Processing*, Vol. 3, pp. 1049–1052.

Tsang, W. H. & Tsang, P. W. M. (1997). Suppression of false edge detection due to specular reflection in color images, *Pattern Recognition Letters* 18(2): 165–171.

Twardowski, T., Cyganek, B. & Borgosz, J. (2004). Gradient based dense stereo matching., *International Conference of Image Analysis and Recognition*, pp. 721–728.

van der Mark, W. & Gavrila, D. (2006). Real-time dense stereo for intelligent vehicles, *IEEE Transactions on Intelligent Transportation Systems*, Vol. 7, pp. 38–50.

Veksler, O. (2007). Graph cut based optimization for mrfs with truncated convex priors, *Proceedings of the IEEE Computer Society Conference on Computer Vision and Pattern Recognition*

Weeks, A., Felix, C. & Myler, H. (1995). Edge detection of color images using the hsl color space, *in* E. R. Dougherty, J. T. Astola, H. G. Longbotham, N. M. Nasrabadi & A. K. Katsaggelos (eds), *Proc. SPIE Vol. 2424, p. 291-301, Nonlinear Image Processing VI*, Vol. 2424 of *Presented at the Society of Photo-Optical Instrumentation Engineers (SPIE) Conference*, pp. 291–301.

Wen, F., Hu, M. & Yuan, B. (2002). A comparative study on color edge detection, *In Proc. IEEE Region 10 Conf. Comput., Commun., Contr. Power Eng.*, Vol. 1, pp. 511–514.

Woodfill, J. I., Buck, R., Jurasek, D., Gordon, G. & Brown, T. (2007). 3d vision: Developing an embedded stereo-vision system, *Computer* 40(5): 106–108.

Xu, F. & Fujimura, K. (2002). Pedestrian detection and tracking with night vision, *Proceedings of the IEEE Intelligent Vehicles Symposium, Versailles, France.*

Yang, C. & Tsai, W. (1996). Reduction of color space dimensionality by moment-preserving thresholding and its application for edge-detection in color images, *Pattern Recognition Letters* 17(5): 481–490.

Zhu, Y., Comaniciu, D., Pellkofer, M. & Koehler, T. (2006). Reliable detection of overtaking vehicles using robust information fusion, *IEEE Transactions on Intelligent Transportation Systems* 7(4): 401–414.

Zugaj, D. & Lattuati, V. (1998). A new approach of color images segmentation based on fusing region and edge segmentations outputs, *Pattern Recognition* 31(2): 105–113.

16

A Bio-Inspired Stereo Vision System for Guidance of Autonomous Aircraft

Richard J. D. Moore,
Saul Thurrowgood, Dean Soccol, Daniel Bland and Mandyam V. Srinivasan
University of Queensland
Australia

1. Introduction

Unmanned aerial vehicles (UAVs) are increasingly replacing manned systems in situations that are either too dangerous, too remote, or too difficult for manned aircraft to access. Modern UAVs are capable of accurately controlling their position and orientation in space using systems such as the Global Positioning System (GPS) and the Attitude and Heading Reference System (AHRS). However, they are unable to perform crucial guidance tasks such as obstacle avoidance, low-altitude terrain or gorge following, or landing in an uncontrolled environment using these systems only. For such tasks, the aircraft must be able to continuously monitor its surroundings. Active sensors, such as laser range finders or radar can be bulky, low-bandwidth, and stealth-compromising. Therefore, there is considerable benefit to be gained by designing guidance systems for UAVs that utilise passive sensing, such as vision.

Over the last two decades, a significant amount of research has shown that biological visual systems can inspire novel, vision-based solutions to some of the challenges facing autonomous aircraft guidance. A recent trend in biologically inspired vision systems has been to exploit optical flow information for collision avoidance, terrain and gorge following, and landing. However, systems that rely on optical flow for extracting range information need to discount the components of optical flow that are induced by rotations of the aircraft. Furthermore, altitude cannot be controlled in a precise manner using measurements of optical flow only, as optical flow also depends upon the aircraft's velocity.

Stereo vision, on the other hand, allows the aircraft's altitude to be directly computed and controlled, irrespective of the attitude or ground speed of the aircraft, and independently of its rotations about the roll, pitch, and yaw axes. Additionally, we will show that a stereo vision system can also allow the computation and control of the orientation of the aircraft with respect to the ground. Stereo vision therefore provides an attractive approach to solving some of the problems of providing guidance for autonomous aircraft operating in low-altitude or cluttered environments.

In this chapter, we will explore how stereo vision may be applied to facilitate the guidance of an autonomous aircraft. In particular, we will discuss a wide-angle stereo vision system that has been tailored for the specific needs of aircraft guidance, such as terrain following, obstacle avoidance, and landing. Finally, results from closed-loop flight tests conducted using this system will be presented to demonstrate how stereo vision can be successfully utilised to provide guidance for an autonomous aircraft performing real-world tasks.

2. Relevant background

In this section we will briefly discuss the motivations for designing guidance systems for autonomous aircraft and also review some of the techniques used by state-of-the-art systems.

2.1 Unmanned aerial vehicles

Unmanned aerial vehicles (UAVs) have seen unprecedented levels of growth in both military and civilian application domains since their inception during World War I. So much so, in fact, that the Joint Strike Fighter[1], which is currently under production, is predicted to be the last manned aircraft produced by the US Armed Forces (Valavanis, 2007). The first pilotless aircraft were intended for use as aerial torpedoes. Today, however, autonomous or semi-autonomous fixed-wing aircraft, airships, or helicopters and vertical take-off and landing (VTOL) rotorcraft are increasingly being used for applications such as surveillance and reconnaissance, mapping and cartography, border patrol, inspection, military and defense missions, search and rescue, law enforcement, fire detection and fighting, agricultural and environmental imaging and monitoring, traffic monitoring, *ad hoc* communication networks, and extraterrestrial exploration, to name just a few.

The reason that UAVs are increasingly being preferred for these roles is that they are able to operate in situations that are either too dangerous, too remote, too dull, or too difficult for manned aircraft (Valavanis, 2007). Typically, today's UAVs are flown remotely by a human pilot. However, with the expanding set of roles there is an increasing need for UAVs to be able to fly with a degree of low-level autonomy, thus freeing up their human controllers to concentrate on high level decisions.

2.2 Short range navigation

Modern UAVs are capable of controlling their position and orientation in space accurately using systems such as the Global Positioning System (GPS) and Attitude and Heading Reference Systems (AHRS). This is sufficient when navigating over large distances at high altitude or in controlled airspaces. However, the expanding set of roles for UAVs increasingly calls for them to be able to operate in near-earth environments, and in environments containing 3D structures and obstacles. In such situations, the UAV must know its position in the environment accurately, which can be difficult to obtain using GPS due to occlusions and signal reflections from buildings and other objects. Additionally, the UAV must know *a priori* the 3D structure of the surrounding environment in order to avoid obstacles. Obviously such a scheme presents severe difficulties in situations where there is no foreknowledge of the 3D structure of the environment, or where this structure can change unpredictably. A more efficient approach would be for the aircraft to monitor its surroundings continuously during flight. The use of active proximity sensors such as ultrasonic or laser range finders, or radar has been considered for this purpose (Scherer et al., 2007). However, such systems can be bulky, expensive, stealth-compromising, high power, and low-bandwidth – limiting their utility for small-scale UAVs. Therefore, there is considerable benefit to be gained by designing guidance systems for UAVs that utilise passive sensing, such as vision.

2.3 Biological vision

The importance of vision for short range navigation was realised many decades ago. However, it is not until recently that vision-based guidance systems have been able to be

[1] Lockheed Martin F-35 Lightning II.

demonstrated successfully onboard real robots outside controlled laboratory environments (see (DeSouza & Kak, 2002) for a review). The difficulty is that visual systems provide such a wealth of information about the surrounding environment and the self-motion of the vehicle, that it is a laborious task to extract the information necessary for robot guidance. For many animals, however, vision provides the primary sensory input for navigation, stabilisation of flight, detection of prey or predators, and interaction with other conspecifics. Insects in particular provide a good study model because they have seemingly developed efficient and effective visual strategies to overcome many of the challenges facing UAV guidance. For instance, the humble housefly is often able to outwit even the most determined swatter, despite its small brain and relatively simple nervous system. In fact, many flying insects have attained a level of skill, agility, autonomy, and circuit miniaturisation that greatly outperforms present day aerial robots (Franceschini, 2004).

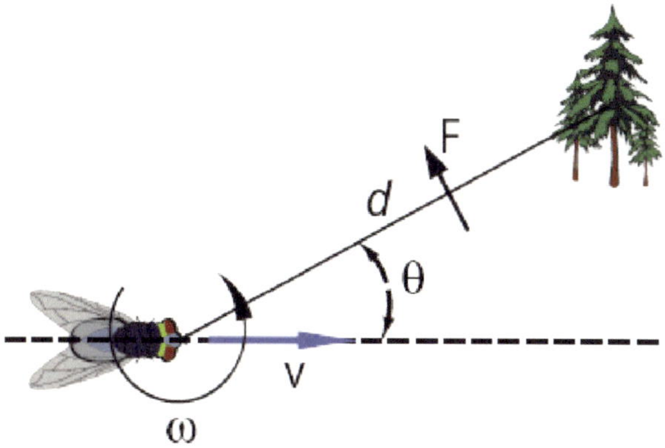

Fig. 1. The optical flow, F, produced by an object as observed by an animal or robot in motion. Reproduced from (Hrabar et al., 2005), with permission.

Unlike vertebrates or humans, insects have immobile eyes with fixed focus optics. Therefore, they cannot infer the distances to objects in the environment using cues such as the gaze convergence or refractive power required to bring an object into focus on the retina. Furthermore, compared with human eyes, the eyes of insects possess inferior spatial acuity, and are positioned much closer together with limited overlapping fields of view. Therefore, the precision with which insects could estimate range through stereopsis would be limited to relatively small distances (Srinivasan et al., 1993). Not surprisingly then, insects have evolved alternative strategies for overcoming the problems of visually guided flight. Many of these strategies rely on using image motion, or *optical flow*, generated by the insect's self-motion, to infer the distances to obstacles and to control various manoeuvres (Gibson, 1950; Nakayama & Loomis, 1974; Srinivasan et al., 1993). The relationship between optical flow and the range to objects in the environment is remarkably simple, and depends only upon the translational speed of the observer, the distance to the obstacle, and the azimuth of the obstacle with respect to the heading direction (Nakayama & Loomis, 1974) (see Fig. 1). The optical flow that is generated by the rotational motion of the insect does not encode any information on the range to objects and so must be discounted from the calculation. Alternatively, rotational movements of the vision system must be prevented and the optical flow measured when the vision system is undergoing pure translation.

For an observer translating at a speed v, and rotating at an angular velocity ω, the optical flow F, generated by a stationary object at a distance d, and angular bearing θ, is given by

$$F = \frac{v \times \sin(\theta)}{d} - \omega. \quad (1)$$

A significant amount of research over the past two decades has shown that biological vision systems can inspired novel, vision-based solutions to many of the challenges that must be overcome when designing guidance systems for autonomous aircraft (see (Srinivasan et al., 2004; Franceschini, 2004; Floreano et al., 2009) for reviews). It has been shown, for example, that honeybees use optical flow for negotiating narrow gaps and avoiding obstacles, regulating their flight speed and altitude, performing smooth landings, and estimating their distance flown (Srinivasan et al., 2000; Srinivasan & Zhang, 2004). A recent trend in biologically inspired vision systems for UAVs, therefore, has been to exploit optical flow information for collision avoidance, terrain and gorge following, and landing (Srinivasan et al., 2004; 2009; Barrows et al., 2003).

2.4 Existing bio-inspired vision-based guidance systems for UAVs

The magnitude of the optical flow gives a measure of the ratio of the aircraft's speed to its distance to objects in the environment. It has been demonstrated that both forward speed and altitude can be regulated using a single optical flow detector that was artificially maintained vertical (Ruffier & Franceschini, 2005). Altitude control for cruise flight has also been demonstrated onboard real UAV platforms (Barrows & Neely, 2000; Barrows et al., 2003; Green et al., 2003; 2004; Oh et al., 2004; Chahl et al., 2004) by regulating the ventral, longitudinal optical flow observed from the aircraft. While functional, the results of these early experiments were limited however, due to the failure to take the pitching motions of the aircraft into account and the passive or artificial stabilisation of roll. (Garratt & Chahl, 2008) also control altitude via optical flow and additionally correct for the pitching motions of the aircraft using an inertial measurement unit (IMU), but do not take the attitude of the aircraft into consideration. (Neumann & Bulthoff, 2001; 2002) use a similar strategy in simulation but regulate the UAV's attitude using colour gradients present in the simulated test environment. Using similar principles, (Thurrowgood et al., 2009; Todorovic & Nechyba, 2004) demonstrate methods for controlling UAV attitude based on the apparent orientation of the horizon and (Thakoor et al., 2003; 2002) use an attitude regulation scheme based on insect *ocelli*.

It has been proposed that insects, such as honeybees, navigate through narrow openings and avoid obstacles by balancing the optical flow observed on both sides of the body (Srinivasan et al., 1991), and by turning away from regions of high optical flow (Srinivasan & Lehrer, 1984; Srinivasan, 1993; Srinivasan & Zhang, 1997). Similar strategies have been employed by (Zufferey & Floreano, 2006; Zufferey et al., 2006; Green et al., 2004; Green, 2007; Oh et al., 2004; Hrabar & Sukhatme, 2009) to demonstrate lateral obstacle avoidance in aircraft. (Beyeler et al., 2007; Beyeler, 2009; Zufferey et al., 2008) steer to avoid obstacles in three dimensions and additionally incorporate rate gyroscopes and an anemometer to account for the motions of the aircraft and the measure the airspeed of the aircraft respectively. The study of insect behaviour has also revealed novel strategies which may be used to control complex flight manoeuvres. It has been observed that as honeybees land they tend to regulate their forward speed proportionally to their height such that the optical flow produced by the landing surface remains constant (Srinivasan et al., 2000). As their height approaches zero, so does their forward speed, ensuring a safe, low speed at touch down for the bee. Similar strategies have

been employed by (Beyeler, 2009; Chahl et al., 2004; Green et al., 2003; 2004; Oh et al., 2004) to demonstrate autonomous take-off and landing of small scale UAVs.
Obviously, therefore, measuring the optical flow produced by the motion of the aircraft through the environment is a viable means of providing guidance information for an autonomous aircraft, as is attested by the success of the approaches described above. However, extracting the necessary information from the observed optical flow is not without its difficulties.

2.5 Stereo vision

Optical flow is inherently noisy, and obtaining dense and accurate optical flow images is computationally expensive. Additionally, systems that rely on optical flow for extracting range information need to discount the components of optical flow that are induced by rotations of the aircraft, and use only those components that are generated by the translational motion of the vehicle (see Equation 1). This either requires an often noisy, numerical estimate of the roll, pitch, and yaw rates of the aircraft, or additional apparatus for their explicit measurement, such as a three-axis gyroscope. Furthermore, the range perceived from a downward facing camera or optical flow sensor is not only dependent upon altitude and velocity, but also the aircraft's attitude. This is particularly relevant to fixed-wing aircraft in which relatively high roll and pitch angles are required to perform rapid manoeuvres. A method for overcoming these shortcomings is described in (Beyeler et al., 2006), however the technique proposed there is too limited to be implemented in practice as it fails to include the roll angle of the aircraft. Finally, as with all optical flow-based approaches, to retrieve an accurate estimate of range, the ground-speed of the aircraft must be decoupled from the optical flow measurement. In practice this requires additional sensors, such as high-precision GPS or a Pitot tube. Moreover, in the case of the latter, the variable measured is actually airspeed, which would lead to incorrect range estimates in all but the case of low altitude flight in still air.
Stereo vision, on the other hand, allows the aircraft's altitude to be directly measured and controlled, irrespective of the attitude or ground-speed of the aircraft, and independently of its rotations about the roll, pitch, and yaw axes. Additionally, for stereo systems the visual search is constrained to a single dimension, hence reducing the complexity and increasing the accuracy of the computation. Furthermore, we will show that a wide-angle stereo vision system can also allow the computation and control of the orientation of the aircraft with respect to the ground. Stereo vision therefore provides an attractive approach to solving some of the problems of providing guidance for autonomous aircraft operating in low-altitude or cluttered environments.
Stereo vision systems have previously been designed for aircraft. An altitude regulation scheme is presented by (Roberts et al., 2002; 2003) who use a downwards facing stereo system to measure the height of an aircraft, although they require that the attitude is regulated via an onboard IMU. (Hrabar & Sukhatme, 2009) also require that the attitude of their aircraft is externally regulated and they utilise a combined stereo and optical flow approach to navigate urban canyons and also avoid frontal obstacles. Wide-angle stereo vision systems have also been investigated (Thurrowgood et al., 2007; Tisse et al., 2007), but they have rarely been tailored to the specific needs of aircraft guidance, such as terrain and gorge following, obstacle avoidance, and landing. In this chapter, we describe a stereo vision system that is specifically designed to serve these requirements.

3. A bio-inspired stereo vision system for UAV guidance

In this section we introduce a wide-angle stereo vision system that is tailored to the specific needs of aircraft guidance. The concept of the vision system is inspired by biological vision systems and its design is intended to reduce the complexity of extracting appropriate guidance commands from the visual data. The vision system was originally designed to simplify the computation of optical flow, but this property also makes it well suited to functioning as a coaxial stereo system. The resultant vision system therefore makes use of the advantages of stereo vision whilst retaining the simplified control schemes enabled by the bio-inspired design of the original vision system. In this section we will discuss the design, development, and implementation of the vision system, and also present results that demonstrate how stereo vision may be utilised to provide guidance for an autonomous aircraft.

3.1 Conceptual design

The concept of the vision system is best described by considering an assembly in which a camera views a specially shaped reflective surface (the mirror). As well as increasing the field of view (FoV) of the camera, the profile of the mirror is designed such that equally spaced points on the ground, on a line parallel to the camera's optical axis, are imaged to points that are equally spaced in the camera's image plane. This has the effect of removing the perspective distortion (and therefore the distortion in image motion) that a camera experiences when viewing a horizontal plane that stretches out to infinity in front of the aircraft. The mapping produced by the mirror is illustrated in Fig. 2. It is clear that equal distances along the ground, parallel to the optical axis of the system, are mapped to equal distances on the image plane, validating the design of the mirror. The full derivation of the mirror profile is given in (Srinivasan et al., 2006).

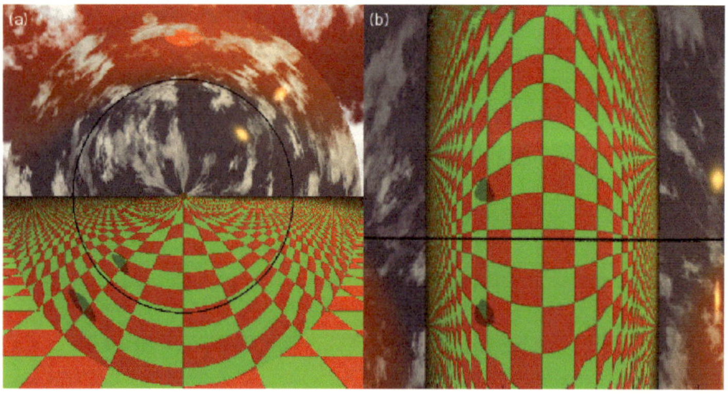

Fig. 2. Illustration of the imaging properties of the mirror. The raw image as viewed by the camera (left), and the remapped image (right). The dark line indicates viewing directions at 90° to the camera's optical axis. Reproduced from (Srinivasan et al., 2006).

The special geometric remapping afforded by the mirror means that, for a given vehicle speed, the motion in the camera's imaging plane of the image of an object in the environment is inversely proportional to the radial distance of that object from the optical axis of the vision system. Therefore, surfaces of constant image motion, when reprojected into the environment, are cylindrical, as is illustrated in Fig. 3. This property makes the system particularly useful for aircraft guidance. For any given aircraft speed, the maximum image velocity that is observed

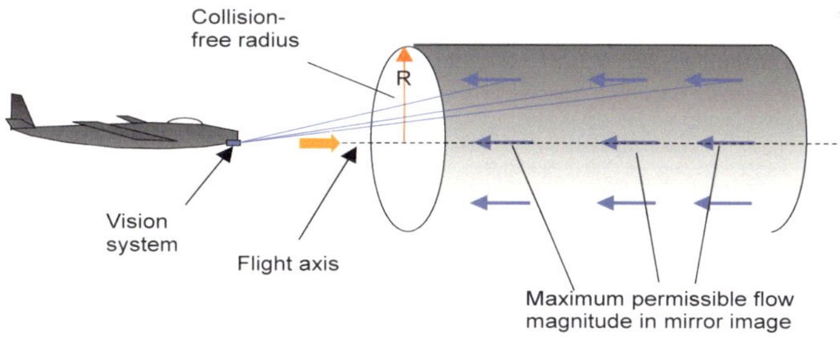

Fig. 3. Illustration of the clear-space mapping provided by the vision system. Reproduced from (Srinivasan et al., 2006).

in the remapped image specifies the radius of a cylinder of space in front of the aircraft, through which collision-free flight can occur. This approach of characterising the collision-free space in front of the aircraft by a virtual cylinder simplifies the problem of determining in advance whether an intended flight trajectory through the environment will be collision-free, and of making any necessary course corrections to facilitate this.

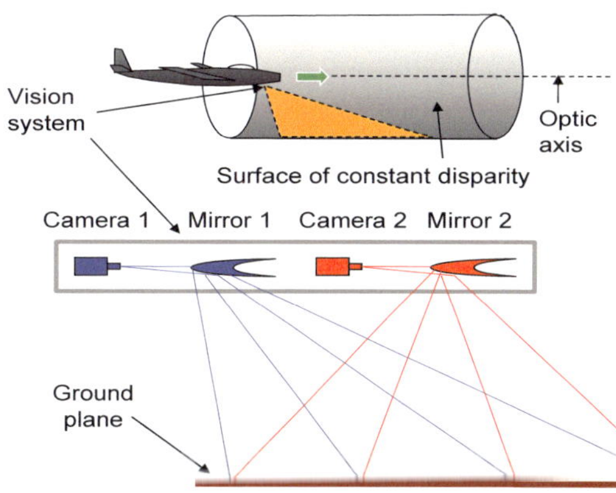

Fig. 4. Schematic illustration of the conceptual stereo vision system, surface of constant disparity, and collision-free cylinder. Reproduced from (Moore et al., 2010).

Now consider a system in which two such camera-mirror assemblies are arranged coaxially, as illustrated in Fig. 4. Each camera views the environment through a mirror that has the imaging properties described above. It follows that the pixel disparity, D_{pixel}, produced by a point imaged in both cameras is inversely proportional to the radial distance, d_{radial}, of that point from the common optical axis of the two camera-mirror assemblies. The relationship is given by

$$D_{pixel} = \frac{d_{baseline} \times h_{image}}{r} \times \frac{1}{d_{radial}}, \tag{2}$$

where $d_{baseline}$ is the stereo baseline, h_{image} is the vertical resolution of the remapped images and r, the forward viewing factor, is the ratio of the total forward viewing distance to the height of the aircraft.

The first term in Equation 2 is simply a constant which depends on the system configuration (see Table 1 for representative values). Therefore, the maximum image disparity, in a

Stereo baseline ($d_{baseline}$)	200mm
Remap image cols / rows (h_{img})	200px / 288px
Vertical FoV	$0°$ to $74°$ from vertical
Horizontal FoV	$-100°$ to $100°$ from vertical
Forward viewing factor (r)	3.5
Detectable disparity (D_{pixel})	0px to 10px
Operational altitude (d_{radial})	1.5m $\sim$ 50m+

Table 1. System parameters and their typical values.

given stereo pair, directly defines the radius of the collision-free cylinder that surrounds the optical axis, independent of the speed of the aircraft. Thus, a simple control loop may be implemented in which the aircraft is repelled from objects penetrating the notional flight cylinder required by the aircraft for collision-free flight. Furthermore, the image disparity will be one dimensional only, thereby reducing the complexity of the computation. The system is therefore well suited to providing real-time information for visual guidance in the context of tasks such as terrain and gorge following, obstacle detection and avoidance, and landing.

3.2 Hardware and implementation

In recent implementations of the vision system (Moore et al., 2009; 2010), the function of the specially shaped mirrors is simulated using software lookup tables. This requires calibrated camera-lens assemblies in order to generate the lookup tables but reduces the physical bulk and cost of the system and avoids aberrations due to imperfections in the mirror surfaces. The software remapping process is illustrated in Fig. 5. In this example an image of a rendered scene is captured through a rectilinear lens with a 120° FoV. The shaded area of the raw image is unwrapped and transformed to produce the remapped image. A comparison with Fig. 2 indicates that the image remapped in software shares the same properties with the image remapped in hardware (simulation), as expected.

Fig. 5. Illustration of the software remapping process. The shaded area in the raw image (a) is remapped to (b). Reproduced from (Moore et al., 2009).

The centre of the raw image (Fig. 5) is not remapped because, in this region, equal distances along the ground plane project onto infinitesimally small distances on the cameras' image planes. Therefore, if remapped, the resolution in this region would be negligible. Using the representative system parameters listed in Table 1, the central unmapped region is a conic section surrounding the optical axis with radius approximately 16°. Thus, by situating the cameras coaxially, the field of view of the system is not compromised as this region is not remapped in any case[2]. The outer diameter of the area to be remapped is limited by the FoV of the camera-lens assemblies.

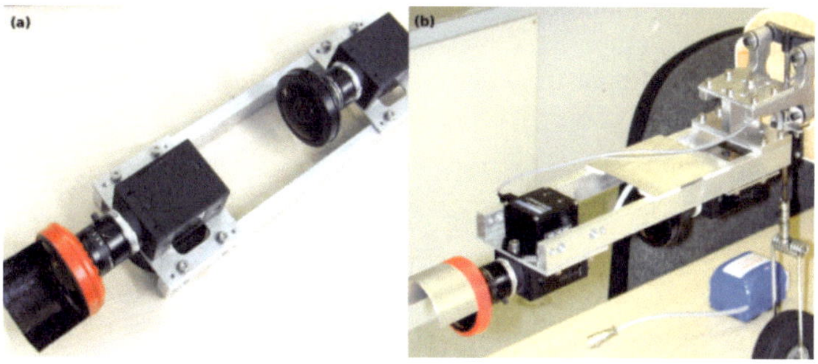

Fig. 6. (a) Implementation of the stereo vision system from (Moore et al., 2009) and (b) mounted on the aircraft. Reproduced from (Moore et al., 2009).

The two cameras are rigidly mounted in a coaxial stereo configuration (Fig. 6) to minimise measurement errors resulting from relative motion between the two camera-lens assemblies during flight. In the implementation described in (Moore et al., 2009), we use high resolution video cameras (PGR GRAS-20S4M) equipped with wide-angle fish-eye lenses (Fujinon FE185C057HA-1), to provide good spatial resolution whilst maintaining a large FoV. However, in (Moore et al., 2010) we found it necessary to use lightweight miniature fish-eye lenses (Sunex DSL215) to reduce the vibration-induced motion of the lenses relative to the camera sensors, without compromising the FoV. In both implementations the stereo cameras are synchronised to within 125μs across the IEEE 1394b bus interface.

Each camera-lens assembly is calibrated according to the generic camera model described in (Kannala & Brandt, 2006). The two assemblies are also calibrated as a stereo pair so that any rotational misalignment can be compensated for during the remapping process. This stereo calibration is performed on the calibrated raw images from each camera. The sum of absolute pixel differences between the two stereo images of a distant scene is minimised by applying a three-degrees-of-freedom (3DOF) rotation to one of the camera models. The optimal corrective 3DOF rotation is found using the NLopt library (Johnson, 2009) implementation of the BOBYQA algorithm (Powell, 2009).

The image disparity between stereo pairs is computed using an algorithm based on the sum of absolute pixel differences (SAD) between images and is implemented using the Intel Integrated Performance Primitives library (Intel, 2009). To remove low frequency image intensity gradients, which can confuse the SAD algorithm, the remapped images are convolved with a Scharr filter kernel before the disparity is computed. The SAD algorithm gives the image offset for a window surrounding each pixel for which the computed SAD score is a minimum. An equiangular fit, as described in (Shimizu & Okutomi, 2003), is applied to the minimum and neighbouring SAD scores for each window to obtain sub-pixel disparity estimates. Incorrect matches are rejected by re-computing the disparity for the

[2]This is also true if physical mirrors are used, as this region would be obscured by the self-reflection of each camera. This phenomenon is not visible in Fig. 2, as the camera body is not rendered in this case.

reverse image order and discarding disparities that differ from the initial estimate. This bidirectional technique is effective at rejecting mismatches but doubles the execution time of the algorithm. Further details on the specific implementations can be found in (Moore et al., 2009; 2010).
Stereo disparities are extracted from the remapped images via the process described above. The radial distances to objects in the environment can then be calculated from the stereo disparities according to Equation 2. Values for the system parameters can be selected depending on the desired operational range envelope, the required resolution of the range estimates, or the computational time available for processing disparities. Representative values used in (?) for flight testing are listed in Table 1.

Fig. 7. The aircraft used for flight testing was a Super Frontier Senior-46 (wingspan 2040mm), modified so that the engine and propeller assembly is mounted above the wing.

All image processing and higher order functions are performed on the aircraft (Fig. 7) by the onboard computer (Digital-Logic MSM945 which incorporates an Intel Core2 Duo 1.5GHz processor). Flight commands are sent continuously to the aircraft's control surfaces through an interface which allows a ground-based human pilot to select between computer controlled autonomous flight and radio controlled manual flight.

3.3 Range testing

The performance and accuracy of the stereo system were evaluated in (Moore et al., 2009) using an artificially textured arena. A cropped image of the arena as viewed by the front camera is displayed in Fig. 8. The texture used to line the arena is composed of black circles of varying diameter (65mm $\rightarrow$ 150mm) on a white background. The dimensions of the arena are 3200mm $\times$ 2350mm $\times$ 1150mm. The stereo rig was positioned in the centre of the arena with the optical axis parallel to the longest dimension of the arena. Also displayed in Fig. 8 is the remapped view of the testing arena overlayed with the computed stereo disparities. It can be seen that the disparity vectors have a constant magnitude in any given column[3]. This verifies the expected result – that image disparity between stereo pairs depends only on the radial distance of the viewed points from the optical axis.
Estimates of the radial distance to observed points can be calculated from the disparities via Equation 2. In order to quantify the accuracy of the stereo system, the relationship between the estimated radial distance to the arena and the viewing angle was plotted against the actual relationship (Fig. 9). The actual relationship was calculated from the known geometry of the arena. The viewing angle in this case corresponds to the vertical elevation of the viewing ray –

[3]Note that the disparity vectors that correspond to the rear wall of the arena are large in magnitude compared with surrounding vectors as these areas lie close to the optical axis of the vision system. These vectors are omitted from the following discussion to simplify analysis.

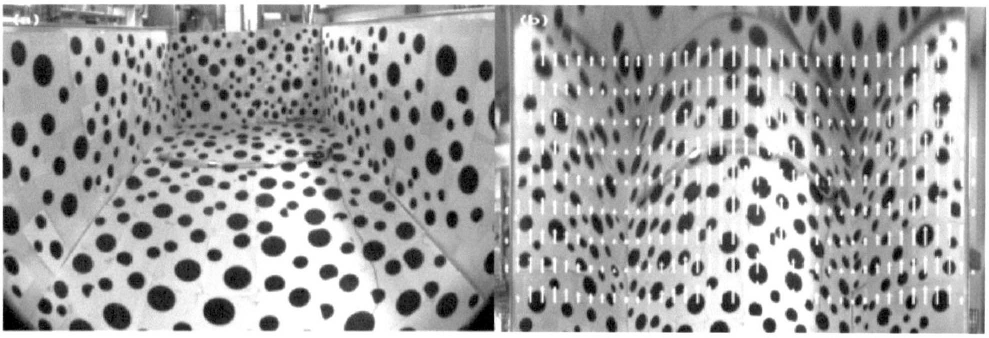

Fig. 8. (a) Cropped image of the testing arena as seen by the front camera and (b) the same view of the arena after remapping. The computed stereo disparities are overlayed in white. The disparity vectors have been scaled to aid visualisation. Reproduced from (Moore et al., 2009).

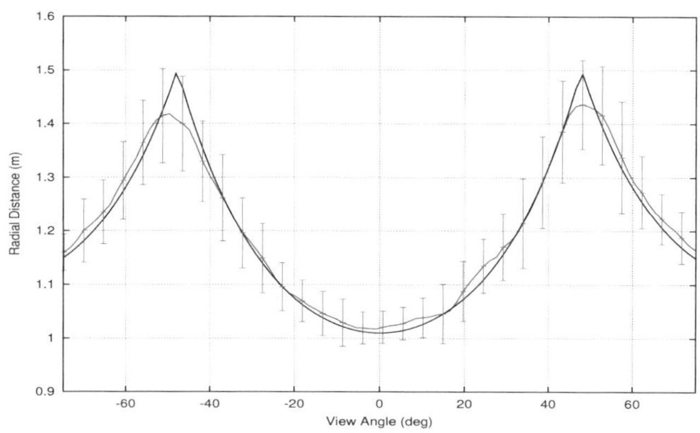

Fig. 9. Profile of the estimated radial distance to the arena wall and floor (blue) shown alongside the actual radial distance at each viewing angle (black). Error bars represent $\pm 2\sigma$ at each viewing angle. Reproduced from (Moore et al., 2009).

i.e. points that lie in the same column in the remapped image (Fig. 8) share the same viewing elevation. The error in the estimated radial distance at each viewing angle in Fig. 9 thus represents the variance from the multiple estimates at each viewing elevation. It can be seen that the errors in the estimated radial distances are most significant for viewing elevations that correspond to where the walls of the arena join the floor. This is a result of the non-zero size of the window used to compute the stereo disparity. A window size larger than one pixel would be expected to cause an underestimation of the radial distance to the corners of the arena, where surrounding pixels correspond to closer surfaces. Indeed this is observed in Fig. 9. Similarly, it would be expected to observe a slight overestimation in the radial distance to the arena floor directly beneath the vision system, where surrounding pixels correspond to surfaces that are further away, and this is also observed in Fig. 9.

The data presented in Fig. 9 is computed from a single typical stereo pair and is unfiltered, however a small number of points were rejected during the disparity computation. Small errors in the reprojected viewing angles may arise from inaccurate calibration of the camera-lens assemblies but are presumed to be negligible in this analysis. Therefore, the total error in the reconstruction can be specified as the error in the radial distance to the arena at each viewing angle. The standard deviation of this error, measured from approximately 2.5×10^4 reprojected points, was $\sigma = 3.5 \times 10^{-2}$m, with very little systematic bias (systematic variance amongst points at the same viewing elevation). Represented as a percentage of the estimated radial distance at each viewing angle, the absolute (unsigned) reprojection error was calculated as having a mean of 1.2% and a maximum of 5.6%. This error is a direct consequence of errors in the computed stereo disparities.

4. UAV attitude and altitude stabilisation

In section 3, a closed-loop control scheme using a stereo vision system was described in which the aircraft was repelled from objects that penetrate a notional flight cylinder surrounding the flight trajectory. This control scheme provides an effective collision avoidance strategy for an autonomous UAV and also provides the ability to demonstrate behaviours such as terrain and gorge following. In this section we will show that the attitude and altitude of the aircraft with respect to the ground may also be measured accurately using the same stereo vision system. This enhancement provides for more precise attitude and altitude control during terrain following, and also allows for other manoeuvres such as constant altitude turns and landing. We will present results from recent closed-loop flight tests that demonstrate the ability of this vision system to provide accurate and real-time control of the attitude and altitude of an autonomous aircraft.

4.1 Estimating attitude and altitude

If it is assumed that the ground directly beneath and in front of the aircraft can be modelled as a planar surface, then the attitude of the aircraft can be measured with respect to the plane normal. Also, the altitude of the aircraft can be specified as the distance from the nodal point of the vision system to the ground plane, taken parallel to the plane normal. The attitude and altitude of the aircraft can therefore be measured from the parameters of a planar model fitted to the observed disparity points.

Two approaches for fitting the model ground plane to the observed disparities have been considered in this study. In (Moore et al., 2009) we fit the model ground plane in disparity space and in (Moore et al., 2010) we apply the fit in 3D space. The first approach is more direct but perhaps unintuitive. Given the known optics of the vision system, the calibration parameters of the cameras and the attitude and altitude of the aircraft carrying the vision system, the magnitudes and directions of the view rays that emanate from the nodal point of the vision system and intersect with the ideal infinite ground plane can be calculated. By reformulating the ray distances as radial distances from the optical axis of the vision system, the ideal disparities may be calculated via Equation 2. Thus, the disparity surface that should be measured by the stereo vision system at some attitude and altitude above an infinite ground plane can be predicted. Conversely, given the measured disparity surface, the roll, pitch, and height of the aircraft with respect to the ideal ground plane can be estimated by iteratively fitting the modelled disparity surface to the measurements. This is a robust method for estimating the attitude and altitude of the aircraft because the disparity data is used directly, hence the data points and average error will be distributed evenly over the fitted surface.

In order to fit the modelled disparity surface to the observed data, we must parameterise the disparity model using the roll, pitch, and height of the aircraft above the ground plane. We start by calculating the intersection between our view vectors and the ideal plane. A point on a line can be parameterised as $\mathbf{p} = t\hat{\mathbf{v}}$, where in our case $\hat{\mathbf{v}}$ is a unit view vector and t is the distance to the intersection point from the origin (nodal point of the vision system), and a plane can be defined as $\mathbf{p} \cdot \hat{\mathbf{n}} + d = 0$. Solving for t gives

$$t = \frac{-d|\mathbf{v}|}{\mathbf{v} \cdot \hat{\mathbf{n}}}. \tag{3}$$

Now, in the inertial frame[4], our ideal plane will remain stationary (our aircraft will rotate), so we define $\hat{\mathbf{n}} = \begin{bmatrix} 0 & 0 & -1 \end{bmatrix}$. Therefore, $d = d_{height}$ is the distance from the ideal plane to the origin and, conversely, the height of the aircraft above the ground plane. So, making the substitutions,

$$t = \frac{-d_{height}|\mathbf{v}|}{\mathbf{v} \cdot \begin{bmatrix} 0 & 0 & -1 \end{bmatrix}} = \frac{d_{height}|\mathbf{v}|}{\mathbf{v}_z}, \tag{4}$$

thus we must only find the z component of our view vector in the inertial frame.
In the camera frame, the z axis is parallel with the optical axis and the x and y axes are parallel with the rows and columns of the raw images respectively. Thus, our view vector is defined by the viewing angle, ν, taken around the positive z axis from the positive x axis, and the forward viewing ratio, r. Thus, $\mathbf{v}_{cam} = \begin{bmatrix} \cos\nu & \sin\nu & r \end{bmatrix}$. To find the view vector in the inertial frame, we first transpose our view vector from the camera frame to the body frame, $\mathbf{v}_{body} = \begin{bmatrix} r & -\cos\nu & -\sin\nu \end{bmatrix}$ (our cameras are mounted upside down), and then we rotate from the body frame to the inertial frame (we neglect yaw since our ideal ground plane does not define a heading direction).

$$\mathbf{R}_x(\phi) = \begin{bmatrix} 1 & 0 & 0 \\ 0 & \cos\phi & -\sin\phi \\ 0 & \sin\phi & \cos\phi \end{bmatrix}$$, represents a rolling motion, ϕ, about the x axis.

$$\mathbf{R}_y(\theta) = \begin{bmatrix} \cos\theta & 0 & \sin\theta \\ 0 & 1 & 0 \\ -\sin\theta & 0 & \cos\theta \end{bmatrix}$$, represents a pitching motion, θ, about the y axis.

Therefore,

$$\mathbf{R}_{body\rightarrow world}(\phi,\theta) = \mathbf{R}_y(\theta) \times \mathbf{R}_x(\phi) = \begin{bmatrix} \cos\theta & \sin\theta\sin\phi & \sin\theta\cos\phi \\ 0 & \cos\phi & -\sin\phi \\ -\sin\theta & \cos\theta\sin\phi & \cos\theta\cos\phi \end{bmatrix},$$

and

$$\mathbf{v}_{world} = \mathbf{R}_{body\rightarrow world}(\phi,\theta) \times \mathbf{v}_{body}. \tag{5}$$

Now, we are only interested in $\mathbf{v}_z$, the z component of the view vector, $\mathbf{v}_{world}$. Therefore, multiplying out Equation 5 gives

$$\mathbf{v}_z^i = -\cos(\theta)\sin(\nu^i + \phi) - r^i\sin(\theta), \tag{6}$$

where we have included the superscript i to indicate that this is the view vector corresponding to the ith pixel in the remapped image. Substituting Equation 6 back into Equation 4 gives

$$t^i = \frac{d_{height}|\mathbf{v}^i|}{-\cos(\theta)\sin(\nu^i + \phi) - r^i\sin(\theta)}, \tag{7}$$

[4]We use the common aeronautical North-East-Down (NED) inertial frame.

where t^i is the direct ray distance to the ideal ground plane along a particular view vector. Now, the stereo vision system actually measures the radial distance to objects from the optical axis. Therefore to convert t in Equation 7 from ray distance to radial distance, we drop the scale factor $|\mathbf{v}|$. So finally, substituting Equation 7 back into Equation 2, we get the expected disparity surface measured by the stereo vision system for a particular attitude and altitude above an ideal ground plane,

$$D^i_{pixel} = \frac{d_{baseline} \times h_{image}}{r_{tot}} \times \frac{1}{d_{height}} \times \left[-\cos(\theta)\sin(\nu^i + \phi) - r^i \sin(\theta) \right], \tag{8}$$

where the first term is a system constant as described before, and the radial distance has been replaced by d_{height}, the vertical height (in the inertial frame) of the aircraft above the ideal ground plane. The bracketed term describes the topology of the disparity surface and depends on the roll, ϕ, and pitch, θ, of the aircraft as well as two parameters ν^i and r^i, that determine the viewing angles in the x and z (camera frame) planes respectively for the ith pixel in the remapped image.

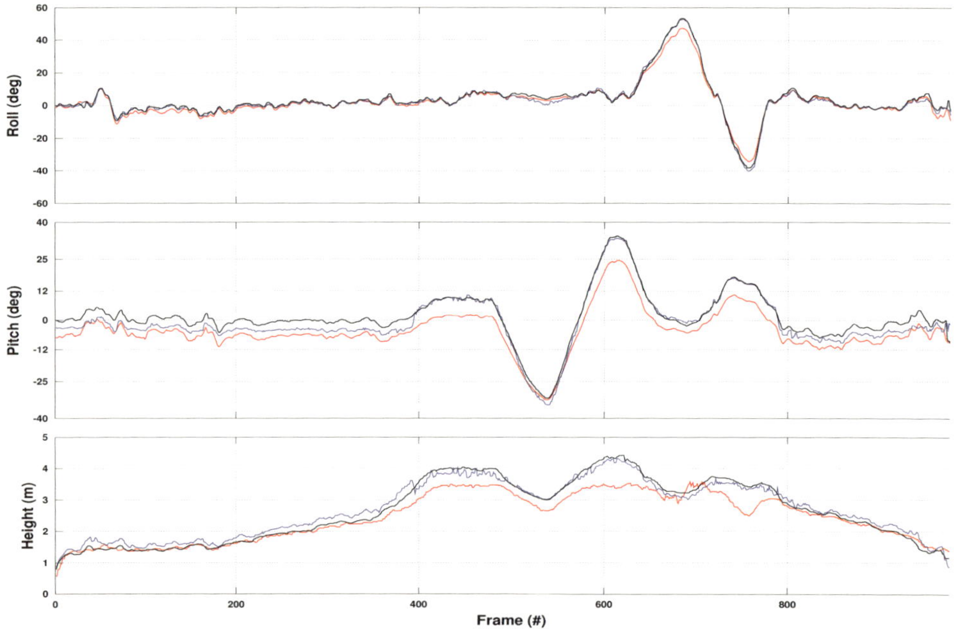

Fig. 10. Attitude and altitude of the aircraft during an outdoor test as estimated via fitting the disparity surface (black, solid), and fitting the 3D point cloud (blue, dashed). Also shown for comparison (red, dotted) are the roll and pitch angles as reported by an IMU and the depth measurement reported by an acoustic sounder. Frames were captured at approximately 12Hz.

In order to obtain the roll, pitch, and height of the aircraft, we minimise the sum of errors between Equation 8 and the measured disparity points using a non-linear, derivative-free optimisation algorithm. Currently, we use the NLopt library (Johnson, 2009) implementation of the BOBYQA algorithm (Powell, 2009). This implementation typically gives minimisation times in the order of 10ms (using $\sim 6 \times 10^3$ disparities on a 1.5GHz processor). To analyse the performance of this approach, an outdoor test was conducted in which the lighting and texture conditions were not controlled. The attitude and altitude estimates computed using this approach are shown in Fig. 10 plotted alongside the measurements from an IMU (MicroStrain 3DM-GX2) and a depth sounder, which were installed onboard the aircraft to provide distinct measurements of the attitude and altitude. It can be seen that the visually estimated motions of the aircraft correlate well with the values used for comparison.

The second approach for determining the attitude and altitude of the aircraft with respect to an ideal ground plane is to re-project the disparity points into 3D coordinates relative to the nodal point of the vision system and fit the ideal ground plane in 3D space. While this procedure does not sample data points uniformly in the plane, it leads to a single-step, non-iterative optimisation that offers the advantage of low computational overheads and reliable real-time operation. This is the approach taken in (Moore et al., 2010) to achieve real-time, closed-loop flight.

To re-project the disparity points into 3D space, we use the radial distances computed directly from the disparities via Equation 2,

$$\mathbf{p}^i = \frac{d^i_{rad}}{\sin \alpha^i} \cdot \hat{\mathbf{u}}^i, \tag{9}$$

where $\mathbf{p}^i$ is the reprojected location of the ith pixel in 3D coordinates relative to the nodal point of the vision system, $\hat{\mathbf{u}}^i$ is the unit view vector for the ith pixel (derived from the calibration parameters of the cameras) and α^i is the angle between the view vector and the optical axis.

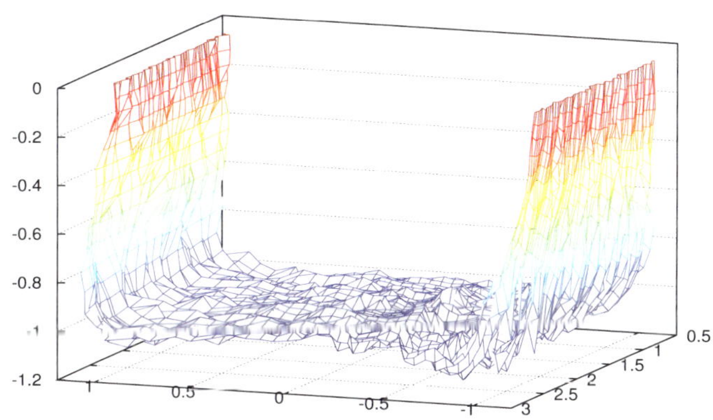

Fig. 11. 3D reconstruction of the test arena. Measurements are in metres relative to the nodal point of the vision system. Reproduced from (Moore et al., 2009).

The radial distances computed from the stereo image pair of the test arena (seen in Fig. 8) were used to reconstruct the arena in 3D space (Fig. 11). It was found in (Moore et al., 2009) that the mean error in the radial distance estimates was approximately 1.2% for the test conducted in the indoor arena. It can be seen from Fig. 11 that this error leads to an accurate 3D reconstruction of the simple test environment. However, this reprojection error is directly attributable to the errors in the computed stereo disparities – which are approximately constant for any measurable disparity. Therefore, for the system parameters used during range testing (see (Moore et al., 2009)), the mean radial distance error of 1.2% actually indicates a mean error in the computed stereo disparities of approximately $\frac{1}{4}$ pixel.

The (approximately constant) pixel noise present in the disparity measurements means that at higher altitudes the range estimates will be increasingly noisy. This phenomena is responsible for the maximum operational altitude listed in Table 1, for at altitudes higher than this maximum, the disparity generated by the ground is less than the mean pixel noise. Thus, for altitudes within the operational range, fitting the ideal ground plane model to the reprojected 3D point cloud, rather than fitting the model to the disparities directly, results in less well constrained estimates of the orientation of the ideal plane, and hence less well constrained estimates of the attitude and altitude of the aircraft. However, it can be seen from Fig. 10 that this approach is still a viable means of estimating the state of the aircraft, particularly at altitudes well below the operational limit of the system. Furthermore, this approach results in an optimisation that is approximately two orders of magnitude faster than the first approach discussed above. This is because the optimisation can be performed in a single-step using a least-squares plane fit on the 3D point cloud. In (Moore et al., 2010) we use a least-squares algorithm from the WildMagic library (Geometric Tools, 2010) and achieve typical optimisation times in the order of < 1ms (using $\sim 6 \times 10^3$ reprojected points on a 1.5GHz processor).

Applying the planar fit in 3D space therefore offers lower computational overheads at the cost of reduced accuracy in the state estimates. However, the least-squares optimisation may be implemented within a RANSAC[5] framework to reject outliers and improve the accuracy of the state estimation. This is the approach taken in (Moore et al., 2010) to achieve closed-loop control of an aircraft performing time-critical tasks such as low-altitude terrain following.

4.2 Closed-loop terrain following

During flight, the stereo vision system discussed in this chapter can provide real-time estimates of the attitude and altitude of an aircraft with respect to the ground plane using the methods described above. However, for autonomous flight, the aircraft must also generate control commands appropriate for the desired behaviour. In (Moore et al., 2010), we use cascaded proportional-integral-derivative (PID) feedback control loops to generate the flight commands whilst attempting to minimise the error between the visually estimated altitude and attitude and their respective setpoints. The closed-loop control scheme is depicted in Fig. 12. Roll and pitch are controlled independently and so full autonomous control is achieved using two feedback control subsystems. Additionally, within each control subsystem, multiple control layers are cascaded to improve the stability of the system.

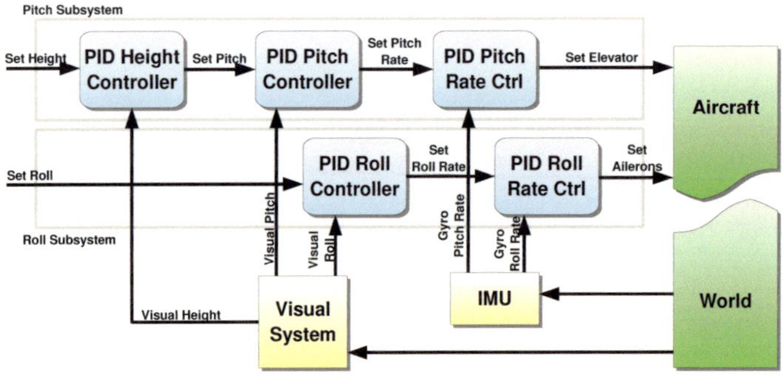

Fig. 12. Block diagram illustrating the closed-loop control scheme used for closed-loop flight testing. Reproduced from (Moore et al., 2010).

[5]RANdom SAmple Consensus. An iterative method for estimating function parameters in the presence of outliers.

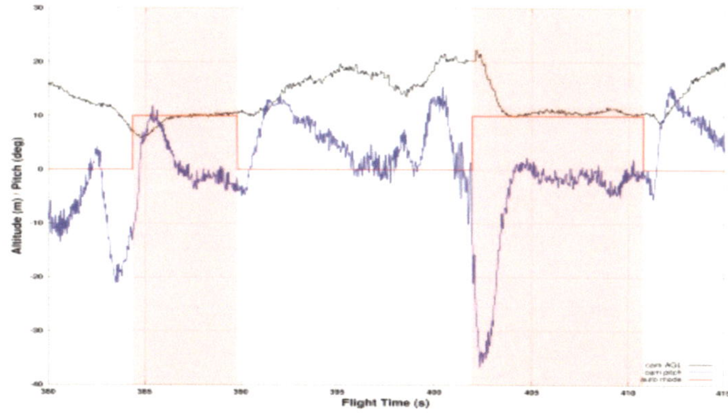

Fig. 13. Visually estimated height (black, solid) and pitch angle (blue, dashed) during a segment of flight. Also shown is a scaled binary trace (red, shaded) that indicates the periods of autonomous control, during which the aircraft was programmed to hold an altitude of 10m AGL. Reproduced from (Moore et al., 2010).

The control subsystem for stabilising the roll of the aircraft comprises two cascaded PID controllers. The highest level controller measures the error in the roll angle of the aircraft and delivers an appropriate roll rate command to the lower level controller, which implements the desired roll rate. The pitch control subsystem functions identically to the roll subsystem, although it includes an additional cascaded PID controller to incorporate altitude stabilisation. Shown in Fig. 12, aircraft altitude is regulated by the highest level PID controller, which feeds the remainder of the pitch control subsystem. Measurements of the absolute attitude and altitude of the aircraft are made by the stereo vision system and are used to drive all other elements of the closed-loop control system. Low level control feedback for the roll rate and pitch rate is provided by an onboard IMU. The multiple control layers allow the aircraft to be driven towards a particular altitude, pitch angle, and pitch rate simultaneously. This allows for stable control without the need for accurately calibrated integral and derivative gains. It is observed that a more responsive control system may be produced by collapsing the absolute angle and rate controllers into a single PID controller for each subsystem (where the rate measurements from the IMU are used by the derivative control component). However, the closed-loop data presented in this section was collected using the control system described by Fig. 12.

The closed-loop performance of the vision system was evaluated in (Moore et al., 2010) by piloting the test aircraft (Fig. 7) in a rough racetrack pattern. During each circuit the aircraft was piloted to attain an abnormal altitude and attitude, and then automatic control was engaged for a period of approximately 5s – 10s. A quantitative measure of the performance of the system was then obtained by analysing the ability of the aircraft to restore the set attitude and altitude of 0° roll angle and 10m above ground level (AGL) respectively. This procedure was repeated 18 times during a test flight lasting approximately eight minutes. A typical segment of flight (corresponding to 380s $\sim$ 415s in Fig. 15) during which the aircraft made two autonomous passes is shown in Figs. 13 & 14. It can be seen that on both passes, once autonomous control was engaged, the aircraft was able to attain and hold the desired attitude and altitude within approximately two seconds. It can also be seen that the visually estimated roll angle closely correlates with the measurement from the IMU throughout the flight segment. Temporary deviations between the estimated roll and pitch angles and the

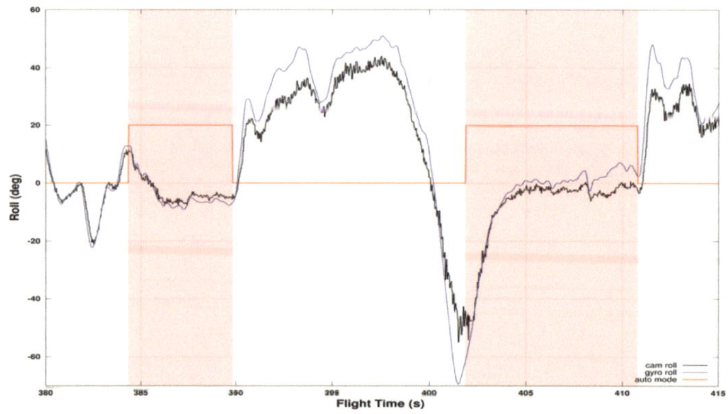

Fig. 14. Visually estimated roll angle (black, solid) during a segment of flight. For comparison, the roll angle reported by an onboard IMU is shown (blue, dashed). Also shown is a scaled binary trace (red, shaded) that indicates the periods of autonomous control, during which the aircraft was programmed to hold a roll angle of 0° with respect to the ground plane. Reproduced from (Moore et al., 2010).

values reported by the IMU are to be expected, however, due to the inherent difference between the measurements performed by the stereo vision system, which measures attitude with respect to the local orientation of the ground plane, and the IMU, which measures attitude with respect to gravity.

The visually estimated altitude of the aircraft throughout the full flight test is displayed in Fig. 15. It can be seen that in every autonomous pass the aircraft was able to reduce the absolute error between its initial altitude and the setpoint (10m AGL), despite initial altitudes varying between 5m and 25m AGL. The performance of the system was measured by considering two metrics: the time that elapsed between the start of each autonomous segment and the aircraft first passing within one metre of the altitude setpoint; and the average altitude of the aircraft during the remainder of each autonomous segment (*i.e.* not including the initial response phase). These metrics were used to obtain a measure of the response time and steady-state accuracy of the system respectively. From the data presented in Fig. 15, the average response time of the system was calculated as $1.45s \pm 1.3s$, where the error bounds represent 2σ from the 18 closed-loop trials. The relatively high variance of the average response time is due to the large range of initial altitudes. Using the second metric defined above, the average unsigned altitude error was calculated as 6.4×10^{-1}m from approximately 92s of continuous segments of autonomous terrain following. These performance metrics both indicate that the closed-loop system is able to quickly respond to sharp adjustments in altitude and also that the system is able to accurately hold a set altitude, validating its use for tasks such as autonomous terrain following.

5. Conclusions

This chapter has introduced and described a novel, wide-angle stereo vision system for the autonomous guidance of aircraft. The concept of the vision system is inspired by biological vision systems and its design is intended to reduce the complexity of extracting appropriate guidance commands from visual data. The vision system takes advantage of the accuracy and reduced computational complexity of stereo vision, whilst retaining the simplified control

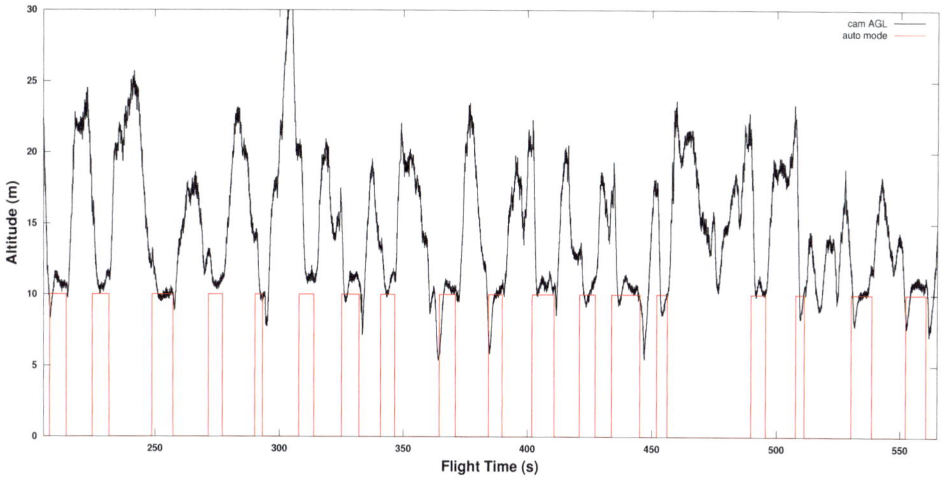

Fig. 15. The visually estimated altitude (black, solid) of the aircraft during the flight test. Also shown is a scaled binary trace (red, dashed) that indicates the periods of autonomous control, during which the aircraft was programmed to hold an altitude of 10m AGL. Reproduced from (Moore et al., 2010).

schemes enabled by its bio-inspired design. Two coaxially aligned video cameras are used in conjunction with two wide-angle lenses to capture stereo imagery of the environment, and a special geometric remapping is employed to simplify the computation of range. The maximum disparity, as measured by this system, defines a collision-free cylinder surrounding the optical axis through which the aircraft can fly unobstructed. This system is therefore well suited to providing visual guidance for an autonomous aircraft in the context of tasks such as terrain and gorge following, obstacle detection and avoidance, and take-off and landing. Additionally, it was shown that this stereo vision system is capable of accurately measuring and representing the three dimensional structure of simple environments, and two control schemes were presented that facilitate the measurement of the attitude and altitude of the aircraft with respect to the local ground plane. It was shown that this information can be used by a closed-loop control system to successfully provide real-time guidance for an aircraft performing autonomous terrain following. The ability of the vision system to react quickly and effectively to oncoming terrain has been demonstrated in closed-loop flight tests. Thus, the vision system discussed in this chapter demonstrates how stereo vision can be effectively and successfully utilised to provide visual guidance for an autonomous aircraft.

6. Acknowledgments

This work was supported partly by US Army Research Office MURI ARMY-W911NF041076, Technical Monitor Dr Tom Doligalksi, US ONR Award N00014-04-1-0334, ARC Centre of Excellence Grant CE0561903, and a Queensland Smart State Premier's Fellowship. The authors are associated with the Queensland Brain Institute & School of Information Technology and Electrical Engineering, University of Queensland, St Lucia, Australia and ARC Centre of Excellence in Vision Science, Australia. Finally, sincere thanks to Mr. David Brennan, who owns and maintains the airstrip at which the flight testing was done.

7. References

Barrows, G. L., Chahl, J. S. & Srinivasan, M. V. (2003). Biologically inspired visual sensing and flight control, *The Aeronautical Journal* 107(1069): 159–168.

Barrows, G. L. & Neely, C. (2000). Mixed-mode VLSI optic flow sensors for in-flight control of a micro air vehicle, *Proc. SPIE*, Vol. 4109, pp. 52–63.

Beyeler, A. (2009). *Vision-based control of near-obstacle flight*, PhD thesis, Ecole Polytechnique Federale de Lausanne, Lausanne, Switzerland.

Beyeler, A., Mattiussi, C., Zufferey, J.-C. & Floreano, D. (2006). Vision-based altitude and pitch estimation for ultra-light indoor aircraft, *Proc. IEEE International Conference on Robotics and Automation (ICRA'06)*, pp. 2836–2841.

Beyeler, A., Zufferey, J.-C. & Floreano, D. (2007). 3D vision-based navigation for indoor microflyers, *Proc. IEEE International Conference on Robotics and Automation (ICRA'07)*, Roma, Italy.

Chahl, J. S., Srinivasan, M. V. & Zhang, S. W. (2004). Landing strategies in honeybees and applications to uninhabited airborne vehicles, *The International Journal of Robotics Research* 23(2): 101–110.

DeSouza, G. N. & Kak, A. C. (2002). Vision for mobile robot navigation: A survey, 24(2).

Floreano, D., Zufferey, J.-C., Srinivasan, M. V. & Ellington, C. P. (2009). *Flying Insects and Robots*, Springer. In press.

Franceschini, N. (2004). Visual guidance based on optic flow: A biorobotic approach, *Journal of Physiology* 98: 281–292.

Garratt, M. A. & Chahl, J. S. (2008). Vision-based terrain following for an unmanned rotorcraft, *Journal of Field Robotics* 25: 284–301.

Geometric Tools (2010). Wildmagic library. URL:*http://www.geometrictools.com/LibMathematics/Approximation/Approximation.html*

Gibson, J. J. (1950). *The Perception of the Visual World*, Houghton Mifflin.

Green, W. E. (2007). *A Multimodal Micro Air Vehicle for Autonomous Flight in Near-Earth Environments*, PhD thesis, Drexel University, Philadelphia, PA.

Green, W. E., Oh, P. Y. & Barrows, G. L. (2004). Flying insect inspired vision for autonomous aerial robot maneuvers in near-earth environments, *Proc. IEEE International Conference on Robotics and Automation (ICRA'04)*, New Orleans, LA.

Green, W. E., Oh, P. Y., Sevcik, K. & Barrows, G. (2003). Autonomous landing for indoor flying robots using optic flow, *Proc. ASME International Mechanical Engineering Congress*, Washington, D.C.

Hrabar, S. & Sukhatme, G. (2009). Vision-based navigation through urban canyons, *Journal of Field Robotics* 26(5): 431–452.

Hrabar, S., Sukhatme, G. S., Corke, P., Usher, K. & Roberts, J. (2005). Combined optic-flow and stereo-based navigation of urban canyons for a UAV, *Proc. IEEE International Conference on Intelligent Robots and Systems (IROS'05)*, Edmonton, Canada.

Intel (2009). Integrated performance primitives library. URL:*http://software.intel.com/sites/products/collateral/hpc/ipp/ippindepth.pdf*

Johnson, S. G. (2009). The NLopt nonlinear-optimization package. URL:*http://ab-initio.mit.edu/nlopt*

Kannala, J. & Brandt, S. S. (2006). A generic camera model and calibration method for conventional, wide-angle, and fish-eye lenses, 28(8): 1335–1340.

Moore, R. J. D., Thurrowgood, S., Bland, D., Soccol, D. & Srinivasan, M. V. (2009). A stereo vision system for UAV guidance, *Proc. IEEE International Conference on Intelligent*

Robots and Systems (IROS'09), St Louis, MO.

Moore, R. J. D., Thurrowgood, S., Bland, D., Soccol, D. & Srinivasan, M. V. (2010). UAV altitude and attitude stabilisation using a coaxial stereo vision system, *Proc. IEEE International Conference on Robotics and Automation (ICRA'10)*, Anchorage, AK.

Nakayama, K. & Loomis, J. M. (1974). Optical velocity patterns, velocity-sensitive neurons, and space perception: A hypothesis, *Perception* 3(1): 63–80.

Neumann, T. & Bulthoff, H. H. (2001). Insect inspired visual control of translatory flight, *Proc. 6th European Conference on Artificial Life (ECAL'01)*, Prague, Czech Republic.

Neumann, T. & Bulthoff, H. H. (2002). Behaviour oriented vision for biomimetic flight control, *Proc. EPSRC/BBSRC International Workshop on Biologically Inspired Robotics*, Bristol, UK.

Oh, P. Y., Green, W. E. & Barrows, G. L. (2004). Neural nets and optic flow for autonomous micro-air-vehicle navigation, *Proc. ASME International Mechanical Engineering Congress and Exposition*, Anaheim, CA.

Powell, M. (2009). The BOBYQA algorithm for bound constrained optimization without derivatives, *Cambridge NA Report NA2009/06, University of Cambridge, Cambridge, Reino Unido* .

Roberts, J. M., Corke, P. I. & Buskey, G. (2002). Low-cost flight control system for a small autonomous helicopter, *Proc. Australasian Conference on Robotics and Automation (ACRA'02)*, Auckland, New Zealand.

Roberts, J. M., Corke, P. I. & Buskey, G. (2003). Low-cost flight control system for a small autonomous helicopter, *Proc. IEEE International Conference on Robotics and Automation (ICRA'03)*, Taipei, Taiwan.

Ruffier, F. & Franceschini, N. (2005). Optic flow regulation: the key to aircraft automatic guidance, *Robotics and Autonomous Systems* 50: 177–194.

Scherer, S., Singh, S., Chamberlain, L. & Saripalli, S. (2007). Flying fast and low among obstacles, *Proc. IEEE International Conference on Robotics and Automation (ICRA'07)*, Roma, Italy.

Shimizu, M. & Okutomi, M. (2003). Significance and attributes of subpixel estimation on area-based matching, *Systems and Computers in Japan* 34(12).

Srinivasan, M. V. (1993). How insects infer range from visual motion, *Reviews of Occulomotor Research* 5: 139–156.

Srinivasan, M. V. & Lehrer, M. (1984). Temporal acuity of honeybee vision: behavioural studies using moving stimuli, *Journal of Comparitive Physiology* 155: 297–312.

Srinivasan, M. V., Lehrer, M., Kirchner, W. H. & Zhang, S. W. (1991). Range perception through apparent image speed in freely-flying honeybees, *Visual Neuroscience* 6: 519–535.

Srinivasan, M. V., Thurrowgood, S. & Soccol, D. (2006). An optical system for guidance of terrain following in UAV's, *Proc. IEEE International Conference on Advanced Video and Signal Based Surveillance (AVSS'06)*, Sydney, Australia, pp. 51–56.

Srinivasan, M. V., Thurrowgood, S. & Soccol, D. (2009). From flying insects to autonomously navigating robots, 16(3): 59–71.

Srinivasan, M. V. & Zhang, S. (2004). Visual motor computations in insects, *Annual Review of Neuroscience* 27: 679–696.

Srinivasan, M. V. & Zhang, S. W. (1997). Visual control of honeybee flight, *Orientation and Communication in Arthropods* 84: 95–113.

Srinivasan, M. V., Zhang, S. W., Chahl, J. S., Barth, E. & Venkatesh, S. (2000). How honeybees make grazing landings on flat surfaces, *Biological Cybernetics* 83(3): 171–183.

Srinivasan, M. V., Zhang, S. W., Chahl, J. S., Stange, G. & Garratt, M. (2004). An overview of insect inspired guidance for application in ground and airborne platforms, *Proc. Inst. Mech. Engnrs. Part G* 218: 375–388.

Srinivasan, M. V., Zhang, S. W. & Chandrashekara, K. (1993). Evidence for two distinct movement-detecting mechanisms in insect vision, *Naturwissenschaften* 80: 38–41.

Thakoor, S., Chahl, J., Srinivasan, M. V., Young, L., Werblin, F., Hine, B. & Zornetzer, S. (2002). Bioinspired engineering of exploration systems for NASA and DoD, *Artificial life* 8(4): 357–369.

Thakoor, S., Zornetzer, S., Hine, B., Chahl, J. & Stange, G. (2003). Bioinspired engineering of exploration systems: a horizon sensor/attitude reference system based on the dragonfly ocelli for mars exploration applications, *Journal of Robotic Systems* 20(1): 35–42.

Thurrowgood, S., Soccol, D., Moore, R. J. D., Bland, D. & Srinivasan, M. V. (2009). A vision based system for attitude estimation of UAVs, *Proc. IEEE International Conference on Intelligent Robots and Systems (IROS'09)*, St Louis, MO.

Thurrowgood, S., Stuerzl, W., Soccol, D. & Srinivasan, M. V. (2007). A panoramic stereo imaging system for aircraft guidance, *Proc. Ninth Australasian Conference on Robotics and Automation (ACRA'07)*, Brisbane, Australia.

Tisse, C. L., Frank, O. & Durrant-Whyte, H. (2007). Hemispherical depth perception for slow-flyers using coaxially aligned fisheye cameras, *Proc. International Symposium on Flying Insects and Robots*, Ascona, Switzerland, p. 123.

Todorovic, S. & Nechyba, M. C. (2004). A vision system for intelligent mission profiles of micro air vehicles, *IEEE Transactions on Vehicular Technology* 53(6): 1713–1725.

Valavanis, K. P. (2007). *Advances in Unmanned Aerial Vehicles: State of the Art and the Road to Autonomy*, Springer.

Zufferey, J.-C., Beyeler, A. & Floreano, D. (2008). Near-obstacle flight with small UAVs, *Proc. International Symposium on Unmanned Aerial Vehicles (UAV'08)*, Orlando, FL.

Zufferey, J.-C. & Floreano, D. (2006). Fly-inspired visual steering of an ultralight indoor aircraft, 22: 137–146.

Zufferey, J.-C., Klaptocz, A., Beyeler, A., Nicoud, J.-D. & Floreano, D. (2006). A 10-gram microflyer for vision-based indoor navigation, *Proc. IEEE International Conference on Intelligent Robots and Systems (IROS'06)*, Beijing, China.

17

Stereovision Algorithm to be Executed at 100Hz on a FPGA-Based Architecture

Michel Devy[1] *, Jean-Louis Boizard[2], Diego Botero Galeano[3], Henry Carrillo Lindado[4], Mario Ibarra Manzano[5], Zohir Irki[6], Abdelelah Naoulou[7], Pierre Lacroix[8], Philippe Fillatreau[9], Jean-Yves Fourniols[10], Carlos Parra[11]
[1,2,3,5,6,7,8,10]*CNRS; LAAS; 7 avenue du Colonel Roche, F-31077 Toulouse*
Université de Toulouse; UPS, INSA, INP, ISAE; LAAS-CNRS : F-31077 Toulouse
[3,4,11]*Pontificia Universidad Javeriana; Carrera 7 No. 40-62; Bogotá*
[9]*Delta Technologies Sud Ouest; 2 Impasse Michel Labrousse, 31036 Toulouse*
[1,2,3,5,6,7,8,9,10]*France*
[3,4,11]*Columbia*

1. Introduction

This chapter describes the development of an integrated stereovision sensor intended to be embedded on mobile platforms like robots or intelligent vehicles. Such a sensor is required for the motion control of these platforms. Navigation can be either autonomous (e.g. for a robot executing tasks in dangerous environments), or supervised by a human driver (typically for intelligent transportation systems).

Motion control of a mobile vehicle requires to integrate on the platform, a system generally structured in several levels. At the lower level, functions are encapsulated in modules directly connected to sensors and actuators; the next level, named generally the supervision level, controls the execution of these functions, recovers from internal errors or from unexpected events in the environment; finally the upper level, or decision-making level, generates tasks or adapts existing scritps with respect to missions which are generally transmitted by an operator through a communication medium. Tasks and scripts activate sequentially or in parallel several functions at the lower level. Depending on the complexity of the platform (number of sensors and actuators), of the environment (static vs dynamic, structured vs unstructured, a priori known vs unknown...) and of the missions to be executed, the system embedded on a mobile platform, is implemented on one or several processors, and could take advantage of dedicated subsystems, e.g. smart sensors equipped by its own processing unit, or smart actuators fitted with micro-controllers.

Our project deals with the design and the implementation of a smart sensor that could execute complex perceptual functions, while satisfying very demanding real-time constraints. As soon as a motion must be executed by a mobile platform, perception functions provide environment modelling and monitoring, human-machine interface, sensor-based servoing, obstacle detection ...Real time execution is required when tasks are executed in dynamic

*Authors contact: michel.devy@laas.fr.

environments, i.e. when several mobile platforms act in the same area (multi-robots applications or several vehicles on roads) or when these platforms act in human environments (pedestrians in urban scenes, human operators for service robots...). Real time constraints depend on the relative speeds between mobile entities: for example, obstacle detection on an intelligent transportation system, must be executed at 100Hz, so that (1) several detections could be fused before activating an avoidance or an alarm action and (2) Time To Collision remains compatible with the system or the driver reaction time.
Sensory data must be acquired on the environment, in order to feed perceptual functions devoted to detection, tracking, identification or interpretation of events, environment modelling, visual odometry or self-localization ... Vehicles or robots are equipped with cameras, telemeters (radar, laser, sonar...) or with more specific devices (RFID readers, magnetic sensors...). Vision is the more popular, not only for biologically or human inspired apriorism, but because it has many advantages: high resolution, cheap sensors, acquisition of both photometric and geometric information ... Nevertheless, vision (especially 3D vision) is known to be very computationally demanding: it is why adapted visual algorithms and dedicated hardware subsystems must be jointly designed and evaluated for these applications.
In the section 2, some works related to obstacle detection are recalled, as a justification for our hardware implementation of the stereovision algorithm. Then the classical stereovision algorithm is described in section 3, before presenting the state of the art for real time stereovision systems in section 4. The FPGA-based architecture for our hardware stereovision implementation is described in section 5. Our real time stereovision system is presented in section 6 and is evaluated in section 7. Finally, conclusions and perspectives are discussed in section 8.

2. Stereovision for ITS applications

Companies which make Intelligent Transportation Systems (ITS), are eager to integrate sensors and perceptual algorithms on cars, for different applications: obstacle detection on motorway or in urban traffic, lane departure detection, parking assistance, navigation, cockpit and driver monitoring... Different sensors have been evaluated for these applications: only vision is considered in this paper.

- monocular vision has been proposed to detect obstacles (cars or pedestrians) in urban scenes, but without assumptions on the environment (no "flat road" approximation for example). Monocular vision does not allow to cope with complex situations and is generally coupled with other kind of sensors (e.g. radar or laser devices).
- stereovision is widely used in the robotics community, typically to evaluate the terrain navigability at short distances (Matthies (1992)). Several companies (*Videre Design Company* (n.d.)) propose stereo rigs with a short baseline (10cm), well suited for indoor perception; K.Konolige (Konolige (1997)) has developed the SVS library, with a real-time version of the stereo correlation algorithm (30Hz); VIDERE has also implemented this algorithm on a FPGA-based architecture.
- stereovision has been also evaluated in ITS applications for many years, but the real-time requirements, the limitations of the depth field, the lack of robustness... makes difficult to use stereovision in changing contexts.

In the LAAS robotics team, stereo is the main sensor used for outdoor terrestrial robot (figure 1 (top left)). It has been evaluated for several ITS applications:

Fig. 1. Example of stereo setups, on a robot (top left) or inside a vehicle for cockpit monitoring (top right) or road perception (bottom)

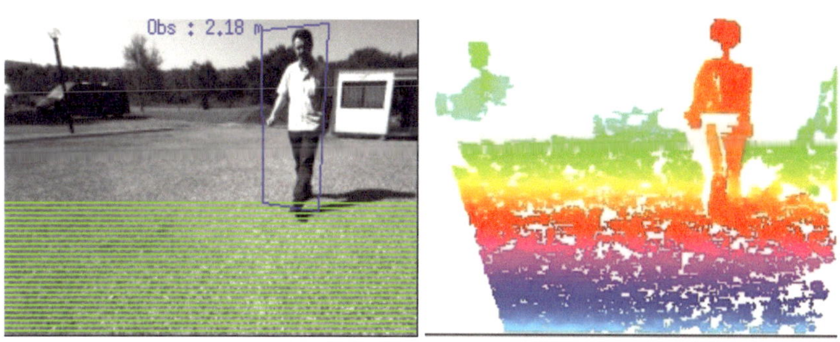

Fig. 2. Obstacle detection in a urban scene

- monitoring of the passenger seat (Devy et al. (2000)) with Siemens VDO. Figure 1 (top right) shows the sensor integrated in an experimental car [1]);
- detection of a free parking slot and assistance for the parking manoeuvre (Lemonde et al. (2005)). Figure 3 shows the rectified image built from the left camera of the stereovision sensor (left) and the disparity image (right);
- pedestrian detection in urban scene (see figure 2, where it can be seen dense disparity information on the ground) or obstacle detection on motorway (Lemonde et al. (2004))

[1] Test vehicle of Continental in Toulouse, France

Fig. 3. Obstacle detection to find a parking slot

(figure 4, where the road cannot be detected, due to the lack of texture). For this latter application, images have been acquired from a large baseline stereo rig presented on figure 1 (bottom) [2].

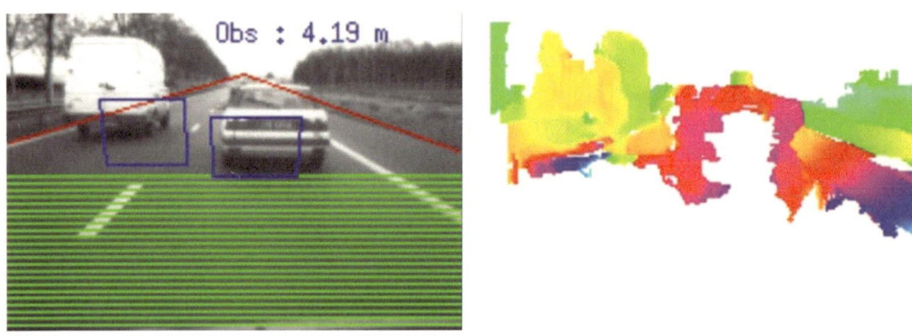

Fig. 4. Obstacle detection on a highway

Figures 2, 3 and 4 (left) present images acquired by the left camera of the stereovision sensor, after rectification: on figures 2 and 4, the green lines on the bottom of the images, indicate the free space before the detected obstacle. On the right, these figures show disparity maps, with progressive color variations with respect to the disparity value.

The next section recalls the main steps of the stereovision algorithm, on which our developments are based. Inputs are images acquired from left and right cameras; the output is the disparity image.

3. The stereovision algorithm

Our stereovision algorithm is classical. It requires an a priori calibration of the stereo rig. The main steps are presented on figure 5.

Initially the original right and left images I_d and I_g are processed independently. The distortion correction and rectification step allows to provide two aligned rectified images IR_d and IR_g: this step consists in applying a warping transform, using tables to transform (u, v) pixel coordinates from the original image frame to the rectified one: here u and v correspond respectively to the line number, and to the column number.
Then a preprocessing is applied on each rectified image, before looking for the best matching between a left pixel (u, v), with a right pixel $(u, v - D)$, where D is the disparity. The

[2] Test vehicle of the LIVIC lab in Satory, France

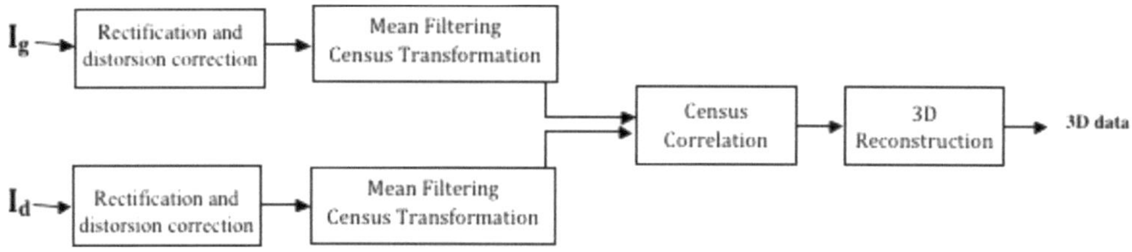

Fig. 5. The description of the stereovision algorithm.

pre-processing function depends on the score used in the matching function. Figure 6 shows a rectified stereo system, i.e. the two image planes are coplanar and lines are collinear. The disparity is equal to zero for two pixels corresponding to a 3D point located at an infinite distance; the maximal disparity D_{max} is tuned according to the minimal 3D points distance that the sensor must detect, e.g. the minimal distance between a vehicle and an obstacle.

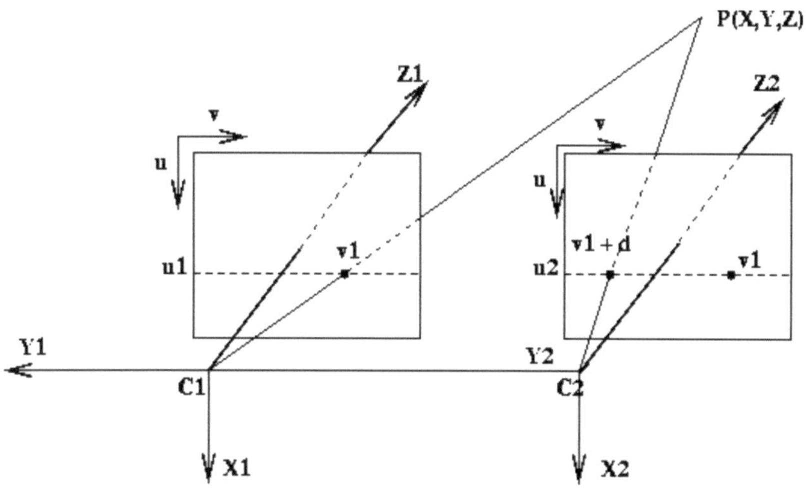

Fig. 6. 3D reconstruction from rectified images.

Several correlation scores -SAD, SSD, ZNCC...- could be used to compare the correlation windows around the left pixel and around every right candidate (figure 7). Here the Census score (Zabih et al. (1994)) is exploited because it does not require floating-point computations and thus is better suited for an hardware implementation. Moreover it is a non-parametric technique based on the relative ordering of pixel intensities within a window W, rather than the intensity values themselves. Consequently, such a technique is robust with respect to the radiometric distortion.

As mentionned here above, before computing the Census transform from the rectified images, a preprocessing, i.e. an arithmetic mean filter, is executed on both images. Let S_{uv} be the set of coordinates in a rectangular sub image window of size $m \times n$ pixels and that is centered on the (u, v) pixel. The arithmetic mean filtering process computes the average value of the original rectified image $IR(u, v)$ in the area defined by S_{uv}. The value of the filtered image $\hat{IR}$ at any point (u, v) is simply the arithmetic mean of all pixels in the region defined by S_{uv}. The formula of this arithmetic mean is given by equation 1.

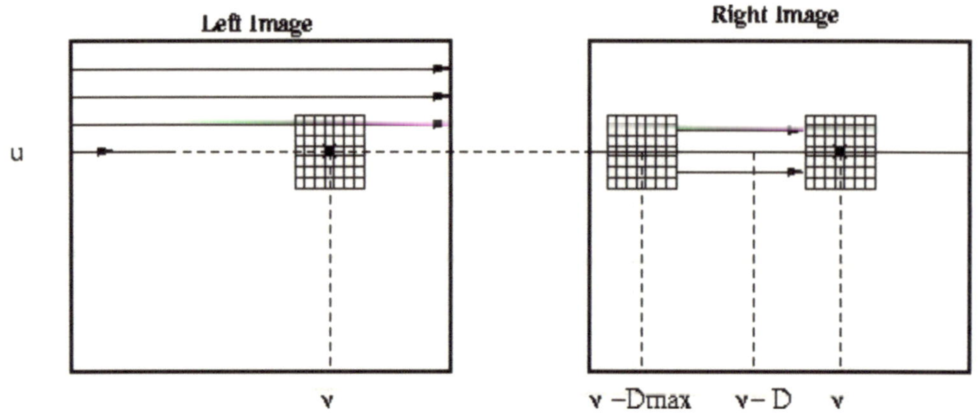

Fig. 7. Stereo matching on rectified images: the correlation principle

$$\hat{IR}(u,v) = \frac{1}{mn} \sum_{(i,j)\in S_{uv}} IR(i,j) \tag{1}$$

This operation can be implemented without using the $1/mn$ scaling factor, only if the correct rank of the filtered pixels is considered. The mean filter simply smoothes local variations in an image. Also in this operation, noise is reduced as a result of blurring.

The Census score is computed from the left and right rectified and filtered images, modified by the Census transform (CT) expressed on equation 2, and illustrated on figure 8.

$$I\hat{R}T(u,v) = \bigotimes_{(i,j)\in S_{uv}} \xi\left(\hat{IR}(u,v), \hat{IR}(i,j)\right) \tag{2}$$

In these transformed images, the intensity value on each pixel (u,v) is replaced by a bit string computed by comparing the intensity $\hat{IR}(u,v)$ with the intensity of neighbour pixels selected in the area defined by S_{uv}, i.e. a F_c x F_c correlation window centered on (u,v), where F_c is a odd number. The function ξ computes the relationship between a pixel (u,v) and its nearest neighbors in D_{uv}. This function returns a bit, that is set to one, when the intensity of the point (i,j) is lower than the intensity of the point (u,v), otherwise the bit is set to zero. The operator $\otimes$ denotes concatenation. Finally, $I\hat{R}T(u,v)$ represents the Census transform of the (u,v) pixel: it is a bit string with a length equal to $F_c^2 - 1$.

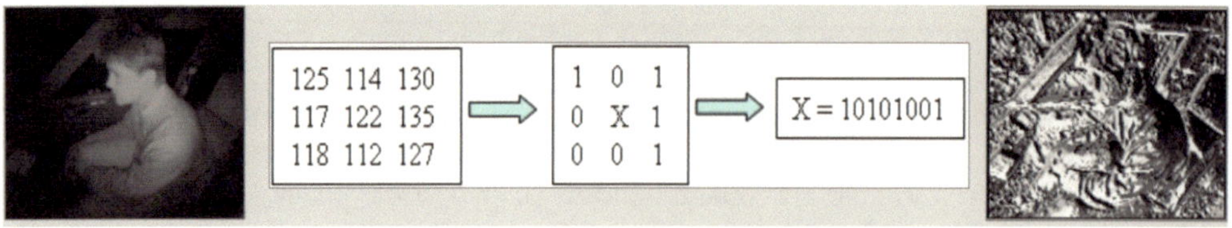

Fig. 8. The CENSUS transform.

The Census score between a left pixel (u,v) and a right one $(u,v-D)$, is evaluated using the Hamming distance, i.e. the binary comparison between two bit strings provided by the Census transform applied independently on the two images. It is given by the number of equal bits between $IRT_g(u,v)$ and $IRT_d(u,v-D)$, so this score is normalized, from an integer

included between 0 and $F_c^2 - 1$. Equation 3 shows how this score is computed: $I\hat{R}T_l$ and $I\hat{R}T_r$ represent the two Census transformed images (left and right images respectively), $\bar{\otimes}$ denotes the binary XNOR operation, applied for each bit of the bit string (index i).
For every (u, v) left pixel, all scores are computed with all $(u, v - D)$ right pixels on the same epipolar line for all D in $[0, D_{max}]$. Then, for the (u, v) left pixel, the disparity $D_H(u, v)$ corresponds to the maximum of these Census scores. How to find this maximum? Several classical tests could be used, like it is shown on figure 9 (left): a maximum is valid only if it is discriminant (i.e. high enough), not flat (i.e. sharp enough) and not ambiguous (i.e. the difference between the two first maximal scores is higher than a given threshold). If the maximal score is not valid (lack of texture, ambiguity...), the (u, v) pixel is unmatched.
An error during this matching step, could create false points in the 3D image; a good verification method to avoid these errors, consists in performing pixel correlation first from the left image to the right one, then from the right image to the left one, and to select the best common matching. In the software version, this verification does not increase the computation time. Scores are computed during the left-right run, a potential disparity D is found for each left pixel, and then scores are recorded to be used again during the right-left run. The verification is performed when the left-right run has been processed for a complete line; it is controlled that the same D disparity is found when starting from the right pixel, looking for a maximal score in the left image. If not, the potential disparity D is cancelled in the disparity map.

$$D_H(u, v) = \max_{D \in [0, D_{max}]} \left(\frac{1}{N} \sum_{i=1}^{N} I\hat{R}T_l(u, v)_i \bar{\otimes} I\hat{R}T_r(u, v - D)_i \right) \quad (3)$$

Finally, the $D_H(u, v)$ disparity is an integer between 0 and D_{max}: two improvements are possible. First a sub pixel accuracy could be obtained by an interpolation method applied on the score function; on figure 9 (right),the maximal score has been found in $i + 1$; the sub pixel *imax* value is computed from a parabolic interpolation of the score function. Secondly, a filtering function could be applied to remove potential errors in the disparity image: it consists in segmenting this image in regions, and to remove the very small regions.

Fig. 9. The disparity validation and computation

Once the Census correlation step has been completed, the 3D reconstruction is computed in the left camera reference frame, as shown in figure 6: the Z axis corresponds to the optical axis, the Y axis is parallel to the image line and oriented towards the left, while the X axis is parallel to the image column and oriented downwards. The 3D reconstruction step requires the calibration data, i.e. the baseline B (distance between the two optical centers) and similar intrinsic parameters for the rectified ilatinmages $(\alpha_u, \alpha_v, u_0, v_0)$. If a (u_1, v_1) left pixel matched with a $(u_1, v_1 + D)$ right pixel (D negative), it corresponds to a (X, Y, Z) 3D point with the following coordinates:

$$X = \frac{\alpha_v.B.(u_1 - u_0)}{\alpha_u.D}; \quad Y = \frac{B.(v_1 - v_0)}{D}; \quad Z = \frac{\alpha_v.B}{D}$$

These equations show that (1) the disparity is constant for pixels located at a fixed depth Z with respect to the cameras, and (2) the Z error increases as Z^2, so that the stereo measurements are very noisy for long distances.

Depending on the available computation power, and on the optimization of the code, this algorithm could provide low resolution (320x240 or 160x120) 3D images at video rate; it could be sufficient for robotics application, with a weak robot speed. It does not satisfy real-time requirements for ITS applications or for safety issues when service robots navigate in human environments.

4. Real time stereovision: state of the art

In vision, the term *real time* is generally understood as video-rate (Brown et al. (2003)), i.e. 30 frames per second or higher . Our challenge is real time stereovision at more than 100Hz, for a 640x480 resolution (nb of pixels per line W = 640). Using Camera Link connections with two synchronized cameras, images are transmitted with a 40MHz pixel rate (pixel period T = 25ns), giving 130 images per second at this resolution. We aim at a 100Hz image rate, so pixels must be processed on the fly, with a possible delay between successive images if required.
It is yet beyond the possibility of the software implementation, that are generally limited to a video-rate performance with this VGA resolution; several authors proposed in the 90's, such implementations, e.g. the SVS library implemented by K.Konolige (Konolige (1997)), or the stereo machine of T.Kanade (Kanade et al. (1996)).
Only an FPGA implementation can reach a 100Hz performance, and can also meet cost and size requirements. As soon as powerful enough FPGAs appeared, stereovision architectures (Corke et al. (1999)) have been proposed. A variety of architectures able to provide dense disparity maps have been reported since 1995. Most of the integrated real-time stereo system, are based on Field Programmable Gate Array (FPGA) because of the flexibility given by FPGAs at the moment to realize dedicated hardware architecture, a reasonable low cost (e.g. against ASIC) and an higher processing speed (e.g. against PC).
In 2001, Arias-Estrada et al. (Arias-Estrada et al. (2001)) reported a stereo system able to process 320x240 images at a rate of 71 FPS using SAD scores for stereo matching. The system does not perform any rectification nor distortion correction and uses a Xilinx Virtex FPGA valued at $2,000 dollars. Darabiha et al. (Darabiha et al. (2003)) developed a four FPGA based system with an estimate cost of $10,328 dollars able to provide 256 x360 dense disparity map at 30 FPS. A complete stereo vision system with radial distortion correction, Laplacian of Gaussian Filtering and disparity map computation via SAD is proposed by Jia et al. Jia et al. (2004). This system can produce 640 x 480 dense disparity maps with 64 levels of disparity at 30 FPS and has an estimated cost of $2,582 dollars. Two systems able to process more than 200 images per second, are presented by Georgoulas et al. (Georgoulas et al. (2008)) and Jin et al. (Jin et al. (2010)) respectively. The first system used SAD and the second is based on

Census for computing the disparity map, both system process 640 x 480 images and both of them have a price higher than a thousand dollars.
These systems (Chonghun et al. (2004)) (Sunghwan et al. (2005)) are compared with our own architecture in table 1, considering the FPGA family, the estimated cost (in $), the resolution of input and output images (Res in $pixel^2$), the frame rate (in Frame Per Second), the score used by the matching method, the maximal disparity (Max in pixels) and finally, the size of the neighbourhood used to compute scores (Win in pixels). The architecture presented in this paper can produced 640 x 480 dense disparity maps at maximum rate of 491 FPS. This stereo vision system performs rectification and distortion correction functions on images acquired from two cameras, and then the correlation function on the transformed images, with a 3 FPGAs pipeline architecture. The overall cost of the proposed hardware, is about $120, thus making this architecture a good choice for low cost system.

Author	FPGA family	Cost	Resolution	FPS	Score	Max	Win
Arias Estrada	Xilinx Virtex2	2000	320 x 240	71	SAD	16	7 x 70
Darabiha	4 Xilinx Virtex2	10328	256 x 360	30	LWPC	20	N/A
Jia	Xilinx Virtex2	2582	640 x 480	30	SAD	64	9 X 9
Chonghun	Xilinx Virtex2	2983	1024 x 1024	47	SAD	32	16 x 16
Lee	Xilinx Virtex2	7567	640 x 480	30	SAD	64	32 x 32
Georgulas	Altera Stratix2	10797	640 X 480	275	SAD	80	7 X 7
Jin	Xilinx Virtex4	7261	640 x 480	230	Census	64	11 x 11
Our system	3 Altera Cyclone2	120	640 x 480	491	Census	64	7 x 7

Table 1. Comparisons between integrated stereovision algorithms.

Some authors have used FPGA platforms only as a preliminary validation for a ASIC-based implementation: several ones have been developed, e.g. at Zurich ETH Institute ((Kuhn et al.(n.d.)) (50Hz for 256x192 images), (Hamette et al. (2006)) (pixel clock limited to 5MHz) or at Daejeon University in Korea (Han et al. (2009)) (30hz for 320x240 images).

5. Real time stereovision: our architecture

Even though its software implementation requires a lot of memory, our stereo algorithm is well adapted for integration on a dedicated architecture: no floating-point computations, boolean operations on bit strings..., even if the software implementation requires a lot of memory. The FPGA implementation has been presented in (Boizard et al. (2005)) (Naoulou et al. (2006)) (Naoulou (2006)). In (Ibarra-Manzano et al. (2009)) and (Ibarra-Manzano et al. (2009)) it is discussed how to generate such an architecture, from tools dedicated to high level synthesis from C programs. Actually, these tools have been used in order to test and evaluate several possible architectures: once these preliminary choices have been done, actual architectures have been generated using classical tools, i.e. QUARTUS for our ALTERA implementation.
Figure 10 presents the general architecture, which is made with five main modules: the acquisition of original left and right images, the rectification, the mean operator, the Census transformation and the Census correlation. Images are not stored completely; pixels are processed on the fly, with a pixel clock defined by the cameras or the communication protocol with the cameras (here CamLink). So the pixel clock is 40MHz, i.e. every module must execute its task every 25ns.

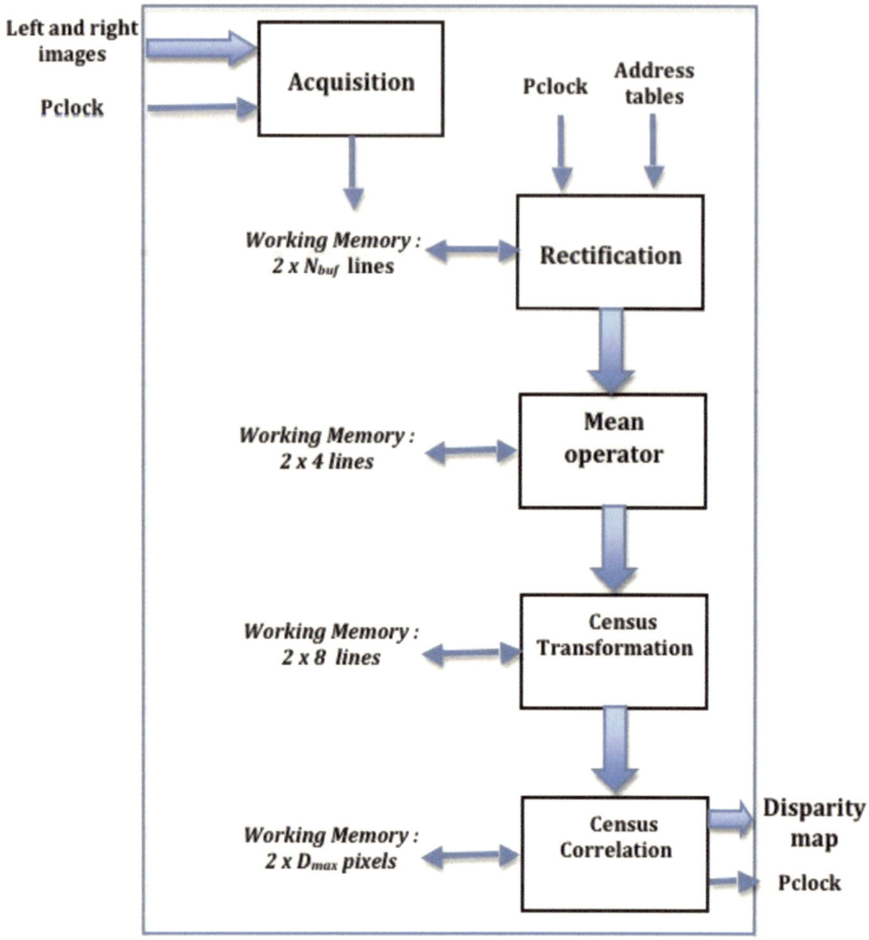

Fig. 10. General architecture.

- Two *Acquisition modules* acquire the two left and right images, here at a 40MHz pixel clock. A given number N_{buf} of lines acquired directly from the cameras, have to be memorized, before executing the next processings; this number depends on the images distortion or misalignment ranges. Cameras are synchronized, so that pixels with the same image coordinates (u, v) are received at the same clock front edge.
- Two *Rectification modules* generate intensities for the rectified left and right pixels, using precomputed address tables. These tables are built offline, from calibration data. The rectified left and right pixels with coordinates $(0, 0)$ are generated with a delay of N_{buf} lines with respect to the acquisition.
- Then two *Mean operator modules* apply a mean filter independently on the two images. This computation is based on the sum of 3*x*3 window centered around every pixel. Every mean module requires a working memory of 4 lines, avoiding read-write conflicts. The mean pixels are provided with a latency of 3 lines (plus 2 pixels) with respect to the input.
- Outputs from the *Mean operator modules* are inputs for the *Census Transformation (CT) modules* which compute census images; every pixel is replaced by a bitstring computed

from comparisons with their neighbours, in a 7x7 window. So every CT module requires a working memory of 8 lines, and provides the result as a string of 49 bits for every pixel, with a latency of 7 lines (plus 3 pixels) with respet to the input.

- Finally from these left and right CT pixels, the correlation scores are computed and maximum scores are selected by a *Census Correlation module*. When starting from the left image, due to the configuration (see figure 6), the left pixel (u, v) can be matched with right pixels from $(u, v - D_{max})$ to (u, v). So scores are computed for $(D_{max} + 1)$ couples of pixels; if the maximum score is found for the position $(u, v - D)$, then the output of the module is equal to the disparity D corresponding to the (u, v) coordinates in the disparity map.
- In our implementation, the disparity is directly sent to a CamLink output generator, so that the disparity map is sent at the same frequency than the original images, towards a client system, here a PC only used in order to display the stereo result.

The architecture performance depends on the way scores are computed. Figure 11 presents several options:

- at the top, a sequential architecture is shown. It is a software-like strategy, where $(D_{max} + 1)$ scores are computed in sequence before looking for the maximum: it does not take advantage of the potential parallelization on an hardware implementation.
- in the middle, the scores computation is parallelized only to match left pixels with right ones; it is typically a SIMD operation, so that $(D_{max} + 1)$ identical and synchronous processes can provide all scores in parallel. It is the simpler strategy, because when the left CT pixel (u, v) is available, its corresponding one in the right image is already computed in the right image. The search for the maximum, exploits a dichotomy strategy.
- on the bottom, a dual approach is proposed. Left-right scores are computed and the maximum score is looked for like in the previous case, but a verification is made using right-left scores and right-left matchings.

The dual approach using both the right-left and the left-right stereo matching, requires more memory and more delay. In the software implementation, verifications are applied between every line u; all scores are memorized when applying the left-right stereo matching for every (u, v) pixel on this line; so scores are stored in a $(D_{max} + 1)x640$ 2D table; the left-right matching for a (u, v) left pixel consists in finding the maximum score on the line v of the score table; the right-left matching for a $(u\prime, v\prime)$ right pixel consists in finding the maximum score for a diagonal of the score table. These two maximums (on the line and the diagonal), must be the same. This approach is sequential, thus not adapted to hardware implementation; a dedicated architecture is proposed hereafter, based on parallel searching for the left-right and the right-left matchings. Results presented in the section 7 are obtained with the parallel architecture, without right-left verification.
At the end, the final latency between the original acquisition and the generation of the disparity for a (u, v) pixel, can be approximated by $(N_{buf} + 10)$ lines, plus 5 pixels:

- the number of lines is given both by the distortion factor of the original images, and by the window size used to compute the Mean operator and the Census Transformation;
- the extra delay of 5 pixels, is given also by the window size, and also by pipeline stage required in order to compute the maximal score.

Each module is detailed in the following subsections.

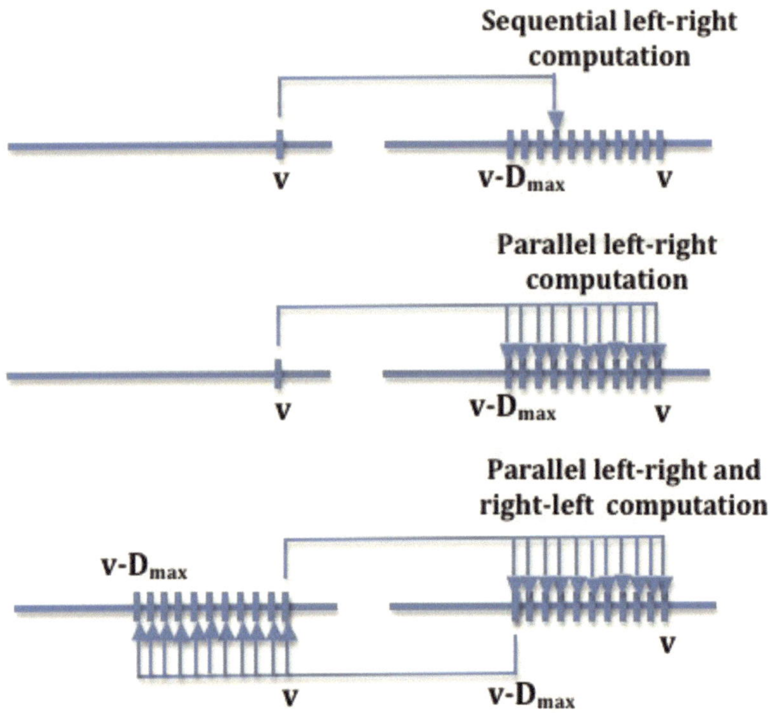

Fig. 11. Sequential vs parallel architectures.

5.1 The rectification.

This function applies an homography to the two images, and correct distortions if they cannot be neglected. So, it is a simple coordinate transform, using for every image, two address tables generated off line, one for u, one for v. These tables give the correspondance between the (u, v) coordinates in the original image and the (u_{rect}, v_{rect}) ones in the rectified image. Two solutions could be implemented:

- N_{buf} lines of the original image are recorded before activating the stereo algorithm on successive rectified pixels; first "inverse" address tables are used to transform every rectified pixel coordinates and to pick up its intensity in the buffer.
- N_{buf} lines of the rectified image are initialized from the pixels of the original image using "direct" address tables. Some rectified pixels could remain not initialized, creating artificial "holes" in the rectified image (Irki et al. (2007)).

The two solutions have been implemented; the first one is the more efficient.
The resolution of the rectified images could be reduced with respect to the original one; in our implementation, the pixel clock is 40MHz for the *acquisition module* of 640x480 images (25ns between two pixels of the original images). The frequency could be reduced to 10MHz (100ns between two pixels) if rectified images are generated with a 320x240 resolution. Here the same frequency is used for all modules, so that the final disparity map has the same resolution than original images.
Address tables are generated especially to correct image distortions. Figure 12 presents possible configurations for the rectified images with respect to the corrected original ones.

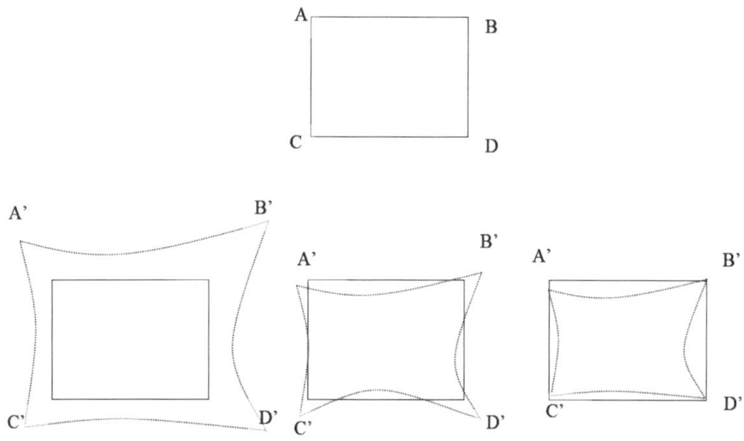

Fig. 12. Possible configurations for the rectified and corrected images.

Let us note (A, B, C, D) the four original image corners in pixel coordinates, so $A = (0, 0); B = (0, 639); C = (479, 0); D = (639, 479)$. Let us note $(A\prime, B\prime, C\prime, D\prime)$ the four rectified image corners. Generally wide-angle lenses are used on our robotics application, so that images are mainly warped due to barrel radial distortions. So the distortion correction deplaces every pixel of the original images on its image radius, creating a zooming effect, i.e. pixels are further from the image center. The corrected images could be selected as shown on the bottom line: on the left, the rectified cameras have a smaller view field than the original ones and the resolution is higher; on the right, the view field is the same, but keeping the same image size, the resolution is smaller.

So address tables are implemented as a 2D array; for every (u_{rect}, v_{rect}) pixel of the rectified image, a 32 bits word is read in the address table. This word encodes for each rectified pixel, the position of the corresponding one in the original image. It is given as a position in the current circular buffer of N_{buf} lines, (U_{int}, V_{int}), plus four factors $(\Delta a, \Delta b, \Delta c, \Delta d)$ required to apply a bilinear interpolation. The intensity in the position (u_{rect}, v_{rect}) of the rectified image, is computed as:

$$\begin{aligned} Irect(u_{rect}, v_{rect}) \quad = \quad & \Delta a \; Ibuf(U_{int}, V_{int}) \quad + \quad \Delta b \; Ibuf(U_{int}, V_{int}+1) \quad + \\ & \Delta c \; Ibuf(U_{int}+1, V_{int}) \quad + \quad \Delta d \; Ibuf(U_{int}+1, V_{int}+1) \end{aligned} \tag{4}$$

The size N_{buf} of the circular buffer filled by the *Acquisition module* must be selected so that the required original pixels are in the buffer when applying this interpolation. In our implementation, using wide-angle lenses, $N_{buf} = 30$.

5.2 The arithmetic mean filter.

Rectified pixels are processed on the fly, synchronously with the acquisition of the original pixels, but with a latency of $N_{buf} * W * T$ns (480μs with $N_{buf} = 30; W = 640; T = 25ns$). Once initialized, a rectified pixel is transformed by a simple mean filter, using a 3x3 window. The filtering process requires to record 4 lines (3 to compute the mean, one to memorize the incoming pixels of the next line). A filtered pixel is generated with a latency of $(2W + 2) * T$ns. The mean computation is achieved in two steps; namely horizontal and vertical additions. The architecture of the corresponding module is shown on Fig. 13. Three registers as shown in figure 14, are used to perform the horizontal addition. Three successive pixels are stored in three shift registers. These shift registers are connected to two parallel adders of eight bits so that the result is coded in ten bits. The result of horizontal addition is stored in a memory, which is twice as large as the image width. The vertical addition is computed by taking the current horizontal addition result plus the stored horizontal addition of the two previous lines. The arithmetic mean of the nine pixels window is coded in 12 bits. The normalization (division by 9) is not required here, because the next function only compares pixel intensities.

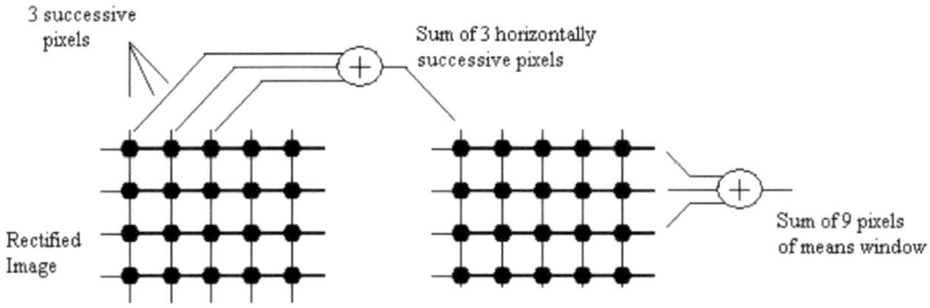

Fig. 13. Architecture for the module *Arithmetic mean filter*.

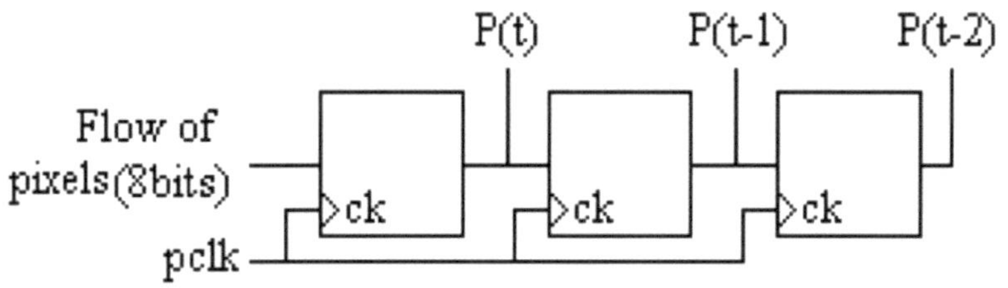

Fig. 14. Shift registers in order to memorize 3 successive pixels.

5.3 The Census transform.

Pixels filtered by the mean operator are provided by the previous step at every pixel clock; they are used as inputs for the Census transform module. This transformation encodes all the intensity values contained in a F_cxF_c window as a function of its intensity central value. The process is very simple, but it generates long bit strings if F_c is increased. After analysis on synthetic and real images, F_c was set to 7, giving for every Census pixel, a string of 48 bits; fortunately only a circular buffer of D_{max} strings computed from the left and right images, must be recorded before executing the *Census Correlation module*. The Census Transform requires to record $F_c + 1$ lines, and a transformed pixel is generated with a latency of three lines plus four pixels, $(4W + 4) * T$ns.
The architecture of this module is decribed on Fig. 15. This module requires a circular buffer of 8 lines in order to store results of the Mean operator, that is to say 12 bits pixels. The size of the working memory is equal to the image width ($W = 640$) minus the width of the searching window (7 pixels in our case), because Census bitstring cannot be computed for pixels close to the image limits, so 60,8Kbits. Moreover this module requires a matrix of 7x7 shift registers, so that at every pixel clock, seven successive pixels on seven successive lines centered on a (u, v) pixel are stored synchronously. Let us note that at this same period, the $(u + 4, v + 4)$ pixel is computed by the *Rectification module*.

Once pixels of the 7x7 Census window are stored in registers, then the central procedure of the Census transform is executed: the central pixel of the Census window is compared with its 48 local neighbours. It requires that all corresponding registers are connected to comparators activated in parallel as shown on Fig. 15. Finally, the Census result is coded on 48 bits, where each bit corresponds to a comparator output.

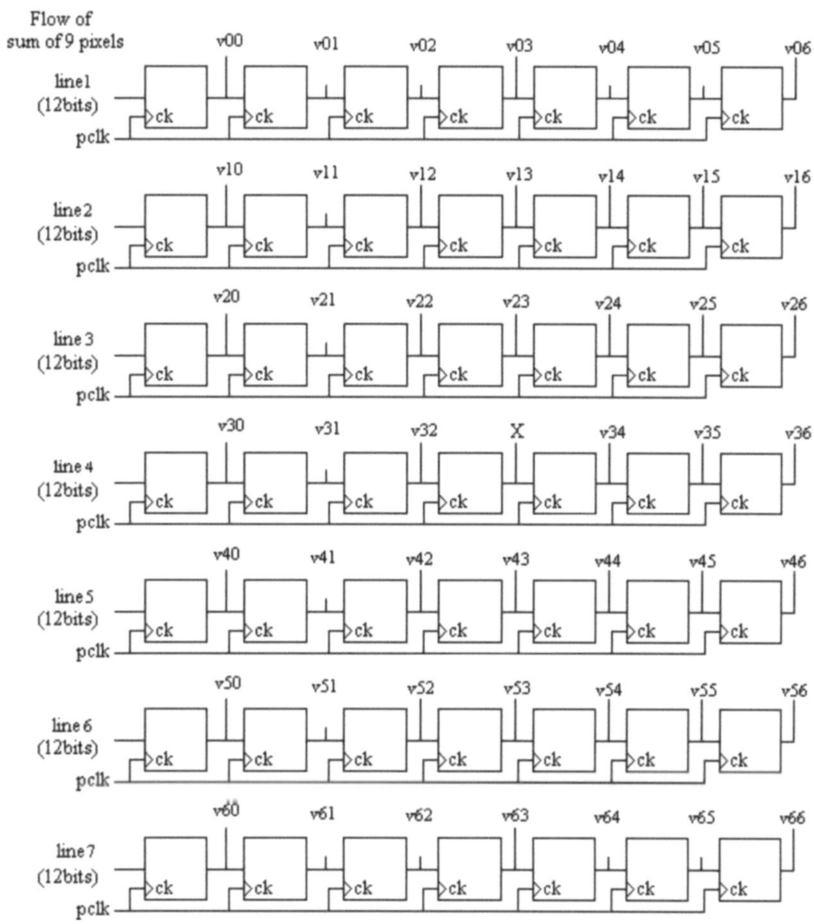

Fig. 15. Architecture for the module *Census transform*.

5.4 The Census correlation.

Correlation task is intended to link up right Census image with left one or vice versa, taking into account that, images contain objects that are common between them. As it is well known, correlation task serves to find the object apparent displacement, called disparity measurement. Stereo matching must compute similarity measurements (or scores), between left and right pixels that could be matched; matchings are selected maximizing the similarity scores. So the module consists of two main steps: in one hand, the computation of the similarity scores, in another hand, the maximum score search.

As shown on figure 7, the *Census Correlation module* has been designed at first from the left image to the right one, because it allows to minimize the latency time.

Figure 16 shows the corresponding module architecture for the left-right correlation. Firstly all $D_{max} + 1$ scores are computed in parallel; the last 64 Census codes computed by the previous module in the right image, are synchronously stored in shift registers (each one is a word of 48 bits), depicted as D_0 (for (u, v)), D_1 (for $(u, v-1)$), D_2 (for $(u, v-2)$)... on the left of Fig. 16. Both registers and the left Census code computed for the current processed pixel in (u, v) position, are the inputs of *XNOR* binary operator which delivers 48 bits as output; if a bit in the right Census code is the same than the corresponding one in the left Census code, the resulting bit given of the *XNOR* operation will be set to one; on the contrary, if compared bits are different, the *XNOR* operation returns zero. The 48 bits returned by every *XNOR* operator, are summed, in order to find the number of equal bits in the compared Census codes. This number add_i gives the similarity score between the (u, v) left pixel with the $(u, v-i)$ right one. So scores are integer numbers from 0 (if all bits of the Census codes are different) to 48 (identical Census codes).

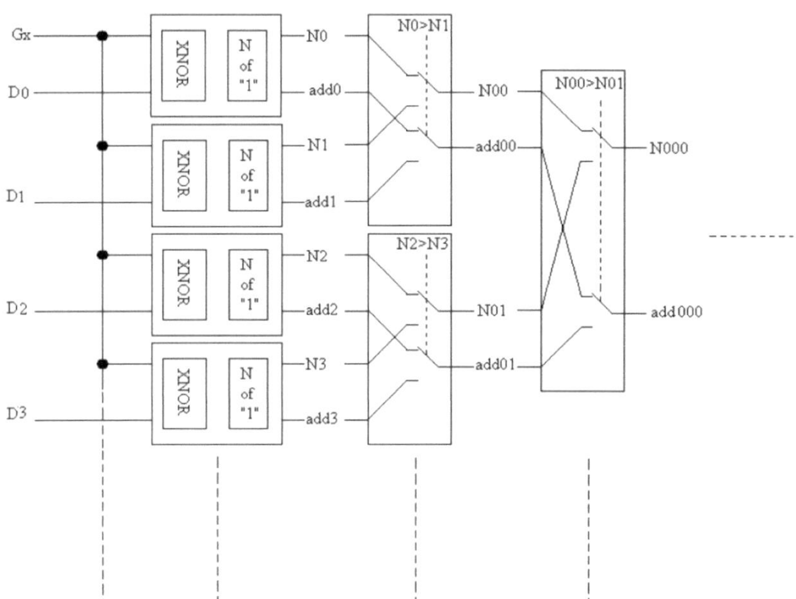

Fig. 16. Architecture for the module *Census correlation*.

Then these scores are compared in order to find the N_i position for the add_i maximum score; it is done by comparing scores for adjacent potential matches. The search for the maximum score is processed by pyramidal comparisons; for a 2^N array, it requires N cycles. Here $D_{max} = 64$, so the search for the maximum score, requires 6 steps.

5.5 The left-right verification.

The Census correlation could be made in parallel from the left image to the right one and from the right image to the left one, but not synchronously. With rectified and non convergent cameras, when a left pixel is read, the matched one in the right image is already recorded amongst the D_{max} circular buffer. On the contrary, when a right pixel is read, the matched one in the left image will be acquired during the D_{max} next periods. This time-lag makes the architecture more complex, and adds a latency of D_{max} periods.

Nevertheless, the result is improved using this left-right verification. Indeed, when we search for the maximum scores, several scores could be identical for different disparities. In the software version, basic verification tests on the found maximum, are made to filter bad matchings (see figure 9(left)). These tests are not implemented in the previous module. So a verification step allows to eliminate these false disparities, comparing disparities provided by the left-right and right-left Correlation processes.
Figure 17 presents the proposed architecture. Two *Census Correlation modules* are executed in parallel; the first one has been described in the previous section. The second one is identical, but a right Census code is compared with the $D_{max} + 1$ next computed left Census codes. So this right-left search requires an extra latency (here 64 pixel periods more). All computed disparities are stored in shift registers: so this module requires $2xD_{max}$ registers (here 6 bits registers, because disparity is between 0 and 63). The verification consists in comparing disparities given by the two approaches: if disparity d is given by the left-right search, a disparity $D_{max} - d$ must be given by the right-left search. If this test is not satisfied, the disparity is not valid.

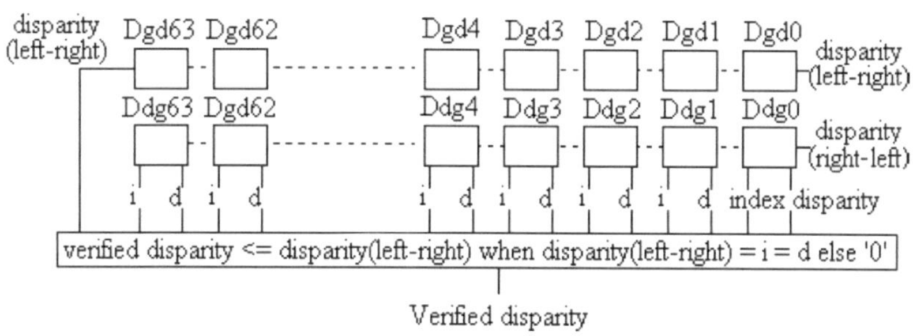

Fig. 17. Architecture for the module *left-right verification*.

Finally, a disparity is generated for a given pixel with a latency of $(N_{buf} * W + (2W + 2) + (4W + 4) + 2 * D_m ax) * T$ns with all steps. By now the filtering algorithm used in the software version, is not integrated on a FPGA.

6. Real time stereovision: our FPGA-based implementation

6.1 First validations without rectification

The stereovision algorithm has been firstly implemented in VHDL on the QUARTUS development tool (*Altera Quartus reference manual* (n.d.)), and then loaded and executed on the evaluation kit NIOS-DEVKIT-1S40 (*Altera Stratix reference manual* (n.d.)), equipped with a STRATIX 1S40 with 41250 logic elements (LEs) and 3.4Mbits of embedded RAM memory. The embedded memory was not sufficient to test the rectification function. So it was not implemented in this first implementation. Cameras were aligned thanks to mechanical devices shown with our preliminary acquisition setup on figure 18 presents :

- the evaluation kit was connected to two JAI cameras, mounted on micro-actuators, so that an expert operator could manually align the two image planes.
- Images with a 640x480 resolution, are transferred to the evaluation kit at 40MHz, using CameraLink serial communication protocol.
- it was intended to study a multispectral version of this perceptual method, fusing sensory data provided by classical CMOS cameras with FIR ones (far infrared, using micro

Fig. 18. Three cameras (the central FIR) connected to the computing unit.

bolometers).

The Census Transform and the Census Correlation functions have been evaluated on this first setup; this system allowed to learn about the required ressources in LEs, in memory and in EABs (Embedded Array Blocks). Figure 19 shows the relationships between numbers of used LEs (left) and of used memory bits (right) with the F_c and W parameters, considering a maximal distortion of $H/4$ (with generally $H = 2/3W$) and a maximal disparity $D_{max} = 63$. It appears clearly that the most critical requirement comes from the memory consumption, and especially, from the number of available EABs, due to the fact that one EAB (4096 bits) allows to record only one image line only if $W < 512$.

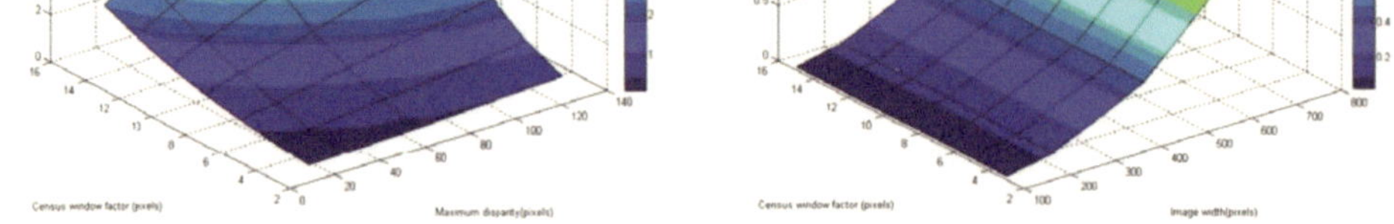

Fig. 19. The ressource requirements with respect to the image size and the size of the correlation window.

This static analysis about the resources requirements, allowed us to select what could be the most well suited FPGA in the ALTERA family, in order to implement our stereo algorithm. Due to economic requirements (low cost, low power consumption), the Cyclone family was mainly considered: the number of LEs available on the 1C20 chip (20000) could be sufficient, but not the number of EABs (64). The CycloneII family has been selected (1.1Mbits of embedded memory, up to 64000 LEs) to design a computing unit adapted for the stereovision algorithm.

6.2 A multi-FPGAs computing box for stereovision

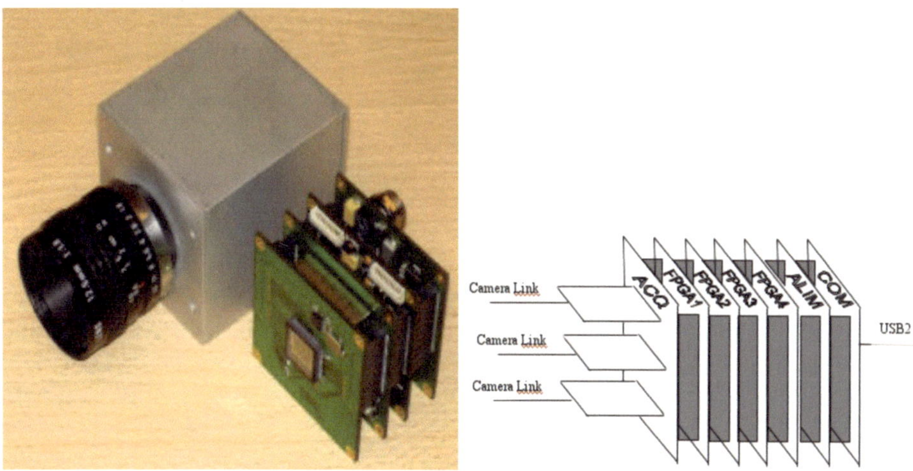

Fig. 20. The developed multi-FPGAs platform (right), inspired from the DTSO camera (left)

A modular electronic computing board based on a CycloneII FPGA, was designed by Delta Technologies Sud Ouest (*Delta Technologie Sud-Ouest Company* (n.d.)), for this project about stereovision, but also, for high-speed vision applications using smart cameras. DTSO has designed an intelligent camera called ICam (figure 20), made of at least 4 boards: (1) the sensor board, equipped with a 1280x1024 CMOS array, (2) the computing board, equipped with a CycloneII FPGA with only 18000 LEs, but with two 1MBytes banks of external memories (read access time: 50ns, with the possibility to read two bytes in parallel), (3) the power supplying board and (4) an interface board, allowing an USB2 connection (8MBytes/s) between the camera and a client computer. Recently a Ethernet version (Wifi or wired) has been designed, integrating in the camera a PowerPC on Linux, in order to manage the TCP/IP protocol, and to allow to use a network of communicating iCam cameras.

Depending on the application, it is possible to integrate in ICam several computing boards, connected by a chained parallel bus: an algorithm could be parallelized according to a functional repartition (sequences of functions executed in pipeline) or a data distribution between the computing boards.

ICam is a smart modular camera: how to convert this design in order to deal with stereovision? Depending on the sensor baseline, two configurations could be considered to implement a real-time stereovision sensor.

- For applications involving small view fields, like cockpit monitoring in a car (figure 1(top right)), the stereo baseline could be less than 10cm, like for on-the-shelf stereo sensors (*Videre Design Company* (n.d.)) (*Point Grey Design Company* (n.d.)). The ICam architecture

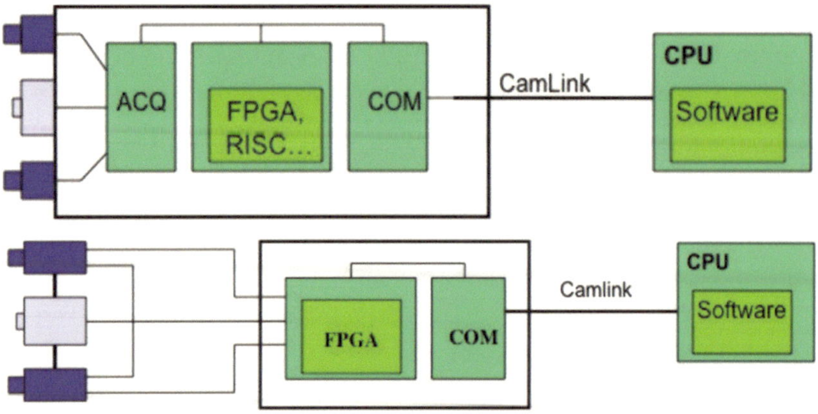

Fig. 21. Two possible configurations, with or without sensor integration.

could be adapted by rigidly coupling two sensor boards (figure 21(top)) and to map four computing boards to the functional decomposition presented on figure 5. Thanks to the rigidity, such a stereo sensor could be calibrated off line.

- A larger baseline could be required for applications like obstacle detection on a motorway with a view field up to 50m. (figure 1(bottom)). For such applications, only a computing box is integrated using the ICam architecture without the sensor board: a Camera Link interface has been developed to connect up to three cameras to this box (figure 21(bottom)). With large baselines, self-calibration methods will have to be integrated to make on line estimation or on line correction (Lemonde (2005)) of the sensor parameters, especially of the relative situation between left and right cameras.

The stereovision computing box is presented on figure 22; only three FPGA boards are integrated by now, because like it will be seen in the section 7, the CycloneII resources provided by three boards are sufficient with a wide margin. As presented on figure 23, our system has a pipeline architecture; two image flows go through all FPGAs:

- FPGA1 receives the two original images; it performs the rectification function on the left one; outputs are the rectified left image, and the original right one.
- FPGA2 performs the rectification function on the right original image; outputs are the two rectified images.
- FPGA3 performs the correlation function; outputs can be selected, using jumpers. Generally it is the disparity map, and the left rectified image (for display purpose on the PC).

7. Real time stereovision: evaluations

7.1 Benchmarking on the Middlebury data set

The performance of our integrated stereo architecture has been evaluated using two methods. First, a simulation of the HDL code has been performed on images *Tsukuba, Teddy, Venus and Cones* extracted from the Middlebury stereo dataset (Scharstein et al. (2002)). Percentages of bad pixels are computed on different regions (all, non-occluded, discontinuity) of the disparity images, according to the method proposed for benchmarking stereo algorithms in (Scharstein et al. (2002)):

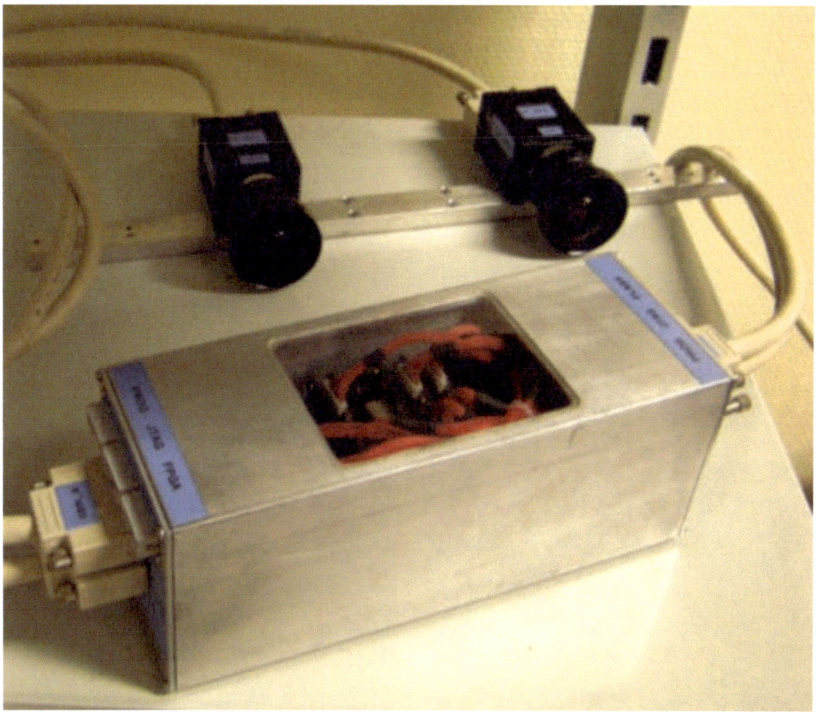

Fig. 22. An integrated version on a multi-FPGAs architecture.

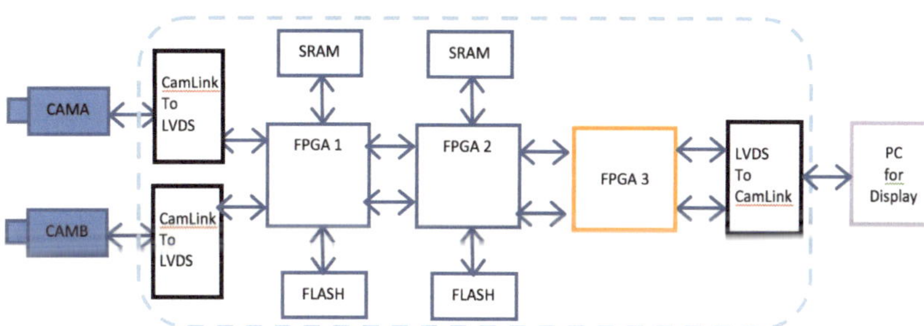

Fig. 23. The hardware computing box for the stereovision algorithm.

$$B = \frac{1}{N}\Sigma_{(x,y)}(d_C(x,y) - d_T(x,y) > \epsilon_d)$$

where N is the number of pixels in the disparity map, $d_C(x,y)$ is the computed disparity, $d_T(x,y)$ is the ground truth disparity, and ϵ_d is the disparity error tolerance.

Table 2 presents on the three first columns, these percentages for the raw disparity images; the mean percentage of bad pixels for all images is 37,5%. Then a filtering operation is applied on the raw disparity images, using a median filter on a 5x5 window, followed by a erode operation on a 5x5 structuring element. Table 2 presents on the three last columns, these percentages for the filtered disparity images; the mean percentage of bad pixels is decreased to 29,4%.

Image name	nonocc	disc	all	nonocc	disc	all
Tsukuba	36.0	43.1	37.4	26.0	27.7	33.9
Teddy	36.4	37.5	47.9	28.1	29.3	42.3
Venus	36.6	42.8	48.5	28.2	35.3	40.5
Cones	19.6	28.4	36.1	12.2	21.8	27.3

Table 2. Percentages of errors for the raw and filtered disparities, computed on the four images extracted from the Middlebury data set.

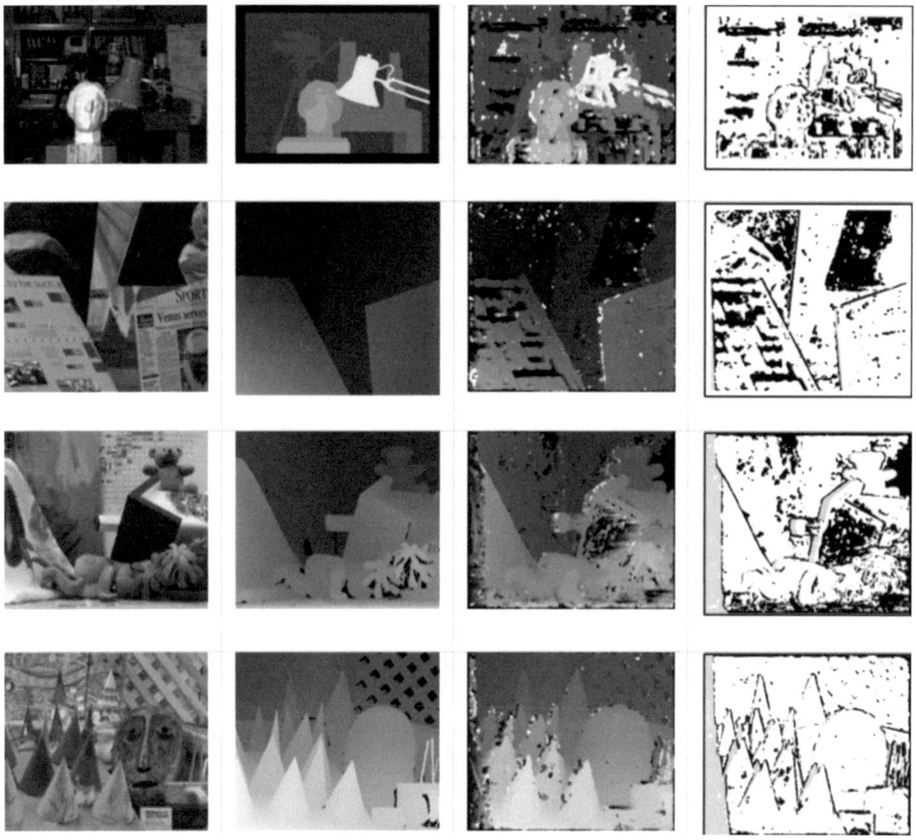

Fig. 24. Results provided by our architecture with a Post-Processing applied to images from the Middlebury data set

7.2 Evaluation from real-time experiments

Second, performances are evaluated from real-time image sequences acquired on indoor scenes with a stereo rig connected to the multi-FPGAs system presented on figure 22. A result is presented on figure 25. This figure shows the left stereo image (top) and the raw disparity image (bottom left) sent by the multi-FPGAs system on a CameraLink connection to a PC, and the filtered disparity image (bottom right) processed by software. The PC can filter and display these disparity images only at 15Hz; the filtering method will be soon implemented on a fourth FPGA board which will be integrated on our system.

Table 3 shows how many resources are used on the three FPGAs on which our architecture is integrated. The synthesis process is carried out thanks to Altera Quartus II v 9.0 Web

Fig. 25. Results provided by our architecture implemented on a multi-fpgas configuration: (top) original image, (bottom) disparity images before and after filtering

Board	Used LEs	Available LEs	% Used LEs	% Used Memory	Max Frequency
FPGA 1	868	18752	5%	31%	160 MHz
FPGA 2	868	18752	5%	31%	160 MHz
FPGA 3	13582	18752	72%	37%	151.31 MHz

Table 3. Resources required for the presented algorithm.

Edition. Theoretically, the maximal frames per second rate of our stereo implementation, could be 490 FPS, taking 151.31 MHz as the maximal frequency for the pixel clock: $N_{images/s} = N_{pixels/s}/size_{image}$ (so 491 151310000/640x480). Our real tests are based on JAI cameras which have a 40MHz pixel clock; so now our system provides 130 disparity images/s. The CameraLink connection is sufficient in order to send this data flow to an host computer; by now, it is a PC which only displays disparity images at 15Hz.

Furthermore, another relevant fact is that FPGAs 1 and 2 on which the rectification architectures are implemented, are underused according to the percentage of used logic elements (LEs), so it could be possible to use a smaller and cheaper FPGA for these tasks.

8. Conclusions

This paper has described the current results of a project about the design and the implementation of a smart perceptual subsystem, that could be mounted on a mobile platform in order to execute very computationnaly demanding functions, like obstacle detection. Up to now only the acquisition of 3D data from visual sensors has been considered, using the integration of a classical correlation-based stereovision algorithm on a processing unit made of connected FPGA-based boards. This processing unit is fed at 40MHz by images acquired by two or three cameras through Camera Link connections, and can provide disparity images at more than 100Hz with a 640x480 resolution on a Camera Link output connected to a client computer. By now, other perceptual functions must be executed on the client computer because either they are too complex (like image segmentation) or they require too many

floating-point computations : filtering of the disparity map, 3D reconstruction, obstacle detection either directly from the disparity map or from the 3D image...
Up to now, because of some simplifications made on the original stereovision algorithm, disparity maps acquired by our stereo sensor, are very noisy and contain too many artefacts. We are currently improving these results, by implementing on FPGA, interpolations and verifications already validated on the software version.
Moreover, assuming that the ground is planar, disparity maps can be directly exploited to detect obstacles on the ground, using the v-disparity concept (Labayrade et al. (2002)), so that a probabilistic obstacle map could be provided to the client computer. It is intended to estimate also on the smart sensor, the relative speed of the detected obstacles. Finally other

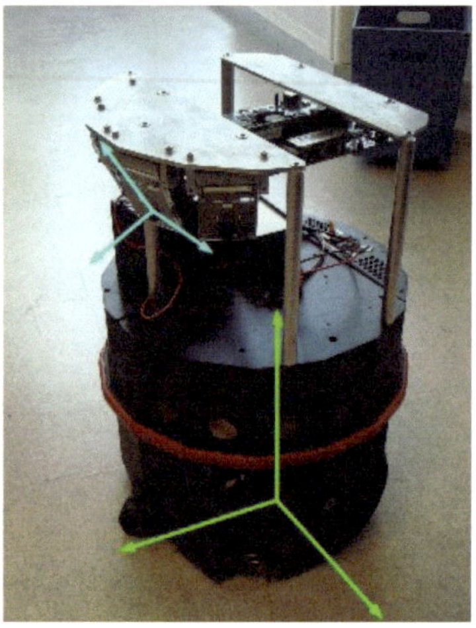

Fig. 26. A demonstrator for a smart multi-cameras sensor for obstacle detection.

algorithms, not directly based on stereovision, are currently studied, in order to design and implement smart sensors for obstacle detection. First a multi-cameras system, devoted to ground-obstacle segmentation (Devy et al. (2009)) has been developed for service robotics: figure 26 presents our demonstrator, currently equipped with four cameras. Then we develop an heterogeneous multi-cameras system, made with a classical CMOS camera and an infrared sensor (in the 8-12μm bandwidth), devoted to obstacle detection in bad visibility conditions.

9. Acknowledgments

This work has been funded by a Midi-Pyrénées region project in France and by the ECOS Nord action C07M01 about the international scientific cooperation between France and Columbia.
• Mario Ibarra Manzano was supported by the scholarship 183807 granted by CONACYT and SEP administration in Mexico.
• Diego Botero Galeano is supported by the FUI project SART, funded by the french ministry of Industry.
• Zohir Irki is supported by the *Laboratoire des Systèmes Numériques (LSN/UERAuto), Ecole Militaire Polytechnique (EMP)*, Alger, Algeria.
• Philippe Fillatreau is currently Assistant Professor at the Laboratoire Genie de Production (LGP) of the *Ecole Nationale d'Ingénieurs de Tarbes (ENIT).*

10. References

Altera Quartus reference manual (n.d.). URL: *http://www.altera.com/literature/lit-qts.jsp.*

Altera Stratix reference manual (n.d.). URL: *http://www.altera.com/products/devices/stratix /features /stx-architecture.html.*

Arias-Estrada, M. & Xicotencatl, J. M. (2001). Multiple stereo matching using an extended architecture, *Proc. 11th Int. Conf. on Field-Programmable Logic and Applications (FPL), G. Brebner and R. Woods, Eds. London, UK: Springer-Verlag*, pp. 203–212.

Boizard, J.L., Naoulou, A., Fourniols, J., Devy, M., Sentenac, T. & Lacroix, P. (2005). Fpga based architectures for real time computation of the census transform and correlation in various stereovision contexts, *7th International workshop on Electronics, Control, Modelling, Measurement and Signals (ECMS'2005), 7p.*

Brown, M., Burschka, D. & Hager, G. (2003). Advances in computational stereo., *IEEE Trans. on Pattern Analysis and Machine Intelligence*, Vol. 25(8), pp. 993–1008.

Chonghun, R., Taehyun, H., Sungsik, K. & Jaeseok, K. (2004). Symmetrical dense disparity estimation: algorithms and fpgas implementation, *Consumer Electronics, 2004 IEEE International Symposium on . Sept. 1-3*, pp. 452–456.

Corke, P. & Dunn, P. (1999). Frame-rate stereopsis using non-parametric transforms and programmable logic, *Proc. IEEE Int. Conf. on Robotics and Automation (ICRA).*

Darabiha, A., Rose, J. & MacLean, W. (2003). Video-rate stereo depth measurement on programmable hardware, *Proc. IEEE Conf. on Vision and Pattern recognition (CVPR2003), Madison (USA).*

Delta Technologie Sud-Ouest Company (n.d.). URL: *http://www.delta-technologies.fr.*

Devy, M., Giralt, A. & Hernandez, A. M. (2000). Detection and classification of passager seat occupancy using stereovision, *Proc.IEEE Symp. on Intelligent Vehicles (IV2000), Dearborn (USA)*, pp.714-719.

Devy, M., Ibarra Manzano, M., Boizard, J.L., Lacroix, P., Filali, W. & Fourniols, J. (2009). Integrated subsystem for obstacle detection from a belt of micro-cameras, *14th International Conference on Advanced Robotics (ICAR 2009), Munich (Germany), 6p..*

Georgoulas, C., Kotoulas, L., Sirakoulis, G., Andreadis, I. & Gasteratos, A. (2008). Real-time disparity map computation module, *Microprocessors And Microsystems*, Vol. 32(3), pp. 159–170.

Hamette, P. L. & Troster, G. (2006). Fingermouse - architecture of an asic-based mobile stereovision smart camera, *Wearable Computers, IEEE International Symposium*, Vol. 0, pp. 121–122.

Han, S., Woo, S., Jeong, M. & You, B. (2009). Improved-quality real-time stereo vision processor, *VLSI Design, International Conference on*, Vol. 0, pp. 287–292.

Ibarra-Manzano, M., Almanza-Ojeda, D., Devy, M., Boizard, J.L. & Fourniols, J. (2009). Stereo vision algorithm implementation in fpga using census transform for effective resource optimization, *Proc. 12th Euromicro Conference on Digital System Design, Architectures, Methods and Tools (DSD'2009), Patras (Greece)*, pp. 799–805.

Ibarra-Manzano, M., Devy, M., Boizard, J.L., Lacroix, P. & Fourniols, J. (2009). An efficient reconfigurable architecture to implement dense stereo vision algorithm using high-level synthesis, *Proc. 19th Int. Conf. on Field Programmable Logic and Applications (FPL 2009), Prague (Czech Republic).*

Irki, Z., Devy, M., Fillatreau, P. & Boizard, J.L. (2007). An approach for the real time correction of stereoscopic images, *8th International Workshop on Electronics, Control, Modelling,*

Measurement and Signals (ECMS 2007) & Doctoral School (EDSYS, GEET), Liberec (Czech Republic).

Jia, Y., Zhang, X., Li, M., & An, L. (2004). A miniature stereo vision machine (msvm-iii) for dense disparity mapping, *Proc. 17th Int. Conf. Pattern Recognition (ICPR), Cambridge, U.K.*, Vol. 1, p. 728–731.

Jin, S., Cho, J., Pham, X., Lee, K., Park, S., Kim, M. & Jeon, J. (2010). Fpga design and implementation of a real-time stereo vision system, *IEEE Trans. on circuits and systems for video technology* Vol. 20(1), p. 15–26.

Kanade, T., Yoshida, A., Oda, K., Kano, H. & Tanaka, M. (1996). A stereo machine for video-rate dense depth mapping and its new applications, *Proc IEEE Int. Conf. on Computer Vision and Pattern Recognition (CVPR).*

Konolige, K. (1997). Small vision systems : Hardware and implementation, *Proc. 8th Int.Symp. on Robotics Research (ISRR), Hayama (Japan).*

Kuhn, M., Moser, S., Isler, O., Gurkaynak, F. K., Burg, A., Felber, N., Kaeslin, H. & Fichtner, W. (2003). Efficient asic implementation of a real-time depth mapping stereo vision system, *Proc. IEEE Int. Symp. Micro-Nano Mechatronics and Human Science*, Vol. 3, pp. 1478–1481.

Labayrade, R., Aubert, D. & Tarel, J. (2002). Real time obstacle detection in stereo vision on non flat road geometry through v-disparity representation, *Proc. IEEE Symp. on Intelligent Vehicle (IV2004), Versailles (France).*

Lemonde, V. (2005). Stéréovision embarquée sur véhicule : de l'auto-calibrage Ãă la détection d'obstacles, *Phd report, institut national des sciences appliquées, Toulouse (France)*, Laboratoire d'Architecture et d'Analyse des Systèmes (C.N.R.S.).

Lemonde, V. & Devy, M. (2004). Obstacle detection with stereovision, *Mechatronics & Robotics 2004 (MECHROB'04), Aachen (Allemagne)*, Vol.3, pp. 919–924.

Lemonde, V. & Devy, M. (2005). Obstacle detection with stereovision for parking modeling, *Proc. European Congress Sensors & Actuators for Advanced Automotive Applications (SENSACT'2005), Noisy-Le-Grand (France), 10p.*

Matthies, L. (1992). Stereo vision for planetary rovers: Stochastic modelling to near-real tim e implementation, *Int. Journal on Computer Vision*, Vol. 8(1).

Naoulou, A. (2006). Architectures pour la stéréovision passive dense temps réel : application àă la stéréo-endoscopie, *Phd report, Université Paul Sabatier, Toulouse (France)*, Laboratoire d'Architecture et d'Analyse des Systèmes (C.N.R.S.).

Naoulou, A., Boizard, J.L., Fourniols, J. & Devy, M. (2006). An alternative to sequential architectures to improve the processing time of passive stereovision algorithms, *Proc. 16th Int. Conf. on Field Programmable Logic and Applications (FPL'2006), Madrid (Spain), 4p.*, pp. 821–824.

Point Grey Design Company: BumbleBee2 sensor (n.d.). URL: *http://www.dnai.com/mclaughl.*

Scharstein, D. & Szeliski, R. (2002). A taxonomy and evaluation of dense two-frame stereo correspondence algorithms, *Int. Journal on Computer Vision*, Vol. 47(1-3), pp. 7–42.

Sunghwan, L., Jongsu, Y. & Junseong, K. (2005). Real-time stereo vision on a reconfigurable system, *Proc. Int. Conf. SAMOS, Lecture notes in computer science, ISSN 0302-9743*, pp. 299–307.

Videre Design Company (n.d.). URL: *http://www.dnai.com/mclaughl.*

Zabih, R. & Woodfill, J. (1994). Non-parametric local transforms for computing visual correspondence, *Third European Conf. on Computer Vision (ECCV), Stockholm (Sweden).*